# First Workshop on Speech and Language Technologies for Dravidian Languages (DravidianLangTech 2021)



Online
19 April 2021

ISBN: 978-1-7138-2959-1

**Printed from e-media with permission by:**

Curran Associates, Inc.
57 Morehouse Lane
Red Hook, NY 12571

**Some format issues inherent in the e-media version may also appear in this print version.**



Printed with permission by Curran Associates, Inc. (2021)

For permission requests, please contact the Association for Computational Linguistics at the address below.

Association for Computational Linguistics
209 N. Eighth Street
Stroudsburg, Pennsylvania 18360

Phone: 1-570-476-8006
Fax: 1-570-476-0860

acl@aclweb.org

**Additional copies of this publication are available from:**

Curran Associates, Inc.
57 Morehouse Lane
Red Hook, NY 12571 USA
Phone: 845-758-0400
Fax: 845-758-2633
Email: curran@proceedings.com
Web: www.proceedings.com

DravidianLangTech EACL 2021

# 16th conference of the European Chapter of the Association for Computational Linguistics (EACL)

# Proceedings of the First Workshop on Speech and Language Technologies for Dravidian Languages

April 19,2021

# Preface

The development of technology increases our internet use, and most of the global languages have adapted themselves to the digital era. However, many regional, under-resourced languages face challenges as they still lack developments in language technology. One such language family is the Dravidian (Tamil) family of languages. Dravidian is the name for the Tamil languages or Tamil people in Sanskrit, and all the current Dravidian languages were called a branch of Tamil in old Jain, Bhraminic, and Buddhist literature (Caldwell, 1875). Tamil languages are primarily spoken in south India, Sri Lanka, and Singapore. Pockets of speakers are found in Nepal, Pakistan, Malaysia, other parts of India, and elsewhere globally. The Tamil languages, which are 4,500 years old and spoken by millions of speakers, are under-resourced in speech and natural language processing. The Dravidian languages were first documented in Tamili script on pottery and cave walls in the Keezhadi (Keeladi), Madurai and Tirunelveli regions of Tamil Nadu, India, from the 6th century BCE.

The Tamil languages are divided into four groups: South, South-Central, Central, and North groups. Tamil morphology is agglutinating and exclusively suffixal. Syntactically, Tamil languages are head-final and left-branching. They are free-constituent order languages. To improve access to and production of information for monolingual speakers of Dravidian (Tamil) languages, it is necessary to have speech and languages technologies. These workshops aim to save the Dravidian languages from extinction in technology. This is the first workshop on speech and language technologies for Dravidian languages.

The broader objective of DravidianLangTech-2021 was

- To investigate challenges related to speech and language resource creation for Dravidian languages.
- To promote a research in speech and language technology in Dravidian languages.
- To adopt appropriate language technology models which suit Dravidian languages
- To provide opportunities for researchers from the Dravidian language community from around the world to collaborate with other researchers.

## Organizing Committee

- Bharathi Raja Chakravarthi, Insight SFI Research Centre for Data Analytics, Data Science Institute, National University of Ireland Galway
- Ruba Priyadharshini, Saraswathi Narayanan College, Madurai, India
- Anand Kumar M, Department of Information Technology, National Institute of Technology Karnataka Surathkal, India.
- Parameswari Krishnamurthy, Centre for Applied Linguistics and Translation Studies, University of Hyderabad, Telangana, India.
- Elizabeth Sherly, Indian Institute of Information Technology and Management-Kerala, India

## Programme Committee

- Adeep Hande, Indian Institute of Information Technology Tiruchirappalli, Tamil Nadu, India
- Bharathi B, SSN College of Engineering, Tamil Nadu, India
- Barry Haddow, University of Edinburgh, United Kingdom
- Charangan Vasantharajan, University of Moratuwa, Sri Lanka
- Deepak Padmanabhan, Queen's University Belfast, United Kingdom
- Dhanalakshmi V, Tamil Virtual Academy, Tamil Nadu, India
- Dhivya Chinnappa, Thomson Reuters, United States of America
- Eswari Rajagopal, National Institute of Technology Tiruchirappalli, Tamil Nadu, India
- Fausto Giunchiglia, Universit di Trento, Italy
- Gihan Dias, University of Moratuwa, SriLanka
- Hema A Murthy, Indian Institute of Technology Madras, Tamil Nadu, India
- Marcos Zampieri, Rochester Institute of Technology, United States of America
- Manikandan Ravikiran, Hitachi Research and Development, India
- Melvin Johnson, Google, United States of America
- Mihael Arcan, National University of Ireland Galway
- Navya Jose, Indian Institute Of Information Technology and Management Kerala, India
- Premjith, Amrita Vishwa Vidyapeetham, Kerala, India
- Prem Kumar, Central Institute of Indian Languages, Mysore, India
- Punyajoy Saha, Indian Institute of Technology, Kharagpur
- Rajendran Sankaravelayuthan, Amrita Vishwa Vidyapeetham, India
- Sai Krishna Rallabandi, Carnegie Mellon University, United States of America

- Sai Muralidhar Jayanthi, Carnegie Mellon University, United States of America
- Sainik Kumar Mahata, Institute of Engineering and Management, India
- Sara Renjit, Cochin University of Science and Technology, Kerala, India
- S. Sangeetha, National Institute of Technology-Trichy, Tamil Nadu, India
- Sinnathamby Mahesan, University of Jaffna, Sri Lanka
- Subalalitha N, SRM Institute of Science and Technology, India
- Sudheer Kolachina, Amazon, United Kingdom
- Thavareesan Sajeetha, Eastern University, Sri Lanka
- Thenmozhi D, Sri Sivasubramaniya Nadar College of Engineering, Tamil Nadu, India
- Thomas Mandl, Universitt Hildesheim, Germany
- Tony McEnery, Lancaster University, United Kingdom
- Uma Maheshwar Rao, University of Hyderabad, India
- Uthayasanker Thayasivam, University of Moratuwa, SriLanka
- Vasu Renganathan, UPenn University of Pennsylvania, United State of America

# Table of Contents

*Tamil Lyrics Corpus: Analysis and Experiments*
Dhivya Chinnappa and Praveenraj Dhandapani ............ 1

*DOSA: Dravidian Code-Mixed Offensive Span Identification Dataset*
Manikandan Ravikiran and Subbiah Annamalai ............ 10

*Towards Offensive Language Identification for Dravidian Languages*
Siva Sai and Yashvardhan Sharma ............ 18

*Sentiment Classification of Code-Mixed Tweets using Bi-Directional RNN and Language Tags*
Sainik Mahata, Dipankar Das and Sivaji Bandyopadhyay ............ 28

*Offensive language identification in Dravidian code mixed social media text*
SUNIL SAUMYA, Abhinav Kumar and Jyoti Prakash Singh ............ 36

*Sentiment Analysis of Dravidian Code Mixed Data*
Asrita Venkata Mandalam and Yashvardhan Sharma ............ 46

*Unsupervised Machine Translation On Dravidian Languages*
Sai Koneru, Danni Liu and Jan Niehues ............ 55

*Graph Convolutional Networks with Multi-headed Attention for Code-Mixed Sentiment Analysis*
Suman Dowlagar and Radhika Mamidi ............ 65

*Task-Specific Pre-Training and Cross Lingual Transfer for Sentiment Analysis in Dravidian Code-Switched Languages*
Akshat Gupta, Sai Krishna Rallabandi and Alan W Black ............ 73

*Analysis of Uvama Urubugal in Tamil Sangam Literatures*
SUBALALITHA CN ............ 80

*Task-Oriented Dialog Systems for Dravidian Languages*
Tushar Kanakagiri and Karthik Radhakrishnan ............ 85

*A Survey on Paralinguistics in Tamil Speech Processing*
Anosha Ignatius and Uthayasanker Thayasivam ............ 94

*Is this Enough?-Evaluation of Malayalam Wordnet*
Nandu Chandran Nair, Maria-chiara Giangregorio and Fausto Giunchiglia ............ 100

*LA-SACo: A Study of Learning Approaches for Sentiments Analysis inCode-Mixing Texts*
Fazlourrahman Balouchzahi and H L Shashirekha ............ 109

*Findings of the Shared Task on Machine Translation in Dravidian languages*
Bharathi Raja Chakravarthi, Ruba Priyadharshini, Shubhanker Banerjee, Richard Saldanha, John P. McCrae, Anand Kumar M, Parameswari Krishnamurthy and Melvin Johnson ............ 119

*Findings of the Shared Task on Troll Meme Classification in Tamil*
Shardul Suryawanshi and Bharathi Raja Chakravarthi ............ 126

*Findings of the Shared Task on Offensive Language Identification in Tamil, Malayalam, and Kannada*
Bharathi Raja Chakravarthi, Ruba Priyadharshini, Navya Jose, Anand Kumar M, Thomas Mandl, Prasanna Kumar Kumaresan, Rahul Ponnusamy, Hariharan R L, John P. McCrae and Elizabeth Sherly 133

*GX@DravidianLangTech-EACL2021: Multilingual Neural Machine Translation and Back-translation*
Wanying Xie . . . . . . . . . . 146

*OFFLangOne@DravidianLangTech-EACL2021: Transformers with the Class Balanced Loss for Offensive Language Identification in Dravidian Code-Mixed text.*
Suman Dowlagar and Radhika Mamidi . . . . . . . . . . 154

*Simon @ DravidianLangTech-EACL2021: Detecting Offensive Content in Kannada Language*
Qinyu Que . . . . . . . . . . 160

*Codewithzichao@DravidianLangTech-EACL2021: Exploring Multilingual Transformers for Offensive Language Identification on Code Mixing Text*
Zichao Li . . . . . . . . . . 164

*JudithJeyafreedaAndrew@DravidianLangTech-EACL2021:Offensive language detection for Dravidian Code-mixed YouTube comments*
Judith Jeyafreeda Andrew . . . . . . . . . . 169

*professionals@DravidianLangTech-EACL2021: Malayalam Offensive Language Identification - A Minimalistic Approach*
Srinath Nair and Dolton Fernandes . . . . . . . . . . 175

*UVCE-IIITT@DravidianLangTech-EACL2021: Tamil Troll Meme Classification: You need to Pay more Attention*
Siddhanth U Hegde, Adeep Hande, Ruba Priyadharshini, Sajeetha Thavareesan and Bharathi Raja Chakravarthi . . . . . . . . . . 180

*IIITT@DravidianLangTech-EACL2021: Transfer Learning for Offensive Language Detection in Dravidian Languages*
Konthala Yasaswini, Karthik Puranik, Adeep Hande, Ruba Priyadharshini, Sajeetha Thavareesan and Bharathi Raja Chakravarthi . . . . . . . . . . 187

*Hypers@DravidianLangTech-EACL2021: Offensive language identification in Dravidian code-mixed YouTube Comments and Posts*
Charangan Vasantharajan and Uthayasanker Thayasivam . . . . . . . . . . 195

*HUB@DravidianLangTech-EACL2021: Identify and Classify Offensive Text in Multilingual Code Mixing in Social Media*
Bo Huang and Yang Bai . . . . . . . . . . 203

*HUB@DravidianLangTech-EACL2021: Meme Classification for Tamil Text-Image Fusion*
Bo Huang and Yang Bai . . . . . . . . . . 210

*ZYJ123@DravidianLangTech-EACL2021: Offensive Language Identification based on XLM-RoBERTa with DPCNN*
Yingjia Zhao and Xin Tao . . . . . . . . . . 216

*IIITK@DravidianLangTech-EACL2021: Offensive Language Identification and Meme Classification in Tamil, Malayalam and Kannada*
Nikhil Ghanghor, Parameswari Krishnamurthy, Sajeetha Thavareesan, Ruba Priyadharshini and Bharathi Raja Chakravarthi . . . . . 222

*cs@DravidianLangTech-EACL2021: Offensive Language Identification Based On Multilingual BERT Model*
shi chen and bing kong . . . . . 230

*CUSATNLP@DravidianLangTech-EACL2021:Language Agnostic Classification of Offensive Content in Tweets*
Sara Renjit and Sumam Mary Idicula . . . . . 236

*IIIT_DWD@EACL2021: Identifying Troll Meme in Tamil using a hybrid deep learning approach*
Ankit Kumar Mishra and SUNIL SAUMYA . . . . . 243

*Amrita_CEN_NLP@DravidianLangTech-EACL2021: Deep Learning-based Offensive Language Identification in Malayalam, Tamil and Kannada*
Sreelakshmi K, Premjith B and Soman KP . . . . . 249

*NLP-CUET@DravidianLangTech-EACL2021: Offensive Language Detection from Multilingual Code-Mixed Text using Transformers*
Omar Sharif, Eftekhar Hossain and Mohammed Moshiul Hoque . . . . . 255

*IRLAB-DAIICT@DravidianLangTech-EACL2021: Neural Machine Translation*
Raj Prajapati, Vedant Vijay Parikh and Prasenjit Majumder . . . . . 262

*IRNLP_DAIICT@DravidianLangTech-EACL2021:Offensive Language identification in Dravidian Languages using TF-IDF Char N-grams and MuRIL*
Bhargav Dave, Shripad Bhat and Prasenjit Majumder . . . . . 266

*Hate-Alert@DravidianLangTech-EACL2021: Ensembling strategies for Transformer-based Offensive language Detection*
Debjoy Saha, Naman Paharia, Debajit Chakraborty, Punyajoy Saha and Animesh Mukherjee . . 270

*TrollMeta@DravidianLangTech-EACL2021: Meme classification using deep learning*
Manoj Balaji J and Chinmaya HS . . . . . 277

*Maoqin @ DravidianLangTech-EACL2021: The Application of Transformer-Based Model*
Maoqin Yang . . . . . 281

*Simon @ DravidianLangTech-EACL2021: Meme Classification for Tamil with BERT*
Qinyu Que . . . . . 287

*Bitions@DravidianLangTech-EACL2021: Ensemble of Multilingual Language Models with Pseudo Labeling for offence Detection in Dravidian Languages*
Debapriya Tula, Prathyush Potluri, Shreyas MS, Sumanth Doddapaneni, Pranjal Sahu, Rohan Sukumaran and Parth Patwa . . . . . 291

*NLP-CUET@DravidianLangTech-EACL2021: Investigating Visual and Textual Features to Identify Trolls from Multimodal Social Media Memes*
Eftekhar Hossain, Omar Sharif and Mohammed Moshiul Hoque . . . . . 300

*SJ_AJ@DravidianLangTech-EACL2021: Task-Adaptive Pre-Training of Multilingual BERT models for Offensive Language Identification*
Sai Muralidhar Jayanthi and Akshat Gupta . . . . . . . . . . 307

*SSNCSE_NLP@DravidianLangTech-EACL2021: Offensive Language Identification on Multilingual Code Mixing Text*
Bharathi B and Agnusimmaculate Silvia A . . . . . . . . . . 313

*JUNLP@DravidianLangTech-EACL2021: Offensive Language Identification in Dravidian Langauges*
Avishek Garain, Atanu Mandal and Sudip Kumar Naskar . . . . . . . . . . 319

*MUCS@DravidianLangTech-EACL2021:COOLI-Code-Mixing Offensive Language Identification*
Fazlourrahman Balouchzahi, Aparna B K and H L Shashirekha . . . . . . . . . . 323

*indicnlp@kgp at DravidianLangTech-EACL2021: Offensive Language Identification in Dravidian Languages*
Kushal Kedia and Abhilash Nandy . . . . . . . . . . 330

*SSNCSE_NLP@DravidianLangTech-EACL2021: Meme classification for Tamil using machine learning approach*
Bharathi B and Agnusimmaculate Silvia A . . . . . . . . . . 336

*MUCS@ - Machine Translation for Dravidian Languages using Stacked Long Short Term Memory*
Asha Hegde, Ibrahim Gashaw and Shashirekha H.L. . . . . . . . . . . 340

*OffTamil@DravideanLangTech-EASL2021: Offensive Language Identification in Tamil Text*
Disne Sivalingam and Sajeetha Thavareesan . . . . . . . . . . 346

*Codewithzichao@DravidianLangTech-EACL2021: Exploring Multimodal Transformers for Meme Classification in Tamil Language*
Zichao Li . . . . . . . . . . 352

*DLRG@DravidianLangTech-EACL2021: Transformer based approachfor Offensive Language Identification on Code-Mixed Tamil*
Ratnavel Rajalakshmi, Yashwant Reddy and Lokesh Kumar . . . . . . . . . . 357

# Conference Program

**Tuesday, April 20, 2021**

**09:00–09:30 Keynote: Vasu Renganathan (Dravidian Languages)**

**09:30–10:00 Keynote: John P McCrae (Under-resourced Languages)**

**10:00–11:00 Paper Session I**

10:00–10:15 *Tamil Lyrics Corpus: Analysis and Experiments*
Dhivya Chinnappa and Praveenraj Dhandapani

10:15–10:30 *DOSA: Dravidian Code-Mixed Offensive Span Identification Dataset*
Manikandan Ravikiran and Subbiah Annamalai

10:30–10:45 *Towards Offensive Language Identification for Dravidian Languages*
Siva Sai and Yashvardhan Sharma

10:45–11:00 *Sentiment Classification of Code-Mixed Tweets using Bi-Directional RNN and Language Tags*
Sainik Mahata, Dipankar Das and Sivaji Bandyopadhyay

**11:00–11:30 Break**

**Tuesday, April 20, 2021 (continued)**

**11:30–13:00 Paper Session II**

11:30–11:45 *Offensive language identification in Dravidian code mixed social media text*
SUNIL SAUMYA, Abhinav Kumar and Jyoti Prakash Singh

11:45–12:00 *Sentiment Analysis of Dravidian Code Mixed Data*
Asrita Venkata Mandalam and Yashvardhan Sharma

12:00–12:15 *Unsupervised Machine Translation On Dravidian Languages*
Sai Koneru, Danni Liu and Jan Niehues

12:15–12:30 *Graph Convolutional Networks with Multi-headed Attention for Code-Mixed Sentiment Analysis*
Suman Dowlagar and Radhika Mamidi

12:30–12:45 *Task-Specific Pre-Training and Cross Lingual Transfer for Sentiment Analysis in Dravidian Code-Switched Languages*
Akshat Gupta, Sai Krishna Rallabandi and Alan W Black

12:45–13:00 *Analysis of Uvama Urubugal in Tamil Sangam Literatures*
SUBALALITHA CN

**13:00–14:00 Lunch Break**

**Tuesday, April 20, 2021 (continued)**

**14:00–15:00 Paper Session III**

14:00–14:15 *Task-Oriented Dialog Systems for Dravidian Languages*
Tushar Kanakagiri and Karthik Radhakrishnan

14:15–14:30 *A Survey on Paralinguistics in Tamil Speech Processing*
Anosha Ignatius and Uthayasanker Thayasivam

14:30–14:45 *Is this Enough?-Evaluation of Malayalam Wordnet*
Nandu Chandran Nair, Maria-chiara Giangregorio and Fausto Giunchiglia

14:45–15:00 *LA-SACo: A Study of Learning Approaches for Sentiments Analysis inCode-Mixing Texts*
Fazlourrahman Balouchzahi and H L Shashirekha

**15:00–16:00 Session Poster: Poster Session**

15:00–16:00 *Findings of the Shared Task on Machine Translation in Dravidian languages*
Bharathi Raja Chakravarthi, Ruba Priyadharshini, Shubhanker Banerjee, Richard Saldanha, John P. McCrae, Anand Kumar M, Parameswari Krishnamurthy and Melvin Johnson

15:00–16:00 *Findings of the Shared Task on Troll Meme Classification in Tamil*
Shardul Suryawanshi and Bharathi Raja Chakravarthi

15:00–16:00 *Findings of the Shared Task on Offensive Language Identification in Tamil, Malayalam, and Kannada*
Bharathi Raja Chakravarthi, Ruba Priyadharshini, Navya Jose, Anand Kumar M, Thomas Mandl, Prasanna Kumar Kumaresan, Rahul Ponnusamy, Hariharan R L, John P. McCrae and Elizabeth Sherly

15:00–16:00 *GX@DravidianLangTech-EACL2021: Multilingual Neural Machine Translation and Back-translation*
Wanying Xie

15:00–16:00 *OFFLangOne@DravidianLangTech-EACL2021: Transformers with the Class Balanced Loss for Offensive Language Identification in Dravidian Code-Mixed text.*
Suman Dowlagar and Radhika Mamidi

15:00–16:00 *Simon @ DravidianLangTech-EACL2021: Detecting Offensive Content in Kannada Language*
Qinyu Que

**Tuesday, April 20, 2021 (continued)**

15:00–16:00 *Codewithzichao@DravidianLangTech-EACL2021: Exploring Multilingual Transformers for Offensive Language Identification on Code Mixing Text*
Zichao Li

15:00–16:00 *JudithJeyafreedaAndrew@DravidianLangTech-EACL2021:Offensive language detection for Dravidian Code-mixed YouTube comments*
Judith Jeyafreeda Andrew

15:00–16:00 *professionals@DravidianLangTech-EACL2021: Malayalam Offensive Language Identification - A Minimalistic Approach*
Srinath Nair and Dolton Fernandes

15:00–16:00 *UVCE-IIITT@DravidianLangTech-EACL2021: Tamil Troll Meme Classification: You need to Pay more Attention*
Siddhanth U Hegde, Adeep Hande, Ruba Priyadharshini, Sajeetha Thavareesan and Bharathi Raja Chakravarthi

15:00–16:00 *IIITT@DravidianLangTech-EACL2021: Transfer Learning for Offensive Language Detection in Dravidian Languages*
Konthala Yasaswini, Karthik Puranik, Adeep Hande, Ruba Priyadharshini, Sajeetha Thavareesan and Bharathi Raja Chakravarthi

15:00–16:00 *Hypers@DravidianLangTech-EACL2021: Offensive language identification in Dravidian code-mixed YouTube Comments and Posts*
Charangan Vasantharajan and Uthayasanker Thayasivam

15:00–16:00 *HUB@DravidianLangTech-EACL2021: Identify and Classify Offensive Text in Multilingual Code Mixing in Social Media*
Bo Huang and Yang Bai

15:00–16:00 *HUB@DravidianLangTech-EACL2021: Meme Classification for Tamil Text-Image Fusion*
Bo Huang and Yang Bai

15:00–16:00 *ZYJ123@DravidianLangTech-EACL2021: Offensive Language Identification based on XLM-RoBERTa with DPCNN*
Yingjia Zhao and Xin Tao

15:00–16:00 *IIITK@DravidianLangTech-EACL2021: Offensive Language Identification and Meme Classification in Tamil, Malayalam and Kannada*
Nikhil Ghanghor, Parameswari Krishnamurthy, Sajeetha Thavareesan, Ruba Priyadharshini and Bharathi Raja Chakravarthi

15:00–16:00 *cs@DravidianLangTech-EACL2021: Offensive Language Identification Based On Multilingual BERT Model*
shi chen and bing kong

15:00–16:00 *CUSATNLP@DravidianLangTech-EACL2021:Language Agnostic Classification of Offensive Content in Tweets*
Sara Renjit and Sumam Mary Idicula

**Tuesday, April 20, 2021 (continued)**

15:00–16:00 *IIIT_DWD@EACL2021: Identifying Troll Meme in Tamil using a hybrid deep learning approach*
Ankit Kumar Mishra and SUNIL SAUMYA

15:00–16:00 *Amrita_CEN_NLP@DravidianLangTech-EACL2021: Deep Learning-based Offensive Language Identification in Malayalam, Tamil and Kannada*
Sreelakshmi K, Premjith B and Soman KP

15:00–16:00 *NLP-CUET@DravidianLangTech-EACL2021: Offensive Language Detection from Multilingual Code-Mixed Text using Transformers*
Omar Sharif, Eftekhar Hossain and Mohammed Moshiul Hoque

15:00–16:00 *IRLAB-DAIICT@DravidianLangTech-EACL2021: Neural Machine Translation*
Raj Prajapati, Vedant Vijay Parikh and Prasenjit Majumder

15:00–16:00 *IRNLP_DAIICT@DravidianLangTech-EACL2021:Offensive Language identification in Dravidian Languages using TF-IDF Char N-grams and MuRIL*
Bhargav Dave, Shripad Bhat and Prasenjit Majumder

15:00–16:00 *Hate-Alert@DravidianLangTech-EACL2021: Ensembling strategies for Transformer-based Offensive language Detection*
Debjoy Saha, Naman Paharia, Debajit Chakraborty, Punyajoy Saha and Animesh Mukherjee

15:00–16:00 *TrollMeta@DravidianLangTech-EACL2021: Meme classification using deep learning*
Manoj Balaji J and Chinmaya HS

15:00–16:00 *Maoqin @ DravidianLangTech-EACL2021: The Application of Transformer-Based Model*
Maoqin Yang

15:00–16:00 *Simon @ DravidianLangTech-EACL2021: Meme Classification for Tamil with BERT*
Qinyu Que

15:00–16:00 *Bitions@DravidianLangTech-EACL2021: Ensemble of Multilingual Language Models with Pseudo Labeling for offence Detection in Dravidian Languages*
Debapriya Tula, Prathyush Potluri, Shreyas MS, Sumanth Doddapaneni, Pranjal Sahu, Rohan Sukumaran and Parth Patwa

15:00–16:00 *NLP-CUET@DravidianLangTech-EACL2021: Investigating Visual and Textual Features to Identify Trolls from Multimodal Social Media Memes*
Eftekhar Hossain, Omar Sharif and Mohammed Moshiul Hoque

15:00–16:00 *SJ_AJ@DravidianLangTech-EACL2021: Task-Adaptive Pre-Training of Multilingual BERT models for Offensive Language Identification*
Sai Muralidhar Jayanthi and Akshat Gupta

**Tuesday, April 20, 2021 (continued)**

15:00–16:00 *SSNCSE_NLP@DravidianLangTech-EACL2021: Offensive Language Identification on Multilingual Code Mixing Text*
Bharathi B and Agnusimmaculate Silvia A

15:00–16:00 *JUNLP@DravidianLangTech-EACL2021: Offensive Language Identification in Dravidian Langauges*
Avishek Garain, Atanu Mandal and Sudip Kumar Naskar

15:00–16:00 *MUCS@DravidianLangTech-EACL2021:COOLI-Code-Mixing Offensive Language Identification*
Fazlourrahman Balouchzahi, Aparna B K and H L Shashirekha

15:00–16:00 *indicnlp@kgp at DravidianLangTech-EACL2021: Offensive Language Identification in Dravidian Languages*
Kushal Kedia and Abhilash Nandy

15:00–16:00 *SSNCSE_NLP@DravidianLangTech-EACL2021: Meme classification for Tamil using machine learning approach*
Bharathi B and Agnusimmaculate Silvia A

15:00–16:00 *MUCS@ - Machine Translation for Dravidian Languages using Stacked Long Short Term Memory*
Asha Hegde, Ibrahim Gashaw and Shashirekha H.L.

15:00–16:00 *OffTamil@DravideanLangTech-EASL2021: Offensive Language Identification in Tamil Text*
Disne Sivalingam and Sajeetha Thavareesan

15:00–16:00 *Codewithzichao@DravidianLangTech-EACL2021: Exploring Multimodal Transformers for Meme Classification in Tamil Language*
Zichao Li

15:00–16:00 *DLRG@DravidianLangTech-EACL2021: Transformer based approachfor Offensive Language Identification on Code-Mixed Tamil*
Ratnavel Rajalakshmi, Yashwant Reddy and Lokesh Kumar

**Tuesday, April 20, 2021 (continued)**

**16:00–17:00 Closing Remarks**

# Tamil lyrics corpus: Analysis and Experiments

**Dhivya Chinnappa**
Thomson Reuters
dhivya.infant@gmail.com

**Praveenraj Dhandapani**
Intellect Design Arena Ltd.
praveenraj0904@gmail.com

## Abstract

In this paper, we present a new Tamil lyrics corpus extracted from Tamil movies captured across a range of 65 years (1954 to 2019). We present a detailed corpus analysis showing the nature of Tamil lyrics with respect to lyricists and the year which it was written. We also present similarity score across different lyricists based on their song lyrics. We present experimental results based on the SOTA BERT Tamil models to identify the lyricists of a song. Finally, we present future research directions encouraging researchers to pursue Tamil NLP research.

## 1 Introduction

Tamil is a classical Dravidian language spoken in the states Tamil Nadu and Pondicherry, India. It is also widely spoken in Srilanka and is one of the official languages of the country. There are considerable Tamil speaking people in countries like Singapore, Malaysia, Canada, and Mauritius.

Historians note that Tamil is as old as 2600 years. The earliest identified Tamil literature known as the *Sangam literature* dates back to 600 B.C. (Abraham, 2003). Tamilians as an ethnic group appreciate literary works and refer to literary excerpts in their daily lives. For example, *Thirukkural*[1], one of the popular literary works, also called the *Ulaga Pothu Marai* (translation: Universal book of principles) includes short literary phrases emphasizing on principles for a prosperous life. Schools teach *Thirukkural* to their students as early as kindergarten. *Thirukkural* excerpts are often found in public transportations and government buildings in Tamil Nadu, India. Political leaders, orators and even common people quote *Thirukkural* excerpts in their daily lives.

Since the inception of the Tamil movie industry in the early 1930s, Tamil literary works have taken a different form. From the very beginning, Tamil movies used the platform to showcase the language's rich literature through movie dialogues and song lyrics. Tamil literary works as old as *Sangam literature* have been depicted in early movies, and the recent movies showcase a mix of old and contemporary literary works. Thus, Tamil movies have become an inseparable part of most Tamilians' lives. While independent literary works (poems, hykoos, novels, etc.) exist, Tamil movies consistently act as important medium in showcasing rich Tamil literary works.

The ideologies portrayed in Tamil movies closely reflect Tamilians' lifestyles. Tamil movies and Tamil politics go hand in hand (Kalorth, 2021). There are several people in the Tamil movie industry with strong political opinions, and it is not uncommon for Tamil movie dialogues and Tamil songs to reflect their political ideologies.

The Tamil movie industry releases a movie every four days (Krishnan and Sakkthivel, 2010). That is, on average there are 90 movies released every year. Similar to other Indian language movies, Tamil movies include several songs. Each song in a Tamil movie is written by a lyricist coordinating with the movie director and the music director. The movie director usually describes the situation and the emotion where the song is supposed to fit in. Depending on the given situation by the movie director, the lyricist writes the song lyrics, and the music director composes the music for the

[1] https://thirukkural133.wordpress.com/contents/



*Proceedings of the First Workshop on Speech and Language Technologies for Dravidian Languages*, pages 1–9
April 20, 2021 ©2021 Association for Computational Linguistics

song. Though the lyrics of a Tamil movie song can stand alone, they are usually an integral part of the movie enhancing an emotion.

In this paper, we introduce a new Tamil lyrics corpus[2]. Specifically, we focus only on Tamil movie lyrics and not Tamil lyrics by independent lyricists. The main contributions of this paper are (a) a corpus including Tamil song lyrics, lyricists, and other details; (b) a detailed corpus analysis focusing on Tamil lyrics; (c) experimental results to identify the lyricist of a given song lyric; and (d) future research directions about how to utilize the Tamil lyrics dataset.

## 2 Background

Songs are an integral part of Tamil movies. They represent, enhance, and complement an emotion in the movie. We explain the role of these songs and exemplify with some recent Tamil movie songs.

One of the most common emotion expressed in Tamil songs is romance. This includes *falling in love, breakup, marriage*, etc. For example, the song *Nenjukul peidhidum*[3] from the movie *Vaaranam Aayiram* describes a situation when a man meets a woman for the first time. This song emphasizes the emotion of *love at first sight*. The visualization and the lyrics are dramatic, and do not depict the actual story of the movie. While the flow of the movie is not affected by the song, it plays a vital role in emphasizing a man's emotion towards a woman the first time he sees her.

Some Tamil movie songs are created to complement the scenes in the movie. The movie would not be complete without the song. These songs include sequential scenes from the movie. For instance, the song *Kadhaipoma*[4] from the movie *Oh my kadavulae* describes the emotion of *taking someone for granted* while aptly fitting in the movie scenes.

There are several Tamil movie songs written with political and social intentions. Tamil actors with political ideologies often hint their political intentions in their songs. Recently, there are several songs released emphasizing on social equity. The song *Aalaporan Thamizhan*[5] from the movie *Mersal* describes the beauty of the language Tamil and glorifies Tamilians life styles.

Recently with the advent of youtube, there are several songs that get popular even before the movie release. While releasing songs before releasing a movie has been a practice in the Tamil movie industry for a while, youtube has taken these songs sooner to the audience than ever before. Until recently, all movie songs were released together in a Compact Disk, cassette tape or an online streaming site. However, in the past few years Tamil movies have started releasing singles from movies. These songs typically include a catchy lyric, music or dance moves. They act as a promotion for the movie and usually have millions of views before the movie release. Kutty story[6] from the movie *Master* and *Bujji*[7] from the movie *Jagamae thanthiram* fall under this category. Interestingly, the song *Kutty story* has large amount of English songs, which is a phenomena observed in many recent Tamil songs.

We present youtube links in the footnote to each song exemplified in this section. The English translation of the song lyrics can be viewed by turning on the subtitles in the youtube video.

**How are Tamil song lyrics written?** In most cases, the movie director comes up with a situation in the movie.. The music director composes a tune capturing the emotion of this situation. The lyricist writes the lyrics, given the tune. However, there are few music directors who compose tune to a given lyric.

## 3 Related work

There exists a Tamil lyrics dataset (Subramanian, 2020) in Kaggle for Tamil lyrics. The dataset includes the lyrics of Tamil songs, alongside song name and movie name. However, we could not track any further experiments or research related to this dataset. It does not include the name of the lyricist or other details. Unlike this dataset, our corpus includes the name of the lyricist, the name of the music director, and the year the song was released. We also include the English translit-

[2]https://github.com/praveenraj0904/tamillyricscorpus
[3]Nenjukul peithidum
[4]Kadhaipoma
[5]Aalaporan Thamizhan
[6]Kutty Story
[7]Bujji

erated song lyrics. We believe these information would be useful to researchers.

There are some prominent Tamil NLP works associated with Tamil lyrics. Sundara Kanchana and Ganapathy (2017) work with 1, 000 Tamil songs to identify three aspects for a given Tamil song lyric. The three aspects are base, mood, and style. The base aspect includes the types *character, festival, nature, relationship, romance, occasion, spiritual, patriotic and misc.* The emotion aspect includes the types *happy, sad, excited, tender, scared and angry.* The styles aspect includes *traditional, folk, contemporary and mixed.* Their work is word based, and they use TF-IDF as a feature in their classifier to predict these aspects.

Ramakrishnan A et al. (2009) work on automatically generating Tamil lyrics for melodies. They approach the problem as a sequence labeling problem targeting to guess the syllabic pattern. Then they forward this pattern to a sentence generation module, where they use Dijkstra's algorithm to choose a meaningful phrase. In their latter work Ramakrishnan A and Lalitha Devi (2010), follow a mapping scheme for matching melody with words. They also use a knowledge-based text generation algorithm on an existing Ontology and Tamil Morphology Generator.

E. et al. (2011) design a pleasantness scoring model based not only based on phonetic aspects. Ranganathan et al. (2011) present analysis over a given set of lyrics. In their later work, they (Ranganathan et al., 2013) present a visualization tool for lyrics based on the characteristics of the lyrics.

Sridhar et al. (2013) have extensively worked in automatic Tamil lyrics generation. In their first work, (Sridhar et al., 2013) they follow a trigram approach using the emotion of a given scene. The use this emotion as a seed word and follow Tamil grammatical rules to generate lyrics. In their next work, Sridhar et al. (2014) they follow a similar approach getting 77% accuracy. Following that, they (Sridhar et al., 2015) intend to generate Tamil lyrics given a sequence of images and a derived tune. They generate a tune automatically based on carnatic music. Their system generates two sets of Tamil lyrics based on (i) context text and tune; and (ii) context text and images. In their next work (Sridhar et al., 2016) they follow a neuro-linguistic approach for lyric generation intending to add dialect, image, and author specific features. In their recent work (Sridhar et al., 2018) they generate lyrics, combining their two previous works. They make use of visual images, derived tune, and other specification such as the dialect of the speaker.

| Statistics | |
|---|---|
| Songs | 5,449 |
| Lyricists | 324 |
| Music directors | 151 |
| Movies | 1,147 |
| Words | 1,309,425 |
| Unique words | 129,614 |
| Years range | 1954-2019 |
| Maximum words/song | 653 |
| Minimum words/song | 17 |
| Average words/song | 188 |

Table 1: Statistics of the Tamil lyrics dataset

Unlike the works described, our work tries to capture the characteristics of the lyric and the lyricist. In an analysis perspective, our work is analogous to (Ranganathan et al., 2011). We go beyond, and present analysis with respect to the year the lyrics were written, and similarity between pairs of lyricists.

## 4 Corpus creation

We create a corpus of Tamil lyrics from www.allnewlyrics.com. The corpus consists of 5,449 Tamil songs lyrics and their English transliteration. Apart from the lyrics of a song, the corpus includes the name of the lyricist, music director, movie, and the year the song was released. We also present a link to the web page where the data was extracted. The statistics of the corpus are presented in Table 1. The corpus includes songs written by 324 lyricists across 1,147 movies for which the music was composed by 151 music directors.

From a linguistics perspective, lyrics are the most interesting. The lyrics of a song reflects the (i) situation in the movie, (ii) writing style of the lyricist, (iii) language style during which the lyrics were released, and (iv) the emotion of the song. On an average each song includes 188 words ranging from minimum 17 words to

| | Lyricist | Music director | Movie | Year |
|---|---|---|---|---|
| | Vaali | M.S. Vishwanathan | Kasethan Kadavulada | 1972 |
| Tamil | மெல்ல பேசுங்கள் பிறர் கேட்க கூடாது சொல்லித் தாருங்கள் யாரும் பார்க்க கூடாது [...] | | | |
| English | Mella pesungal pirar ketkka koodadhu solli thaarungal yaarum paarkka koodadhu [...] | | | |

| | Lyricist | Music director | Movie | Year |
|---|---|---|---|---|
| | Vairamuthu | A. R. Rahman | Love Birds | 1996 |
| Tamil | மலர்களே மலர்களே இது என்ன கனவா மலைகளே மலைகளே இது என்ன நினைவா [...] | | | |
| English | Malargalae malargalae idhu enna kanavaa malaigalae malaigalae idhu enna ninaivaa aa... [...] | | | |

| | Lyricist | Music director | Movie | Year |
|---|---|---|---|---|
| | Na. Muthu Kumar | Yuvan Shankar Raja | Kaadhal kondein | 2003 |
| Tamil | நெஞ்சோடு கலந்திடு உறவாலே காலங்கள் மறந்திடு அன்பே நிலவோடு தென்றலும் வரும் வேளை காயங்கள் மறந்திடு அன்பே [...] | | | |
| English | Nenjodu kalanthidu uravaalae kaalangal maranthidu anbae nilavodu thendralum varum velai kaayangal maranthidu anbae [...] | | | |

| | Lyricist | Music director | Movie | Year |
|---|---|---|---|---|
| | Gangai Amaran | Ilayaraja | Paneer Pushpangal | 1981 |
| Tamil | கோடைக்கால காற்றே குளிர்த்தென்றல் பாடும் பாட்டே மனம் தேடும் சுவையோடு தினம்தோறும் இசைபாடு [...] | | | |
| English | Kodai kaala kaatrae kulir thendral paadum paattae manam thedum suvaiyodu dhinandhorum isai paadu [...] | | | |

| | Lyricist | Music director | Movie | Year |
|---|---|---|---|---|
| | Thamarai | Darbuka Siva | Enai Noki Paayum Thota | 2019 |
| Tamil | எதுவரை போகலாம் என்று நீ சொல்லவேண்டும் என்றுதான் விடாமல் கேட்கிறேன் [...] | | | |
| English | Ethuvarai pogalaam endru nee sollavendum endruthaan... vidamal ketkiren... [...] | | | |

Table 2: Examples from the Tamil lyrics corpus. Each instance includes the name of the lyricist, music director, movie, and the year the movie was released. Additionally, the Tamil lyrics and the equivalent English transliterated lyrics is also available.

maximum 653 words. The total number of Tamil words for all songs combined in the corpus is more than a million. The total number of unique Tamil words in the corpus is close to 130, 000. Table 2 presents examples from the corpus.

## 5 Corpus Analysis

We present detailed corpus analysis focusing on the Tamil lyrics our corpus. All statistics presented in this paper represent the distribution of the data in our corpus and may not reflect the contribution of a lyricist to the Tamil movie or music industry[8].

Figure 1 depicts the number of songs written by a lyricist across different years. Evidently, Vaali has written songs across a wide range of years starting from the mod 1960s to the late 2010s. Vairamuthu has reached the peak of his lyric writing in the early 2000s. Interest-

[8]All statistics correspond to the corpus, and may not reflect the contribution of a lyricist in real time.

| Lyricist | No. songs | Top 10 words |
|---|---|---|
| All (with stopwords) | 5449 | நீ, என், நான், உன், ஒரு, என்ன, காதல், வா, தான், என்னை |
| All (No stopwords) | 5449 | தா, போது, மேலே, பார்த்து, பொண்ணு, இவன், உலகம், தேன், கண்ணே, சுகம் |
| Vaali | 873 | தா, வந்தது, நாளும், தேன், மாமா, தொட்டு, மெல்ல, பிள்ளை, வாழும், அவன் |
| Kannadasan | 797 | கண்டேன், உள்ளம், கொண்ட, வந்தது, அவள், ஆட, கண்ணா, பிள்ளை, கண்டு, ஒரே |
| Vairamuthu | 390 | நோ, முத்தம், கண்ணே, கண்டு, ஆண், உலகம், கிளி, பூமி, சிரி, சத்தம் |
| Na. Muthu Kumar | 340 | இதயம், உயிரே, இவன், உலகம், ராஜா, அவள், பறக்குது, எங்கும், வேணும், முன்னே |
| Gangai Amaran | 279 | மாமா, ஊரு, பொண்ணு, கேட்டு, குயிலே, கேளு, கதை, ஒண்ணு, ராகம், ராசா |
| Pa.Vijay | 263 | பேபி, முதல், நோ, போடு, வாவ், சும்மா, தானா, தில், முனி, தீண்ட |
| Yugabharathi | 179 | ஜிக்கி, அழகு, புள்ள, அவ, போ, பேச, கண்ணு, ஆச, வாழ, அப்பா |
| Madhan Karky | 163 | வெறி, மை, ராஜா, ராஜ, அவள், சச்சின், மேலே, தல, ஏத்திக்க, நாம் |
| Thamarai | 107 | ஏனோ, யாரோ, அவள், முதல், நிலா, என, எனை, மேகம், மேலே, தாண்டி |
| Viveka | 105 | ரக்கரா, கபடி, சிக்கு, டக்குனக்கா, மட்டக்கு, கோ, கைய, ஒய்ய, மியாவ், சக்கான் |

Table 3: Number of songs written by a lyricist and the most frequent 10 words by them are presented. The most frequent 10 words are obtained after removing the stop words. The most frequent 100 words from the entire corpus are treated as stop words.

ingly, Na. Muthukumar has written the most number of songs in the shortest span of years.

We treat each word in the corpus as the simplest unit for our analysis. That is, we do not conduct analysis based on lemmas or stems of words. The top 10 lyricists with the highest number of songs and their most frequent 10 words are presented in Table 3. Vaali ranks first with 873 songs followed by Kannadasan (797 songs), and Vairamuthu (390 songs).

We noticed that the top 10 most frequent words across the entire corpus (Table:3, $1^{st}$ row), and the top 10 most frequent words per lyricist were all pronouns or interrogative words. Our further investigation revealed that the top 100 words mostly included pronouns, interrogative words, prepositions, and conjunctions which are considered as stop words in English. Thus we decided to treat the top 100 most frequent words as stop words. We acknowledge that this process is not perfect, as there are a few non stop words in the top 100 words, and few stop words after the most frequent 100 words. The top 10 most frequent words per lyricist (Table 3) are extracted after removing the stop words. Interestingly, the word காதல் (love) always is present in the top 10 words despite not being a traditional stop word. We attribute this to the nature of Tamil movie songs which usually circles around the emotion, romance or love (காதல்).

Table 4 presents the number of songs per decade and the top 10 most frequent words per decade. For example, there are 312 songs included in the corpus belonging to the decade (1970), that is from the year 1961 to 1970. The top 10 words for the decade 1970 are also given. The top 10 most frequent words are extracted after removing the stop words.

In Table 5, we present similarity scores between pairs of lyrics among the top 5 artists. The Jaccard similarity computes similarity between two sets by calculating the intersection over union. First, we combine all songs by

| Year | No. songs | Top 10 words |
|---|---|---|
| 1960 | 71 | கண்டேன், கனவு, எங்கள், சிவகங்கை, சீமை, சொந்தம், வாழும், அப்பா, மொழி, சுகம் |
| 1970 | 312 | உள்ளம், அவள், கொண்ட, பார்த்து, நிலா, ஆட, அவன், பார், கண்டு, கண்டேன் |
| 1980 | 296 | சுகம், பிள்ளை, வந்தது, ஆடும், இரு, கண்ணன், உள்ளம், மெல்ல, ராகம், பா |
| 1990 | 820 | ராகம், கதை, மானே, மாமா, தேன், தேகம், நாளும், பாட, வந்தது, சுகம் |
| 2000 | 1071 | நோ, பூவே, தா, பொண்ணு, நிலா, கிளி, கண்ணே, தேன், மாமா, ஒன்னு |
| 2010 | 1087 | முதல், வாவ், போடு, ஏதோ, தொட்டு, இதயம், போது, பார்த்து, மேலே, மெல்ல |
| 2020 | 1593 | இவன், போ, நாங்க, இதயம், அவ, வாடி, ராஜா, அவன், நாம், போக |

Table 4: Number of songs written in a decade and the most frequent 10 words per decade is given. The most frequent 10 words are obtained after removing the stop words. The most frequent 100 words from the entire corpus are treated as stop words.

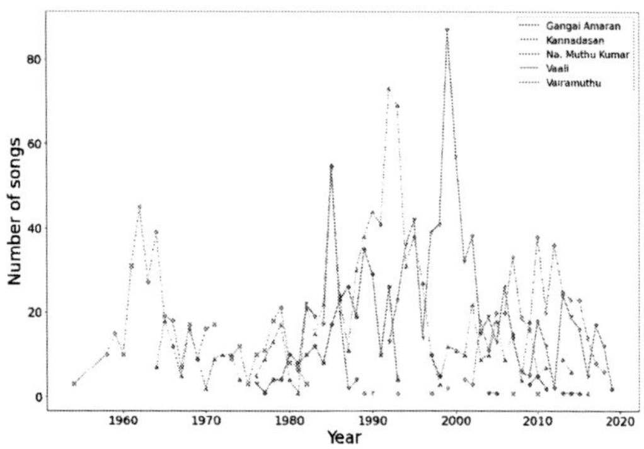


Figure 1: The number of songs written by a lyricist across 65 years (1954 to 2019) is presented. Vaali has written Tamil song lyrics covering the widest range of years. Na. Muthukumar has written the most number of songs in the shortest span of years.

each lyricist into a large text. Thus we obtain five large texts for the top 5 lyricists. We remove duplicate words from each text to create a set for each lyricist. We calculate the Jaccard similarity over these sets to measure their similarity. Results show that there is higher overlap between the words used by Vaali and Vairamuthu (Jacc. sim.: 0.94), and Vairamuthu and Na. Muthu Kumar (Jacc. sim.: 0.9)

We also present the cosine similarity between the TF-IDF representations of the lyrics by the top 5 lyricists. We process the lyrics similar to the processing for calculating Jaccard similarity, but do not form a unique set of words for each lyricist. First, we combine all songs by each lyricist into a large text. Next,

| | | Jacc. sim. | TFIDF cos sim |
|---|---|---|---|
| Vaali | Kannadasan | 0.76 | 0.956 |
| | Vairamuthu | 0.94 | 0.972 |
| | Na. Muthu Kumar | 0.89 | 0.956 |
| | Gangai Amaran | 0.76 | 0.969 |
| Kannadasan | Vairamuthu | 0.71 | 0.948 |
| | Na. Muthu Kumar | 0.77 | 0.910 |
| | Gangai Amaran | 0.85 | 0.922 |
| Vairamuthu | Na. Muthu Kumar | 0.9 | 0.964 |
| | Gangai Amaran | 0.74 | 0.939 |
| Na. Muthu Kumar | Gangai Amaran | 0.81 | 0.924 |

Table 5: Words based similarity between pairs of the top 5 lyricists from the corpus. Both Jaccard similarity and cosine similarity on the TF-IDF vectors indicate that the lyrics of Vaali and Vairamuthu are the most similar.

we represent these texts using their TF-IDF vector. We calculate the cosine similarity between these vectors to measure their similarity. Based on this TF-IDF cosine similarity measure, the lyrics Vaali and Vairamuthu (TF-IDF cos. sim: 0.972 ) are very similar which is observed in the Jaccard similarity score (Jacc. sim.: 0.94) as well. Similarly Vaali and Gangai Amaran (TFIDF cos. sim: 0.969 ), and

| | Multingual BERT uncased | | | Indic-NLP AI4Bharat | | | Tamillion BERT | | |
|---|---|---|---|---|---|---|---|---|---|
| | P | R | F1 | P | R | F1 | P | R | F1 |
| Vaali | 0.62 | 0.57 | 0.59 | 0.65 | 0.75 | 0.69 | 0.68 | 0.74 | 0.70 |
| Kannadasan | 0.56 | 0.62 | 0.59 | 0.67 | 0.55 | 0.60 | 0.68 | 0.61 | 0.64 |
| W.Avg | 0.59 | 0.59 | 0.59 | 0.66 | 0.66 | 0.65 | 0.68 | 0.68 | 0.68 |

Table 6: Results of binary classifiers to classify between Vaali and Kannadasan given a song Tamil lyric is presented. All models are fine tuned to obtain the results.

Vairamuthu and Na. Muthu Kumar (TFIDF cos. sim: 0.964 ). also have high TFIDF cosine similarity scores.

## 6 Experiments and Results

We conduct experiments to identify the lyricist of a given lyric. We formulate a binary classification problem by generating a dataset including only the top two lyricists with the most number of songs, Vaali and Kannadasan. This dataset consists of 1,670 instances from the Tamil lyrics corpus, where 873 instances correspond to Vaali and 797 instances correspond to Kannadasan. We used 80% of this dataset for training and withheld the remaining 20% for testing. We ensured the lyricists distribution is stratified across the train and test sets.

### 6.1 Experiments

In an era where BERT (Devlin et al., 2019) models are used as a baseline, we present results using three BERT models supporting Tamil. We conducted all our experiments using the simpletransformers (Rajapakse, 2019) python package. First, we fine tuned the multilingual uncased BERT (Reimers and Gurevych, 2020) model. We obtained the best results at a learning rate of $1e^{-5}$ with 3 epochs. Next, we fine tuned with the indic-bert model from AI4Bharat (Kunchukuttan et al., 2020). Here we obtained the best results at a learning rate of $1e^{-5}$ with 2 epochs. Finally, we fine tuned the Tamillion BERT (Doiron, 2020) model. We reached the best results in this model at learning rate of $1e^{-5}$ with 7 epochs.

### 6.2 Results

We present results in Table 6. The results obtained using multilingual BERT is lower than Indic-NLP and Tamillion BERT (F1: .59 vs. .65 vs. .68). The results obtained using Indic-NLP and Tamillion BERT are comparable (F1: .65 vs. .68).

Regarding the results for *Vaali*, Tamillion BERT obtains the highest precision (.68), and Indic-NLP obtains the highest recall (.75). Overall, the performance for *Vaali* is better when using the Tamillion BERT (F1: .70).

In case of the results for *Kannadasan*, the highest performance is obtained both for precision and recall by fine tuning the Tamillion BERT model (P: .68, R: .61). We note that there is still room for improvement in this binary lyricist identification task. The task becomes even more challenging when the number of lyricists are increased changing the binary classification task into a multi class classification task.

## 7 Future research

We use the Tamil lyrics corpus to identify lyricists formulating a binary classification task. The same corpus could be used for several other tasks. We discuss the previous works relating to Tamil lyrics in Section 3. In this section, we describe a few possible research that could conducted using the Tamil lyrics corpus.

### 7.1 Language trend analysis

Language trend analysis intends to capture the change in a language over years. As Tamil song lyrics are closely tied to the political and personal lives of Tamilians, we expect the change of language style in the lyrics to reflect the lives of Tamilians. We hypothesize that the songs released after the year 2000 would include more English words (code-switching) than the songs from the 1960s. For instance, the song *Why this kolaveri?* has more than 50% English words. Additionally, as Tamilians have moved across the world, Tamil songs have gained international attention, enabling changes in Tamil music.

We also hypothesize that the songs released after the year 2000 would include several meaningless words, whereas the songs released around the 1960s followed strict literary style. For example, phrases like jimjikka, rangu rakkara, tasaku tasaku, etc. have no meaning (also called *Rettai Kilavi* in Tamil grammar) are often used in Tamil songs, as they are fun and catchy.

### 7.2 Emotion detection

As Tamil song lyrics are usually written for an emotion in the movie, it is possible to use the Tamil lyrics dataset to identify the emotion in them. This task would require an additional layer of annotations for emotions. We also believe a distant supervision mechanism to annotate for the labels should be possible. The possible emotions would include, but not limit to *love, breakup, hero introduction, happy,* and *sorrow*. While the work by (Sundara Kanchana and Ganapathy, 2017) closely relates to the emotion detection space, we believe there is so much to be explored in this area.

### 7.3 Evaluating transliteration models

There are many works relating to English transliteration of Tamil (Chinnakotla and Damani, 2009; Vijayanand, 2009). As our corpus includes the English transliterated text of the Tamil lyrics, it could be used as a validation set to evaluate a transliteration model.

We hypothesize that Tamil lyrics are rich in linguistic phenomena such as cliches, metaphors, etc. A model identifying such phenomena in the Tamil corpus would be interesting.

## 8 Conclusion

In this paper, we introduce a new Tamil lyrics dataset. We collect Tamil movie lyrics along with the names of the lyricist, the movie, and the music director over a range of 65 years. We also present the English transliteration of the Tamil lyrics. We present an elaborate literature review on studies relating to Tamil lyrics. We conduct detailed corpus analysis revealing the top 10 frequent words per decade, and top 10 frequent words per lyricist. We also study the similarity of the lyrics between different lyricists using standard similarity approaches. Next, we formulate a binary classification task to identify the lyricist, given a song lyric. We fine tuned the state-of-the-art BERT models to predict the lyricists. Our experimental results show that identifying lyricists is a challenging task, and there is scope for improvement. We go beyond the experiments, and elaborate on the possible future research directions with the Tamil lyrics corpus. We intend to add more instances to our corpus to encourage research on Tamil lyrics.

## References


Shinu Anna Abraham. 2003. Chera, chola, pandya: Using archaeological evidence to identify the tamil kingdoms of early historic south india. In *Asian Perspectives*, volume 42, pages 207–223. University of Hawai'i Press.

Manoj Kumar Chinnakotla and Om P. Damani. 2009. Experiences with English-Hindi, English-Tamil and English-Kannada transliteration tasks at NEWS 2009. In *Proceedings of the 2009 Named Entities Workshop: Shared Task on Transliteration (NEWS 2009)*, pages 44–47, Suntec, Singapore. Association for Computational Linguistics.

Jacob Devlin, Ming-Wei Chang, Kenton Lee, and Kristina Toutanova. 2019. BERT: Pre-training of deep bidirectional transformers for language understanding. In *Proceedings of the 2019 Conference of the North American Chapter of the Association for Computational Linguistics: Human Language Technologies, Volume 1 (Long and Short Papers)*, pages 4171–4186, Minneapolis, Minnesota. Association for Computational Linguistics.

Nick Doiron. 2020. Tamillion bert. `https://huggingface.co/monsoon-nlp/tamillion`.

Giruba Beulah S. E., Madhan Karky V., Karthika Ranganathan, and Suriyah M. 2011. Pleasantness scoring models for tamil lyrics. In *Proceedings of the 5th Indian International Conference on Artificial Intelligence, IICAI 2011, Tumkur, Karnataka State, India, December 14-16, 2011*, pages 1561–1571. IICAI.

Nithin Kalorth. 2021. Identities and ideologies in tamil cinema understanding within the framwork of socio political movements in tamil nadu. In *Into the Nuances of Cultural - Essays on Cultural Studies*, pages 95–103. Yking books.

Trichy V. Krishnan and A.M. Sakkthivel. 2010. To push for stardom or not: A rookie's dilemma in the tamil movie industry. *IIMB Management Review*, 22(3):80–92.

Anoop Kunchukuttan, Divyanshu Kakwani, Satish Golla, Gokul N.C., Avik Bhattacharyya, Mitesh M. Khapra, and Pratyush Kumar. 2020. Ai4bharat-indicnlp corpus: Monolingual corpora and word embeddings for indic languages. *arXiv preprint arXiv:2005.00085*.

T. C. Rajapakse. 2019. Simple transformers. `https://github.com/ThilinaRajapakse/simpletransformers`.

Ananth Ramakrishnan A, Sankar Kuppan, and Sobha Lalitha Devi. 2009. Automatic generation of tamil lyrics for melodies. In *Proceedings of the NAACL HLT Workshop on Computational Approaches to Linguistic Creativity*, pages 40–46, Boulder, Colorado. Association for Computational Linguistics.

Ananth Ramakrishnan A and Sobha Lalitha Devi. 2010. An alternate approach towards meaningful lyric generation in Tamil. In *Proceedings of the NAACL HLT 2010 Second Workshop on Computational Approaches to Linguistic Creativity*, pages 31–39, Los Angeles, California. Association for Computational Linguistics.

K. Ranganathan, T. V. Geetha, R. Parthasarathi, and Madhan Karky. 2011. Lyric mining : Word , rhyme & concept co-occurrence analysis.

Karthika Ranganathan, B. Barani, and T. V. Geetha. 2013. A tamil lyrics search and visualization system. volume 8281, pages 513–527. Lecture Notes in Computer Science.

Nils Reimers and Iryna Gurevych. 2020. Making monolingual sentence embeddings multilingual using knowledge distillation. In *Proceedings of the 2020 Conference on Empirical Methods in Natural Language Processing*. Association for Computational Linguistics.

R. Sridhar, N. Dharmaraj, J. Damodaran, and S. Sampath. 2015. Automatic tamil lyric generation based on image sequence and derived tune. In *2015 IEEE International Advance Computing Conference (IACC)*, pages 861–866.

R. Sridhar, S. Venkatsubhramaniyen, and S. S. Rashmi. 2018. Automatic singable tamil lyric generation for a situation and tune based on causal effect. In *2018 International Conference on Advances in Computing, Communications and Informatics (ICACCI)*, pages 1152–1159.

Rajeswari Sridhar, S. R. Surya Dev, V. Sankar, and K. Sivakumar. 2016. Automatic tamil lyric generation based on neuro-linguistics. In *Proceedings of the International Conference on Informatics and Analytics*, ICIA-16, New York, NY, USA. Association for Computing Machinery.

Rajeswari Sridhar, G Jalin Gladis, K Ganga, and G Dhivya Prabha. 2013. N-gram based approach to automatic tamil lyric generation by identifying emotion. pages 919–926. Proceedings of International Conference on Advances in Computing.

Rajeswari Sridhar, G Jalin Gladis, K Ganga, and G Dhivya Prabha. 2014. Automatic tamil lyric generation based on ontological interpretation for semantics. pages 97–121. Academy Proceedings in Engineering Sciences.

Siva Subramanian. 2020. Tamil songs lyrics dataset. Data retrieved from Kaggle `http://www.kaggle.com/sivaskvs/tamil-songs-lyrics-dataset`.

Meenakshi K Sundara Kanchana and Velappa Ganapathy. 2017. Comparison of genre based tamil songs classification using term frequency and inverse document frequency. *Research Journal of Pharmacy and Technology*, 5:80–92.

Kommaluri Vijayanand. 2009. Testing and performance evaluation of machine transliteration system for Tamil language. In *Proceedings of the 2009 Named Entities Workshop: Shared Task on Transliteration (NEWS 2009)*, pages 48–51, Suntec, Singapore. Association for Computational Linguistics.

# DOSA: Dravidian Code-Mixed Offensive Span Identification Dataset

**Manikandan Ravikiran***
OMSCS Program
Bangalore, Karnataka, India
mravikiran3@gatech.edu

**Subbiah Annamalai***
OMSCS Program
Columbus, Ohio, USA
sannamali@gatech.edu

## Abstract

This paper presents the Dravidian Offensive Span Identification Dataset (DOSA) for under-resourced Tamil-English and Kannada-English code-mixed text. The dataset addresses the lack of code-mixed datasets with annotated offensive spans by extending annotations of existing code-mixed offensive language identification datasets. It provides span annotations for Tamil-English and Kannada-English code-mixed comments posted by users on YouTube social media. Overall the dataset consists of 4786 Tamil-English comments with 6202 annotated spans and 1097 Kannada-English comments with 1641 annotated spans, each annotated by two different annotators. We further present some of our baseline experimental results on the developed dataset, thereby eliciting research in under-resourced languages, leading to an essential step towards semi-automated content moderation in Dravidian languages. The dataset is available in https://github.com/manikandan-ravikiran/DOSA.

## 1 Introduction

Fighting offensive content is imperative for social media companies and other entities involved in content moderation. Currently, much of moderation is relatively limited on most community platforms (Jhaver et al., 2019) with most of them relying on detection of repeatedly used words[1] and block-lists (Jhaver et al., 2018). Additionally, most social media companies employ human content moderators, who are frequently swamped by offensive mentions and their volume (Arsht and Etcovitch, 2018). On the other hand, precise moderation leads to content delay leading to user attrition. Furthermore, smaller entities cannot utilize human moderators on a large scale due to their sheer cost. As a result, they shut down their comments sections entirely. Although content moderation to some degree has utilized semi-automated approaches (Jhaver et al., 2019), most of them are not yet available for Non-English languages and code-mixed texts.

Code-switching or code-mixing is a mixing of linguistic units from two or more languages in a single conversation or sometimes even a single utterance and is widely used across the world (Sitaram et al., 2019). In India, due to widely employed educational and cultural guidelines, English largely influences all the Indian spoken languages, including Dravidian languages like Kannada and Tamil (Chakravarthi et al., 2020). However, with the advent of social media, code-switching has permeated to mediums with informal contexts like forums and messaging platforms. As a result, code-switching is part and parcel of offensive conversations in social media.

Despite many recent NLP advancements, handling code-mixed offensive content is still a challenge in Dravidian Languages (Sitaram et al., 2019). The primary reason is data scarcity, as it appears relatively less in standard textual resources and instead spread across the World Wide Web. However, recently the research of offensive code-mixed texts in Dravidian languages has seen traction (Chakravarthi et al., 2020; Hande et al., 2020). However, these are restricted to the whole comment's classification for offensiveness and do not identify the spans that make a text offensive. But emphasizing such offensive spans can assist human moderators who often deal with lengthy comments and prefer attribution instead of just a system-generated unexplained score per post. Accordingly, the contributions of this paper are as follows

- We first present DOSA, a code-mixed Tamil-English, and Kannada-English dataset annotated for offensive spans. We describe our

*Equal Contribution
[1]https://www.reddit.com/wiki/automoderator



*Proceedings of the First Workshop on Speech and Language Technologies for Dravidian Languages*, pages 10–17
April 20, 2021 ©2021 Association for Computational Linguistics

annotation scheme in the due process and examine the dataset properties, and brief about annotator-related information[2].

- We also provide an experimental baseline over state-of-the-art multilingual language models of BERT (Devlin et al., 2019), DistillBERT (Sanh et al., 2019), and XLM-RoBERTA (Conneau et al., 2020) on the developed offensive span identification dataset.

The rest of the paper is organized as follows. In section 2, we discuss literature on offensive language and span identification. Following this in section 3, we present the dataset collection and annotation process. Section 4 offers the experimental setting used for the baseline creation. In section 5, we discuss our results and errors so identified. Finally, in section 6, we conclude with a summary and possible directions for future work.

## 2 Related Work

### 2.1 Offensive language & Span Identification:

Offensive language identification (OLID) problem is widely investigated in the literature via multiple facets of works ranging from hierarchical OLID annotation scheme (Zampieri et al., 2019a,b), release of large-scale semi-supervised training dataset with over nine million English tweets (Rosenthal et al., 2020), extension of OLID to languages of Arabic (Mubarak et al., 2020), Danish (Sigurbergsson and Derczynski, 2020), Greek (Pitenis et al., 2020), and Turkish (Çöltekin, 2020) and development of multiple systems (Zampieri et al., 2020; Ravikiran et al., 2020). In parallel, there are more course-grained works on Hate Speech Identification (Kumar et al., 2018), Aggressiveness Detection (Aroyehun and Gelbukh, 2018), Bullying Detection (Xu et al., 2012) etc. In this work, we restrict ourselves to offensive comments only[3]. Unlike OLID, span identification is still in the nascent stage. To the best of our knowledge work by Pavlopoulos et al. 2021 which introduces a toxic span dataset and shared task with 10k comments is the only work in this line. Our work extends span identification to Youtube comments in code-mixed Dravidian languages.

### 2.2 Code-Mixing in Offensive Language and Span Identification:

Offensive language identification with code mixed texts have seen most works in Hindi-English (Srivastava et al., 2020; Bohra et al., 2018; Santosh and Aravind, 2019; Rajput et al., 2020; Chopra et al., 2020). Recently there are works in Bangla (Jahan et al., 2019), Kannada (Hande et al., 2020) and Tamil (Chakravarthi et al., 2020). To the best of our knowledge, there are no works on span identification with Dravidian code-mixed datasets. Our work addresses this gap, by emphasizing the creation of code-mixed offensive span identification inline with Pavlopoulos et al. 2021.

## 3 Dataset Collection and Annotation

In this work, we reuse TamilMixSentiment (Chakravarthi et al., 2020), and KanCMD (Hande et al., 2020) datasets consisting of 15k and 7k YouTube code-mixed comments respectively in Tamil-English and Kannada-English languages. Reusing the existing dataset is beneficial. It encourages the development of multitask models with span identification as one of the tasks, analysis of model interpretability during offensive language identification, and developing a unified benchmark dataset for multiple NLP tasks in code-mixed Dravidian languages.

In this work, we considered only a subset of the comments that were already annotated as offensive[4] for our span annotation process. Out of this subset, we rechecked and removed non-code mixed comments resulting in 9049 and 1311 comments in Tamil-English and Kannada-English, respectively. For the final annotation process, we considered all of the code-mixed Kannada-English comments and 5000 Tamil-English comments.

### 3.1 Annotation Setup

For annotation, we follow earlier works on span identification (Pavlopoulos et al., 2021) where two annotators annotated every comment according to the guidelines from section 3.2.

[2]**Disclaimer**: This paper contains examples that may be considered profane, vulgar, or offensive. These contents do not reflect the authors' views or the graduate schools/employed organization with which they are associated and exclusively serve to explain linguistic research challenges.

[3]The relationship between offensiveness, Hate-speech, agreesiveness etc. is presented in `https://link.springer.com/article/10.1007/s10579-020-09502-8`

[4]Released as part of `https://competitions.codalab.org/competitions/27654`

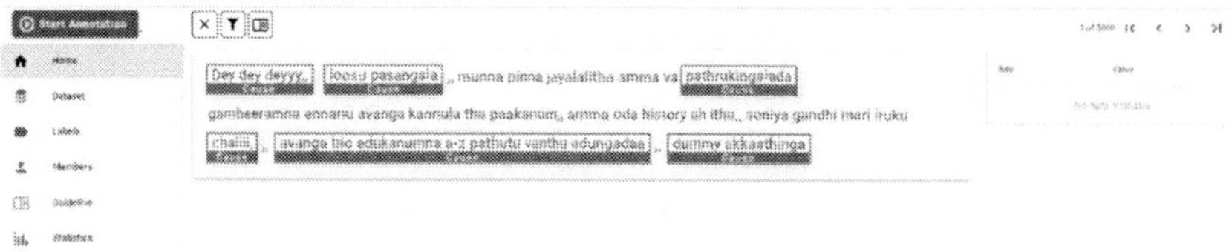


Figure 1: Annotation of offensive spans using Doccano.

Since the original comments are from the public domain, we anonymized all the personal information and user-related tags to protect actual users' privacy during our annotation process. Besides, no personal information of annotators was collected except their educational background and expertise in the language they volunteered to annotate.

Moreover, all the annotators were informed that the contents to be annotated are profane, vulgar, or offensive and can withdraw from the annotation process if necessary. For annotation, we use doccano (Nakayama et al., 2018) which was locally hosted by each individual annotator, and the annotations were finally merged separately once all annotations were obtained. Within doccano, all the annotators were explicitly asked to create a single label called **CAUSE** with label id of 1, thus maintaining consistency of annotation labels. (See Figure 1)

### 3.2 Annotation Guidelines

The annotators have explained the meaning of offensiveness with illustrative examples. Annotators who agreed that they understood this were given the following instructions:

- Extract the offensive word sequences (spans) of the comment by highlighting each such span and labeling them as **CAUSE** as shown in Figure 1.
- If the comment is not offensive or if the offensiveness is context-dependent, do not highlight any span.
- If the whole comment should be annotated, then annotate the whole comment and convey the annotation verifier about the same after completion.

### 3.3 Annotators

To start with, we selected a total of 15 annotators, all of whom had minimal education of Bachelors Degree with either medium of schooling to be one of the English, Tamil, and Kannada languages or proficient in both speaking and writing of one or both the Dravidian languages. Further, the annotation was done iteratively in a cycle of 500 sentences where each of the annotators was asked to report back to verify the quality of annotations and receive their next batch of 500 sentences. Each batch was manually verified by an annotation verifier, which allowed us to control the quality of annotations. This, in turn, permitted us to remove annotators who did not annotate well or had a significant delay in annotations. At the end of this process, we had six annotators, out of which all of the annotators were native speakers or writers of either Kannada or Tamil or both. Also, two of the annotators acted as annotation verifiers. Table 1 shows details of the annotators with educational qualification, gender diversity, Medium of instruction in schooling, miscellaneous qualities, including knowledge of multiple accents of Kannada/Tamil. Each YouTube comment was initially sent to two annotators for span annotation without revealing that the comment was offensive. If there was a disagreement in annotation, then the comment was sent to the third annotator. If all the three disagreed, then we skipped the annotation of that particular comment. Overall this leads to the annotation of each comment by two annotators.

| Annotator Identity | Educational Background | Medium of Schooling | Bilingual | Accent Knowledge |
|---|---|---|---|---|
| 1 | Masters ♂ ✡ | English | ✗ | ✗ |
| 2 | Masters ♂ ✡ | English | ✓ | ✗ |
| 3 | Master (Tamil) ♀ | Tamil | ✗ | ✓ |
| 4 | Bachelors ♀ | Kannada | ✓ | ✗ |
| 5 | Masters (Kannada) ♂ | Kannada | ✓ | ✓ |
| 6 | Masters ♂ | English | ✗ | ✗ |

Table 1: Annotators and their characteristics. ✡ indicates annotation verifiers.

### 3.4 Ground Truth Creation

For ground truth creation, we follow a strategy in line with works of Pavlopoulos et al. 2021 where for each comment, we obtain character offset of the identified span using doccano. We then retained only the overlapping annotations, i.e., both annotators must have included each character offset in their spans for the offset to be included in the ground truth. The annotation verifiers resolved any discrepancy in considering the non-overlapping part of the annotations.

### 3.5 Corpus Statistics

| Language-Pair | Tamil-English | Kannada-English |
|---|---|---|
| Number of Sentences | 4786 | 1097 |
| Number of unique tokens | 22096 | 7781 |
| Number of annotated spans | 6202 | 1641 |
| Average size of spans (# of characaters) | 21 | 20 |
| Min size of spans (# of characaters) | 4 | 2 |
| Max size of spans (# of characaters) | 82 | 160 |
| Number of unique tokens in spans | 10737 | 3742 |

Table 2: DOSA corpus statistics

Corpus statistics is given in the Table 2. Compared to Tamil-English, we can see Kannada-English has a significantly lesser number of samples. This is because of the inherent nature of the KanCMD dataset (Hande et al., 2020) which consists of only 1472 comments annotated as offensive. While the dataset is minimal, we release this along with Tamil-English to empower more annotation and subsequently build better offensive span identification models for the Kannada-English language. Moreover, we can see that the maximum size of the annotation is 82 and 102, respectively, across the datasets, but it can be seen from Figure 2 and 3 that these have very few occurrences.

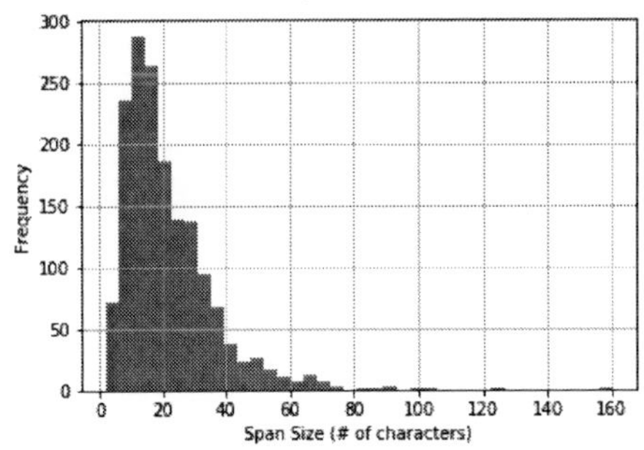


Figure 2: Histogram of annotated Span size in Kannada-English dataset.

### 3.6 Inter annotator Agreement

Since two annotators annotated each sentence, and the focus is only on the offensive contents, the annotation quality is validated using Cohens Kappa on annotated tokens only. In our case, we saw this value to be 0.6.

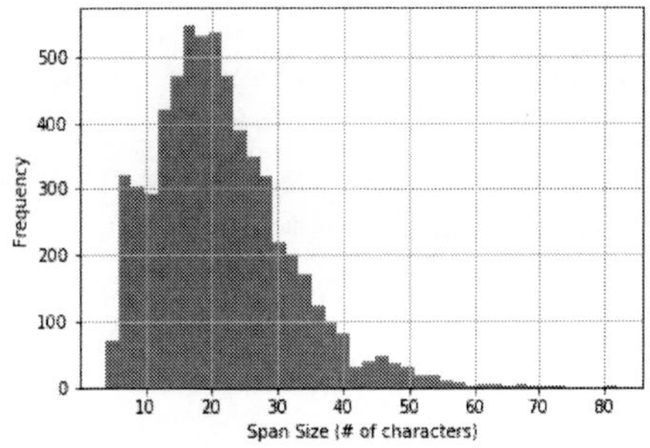


Figure 3: Histogram of annotated Span size in Tamil-English dataset.

## 4 Experimental Settings

To establish a baseline performance, we applied multiple state-of-the-art multilingual language models to determine the span of offensive comments. In this section, we present various models, hyperparameters, and other experimental settings used as part of the baseline estimation.

### 4.1 Models

Since the task focuses on identifying spans of offensive word sequences, we treat the problem of identification of span as the task of sequence labeling where we tag words that contribute to offensiveness. In this work, we use the following language models available through HuggingFace's Transformer Library (Wolf et al., 2019).

- **Mulitlingual BERT:** Multilingual BERT (M-BERT) is a language model pre-trained from monolingual corpora in 104 languages where task-specific annotations in one language are used to finetune the model for evaluation in another language. We use two variants of BERT, namely **BERT-M1**[5] which is trained on Wikipedia corpus and **BERT-M2**[6] which is original BERT finetuned first on XQUAD and Tydi QA dataset.
- **Mulitlingual DistilBERT:** We also use a smaller general-purpose language representation model, DistilBERT, which upon finetuning offers better performance on downstream tasks. Again we use two variants of DistilBERT namely DBERT-M1 [7] which is the original model developed as part of (Sanh et al.,

[5] bert-base-multilingual-uncased
[6] bert-multi-cased-finedtuned-xquad-tydiqa-goldp
[7] distilbert-base-multilingual-cased

2019) and **DBERT-M2** [8] which is similar to the earlier case of BERT where the model is again finetuned on XQUAD and Tydi QA dataset.

- **Mulitlingual XML-RoBERTA:** This is a masked language model trained on a multilingual language modeling objective using only monolingual data. Here again we use two variants namely **XBERT-M1**[9] and **XBERT-M2** [10] with former being the base model released as part of (Conneau et al., 2020) and later being a larger model which is finetuned on multiple NLI datasets.

### 4.2 Hyperparameters

For our experiments, we trained all of our models under a common setting. The various parameter setting is as shown in Table 3. Considering the effect of the presence of specific offensive terms and the size of the overall dataset, rather than creating a random train-test split in this work, we employed 3-fold cross-validation for all the experiments.

| Parameters | Values |
|---|---|
| Learning Rate | $4x10^{-5}$ |
| Maximum Sequence Length | 128 |
| Batch Size | 16 |
| Epochs | 100 |
| Weight Decay | 0.01 |
| Adam $\epsilon$ | $1x10^{-8}$ |

Table 3: Hyperparameters used across experiments.

## 5 Experiments, Results, and Discussion

The experimental results for various state-of-the-art multilingual language models are as shown in Tables 4-9. Since the focus of these experiments is to just establish baselines and provide some starting pointers for further exploration, we restrict ourselves from in-depth error analysis and instead focus on unique errors which we came across during the experiments. To start with, we compute results for each of the fold where we identify span/entity level Precision (P), Recall (R), and F1-Score (F1) inline with past works (Wang and Iwaihara, 2019; Yamada et al., 2020). Computing entity level P, R, and F1 measures consider only those word sequences which precisely match the annotation, thus eliminating partially identified offensive spans. This measure is also in line with Pavlopoulos et al. 2021.

[8]distilbert-multi-finetuned-for-xqua-on-tydiqa

[9]xlm-roberta-base

[10]xlm-roberta-large-xnli-anli

| Model | | Kannada-English | | | Tamil-English | | |
|---|---|---|---|---|---|---|---|
| | Fold # | P | R | F1 | P | R | F1 |
| BERT-M1 | 1 | 0.369 | 0.387 | 0.377 | 0.374 | 0.397 | 0.385 |
| | 2 | 0.381 | 0.432 | 0.406 | 0.309 | 0.356 | 0.331 |
| | 3 | 0.397 | 0.419 | 0.408 | 0.400 | 0.416 | 0.408 |
| | Average | **0.382** | **0.413** | **0.397** | **0.361** | **0.390** | **0.375** |

Table 4: Results of BERT-M1 for offensive span identification.

| Model | | Kannada-English | | | Tamil-English | | |
|---|---|---|---|---|---|---|---|
| | Fold # | P | R | F1 | P | R | F1 |
| BERT-M2 | 1 | 0.394 | 0.394 | 0.394 | 0.382 | 0.391 | 0.387 |
| | 2 | 0.397 | 0.441 | 0.418 | 0.349 | 0.397 | 0.372 |
| | 3 | 0.386 | 0.408 | 0.396 | 0.387 | 0.406 | 0.396 |
| | Average | **0.392** | **0.414** | **0.403** | **0.373** | **0.398** | **0.385** |

Table 5: Results of BERT-M2 for offensive span identification.

| Model | | Kannada-English | | | Tamil-English | | |
|---|---|---|---|---|---|---|---|
| | Fold # | P | R | F1 | P | R | F1 |
| DBERT-M1 | 1 | 0.380 | 0.412 | 0.395 | 0.408 | 0.420 | 0.414 |
| | 2 | 0.349 | 0.364 | 0.356 | 0.363 | 0.417 | 0.389 |
| | 3 | 0.413 | 0.417 | 0.415 | 0.393 | 0.436 | 0.414 |
| | Average | **0.381** | **0.398** | **0.389** | **0.388** | **0.425** | **0.405** |

Table 6: Results of DBERT-M1 for offensive span identification.

| Model | | Kannada-English | | | Tamil-English | | |
|---|---|---|---|---|---|---|---|
| | Fold # | P | R | F1 | P | R | F1 |
| DBERT-M2 | 1 | 0.372 | 0.391 | 0.381 | 0.378 | 0.387 | 0.382 |
| | 2 | 0.295 | 0.365 | 0.328 | 0.382 | 0.440 | 0.409 |
| | 3 | 0.370 | 0.378 | 0.374 | 0.396 | 0.434 | 0.414 |
| | Average | **0.346** | **0.378** | **0.361** | **0.385** | **0.420** | **0.402** |

Table 7: Results of DBERT-M2 for offensive span identification.

| Model | | Kannada-English | | | Tamil-English | | |
|---|---|---|---|---|---|---|---|
| | Fold # | P | R | F1 | P | R | F1 |
| XBERT-M1 | 1 | 0.405 | 0.432 | 0.418 | 0.379 | 0.395 | 0.387 |
| | 2 | 0.364 | 0.397 | 0.380 | 0.395 | 0.420 | 0.407 |
| | 3 | 0.407 | 0.415 | 0.411 | 0.374 | 0.391 | 0.382 |
| | Average | **0.392** | **0.415** | **0.403** | **0.383** | **0.402** | **0.392** |

Table 8: Results of XBERT-M1 for offensive span identification.

| Model | | Kannada-English | | | Tamil-English | | |
|---|---|---|---|---|---|---|---|
| | Fold # | P | R | F1 | P | R | F1 |
| XBERT-M2 | 1 | 0.365 | 0.381 | 0.372 | 0.249 | 0.308 | 0.275 |
| | 2 | 0.379 | 0.438 | 0.405 | 0.216 | 0.254 | 0.234 |
| | 3 | 0.336 | 0.408 | 0.369 | 0.263 | 0.317 | 0.289 |
| | Average | **0.360** | **0.409** | **0.382** | **0.243** | **0.293** | **0.266** |

Table 9: Results of XBERT-M2 for offensive span identification.

To start with, for both Tamil-English and Kannada-English code-mixed text, all the models perform poorly with the best average F1 of 0.403 for BERT-M2 and XBERT-M2, respectively for Kannada-English. Meanwhile, for Tamil-English comments, we found the maximum average F1 of 0.405 for DBERT-M1. Besides, across all the folds on each language model, the results are in similar ranges. Such poor performance can be attributed to two reasons: the training process and the complexity of the code-mixed text.

During our experiments, for Kannada-English, we found most models tend to overfit, and in some cases, the model training saturated at a training loss of 0.1. For the former case, we employed precision control of the learning rate to control overfitting; however, the net effect was relatively limited due to the small dataset size. However, the latter case tends to be more challenging to handle even after significant learning rate changes. Additionally, since the experiment was a baseline, we didn't perform any hyperparameter tuning for other parameters, leaving them for future work.

Furthermore, unlike Kannada-English experiments, we found overfitting for Tamil-English only in the case of XLM-RoBERTA models. Moreover, for both Kannada-English and Tamil-English, we found that comments with only one or more profane words causing offensiveness were correctly identified in their spans. However, for both Tamil-English and Kannada-English, we can see overall lower results for which one of the reasons we thought was the nature of code-mixed text themselves. To verify this, we cross-check the errors and found the following issues.

**Complete Sentence annotations** - For cases where the complete comment or more than 70% of the characters are accounted in offensive span, we found the errors to be highest where one or more words are not tagged as offensive, leading to a drop in span level F1. Example sentences with ground truth and predicted spans are as shown below.

**Ground Truth:** *Sir intha cinema madida mele dodda mattadalli prachara madbekittu. nNodi prem avru dabba film madudru hype build-up create madodralli etthida kai.*

**Prediction:** *Sir intha cinema madida mele dodda mattadalli prachara madbekittu. nNodi prem avru dabba film madudru hype build-up create madodralli etthida kai.*

***Translation:*** *Sir, after making this kind of movie, there was need of more publicity. Please see Mr. Prem, even after making useless movie still he is king in creating hype.*

**Word Pronunciation** - Another unique case of errors involves words that are the same except the texts are written differently. These are again not correctly identified as offensive. In the example below both Devidya and Thevidya translates to *whore*, which is often used as an abuse word.

**Example 1:** *...Dai unga ammayepdi da unna petha **Devidiya** intha comments ku.*

**Example 2:** *Otha **Thevidiya** Pasangala Neenga Nalla Padam Edukkanumnu Yenda...*

**Noisy texts** - Occasionally, we also found span errors where the sentence is full of hashtags that were annotated as offensive, but the model only identifies part of them. Examples are shown below.

**Example 1:** *#BoycottComali #BoycottComali #BoycottComali #BoycottComali #BoycottComali #BoycottComali #BoycottComali #BoycottComali #BoycottComali #BoycottComali ....*

**Example 2:** *Disaster.... disaster .... disaster.....Disaster.... disaster .... disaster.....Disaster.... disaster.*

**Sarcastic Sentences:** Sarcastic comments where the complete sentence is annotated for spans were also cases where the model fails to work. One such example is as shown with ground truth and prediction.

**Ground Truth:** *puratchi thalavi kamika sona tun tun aunty kamikerenga.*

**Prediction:** *puratchi thalavi kamika sona tun tun aunty kamikerenga*

**Translation**: Rather than showing purtachi thalavi (Honorable Nick Name given to former Tamil Nadu CM), why are you showing Tun Tun Aunty (A Cartoon character in Chota Bheem).

## 6 Conclusion

In this paper, we presented DOSA, a dataset for offensive span identification for Tamil-English and Kannada-English code mixed texts. We also achieved an inter-annotator agreement of 0.6 for the annotations. We also created baselines and reported P, R, and F1 for span identification using the developed dataset and state-of-the-art multilingual language models. In the due process, we presented some of the challenges in the training language model-based baselines, which is a possible future work. Moreover, in this work, we did not present results on simpler models like LSTM-CRF and its variants, which is also a possible exploration. Most importantly, we could see cases where the complete comment was annotated either due to their sarcastic nature or because they had only offensive terms. In this regard, a possible question to explore includes evaluating the need for such annotations by considering larger datasets and improving models' performance under such conditions. Additionally, we think this resource is useful for multitask learning and interpretability for code-mixed offensive language models.

## Acknowledgments

We thank our anonymous reviewers for their valuable feedback. Any opinions, findings, and conclusion or recommendations expressed in this material are those of the authors only and does not reflect the view of their employing organization or graduate schools. The work is the result of continuous study group discussions during and after the CS7646-ML4T course (OMSCS Program, Georgia Tech) done at MLSG - An online machine learning study group formed to discuss interesting papers and open research problems in areas of NLP focus on South Indian Languages. Further, MLSG is a random name generated for the representation purpose of our reading-discussion group. We would also like to thank all of our annotators for their effort in annotation and review.

## References

Segun Taofeek Aroyehun and Alexander F. Gelbukh. 2018. Aggression detection in social media: Using deep neural networks, data augmentation, and pseudo labeling. In *Proceedings of the First Workshop on Trolling, Aggression and Cyberbullying, TRAC@COLING 2018, Santa Fe, New Mexico, USA, August 25, 2018*, pages 90–97. Association for Computational Linguistics.

Andrew Arsht and Daniel Etcovitch. 2018. The human cost of online content moderation. *Harvard Journal of Law & Technology*.

Aditya Bohra, Deepanshu Vijay, Vinay Singh, Syed Sarfaraz Akhtar, and Manish Shrivastava. 2018. A dataset of hindi-english code-mixed social media text for hate speech detection. In *Proceedings of the Second Workshop on Computational Modeling of People's Opinions, Personality, and Emotions in Social Media, PEOPLES@NAACL-HTL 2018, New Orleans, Louisiana, USA, June 6, 2018*, pages 36–41. Association for Computational Linguistics.

Bharathi Raja Chakravarthi, Vigneshwaran Muralidaran, Ruba Priyadharshini, and John Philip McCrae. 2020. Corpus creation for sentiment analysis in code-mixed tamil-english text. In *Proceedings of the 1st Joint Workshop on Spoken Language Technologies for Under-resourced languages and Collaboration and Computing for Under-Resourced Languages, SLTU/CCURL@LREC 2020, Marseille, France, May 2020*, pages 202–210. European Language Resources association.

Shivang Chopra, Ramit Sawhney, Puneet Mathur, and Rajiv Ratn Shah. 2020. Hindi-english hate speech detection: Author profiling, debiasing, and practical perspectives. In *The Thirty-Fourth AAAI Conference on Artificial Intelligence, AAAI 2020, The Thirty-Second Innovative Applications of Artificial Intelligence Conference, IAAI 2020, The Tenth AAAI Symposium on Educational Advances in Artificial Intelligence, EAAI 2020, New York, NY, USA, February 7-12, 2020*, pages 386–393. AAAI Press.

Çagri Çöltekin. 2020. A corpus of turkish offensive language on social media. In *Proceedings of The 12th Language Resources and Evaluation Conference, LREC 2020, Marseille, France, May 11-16, 2020*, pages 6174–6184. European Language Resources Association.

Alexis Conneau, Kartikay Khandelwal, Naman Goyal, Vishrav Chaudhary, Guillaume Wenzek, Francisco Guzmán, Edouard Grave, Myle Ott, Luke Zettlemoyer, and Veselin Stoyanov. 2020. Unsupervised cross-lingual representation learning at scale. In *Proceedings of the 58th Annual Meeting of the Association for Computational Linguistics, ACL 2020, Online, July 5-10, 2020*, pages 8440–8451. Association for Computational Linguistics.

Jacob Devlin, Ming-Wei Chang, Kenton Lee, and Kristina Toutanova. 2019. BERT: pre-training of deep bidirectional transformers for language understanding. In *Proceedings of the 2019 Conference of the North American Chapter of the Association for Computational Linguistics: Human Language Technologies, NAACL-HLT 2019, Minneapolis, MN, USA, June 2-7, 2019, Volume 1 (Long and Short Papers)*, pages 4171–4186. Association for Computational Linguistics.

Adeep Hande, R. Priyadharshini, and Bharathi Raja Chakravarthi. 2020. Kancmd: Kannada codemixed dataset for sentiment analysis and offensive language detection. In *PEOPLES*.

Maliha Jahan, Istiak Ahamed, Md. Rayanuzzaman Bishwas, and Swakkhar Shatabda. 2019. Abusive comments detection in bangla-english code-mixed and transliterated text. *2019 2nd International Conference on Innovation in Engineering and Technology (ICIET)*, pages 1–6.

Shagun Jhaver, Iris Birman, Eric Gilbert, and Amy S. Bruckman. 2019. Human-machine collaboration for content regulation: The case of reddit automoderator. *ACM Trans. Comput. Hum. Interact.*, 26(5):31:1–31:35.

Shagun Jhaver, Sucheta Ghoshal, Amy S. Bruckman, and Eric Gilbert. 2018. Online harassment and content moderation: The case of blocklists. *ACM Trans. Comput. Hum. Interact.*, 25(2):12:1–12:33.

Ritesh Kumar, Atul Kr. Ojha, Shervin Malmasi, and Marcos Zampieri. 2018. Benchmarking aggression identification in social media. In *Proceedings of the First Workshop on Trolling, Aggression and Cyberbullying, TRAC@COLING 2018, Santa Fe, New*

*Mexico, USA, August 25, 2018*, pages 1–11. Association for Computational Linguistics.

Hamdy Mubarak, Ammar Rashed, Kareem Darwish, Younes Samih, and Ahmed Abdelali. 2020. Arabic offensive language on twitter: Analysis and experiments. *CoRR*, abs/2004.02192.

Hiroki Nakayama, Takahiro Kubo, Junya Kamura, Yasufumi Taniguchi, and Xu Liang. 2018. doccano: Text annotation tool for human. Software available from `https://github.com/doccano/doccano`.

John Pavlopoulos, Lo Laugier, Jeffrey Sorensen, and Ion Androutsopoulos. 2021. Semeval-2021 task 5: Toxic spans detection (to appear). In *Proceedings of the 15th International Workshop on Semantic Evaluation*.

Zeses Pitenis, Marcos Zampieri, and Tharindu Ranasinghe. 2020. Offensive language identification in greek. In *Proceedings of The 12th Language Resources and Evaluation Conference, LREC 2020, Marseille, France, May 11-16, 2020*, pages 5113–5119. European Language Resources Association.

Kshitij Rajput, Raghav Kapoor, Puneet Mathur, Hitkul, Ponnurangam Kumaraguru, and Rajiv Ratn Shah. 2020. *Transfer Learning for Detecting Hateful Sentiments in Code Switched Language*, pages 159–192. Springer Singapore, Singapore.

Manikandan Ravikiran, Amin Ekant Muljibhai, Toshinori Miyoshi, Hiroaki Ozaki, Yuta Koreeda, and Sakata Masayuki. 2020. Hitachi at semeval-2020 task 12: Offensive language identification with noisy labels using statistical sampling and post-processing. pages 1961–1967.

Sara Rosenthal, Pepa Atanasova, Georgi Karadzhov, Marcos Zampieri, and Preslav Nakov. 2020. A large-scale semi-supervised dataset for offensive language identification. *CoRR*, abs/2004.14454.

Victor Sanh, Lysandre Debut, Julien Chaumond, and Thomas Wolf. 2019. Distilbert, a distilled version of bert: smaller, faster, cheaper and lighter. *ArXiv*, abs/1910.01108.

T. Y. S. S. Santosh and K. V. S. Aravind. 2019. Hate speech detection in hindi-english code-mixed social media text. pages 310–313.

Gudbjartur Ingi Sigurbergsson and Leon Derczynski. 2020. Offensive language and hate speech detection for danish. In *Proceedings of The 12th Language Resources and Evaluation Conference, LREC 2020, Marseille, France, May 11-16, 2020*, pages 3498–3508. European Language Resources Association.

Sunayana Sitaram, Khyathi Raghavi Chandu, Sai Krishna Rallabandi, and A. Black. 2019. A survey of code-switched speech and language processing. *ArXiv*, abs/1904.00784.

Abhishek Srivastava, Kalika Bali, and Monojit Choudhury. 2020. Understanding script-mixing: A case study of hindi-english bilingual twitter users. In *Proceedings of the The 4th Workshop on Computational Approaches to Code Switching, CodeSwitch@LREC 2020, Marseille, France, May, 2020*, pages 36–44. European Language Resources Association.

Qianwen Wang and Mizuho Iwaihara. 2019. Deep neural architectures for joint named entity recognition and disambiguation. In *IEEE International Conference on Big Data and Smart Computing, BigComp 2019, Kyoto, Japan, February 27 - March 2, 2019*, pages 1–4. IEEE.

Thomas Wolf, Lysandre Debut, Victor Sanh, Julien Chaumond, Clement Delangue, Anthony Moi, Pierric Cistac, Tim Rault, R'emi Louf, Morgan Funtowicz, and Jamie Brew. 2019. Huggingface's transformers: State-of-the-art natural language processing. *ArXiv*, abs/1910.03771.

Jun-Ming Xu, Kwang-Sung Jun, Xiaojin Zhu, and Amy Bellmore. 2012. Learning from bullying traces in social media. In *Human Language Technologies: Conference of the North American Chapter of the Association of Computational Linguistics, Proceedings, June 3-8, 2012, Montréal, Canada*, pages 656–666. The Association for Computational Linguistics.

Ikuya Yamada, Akari Asai, Hiroyuki Shindo, H. Takeda, and Yuji Matsumoto. 2020. Luke: Deep contextualized entity representations with entity-aware self-attention. *ArXiv*, abs/2010.01057.

Marcos Zampieri, Shervin Malmasi, Preslav Nakov, Sara Rosenthal, Noura Farra, and Ritesh Kumar. 2019a. Predicting the type and target of offensive posts in social media. In *Proceedings of the 2019 Conference of the North American Chapter of the Association for Computational Linguistics: Human Language Technologies, NAACL-HLT 2019, Minneapolis, MN, USA, June 2-7, 2019, Volume 1 (Long and Short Papers)*, pages 1415–1420. Association for Computational Linguistics.

Marcos Zampieri, Shervin Malmasi, Preslav Nakov, Sara Rosenthal, Noura Farra, and Ritesh Kumar. 2019b. Semeval-2019 task 6: Identifying and categorizing offensive language in social media (offenseval). In *Proceedings of the 13th International Workshop on Semantic Evaluation, SemEval@NAACL-HLT 2019, Minneapolis, MN, USA, June 6-7, 2019*, pages 75–86. Association for Computational Linguistics.

Marcos Zampieri, Preslav Nakov, Sara Rosenthal, Pepa Atanasova, Georgi Karadzhov, Hamdy Mubarak, Leon Derczynski, Zeses Pitenis, and Çagri Çöltekin. 2020. Semeval-2020 task 12: Multilingual offensive language identification in social media (offenseval 2020). In *Proceedings of the Fourteenth Workshop on Semantic Evaluation, SemEval@COLING 2020, Barcelona (online), December 12-13, 2020*, pages 1425–1447. International Committee for Computational Linguistics.

# Towards Offensive Language Identification for Dravidian Languages

**Siva Sai**
Birla Institute of Technology and Science Pilani, India.
f20170779@pilani.bits-pilani.ac.in

**Yashvardhan Sharma**
Birla Institute of Technology and Science Pilani, India.
yash@pilani.bits-pilani.ac.in

## Abstract

Offensive speech identification in countries like India poses several challenges due to the usage of code-mixed and romanized variants of multiple languages by the users in their posts on social media. The challenge of offensive language identification on social media for Dravidian languages is harder, considering the low resources available for the same. In this paper, we explored the zero-shot learning and few-shot learning paradigms based on multilingual language models for offensive speech detection in code-mixed and romanized variants of three Dravidian languages - Malayalam, Tamil, and Kannada. We propose a novel and flexible approach of selective translation and transliteration to reap better results from fine-tuning and ensembling multilingual transformer networks like XLM-RoBERTa and mBERT. We implemented pre-trained, fine-tuned, and ensembled versions of XLM-RoBERTa for offensive speech classification. Further, we experimented with inter-language, inter-task, and multi-task transfer learning techniques to leverage the rich resources available for offensive speech identification in the English language and to enrich the models with knowledge transfer from related tasks. The proposed models yielded good results and are promising for effective offensive speech identification in low resource settings.[1]

## 1 Introduction

Offensive speech is defined as speech that causes a person to feel upset, resentful, annoyed, or insulted. In recent years, social media such as Twitter, Facebook and Reddit have been increasingly used for the propagation of offensive speech and the organization of hate and offense-based activities (Mandl et al., 2020; Chakravarthi et al., 2020e). In a country like India with multiple native languages, users prefer to use their regional language in their social media interactions (Thavareesan and Mahesan, 2019, 2020a,b). It has also been identified that users tend to use roman characters for texting instead of the native script. This poses a severe challenge for the identification of offensive speech, considering the under-developed methodologies for handling code-mixed and romanized text (Jose et al., 2020; Priyadharshini et al., 2020).

Until a few years ago, hate and offensive speech were identified manually which is now an impossible task due to the enormous amounts of data being generated daily on social media platforms. The need for scalable, automated methods of hate speech detection has attracted significant research from the domains of natural language processing and machine learning. A variety of techniques and tools like bag of words models, N-grams, dictionary-based approaches, word sense disambiguation techniques are developed and experimented with by researchers. Recent developments in multilingual text classification are led by Transformer architectures like mBERT (Devlin et al., 2018) and XLM-RoBERTa (Conneau et al., 2019). An additional advantage of these architectures, particularly XLM-RoBERTa, is that it yields good results even with lower resource languages and this particular aspect is beneficial to Indian languages which do not have properly established datasets. In our work, we focused on using these architectures in multiple ways. However, there is a caveat in directly using the models on the romanized or code-mixed text: the transformer models are trained on languages in their native script, not in the romanized script in which users prefer to write online. We solve this problem by using a novel way to convert the romanized sentences into their native language while preserving their semantic meaning - selective translation and transliteration.

[1] https://github.com/SivaAndMe/TOLIDL_DravidianLangTech_EACL_2021



*Proceedings of the First Workshop on Speech and Language Technologies for Dravidian Languages*, pages 18–27
April 20, 2021 

This work is an extension of (Sai and Sharma, 2020). Our important contributions are as follows 1) Proposed selective translation and transliteration for text conversion in romanized and code-mixed settings which can be extended to other romanized and code-mixed contexts in any language. 2) Experimented and analyzed the effectiveness of finetuning and ensembling of XLM-RoBERTa models for offensive speech identification in code-mixed and romanized scripts. 3) Investigated the efficacy of inter-language, inter-task, and multi-task transfer learning techniques and demonstrated the results with t-SNE (Maaten and Hinton, 2008) visualizations.

The rest of the paper is organized as follows: In section 2, we discuss related work followed by datasets' description in section 3. Section 4 describes methodology and section 5 discusses about results. Finally, we conclude the paper in section 6.

## 2 Related works

Two major shared tasks organized in offensive language identification are OffensEval 2019 (Zampieri et al., 2019) and GermEval (Struß et al., 2019). Other tasks related to offensive speech identification include HASOC-19 (Mandl et al., 2019) which dealt with hate speech and offensive content identification in Indo-European languages, TRAC-2020 (Kumar et al., 2020), which dealt with aggression identification in Bangla, Hindi and English. While HASOC-19 and TRAC 2020 dealt with offensive speech identification in Indian languages of Bangla and Hindi, HASOC-Dravidian-CodeMix - FIRE 2020 (Chakravarthi et al., 2020b) is the first shared task to conduct offensive speech identification task in Dravidian languages.

Researchers used a wide variety of techniques for the identification of offensive language. Recently, (Ranasinghe and Zampieri, 2020)(work published after the first version of this paper was submitted) used the XLM-RoBERTa model for offensive language identification in Bengali, Hindi, and Spanish. They show that the XLM-R model beats all other previous approaches for offensive language detection. (Saha et al., 2019), used the LGBM classifier on top of the combination of multilingual BERT and LASER pre-trained embeddings in HASOC-19. (Mishra and Mishra, 2019) fine-tuned monolingual and multilingual BERT based network models to achieve good results in identifying hate speech. (Risch and Krestel, 2020) used an ensemble of BERT models with different random seeds for aggression detection on social media text, which is the inspiration behind our ensembling strategy with XLM-RoBERTa models. There has been less research on text classification in Dravidian languages and there is no research in offensive speech identification for Dravidian languages so far. (Thomas and Latha, 2020) uses a simple LSTM model for sentiment analysis in the Malayalam language. Our work adresses this gap of less research in offensive speech identification methods for Dravidian languages and the systems proposed can be extended to other Indian and foreign languages as well.

## 3 Datasets

The datasets used in this work were taken from three competitions - HASOC-Dravidian-CodeMix - FIRE 2020 (Chakravarthi et al., 2020a,c,b,d; Chakravarthi, 2020) (henceforth HDCM), Sentiment Analysis for Dravidian Languages in Code-Mixed Text (Chakravarthi et al., 2020a,d)(henceforth SADL) and Offensive Language Identification in Dravidian Languages (Chakravarthi et al., 2021; Hande et al., 2020; Chakravarthi et al., 2020d,a)(henceforth ODL). As a part of HDCM, there were two binary classification tasks, with the second task having two subtasks. The objective of all of the tasks was the same: given a Youtube comment, classify it as offensive or not offensive. But the format and language of data provided to different tasks were different: Code-mixed Malayalam for Task-1(henceforth referred to as Mal-CM), Tanglish for Task- 2a(henceforth referred to as Tanglish), and Manglish for Task-2b(henceforth referred to as Manglish). From ODL, we used the Kanglish dataset provided. Originally, the task proposed in ODL is a multi-class classification problem with multiple offensive categories. However, to maintain uniformity among the datasets, we divided the classes into two - offensive and not offensive. Offensive-Targeted-Insult-Individual, Offensive-Targeted-Insult-Group, Offensive-Untargeted, and Offensive-Targeted-Insult-Other classes in the dataset are renamed as offensive, and all the non-Kannada posts are removed from the dataset. As far as SADL is concerned, we used the given sentiment analysis datasets as helper datasets in inter-task transfer learning technique(4.5). OLID (Zampieri et al., 2019) is a dataset for offensive language iden-

| Task | Train | | Dev | Test |
|---|---|---|---|---|
| | OFF | NOT | | |
| Mal-CM | 567 | 2633 | 400 | 400 |
| Tanglish | 1980 | 2020 | - | 940 |
| Manglish | 1952 | 2048 | - | 951 |
| Kanglish | 1151 | 3544 | 586 | 778 |
| OLID | 4400 | 8840 | - | 860 |

Table 1: Statistics of the offensive speech datasets used in this work.

tification in the English language and we used it as a helper dataset for inter-language transfer learning technique (4.4). It consists of 14,100 tweets as stated before; each tweet is annotated as offensive or not-offensive(subtask-A). The statistics of the offensive speech datasets used in this work are provided in table 1.

## 4 System description

### 4.1 Preprocessing

Further, we have done following pre-processing on text for all the datasets: a) Lower case the romanized words. This step is not performed for words written in Malayalam script in Mal-CM as there is no such casing used in Malayalam script. b) Remove emojis from text. c) Remove all special characters, numbers and punctuation. d) Remove user mentions as they generally do not carry any semantic meaning.

### 4.2 Selective translation and transliteration(STT)

This is a novel idea we have used to get a proper representation of text in the native script for the final neural architecture training. The pseudo-code for the proposed algorithm is given in Algorithm 1. The primary need for this step is as follows: Recent advancements in state-of-the-art multilingual NLP tasks are led by Transformer architectures like mBERT and XLM-RoBERTa which are trained on multiple languages in the native script but not in the romanized script[2]. Hence to reap better results by fine-tuning these architectures, the text is to be in a native script(for example, Tamil text in Tamil script).

To convert text into the native script, we cannot rely on neural translation systems, particularly in tweets where users tend to write informally using multiple languages. Also, translating romanized non-English language words into that particular language does not make any sense in our context. For example, translating the word "Maram"(which means tree in Tamil) directly into Tamil would seriously affect the entire sentence's semantics in which the word is present because "Maram" will be treated as an English word. In many cases, valid translations from English to a non-English language would not be available for words.

So, as a solution to this problem, we propose selective transliteration and translation of the text. In effect, this process of conversion of romanized or code-mixed text(for example, Tanglish) is to transliterate the romanized native language(Tamil) words in the text into Tamil and translate the English words in the text into Tamil selectively. The segregation of English words and native language words in a given sentence is done using a big corpus of English words from NLTK-corpus[3]. The idea of this selective conversion is based on the observation that in romanized native language comments(like Tanglish), users tend to use English words only when they can convey the meaning better with the English word or when the corresponding native language word is not much used in regular conversations. For example, the word "movie" is preferred by Tamil-users than its corresponding Tamil word.

The translation of words is done using Google Translate API[4], and transliteration is done with the help of BrahmiNet API[5]. The detection of language script is carried out with the help of langdetect API[6].

#### 4.2.1 Variation of STT algorithm

In some tweets, the direct translation of intermediate English words present in them can affect the semantics negatively, and it may be better to keep them as they are. So, we have experimented with this variation of the STT algorithm - only transliterate the non-English words into their corresponding language and keep the English words as they are. We observed that the cross-lingual nature of the XLM-RoBERTa model can efficiently handle these types of mixed script sentences.

[2]except few languages like Telugu, Tamil and Urdu for XLM-RoBERTa.

[3]https://www.nltk.org/

[4]https://pypi.org/project/googletrans/

[5]http://www.cfilt.iitb.ac.in/brahminet/static/rest.html

[6]https://pypi.org/project/langdetect/

**Algorithm 1:** Algorithm for Selective Translation and Transliteration of code mixed and romanized languages

```
Input  : Romanized or Code-mixed text T
         and desired native language for the
         final script L
Output : Text in native script
Initialization: EngWords = Set of all english
  words
words = splitSentIntoWords(T)
LOOP Process
for i=0 to len(words) do
    word = words[i]
    if(detectLanguageScript(word)==L)
  then
        continue
    else if(word in EngWords) then
        words[i] = translate(word,L)
    else
        words[i] = transliterate(word,L)
    endif
end for
return joinWordsToSent(words)
```

### 4.3 Models

Recent studies show that pre-trained word embeddings and fine-tuning of state-of-the-art Transformer architectures show better performance in text classification compared to classical machine learning approaches like N-gram features with bag of words models (Saha et al., 2019). So we directed our entire focus on using the word-embeddings of transformer architectures both pre-trained and fine-tuned for text classification. The text obtained using selective translation and transliteration is used in further steps.

#### 4.3.1 XLM-RoBERTa

XLM-RoBERTa (Conneau et al., 2019) is a large multilingual model trained on 2.5TB of CommonCrawl data in 100 different languages. It shows improved performance on low-resource languages and outperforms other transformer models like mBERT on cross-lingual benchmarks. The model gives good performance on multilingual datasets without losing the competitive edge on monolingual benchmarks.The base version of the XLM-RoBERTa model consists of 12 hidden layers, 250k parameters, and 12 attention heads.

#### 4.3.2 Pre-trained word embeddings

Transfer learning using pre-trained word embeddings is proved to be useful for offensive speech detection tasks (Saha et al., 2019). So we experimented with XLM-RoBERTa pre-trained embeddings in our work. The pre-trained XLM-R model takes text as input and outputs feature vector of size 1024 for each token in the sentence. We take the average of the feature vectors for all tokens as the final feature vector for the entire sentence.

The pretrained feature vectors of size 1024 are given as input to classical classification algorithms like Logistic Regression. We performed an exhaustive classifier search among 16 classifiers like DecisionTreeClassifier, XGBoostClassifier, etc., to find the classifier that performs better for each task. Our observations show that Logistic Regression outperforms others for Tanglish and Manglish datasets, whereas MLP classifier shows better performance for Mal-CM. We also experimented with a neural network classifier on top of the word embeddings in place of classical algorithms. However, it did not improve the performance much. We have used the Pytorch[7] framework to obtain pre-trained XLM-R embeddings and Sklearn[8] for classifiers.

#### 4.3.3 Fine-tuning Transformer architectures

When we extract features from the pre-trained model, we are using the base model as it is. However, we can fine-tune the base model to customize on our dataset to improve performance. We used Multilingual BERT(uncased) (Devlin et al., 2018), XLM-RoBERTa(both base and large versions) for fine-tuning. For both mBERT and XLM-R, the final hidden state of first token [CLS] (which represents the entire sentence) is fed to a softmax layer for text classification. We performed minimal hyperparameter tuning. Early stopping with a patience of 10 is used targeting the f1-weighted score. A maximum sequence tokens length of 70 is used for all the models based on the observation that around 95% of posts have lesser than 70 tokens. AdamW optimizer with a weight decay of 0.01 is utilized. Cross entropy loss is used as the loss function. We have evaluated the model once for every 100 batches during fine-tuning with 50 as maximum number of epochs. It implies that the model is evaluated once for every 1.25 epochs. All the experiments in this work are performed using

[7] https://pytorch.org/

[8] https://scikit-learn.org/

Google Colab GPU runtime[9].

#### 4.3.4 Ensembling Transformer architectures

The instability and variance of the transformer architectures' performance is the motivation behind this ensembling strategy (Risch and Krestel, 2020). (Devlin et al., 2018) show that the performance(accuracy score) of the BERT model on small datasets, such as the Microsoft Research Paraphrase Corpus (MRPC), varies between 84% and 88%. In our experiments with XLM-R base models, we observed a similar pattern:± 5% F1-weighted score for Mal-CM and Manglish, and ±4% F1-weighted score for Tanglish on validation data. This variance can be created by slight changes in hyperparameters(random seed particularly) and training data. The random seed of a model affects the initialization of weights of the final classification layer. Furthermore, change in random seed while splitting the data into train and validation sets decide which samples go into each of them. This also affects the ordering of the samples in a particular set.

We experimented with 10 different random seeds on XLM-R base model. (Risch and Krestel, 2020) reports that 15 is the optimal number of BERT models for ensembling and that the performance plateaus above that number. In our experiments with XLM-R base, we observed that ensembling 10 models is optimal, where each model corresponds to a different random seed. All other hyperparameters are kept the same as that of 4.3.3 for ensembling. We used soft-majority voting to combine predictions of these ten models. Soft majority voting simply adds the probabilities of each class from all the models and chooses the one with highest probability as the predicted class.

Apart from ensembling of same XLM-RoBERTa models, we also experimented with ensembles of different models : XLM-RoBERTa base + XLM-RoBERTa large and XLM-RoBERTa base + mBERT to analyse the effect of diversity of architectures on the performance.

### 4.4 Inter-language transfer learning

The intuition behind this transfer learning technique is as follows: the patterns of expression of offensive content can have similarities across different languages. Hence, fine-tuning the neural network first on a large scale dataset and using its

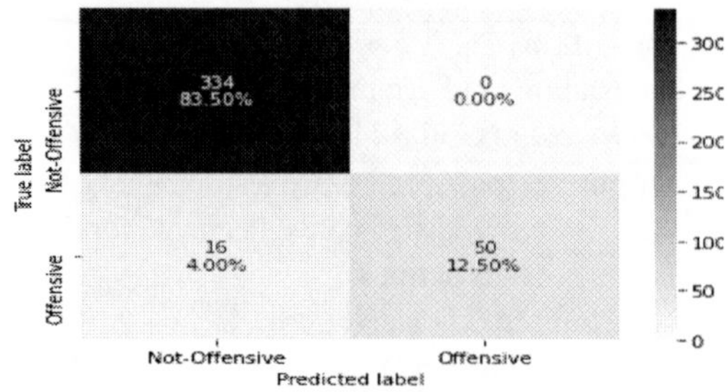


Figure 1: Mal-CM - STT variant XLM-R - confusion matrix

knowledge(weights) to fine-tune the model on another smaller or under-resourced language dataset can improve the performance. The size of OLID dataset is large as compared to the datasets that we are targeting in our work. We first fine-tune the XLM-RoBERTa model (base version) on the OLID dataset. After this first fine-tuning step, the weights of all layers except the pre-final fully connected layer and the final softmax layer are used for initializing the XLM-RoBERTa model, which is to be fine-tuned for offensive speech classification in a Dravidian language.

### 4.5 Inter-task transfer learning

In this type of transfer learning technique, the knowledge learned by fine-tuning a language model with a particular objective is transferred to another language model for achieving a different objective. In our work, we keep the language of the datasets for the two tasks the same. However, it can be different, as well. Firstly, we fine-tune the XLM-RoBERTa model for multi-label multi-class sentiment analysis in a particular code-mixed and romanized language and use the final weights of the neural network layers for initializing weights for another XLM-RoBERTa model, which is used for offensive speech identification in the same code-mixed language. The weights of the final softmax layer are not transferred, as it is evident that two different tasks are being dealt with here. We used this technique for Tanglish and Manglish datasets because the corresponding sentiment analysis datasets are available only for these languages. We used datasets from SADL for the initial fine-tuning. We show that the first model's knowledge in dealing with code-mixed languages is helpful for the second model.

[9] https://colab.research.google.com/

| Task | XLMR-pretrained+clf | mBERT | XLMR-B | XLMR-B+ mBERT | XLMR-B + XLMR-L |
|---|---|---|---|---|---|
| Mal-CM | 0.88 | 0.91 | **0.93** | **0.93** | 0.93 |
| Tanglish | 0.78 | 0.83 | 0.86 | **0.88** | 0.85 |
| Manglish | 0.67 | 0.60 | **0.69** | **0.69** | **0.69** |
| Kanglish | 0.80 | 0.81 | **0.82** | **0.82** | **0.82** |

Table 2: Results on Validation data - F1-Weighted score

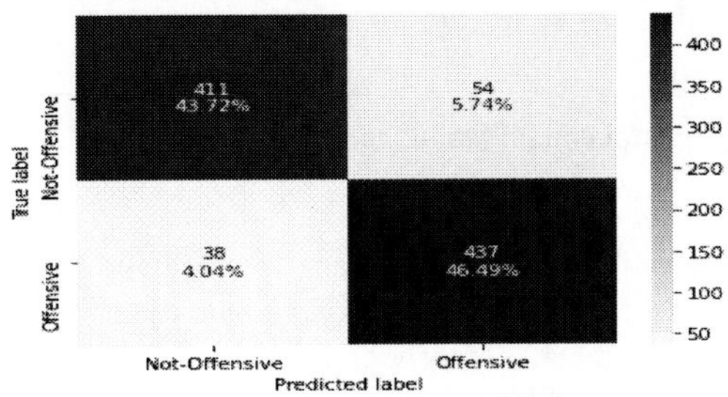


Figure 2: Tanglish - Ensemble of XLMR models - confusion matrix

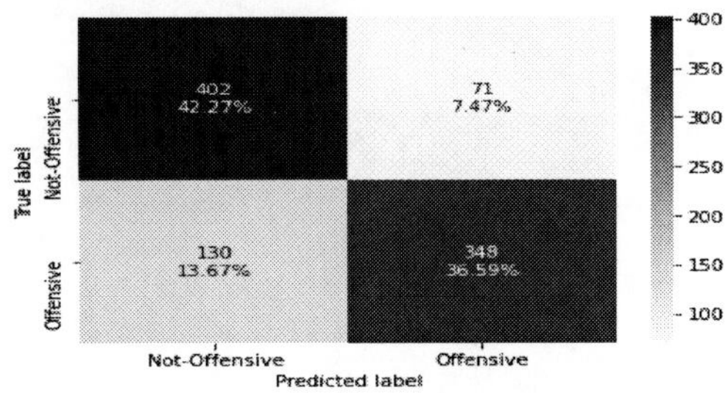


Figure 3: Manglish - Ensemble of XLMR models - confusion matrix

### 4.6 Multi-task transfer learning(MTL)

As the name implies, the neural network learns two or more tasks simultaneously in this type of transfer learning technique. The intuition behind this technique is that the learning of the model is enhanced by dealing simultaneously with multiple tasks due to the inherent similarities and differences present in data and the learning approach. (Caruana, 1998) states that the goal of MTL is to improve the generalization capability of the model by leveraging domain specific knowledge present in the training data of related tasks. In our work, we experimented with MTL on the Kanglish dataset, with two related tasks - fine-grained and coarse-grained identification of offensive speech. To implement MTL, two separate fully connected layers are added on top of the same XLM-R model for final classification. The loss is an aggregate of the individual losses of two tasks. In our context, the goal is to improve the coarse-grained classification(offensive or not-offensive) with the help of fine-grained classification(not-offensive or offensive-targeted-insult-individual or offensive-targeted-insult-group or offensive-untargeted or offensive-targeted-insult-other).

## 5 Results and discussion

To test the performance of our proposed models, we had evaluated them on validation data before the test set was made available by the concerned task organizers. When unlabeled test data was released, we used the above-mentioned validation data as dev set to develop the model, and final predictions are made using these models. Ensemble of XLM-RoBERTa models is not experimented on dev data due to computational limitations. Nevertheless, we verified the better performance of Ensemble models with few random seeds and directly used them for final training.

### 5.1 Results on validation data

We created stratified dev sets from training data for Tanglish and Manglish. The dev sets for Mal-CM and Kanglish are provided by the organizers of HDCM and ODL respectively. And these dev sets are used for final internal valuation as test sets. A 10% of training data was used as dev data for training for all the tasks. The results are shown in table 2. In the case of pre-trained embeddings, clf(classifier) used is Logistic Regression for Tanglish, Kanglish and Manglish tasks and MLP for Mal-CM. Because XLM-RoBERTa is also trained on Tamil dataset in roman script, we experimented with directly feeding the pre-processed Tanglish text to the model without STT. But, the performance is significantly lower than the model which follows entire pipeline.

It can be observed from the table 2 that fine-tuning models gave better results than directly using off-the-shelf embeddings. But for Manglish and Kanglish, pre-trained embeddings come closer to fine-tuned models in performance. The superior

| Model | Mal-CM | Tanglish | Manglish | Kanglish |
|---|---|---|---|---|
| STT + XLMR | 0.92 | 0.90 | 0.73 | 0.82 |
| STT variant + XLMR | **0.96** | 0.90 | 0.75 | **0.82** |
| Ensemble of XLMR models | 0.95 | **0.90** | **0.79** | – |
| Inter-language Transfer Learning | 0.94 | 0.87 | 0.75 | 0.81 |
| Inter-task Transfer Learning | 0.94 | 0.90 | 0.71 | – |
| Multi-task Transfer Learning | – | – | – | 0.78 |

Table 3: Results on test data - F1-Weighted

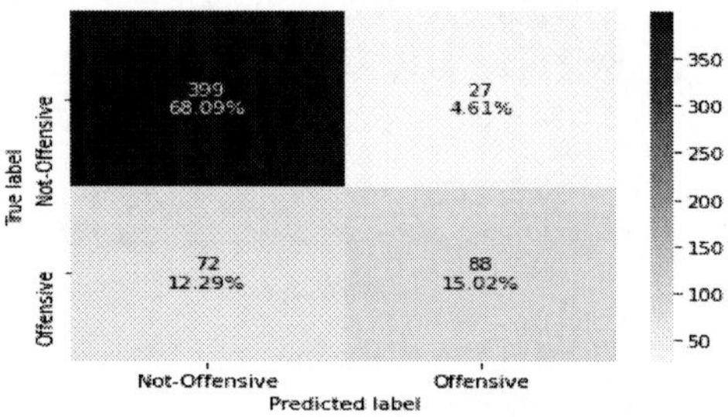


Figure 4: Kanglish - STT XLMR - confusion matrix

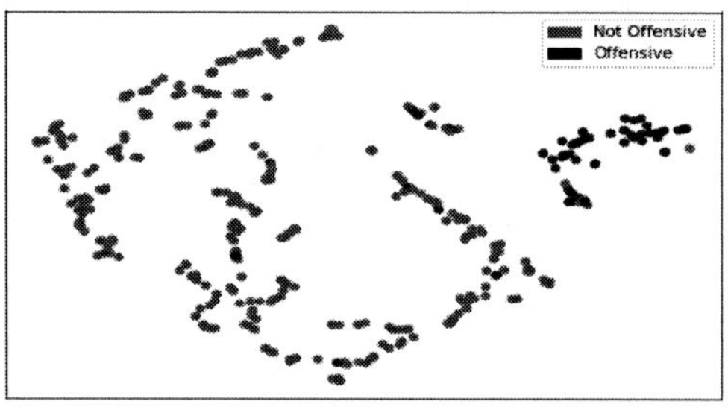


Figure 5: t-SNE visualization for Mal-CM on test data

performance of XLMR-base model in all the tasks can also also be inferred. This is the reason, we chose XLMR-base for ensembling strategy.

### 5.2 Results on test data

We submitted the models proposed for Mal-CM, Tanglish, and Manglish to HDCM and the results were encouraging. Our submissions topped two out of three tasks(Mal-CM and Tanglish) and stood second in the third task lagging the top model only by 0.01 points(Manglish). We can see that the test F1-weighted scores are slightly better than validation results for Mal-CM and Tanglish tasks (table 3). And the results on test data are significantly higher than results on dev data for Manglish task(8% higher). It can be inferred that performance scores for Manglish are significantly less than those of Tanglish task(10% lower). We attribute this to agglutinative and inflectional nature of Malayalam language.

**STT v/s STT variant**
From the results, it can also be observed that the XLM-R model using STT variant algorithm performed better than(or at par with) XLM-R model using STT on all datasets. We attribute this to the efficiency of XLM-R model to handle cross-lingual sentences(Conneau et al., 2019). Moreover, in some instances, the STT may give bad translations. For instance, when the sentence is entirely in English, STT algorithm translates every word, affecting the meaning of the sentence because, in general, the word-to-word translation of a sentence will not give the correct meaning in the target language. This is a drawback of STT. But the assumption that most of the corpus text is in code-mixed and romanized format reduces the issues from this drawback. Notably, the STT variant based model performs even better than the ensemble of XLMR models(which is computationally intensive) on some datasets.

**Inter-language and inter-task transfer learning**
The initialization of weights from OLID based XLM-R model(inter-language transfer learning technique) helped Mal-CM and Manglish compared to the basic XLM-R model(with STT) while decreasing the performance for Tanglish. The initialization of weights from SADL based XLM-R model(inter-task transfer learning technique) increased the performance for Mal-CM and decreased the performance for Manglish compared to the basic XLM-R model.

Although the inter-language and inter-task transfer learning did not improve the results largely, we observed that the initial validation scores while training are significantly higher for those with SADL or OLID based initialization compared to a model initialized with random weights. We attribute this to the initial transfer of useful knowledge from the SADL and OLID tasks.

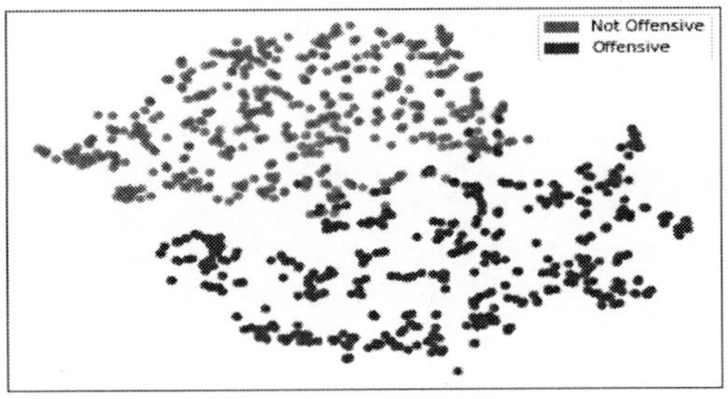


Figure 6: t-SNE visualization for Tanglish on test data

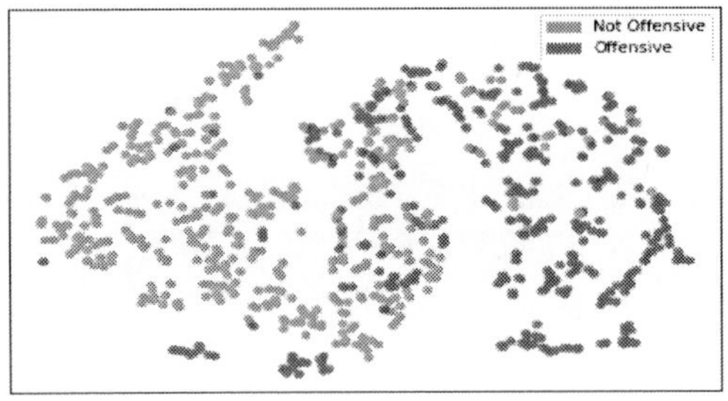


Figure 7: t-SNE visualization for Manglish on test data

**Multi-task transfer learning**
The notable decrease of F1-weighted score for multi-task learning based XLM-R model for Kanglish corroborates with the findings of (Sun et al., 2019). Although the task of coarse-grained classification (as a part of MTL) did not gain anything, the fine-grained classification has substantial gains in terms of performance. This second task achieved an F1-weighted score of 72.8% for fine-grained classification with five classes, which is fair enough considering that the best F1-weighted score for two-way classification is 82%(as shown in table 3).

We could not perform certain experiments(refer table 3) like SADL-based weight initialization for Kanglish and MTL with datasets other than Kanglish because of lack of suitable datasets.

**t-SNE Visualizations and Confusion matrices**
We projected the 768-dimensional feature vectors obtained from the final layer of XLM-RoBERTa model(with STT) onto a two-dimensional space using t-SNE algorithm (Maaten and Hinton, 2008) for all the tasks on test data (refer figures 5,6,7 and 8 ). The distinction between two clusters in all of the t-SNE visualizations are clearly in line with the results given in table 3. For example, the clusters for Tanglish(figure 6) and Mal-CM(figure 5) are almost well segregated, but the clusters for Manglish(figure 7) are overlapping. We have also provided the confusion matrices for best performing models on each dataset - STT variant XLMR model for Mal-CM(figure 1), ensemble of XLMR models for Tanglish(figure 2) and Manglish(figure 3), and STT XLMR model for Kanglish(figure 4).

## 6 Conclusion

In this paper, we have presented various techniques and neural network models to identify offensive language in social media text for code mixed and romanized Dravidian languages. A novel technique of selective translation and transliteration is proposed to deal with code-mixed and romanized offensive speech classification in Dravidian languages. This technique is flexible and can be extended to other languages as well. For classification, classical classifiers on top of pre-trained embeddings, fine-tuned XLM-RoBERTa models, and an ensemble of XLM-RoBERTa models are used. We experimented with different transfer learning techniques to leverage the offensive speech datasets from resource-rich languages. Our work also points to the usefulness of Transformer architectures, particularly XLM-RoBERTa, for low resource languages like Tamil and Malayalam. Our proposed models show an average performance of 85% F1-weighted score across all datasets.

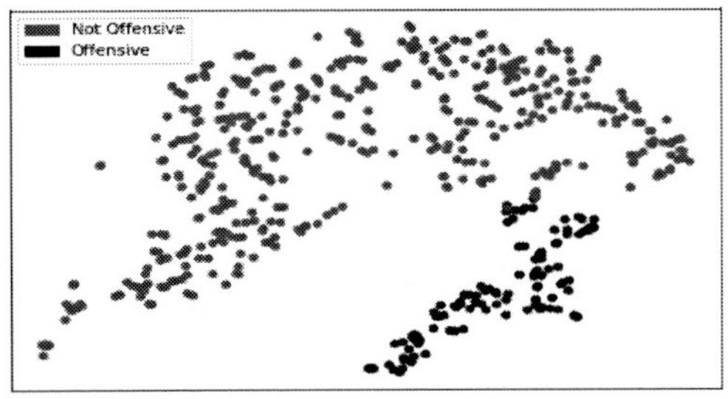


Figure 8: t-SNE visualization for Kanglish on test data

## 7 Acknowledgement

The authors would like to convey their sincere thanks to the Department of Science and Technology (ICPS Division), New Delhi, India, for providing financial assistance under the Data Science (DS) Research of Interdisciplinary Cyber Physical Systems (ICPS) Programme [DST /ICPS /CLUSTER /Data Science/2018/Proposal-16:(T-856)] at the department of computer science, Birla Institute of Technology and Science, Pilani, India.

## References


R Caruana. 1998. Multitask learning. autonomous agents and multi-agent systems.

Bharathi Raja Chakravarthi. 2020. *Leveraging orthographic information to improve machine translation of under-resourced languages*. Ph.D. thesis, NUI Galway.

Bharathi Raja Chakravarthi, Navya Jose, Shardul Suryawanshi, Elizabeth Sherly, and John Philip McCrae. 2020a. A sentiment analysis dataset for code-mixed Malayalam-English. In *Proceedings of the 1st Joint Workshop on Spoken Language Technologies for Under-resourced languages (SLTU) and Collaboration and Computing for Under-Resourced Languages (CCURL)*, pages 177–184, Marseille, France. European Language Resources association.

Bharathi Raja Chakravarthi, M Anand Kumar, John Philip McCrae, Premjith B, Soman KP, and Thomas Mandl. 2020b. Overview of the track on HASOC-Offensive Language Identification-DravidianCodeMix. In *Working Notes of the Forum for Information Retrieval Evaluation (FIRE 2020). CEUR Workshop Proceedings. In: CEUR-WS. org, Hyderabad, India.*

Bharathi Raja Chakravarthi, M Anand Kumar, John Philip McCrae, Premjith B, Soman KP, and Thomas Mandl. 2020c. Overview of the track on "HASOC-Offensive Language Identification-DravidianCodeMix". In *Proceedings of the 12th Forum for Information Retrieval Evaluation*, FIRE '20.

Bharathi Raja Chakravarthi, Vigneshwaran Muralidaran, Ruba Priyadharshini, and John Philip McCrae. 2020d. Corpus creation for sentiment analysis in code-mixed Tamil-English text. In *Proceedings of the 1st Joint Workshop on Spoken Language Technologies for Under-resourced languages (SLTU) and Collaboration and Computing for Under-Resourced Languages (CCURL)*, pages 202–210, Marseille, France. European Language Resources association.

Bharathi Raja Chakravarthi, Ruba Priyadharshini, Navya Jose, Anand Kumar M, Thomas Mandl, Prasanna Kumar Kumaresan, Rahul Ponnusamy, Hariharan V, Elizabeth Sherly, and John Philip McCrae. 2021. Findings of the shared task on Offensive Language Identification in Tamil, Malayalam, and Kannada. In *Proceedings of the First Workshop on Speech and Language Technologies for Dravidian Languages*. Association for Computational Linguistics.

Bharathi Raja Chakravarthi, Ruba Priyadharshini, Vigneshwaran Muralidaran, Shardul Suryawanshi, Navya Jose, Elizabeth Sherly, and John P. McCrae. 2020e. Overview of the Track on Sentiment Analysis for Dravidian Languages in Code-Mixed Text. In *Forum for Information Retrieval Evaluation*, FIRE 2020, page 21–24, New York, NY, USA. Association for Computing Machinery.

Alexis Conneau, Kartikay Khandelwal, Naman Goyal, Vishrav Chaudhary, Guillaume Wenzek, Francisco Guzmán, Edouard Grave, Myle Ott, Luke Zettlemoyer, and Veselin Stoyanov. 2019. Unsupervised cross-lingual representation learning at scale. *arXiv preprint arXiv:1911.02116*.

Jacob Devlin, Ming-Wei Chang, Kenton Lee, and Kristina Toutanova. 2018. Bert: Pre-training of deep bidirectional transformers for language understanding. *arXiv preprint arXiv:1810.04805*.

Adeep Hande, Ruba Priyadharshini, and Bharathi Raja Chakravarthi. 2020. KanCMD: Kannada CodeMixed dataset for sentiment analysis and offensive language detection. In *Proceedings of the Third Workshop on Computational Modeling of People's Opinions, Personality, and Emotion's in Social Media*, pages 54–63, Barcelona, Spain (Online). Association for Computational Linguistics.

Navya Jose, Bharathi Raja Chakravarthi, Shardul Suryawanshi, Elizabeth Sherly, and John P. McCrae. 2020. A Survey of Current Datasets for Code-Switching Research. In *2020 6th International Conference on Advanced Computing and Communication Systems (ICACCS)*, pages 136–141.

Ritesh Kumar, Atul Kr. Ojha, Bornini Lahiri, Marcos Zampieri, Shervin Malmasi, Vanessa Murdock, and Daniel Kadar, editors. 2020. *Proceedings of the Second Workshop on Trolling, Aggression and Cyberbullying*. European Language Resources Association (ELRA), Marseille, France.

Laurens van der Maaten and Geoffrey Hinton. 2008. Visualizing data using t-sne. *Journal of machine learning research*, 9(Nov):2579–2605.

Thomas Mandl, Sandip Modha, Anand Kumar M, and Bharathi Raja Chakravarthi. 2020. Overview of the HASOC Track at FIRE 2020: Hate Speech and Offensive Language Identification in Tamil, Malayalam, Hindi, English and German. In *Forum for Information Retrieval Evaluation*, FIRE 2020, page 29–32, New York, NY, USA. Association for Computing Machinery.

Thomas Mandl, Sandip Modha, Prasenjit Majumder, Daksh Patel, Mohana Dave, Chintak Mandlia, and Aditya Patel. 2019. Overview of the hasoc track at fire 2019: Hate speech and offensive content identification in indo-european languages. In *Proceedings of the 11th Forum for Information Retrieval Evaluation*, pages 14–17.

Shubhanshu Mishra and Sudhanshu Mishra. 2019. 3idiots at hasoc 2019: Fine-tuning transformer neural networks for hate speech identification in Indo-European languages. In *FIRE (Working Notes)*, pages 208–213.

Ruba Priyadharshini, Bharathi Raja Chakravarthi, Mani Vegupatti, and John P. McCrae. 2020. Named Entity Recognition for Code-Mixed Indian Corpus using Meta Embedding. In *2020 6th International Conference on Advanced Computing and Communication Systems (ICACCS)*, pages 68–72.

Tharindu Ranasinghe and Marcos Zampieri. 2020. Multilingual offensive language identification with cross-lingual embeddings. *arXiv preprint arXiv:2010.05324*.

Julian Risch and Ralf Krestel. 2020. Bagging bert models for robust aggression identification. In *Proceedings of the Second Workshop on Trolling, Aggression and Cyberbullying*, pages 55–61.

Punyajoy Saha, Binny Mathew, Pawan Goyal, and Animesh Mukherjee. 2019. Hatemonitors: Language agnostic abuse detection in social media. *arXiv preprint arXiv:1909.12642*.

Siva Sai and Yashvardhan Sharma. 2020. Siva@HASOC-Dravidian-CodeMix-FIRE-2020: Multilingual Offensive Speech Detection in Code-mixed and Romanized text. FIRE.

Julia Maria Struß, Melanie Siegel, Josef Ruppenhofer, Michael Wiegand, Manfred Klenner, et al. 2019. Overview of germeval task 2, 2019 shared task on the identification of offensive language.

Chi Sun, Xipeng Qiu, Yige Xu, and Xuanjing Huang. 2019. How to fine-tune bert for text classification? In *China National Conference on Chinese Computational Linguistics*, pages 194–206. Springer.

Sajeetha Thavareesan and Sinnathamby Mahesan. 2019. Sentiment Analysis in Tamil Texts: A Study on Machine Learning Techniques and Feature Representation. In *2019 14th Conference on Industrial and Information Systems (ICIIS)*, pages 320–325.

Sajeetha Thavareesan and Sinnathamby Mahesan. 2020a. Sentiment Lexicon Expansion using Word2vec and fastText for Sentiment Prediction in Tamil texts. In *2020 Moratuwa Engineering Research Conference (MERCon)*, pages 272–276.

Sajeetha Thavareesan and Sinnathamby Mahesan. 2020b. Word embedding-based Part of Speech tagging in Tamil texts. In *2020 IEEE 15th International Conference on Industrial and Information Systems (ICIIS)*, pages 478–482.

Merin Thomas and CA Latha. 2020. Sentimental analysis of transliterated text in malayalam using recurrent neural networks. *Journal of Ambient Intelligence and Humanized Computing*, pages 1–8.

Marcos Zampieri, Shervin Malmasi, Preslav Nakov, Sara Rosenthal, Noura Farra, and Ritesh Kumar. 2019. Semeval-2019 task 6: Identifying and categorizing offensive language in social media (offenseval). *arXiv preprint arXiv:1903.08983*.

# Sentiment Classification of Code-Mixed Tweets using Bi-Directional RNN and Language Tags

**Sainik Kumar Mahata[1], Dipankar Das[2], Sivaji Bandyopadhyay[3]**
[1]Institute of Engineering and Management, Kolkata, India
[2,3]Jadavpur University, Kolkata, India
[1]sainik.mahata@gmail.com, [2]dipankar.dipnil2005@gmail.com
[3]sivaji.cse.ju@gmail.com

## Abstract

Sentiment analysis tools and models have been developed extensively throughout the years, for European languages. In contrast, similar tools for Indian Languages are scarce. This is because, state-of-the-art pre-processing tools like POS tagger, shallow parsers, etc., are not readily available for Indian languages. Although, such working tools for Indian languages, like Hindi and Bengali, that are spoken by the majority of the population, are available, finding the same for less spoken languages like, Tamil, Telugu, and Malayalam, is difficult. Moreover, due to the advent of social media, the multi-lingual population of India, who are comfortable with both English ad their regional language, prefer to communicate by mixing both languages. This gives rise to massive code-mixed content and automatically annotating them with their respective sentiment labels becomes a challenging task. In this work, we take up a similar challenge of developing a sentiment analysis model that can work with English-Tamil code-mixed data. The proposed work tries to solve this by using bi-directional LSTMs along with language tagging. Other traditional methods, based on classical machine learning algorithms have also been discussed in the literature, and they also act as the baseline systems to which we will compare our Neural Network based model. The performance of the developed algorithm, based on Neural Network architecture, garnered precision, recall, and F1 scores of 0.59, 0.66, and 0.58 respectively.

## 1 Introduction

Sentiment analysis is the interpretation and classification of emotions (positive, negative, and neutral) within text data using text analysis techniques. It is one of the most important research areas in the domain of Natural Language Processing (NLP) and has garnered much attention in the recent past. Throughout the years, multiple state-of-the-Art sentiment analysis models have been developed for the well known European languages, using classical Machine Learning (ML) algorithms as well as the recently developed Neural Network (NN) models. In contrast, very few such models have been developed for Indian languages, due to their lower digital footprint, which results in the lack of annotated data. Also, various pre-processing tools like Parts-of-Speech (POS) taggers, tokenizers, parsers, etc., for Indian languages, are not readily available or are not of competitive quality. Although, recent advances have been made for the Indian languages that are spoken by the majority of the population, like Hindi and Bengali, the same cannot be said for under-resourced languages such as, Tamil, Telugu, and Malayalam. For over 2600 years, recorded Tamil literature has been documented. Sangam literature, the earliest period of Tamil literature, is dated from around 600 BC- 300 AD. Among the Dravidian languages, Tamil has the oldest existing literature. Tamil is the oldest living language in India.

Moreover, with the advent of social media, sentiment analysis research has become even more wide-spread (Mahata et al., 2020; Garain et al., 2020) as it takes into account conversations of customers around the social space and puts them into context. But, in the context of the Indian subcontinent, social media texts are not in one language and are largely code-mixed in nature. This is because India, has had much foreign acquaintance historically, and this has led the diaspora to adopt English as one of their official languages. Due to this, much of the Indian population are familiar with English as well as one or more regional languages (Mahata et al., 2019). This leads to communication in sentences, which contain more than one language in the same phrase (Soumil Mandal and Das, 2018).

Furthermore, in a code-mixed communication,



*Proceedings of the First Workshop on Speech and Language Technologies for Dravidian Languages*, pages 28–35
April 20, 2021 ©2021 Association for Computational Linguistics

words of different languages are generally written in Roman script, which leads to the formation of complex syntactical structures that are difficult to parse with traditional NLP tools. While traditional sentiment analysis models can model themselves on social media texts in one language, the same cannot be said for texts that are code-mixed in nature and also comprised of Indian low-resourced languages.

The proposed approach aims to mitigate this research problem for English-Tamil code-mixed texts and uses Bi-Directional Long-Short-term-Memory (LSTM)s (Hochreiter and Schmidhuber, 1997) to tag the texts with their respective sentiment. Language tagging of individual words was used as additional features while training the classification model. Moreover, the training corpus was passed through FastText (Bojanowski et al., 2016) embedding, to map the semantically similar words in a common 3D space. This mapping was also used to build the classification system. The designed model, when evaluated on test data, garnered an F1 score of 0.58.

Other baseline sentiment analysis models were also developed using classical ML algorithms and were used to compare the quality of the proposed algorithm developed by using NNs.

The rest of the paper is organized as follows. Section 2 describes some of the previous research work conducted on the domain of language identification and sentiment analysis of code-mixed texts. Section 3 describes the training and the test data used to develop and analyze our model. Section 4 introduces the model developed for identifying languages of individual words in a code-mixed sentence. Also, it describes our developed model and all the baseline models that were developed using traditional ML algorithms.Finally, section 5 and 6 deals with the evaluation of our model and the concluding remarks.

## 2 Related Work

Social media has become the voice of many people over the decades and it has special relations with real-time events. With its rise, a lot of data is being generated every day and information extraction from such data has become an important research area. Also, the multi-lingual speaker, who prefers to communicate in more than one language, when expressing their opinions, generates a new kind of language, known as code-mixed language. Since, these kinds of data are more or less always written in the Roman script, analyzing these kinds of data, with help of NLP tools, becomes even more difficult.

Over the years, many experiments have been performed on code-mixed data. These include language identification, sentiment analysis, etc., to name a few. Language identification tasks have been earlier performed on various language pairs, such as Spanish-English (Negrón Goldbarg, 2009), French-English (Voss et al., 2014), Hindi-English (Vyas et al., 2014; Das and Gambäck, 2014) and Bengali-English (Das and Gambäck, 2014). While these experiments were conducted with the help of dictionary word matching and ML-based algorithms such as Support Vector Machines (SVM), word-based logistic regression classifiers, and Latent Direchlet Allocation (LDA) (Blei et al., 2003), we use more state-of-the-art deep learning approaches to achieve the same.

Also, sentiment analysis or opinion mining from code-mixed data is a trivial task because

- Generally, code-mixed data is noisy in nature and requires cleaning and normalization.
- It needs several steps such as language identification and POS tagging.
- There is no sentiment annotated code-mixed lexicon available for any language pairs.
- The available code-mixed datasets are small in size to perform any unsupervised classification.

Sentiment analysis of Hindi-English code-mixed was performed by Joshi et al. (2016) which used sub-word level representations in LSTM architecture to perform it. Shalini et. al. (Shalini et al., 2018), attempted a case-study on sentiment analysis of English-Kannada, English-Hindi, and English-Bengali texts using various machine and deep learning methods settings, like i. Doc2Vec+SVM, ii. FastText+Softmax, iii. Bi-LSTM+SoftMax and iv. CNN+SoftMax. Their reported results showed better accuracy when using deep learning methods as compared to traditional machine learning methods.

Our work, on the other hand, is an amalgamation of all the methods pointed out earlier and incorporates language identification modules, the usage of FastText embeddings, and Bi-LSTM cells to develop the deep learning model.

## 3 Data

The data for building the sentiment analysis model for English-Tamil code-mixed data was collected from the "Dravidian-CodeMix - FIRE 2020"[1] shared task. The organizers of the task provided us with Tamil-English and Malayalam-English code-mixed text data, derived from YouTube video comments. The dataset contained all the three types of code-mixed sentences – Inter-Sentential switch, Intra-Sentential switch, and Tag switching and had five output labels; Positive, Negative, Mixed Feelings, Not Tamil, and Unknown State. Most comments were written in Roman script with either Tamil / Malayalam grammar with English lexicon or English grammar with Tamil / Malayalam lexicon. Some comments were written in Tamil / Malayalam script with English expressions in between. Further, the English-Tamil dataset was divided into training, validation, and test data which had 11,335, 1,260, and 3,149 code-mixed sentence instances respectively.

## 4 Framework

After we collected the English-Tamil code-mixed labeled dataset, the initial pre-processing steps included the removal of extra characters to clean the data. The extra characters that were removed/cleaned included

- Removing mentions
- Removing punctuation
- Removing URLs
- Contracting extra white space
- Extracting words from hashtags

After the pre-processing step, we proceeded with tokenizing the cleaned sentences using the NLTK[2] library. Subsequently, we used this data to train FastText embedding. This was done, to map the words with similar meaning and context, close to each other in a 3D space. The skip-gram model was used instead of the continuous-bag-of-words (CBOW) model as skip-gram works best for low data sizes. The model took into account character n-grams from 3 to 6 characters. Using the trained model, we were able to extract word vectors of size 100. These word vectors were preserved to be used as input for our sentiment analysis model.

### 4.1 Language Identification

Apart from providing our model, with the sequential word vectors of sentences, we also decided on providing an extra input in the form of language tags of every word of the sentences. For this, we developed a language identification system, that was trained to classify individual words, written in Roman script, as either English or Tamil. To achieve this, we used the character-level LSTM architecture put forward by Mandal et al. (2018). This is a model having stacked LSTM of sizes 193-128-128-1, in order where 193 is the input dimension while 1 is the output dimension.

The training data was acquired by concatenating different datasets for both English and Tamil. For the English data, we used the words from the NLTK corpus, that contained 2,34,377 unique English words. For the Tamil data, we used the data from Google Dakshina Dataset[3]. This dataset contained 48,998 Tamil words, transliterated in Roman script. After adding up both the datasets, we were able to gather 2,83,332 words. Of this, 3,35,792 words were used for the training data and the rest 5,000 words were used as the test data. Also, since the data labels were imbalanced, we used the class_weight feature of sklearn[4] package to assign class weights.

The schematic of the developed language identification model is shown in Figure 1. After testing the model with 5,000 words, the model returned an accuracy of 96.89%. The other metrics for the model are shown in Table 1.

| Metrics | Value |
|---|---|
| **Accuracy** | 96.89% |
| **Precision** | 0.94 |
| **Recall** | 0.96 |
| **F1-Score** | 0.95 |

Table 1: Accuracy metrics of the Language Identification model.

[1] https://dravidian-codemix.github.io/2020/

[2] https://www.nltk.org/

[3] https://github.com/google-research-datasets/dakshina

[4] https://scikit-learn.org/stable/modules/generated/sklearn.utils.\class_weight.compute_class_weight.html

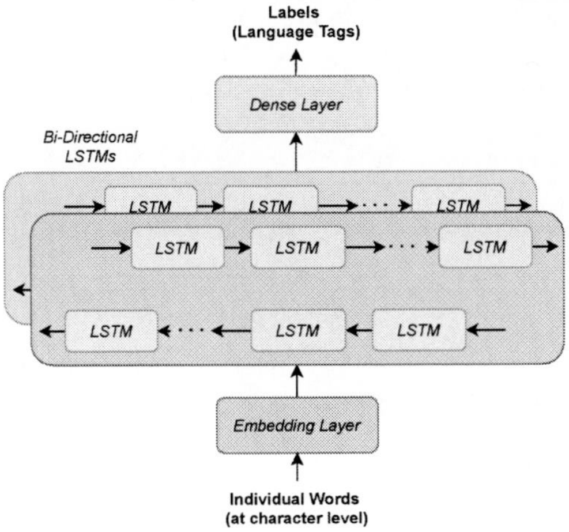


Figure 1: Classification model for language identification.

## 4.2 Sentiment Classification

Using the language identification model, we were able to classify the words of the validation and the training data into either English or Tamil. Now, the next step was to develop the sentiment classification model which was to be designed for taking two inputs; i. the individual words of the code-mixed tweets and ii. the language tags of the individual words in the code-mixed tweets. The vectors of the individual words of the training data, as discussed earlier, were extracted from the already trained FastText embedding file. Thereafter, vectors of sentences of the train and validation dataset were extracted from the trained embedding. The language tags and the word vectors were merged using a Concatenation layer and were given as input to a Bi-Directional LSTM cell. The context vector was then mapped to the output labels with the help of a Dense layer.
The schematic of the model is shown in Figure 2. Other parameters of the model are as follows.

- batch size: 32
- epochs: 50
- optimizer: adam
- loss: sparse categorical cross-entropy
- validation split: 0.1

On validating the developed model using a validation split of 0.1 (1,260 sentences), it garnered

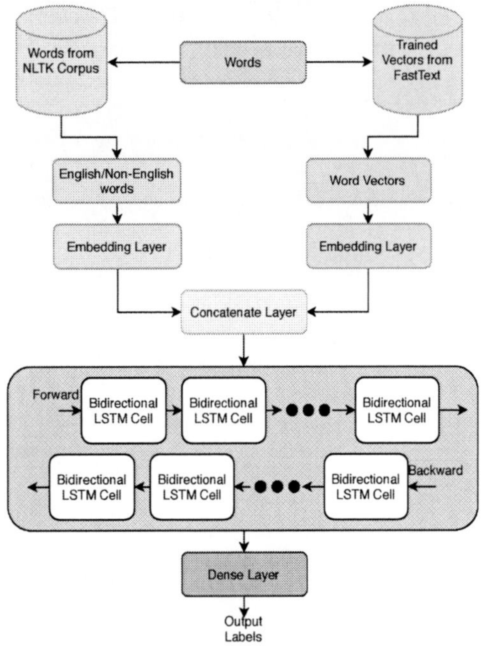


Figure 2: Code-Mixed Sentiment Analysis model.

accuracy and F1-Score of 70.42% and 0.63 respectively. We also trained three other models, where the basic architecture was the same, the difference being the usage of LSTM/Bi-Directional LSTM and language tag features. The models were

- Bidirectional LSTM without the language tag feature.
- LSTM with the language tag feature.
- LSTM without the language tag feature.

The accuracy and F1-Score of every model are shown in Table 2.

## 4.3 Baseline Models

For developing the baseline models, we decided on using traditional ML algorithms. The algorithms chosen were,

- Naive Bayes algorithm
- Logistic Regression algorithm
- Support Vector Machine algorithm
- Random Forest algorithm

Four types of models with different features were selected to develop the models. Count Vectorizer, which converts a collection of text documents to a

| Model | Bi-LSTM+ln tag | Bi-LSTM | LSTM+ln tag | LSTM |
|---|---|---|---|---|
| Accuracy | 70.42% | 70.82% | 70.62% | 70.22% |
| F1-Score | 0.63 | 0.61 | 0.62 | 0.62 |
| Precision | 0.62 | 0.59 | 0.63 | 0.62 |
| Recall | 0.70 | 0.71 | 0.71 | 0.70 |

Table 2: Comparison of accuracy scores of the developed models built using NN architecture.

| Model | Algorithm | Features | Accuracy | Precision | Recall | F1-Score |
|---|---|---|---|---|---|---|
| NB | CV | Word | 65.23% | 0.52 | 0.65 | 0.58 |
| | | Word+Ln Tag | 69.20% | 0.55 | 0.69 | 0.61 |
| | TF-IDF | Word | 64.96% | 0.51 | 0.65 | 0.57 |
| | | Word+Ln Tag | 69.68% | 0.56 | 0.70 | 0.62 |
| LR | CV | Word | 65.22% | 0.51 | 0.65 | 0.57 |
| | | Word+Ln Tag | 68.65% | 0.53 | 0.69 | 0.60 |
| | TF-IDF | Word | 66.54% | 0.53 | 0.67 | 0.59 |
| | | Word+Ln Tag | 70.23% | 0.56 | 0.70 | 0.62 |
| SVM | CV | Word | 65.34% | 0.52 | 0.65 | 0.58 |
| | | Word+Ln Tag | 68.88% | 0.53 | 0.69 | 0.60 |
| | TF-IDF | Word | 65.89% | 0.52 | 0.66 | 0.58 |
| | | Word+Ln Tag | 69.44% | 0.53 | 0.69 | 0.60 |
| RF | CV | Word | 65.12% | 0.49 | 0.65 | 0.56 |
| | | Word+Ln Tag | 69.76% | 0.54 | 0.70 | 0.61 |
| | TF-IDF | Word | 64.27% | 0.51 | 0.64 | 0.57 |
| | | Word+Ln Tag | 69.60% | 0.53 | 0.70 | 0.60 |

Table 3: Comparison of accuracy scores of the developed models built using ML algorithms.

matrix of token counts was used as a feature. This implementation produces a sparse representation of the counts. Since we did not provide an a-priori dictionary and did not use an analyzer that does some kind of feature selection, the number of features was equal to the vocabulary size found by analyzing the data.

For the second model, we used the TF-IDF Vectorizer, with maximum features of 5000, where it converts a collection of raw documents to a matrix of TF-IDF features. We used the 2-gram and 3-gram range for this.

Also, for the third and the fourth model, the same features, Count Vectorizer and TF-IDF Vectorizer were used but in this case, we went for data augmentation, where the input was changed from words only to the form of $Word\_LanguageTag$.

On validation, the accuracy metrics garnered by the developed models, are shown in Table 3.

## 5 Evaluation

From Tables 2 and 3, we can see that though the ML and DL models perform neck-in-neck, but still, we preferred the DL model, developed using Bidirectional LSTM's and language tag feature as it garnered the highest F1-Score. This model was then tested using 3,149 test data, provided by the shared task organizers. The results of the testing phase of the selected model are quantified in Table 4.

| Model | Precision | Recall | F1-Score |
|---|---|---|---|
| Bi-LSTM+ ln tag | 0.59 | 0.66 | 0.58 |

Table 4: Final evaluation of the model, developed using Bidirectional LSTMs and Language Tag features.

## 6 Conclusion

In the current work, we attempted to solve the problem of Sentiment Analysis of code-mixed English-Tamil sentences. Our system was based on using Bi-Directional LSTM along with Language Tag features. Also, FastText embedding was used to generate word vectors to train the model. For predicting the language tags, another deep learning system, based on character embedding was also developed. Other models, based on traditional ML algorithms were also developed that was used to compare our developed model. Our system, when evaluated on the test data, garnered an F1 score of 0.58. As future work, we would like to increase this data, as deep learning algorithms tend to work well with higher amount of data and use state-of-the-art Neural Network architectures, like BERT, RoBERTa, etc., on this data, taking into advantage the concept of matrix and embedded language, SentiWordNet, and other NLP features.

## References


Alfred V. Aho and Jeffrey D. Ullman. 1972. *The Theory of Parsing, Translation and Compiling*, volume 1. Prentice-Hall, Englewood Cliffs, NJ.

American Psychological Association. 1983. *Publications Manual*. American Psychological Association, Washington, DC.

Rie Kubota Ando and Tong Zhang. 2005. A framework for learning predictive structures from multiple tasks and unlabeled data. *Journal of Machine Learning Research*, 6:1817–1853.

Galen Andrew and Jianfeng Gao. 2007. Scalable training of L1-regularized log-linear models. In *Proceedings of the 24th International Conference on Machine Learning*, pages 33–40.

David M Blei, Andrew Y Ng, and Michael I Jordan. 2003. Latent dirichlet allocation. *Journal of machine Learning research*, 3(Jan):993–1022.

Piotr Bojanowski, Edouard Grave, Armand Joulin, and Tomas Mikolov. 2016. Enriching word vectors with subword information. *arXiv preprint arXiv:1607.04606*.

Bharathi Raja Chakravarthi. 2020a. HopeEDI: A multilingual hope speech detection dataset for equality, diversity, and inclusion. In *Proceedings of the Third Workshop on Computational Modeling of People's Opinions, Personality, and Emotion's in Social Media*, pages 41–53, Barcelona, Spain (Online). Association for Computational Linguistics.

Bharathi Raja Chakravarthi. 2020b. *Leveraging orthographic information to improve machine translation of under-resourced languages*. Ph.D. thesis, NUI Galway.

Bharathi Raja Chakravarthi, Mihael Arcan, and John P. McCrae. 2018. Improving wordnets for under-resourced languages using machine translation. In *Proceedings of the 9th Global Wordnet Conference*, pages 77–86, Nanyang Technological University (NTU), Singapore. Global Wordnet Association.

Bharathi Raja Chakravarthi, Mihael Arcan, and John P. McCrae. 2019. WordNet gloss translation for under-resourced languages using multilingual neural machine translation. In *Proceedings of the Second Workshop on Multilingualism at the Intersection of Knowledge Bases and Machine Translation*, pages 1–7, Dublin, Ireland. European Association for Machine Translation.

Bharathi Raja Chakravarthi, Navya Jose, Shardul Suryawanshi, Elizabeth Sherly, and John Philip McCrae. 2020a. A sentiment analysis dataset for code-mixed Malayalam-English. In *Proceedings of the 1st Joint Workshop on Spoken Language Technologies for Under-resourced languages (SLTU) and Collaboration and Computing for Under-Resourced Languages (CCURL)*, pages 177–184, Marseille, France. European Language Resources association.

Bharathi Raja Chakravarthi, M Anand Kumar, John Philip McCrae, Premjith B, Soman KP, and Thomas Mandl. 2020b. Overview of the track on HASOC-Offensive Language Identification-DravidianCodeMix. In *Working Notes of the Forum for Information Retrieval Evaluation (FIRE 2020). CEUR Workshop Proceedings. In: CEUR-WS. org, Hyderabad, India*.

Bharathi Raja Chakravarthi and Vigneshwaran Muralidaran. 2021. Findings of the shared task on Hope Speech Detection for Equality, Diversity, and Inclusion. In *Proceedings of the First Workshop on Language Technology for Equality, Diversity and Inclusion*. Association for Computational Linguistics.

Bharathi Raja Chakravarthi, Vigneshwaran Muralidaran, Ruba Priyadharshini, and John Philip McCrae. 2020c. Corpus creation for sentiment analysis in code-mixed Tamil-English text. In *Proceedings of the 1st Joint Workshop on Spoken Language Technologies for Under-resourced languages (SLTU) and Collaboration and Computing for Under-Resourced Languages (CCURL)*, pages 202–210, Marseille, France. European Language Resources association.

Bharathi Raja Chakravarthi, Ruba Priyadharshini, Shubhanker Banerjee, Richard Saldhana, John Philip McCrae, Anand Kumar M, Parameswari Krishnamurthy, and Melvin Johnson. 2021a. Findings of the shared task on Machine Translation in Dravidian languages. In *Proceedings of the First Workshop on Speech and Language Technologies for Dravidian Languages*. Association for Computational Linguistics.

Bharathi Raja Chakravarthi, Ruba Priyadharshini, Navya Jose, Anand Kumar M, Thomas Mandl, Prasanna Kumar Kumaresan, Rahul Ponnusamy, Hariharan V, Elizabeth Sherly, and John Philip McCrae. 2021b. Findings of the shared task on Offensive Language Identification in Tamil, Malayalam, and Kannada. In *Proceedings of the First Workshop on Speech and Language Technologies for Dravidian Languages*. Association for Computational Linguistics.

Bharathi Raja Chakravarthi, Ruba Priyadharshini, Vigneshwaran Muralidaran, Shardul Suryawanshi, Navya Jose, Elizabeth Sherly, and John P. McCrae. 2020d. Overview of the Track on Sentiment Analysis for Dravidian Languages in Code-Mixed Text. In *Forum for Information Retrieval Evaluation*, FIRE 2020, page 21–24, New York, NY, USA. Association for Computing Machinery.

Bharathi Raja Chakravarthi, Ruba Priyadharshini, Vigneshwaran Muralidaran, Shardul Suryawanshi, Navya Jose, Elizabeth Sherly, and John Philip McCrae. 2020e. Overview of the track on Sentiment Analysis for Dravidian Languages in Code-Mixed Text. In *Proceedings of the 12th Forum for Information Retrieval Evaluation*, FIRE '20.

Bharathi Raja Chakravarthi, Ruba Priyadharshini, Vigneshwaran Muralidaran, Shardul Suryawanshi, Navya Jose, and John Philip Sherly, Elizabeth McCrae. 2020f. Overview of the track on Sentiment Analysis for Dravidian Languages in Code-Mixed Text. In *Working Notes of the Forum for Information Retrieval Evaluation (FIRE 2020). CEUR Workshop Proceedings. In: CEUR-WS. org, Hyderabad, India.*

Bharathi Raja Chakravarthi, Navaneethan Rajasekaran, Mihael Arcan, Kevin McGuinness, Noel E. O'Connor, and John P. McCrae. 2020g. Bilingual lexicon induction across orthographically-distinct under-resourced Dravidian languages. In *Proceedings of the 7th Workshop on NLP for Similar Languages, Varieties and Dialects*, pages 57–69, Barcelona, Spain (Online). International Committee on Computational Linguistics (ICCL).

Ashok K. Chandra, Dexter C. Kozen, and Larry J. Stockmeyer. 1981. Alternation. *Journal of the Association for Computing Machinery*, 28(1):114–133.

Amitava Das and Björn Gambäck. 2014. Identifying languages at the word level in code-mixed indian social media text.

Avishek Garain, Sainik Kumar Mahata, and Dipankar Das. 2020. JUNLP at SemEval-2020 task 9:Sentiment Analysis of Hindi-English code mixed data using Grid Search Cross Validation. In *Proceedings of the 14th International Workshop on Semantic Evaluation (SemEval-2020)*, Barcelona, Spain. Association for Computational Linguistics.

Nikhil Kumar Ghanghor, Parameswari Krishnamurthy, Sajeetha Thavareesan, Ruba Priyadharshini, and Bharathi Raja Chakravarthi. 2021a. IIITK@DravidianLangTech-EACL2021: Offensive Language Identification and Meme Classification in Tamil, Malayalam and Kannada. In *Proceedings of the First Workshop on Speech and Language Technologies for Dravidian Languages*, Online. Association for Computational Linguistics.

Nikhil Kumar Ghanghor, Rahul Ponnusamy, Prasanna Kumar Kumaresan, Ruba Priyadharshini, Sajeetha Thavareesan, and Bharathi Raja Chakravarthi. 2021b. IIITK@LT-EDI-EACL2021: Hope Speech Detection for Equality, Diversity, and Inclusion in Tamil, Malayalam and English. In *Proceedings of the First Workshop on Language Technology for Equality, Diversity and Inclusion*, Online.

Dan Gusfield. 1997. *Algorithms on Strings, Trees and Sequences*. Cambridge University Press, Cambridge, UK.

Adeep Hande, Ruba Priyadharshini, and Bharathi Raja Chakravarthi. 2020. KanCMD: Kannada CodeMixed dataset for sentiment analysis and offensive language detection. In *Proceedings of the Third Workshop on Computational Modeling of People's Opinions, Personality, and Emotion's in Social Media*, pages 54–63, Barcelona, Spain (Online). Association for Computational Linguistics.

Siddhanth U Hegde, Adeep Hande, Ruba Priyadharshini, Sajeetha Thavareesan, and Bharathi Raja Chakravarthi. 2021. UVCE-IIITT@DravidianLangTech-EACL2021: Tamil Troll Meme Classification: You need to Pay more Attention. In *Proceedings of the First Workshop on Speech and Language Technologies for Dravidian Languages*. Association for Computational Linguistics.

Sepp Hochreiter and Jürgen Schmidhuber. 1997. Long short-term memory. *Neural Comput.*, 9(8):1735–1780.

Navya Jose, Bharathi Raja Chakravarthi, Shardul Suryawanshi, Elizabeth Sherly, and John P. McCrae. 2020. A Survey of Current Datasets for Code-Switching Research. In *2020 6th International Conference on Advanced Computing and Communication Systems (ICACCS)*, pages 136–141.

Sainik Kumar Mahata, Sushnat Makhija, Ayushi Agnihotri, and Dipankar Das. 2020. Analyzing code-switching rules for english–hindi code-mixed text. In *Emerging Technology in Modelling and Graphics*, pages 137–145, Singapore. Springer Singapore.

Sainik Kumar Mahata, Soumil Mandal, Dipankar Das, and Sivaji Bandyopadhyay. 2019. Code-mixed to monolingual translation framework. In *Proceedings of the 11th Forum for Information Retrieval Evaluation*, FIRE '19, page 30–35, New York, NY, USA. Association for Computing Machinery.

Soumil Mandal, Sourya Dipta Das, and Dipankar Das. 2018. Language identification of bengali-english code-mixed data using character & phonetic based lstm models. *arXiv preprint arXiv:1803.03859*.

Thomas Mandl, Sandip Modha, Anand Kumar M, and Bharathi Raja Chakravarthi. 2020. Overview of the HASOC Track at FIRE 2020: Hate Speech and Offensive Language Identification in Tamil, Malayalam, Hindi, English and German. In *Forum for Information Retrieval Evaluation*, FIRE 2020, page

29–32, New York, NY, USA. Association for Computing Machinery.

Rosalyn Negrón Goldbarg. 2009. Spanish-english codeswitching in email communication. *Language@ internet*, 6(3).

Ruba Priyadharshini, Bharathi Raja Chakravarthi, Mani Vegupatti, and John P. McCrae. 2020. Named Entity Recognition for Code-Mixed Indian Corpus using Meta Embedding. In *2020 6th International Conference on Advanced Computing and Communication Systems (ICACCS)*, pages 68–72.

Karthik Puranik, Adeep Hande, Ruba Priyadharshini, Sajeetha Thavareesan, and Bharathi Raja Chakravarthi. 2021. IIITT@LT-EDI-EACL2021-Hope Speech Detection: There is always hope in Transformers. In *Proceedings of the First Workshop on Language Technology for Equality, Diversity and Inclusion*. Association for Computational Linguistics.

Mohammad Sadegh Rasooli and Joel R. Tetreault. 2015. Yara parser: A fast and accurate dependency parser. *Computing Research Repository*, arXiv:1503.06733. Version 2.

K. Shalini, H. B. Ganesh, M. A. Kumar, and K. P. Soman. 2018. Sentiment analysis for code-mixed indian social media text with distributed representation. In *2018 International Conference on Advances in Computing, Communications and Informatics (ICACCI)*, pages 1126–1131.

Sainik Kumar Mahata Soumil Mandal and Dipankar Das. 2018. Preparing bengali-english code-mixed corpus for sentiment analysis of indian languages. In *Proceedings of the Eleventh International Conference on Language Resources and Evaluation (LREC 2018)*, Paris, France. European Language Resources Association (ELRA).

Shardul Suryawanshi and Bharathi Raja Chakravarthi. 2021. Findings of the shared task on Troll Meme Classification in Tamil. In *Proceedings of the First Workshop on Speech and Language Technologies for Dravidian Languages*. Association for Computational Linguistics.

Shardul Suryawanshi, Bharathi Raja Chakravarthi, Mihael Arcan, and Paul Buitelaar. 2020. Multimodal meme dataset (MultiOFF) for identifying offensive content in image and text. In *Proceedings of the Second Workshop on Trolling, Aggression and Cyberbullying*, pages 32–41, Marseille, France. European Language Resources Association (ELRA).

Sajeetha Thavareesan and Sinnathamby Mahesan. 2019. Sentiment Analysis in Tamil Texts: A Study on Machine Learning Techniques and Feature Representation. In *2019 14th Conference on Industrial and Information Systems (ICIIS)*, pages 320–325.

Sajeetha Thavareesan and Sinnathamby Mahesan. 2020a. Sentiment Lexicon Expansion using Word2vec and fastText for Sentiment Prediction in Tamil texts. In *2020 Moratuwa Engineering Research Conference (MERCon)*, pages 272–276.

Sajeetha Thavareesan and Sinnathamby Mahesan. 2020b. Word embedding-based Part of Speech tagging in Tamil texts. In *2020 IEEE 15th International Conference on Industrial and Information Systems (ICIIS)*, pages 478–482.

Clare R Voss, Stephen Tratz, Jamal Laoudi, and Douglas M Briesch. 2014. Finding romanized arabic dialect in code-mixed tweets. In *LREC*, pages 2249–2253.

Yogarshi Vyas, Spandana Gella, Jatin Sharma, Kalika Bali, and Monojit Choudhury. 2014. Pos tagging of english-hindi code-mixed social media content. In *Proceedings of the 2014 Conference on Empirical Methods in Natural Language Processing (EMNLP)*, pages 974–979.

Konthala Yasaswini, Karthik Puranik, Adeep Hande, Ruba Priyadharshini, Sajeetha Thavareesan, and Bharathi Raja Chakravarthi. 2021. IIITT@DravidianLangTech-EACL2021: Transfer Learning for Offensive Language Detection in Dravidian Languages. In *Proceedings of the First Workshop on Speech and Language Technologies for Dravidian Languages*. Association for Computational Linguistics.

# Offensive language identification in Dravidian code mixed social media text

**Sunil Saumya**[1], **Abhinav Kumar**[2] and **Jyoti Prakash Singh**[2]
[1]Indian Institute of Information Technology Dharwad, Karnataka, India
[2]National Institute of Technology Patna, Bihar, India
sunil.saumya@iiitdwd.ac.in,
abhinavanand05@gmail.com, jps@nitp.ac.in

## Abstract

Hate speech and offensive language recognition in social media platforms have been an active field of research over recent years. In non-native English spoken countries, social media texts are mostly in code mixed or script mixed/switched form. The current study presents extensive experiments using multiple machine learning, deep learning, and transfer learning models to detect offensive content on Twitter. The data set used for this study are in Tanglish (Tamil and English), Manglish (Malayalam and English) code-mixed, and Malayalam script-mixed. The experimental results showed that 1 to 6-gram character TF-IDF features are better for the said task. The best performing models were naive bayes, logistic regression, and vanilla neural network for the dataset Tamil code-mix, Malayalam code-mixed, and Malayalam script-mixed, respectively instead of more popular transfer learning models such as BERT and ULMFiT and hybrid deep models.

## 1 Introduction

The hate speech is generally defined as any communication which humiliates or denigrates an individual or a group based on the characteristics such as colour, ethnicity, sexual orientation, nationality, race and religion. Due to huge volume of user-generated content on the web, particularly social networks such as Twitter, Facebook, and so on, the problem of detecting and probably restricting Hate Speech on these platforms has become a very critical issue (Del Vigna12 et al., 2017). Hate speech lasts forever on these social platforms compared to physical abuse and terribly affects the individual on the mental status creating depression, sleeplessness and even suicide (Ullmann and Tomalin, 2020).

Owing to the high frequency of posts, detecting hate speech on social media manually is almost impossible. Some recent researches have indicated that the automation of hate speech detection is a more reliable solution. (Davidson et al., 2017) extracted N-gram TF-IDF features from tweets using logistical regression to classify each tweet in hate, offensive and non-offensive classes. Another model for the detection of the cyberbullying instances was presented by (Kumari and Singh, 2020) with a genetic algorithm to optimize the distinguishing features of multimodal posts. (Agarwal and Sureka, 2017) used the linguistic, semantic and sentimental feature to detect racial content. The LSTM and CNN based model for recognising hate speech in the social media posts were explored by (Kapil et al., 2020). (Badjatiya et al., 2017) exploited the semantic word embedding to classify each tweet into racist, sexist and neither class. Another deep learning model for the detection of hate speech was proposed by (Paul et al., 2020). However, most of the works for hate speech detection were validated with English datasets only.

In a country such as India, the majority of people in social media use at least two languages, primarily English and Hindi (or say Hinglish). These texts are considered bilingual. In a bilingual setting, the script of the entire post may be same with words coming from both of these languages termed as mixed-code (or code mix) text. A few popular code mixed posts in India are English and Hindi (or say Hinglish), Tanglish (Tamil and English) (Chakravarthi et al., 2020c), Manglish (Malayalam and English) (Chakravarthi et al., 2020a), Kanglish (Kannada and English) (Hande et al., 2020), and so on. The Tamil language is one of the world's longest-enduring traditional languages, with a set of experiences tracing all the way back to 600 BCE. Tamil writing is overwhelmed by verse, particularly Sangam writing, which is made out of sonnets formed between 600 BCE and 300 CE. The main Tamil creator was the writer and thinker Thiruvalluvar, who composed the Tirukkua, a gathering of



*Proceedings of the First Workshop on Speech and Language Technologies for Dravidian Languages*, pages 36–45
April 20, 2021 ©2021 Association for Computational Linguistics

compositions on morals, legislative issues, love and ethical quality broadly thought to be the best work of Tamil writing. Tamil has the oldest extant literature among Dravidian languages. All Dravidian languages evolved from classical Tamil language (Thavareesan and Mahesan, 2019, 2020a,b). Even though they have their own scripts still in the Internet code-mixing comments can be found in these languages (Chakravarthi, 2020b). Identifying hate content in such bilingual or code mixed language is a very challenging task (Jose et al., 2020; Priyadharshini et al., 2020; Chakravarthi, 2020a). An automatic model which is trained in a monolingual context to detect hate posts may not yield the same result when tested bilingually or with a code-mix (Puranik et al., 2021; Hegde et al., 2021; Yasaswini et al., 2021; Ghanghor et al., 2021b,a). This is because each system learns and recognises words in the given vocabulary. When a new word is encountered, which is not in the vocabulary, it is marked as an undefined token that makes no difference in the estimation of the model. Therefore, when checked with the language in other scripts the model's performance decreases.

The current study identifies the hate content in Tanglish, Manglish and Malayalam script mixed in tweets and validated with the dataset provided in *HASOC-Dravidian-CodeMix-FIRE2020 challenge* (Chakravarthi et al., 2020b). The dataset proposed in the challenge was collected from Twitter. A variety of deep learning models have been examined in the current paper to distinguish offensive posts from script-mixed posts. Along with that we also examined a few transfer learning models like BERT (Devlin et al., 2018a) and ULMFit (Howard and Ruder, 2018) for the classification task.

The rest of the article is summarized as follows: Section 2 presents the overview of articles proposed in the domain of hate or offensive speech. The task and dataset description is explained in Section 3. This followed by the explanation of the proposed methodology in Section 4. The experimental results and discussion are explained in Section 5 and 6. The paper concludes by highlighting the main findings in Section 7.

## 2 Related works

The hate speech identification in social media texts suffers from many challenges; such as code-mixed social media content, script-mixed social media contents, and so on. This section sheds light on a few state-of-art techniques presented to handle such issues.

Most of the analysis proposed for the detection of hate contents were validated with monolingual datasets. It is relatively easy to build a monolingual model, since (i) it is readily accessible, (ii) it learns a single language dictionary, and (iii) unknown token frequency is lower in the test data. (Davidson et al., 2017) worked on 25000 tweets in English and reported that tweets that contained racism and homophobic contexts were hate speech and tweets that contained sexism contexts were offensive contents. Other work, on English data, was proposed by (Waseem and Hovy, 2016) where n-gram features were extracted for identifying sexiest, racism, and none class.

Apart from this, some works were reported on a multilingual dataset where scripts of two or more languages are mixed. (Kumar et al., 2018) proposed a model for multi-lingual datasets containing aggressive and non-aggressive comments in English as well as Hindi from Facebook and Twitter. (Samghabadi et al., 2018) used ensemble learning based on various machine learning classifiers such as Logistic Regression, SVM with word n-gram, character n-gram, word embedding, and sentiment as a feature set. They found that combined words and character n-gram features performed better than an individual feature. (Srivastava et al., 2018) identified online social aggression on the Facebook comment in a multilingual scenario and Wikipedia toxic comments using stacked LSTM units followed by convolution layer and fastText as word representation. They achieved 0.98 AUC for Wikipedia toxic comment classification and a weighted F1 score of 0.63 for the Facebook test set and 0.59 for the Twitter test set. (Mandl et al., 2020; Chakravarthi et al., 2020d) presented several models and their results for English, Hindi, and German datasets. They reported the best model as long short term memory-based network that could capture the multilingual context in a better way. Bohra et al. (2018) extended the earlier research of hate speech detection for code mixed tweets of Hindi and English. (Kumari et al., 2021) presented a Convolutional Neural Network (CNN) and Binary Particle Swarm Optimization (BPSO) based model to classify multimodal posts with images and text into non-aggressive, medium-aggressive and high-aggressive classes. Another multilingual context could be code-mixed where two languages are written in a single script. For example, (Chakravarthi et al., 2021b; Chakravarthi and Muralidaran, 2021; Chakravarthi et al., 2021a; Suryawanshi and Chakravarthi, 2021) proposed a code mixed Dravidian data in Tamil, Malayalam, and Kannada. (Bohra et al., 2018) developed a Hinglish dataset from Twitter. They reported preliminary experiment results of Support Vector Machine (SVM) and Random Forest (RF) classifiers with n-grams and lexicon-based features with an accuracy of 0.71.

Research in hate and offensive language, as described above, is mainly conducted in a monolingual setting. The paper aims to propose a machine learning system for the code-mixed and script-mixed dataset to identify hate contents.

## 3 Task and Data description

The current study performs two tasks; (i) Task 1 includes the development of an offensive and non-offensive classification system for distinguishing *script-mixed Malayalam* comments, and (ii) Task 2 requires to build a classifier to differentiate *Tanglish* and *Manglish* (Tamil and Malayalam have written using Roman Characters) into offensive and not-offensive classes. Table 1 shows the overview of the data set used in this analysis. As can be seen in Table 1, there are three sets of data, out of which in the first sets, Malayalam code-mixed and Tamil code-mixed, the posts were written in a single script English, but in the last set, the posts were written in two different scripts (Malayalam script-mixed).

## 4 Methodology

Three different models were developed to identify hate or offensive contents in Dravidian posts; (i) conventional learning based models, (ii) neural network-based models, and (iii) transfer learning-based models. In this section, we explain the working of each model in detail. A detailed diagram for presented models is shown in Figure 1. The results of the models are explained in Section 5.

### 4.1 Conventional learning based models

In conventional machine learning-based classifications, the current study explored the use of different N-gram TF-IDF word and character features. In the case of character, 1 to 6 gram character TF-IDF features were used, whereas, in case of a word, 1 to 3 gram word TF-IDF features were used. The extracted features were fed to classifiers like Support Vector Machine (SVM), Logistic Regression (LR), Naive Bayes (NB), Random Forest (RF). The detailed performance report of word n-grams and character n-grams are shown in Section 5.

### 4.2 Neural learning-based models

Initially, the character n-grams TF-IDF features (1-6 grams) extracted in previous Section 4.1 were used as an input to a vanilla neural network (VNN) model. For the vanilla neural network, four fully connected layers were sequenced, having 1024, 256, 128, and 2 neurons in first, second, third and fourth layer, respectively. We kept two neurons in the final layer (or output layers) to identify each input in offensive groups. Based on the probabilities of softmax activation with output neurons, the last class was determined. In the intermediate layers, the activation function was ReLu. The proposed vanilla neural network was trained with cross-entropy loss function and Adam optimizer. The training dropout was 0.3 and the batch size was 32.

Consequently, other deep learning models for offensive groups prediction were also developed. A hybrid attention-based Bi-LSTM and CNN network was built as shown in Figure 1. The detailed working of the CNN and attention-based Bi-LSTM network for text classification can be seen in (Jang et al., 2020; Xu et al., 2020; Saumya et al., 2019). To CNN, character embedding was the input, whereas to Bi-LSTM, word embedding was the input. To prepare the character embedding, a one-hot vector representation of characters were used. Every input was padded with a maximum of 200 characters with repetition. The total unique character found in the vocabulary was 70. Therefore, a $(200 \times 70)$ dimensional embedding matrix was given as an input to CNN. To extract the features from the convolution layer, 128 different filters for each 1-gram, 2-gram, 3-gram, and 4-gram were used. The output of the first convolution layer was fed to the second convolution layer with similar filter dimensions. The features extracted from the CNN layers were then represented in a vector having 128 features using a dense layer.

To prepare the word embedding input for Bi-LSTM was we used FastText[1] utilizing the language-specific code-mixed Tamil and Malayalam text for Tamil and Malayalam models, respec-

[1] https://fasttext.cc/

Table 1: Data statistic used in this study

| Language | Class | Not-offensive | Offensive | Total |
|---|---|---|---|---|
| Malayalam code-mixed | Training | 2047 | 1953 | 4000 |
| | Testing | 473 | 478 | 951 |
| Tamil code-mixed | Training | 2020 | 1980 | 4000 |
| | Testing | 465 | 475 | 940 |
| Malayalam script-mixed | Training | 2633 | 567 | 3200 |
| | Development | 328 | 72 | 400 |
| | Testing | 334 | 66 | 400 |

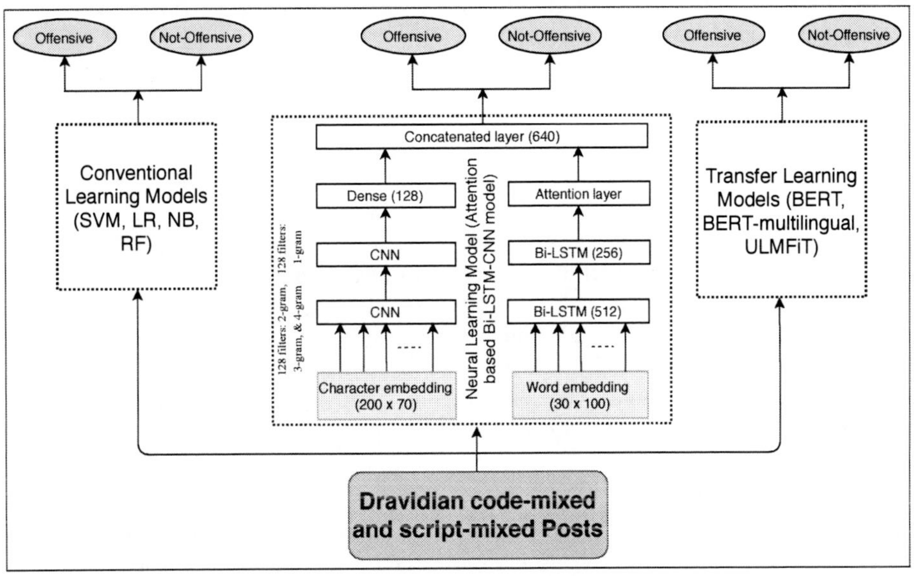


Figure 1: Proposed hybrid attention-based Bi-LSTM and CNN network

tively. The skip-gram architecture was trained for ten epochs to extract the FastText embedding vectors. A maximum of 30 words embedding vectors was given input to the network in a time stamp manner. Every word was represented in a 100-dimensional vector which was extracted from the embedding layer. Finally, a $(30 \times 100)$ dimensional matrix input was given to 2-layered stacked Bi-LSTM layer, followed by an attention layer. Finally, the output of attention-based Bi-LSTM and CNN layer is concatenated and passes through a softmax layer to predict offensive and not-offensive text.

Hyperparameters tuning was done to check the performance of the proposed deep-neural model. We conducted comprehensive experiments by adjusting the learning rate, batch size, optimizer, epoch, loss function and activation function. The system performance was best with the learning rate 0.001, batch size 32, Adam optimizer, epochs 100, loss function as binary cross-entropy, and ReLU activation within the internal layers of the network. At the output layer, the activation was softmax.

### 4.3 Transfer models

The current study used two different transfer models, BERT (Bidirectional Encoder Representations from Transformers ) and ULMFiT (Universal Language Model Fine-tuning for Text Classification) to accomplish the given objectives.

Two different variations of BERT model[2] (Devlin et al., 2018b) is used in the current study; (i) BERT base (*bert-base-uncased*), and (ii) BERT multilingual (*bert-base-multilingual-uncased*). The BERT base model is trained for English language using a masked modelling technique. Whereas, BERT multilingual is trained for 102 languages with masked language modelling. We used

[2] `https://huggingface.co/transformers/pretrained_models.html`

*ktrain*[3] libraries to develop the BERT based models. Both BERT variations are uncased that means it does not make a difference between a word written in upper case lower case. In training BERT-models, we fixed 30-words for the text to input in the model and used a batch size of 32 and a learning rate of $2e^{-5}$ to fine-tune the pre-trained model. The detailed description of the BERT model can be seen in (Sanh et al., 2019). The other transfer model used was ULMFiT. It can be applied to any task in NLP. To train ULMFiT model, we used fastai library[4]. The input and hyper-parameters were the same as we used in BERT.

## 5 Result

This section presents the experimental results of all three aforementioned models explained in Section 4. The results are presented in terms of precision, recall, and $F_1$-score of class offensive and not-offensive. The weighted average of both classes is also presented. A particular model is identified as best if it has reported the highest weighted average of precision, recall, and $F_1$-score. The value in bold represents the highest value for a particular dataset.

The convectional learning experiments were performed using character N-gram (1 to 6-gram) TF-IDF features. The results are shown in the Table 2 for SVM, LR, NB, RF. In the case of Tamil code-mixed text, the NB classifier performed best and achieved a precision, recall, and $F_1$-score of 0.90. In the case of Malayalam code-mixed text, the LR classifier performed best with the precision, recall, and $F_1$-score of 0.78. Similarly, in the case of Malayalam script-mixed RF classifier reported better performance having precision, recall of 0.95, and $F_1$-score of 0.94. Similar experiments were done for word TF-IDF features for 1 to 3 N-grams. The results are shown in the Table 3.

The results of the proposed neural-based models for Tamil code-mixed, Malayalam code-mixed, and Malayalam script-mixed text are listed in Table 4. As can be seen from the Table 4, the vanilla neural network (VNN) model outperformed attention-based Bi-LSTM-CNN for all three datasets. For Tamil code-mixed, VNN reported precision, recall, and $F_1$-score of 0.89 and for Malayalam code-mixed it reported precision, recall, and $F_1$-score of 0.77. Similarly, for Malayalam script-mixed data, the proposed vanilla neural network reported a precision, recall, and $F_1$ score of 0.95.

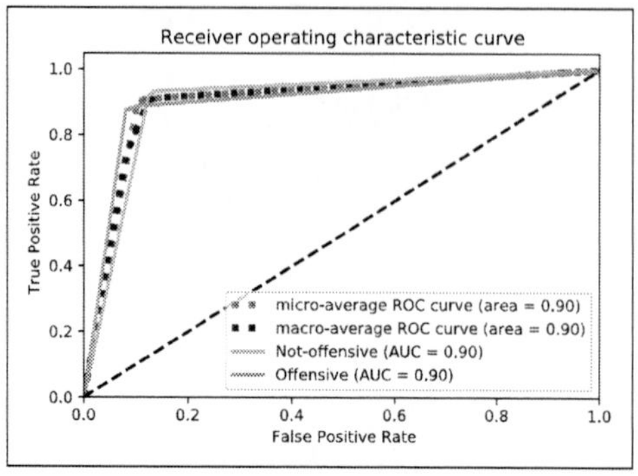


Figure 2: ROC for Naive Bayes (Tamil code-mixed)

Finally, the experimental results of transfer models are shown in Table 5. The table shows the results of three transfer models BERT, BERT-multilingual, and ULMFiT. In Malayalam script-mixed text, the BERT-multilingual model achieved the highest precision, recall, and $F_1$-score of 0.93. Even, for Tamil code-mixed text, BERT-multilingual performed better than others with precision, recall, and $F_1$-score of 0.86. The results of the BERT model was also comparable with precision, recall, and $F_1$-score of 0.89, 0.84, and 0.86. But, for Malayalam code-mixed BERT performance was highest with precision, recall, and $F_1$-score of 0.76.

## 6 Result Comparison and Discussion

Of all the experimental models, conventional learning models with character 1 to 6 gram TF-IDF features showed the best output for the two datasets, Tamil code-mixed and Malayalam code-mixed. For Tamil code-mixed, the best performance was reported by NB model with precision, recall, and $F_1$-score of 0.90. Similarly, for Malayalam code-mixed the LR model reported best with precision, recall, and $F_1$-score of 0.78. However, for the Malayalam Script mixed, Vanilla Neural Network (VNN) reported best results having precision, recall, and $F_1$-score of 0.95, 0.95, and 0.95 respectively. The receiver operating characteristics (ROC) area under curve for all three best models are shown in Figures 2, 3, and 4.

The outcome of this comprehensive study was surprising, given that the performance of all complex models, such as the BiLSTM-CNN hybrid model and Transfer models, was relatively low, but

[3] https://github.com/amaiya/ktrain
[4] https://nlp.fast.ai/

Table 2: Results for the different classifiers with character 1 to 6-gram TF-IDF feature

| Models | Class | Tamil (Code-mixed) | | | Malayalam (Code-mixed) | | | Malayalam (Script-mixed) | | |
|---|---|---|---|---|---|---|---|---|---|---|
| | | Precision | Recall | $F_1$-score | Precision | Recall | $F_1$-score | Precision | Recall | $F_1$-score |
| **SVM** | Offensive | 0.87 | 0.90 | 0.88 | 0.83 | 0.69 | 0.75 | 0.97 | 0.56 | 0.71 |
| | Not-offensive | 0.89 | 0.86 | 0.88 | 0.73 | 0.86 | 0.79 | 0.92 | 1.00 | 0.96 |
| | Weighted Avg. | 0.88 | 0.88 | 0.88 | 0.78 | 0.77 | 0.77 | 0.93 | 0.93 | 0.92 |
| **LR** | Offensive | 0.88 | 0.89 | 0.89 | 0.81 | 0.72 | 0.77 | 0.91 | 0.30 | 0.45 |
| | Not-offensive | 0.89 | 0.88 | 0.88 | 0.75 | 0.83 | 0.79 | 0.88 | 0.99 | 0.93 |
| | Weighted Avg. | 0.89 | 0.89 | 0.89 | **0.78** | **0.78** | **0.78** | 0.88 | 0.88 | 0.85 |
| **NB** | Offensive | 0.92 | 0.88 | 0.90 | 0.79 | 0.63 | 0.70 | 0.49 | 0.73 | 0.59 |
| | Not-offensive | 0.88 | 0.92 | 0.90 | 0.69 | 0.83 | 0.75 | 0.94 | 0.85 | 0.89 |
| | Weighted Avg. | **0.90** | **0.90** | **0.90** | 0.74 | 0.73 | 0.73 | 0.87 | 0.83 | 0.84 |
| **RF** | Offensive | 0.85 | 0.90 | 0.88 | 0.78 | 0.70 | 0.74 | 0.96 | 0.71 | 0.82 |
| | Not-offensive | 0.89 | 0.84 | 0.87 | 0.72 | 0.81 | 0.76 | 0.95 | 0.99 | 0.97 |
| | Weighted Avg. | 0.87 | 0.87 | 0.87 | 0.75 | 0.75 | 0.75 | **0.95** | **0.95** | **0.94** |

Table 3: Results for the different classifiers with word 1 to 3-gram TF-IDF feature

| Models | Class | Tamil (Code-mixed) | | | Malayalam (Code-mixed) | | | Malayalam (Script-mixed) | | |
|---|---|---|---|---|---|---|---|---|---|---|
| | | Precision | Recall | $F_1$-score | Precision | Recall | $F_1$-score | Precision | Recall | $F_1$-score |
| **SVM** | Offensive | 0.64 | 0.94 | 0.76 | 0.75 | 0.55 | 0.63 | 1.00 | 0.53 | 0.69 |
| | Not-offensive | 0.88 | 0.46 | 0.60 | 0.64 | 0.81 | 0.72 | 0.92 | 1.00 | 0.96 |
| | Weighted Avg. | 0.76 | 0.70 | 0.68 | 0.69 | 0.68 | 0.67 | 0.93 | 0.92 | 0.91 |
| **LR** | Offensive | 0.88 | 0.86 | 0.87 | 0.75 | 0.68 | 0.71 | 0.91 | 0.30 | 0.45 |
| | Not-offensive | 0.86 | 0.88 | 0.87 | 0.70 | 0.77 | 0.74 | 0.88 | 0.99 | 0.93 |
| | Weighted Avg. | **0.87** | **0.87** | **0.87** | **0.73** | **0.73** | **0.73** | 0.88 | 0.88 | 0.85 |
| **NB** | Offensive | 0.67 | 0.82 | 0.74 | 0.68 | 0.62 | 0.65 | 0.47 | 0.83 | 0.60 |
| | Not-offensive | 0.76 | 0.59 | 0.67 | 0.65 | 0.71 | 0.68 | 0.96 | 0.81 | 0.88 |
| | Weighted Avg. | 0.72 | 0.71 | 0.70 | 0.67 | 0.66 | 0.66 | 0.88 | 0.81 | 0.83 |
| **RF** | Offensive | 0.78 | 0.89 | 0.83 | 0.70 | 0.66 | 0.68 | 0.94 | 0.67 | 0.78 |
| | Not-offensive | 0.87 | 0.75 | 0.80 | 0.67 | 0.71 | 0.69 | 0.94 | 0.99 | 0.96 |
| | Weighted Avg. | 0.83 | 0.82 | 0.82 | 0.69 | 0.68 | 0.68 | **0.94** | **0.94** | **0.93** |

Table 4: Results for the VNN and attention-based BiLSTM-CNN models

| Models | Class | Tamil (code-mixed) | | | Malayalam (Code-mixed) | | | Malayalam (script-mixed) | | |
|---|---|---|---|---|---|---|---|---|---|---|
| | | Precision | Recall | F1-score | Precision | Recall | F1-score | Precision | Recall | F1-score |
| **Vanilla NN** | Offensive | 0.87 | 0.91 | 0.89 | 0.77 | 0.78 | 0.78 | 0.96 | 0.76 | 0.85 |
| | Not-offensive | 0.91 | 0.86 | 0.88 | 0.78 | 0.76 | 0.76 | 0.95 | 0.99 | 0.97 |
| | Weighted-Avg | **0.89** | **0.89** | **0.89** | **0.77** | **0.77** | **0.77** | **0.95** | **0.95** | **0.95** |
| **Attention-based BiLSTM-CNN** | Offensive | 0.85 | 0.83 | 0.84 | 0.71 | 0.71 | 0.71 | 0.89 | 0.68 | 0.77 |
| | Not-offensive | 0.83 | 0.85 | 0.84 | 0.71 | 0.71 | 0.71 | 0.93 | 0.98 | 0.96 |
| | Weighted-Avg | 0.84 | 0.84 | 0.84 | 0.71 | 0.71 | 0.71 | 0.93 | 0.93 | 0.92 |

Table 5: Results transfer models BERT and ULMFiT

| Models | Class | Tamil (code-mixed) | | | Malayalam (Code-mixed) | | | Malayalam (script-mixed) | | |
|---|---|---|---|---|---|---|---|---|---|---|
| | | Precision | Recall | F1-score | Precision | Recall | F1-score | Precision | Recall | F1-score |
| **BERT** | Offensive | 0.93 | 0.77 | 0.84 | 0.71 | 0.79 | 0.75 | 0.73 | 0.73 | 0.73 |
| | Not-offensive | 0.85 | 0.92 | 0.88 | 0.81 | 0.73 | 0.77 | 0.73 | 0.73 | 0.73 |
| | Weighted-Avg | 0.89 | 0.84 | 0.86 | **0.76** | **0.76** | **0.76** | 0.73 | 0.73 | 0.73 |
| **BERT Muiltilingual** | Offensive | 0.85 | 0.87 | 0.86 | 0.75 | 0.68 | 0.72 | 0.95 | 0.97 | 0.96 |
| | Not-offensive | 0.86 | 0.85 | 0.86 | 0.71 | 0.77 | 0.74 | 0.83 | 0.74 | 0.78 |
| | Weighted-Avg | **0.86** | **0.86** | **0.86** | 0.73 | 0.73 | 0.73 | **0.93** | **0.93** | **0.93** |
| **ULMFit** | Offensive | 0.72 | 0.63 | 0.67 | 0.30 | 0.51 | 0.38 | 0.57 | 0.68 | 0.62 |
| | Not-offensive | 0.56 | 0.57 | 0.57 | 0.71 | 0.50 | 0.59 | 0.72 | 0.56 | 0.63 |
| | Weighted-Avg | 0.65 | 0.60 | 0.62 | 0.59 | 0.50 | 0.52 | 0.66 | 0.61 | 0.63 |

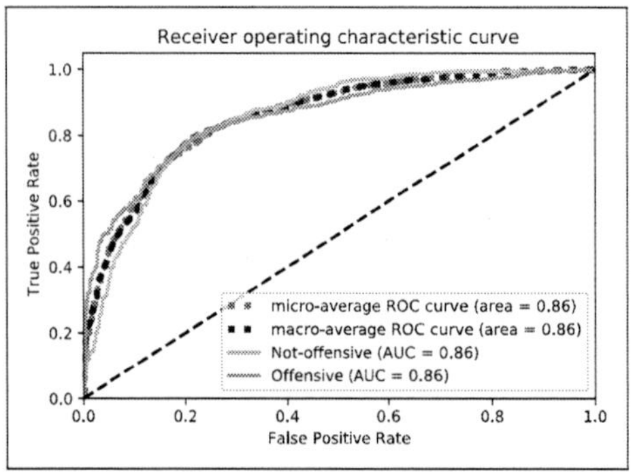


Figure 3: ROC for Logistic Regression (Malayalam code-mixed)

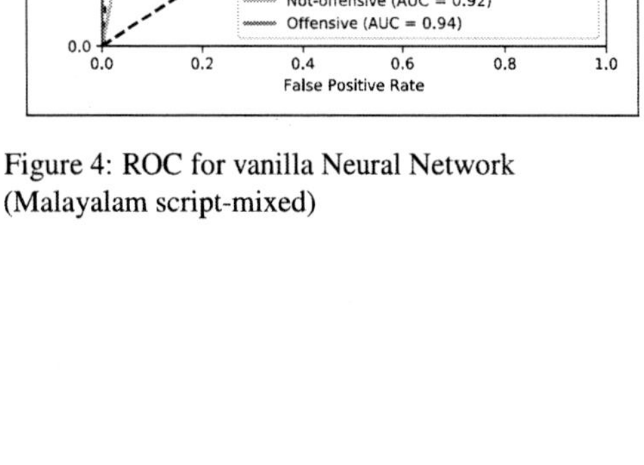


Figure 4: ROC for vanilla Neural Network (Malayalam script-mixed)

for many NLP tasks, such as text classification or language modelling, it was proven better.

The results indicate that the character n-gram TF-IDF features play a very important role for code-mixed and code-script data. Secondly, in the same sense, the performance of the transfer models is not encouraging. BERT, which is trained in the English language, treats most of the token of code-mixed and code-script data as an unknown token which could affect the model performance. The BERT-multilingual which is trained on 102 languages identifies the language of input text first and loads its vocabulary then. Even, for code-mixed and code-script data BERT-multilingual identified a single language and was subsequently processed. In effect, the overall model performance was reduced. Moreover, it was found that the language identified by BERT-multilingual for code-mixed and the code-script dataset was different for different runs. Consequently, the results fluctuated even.

## 7 Conclusion

Hate speech identification in code-mixed and script-mixed context is one of the most challenging tasks in NLP. The current study presented extensive experiments utilizing various conventional learning, deep learning, and transfer learning models. Three datasets used in the study were Tamil code-mixed, Malayalam code-mixed, and Malayalam script-mixed. The results reported by all models clearly show that conventional learning models along with vanilla neural model outperformed other complex deep learning, and transfer learning models. The character N-gram TF-IDF based Naive Bayes classifier performed best with the weighted precision, recall, and $F_1$-score of 0.90 for Tamil code-mixed text. The Logistic regression classifier with character N-gram TF-IDF features performed best with the weighted precision, recall, and $F_1$-score of 0.78 for Malayalam code-mixed text. The Vanilla Neural Network with character N-gram TF-IDF features performed best with the weighted precision of 0.95, recall of 0.95, and $F_1$-score of 0.95 for Malayalam script-mixed text.

## References

Swati Agarwal and Ashish Sureka. 2017. Characterizing linguistic attributes for automatic classification of intent based racist/radicalized posts on tumblr micro-blogging website. *arXiv preprint arXiv:1701.04931*.

Pinkesh Badjatiya, Shashank Gupta, Manish Gupta, and Vasudeva Varma. 2017. Deep learning for hate speech detection in tweets. In *Proceedings of the 26th International Conference on WWW Companion*, pages 759–760.

Aditya Bohra, Deepanshu Vijay, Vinay Singh, Syed Sarfaraz Akhtar, and Manish Shrivastava. 2018. A Dataset of Hindi-English Code-Mixed Social Media Text for Hate Speech Detection. In *Proceedings of the Second Workshop on Computational Modeling of People's Opinions, Personality, and Emotions in Social Media*, pages 36–41.

Bharathi Raja Chakravarthi. 2020a. HopeEDI: A multilingual hope speech detection dataset for equality, diversity, and inclusion. In *Proceedings of the Third Workshop on Computational Modeling of People's Opinions, Personality, and Emotion's in Social Media*, pages 41–53, Barcelona, Spain (Online). Association for Computational Linguistics.

Bharathi Raja Chakravarthi. 2020b. *Leveraging orthographic information to improve machine translation of under-resourced languages*. Ph.D. thesis, NUI Galway.

Bharathi Raja Chakravarthi, Navya Jose, Shardul Suryawanshi, Elizabeth Sherly, and John Philip McCrae. 2020a. A sentiment analysis dataset for code-mixed Malayalam-English. In *Proceedings of the 1st Joint Workshop on Spoken Language Technologies for Under-resourced languages (SLTU) and Collaboration and Computing for Under-Resourced Languages (CCURL)*, pages 177–184, Marseille, France. European Language Resources association.

Bharathi Raja Chakravarthi, M Anand Kumar, John Philip McCrae, Premjith B, Soman KP, and Thomas Mandl. 2020b. Overview of the track on HASOC-Offensive Language Identification-DravidianCodeMix. In *Working Notes of the Forum for Information Retrieval Evaluation (FIRE 2020). CEUR Workshop Proceedings. In: CEUR-WS. org, Hyderabad, India*.

Bharathi Raja Chakravarthi and Vigneshwaran Muralidaran. 2021. Findings of the shared task on Hope Speech Detection for Equality, Diversity, and Inclusion. In *Proceedings of the First Workshop on Language Technology for Equality, Diversity and Inclusion*. Association for Computational Linguistics.

Bharathi Raja Chakravarthi, Vigneshwaran Muralidaran, Ruba Priyadharshini, and John Philip McCrae. 2020c. Corpus creation for sentiment analysis in code-mixed Tamil-English text. In *Proceedings of the 1st Joint Workshop on Spoken Language Technologies for Under-resourced languages (SLTU) and Collaboration and Computing for Under-Resourced Languages (CCURL)*, pages 202–210, Marseille, France. European Language Resources association.

Bharathi Raja Chakravarthi, Ruba Priyadharshini, Shubhanker Banerjee, Richard Saldhana, John Philip McCrae, Anand Kumar M, Parameswari Krishnamurthy, and Melvin Johnson. 2021a. Findings of the shared task on Machine Translation in Dravidian languages. In *Proceedings of the First Workshop on Speech and Language Technologies for Dravidian Languages*. Association for Computational Linguistics.

Bharathi Raja Chakravarthi, Ruba Priyadharshini, Navya Jose, Anand Kumar M, Thomas Mandl, Prasanna Kumar Kumaresan, Rahul Ponnusamy, Hariharan V, Elizabeth Sherly, and John Philip McCrae. 2021b. Findings of the shared task on Offensive Language Identification in Tamil, Malayalam, and Kannada. In *Proceedings of the First Workshop on Speech and Language Technologies for Dravidian Languages*. Association for Computational Linguistics.

Bharathi Raja Chakravarthi, Ruba Priyadharshini, Vigneshwaran Muralidaran, Shardul Suryawanshi, Navya Jose, Elizabeth Sherly, and John P. McCrae. 2020d. Overview of the Track on Sentiment Analysis for Dravidian Languages in Code-Mixed Text. In *Forum for Information Retrieval Evaluation*, FIRE 2020, page 21–24, New York, NY, USA. Association for Computing Machinery.

Thomas Davidson, Dana Warmsley, Michael Macy, and Ingmar Weber. 2017. Automated hate speech detection and the problem of offensive language. *arXiv preprint arXiv:1703.04009*.

Fabio Del Vigna12, Andrea Cimino23, Felice Dell'Orletta, Marinella Petrocchi, and Maurizio Tesconi. 2017. Hate me, hate me not: Hate speech detection on facebook. In *Proceedings of the First Italian Conference on Cybersecurity (ITASEC17)*, pages 86–95.

Jacob Devlin, Ming-Wei Chang, Kenton Lee, and Kristina Toutanova. 2018a. Bert: Pre-training of deep bidirectional transformers for language understanding. *arXiv preprint arXiv:1810.04805*.

Jacob Devlin, Ming-Wei Chang, Kenton Lee, and Kristina Toutanova. 2018b. BERT: pre-training of deep bidirectional transformers for language understanding. *CoRR*, abs/1810.04805.

Nikhil Kumar Ghanghor, Parameswari Krishnamurthy, Sajeetha Thavareesan, Ruba Priyadharshini, and Bharathi Raja Chakravarthi. 2021a. IIITK@DravidianLangTech-EACL2021: Offensive Language Identification and Meme Classification in Tamil, Malayalam and Kannada. In *Proceedings of the First Workshop on Speech and Language Technologies for Dravidian Languages*, Online. Association for Computational Linguistics.

Nikhil Kumar Ghanghor, Rahul Ponnusamy, Prasanna Kumar Kumaresan, Ruba Priyadharshini, Sajeetha Thavareesan, and Bharathi Raja

Chakravarthi. 2021b. IIITK@LT-EDI-EACL2021: Hope Speech Detection for Equality, Diversity, and Inclusion in Tamil, Malayalam and English. In *Proceedings of the First Workshop on Language Technology for Equality, Diversity and Inclusion*, Online.

Adeep Hande, Ruba Priyadharshini, and Bharathi Raja Chakravarthi. 2020. KanCMD: Kannada CodeMixed dataset for sentiment analysis and offensive language detection. In *Proceedings of the Third Workshop on Computational Modeling of People's Opinions, Personality, and Emotion's in Social Media*, pages 54–63, Barcelona, Spain (Online). Association for Computational Linguistics.

Siddhanth U Hegde, Adeep Hande, Ruba Priyadharshini, Sajeetha Thavareesan, and Bharathi Raja Chakravarthi. 2021. UVCE-IIITT@DravidianLangTech-EACL2021: Tamil Troll Meme Classification: You need to Pay more Attention. In *Proceedings of the First Workshop on Speech and Language Technologies for Dravidian Languages*. Association for Computational Linguistics.

Jeremy Howard and Sebastian Ruder. 2018. Universal language model fine-tuning for text classification. *arXiv preprint arXiv:1801.06146*.

Beakcheol Jang, Myeonghwi Kim, Gaspard Harerimana, Sang-ug Kang, and Jong Wook Kim. 2020. Bi-lstm model to increase accuracy in text classification: combining word2vec cnn and attention mechanism. *Applied Sciences*, 10(17):5841.

Navya Jose, Bharathi Raja Chakravarthi, Shardul Suryawanshi, Elizabeth Sherly, and John P. McCrae. 2020. A Survey of Current Datasets for Code-Switching Research. In *2020 6th International Conference on Advanced Computing and Communication Systems (ICACCS)*, pages 136–141.

Prashant Kapil, Asif Ekbal, and Dipankar Das. 2020. Investigating deep learning approaches for hate speech detection in social media. *arXiv preprint arXiv:2005.14690*.

Ritesh Kumar, Guggilla Bhanodai, Rajendra Pamula, and Maheshwar Reddy Chennuru. 2018. Trac-1 shared task on aggression identification: Iit (ism) @ coling'18. In *Proceedings of the First Workshop on Trolling, Aggression and Cyberbullying (TRAC-2018)*, pages 58–65.

Kirti Kumari and Jyoti Prakash Singh. 2020. Identification of cyberbullying on multi-modal social media posts using genetic algorithm. *Transactions on Emerging Telecommunications Technologies*, page e3907.

Kirti Kumari, Jyoti Prakash Singh, Yogesh K Dwivedi, and Nripendra P Rana. 2021. Multi-modal aggression identification using convolutional neural network and binary particle swarm optimization. *Future Generation Computer Systems*.

Thomas Mandl, Sandip Modha, Anand Kumar M, and Bharathi Raja Chakravarthi. 2020. Overview of the HASOC Track at FIRE 2020: Hate Speech and Offensive Language Identification in Tamil, Malayalam, Hindi, English and German. In *Forum for Information Retrieval Evaluation*, FIRE 2020, page 29–32, New York, NY, USA. Association for Computing Machinery.

Sayanta Paul, Sriparna Saha, and Mohammed Hasanuzzaman. 2020. Identification of cyberbullying: A deep learning based multimodal approach. *Multimedia Tools and Applications*, pages 1–20.

Ruba Priyadharshini, Bharathi Raja Chakravarthi, Mani Vegupatti, and John P. McCrae. 2020. Named Entity Recognition for Code-Mixed Indian Corpus using Meta Embedding. In *2020 6th International Conference on Advanced Computing and Communication Systems (ICACCS)*, pages 68–72.

Karthik Puranik, Adeep Hande, Ruba Priyadharshini, Sajeetha Thavareesan, and Bharathi Raja Chakravarthi. 2021. IIITT@LT-EDI-EACL2021-Hope Speech Detection: There is always hope in Transformers. In *Proceedings of the First Workshop on Language Technology for Equality, Diversity and Inclusion*. Association for Computational Linguistics.

Niloofar Safi Samghabadi, Deepthi Mave, Sudipta Kar, and Thamar Solorio. 2018. Ritual-uh at trac 2018 shared task: Aggression identification. In *Proceedings of the First Workshop on Trolling, Aggression and Cyberbullying (TRAC-2018)*, pages 12–18.

Victor Sanh, Lysandre Debut, Julien Chaumond, and Thomas Wolf. 2019. DistilBERT, a distilled version of BERT: smaller, faster, cheaper and lighter. *arXiv preprint arXiv:1910.01108*.

Sunil Saumya, Jyoti Prakash Singh, and Yogesh K Dwivedi. 2019. Predicting the helpfulness score of online reviews using convolutional neural network. *Soft Computing*, pages 1–17.

Saurabh Srivastava, Prerna Khurana, and Vartika Tewari. 2018. Identifying aggression and toxicity in comments using capsule network. In *Proceedings of the First Workshop on Trolling, Aggression and Cyberbullying (TRAC-2018)*, pages 98–105.

Shardul Suryawanshi and Bharathi Raja Chakravarthi. 2021. Findings of the shared task on Troll Meme Classification in Tamil. In *Proceedings of the First Workshop on Speech and Language Technologies for Dravidian Languages*. Association for Computational Linguistics.

Sajeetha Thavareesan and Sinnathamby Mahesan. 2019. Sentiment Analysis in Tamil Texts: A Study on Machine Learning Techniques and Feature Representation. In *2019 14th Conference on Industrial and Information Systems (ICIIS)*, pages 320–325.

Sajeetha Thavareesan and Sinnathamby Mahesan. 2020a. Sentiment Lexicon Expansion using Word2vec and fastText for Sentiment Prediction in Tamil texts. In *2020 Moratuwa Engineering Research Conference (MERCon)*, pages 272–276.

Sajeetha Thavareesan and Sinnathamby Mahesan. 2020b. Word embedding-based Part of Speech tagging in Tamil texts. In *2020 IEEE 15th International Conference on Industrial and Information Systems (ICIIS)*, pages 478–482.

Stefanie Ullmann and Marcus Tomalin. 2020. Quarantining online hate speech: technical and ethical perspectives. *Ethics and Information Technology*, 22(1):69–80.

Zeerak Waseem and Dirk Hovy. 2016. Hateful symbols or hateful people? predictive features for hate speech detection on twitter. In *Proceedings of the NAACL student research workshop*, pages 88–93.

Jingyun Xu, Yi Cai, Xin Wu, Xue Lei, Qingbao Huang, Ho-fung Leung, and Qing Li. 2020. Incorporating context-relevant concepts into convolutional neural networks for short text classification. *Neurocomputing*, 386:42–53.

Konthala Yasaswini, Karthik Puranik, Adeep Hande, Ruba Priyadharshini, Sajeetha Thavareesan, and Bharathi Raja Chakravarthi. 2021. IIITT@DravidianLangTech-EACL2021: Transfer Learning for Offensive Language Detection in Dravidian Languages. In *Proceedings of the First Workshop on Speech and Language Technologies for Dravidian Languages*. Association for Computational Linguistics.

# Sentiment Analysis of Dravidian Code Mixed Data

**Asrita Venkata Mandalam**
Department of CSIS
BITS Pilani, Pilani Campus
Rajasthan, India
f20171179
@pilani.bits-pilani.ac.in

**Yashvardhan Sharma**
Department of CSIS
BITS Pilani, Pilani Campus
Rajasthan, India
yash
@pilani.bits-pilani.ac.in

## Abstract

This paper presents the methodologies implemented while classifying Dravidian code-mixed comments according to their polarity. With datasets of code-mixed Tamil and Malayalam available, three methods are proposed - a sub-word level model, a word embedding based model and a machine learning based architecture. The sub-word and word embedding based models utilized Long Short Term Memory (LSTM) network along with language-specific preprocessing while the machine learning model used term frequency–inverse document frequency (TF-IDF) vectorization along with a Logistic Regression model. The sub-word level model was submitted to the the track 'Sentiment Analysis for Dravidian Languages in Code-Mixed Text' proposed by Forum of Information Retrieval Evaluation in 2020 (FIRE 2020). Although it received a rank of 5 and 12 for the Tamil and Malayalam tasks respectively in the FIRE 2020 track, this paper improves upon the results by a margin to attain final weighted F1-scores of 0.65 for the Tamil task and 0.68 for the Malayalam task. The former score is equivalent to that attained by the highest ranked team of the Tamil track.

## 1 Introduction

Code-mixing usually involves two languages to create another language that consists of elements of both in a structurally understandable manner. It has been noted that bilingual and multilingual societies use multiple languages together in informal speech and text. Dravidian code-mixed languages, including but not limited to Malayalam and Tamil, are increasingly used by younger generations in advertising, entertainment and social media. The language is commonly written in Roman script.

With the rise in the number of non-English and multilingual speakers using social media, there is an interest in analysing the sentiment of the content posted by them. As code-mixed data does not belong to one language and is often written using Roman script, identifying its polarity cannot be done using traditional sentiment analysis models(Puranik et al., 2021; Hegde et al., 2021; Yasaswini et al., 2021; Ghanghor et al., 2021b,a). In social media, low-resourced languages such as Tamil and Malayalam have been increasingly used along with English (Thavareesan and Mahesan, 2019, 2020a,b). Indian government declared Tamil as classical language in 2004, meaning that it meets three criteria: its sources are old; it has an independent tradition; and it has a significant body of ancient literature. The most ancient non-Sanskritic Indian literature is found in Tamil. The earliest existing Tamil literary works and their commentaries commemorate the organisation of long-term Tamil Sangams (600 BCE to 300 CE) by the Pandiyan Rulers, which studied, established and made improvements in the language of Tamil. Identifying the sentiment of this data can prove to be useful in social media monitoring and feedback of users towards other online content.

The 'Sentiment Analysis for Dravidian Languages in Code-Mixed Text' task proposed by FIRE 2020 (Chakravarthi et al., 2020c; Chakravarthi, 2020) contains a code-mixed dataset consisting of comments from social media websites for both Tamil and Malayalam. Each team had to submit a set of predicted sentiments for the Tamil-English and Malayalam-English mixed test sets (Chakravarthi et al., 2020d). Along with language specific preprocessing techniques, the implemented model made use of sub-word level representations to incorporate features at the morpheme level, the smallest meaningful unit of any language. Evaluated by weighted average F1-score, the sub-word level approach achieved the 5th highest score



*Proceedings of the First Workshop on Speech and Language Technologies for Dravidian Languages*, pages 46–54
April 20, 2021 ©2021 Association for Computational Linguistics

in the Tamil task and the 12th rank in the Malayalam task (Sharma and Mandalam, 2020).

This paper presents the aforementioned model and two more models - a word embedding based model and a machine learning model in an attempt to improve upon the submitted weighted F1-scores. The highest scoring model for the Tamil dataset received a score equivalent to the highest scoring model presented at the Sentiment Analysis for Dravidian Languages in Code-Mixed Text track of FIRE 2020. Although they achieved it using a Bidirectional Encoder Representations from Transformers (BERT) based model, the model presented in this paper uses Word2Vec and FastText embeddings to achieve the same score. The implemented models are available on Github[1].

## 2 Related Work

Analysing the sentiment of code-mixed data is important as traditional methods fail when given such data. Barman et al. (2014) concluded that n-grams proved to be useful in their experiments that involved multiple languages with Roman script.

Bojanowski et al. (2017) used character n-grams in their skip-gram model. The lack of preprocessing resulted in a shorter training time and outperformed baselines that did not consider sub-word information. Joshi et al. (2016) outperformed existing systems as well by using a sub-word based LSTM architecture. Their dataset consisted of 15% negative, 50% neutral and 35% positive comments. As their dataset was imbalanced like the one used in this paper, the submitted approach involved morpheme extraction as it would help in identifying the polarity of the dataset. Using a hybrid architecture, Lal et al. (2019) an F1-score of 0.827 on the Hindi-English dataset released by Joshi et al. (2016). After generating the sub-word level information of the input data, they used one Bidirectional LSTM to figure out the sentiment of the given sentence and another to select the sub-words that contributed to the overall sentiment of the sentence.

In more recent work, Jose et al. (2020) surveyed publicly available code-mixed datasets. They noted statistics about each dataset such as vocabulary size and sentence length. Priyadharshini et al. (2020) used embeddings of closely related languages of the code-mixed corpus to predict Named Entities of the same corpus.Yadav and Chakraborty (2020) used multilingual embeddings to identify the sentiment of code-mixed text. As they used an unsupervised approach, they performed sentiment analysis by using the embeddings to transfer knowledge from monolingual text to their code-mixed input. Yadav et al. (2020) designed an ensemble model consisting of four classifiers - Naive Bayes, Support-Vector Machines (SVM), Linear Regression, and Stochastic Gradient Descent (SGD) classifiers. They tested it on a Hindi-English code-mix dataset and managed to surpass the scores attained by the baseline and state-of-art systems.

The proposed models test three approaches - subword analysis, word-level embeddings and machine learning algorithm based classification. The top few submissions submitted at the 'Sentiment Analysis for Dravidian Languages in Code-Mixed Text' task proposed by FIRE 2020 (Chakravarthi et al., 2020c) used BERT-based models. This work aims to attain the same F1-score with help of non-BERT-based approaches. As Dravidian code-mixed languages are under-resourced, this paper also describes the preprocessing methods used to aid in the sentiment classification of comments that contain both Roman and Tamil/Malayalam characters.

## 3 Dataset

The model has been trained, validated and tested using the Tamil (Chakravarthi et al., 2020b) and Malayalam (Chakravarthi et al., 2020a) datasets provided by the organizers of the Dravidian Code-Mix FIRE 2020 task. The Tamil code-mix dataset consists of 11,335 comments for the train set, 1,260 for the validation set and 3,149 comments for testing the model. In the Malayalam code-mix dataset, there are 4,851 comments for training, 541 for validating and 1,348 for testing the model. Table 1 gives the distribution of each sentiment in each dataset.

## 4 Proposed Technique

### 4.1 Sub-word level model

The submitted approach used a sub-word level model as it accounts for words that have a similar morpheme. For example, in the Tamil dataset, *Ivan*, *Ivanga* and *Ivana* have similar meanings due to their root word *Ivan*.

First, the dataset is preprocessed to replace all emojis with their corresponding description in English. As the dataset contains both Roman and

[1] `https://github.com/avmand/SA_Dravidian`

| Dataset | Positive | Negative | Mixed Feelings | Unknown State | Other Languages |
|---|---|---|---|---|---|
| Tamil | 10,559 | 2,037 | 1,801 | 850 | 497 |
| Malayalam | 2,811 | 738 | 403 | 1,903 | 884 |

Table 1: Distribution of Data in the Tamil and Malayalam Dataset

Tamil (or Malayalam) characters, the latter is replaced with its corresponding Roman script representation.

From the preprocessed data, a set of characters was obtained. The input to the model is a set of character embeddings. The sub-word level representation is generated through a 1-D convolution layer with activation as ReLU, size of convolutional window as 5 and number of output filters as 128. After getting a morpheme-level feature map, a 1-D maximum pooling layer is used to obtain its most prominent features. To obtain the connections between each of these features, LSTMs are used due to their ability to process sequences and retain information. The first and second LSTM layers have a dropout of 0.4 and 0.2 respectively. Finally, it is passed to a fully connected layer. Batch normalization has been used in the model to prevent overfitting. While training the model, early stopping has been utilized to stop training when the validation loss shows no improvement after 4 epochs. The training data was shuffled before each epoch.

### 4.2 Word Embedding model

This model utilizes two word embedding architectures - continuous bag of words (CBOW) and FastText. This approach was tested after the track had ended and submissions were no longer accepted.

After replacing all of the emojis with their description, non-Tamil and non-Malayalam characters were replaced with their corresponding Roman script representation. Words with multiple repeating characters were shortened to include only one of those multiple characters.

The CBOW model utilized the Word2Vec (Mikolov et al., 2013) method provided by the *gensim* library. As the average length of each comment was 50, the window size was taken as 15. The minimum frequency of words that were taken into consideration was 2 and the architecture was trained on the training data for 10 epoch cycles. The FastText model was trained for 10 iterations and had a window size of 15 as well. These word vectors were created with a dimensionality of 100 and were concatenated to create an embedding matrix. For the classification of the input data, two LSTM layers were used after the embedding layer. The dimensionality of the output space of the first and second LSTM layers were 64 and 32 repectively. Similar to the previous model, batch normalization and early stopping were used with the model automatically stopping training after 5 epoch cycles.

### 4.3 Machine Learning model

Till now, all of the tested models used deep learning based classifiers. As the input data is skewed and is considerably small, two different machine learning models were used to predict the sentiment of the given code-mixed comments.

Before using the classifier, the data was preprocessed and feature extraction using TF-IDF vectorization. The top 5000 features were extracted. Originally, only 300 features were extracted but increasing the number of features resulted in an increase in the weighted F1-score. The features included both unigrams and bigrams. Sub-linear term frequency scaling was applied.

Two different classifiers were tested with the help of the scikit-learn library- Linear Support Vector Machine Classification (Linear SVC) and Logistic Regression. The tolerance for the Linear SVC model was '1e-6' and the multi-class strategy used was 'crammer_singer'. For the Logistic Regression model, the 'newton-cg' algorithm was used for optimization. A binary problem was fit for each of the labels by using the 'ovr' option for the multi_class parameter. The value for the inverse of regulation strength (C) was tested with values in the range of 1 to 20 inclusive.

## 5 Result

The submitted run achieved a rank of 5 and 12 for the Tamil and Malayalam tasks respectively. There were a total of 32 teams that submitted their results for the Tamil task. For the Malayalam task, 28 teams submitted their solution. The final rank was evaluated based on the weighted average F1-score. The classification report is shown in Table 2. The Tamil task received Precision, Recall and an F1-

score of 0.62, 0.66 and 0.61 respectively. For the Malayalam task, the submission received scores of 0.67, 0.59 and 0.60 respectively.

Out of the models that were tested after the deadline for the FIRE 2020 track, the word embedding model performed the best for the Tamil dataset. It attained a weighted F1-score of 0.65, which is the same as the team that scored the highest in the Dravidian Code-Mix FIRE 2020 track. For the Malayalam dataset, the Logistic Regression based model scored the highest with a weighted F1-score of 0.68. For both datasets, the Linear SVC model performed worse than the Logistic Regression model by at least 1%. It was noted that the optimal value for C was 12 for the Tamil dataset and 5 for the Malayalam dataset.

## 6 Error Analysis

### 6.1 Tamil Task

#### 6.1.1 Sub-word level model

From Table 2, one can see that the F1-score of the positive comments is the highest with a value of 0.80. The next highest score is only at 0.46, attained by the class of comments that are not in Tamil. The order of classes from the highest to the lowest F1-scores are Positive, Not Tamil, Negative, Mixed Feelings and Unknown State. The weighted F1-score is lower than the Precision and Recall as the weighted score takes into account the proportion of each class in the dataset.

Due to the higher number of positive comments in the overall dataset, it is not surprising that the model trains well and produces the best results for that class. Non-Tamil comments get the next highest score due to the different morphemes used in them. These comments are usually in a different Indian language like Hindi or Telugu and are written using the English alphabet. Some comments are written in the script of their respective language. This class does not achieve a higher score due to words that they have in common with the Tamil-English code-mixed comments such as *Rajinikanth* and *Thalaiva*. The same can be concluded for the negative label as well as it had many words that were common with those of the positive comments. Comments from the mixed feelings class were misclassified as either positive or negative. They were not misclassified as comments from the unknown state class possibly due to the relatively lower ratio of unknown comments as compared to the positive and negative classes. As these comments contained both positive and negative sentiments, there was a much higher chance of them being classified into one of those classes. The unknown state class receives the lowest F1-score. Its precision is 0.67 but its recall is very low at 0.01. This implies that there is a high false negative rate and is because all of the comments use words from the Tamil vocabulary. Most of those words are common with those of the positive class. Table 5 gives a representation of the misclassified Tamil comments.

#### 6.1.2 Machine Learning model

The machine learning based model performed better than the sub-word level model for the Tamil dataset. Out of the tested machine learning models, the Logistic Regression model performed better, with a weighted F1-score of 0.62. The detailed result can be seen in Table 4. As the Linear SVC model received poorer results with a weighted F1-score of 0.61, it has not been represented in any of the tables. There has been an improvement in the weighted F1-scores of the negative, non-Tamil and unknown state classes. An interesting improvement is the increase in the F1-score of the unknown class as it jumped from 0.02 to 0.22. Table 7 represents the distribution of predicted classes for each class.

#### 6.1.3 Word Embedding model

The word embedding based model performed the best out of the tested models for this dataset with a weighted F1-score of 0.65, the same score as the highest ranked model submitted to the Sentiment Analysis of Dravidian Code Mixed Data FIRE 2020 track. The result of this model can be seen in Table 3. In this model as well, the positive class performed the best with an F1-score of 0.81. Compared to the other two tested models, this model received a higher F1-score for the mixed feelings, negative, positive and unknown state classes. For the classification of comments that were not in Tamil, this class performed much better than the sub-word model but slightly worse than the machine learning model. Table 6 shows that most of the misclassified comments were classified as positive. For the positive comments, the misclassified comments were mainly misclassified into the negative class. This is because negative and positive words, although they may be opposites, are used in similar sentences with a similar word set. This might have led the word embedding models to assign close vectors for them. Another reason for the same might be the fact that the negative class had

| Language | Report | Precision | Recall | F1-Score | Support |
|---|---|---|---|---|---|
| Tamil | Mixed Feelings | 0.26 | 0.17 | 0.21 | 377 |
| | Negative | 0.42 | 0.22 | 0.29 | 424 |
| | Positive | 0.72 | 0.91 | **0.80** | 2075 |
| | Not Tamil | 0.71 | 0.34 | 0.46 | 100 |
| | Unknown State | 0.67 | 0.01 | 0.02 | 173 |
| | Macro Avg | 0.55 | 0.33 | 0.35 | 3149 |
| | **Weighted Avg** | **0.62** | **0.66** | **0.61** | 3149 |
| Malayalam | Mixed Feelings | 0.21 | 0.51 | 0.30 | 70 |
| | Negative | 0.35 | 0.55 | 0.43 | 138 |
| | Positive | 0.73 | 0.73 | **0.73** | 565 |
| | Not Malayalam | 0.58 | 0.68 | 0.63 | 177 |
| | Unknown State | 0.81 | 0.38 | 0.52 | 398 |
| | Macro Avg | 0.54 | 0.57 | 0.52 | 3149 |
| | **Weighted Avg** | **0.67** | **0.59** | **0.60** | 1348 |

Table 2: Classification report for each dataset and class for the sub-word level model.

| Language | Report | Precision | Recall | F1-Score | Support |
|---|---|---|---|---|---|
| Tamil | Mixed Feelings | 0.19 | 0.36 | 0.25 | 377 |
| | Negative | 0.31 | 0.49 | 0.38 | 424 |
| | Positive | 0.70 | 0.95 | **0.81** | 2075 |
| | Not Tamil | 0.58 | 0.64 | 0.61 | 100 |
| | Unknown State | 0.26 | 0.36 | 0.30 | 173 |
| | Macro Avg | 0.41 | 0.56 | 0.47 | 3149 |
| | **Weighted Avg** | **0.56** | **0.78** | **0.65** | 3149 |
| Malayalam | Mixed Feelings | 0.35 | 0.40 | 0.37 | 70 |
| | Negative | 0.39 | 0.54 | 0.45 | 138 |
| | Positive | 0.58 | 0.87 | **0.70** | 565 |
| | Not Malayalam | 0.55 | 0.85 | 0.67 | 177 |
| | Unknown State | 0.51 | 0.84 | 0.63 | 398 |
| | Macro Avg | 0.47 | 0.70 | 0.56 | 3149 |
| | **Weighted Avg** | **0.52** | **0.80** | **0.63** | 1348 |

Table 3: Classification report for each dataset and class for the word embedding model.

| Language | Report | Precision | Recall | F1-Score | Support |
|---|---|---|---|---|---|
| Tamil | Mixed Feelings | 0.25 | 0.10 | 0.14 | 377 |
| | Negative | 0.40 | 0.26 | 0.32 | 424 |
| | Positive | 0.73 | 0.90 | **0.80** | 2075 |
| | Not Tamil | 0.72 | 0.57 | 0.64 | 100 |
| | Unknown State | 0.35 | 0.16 | 0.22 | 173 |
| | Macro Avg | 0.49 | 0.40 | 0.42 | 3149 |
| | **Weighted Avg** | **0.60** | **0.67** | **0.62** | 3149 |
| Malayalam | Mixed Feelings | 0.65 | 0.34 | 0.45 | 70 |
| | Negative | 0.69 | 0.49 | 0.57 | 138 |
| | Positive | 0.70 | 0.81 | **0.75** | 565 |
| | Not Malayalam | 0.72 | 0.65 | 0.68 | 177 |
| | Unknown State | 0.64 | 0.64 | 0.64 | 398 |
| | Macro Avg | 0.68 | 0.59 | 0.62 | 3149 |
| | **Weighted Avg** | **0.68** | **0.68** | **0.68** | 1348 |

Table 4: Classification report for each dataset and class for the machine learning model.

the next highest count of comments.

## 6.2 Malayalam Task

### 6.2.1 Sub-word level model

The classification report of the Malayalam task can be seen in Table 2. The F1-score of the positive comments is the highest at 0.73. The next highest is at 0.63, for the class of comments that are not in Malayalam. The order of classes from the highest to the lowest F1-scores are Positive, Not Malayalam, Unknown State, Negative and Mixed Feelings.

The Malayalam dataset was more balanced as compared to the Tamil dataset with the second largest class less than 1000 comments behind the largest one. Similar to the Tamil dataset, the positive class has the highest number of comments. This led to the relatively higher F1-score and an equally low false positive and false negative rate. For the class of comments that were not in Malayalam, the classifier identified all of the comments that were not written in the Roman or Malayalam script. However, words that were commonly found in positive comments, such as names of Malayalam actors, and were used with English words were classified incorrectly. For the unknown state class, it is noted that the misclassified comments were majorly assigned a positive, negative or mixed feelings tag. Although the overall sentiment of the sentence was unknown, a portion of that sentence had similarities with one of the other classes. For the mixed feelings class, the same was deduced and most of the wrongly classified comments were assigned either a positive or negative tag. Most of the misclassified comments from the negative class were labelled as comments with mixed feelings. Sarcastic comments that used positive words but implied negative sentiments were not accounted for by the model. The distribution of misclassified comments can be seen in Table 5.

### 6.2.2 Word Embedding model

The Malayalam dataset received a weighted F1-score of 0.63 when tested upon the word embedding model. Although this is higher than the F1-score obtained by the sub-word level model, it did not attain a greater accuracy than that of the Tamil dataset. This is possibly due to the fact that the Tamil dataset was much larger than the Malayalam dataset. The result can be seen in Table 3. Compared to the sub-word level model, this model managed to gain a higher F1-score in all of the classes except for the positive class. Table 6 represents the distribution of misclassified comments across all of the tested classes.

### 6.2.3 Machine Learning model

The classification report of this model can be seen in Table 4. This model performed the best out of the three tested models with a weighted average F1-score of 0.68. It outperformed the rest of the models in terms of the F1-score for each class as well. The positive class received the highest score with a value of 0.75. For this dataset, the Logistic Regression model performed better than the Linear SVC model which attained a weighted F1-score of 0.66 and hence, the result of the Linear SVC model has not been recorded in any of the tables. Table 7 represents the distribution of misclassified comments, organized by the expected classification. It can be seen that not many comments were misclassified as not Malayalam and this is mainly due to the difference in vocabulary. Not many comments were misclassified as negative or mixed-feelings. This is partially due to the fact that the top two classes by count are the positive and unknown state classes.

# 7 Conclusion

This paper presents the submitted approach for the Sentiment Analysis for Dravidian Languages in Code-Mixed Text track of Forum for Information Retrieval Evaluation (FIRE) 2020 and two more models to improve upon the previously attained results. The results show that the positive class in each dataset receives the highest F1-scores, regardless of the model. This is due to the higher ratio of the same as compared to the rest of the classes. Comments that were not in the language of their dataset received the next highest score as their vocabulary included sub-words and words that were not a part of the rest of the datasets. Although, the top ranked submissions (Chakravarthi et al., 2020d) used BERT-based models for the Tamil task of the Dravidian Languages in Code-Mixed Text FIRE 2020 track, the presented work made use of word-embedding modelling and attained a weighted F1-score equal to that achieved by the highest scoring team. For future work, a sarcasm detection feature could be included to avoid misclassification of comments from the positive, negative and mixed-feelings classes.

| | | Predicted | | | | |
|---|---|---|---|---|---|---|
| Language | Actual | Mixed-Feelings | Negative | Positive | Not Tamil/ Malayalam | Unknown State |
| Tamil | Mixed-Feelings | 65 | 37 | 273 | 2 | 0 |
| | Negative | 61 | 92 | 268 | 3 | 0 |
| | Positive | 117 | 69 | 1880 | 8 | 1 |
| | Not Tamil | 3 | 12 | 51 | 34 | 0 |
| | Unknown State | 8 | 11 | 151 | 1 | 2 |
| Malayalam | Mixed-Feelings | 36 | 12 | 18 | 4 | 0 |
| | Negative | 39 | 76 | 12 | 4 | 7 |
| | Positive | 44 | 56 | 413 | 25 | 27 |
| | Not Malayalam | 5 | 8 | 42 | 121 | 1 |
| | Unknown State | 48 | 66 | 77 | 54 | 153 |

Table 5: Error Analysis for each dataset and class for the sub-word level model.

| | | Predicted | | | | |
|---|---|---|---|---|---|---|
| Language | Actual | Mixed-Feelings | Negative | Positive | Not Tamil/ Malayalam | Unknown State |
| Tamil | Mixed-Feelings | 14 | 38 | 311 | 4 | 10 |
| | Negative | 16 | 80 | 315 | 6 | 7 |
| | Positive | 20 | 75 | 1929 | 15 | 36 |
| | Not Tamil | 0 | 1 | 47 | 51 | 1 |
| | Unknown State | 6 | 13 | 130 | 1 | 23 |
| Malayalam | Mixed-Feelings | 21 | 1 | 21 | 3 | 24 |
| | Negative | 3 | 49 | 26 | 3 | 57 |
| | Positive | 8 | 14 | 396 | 20 | 127 |
| | Not Malayalam | 3 | 1 | 35 | 113 | 25 |
| | Unknown State | 6 | 9 | 71 | 21 | 291 |

Table 6: Error Analysis for each dataset and class for the word embedding model.

| | | Predicted | | | | |
|---|---|---|---|---|---|---|
| Language | Actual | Mixed-Feelings | Negative | Positive | Not Tamil/ Malayalam | Unknown State |
| Tamil | Mixed-Feelings | 36 | 46 | 284 | 5 | 6 |
| | Negative | 32 | 112 | 268 | 4 | 8 |
| | Positive | 63 | 101 | 1865 | 10 | 36 |
| | Not Tamil | 1 | 5 | 35 | 57 | 2 |
| | Unknown State | 12 | 14 | 116 | 3 | 28 |
| Malayalam | Mixed-Feelings | 23 | 3 | 28 | 2 | 14 |
| | Negative | 2 | 67 | 41 | 3 | 25 |
| | Positive | 1 | 10 | 463 | 19 | 72 |
| | Not Malayalam | 0 | 4 | 33 | 113 | 27 |
| | Unknown State | 7 | 11 | 101 | 21 | 258 |

Table 7: Error Analysis for each dataset and class for the machine learning model.

## Acknowledgments

The authors would like to convey their sincere thanks to the Department of Science and Technology (ICPS Division), New Delhi, India, for providing financial assistance under the Data Science (DS) Research of Interdisciplinary Cyber Physical Systems (ICPS) Programme [DST/ICPS/CLUSTER/Data Science/2018/Proposal-16:(T-856)] at the department of computer science, Birla Institute of Technology and Science, Pilani, India.

Authors are also thankful to the authorities of Birla Institute of Technology and Science, Pilani, to provide basic infrastructure facilities during the preparation of the paper.

## References

Utsab Barman, Amitava Das, Joachim Wagner, and Jennifer Foster. 2014. Code mixing: A challenge for language identification in the language of social media. In *Proceedings of the First Workshop on Computational Approaches to Code Switching*, pages 13–23, Doha, Qatar. Association for Computational Linguistics.

Piotr Bojanowski, Edouard Grave, Armand Joulin, and Tomas Mikolov. 2017. Enriching word vectors with subword information. *Transactions of the Association for Computational Linguistics*, 5:135–146.

Bharathi Raja Chakravarthi. 2020. *Leveraging orthographic information to improve machine translation of under-resourced languages*. Ph.D. thesis, NUI Galway.

Bharathi Raja Chakravarthi, Navya Jose, Shardul Suryawanshi, Elizabeth Sherly, and John Philip McCrae. 2020a. A sentiment analysis dataset for code-mixed Malayalam-English. In *Proceedings of the 1st Joint Workshop on Spoken Language Technologies for Under-resourced languages (SLTU) and Collaboration and Computing for Under-Resourced Languages (CCURL)*, pages 177–184, Marseille, France. European Language Resources association.

Bharathi Raja Chakravarthi, Vigneshwaran Muralidaran, Ruba Priyadharshini, and John Philip McCrae. 2020b. Corpus creation for sentiment analysis in code-mixed Tamil-English text. In *Proceedings of the 1st Joint Workshop on Spoken Language Technologies for Under-resourced languages (SLTU) and Collaboration and Computing for Under-Resourced Languages (CCURL)*, pages 202–210, Marseille, France. European Language Resources association.

Bharathi Raja Chakravarthi, Ruba Priyadharshini, Vigneshwaran Muralidaran, Shardul Suryawanshi, Navya Jose, Elizabeth Sherly, and John Philip McCrae. 2020c. Overview of the track on Sentiment Analysis for Dravidian Languages in Code-Mixed Text. In *Proceedings of the 12th Forum for Information Retrieval Evaluation*, FIRE '20.

Bharathi Raja Chakravarthi, Ruba Priyadharshini, Vigneshwaran Muralidaran, Shardul Suryawanshi, Navya Jose, Elizabeth Sherly, and John Philip McCrae. 2020d. Overview of the track on Sentiment Analysis for Dravidian Languages in Code-Mixed Text. In *Working Notes of the Forum for Information Retrieval Evaluation (FIRE 2020). CEUR Workshop Proceedings. In: CEUR-WS. org, Hyderabad, India.*

Nikhil Kumar Ghanghor, Parameswari Krishnamurthy, Sajeetha Thavareesan, Ruba Priyadharshini, and Bharathi Raja Chakravarthi. 2021a. IIITK@DravidianLangTech-EACL2021: Offensive Language Identification and Meme Classification in Tamil, Malayalam and Kannada. In *Proceedings of the First Workshop on Speech and Language Technologies for Dravidian Languages*, Online. Association for Computational Linguistics.

Nikhil Kumar Ghanghor, Rahul Ponnusamy, Prasanna Kumar Kumaresan, Ruba Priyadharshini, Sajeetha Thavareesan, and Bharathi Raja Chakravarthi. 2021b. IIITK@LT-EDI-EACL2021: Hope Speech Detection for Equality, Diversity, and Inclusion in Tamil, Malayalam and English. In *Proceedings of the First Workshop on Language Technology for Equality, Diversity and Inclusion*, Online.

Siddhanth U Hegde, Adeep Hande, Ruba Priyadharshini, Sajeetha Thavareesan, and Bharathi Raja Chakravarthi. 2021. UVCE-IIITT@DravidianLangTech-EACL2021: Tamil Troll Meme Classification: You need to Pay more Attention. In *Proceedings of the First Workshop on Speech and Language Technologies for Dravidian Languages*. Association for Computational Linguistics.

Navya Jose, Bharathi Raja Chakravarthi, Shardul Suryawanshi, Elizabeth Sherly, and John P McCrae. 2020. A survey of current datasets for code-switching research. In *2020 6th International Conference on Advanced Computing and Communication Systems (ICACCS)*, pages 136–141.

Aditya Joshi, Ameya Prabhu, Manish Shrivastava, and Vasudeva Varma. 2016. Towards sub-word level compositions for sentiment analysis of Hindi-English code mixed text. In *Proceedings of COLING 2016, the 26th International Conference on Computational Linguistics: Technical Papers*, pages 2482–2491, Osaka, Japan. The COLING 2016 Organizing Committee.

Yash Kumar Lal, Vaibhav Kumar, Mrinal Dhar, Manish Shrivastava, and Philipp Koehn. 2019. De-mixing sentiment from code-mixed text. In *Proceedings of the 57th Annual Meeting of the Association for*

*Computational Linguistics: Student Research Workshop*, pages 371–377, Florence, Italy. Association for Computational Linguistics.

Tomas Mikolov, Kai Chen, Greg Corrado, and Jeffrey Dean. 2013. Efficient estimation of word representations in vector space. *arXiv preprint arXiv:1301.3781*.

Ruba Priyadharshini, Bharathi Raja Chakravarthi, Mani Vegupatti, and John P McCrae. 2020. Named entity recognition for code-mixed indian corpus using meta embedding. In *2020 6th International Conference on Advanced Computing and Communication Systems (ICACCS)*, pages 68–72.

Karthik Puranik, Adeep Hande, Ruba Priyadharshini, Sajeetha Thavareesan, and Bharathi Raja Chakravarthi. 2021. IIITT@LT-EDI-EACL2021-Hope Speech Detection: There is always hope in Transformers. In *Proceedings of the First Workshop on Language Technology for Equality, Diversity and Inclusion*. Association for Computational Linguistics.

Yashvardhan Sharma and Asrita Venkata Mandalam. 2020. bits2020@dravidian-codemix-fire2020: Subword level sentiment analysis of dravidian code mixed data. In *Working Notes of the Forum for Information Retrieval Evaluation (FIRE 2020). CEUR Workshop Proceedings. In: CEUR-WS. org, Hyderabad, India*.

Sajeetha Thavareesan and Sinnathamby Mahesan. 2019. Sentiment Analysis in Tamil Texts: A Study on Machine Learning Techniques and Feature Representation. In *2019 14th Conference on Industrial and Information Systems (ICIIS)*, pages 320–325.

Sajeetha Thavareesan and Sinnathamby Mahesan. 2020a. Sentiment Lexicon Expansion using Word2vec and fastText for Sentiment Prediction in Tamil texts. In *2020 Moratuwa Engineering Research Conference (MERCon)*, pages 272–276.

Sajeetha Thavareesan and Sinnathamby Mahesan. 2020b. Word embedding-based Part of Speech tagging in Tamil texts. In *2020 IEEE 15th International Conference on Industrial and Information Systems (ICIIS)*, pages 478–482.

Konark Yadav, Aashish Lamba, Dhruv Gupta, Ansh Gupta, Purnendu Karmakar, and Sandeep Saini. 2020. Bi-lstm and ensemble based bilingual sentiment analysis for a code-mixed hindi-english social media text. In *2020 IEEE 17th India Council International Conference (INDICON)*, pages 1–6.

Siddharth Yadav and Tanmoy Chakraborty. 2020. Unsupervised sentiment analysis for code-mixed data.

Konthala Yasaswini, Karthik Puranik, Adeep Hande, Ruba Priyadharshini, Sajeetha Thavareesan, and Bharathi Raja Chakravarthi. 2021. IIITT@DravidianLangTech-EACL2021: Transfer Learning for Offensive Language Detection in Dravidian Languages. In *Proceedings of the First Workshop on Speech and Language Technologies for Dravidian Languages*. Association for Computational Linguistics.

# Unsupervised Machine Translation On Dravidian Languages

**Sai Koneru, Danni Liu and Jan Niehues**
Department of Data Science and Knowledge Engineering, Maastricht University
s.koneru@student.maastrichtuniversity.nl
{danni.liu, jan.niehues}@maastrichtuniversity.nl

## Abstract

Unsupervised neural machine translation (UNMT) is beneficial especially for low resource languages such as those from the Dravidian family. However, UNMT systems tend to fail in realistic scenarios involving actual low resource languages. Recent works propose to utilize auxiliary parallel data and have achieved state-of-the-art results. In this work, we focus on unsupervised translation between English and Kannada, a low resource Dravidian language. We additionally utilize a limited amount of auxiliary data between English and other related Dravidian languages. We show that unifying the writing systems is essential in unsupervised translation between the Dravidian languages. We explore several model architectures that use the auxiliary data in order to maximize knowledge sharing and enable UNMT for distant language pairs. Our experiments demonstrate that it is crucial to include auxiliary languages that are similar to our focal language, Kannada. Furthermore, we propose a metric to measure language similarity and show that it serves as a good indicator for selecting the auxiliary languages.

## 1 Introduction

Around 200 million people in the world speak a Dravidian language which has almost 80 varieties (Kolipakam et al., 2018). Given the significant number of speakers, improving translation quality on these languages is an important task to facilitate intercultural communication. While neural machine translation (NMT) systems (Bahdanau et al., 2015; Vaswani et al., 2017) led to great improvements on high resource languages, a major challenge remains when there is little parallel data between the source and target languages. Compared to resource-rich languages like German and French, the amount of high-quality parallel data for Dravidian languages is minimal. As a result, the current translation quality for Dravidian languages is largely lagging behind.

Unsupervised neural machine translation (UNMT; Artetxe et al., 2018, Lample et al., 2018) learns to translate between languages without relying on parallel data. Instead, only monolingual corpora are required. This relieves the need to acquire large parallel datasets, which is especially difficult for low resource languages. Despite this attractive property, existing literature (Marchisio et al., 2020; Kim et al., 2020) suggests that UNMT performs well under the following conditions: 1) Source and target languages are similar; 2) Monolingual data for both the languages belong to the same domain. In most realistic scenarios that call for unsupervised translation, these conditions are rarely fulfilled.

Considering these challenges, one promising research direction to address these conditions is to combine multilingual NMT models with unsupervised translation (Liu et al., 2020; Li et al., 2020b; Garcia et al., 2020b; Guzmán et al., 2019). Incorporating similar high resource languages could alleviate the data scarcity of low resource languages by exploiting the language similarity between them. Fraser (2020) describes this scenario as "unsupervised machine translation with multilingual transfer". For example, Li et al. (2020a) investigate translating between German to Upper Sorbian with no parallel data between them but using parallel data between the high resource languages German and English. Among Dravidian languages, the comparatively better resourced ones are Tamil, Telugu, Malayalam and Kannada. In turn, among these four languages, Kannada is relatively low resource compared to the others (Reddy and Sharoff, 2011). Therefore, we consider a realistic scenario of improving translation quality on Kannada using auxiliary data in the other three languages. We refer to the additional language as *reference language*



*Proceedings of the First Workshop on Speech and Language Technologies for Dravidian Languages*, pages 55–64
April 20, 2021 ©2021 Association for Computational Linguistics

following the terminology in Li et al. (2020b).

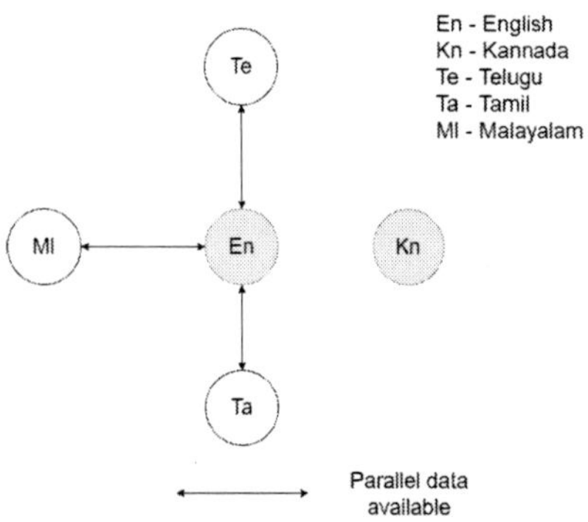


Figure 1: Illustration of the data conditions of the languages in our work. Connected nodes indicate availability of parallel data. We focus on translating between English and Kannada (blue nodes) without any parallel data.

In this work, with a focus on Dravidian languages, we analyze the influence of related languages as auxiliary data in various setups of multilingual UNMT (MUNMT). As shown in Figure 1, we focus on a scenario of translating between Kannada and English with the following conditions: 1) no parallel data for Kannada-English; 2) very limited in-domain parallel data (~30k sentences) between English and three other Dravidian languages; 3) monolingual data for all five languages in a different domain from the test data.

Our main contributions in this paper are:

- We show that transliteration is beneficial in UNMT between related languages that do not share the same writing system.
- We investigated multiple architectures to include reference languages and enable MUNMT for diverse language pair such as English and Kannada.
- We analyze the influence of language similarity and show the importance of using reference languages similar to Kannada.

## 2 Related Work

Initial work on UNMT (Lample et al., 2018) demonstrates the possibility of building unsupervised bilingual systems between similar and high resource languages. However, as shown recently (Guzmán et al., 2019; Marchisio et al., 2020; Kim et al., 2020), purely unsupervised systems perform poorly in situations with low resource and distant language pairs . However, often it is in this very case that unsupervised translation could be helpful. Guzmán et al. (2019) propose a hybrid approach that translates between Nepali and English without parallel data by utilizing parallel data between Hindi and English. Specifically, the model is trained jointly with supervised loss between English and Hindi and unsupervised loss between English and Nepali. In our work, we employ additional loss terms on top of this in order to more tightly connect the languages without parallel data. Moreover, we analyze ways to incorporate auxiliary parallel data and investigate the correlation to language similarity.

The current state-of-the-art UNMT systems build upon multilingual pretraining (Liu et al., 2020; Garcia et al., 2020b) and include a large number of languages from diverse languages families. The high degree of multilinguality is expected to lead to better model generalization. In this work, we zoom in on Dravidian languages and study how we can best utilize the related languages within this particular family. We also study data scenarios with minimal auxiliary parallel data and use a training procedure that relies more on the monolingual data.

The languages in our setup belong to the same family, but have unique scripts. Because of this, there is little vocabulary overlap. Chakravarthi et al. (2018, 2019a,b,c) compare the impact of transliteration in supervised multilingual NMT and shows that it was helpful. Different from Chakravarthi et al. (2019c), the focus of our work is unsupervised translation. We study the role of lexical overlap in a unsupervised training pipeline, including pretraining on monolingual data and supervised training on auxiliary language pairs. We also highlight the information loss caused by transliteration from code-mixing in data from certain domains.

## 3 Background

We define $L_P$ as the set of language pairs with parallel data, and $L_M$ as the set of languages with monolingual data. The sample space of sentences for language $X \in L_M$ is $\phi_X$ following the terminology in (Li et al., 2020c). Similarly, for language pair $X - Y \in L_P$, the sample space of parallel sentences is $\phi_{X-Y}$.

A standard bilingual supervised model translating from language $X$ to $Y$ is trained on parallel dataset $\phi_{X-Y}$. The model parameters $\theta$ are optimized to maximize the likelihood of target sentences in $Y$ given the source sentences in $X$:

$$\mathcal{L}_{MT}(\theta, X, Y) = \mathbf{E}_{(x,y)\sim\phi_{X-Y}}[-\log p_\theta(y|x)]. \quad (1)$$

For unsupervised translation, in absence of parallel sentences, Lample et al. (2018) propose to combine a denoising auto-encoding task with an on-the-fly back-translation task, with the former learning language models from monolingual data, and the latter bridging the two languages.

In the auto-encoding task, the model aims to reconstruct sentences from corrupted inputs. Specifically, a noise model $C(x)$ corrupts an input sentence $x$ by dropping and shuffling the words according to a given probability. The loss function for auto-encoding using a monolingual dataset for language $X$ from the collection $L_M$ is defined as

$$\mathcal{L}_{AE}(\theta, X) = \mathbf{E}_{(x)\sim\phi_X}[-\log p_\theta(x|C(x))]. \quad (2)$$

In the on-the-fly back-translation task, the model only needs monolingual data and its loss function is defined as

$$\mathcal{L}_{BT}(\theta, X, Y) = \mathbf{E}_{(x)\sim\phi_X}[-\log p_\theta(x|\hat{y})], \quad (3)$$

where $\hat{y} = \operatorname{argmax}_y \log p_\theta(y|x)$ is the intermediate translation generated in language $Y$ during training.

The full loss function for unsupervised translation combines the auto-encoding loss in Equation (2) on $X$ and $Y$ respectively and the back-translation loss in Equation (3) between $X$ and $Y$ in both directions:

$$\mathcal{L}_{UMT}(\theta, X, Y) = \mathcal{L}_{AE}(\theta, X) + \mathcal{L}_{AE}(\theta, Y) + \mathcal{L}_{BT}(\theta, X, Y) + \mathcal{L}_{BT}(\theta, Y, X). \quad (4)$$

Cross translation (Garcia et al., 2020a; Li et al., 2020b) is a recently proposed technique that uses a reference language to improve the performance of unsupervised multilingual models. The procedure is similar to on-the-fly back-translation but additionally utilizes parallel dataset with *reference languages*. When training an unsupervised translation model from $X$ to $Y$, we use an additional parallel dataset $X - R$ from the collection $L_P$, where $R$ is the reference language. Beside the UNMT loss, we additionally optimize the following cross translation loss function:

$$\mathcal{L}_{CT}(\theta, X, R, Y) = \mathbf{E}_{(x-r)\sim\phi_{X,R}}[-\log p_\theta(r|\hat{y})], \quad (5)$$

where $\hat{y} = \operatorname{argmax}_y \log p_\theta(y|x)$ is the intermediate translation.

For both on-the-fly back-translation and cross translation, the quality of intermediate translations is essential for the final UNMT model (Li et al., 2020b). High-quality intermediate translations further needs similar encoder outputs for parallel sentences in the source and target language. While the denoising auto-encoding objective is expected to encourage this, achieving this is expected to be easier between similar languages. Therefore, in this work we focus on utilizing similar languages for UNMT.

## 4 Language Similarity in Unsupervised Machine Translation

As outlined in Section 2, distant language pairs pose a great challenge to UNMT systems. In order to apply UNMT between highly dissimilar languages, in our case English and Kannada, we explore several directions to leverage language similarity using other reference languages in the Dravidian family.

First, we investigate the role of transliteration in UNMT, as the languages we work with do not share a common writing system. Secondly, we evaluate multiple model architectures to enable unsupervised translation of dissimilar language pairs. We experiment with using auxiliary data from various related reference languages in each architecture to show the influence of language similarity. Last but not least, we propose a method to measure language similarity using $n$-gram overlap. Based on this metric, we show the benefit of including reference languages with high similarity score.

### 4.1 Transliteration

Unsupervised translation is more difficult when the writings systems differ (Marchisio et al., 2020). Although the languages in our work belong the the Dravidian language family, they do not share a common script. In fact, the ones they we focus on (Kannada, Tamil, Telugu, Malayalam) all have unique scripts. To enable a unified writing system and potentially common cross-lingual representations, we transliterate the Dravidian text into the Latin script. As a result, when translating into Dravidian languages, the model outputs are romanized. To restore the original script, we transliterate once again to convert the outputs back into the respective Dravidian writing system.

While this transliteration procedure is conceptually straightforward, in practice an additional challenge arises due to code-mixed inputs. We illustrate this with the example in Figure 2. As shown in the original Telugu sentence in the first row, the website name is written in the Latin script. The second row shows a perfect translation in the Latin script. However when restoring the original Telugu script in the third row, we incorrectly convert the website name into the wrong writing system, as the transliteration model has no knowledge of the code-mixing in the original sentence. A similar issue occurs with numbers and punctuation marks, which could get converted to the Dravidian versions (e.g. "." mapped to "|" in Figure 2).

Figure 2: Example sentence in Telugu showing information loss from transliteration and partial recovery through post-processing. Orange lines mark the words transliterated into the incorrect script as a result of code-mixing. Blue lines mark the correct forms.

*Original :* ఇలాంటి ఎన్నొ విషయులను నను
thebetterindia.com website లో చదివాను.

*Romanized : ilAMTi ఎnno viSayalanu nenu*
*thebetterindia.com website lo cadivAnu.*

*Deromanized :* ఇలాంట్టి ఎన్నో విషయ్యలను నేను
థెబేత్తేరిన్దిఅ।చోమ్ wఎబ్సితే లో చదివాను।

*Post-processed:* ఇలాంట్టి ఎన్నో విషయ్యలను నేను
థెబేత్తేరిన్దిఅ।చోమ్ wఎబ్సితే లో చదివాను.

To partially cope with the problem described above, we devise a simple post-processing step. When we restore the original script of a Dravidian language, we keep the numbers and punctuation marks in the Latin script. Nevertheless, we still lose information because of code-mixing in the data, such as the website name in Figure 2.

### 4.2 Exploiting Language Similarity

A main focus of this work is to investigate the impact of language similarity in MUNMT. After allowing the model to exploit language similarity by mapping the text to a common script, we analyze the impact of various model architectures on enabling knowledge sharing. We further study the influence of language similarity in each architecture by comparing different reference languages.

In our setup, the goal is to translate between English and Kannada but we do not have parallel data between them. Although, parallel data is available between English and reference languages such as Telugu, Tamil, Malayalam. We explain the different architectures we investigate and training procedure of these models below.

We explore both bilingual and multilingual models to include these reference languages. We build these models by including language embedding to each word embedding as proposed in Conneau and Lample (2019). This is similar to the inclusion of position embedding in the Transformer architecture Vaswani et al. (2017). As a first step, we pretrain a Masked Language Model (MLM; Devlin et al., 2019) on the monolingual corpora for all languages in the model following the procedure proposed by Conneau and Lample (2019). The goal of this step is to get better initialization of word embeddings.

After pretraining, we consider several training setups to utilize auxiliary data, as illustrated in Figure 3 and described next:

**Cascaded** The cascaded system consists of two separate NMT models as shown in Figure 3.1, a supervised one translating English $\leftrightarrow$ reference language, and an unsupervised one translating reference language $\leftrightarrow$ Kannada. The assumption here is that it is easier to learn unsupervised between languages that are in the same family. The reference language will therefore be a Dravidian language. For example, when translating from English to Kannada, we first generate a translation from English to the reference language using the supervised model and pass this intermediate translation to the unsupervised model to get the desired translation.

**Unsupervised, dissimilar languages** A multilingual model is trained to jointly perform supervised translation for reference language $\leftrightarrow$ English and unsupervised translation for English $\leftrightarrow$ Kannada as shown in Figure 3.2. For the former, we use the standard cross-entropy loss from Equation (1). For the latter, we use the unsupervised loss in Equation (4) between English and Kannada.

**Unsupervised, similar languages** The setup is closely related to the previous one. The main difference that the unsupervised translation is between Kannada and another Dravidian language, instead of English as shown in Figure 3.3. Similar to the motivation for the cascaded system, we hope to achieve strong unsupervised model by exploiting the similarity between Kannada and the reference language. During test time, we generate translations between English and Kannada directly unlike the cascaded system, which uses intermediate translations in the reference language.

**Unsupervised, dissimilar languages + cross translation** We add the cross translation loss from Equation (5) in order to generate higher-quality intermediate translations as shown in Figure 3.4. We extend the previous setup for unsupervised between dissimilar languages but also with cross translation loss using Kannada as the language where we generate intermediate translations.

**Unsupervised, similar languages + cross translation** This setup is based on the previous setup with unsupervised between similar languages as shown in Figure 3.5. We add the cross translation loss from Equation (5), with Kannada being the language where we generate the intermediate translations.

**Comparing the approaches** Among the approaches outlined above, the cascaded system consists of two separately-trained NMT models, whereas all the other approaches use a single model. Comparing to the cascaded system provides insights to the benefit of multilinguality within a single model. Furthermore, we will evaluate the impact of using different languages as reference language $R$. This comparison allows us to evaluate whether a certain reference language (e.g. one similar to Kannada) is consistently more beneficial.

### 4.3 Measuring Language Similarity

A main motivation of our approach is to utilize similar languages to improve performance on another language. While a multitude of factors contribute to language similarity, such as morphological, syntactical, and phonetical features, a quantitative indicator could provide us guidance when choosing auxiliary multilingual data.

One way to measure language similarity is to consider the lexical overlap between two languages. As the Dravidian languages we work with are agglutinative, we choose to calculate the overlap based on character $n$-grams rather than at word level. Since our models operate on sub-word level rather than word level, taking character $n$-grams is more appropriate. In addition, we take into account the frequency of the shared character $n$-grams, as overlap between rare character $n$-grams is not as important compared to frequent ones. Below we explain the procedure for calculating the language similarity metric.

Let us consider two languages $A$ and $B$. We create their vocabularies by taking unique character $n$-grams on the monolingual data denoted as $V_A$ and $V_B$ respectively. The union between $V_A$ and $V_B$ is the list of all character $n$-grams denoted as $V$. Let freq$(\cdot)$ be a function that calculates the frequency of a character $n$-grams in the given language. We calculate the overlap of vocabularies between two languages A and B using the following formula

$$\text{overlap} = \frac{\sum_{w \in V} \min(\text{freq}(A, w), \text{freq}(B, w))}{\sum_{w \in V} \max(\text{freq}(A, w), \text{freq}(B, w))}, \tag{6}$$

where $V = V_A \cup V_B$. Consider a scenario of two languages that do not share any common character $n$-grams. The frequency of every character $n$-grams in the union of two vocabularies is 0 in the language that it is not present. Therefore, calculating overlap between two languages without any common character $n$-grams gives a score of 0 as we take the minimum in the numerator. Having minimum frequency in the numerator and maximum frequency in the denominator provides higher score to character $n$-grams that occur frequently in both the languages compared to a common character $n$-grams that occurs frequently in only one language.

## 5 Experiments and Results

First, we analyze the influence of having a unified writing system based on the approach described in Section 4.1. Next, we evaluate multiple architectures with different reference languages described in Section 4.2. We then discuss our results in the context of language similarity.

### 5.1 Datasets

The monolingual datasets we use for Dravidian languages are from AI4Bharat-IndicNLP corpus (Kunchukuttan et al., 2020) while for English we use Wikipedia dumps. The parallel datasets we use from English to Dravidian languages are from the PMIndia dataset (Haddow and Kirefu, 2020). Almost 80% of English sentences are common in any two parallel datasets. We align these common English sentences and extract parallel data between Dravidian languages. The number of sentences in each dataset used for training is shown in Table 1.

### 5.2 Pre-Processing and Training Parameters

We use the *indic-transliteration*[1] toolkit for transliteration between Latin script and Indic script. We then use Byte Pair Encoding (Sennrich et al., 2016)

[1] `https://pypi.org/project/indic-transliteration/`

Figure 3: Pictorial description of multiple architectures to include auxiliary parallel data in reference language $R$. Here $R$ is chosen to be a language similar to Kannada.

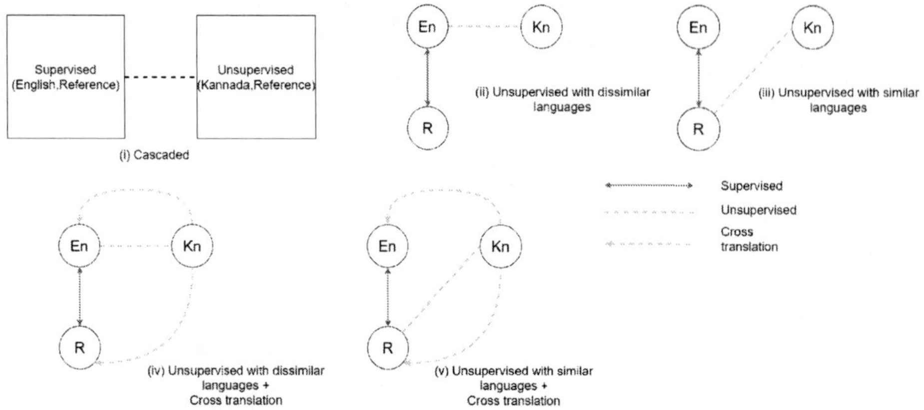


to learn sub-words with 10k merge operations. We tokenize with *Indic NLP Library*[2] for Dravidian languages whereas for English we use Moses (Koehn et al., 2007). All the experiments have been performed using *XLM*[3] toolkit. For our multilingual models, we use the Transformer (Vaswani et al., 2017) architecture with 6 layers and 8 heads whereas for our bilingual supervised model baselines we have 5 layers and 2 heads following the same configuration as in Guzmán et al. (2019). We use a smaller model for the supervised model to avoid overfitting the parallel data amount is minimal. The other parameters are set to default values as they are in *XLM*. The scores are reported in BLEU (Papineni et al., 2002) and characTER (Wang et al., 2016). When translating into Dravidian languages with transliteration, we report the scores after restoring the original scripts. We report detokenized BLEU scores using sacreBLEU[4] (Post, 2018).

### 5.3 Effect of Unifying Writing System

In order to assess the impact of transliteration, we perform experiments in the supervised and unsupervised setup between the following language pairs:

- English and a Dravidian language (dissimilar).
- Two Dravidian languages (similar).

We consider English and Kannada for dissimilar language pair and Kannada and Telugu for similar pair. In Table 2, we report the performance before and after transliteration.

| Languages | Monolingual data | Parallel data to English |
|---|---|---|
| Kannada (Kn) | 14M | 31k* |
| Tamil (Ta) | 21M | 34k |
| Telugu (Te) | 15M | 34k |
| Malayalam (Ml) | 11M | 30k |
| English (En) | 46M | - |

Table 1: The number of sentences in the monolingual and parallel datasets for different languages. *Note that the English-Kannada parallel data is only used to train the supervised model (as performance upper bound). The training of all other models do not involve this set.

First, for the supervised models, romanizing the Dravidian languages has no conclusive effects on translation quality. While there is a drop in BLEU points after transliteration, the characTER scores remain unchanged. Upon inspection of the translation results, we also notice some of the outputs suffer from the information loss described in Section 4.1.

Second, we observe that the purely unsupervised systems perform poorly, especially between English and Kannada, the dissimilar language pair. The scores are nearly zero with or without romanization. This confirms the previous findings (Marchisio et al., 2020; Kim et al., 2020) that unsupervised translation is difficult between distant languages. Between Telugu and Kannada, the unsupervised performance largely improves after romanization. The BLEU scores increase by 3.6 and 2.8 points respectively when translating into and from

[2]https://github.com/anoopkunchukuttan/indic_nlp_library

[3]https://github.com/facebookresearch/XLM

[4]BLEU+case.mixed+numrefs.1+smooth.exp+tok.spm+version.1.4.12. We use the tokenizer "spm" instead of the default "13a" for better tokenization of Indian languages.

| | | Supervised | | | | Unsupervised | | | |
|---|---|---|---|---|---|---|---|---|---|
| | | Original Script | | Romanized | | Original Script | | Romanized | |
| Source | Target | BLEU | characTER | BLEU | characTER | BLEU | characTER | BLEU | characTER |
| En | Kn | **16.4** | 76 | 16 | 76 | 0.1 | 85 | 0.2 | 84 |
| Kn | En | **12.3** | 77 | 11.5 | 77 | 0.3 | 93 | 0.6 | 93 |
| Te | Kn | **20.1** | 69 | 18.9 | 69 | 3.5 | 79 | **7.1** | **74** |
| Kn | Te | **11.9** | 74 | 11.1 | 74 | 2.3 | 86 | **5.1** | **82** |

Table 2: Impact of transliteration with similar and distant language pairs. Scores with noticeable differences to the other writing system are shown in bold. The translation quality is measured in BLEU (↑) and characTER (↓).

Kannada. The characTER scores also decrease by 5 and 4 points absolute. This demonstrates that mapping the text into a common script helps in exploiting the similarity between related languages for UNMT. This finding also contrasts the observations under the supervised model, where transliteration shows no conclusive impact. The difference leads use to conclude that the role of transliteration is scenario-dependent, in this case on the amount of available supervision signals from parallel data.

Furthermore, we use the similarity metric proposed in Section 4.3 to validate this finding. We calculate this by taking character tri-grams on the monolingual data. Indeed, in Table 3, we see that the overlap between Kannada and Telugu increase from 1% to 34% after transliteration, exhibiting the highest similarity scores between Kannada and {Te, Ta, Ml}. This finding is also in line with the close relation between Kannada and Telugu from the linguistic literature (Datta, 1988; Bright, 1996). This evidence shows that transliteration bridges across different writing systems and enables similar representations for related languages. After transliteration, the unsupervised model can more easily leverage the similarity between these related languages and therefore achieve better performance.

| | En | Kn | Te | Ta | Ml |
|---|---|---|---|---|---|
| En | 100 | $0 \rightarrow 6$ | $0 \rightarrow 6$ | $0 \rightarrow 3$ | $0 \rightarrow 6$ |
| Kn | | 100 | $1 \rightarrow$ **34** | $1 \rightarrow 10$ | $1 \rightarrow 26$ |
| Te | | | 100 | $1 \rightarrow 9$ | $1 \rightarrow 27$ |
| Ta | | | | 100 | $1 \rightarrow 11$ |
| Ml | | | | | 100 |

Table 3: Lexical overlap (%; calculated using Equation 6) before and after transliteration (before → after).

### 5.4 Impact of Model Architectures

We evaluate the setups described in Section 4.2 with different reference languages and report these scores in Table 4. Given the previously-found positive impact of unifying the writing systems on unsupervised learning, we transliterate Dravidian languages in all experiment setups here.

First, the unsupervised models on similar languages consistently outperform those with dissimilar languages. This is in line with previous results in Table 2 and further validates our finding on the positive role of language similarity in UNMT.

Second, adding the cross translation loss improves the translation quality into English. The model using Telugu as reference language achieves 5.1 BLEU points when translating into English, the highest among the setups explored so far. However, there is not a similar gain when translating into Kannada. One reason is that cross translation generates more training signals when translating into English but does not explicitly encourage better translation into Kannada.

### 5.5 Impact of Reference Languages

Table 4 provides a clear view of which reference language is more beneficial to a purely unsupervised system. In line with previous observations, when using Telugu as the reference language, the model performance exceeds when using other languages. The only exception is unsupervised dissimilar + cross translation scenario where it falls slightly behind Malayalam. The positive impact of adding Telugu is within expectation given the previous finding on its close relation to Kannada. After Telugu, the next best choices for the reference languages are Malayalam, followed up Tamil. This particular order agrees with the vocabulary overlap with Kannada shown in Table 3, with the highest value on Telugu (34%) followed by Malayalam (26%) and lastly Tamil (10%). Based on our similarity metric, we are able to show the impact of using languages that are more similar.

Given the positive impact of incorporating related reference languages, we extend our investigation to using multiple reference languages. We build upon the best architecture (unsupervised sim-

| | Cascaded | | Unsupervised dissimilar | | Unsupervised similar | | Unsupervised dissimilar + Cross translation | | Unsupervised similar + Cross translation | |
|---|---|---|---|---|---|---|---|---|---|---|
| Reference Language | BLEU | characTER(%) | BLEU | characTER(%) | BLEU | characTER(%) | BLEU | characTER(%) | BLEU | characTER(%) |
| Te | 3.7/**1.6** | 86/**82** | 1.3/2.1 | 89/87 | 3.8/1 | 86/85 | 2.2/0.4 | 87/90 | **5.1**/1.4 | **85**/93 |
| Ml | 2.3/**1.1** | 86/**87** | 1.1/0.6 | 89/92 | 2.0/0.7 | 89/93 | 2.7/0.9 | 85/91 | **3.3**/0.2 | **84**/96 |
| Ta | 1.2/0.2 | 87/**89** | 0.3/**0.4** | 89/93 | 1.4/0.4 | 88/94 | 0.7/0.3 | **86**/94 | **1.8**/0.1 | 87/97 |

Table 4: Unsupervised translation performance between Kannada and English using different reference languages in multiple setups described in Section 4.2. Scores are shown as x/y where x indicates in Kn → En direction and y indicates in En → Kn respectively. The translation quality is measured in BLEU (↑) and characTER (↓). The best scores (BLEU & characTER) for each reference language in both directions are shown in bold.

| | Kn → En | | En→ Kn | |
|---|---|---|---|---|
| | BLEU | characTER(%) | BLEU | characTER(%) |
| Supervised | 11.5 | 77 | 16 | 76 |
| Unsupervised | 0.6 | 93 | 0.2 | 84 |
| MUNMT, Te | 5.1 | 85 | 1.4 | 93 |
| MUNMT, Te+Ml | **5.4** | **84** | 1.6 | 95 |

Table 5: Scores for baselines and proposed model that includes reference languages. MUNMT corresponds to unsupervised similar + cross translation architecture. "MUNMT, Te" uses only Telugu as a reference language whereas "MUNMT, Te+Ml" uses both Telugu and Malayalam as reference languages.

Kannada : ಮಹಾತ್ಮಾ ಗಾಂಧೀ ಅವರು ಕೂಡ ಸಮಾಜದ ಕಟ್ಟಕಡೆಯ ವ್ಯಕ್ತಿಗೆ ಏನಿದೆ ಎಂದು ಹೇಳುತ್ತಿದ್ದರು.
English : And even Mahatma Gandhi used to say that what is there for the last man?
Hypothesis : " Mahatma Gandhi used to say , " No Science has dropped from the skies in a perfect form ."

Kannada : ನೇಪಾಳದಲ್ಲಿನ ಬೆಳವಣಿಗೆಗಳ ಬಗ್ಗೆ ಶ್ರೀ ಬಿಮಲೇಂದ್ರ ನಿಧಿ ಅವರು ಪ್ರಧಾನಮಂತ್ರಿಯವರಿಗೆ ವಿವರಿಸಿದರು.
English : Mr . Bimalendra Nidhi briefed the Prime Minister about developments in Nepal.
Hypothesis : Mr . Bimalendra Nidhi was also briefed on the Prime Minister about the progress achieved in Nepal .

Figure 4: Example outputs when translating Kn→En.

ilar + cross translation) and train it with using auxiliary data of two reference languages. We choose Telugu and Malayalam as they are more related to Kannada and yielded stronger performance than Tamil. The scores for this along with our baselines are in Table 5. By additionally incorporating Malayalam, we see an improvement from 5.1 to 5.4 BLEU points when translating to English. The overlap in the English sentences for the parallel data with the reference languages is more than 80%. Even though we are adding additional data, very few new in-domain English sentences are seen by the model. This might explain the minimal increase in score after adding multiple reference languages. While this performance is still 6.1 points short from supervised model, it is significantly better than the purely unsupervised baseline when translating into English.

### 5.6 Examples of Kn→En Translation

We highlight that our overall task for unsupervised translation remains very challenging, as the auxiliary parallel data amount with the reference languages is also minimal (∼30k sentences). Moreover, there is a domain discrepancy between the monolingual data and the test data from government announcements. In Figure 4, we show example outputs when translating Kn→En using the previous best "MUNMT, Te+Ml" model. The first example shows the problem of hallucination (Koehn and Knowles, 2017), hinting towards negative impacts of domain shifts. Nonetheless, the model sometimes achieves translation with adequate quality such as the last example in Figure 4.

## 6 Conclusion

We focus on the challenging yet realistic scenario of translating between English and Kannada without any parallel data. After confirming the difficulty of purely unsupervised translation between distant language pairs, we show that increasing the lexical overlap by transliteration is necessary for achieving UNMT for our focal language. Moreover, we utilize monolingual and limited amount of auxiliary parallel data in languages related to Kannada. The best performance is achieved by UNMT between similar languages along with cross translation. We show the importance of incorporating languages with high relatedness to the focus language by evaluating different reference languages. Finally, we propose a metric for measuring lexical overlap and show that it serves as a good indicator for selecting the best reference languages.

**Acknowledgement** This work is supported by the Facebook Sponsored Research Agreement "Language Similarity in Machine Translation".

## References

Mikel Artetxe, Gorka Labaka, Eneko Agirre, and Kyunghyun Cho. 2018. Unsupervised neural machine translation. In *International Conference on Learning Representations*.

Dzmitry Bahdanau, Kyung Hyun Cho, and Yoshua Bengio. 2015. Neural machine translation by jointly learning to align and translate. In *International Conference on Learning Representations*.

William Bright. 1996. Kannada and telugu writing. *The world's writing systems*, pages 413–419.

Bharathi Raja Chakravarthi, Mihael Arcan, and John P. McCrae. 2018. Improving wordnets for under-resourced languages using machine translation. In *Proceedings of the 9th Global Wordnet Conference*, pages 77–86, Nanyang Technological University (NTU), Singapore. Global Wordnet Association.

Bharathi Raja Chakravarthi, Mihael Arcan, and John P. McCrae. 2019a. Comparison of Different Orthographies for Machine Translation of Under-Resourced Dravidian Languages. In *2nd Conference on Language, Data and Knowledge (LDK 2019)*, volume 70 of *OpenAccess Series in Informatics (OASIcs)*, pages 6:1–6:14, Dagstuhl, Germany. Schloss Dagstuhl–Leibniz-Zentrum fuer Informatik.

Bharathi Raja Chakravarthi, Mihael Arcan, and John P. McCrae. 2019b. WordNet gloss translation for under-resourced languages using multilingual neural machine translation. In *Proceedings of the Second Workshop on Multilingualism at the Intersection of Knowledge Bases and Machine Translation*, pages 1–7, Dublin, Ireland. European Association for Machine Translation.

Bharathi Raja Chakravarthi, Ruba Priyadharshini, Bernardo Stearns, Arun Jayapal, Sridevy S, Mihael Arcan, Manel Zarrouk, and John P McCrae. 2019c. Multilingual multimodal machine translation for Dravidian languages utilizing phonetic transcription. In *Proceedings of the 2nd Workshop on Technologies for MT of Low Resource Languages*, pages 56–63, Dublin, Ireland. European Association for Machine Translation.

Alexis Conneau and Guillaume Lample. 2019. Cross-lingual language model pretraining. In *Advances in Neural Information Processing Systems*, pages 7059–7069.

Amaresh Datta. 1988. *Encyclopaedia of Indian Literature: devraj to jyoti*, volume 2. Sahitya Akademi.

Jacob Devlin, Ming-Wei Chang, Kenton Lee, and Kristina Toutanova. 2019. BERT: Pre-training of deep bidirectional transformers for language understanding. In *Proceedings of the 2019 Conference of the North American Chapter of the Association for Computational Linguistics: Human Language Technologies, Volume 1 (Long and Short Papers)*, pages 4171–4186, Minneapolis, Minnesota. Association for Computational Linguistics.

Alexander Fraser. 2020. Findings of the WMT 2020 shared tasks in unsupervised MT and very low resource supervised MT. In *Proceedings of the Fifth Conference on Machine Translation*, pages 765–771, Online. Association for Computational Linguistics.

Xavier Garcia, Pierre Foret, Thibault Sellam, and Ankur Parikh. 2020a. A multilingual view of unsupervised machine translation. In *Findings of the Association for Computational Linguistics: EMNLP 2020*, pages 3160–3170, Online. Association for Computational Linguistics.

Xavier Garcia, Aditya Siddhant, Orhan Firat, and Ankur P Parikh. 2020b. Harnessing multilinguality in unsupervised machine translation for rare languages. *arXiv preprint arXiv:2009.11201*.

Francisco Guzmán, Peng-Jen Chen, Myle Ott, Juan Pino, Guillaume Lample, Philipp Koehn, Vishrav Chaudhary, and Marc'Aurelio Ranzato. 2019. The FLORES evaluation datasets for low-resource machine translation: Nepali–English and Sinhala–English. In *Proceedings of the 2019 Conference on Empirical Methods in Natural Language Processing and the 9th International Joint Conference on Natural Language Processing (EMNLP-IJCNLP)*, pages 6098–6111, Hong Kong, China. Association for Computational Linguistics.

Barry Haddow and Faheem Kirefu. 2020. PMIndia–a collection of parallel corpora of languages of india. *arXiv preprint arXiv:2001.09907*.

Yunsu Kim, Miguel Graça, and Hermann Ney. 2020. When and why is unsupervised neural machine translation useless? In *Proceedings of the 22nd Annual Conference of the European Association for Machine Translation*, pages 35–44, Lisboa, Portugal. European Association for Machine Translation.

Philipp Koehn, Hieu Hoang, Alexandra Birch, Chris Callison-Burch, Marcello Federico, Nicola Bertoldi, Brooke Cowan, Wade Shen, Christine Moran, Richard Zens, Chris Dyer, Ondřej Bojar, Alexandra Constantin, and Evan Herbst. 2007. Moses: Open source toolkit for statistical machine translation. In *Proceedings of the 45th Annual Meeting of the Association for Computational Linguistics Companion Volume Proceedings of the Demo and Poster Sessions*, pages 177–180, Prague, Czech Republic. Association for Computational Linguistics.

Philipp Koehn and Rebecca Knowles. 2017. Six challenges for neural machine translation. In *Proceedings of the First Workshop on Neural Machine Translation*, pages 28–39, Vancouver. Association for Computational Linguistics.

Vishnupriya Kolipakam, Fiona M Jordan, Michael Dunn, Simon J Greenhill, Remco Bouckaert, Russell D Gray, and Annemarie Verkerk. 2018. A bayesian phylogenetic study of the dravidian language family. *Royal Society open science*, 5(3):171504.

Anoop Kunchukuttan, Divyanshu Kakwani, Satish Golla, Gokul N.C., Avik Bhattacharyya, Mitesh M. Khapra, and Pratyush Kumar. 2020. AI4Bharat-IndicNLP corpus: Monolingual corpora and word embeddings for indic languages. *arXiv preprint arXiv:2005.00085*.

Guillaume Lample, Alexis Conneau, Ludovic Denoyer, and Marc'Aurelio Ranzato. 2018. Unsupervised machine translation using monolingual corpora only. In *International Conference on Learning Representations*.

Zuchao Li, Hai Zhao, Rui Wang, Kehai Chen, Masao Utiyama, and Eiichiro Sumita. 2020a. SJTU-NICT's supervised and unsupervised neural machine translation systems for the WMT20 news translation task. In *Proceedings of the Fifth Conference on Machine Translation*, pages 218–229, Online. Association for Computational Linguistics.

Zuchao Li, Hai Zhao, Rui Wang, Masao Utiyama, and Eiichiro Sumita. 2020b. Reference language based unsupervised neural machine translation. In *Findings of the Association for Computational Linguistics: EMNLP 2020*, pages 4151–4162, Online. Association for Computational Linguistics.

Zuchao Li, Hai Zhao, Rui Wang, Masao Utiyama, and Eiichiro Sumita. 2020c. Reference language based unsupervised neural machine translation. *arXiv preprint arXiv:2004.02127*.

Yinhan Liu, Jiatao Gu, Naman Goyal, Xian Li, Sergey Edunov, Marjan Ghazvininejad, Mike Lewis, and Luke Zettlemoyer. 2020. Multilingual denoising pre-training for neural machine translation. *Transactions of the Association for Computational Linguistics*, 8:726–742.

Kelly Marchisio, Kevin Duh, and Philipp Koehn. 2020. When does unsupervised machine translation work? In *Proceedings of the Fifth Conference on Machine Translation*, pages 571–583, Online. Association for Computational Linguistics.

Kishore Papineni, Salim Roukos, Todd Ward, and Wei-Jing Zhu. 2002. Bleu: a method for automatic evaluation of machine translation. In *Proceedings of the 40th Annual Meeting of the Association for Computational Linguistics*, pages 311–318, Philadelphia, Pennsylvania, USA. Association for Computational Linguistics.

Matt Post. 2018. A call for clarity in reporting BLEU scores. In *Proceedings of the Third Conference on Machine Translation: Research Papers*, pages 186–191, Brussels, Belgium. Association for Computational Linguistics.

Siva Reddy and Serge Sharoff. 2011. Cross language POS taggers (and other tools) for Indian languages: An experiment with Kannada using Telugu resources. In *Proceedings of the Fifth International Workshop On Cross Lingual Information Access*, pages 11–19, Chiang Mai, Thailand. Asian Federation of Natural Language Processing.

Rico Sennrich, Barry Haddow, and Alexandra Birch. 2016. Neural machine translation of rare words with subword units. In *Proceedings of the 54th Annual Meeting of the Association for Computational Linguistics (Volume 1: Long Papers)*, pages 1715–1725, Berlin, Germany. Association for Computational Linguistics.

Ashish Vaswani, Noam Shazeer, Niki Parmar, Jakob Uszkoreit, Llion Jones, Aidan N Gomez, Łukasz Kaiser, and Illia Polosukhin. 2017. Attention is all you need. *Advances in neural information processing systems*, 30:5998–6008.

Weiyue Wang, Jan-Thorsten Peter, Hendrik Rosendahl, and Hermann Ney. 2016. CharacTer: Translation edit rate on character level. In *Proceedings of the First Conference on Machine Translation: Volume 2, Shared Task Papers*, pages 505–510, Berlin, Germany. Association for Computational Linguistics.

# Graph Convolutional Networks with Multi-headed Attention for Code-Mixed Sentiment Analysis

**Suman Dowlagar**
LTRC
IIIT-Hyderabad
suman.dowlagar
@research.iiit.ac.in

**Radhika Mamidi**
LTRC
IIIT-Hyderabad
radhika.mamidi
@iiit.ac.in

## Abstract

Code-mixing is a frequently observed phenomenon in multilingual communities where a speaker uses multiple languages in an utterance or sentence. Code-mixed texts are abundant, especially in social media, and pose a problem for NLP tools as they are typically trained on monolingual corpora. Recently, finding the sentiment from code-mixed text has been attempted by some researchers in SentiMix SemEval 2020 and Dravidian-CodeMix FIRE 2020 shared tasks. Mostly, the attempts include traditional methods, long short term memory, convolutional neural networks, and transformer models for code-mixed sentiment analysis (CMSA). However, no study has explored graph convolutional neural networks on CMSA. In this paper, we propose the graph convolutional networks (GCN) for sentiment analysis on code-mixed text. We have used the datasets from the Dravidian-CodeMix FIRE 2020. Our experimental results on multiple CMSA datasets demonstrate that the GCN with multi-headed attention model has shown an improvement in classification metrics.

## 1 Introduction

Through the advent of social media, people from around the world can connect and exchange information instantly. The evolution of social media texts from blogs and messaging websites has created many new opportunities for information access worldwide (Thavareesan and Mahesan, 2019, 2020a,b). Multilingual communities often express their thoughts on social media by mixing different languages in the same utterance (Chakravarthi, 2020a). This mixing or alteration of two or more languages is known as code-mixing or code-switching (Wardhaugh, 2011; Chakravarthi, 2020b).

The computational modeling of code-mixed text is challenging due to the linguistic complexity, nature of mixing, the presence of non-standard variations in spellings, grammar, and transliteration (Bali et al., 2014; Jose et al., 2020; Priyadharshini et al., 2020). Because of such non-standard variations, CM poses several unseen difficulties in fundamental fields of natural language processing (NLP) tasks such as language identification, part-of-speech tagging, shallow parsing, Natural language understanding, sentiment analysis, etc.

To encourage research on code-mixing and to solve the problems related to code-mixed text, the NLP community organizes several tasks and workshops such as Task9: SentiMix, SemEval 2020 (Patwa et al., 2020), and 4th Workshop on Computational Approaches for Linguistic Code-Switching (Solorio et al., 2020), Dravidian Code-Mix FIRE 2020 (Chakravarthi et al., 2020c; Mandl et al., 2020). All of these tasks focus on sentiment analysis on code-mixed text.

Some researchers used traditional methods, such as support vector machines (SVM's) (Vapnik, 2013) and Logistic Regression (LR), where the code-mixed text is represented with sparse linguistic features (e.g., bag-of-words and n-grams). Others used deep learning models such as convolutional neural networks (CNN) (Kim, 2014), recurrent neural networks (RNN) (Hochreiter and Schmidhuber, 1997), transformer models (Vaswani et al., 2017), etc. The above deep learning models can capture semantic and syntactic information well in local consecutive word sequences. Such position-dependent models are not suitable for Dravidian languages that follow free word order format.

Recently, an evolving research direction known as graph neural networks (Zhou et al., 2018) or graph representation learning has attracted wide attention. In graph-based approaches, the whole corpus is viewed as a graph (Yao et al., 2019).



*Proceedings of the First Workshop on Speech and Language Technologies for Dravidian Languages*, pages 65–72
April 20, 2021 ©2021 Association for Computational Linguistics

Graph convolutional networks have been effective at tasks for knowledge representation and can preserve global structure information of a graph in graph embeddings.

In this work, we propose the use of the graph neural network for code-mixed sentiment analysis. Our method focuses on constructing a single large graph from an entire corpus. We modeled the graph with a Graph Convolutional Network (GCN) (Kipf and Welling, 2016; Yao et al., 2019) with Multi-headed attention. A graph neural network captures high-order neighborhood information well by using an adjacency matrix. This adjacency matrix helps the graph neural network to not dependent on consecutive word order format. Thus, it is well suited for the Dravidian language datasets that follow a free word order.

The paper is organized as follows. Section 2 provides related work on code-mixed sentiment analysis. Section 3 describes the proposed work. Section 4 presents the experimental setup and the performance of the model. Section 5 concludes our work.

## 2 Related work

In this section, we study the related work in the field of code-mixed sentiment analysis.

### 2.1 Traditional methods for CMSA

Traditional methods for CMSA studies mainly focus on feature engineering and traditional text classification algorithms such as Support Vector Machines (SVMs), Decision Trees (DTs), Logistic Regression (LR) (Chakravarthi et al., 2020c). The most commonly used feature repreentation is the bag-of-words. Some linguistic and complex features have been designed to capture the features, such as n-grams, chunking, capturing phonetics of words, etc.

### 2.2 Deep Learning for CMSA

Deep learning studies focus on using deep neural network classifiers for CMSA. Kumar et al. (2020) used CNN for code-mixed sentiment analysis. Mahata et al. (2020); Lakshmanan and Ravindranath (2020) used LSTM, a specific type of Recurrent neural network, to learn text representation. To further increase the representation ability of neural network models, attention mechanisms, and transformer models have been introduced for code-switched sentiment analysis (Chakravarthi et al., 2020c). These methods mainly focus on the position of the word and local consecutive word sequences and do not explicitly model global word co-occurrence information in a corpus.

### 2.3 Graph Neural Networks

Recently, Graph Neural Networks has received growing attention in the field of natural language processing. The authors used Text GCN (Yao et al., 2019) to construct a heterogeneous graph that helped them in text classification and achieved great results. Graph Neural Networks have also been used in intent slot labeling (Zhang et al., 2020), semantic role labeling (Marcheggiani and Titov, 2017), knowledge base construction (Wang et al., 2019), relation classification (Sahu et al., 2019), and machine translation (Marcheggiani et al., 2018).

The use of graph convolutional networks with undirected graphs to model the free word order languages for CMSA has never been explored before.

## 3 Proposed Work

In this section, we describe our proposed work. First, we present the pre-processing steps to filter the data, and then we describe graph-convolutional networks with multi-headed attention for code-mixed sentiment analysis.

The data we have used for CMSA consists of code-mixed Tamil-English and Malayalam-English youtube comments, and it has many irregularities. Such as the Roman script is used to write Tamil and Malayalam text with variations in the spelling, irregular grammatical structure, mixing of languages at the word level, informal abbreviations, slang, and use of emoticons in text. We can minimize some of these irregularities by using pre-processing methods.

### 3.1 Pre-processing

In pre-processing

- We tokenized the text on whitespaces and symbols, including colons, commas, and semicolons. It was followed by the removal of hashtags, URLs, mentions, numbers.
- In the sentiment analysis scenarios, emoticons help in understanding the polarity of the text. We used the emoji PyPI library to map the emoticons to their corresponding text.

- We know that the code-mixed text document contains multiple scripts involving multiple languages. Each language may or may not use its own native script. When a word is represented in a different script, spelling variations can occur across document(s). This will create unnecessary complexity for the classifier to learn a meaningful representation of a word (that is written in two or more languages in the same document), which results in poor performance of the classifier. In order to resolve such ambiguities, it is necessary to bring the words to a common format. i.e., back transliteration of each word in its native script. We have used AI4Bharat-Transliteration[1] (a python deep transliteration engine for transliteration from roman to native text).

### 3.2 Word embeddings

After transliteration, we have used the pre-trained fastText model (Grave et al., 2018) to obtain the word embeddings. We didn't rely on extracting word-embeddings from the same corpora as its size is small, and we need a large code mixed corpora with cross-lingual mapping or cross-lingual dictionary to obtain better word-embeddings. Even Khanuja et al. (2020) has suggested that we can use pre-trained models to learn representations of words. Their paper has shown an improved performance in accuracy when pre-trained models are used on the code-mixed datasets.

### 3.3 Graph Convolutional Networks (GCN) with Multi-headed Attention

A Graph Convolutional Network is a neural network that operates on graph-like representations. Given a graph with $V$ as the number of vertices and $E$ as the number of edges $G = (V, E)$,

A GCN takes as input an input feature matrix $X$ of size $(N, F^0)$ feature matrix, where $N$ is the number of nodes or vertices, and $F^0$ is the number of input features or node embeddings for each node, and An adjacency matrix $A$ for graph $G$ of size $(N, N)$. A Degree matrix $D$ of size $(1, N)$. A hidden layer in the GCN can be defined as $H^i = f(H^{i-1}, A))$ where $H^0 = X$ and $f$ is a propagation rule. Each layer $H^i$ corresponds to an $(N, F^i)$ feature matrix where each row is a feature representation of a node. The neighboring features are aggregated at each layer to form the next layer's features by using the propagation rule $f$. In this way, features become increasingly more abstract at each consecutive layer.

A simple propagation rule in GCN is given as:

$$f(H^i, A) = \sigma(AH^iW^i) \quad (1)$$

Where $W^i$ is the weight matrix for layer $i$, and $\sigma$ is a non-linear activation function. The weight matrix has dimensions $(F^i, F^{i+1})$. Equation 1 can be explained as a feature transformation that occurs with information borrowed from the neighborhood nodes. But the transformation in the equation 1 focuses only on neighborhood information and ignores its own node features, so we add the identity matrix to the adjacency matrix. Later we normalize the feature representations w.r.t degree of each node. So the initial propagation rule is modified as given in equation 2

$$f(H^i, A) = \sigma(\tilde{A}H^iW^i) \quad (2)$$

where $\tilde{A} = D^{-1/2}(A + I)D^{-1/2}$ is the normalized symmetric adjacency matrix.

The multiheaded attention is applied on the Hidden layer representation of each graph convolutional layer. The multiheaded attention is given by,

$$Attention = softmax\left(\frac{QK^T}{\sqrt{d_k}}\right).V \quad (3)$$

Multi-headed attention gives high weightage to the words of importance for a given query word in a sentence.

### 3.4 GCN with Multi-headed Attention on Text

As mentioned earlier, we use graph-neural networks for code-mixed sentiment analysis. Our approach considers the whole corpus as a graph. Then we perform graph convolutions for CMSA.

In order to construct the whole text as a graph, we use the approach given in the paper Yao et al. (2019). Initially, we build a large corpus graph that contains each word and each document as nodes. The number of nodes or vertices in the text graph $|V|$ is the number of documents plus the number of unique words. We build edges based on word occurrence in documents(document-to-word) and word co-occurrence (word-to-word) in the whole corpus. The weights of edges between word-to-word and document-to-word are given as

[1]https://pypi.org/project/ai4bharat-transliteration/

- **Document-to-word:** The weight of the edge between a document node and a word node is the term frequency-inverse document frequency (TF-IDF) measure of the word in the document.
- **Word-to-word:** We use point-wise mutual information (PMI), to calculate weights between two nodes. A positive PMI value indicates a high semantic correlation of words in a corpus, whereas a negative PMI value indicates little or no semantic correlation in the corpus. As suggested in the paper, we only add edges between word pairs with positive PMI values. Note: There are no direct document-to-document relations in the graph.

Adjacency matrix,

$$A_{ij} = \begin{cases} PMI(i,j) & i,j \text{ are words} \\ TF-IDF_{i,j} & i \text{ is document}, j \text{ is word} \\ 0 & \text{otherwise} \end{cases} \tag{4}$$

where $PMI(i,j) > 0$ and PMI value of a word pair $i, j$ is computed as

$$PMI(i,j) = log\frac{p(i,j)}{p(i)p(j)} \tag{5}$$

where $p(i,j)$ is the probability of sliding window occurences that contains both the words $i$ and $j$. $p(i)$ and $p(j)$ are the individual probability distribution of words $i$ and $j$ respectively.

And Identity matrix is given as,

$$I_{ij} = \begin{cases} 1 & i = j \\ 0 & \text{otherwise} \end{cases} \tag{6}$$

After building the global text graphs, we apply GCN with multilayer GCN as described above. We used a 3-layer of GCN with multi-headed attention, followed by a global max pooling and then a linear layer to obtain the code-mixed text's polarity. A three-layer GCN can allow message passing among neighborhood nodes that are at a maximum of three steps away. This approach resulted in obtaining a better graph representation.

## 4 Experiments

In this section, we compare our method with several baselines. We used only the back transliterated dataset to run all the models.

- **TF-IDF + SVM:** A bag-of-words model with term frequency-inverse document frequency measure. Support Vector machines (SVM) is used as the classifier.
- **CNN:** A Convolutional Neural Network model for CMSA. The CNN model uses pre-trained fastText word embeddings.
- **LSTM:** The LSTM model uses the last hidden state to represent the whole sentence. We used fastText pre-trained word embeddings.
- **ELMO + SVM:** Deep Contextualised Word Representations (Peters et al., 2018) uses a deep, bi-directional LSTM model to create word representations. ELMo obtained the word representations by analyzing words within the context that they are used. It also uses character-based embeddings to model the representations for out-of-vocabulary words.
- **BERT(pre-trained multilingual)**: We used pre-trained multilingual bi-directional encoder representations using transformers (BERT) (Devlin et al., 2018) for CMSA.
- **TextGCN:** It is a graph convolutional network implemented for text classification.

### 4.1 Dataset

For Dravidian code-mixed sentiment analysis, we used the dataset provided by the organizers of Dravidian Code-mixed FIRE-2020. The dataset consists of 15,744 Tamil-English Code-mixed and 6,739 Malayalam-English Code-mixed youtube video comments. The data statistics are given in table 1. Each sentence's sentiment can be classified into five categories: positive, negative, not-Tamil or not-Malayalam, unknown_state, mixed_feelings. The dataset details and the initial benchmarks on the corpus are given in Chakravarthi et al. (2020a,b).

### 4.2 Model parameters and settings

For GCN with multi-headed attention model, we set the embedding size to 300. The embeddings are obtained by using fastText pre-trained models. We used adam optimizer with cross-entropy loss. We tuned other parameters and set the learning rate as 0.02, dropout as 0.25, and we trained the GCN for a maximum of 100 epochs. We stopped the model if the validation loss does not decrease for

| Dataset | #Docs | #Train | #Dev | #Test | #classes |
|---|---|---|---|---|---|
| Tamil-English CM | 15744 | 11335 | 1260 | 3149 | 5 |
| Malayalam-English CM | 6739 | 4851 | 540 | 1348 | 5 |

Table 1: Data Statistics

| Model | Pos | Neg | not-mal | Mixed | Unknown | Macro | Weight | Acc |
|---|---|---|---|---|---|---|---|---|
| TF-IDF+SVM | 0.72 | 0.40 | 0.98 | 0.27 | 0.58 | 0.59 | 0.68 | 0.67 |
| CNN | 0.76 | 0.39 | 0.93 | 0.23 | 0.63 | 0.59 | 0.68 | 0.69 |
| LSTM | 0.74 | 0.44 | 0.93 | 0.26 | 0.63 | 0.60 | 0.68 | 0.69 |
| ELMO+SVM | 0.75 | 0.45 | 0.96 | 0.26 | 0.63 | 0.61 | 0.69 | 0.69 |
| mBERT | 0.77 | 0.53 | **0.99** | 0.26 | **0.69** | 0.65 | 0.72 | 0.72 |
| Text-GCN | 0.79 | **0.55** | 0.98 | **0.30** | 0.67 | **0.66** | 0.74 | **0.73** |
| Our approach | **0.80** | **0.55** | **0.99** | **0.30** | **0.69** | **0.66** | **0.75** | **0.73** |

Table 2: Classification Metrics of our GCN with multi-headed approach when compared to baselines on code-mixed Malayalam-English Dataset

| Model | Pos | Neg | not-Tamil | Mixed | Unknown | Macro | Weight | Acc |
|---|---|---|---|---|---|---|---|---|
| TF-IDF+SVM | 0.80 | 0.19 | 0.93 | 0.06 | 0.12 | 0.42 | 0.56 | 0.68 |
| CNN | **0.81** | 0.04 | 0.82 | 0.01 | 0.00 | 0.34 | 0.56 | 0.68 |
| LSTM | **0.81** | 0.16 | 0.85 | 0.01 | 0.15 | 0.40 | 0.59 | 0.68 |
| ELMO+SVM | **0.81** | 0.17 | 0.88 | 0.04 | 0.15 | 0.43 | 0.58 | 0.69 |
| mBERT | 0.77 | **0.53** | **0.99** | **0.26** | **0.69** | **0.65** | **0.72** | **0.72** |
| Text-GCN | **0.81** | 0.30 | 0.98 | 0.05 | 0.02 | 0.43 | 0.61 | 0.70 |
| Our approach | **0.81** | 0.43 | 0.98 | 0.16 | 0.15 | 0.45 | 0.64 | 0.71 |

Table 3: Classification Metrics of our GCN with multi-headed approach when compared to baselines on code-mixed Tamil-English Dataset

ten consecutive epochs. We used default parameter settings for baseline models as given in their original papers or implementations and used the same pre-trained embeddings obtained from the fastText model. We ran the model more than ten times, and the average metrics are recorded. For baseline models, we used default parameter settings as in their original papers or implementations. For baseline models using pre-trained word embeddings, we used 300-dimensional FastText word embeddings.

We used pytorch-geometric[2] library to implement the graph convolutional networks. Pytorch-geometric library has a set of predefined graph neural network models that can be accessed by calling a simple method. We have used the hugging face transformers library (Wolf et al., 2019) to download the pre-trained multilingual BERT model. The scikit-learn library (Pedregosa et al., 2011) is used to obtain the classification metrics.

[2] https://pytorch-geometric.readthedocs.io/en/latest/index.html

### 4.3 Results and Analysis

Table 3 and 2 presents F1-scores and accuracy of each model on Tamil-English and Malayalam-English datasets respectively. For the Malayalam-English dataset, GCN with Multi-headed attention outperforms all baseline models. It showcases the proposed method's effectiveness on short text datasets. For the Tamil dataset, our model performed competitively when compared to the pre-trained multilingual BERT model and better than all the other baselines. When compared to the BERT introduced in the original paper (Chakravarthi et al., 2020b), our GCN with multi-headed attention achieved better results. We have seen improvement in results in our pre-trained multilingual BERT because we used back transliteration while pre-processing. The back transliteration helped the BERT pre-trained model captured the native word script, thus obtaining better pre-trained sub-word level embeddings. Our model performed better than the Text-GCN because of multi-headed attention. CNN also didn't perform well on both the datasets when compared to the baselines. It might be because there are long-range and implicit dependencies between the text, but CNN only works on exploring the short-range dependencies. LSTM-based models are good at establishing long-range dependencies in the datasets. This helped the LSTM model to perform better when compared to CNN models.

The pre-trained multilingual BERT model has shown a decrease in performance on "positive" polarity of the Tamil-English CM dataset because the model tried to fine-tune the data on other polarities. The original paper reported that there were annotating issues for mixed and unknown sentences as their polarity was similar to the "positive" sentence. Fine-tuning the classifier towards other polarities resulted in a decrease in the classification metrics of the "positive" polarity sentences.

In all the baseline models, We have seen an increase in accuracy compared to the baseline papers on the above datasets (Chakravarthi et al., 2020a,b). It is due to the back-transliteration module used while pre-processing. The back transliteration helped the words retain their native script and helped the words obtain better-pre-trained embeddings from the fastText classification models, and decreased the classifier's training complexity. Especially the accuracy is improved for the "Positive" and "not-tamil/not-malayalam" class. The "not-tamil"/"not-malayalam" class has shown an improved accuracy because we have formulated rules not to transliterate these words into the native script. It helped the classifier to understand them as out-of-context words while training the classifier. Similar to the baseline models, the negative, mixed_feelings, and unknown_state have shown low performance because of their low distribution of data compared to the positive class.

Our graph convolution network with attention mechanism showed good results because

- The weighted label information of document nodes is passed to their neighboring word nodes, then transferred to other word nodes and document nodes that are neighbor to the first step neighboring word nodes. This knowledge transfer helped the graph gather comprehensive word-document information, which helped in learning a better classifier for the given data.

- Using back transliteration with pre-trained fastText word embeddings preserved syntactic and semantic relations among words and provided additional information in classifying the data.

After data analysis, we observed that the negative polarity comments have sarcasm included. The words used in the sarcasm are similar to those of positive comments. It made the classifier identify them as positive words and made sentiment analysis a difficult task. Mixed feelings had both positive and negative sentences. As the classifier was trained on a lot of positive instances, the mixed feelings were tuned to the "positive" class. And the classifier mislabeled them as a "positive" class. It affected the performance of the classifier. More training data or additional labeling of the classifier could help resolve such issues.

## 5 Conclusion

This paper describes the graph convolution networks with multi-headed attention for code mixed sentiment analysis on Dravidian languages. Initially, we transliterate the data and build a word document graph for the whole corpus. This approach considers global dependencies between words and documents in the corpus. A simple three-layer GCN with Multi-headed Attention on CMSA demonstrates encouraging results by outperforming numerous state-of-the-art methods. Our approach obtained the best results on the Malayalam-English CM dataset with a weighted-F1 score and an accuracy of 0.75 and 0.73. We will explore our model's performance on various graph networks with different filtering and smoothing techniques for future work.

## References

Kalika Bali, Jatin Sharma, Monojit Choudhury, and Yogarshi Vyas. 2014. "I am borrowing ya mixing?" An Analysis of English-Hindi Code Mixing in Facebook. In *Proceedings of the First Workshop on Computational Approaches to Code Switching*, pages 116–126.

Bharathi Raja Chakravarthi. 2020a. HopeEDI: A multilingual hope speech detection dataset for equality, diversity, and inclusion. In *Proceedings of the Third Workshop on Computational Modeling of People's Opinions, Personality, and Emotion's in Social Media*, pages 41–53, Barcelona, Spain (Online). Association for Computational Linguistics.

Bharathi Raja Chakravarthi. 2020b. *Leveraging orthographic information to improve machine translation of under-resourced languages*. Ph.D. thesis, NUI Galway.

Bharathi Raja Chakravarthi, Navya Jose, Shardul Suryawanshi, Elizabeth Sherly, and John Philip McCrae. 2020a. A sentiment analysis dataset for code-mixed Malayalam-English. In *Proceedings of the 1st Joint Workshop on Spoken Language Technologies for Under-resourced languages (SLTU) and Collaboration and Computing for Under-Resourced Languages (CCURL)*, pages 177–184, Marseille, France. European Language Resources association.

Bharathi Raja Chakravarthi, Vigneshwaran Muralidaran, Ruba Priyadharshini, and John Philip McCrae. 2020b. Corpus creation for sentiment analysis in code-mixed Tamil-English text. In *Proceedings of the 1st Joint Workshop on Spoken Language Technologies for Under-resourced languages (SLTU) and Collaboration and Computing for Under-Resourced Languages (CCURL)*, pages 202–210, Marseille, France. European Language Resources association.

Bharathi Raja Chakravarthi, Ruba Priyadharshini, Vigneshwaran Muralidaran, Shardul Suryawanshi, Navya Jose, Elizabeth Sherly, and John P. McCrae. 2020c. Overview of the Track on Sentiment Analysis for Dravidian Languages in Code-Mixed Text. In *Forum for Information Retrieval Evaluation*, FIRE 2020, page 21–24, New York, NY, USA. Association for Computing Machinery.

Jacob Devlin, Ming-Wei Chang, Kenton Lee, and Kristina Toutanova. 2018. Bert: Pre-training of deep bidirectional transformers for language understanding. *arXiv preprint arXiv:1810.04805*.

Edouard Grave, Piotr Bojanowski, Prakhar Gupta, Armand Joulin, and Tomas Mikolov. 2018. Learning word vectors for 157 languages. *arXiv preprint arXiv:1802.06893*.

Sepp Hochreiter and Jürgen Schmidhuber. 1997. Long short-term memory. *Neural computation*, 9(8):1735–1780.

Navya Jose, Bharathi Raja Chakravarthi, Shardul Suryawanshi, Elizabeth Sherly, and John P. McCrae. 2020. A Survey of Current Datasets for Code-Switching Research. In *2020 6th International Conference on Advanced Computing and Communication Systems (ICACCS)*, pages 136–141.

Simran Khanuja, Sandipan Dandapat, Anirudh Srinivasan, Sunayana Sitaram, and Monojit Choudhury. 2020. GLUECoS: An Evaluation Benchmark for Code-Switched NLP. *arXiv preprint arXiv:2004.12376*.

Yoon Kim. 2014. Convolutional neural networks for sentence classification. *arXiv preprint arXiv:1408.5882*.

Thomas N Kipf and Max Welling. 2016. Semi-supervised classification with graph convolutional networks. *arXiv preprint arXiv:1609.02907*.

Ayush Kumar, Harsh Agarwal, Keshav Bansal, and Ashutosh Modi. 2020. BAKSA at SemEval-2020 Task 9: Bolstering cnn with self-attention for sentiment analysis of code mixed text. *arXiv preprint arXiv:2007.10819*.

BalaSundaraRaman Lakshmanan and Sanjeeth Kumar Ravindranath. 2020. Theedhum Nandrum@ Dravidian-CodeMix-FIRE2020: ASentiment Polarity Classifier for YouTube Commentswith Code-switching between Tamil, Malayalam and English. *arXiv preprint arXiv:2010.03189*.

Sainik Kumar Mahata, Dipankar Das, and Sivaji Bandyopadhyay. 2020. JUNLP@ Dravidian-CodeMix-FIRE2020: Sentiment Classification of Code-Mixed Tweets using Bi-Directional RNN and Language Tags. *arXiv preprint arXiv:2010.10111*.

Thomas Mandl, Sandip Modha, Anand Kumar M, and Bharathi Raja Chakravarthi. 2020. Overview of the HASOC Track at FIRE 2020: Hate Speech and Offensive Language Identification in Tamil, Malayalam, Hindi, English and German. In *Forum for Information Retrieval Evaluation*, FIRE 2020, page 29–32, New York, NY, USA. Association for Computing Machinery.

Diego Marcheggiani, Joost Bastings, and Ivan Titov. 2018. Exploiting semantics in neural machine translation with graph convolutional networks. *arXiv preprint arXiv:1804.08313*.

Diego Marcheggiani and Ivan Titov. 2017. Encoding sentences with graph convolutional networks for semantic role labeling. In *Proceedings of the 2017 Conference on Empirical Methods in Natural Language Processing*, pages 1506–1515, Copenhagen, Denmark. Association for Computational Linguistics.

Parth Patwa, Gustavo Aguilar, Sudipta Kar, Suraj Pandey, Srinivas PYKL, Björn Gambäck, Tanmoy Chakraborty, Thamar Solorio, and Amitava Das. 2020. Semeval-2020 task 9: Overview of sentiment analysis of code-mixed tweets. *arXiv preprint arXiv:2008.04277*.

F. Pedregosa, G. Varoquaux, A. Gramfort, V. Michel, B. Thirion, O. Grisel, M. Blondel, P. Prettenhofer, R. Weiss, V. Dubourg, J. Vanderplas, A. Passos, D. Cournapeau, M. Brucher, M. Perrot, and E. Duchesnay. 2011. Scikit-learn: Machine learning in Python. *Journal of Machine Learning Research*, 12:2825–2830.

Matthew E Peters, Mark Neumann, Mohit Iyyer, Matt Gardner, Christopher Clark, Kenton Lee, and Luke Zettlemoyer. 2018. Deep contextualized word representations. *arXiv preprint arXiv:1802.05365*.

Ruba Priyadharshini, Bharathi Raja Chakravarthi, Mani Vegupatti, and John P. McCrae. 2020. Named Entity Recognition for Code-Mixed Indian Corpus using Meta Embedding. In *2020 6th International*

*Conference on Advanced Computing and Communication Systems (ICACCS)*, pages 68–72.

Sunil Kumar Sahu, Fenia Christopoulou, Makoto Miwa, and Sophia Ananiadou. 2019. Inter-sentence relation extraction with document-level graph convolutional neural network. *arXiv preprint arXiv:1906.04684*.

Thamar Solorio, Monojit Choudhury, Kalika Bali, Sunayana Sitaram, Amitava Das, and Mona Diab, editors. 2020. *Proceedings of the The 4th Workshop on Computational Approaches to Code Switching*. European Language Resources Association, Marseille, France.

Sajeetha Thavareesan and Sinnathamby Mahesan. 2019. Sentiment Analysis in Tamil Texts: A Study on Machine Learning Techniques and Feature Representation. In *2019 14th Conference on Industrial and Information Systems (ICIIS)*, pages 320–325.

Sajeetha Thavareesan and Sinnathamby Mahesan. 2020a. Sentiment Lexicon Expansion using Word2vec and fastText for Sentiment Prediction in Tamil texts. In *2020 Moratuwa Engineering Research Conference (MERCon)*, pages 272–276.

Sajeetha Thavareesan and Sinnathamby Mahesan. 2020b. Word embedding-based Part of Speech tagging in Tamil texts. In *2020 IEEE 15th International Conference on Industrial and Information Systems (ICIIS)*, pages 478–482.

Vladimir Vapnik. 2013. *The nature of statistical learning theory*. Springer science & business media.

Ashish Vaswani, Noam Shazeer, Niki Parmar, Jakob Uszkoreit, Llion Jones, Aidan N Gomez, Łukasz Kaiser, and Illia Polosukhin. 2017. Attention is all you need. In *Advances in neural information processing systems*, pages 5998–6008.

Qingyun Wang, Lifu Huang, Zhiying Jiang, Kevin Knight, Heng Ji, Mohit Bansal, and Yi Luan. 2019. Paperrobot: Incremental draft generation of scientific ideas. *arXiv preprint arXiv:1905.07870*.

Ronald Wardhaugh. 2011. *An introduction to sociolinguistics*, volume 28. John Wiley & Sons.

Thomas Wolf, Lysandre Debut, Victor Sanh, Julien Chaumond, Clement Delangue, Anthony Moi, Pierric Cistac, Tim Rault, Rémi Louf, Morgan Funtowicz, et al. 2019. Huggingface's transformers: State-of-the-art natural language processing. *ArXiv*, pages arXiv–1910.

Liang Yao, Chengsheng Mao, and Yuan Luo. 2019. Graph convolutional networks for text classification. In *Proceedings of the AAAI Conference on Artificial Intelligence*, volume 33, pages 7370–7377.

Linhao Zhang, Dehong Ma, Xiaodong Zhang, Xiaohui Yan, and Houfeng Wang. 2020. Graph LSTM with Context-Gated Mechanism for Spoken Language Understanding. In *AAAI*, pages 9539–9546.

Jie Zhou, Ganqu Cui, Zhengyan Zhang, Cheng Yang, Zhiyuan Liu, Lifeng Wang, Changcheng Li, and Maosong Sun. 2018. Graph neural networks: A review of methods and applications. *arXiv preprint arXiv:1812.08434*.

# Task-Specific Pre-Training and Cross Lingual Transfer for Code-Switched Data

**Akshat Gupta, Sai Krishna Rallabandi, Alan Black**
Carnegie Mellon University
akshatgu@andrew.cmu.edu, {srallaba, awb}@cs.cmu.edu

**Abstract**

Using task-specific pre-training and leveraging cross-lingual transfer are two of the most popular ways to handle code-switched data. In this paper, we aim to compare the effects of both for the task of sentiment analysis. We work with two Dravidian Code-Switched languages - Tamil-Engish and Malayalam-English and four different BERT based models. We compare the effects of task-specific pre-training and cross-lingual transfer and find that task-specific pre-training results in superior zero-shot and supervised performance when compared to performance achieved by leveraging cross-lingual transfer from multilingual BERT models.

## 1 Introduction

Code-Switching is a common phenomenon which occurs in many bilingual and multilingual communities around the world. It is characterized by the usage of more than one language in a single utterance (Sitaram et al., 2019; Jose et al., 2020; Priyadharshini et al., 2020). India is one such place with many communities using different Code-Switched languages, with Hinglish (Code-Switched Hindi-English) being the most popular one. Dravidian languages like Tamil, Kannada, Malayalam and Telugu are also usually code-mixed with English. For over 2600 years, recorded Tamil literature has been documented. The 500 BCE Tamil script found at the site of Porunthal is situated 12 km southwest of Palani, Tamil Nadu. Tamil was the first to be listed as a classical language of India, one of 22 scheduled languages in the Constitution of India, and is one of the world's longest-surviving classical languages. These code-mixed languages are commonly used to interact with social media, which is why it is essential to be build systems that are able to handle Code-Switched data (Chakravarthi et al., 2021a; Chakravarthi and Muralidaran, 2021; Chakravarthi et al., 2021b; Suryawanshi and Chakravarthi, 2021).

Sentiment analysis poses the task of inferring opinion and emotions of a text query (usually social media comments or Tweets) as a classification problem, where each query is classified to have a positive, negative or neutral sentiment (Thavareesan and Mahesan, 2019, 2020a,b; Nanli et al., 2012). It has various applications like understanding the sentiment of different tweets, facebook and youtube comments, understanding product reviews etc (Puranik et al., 2021; Hegde et al., 2021; Yasaswini et al., 2021; Ghanghor et al., 2021b,a). In times of the pandemic, where the entire world is living online, it has become an even more important tool . Robust systems for sentiment analysis already exist for high resource languages like English (Barbieri et al., 2020), yet progress needs to be made for lower resource and code-switched languages.

One of the major bottlenecks in dealing with Code-Switched languages is the lack of availability of annotated datasets in the Code-Mixed languages. To alleviate this problem for Dravidian languages, datasets have been released for Sentiment Analysis in Tamil-English (Chakravarthi et al., 2020b) and Malayalam-English (Chakravarthi et al., 2020a). Various shared tasks (Patwa et al., 2020) (Chakravarthi et al., 2020c) have also been accompanied by the release of these datasets to advance research in this domain.

Models built on top of contextualized word embeddings have recently received huge amount of success and are used in most state of the art models. Systems built on top of BERT (Devlin et al., 2018) and its multilingual variants mBERT and XLM-RoBERTa (Conneau et al., 2019) have been the top ranking systems in both the above competitions.

In this paper, we train four different BERT based models for sentiment analysis for two different code-switched Dravidian languages. The main con-



*Proceedings of the First Workshop on Speech and Language Technologies for Dravidian Languages*, pages 73–79
April 20, 2021 ©2021 Association for Computational Linguistics

tributions of this paper are:

- Comparing the effects of Task-specific pre-training and cross-lingual transfer for code-switched sentiment analysis. In our experiments, we find that the performance with task-specific pre-training on English BERT models is consistently superior when compared to multilingual BERT models.
- We present baseline results for the Malayalam-English (Chakravarthi et al., 2020a) and Tamil-English (Chakravarthi et al., 2020b) dataset for a three-class sentiment classification problem, classifying each sentence into positive, negative and neutral sentiments. Our results can be used as baselines for future work. Previous work (Chakravarthi et al., 2020c) on these datasets treated the problem as a five-class classification problem.

## 2 Related work

Various datasets for Code-Switched Sentiment Analysis have been released in the last few years, some of which have also been accompanied by shared tasks (Patra et al., 2018) (Patwa et al., 2020) (Chakravarthi et al., 2020c) in the respective languages. The shared task released with (Chakravarthi et al., 2020c) focused on Sentiment Analysis for Tamil-English and Malayalam-English datasets. The best performing systems for both these tasks were built on top of BERT variants. (Chakravarthi et al., 2020b) (Chakravarthi et al., 2020a) have provided baseline results for sentiment analysis with a dataset of Youtube comments in Tamil-Englsih and Malayalam-English datasets respectively, using various classification algorithms including Support Vector Machines, Decision Trees, K-Nearest Neighbours, BERT based models etc. In our paper, we use BERT, mBERT (Devlin et al., 2018), XLM-RoBERTa (Conneau et al., 2019) and a RoBERTa based sentiment classification model (Barbieri et al., 2020) for sentiment classification.

Sentiment classification is usually done by classifying a query into one of three sentiments - positive, negative and neutral. In this work, we perform a three-class classification to be able to leverage the power of the TweetEval sentiment classifier (Barbieri et al., 2020), which was trained on a dataset of English Tweets. The TweetEval model is a monolingual model trained on an out-of-domain dataset for our task ( the Tamil-English and Malayalam-English datasets are made from scraping Youtube comments). We also use mBERT and XLM-RoBERTa (Conneau et al., 2019) models for classification, which are trained on more than 100 languages and are thus able to leverage the power of cross-lingual transfer for sentiment classification. Previous works (Jayanthi and Gupta, 2021) has also shown that mBERT and XLM-RoBERTa based models achieve state of the art performance when dealing with code-switched Dravidian languages.

| Language | Positive | Negative | Neutral |
|---|---|---|---|
| Tam-Eng | 10,559 | 2,037 | 850 |
| Mal-Eng | 2,811 | 738 | 1,903 |
| Hinglish | 6,616 | 5,892 | 7,492 |

Table 1: Dataset statistics for Tamil-English, Malayalam-English and Hinglish (Sentimix) dataset. These numbers for the depict the entire dataset which is then divided into train, development and test sets by respective authors.

## 3 Dataset

In this paper, we primarily test our models on Tamil-English (Chakravarthi et al., 2020b) and Malayalam English (Chakravarthi et al., 2020a). The dataset was collected by scrapping Youtube comments from Tamil and Malayalam movies. All the sentences in the dataset are in the latin script. We also use the Sentimix Hinglish dataset (Patwa et al., 2020) to leverage cross-lingual transfer from Hinglish. The datasets statistics are summarized in Table 1. The numbers shown are for the entire dataset which was then split into train, development and test sets by the respective authors.

## 4 Models

We train sentiment analysis models based on top of four BERT variants:

- **BERT** (Devlin et al., 2018) : The original BERT model was trained using Masked Language Modelling (MLM) and Next Sentence Prediction (NSP) objectives on English Wikipedia and BookCorpus (Zhu et al., 2015) and has approximately 110M parameters. We use the uncased-base implementation from the Hugging Face library for our work.
- **mBERT** (Devlin et al., 2018): This is a multilingual BERT model trained on 104 languages

and has approximately 179M parameters. We again use the uncased-base model for our work.

- **XLM-RoBERTa** (Conneau et al., 2019): This is a multilingual RoBERTa model trained on 100 languages and has approximately 270M parameters. The RoBERTa models were an incremental improvement over BERT models with optimized hyperparameters. The most significant change was the removal of the NSP objective used while training BERT. The XLM-RoBERTa model is trained large multilingual corpus of 2.5TB of webcrawled data. We use the uncased-base XLM-RoBERTa model.

- **TweetEval, a RoBERTa based sentiment classifier**: The paper by (Barbieri et al., 2020) is a benchmark of Tweet classification models trained on top of RoBERTa. We use its sentiment classification model, which is referred to as the TweetEval model in this paper. The sentiment classification model was trained on a dataset of 60M English Tweets. The underlying RoBERTa model was trained on English data and has 160M paramemters.

We use the Hugging Face library implementation of these models. We expect mBERT and XLM-RoBERTa based models to leverage cross-lingual transfer from a large pool of languages it is trained on. The TweetEval model was trained on a dataset of English Tweets for the task of sentiment analysis, but is still out-of domain for Youtube comments datasets. It is important to note that all our chosen models either have a different domain, language or task on which they were initially trained and hence are not directly suitable for the task of code-switched sentiment analysis of Youtube comments.

### 4.1 Metrics

We evaluate our results based on weighted average scores of precision, recall and F1. When calculating the weighted average, the precision, recall and F1 scores are calculated for each class and a weighted average is taken based on the number of samples in each class. This metric is apt as the datasets used are unbalanced. We use the same sklearn implementation [1] of the weighted average metric as used in (Chakravarthi et al., 2020b) (Chakravarthi et al., 2020a). All the numbers shown in the paper are weighted average scores.

| Model | Precision | Recall | F1 |
|---|---|---|---|
| Baseline | 0.76 | **0.80** | **0.78** |
| BERT | 0.74 | 0.78 | 0.75 |
| mBERT | 0.75 | 0.75 | 0.75 |
| XLM-RoBERTa | 0.76 | 0.76 | 0.76 |
| TweetEval | **0.77** | 0.77 | 0.77 |

Table 2: Monolingual Results for Malayalam-English. All scores are weighted average scores.

| Model | Precision | Recall | F1 |
|---|---|---|---|
| Baseline | 0.66 | 0.79 | 0.66 |
| BERT | 0.74 | 0.74 | 0.74 |
| mBERT | 0.75 | 0.77 | 0.76 |
| XLM-RoBERTa | 0.75 | 0.78 | 0.76 |
| TweetEval | **0.76** | **0.79** | **0.76** |

Table 3: Monolingual Results for Tamil-English. All scores are weighted average scores.

## 5 Experiments

In this paper, we aim to understand the effects of task-specific pre-training and cross-lingual transfer in improving performance of BERT based models on code-switched datasets. *Task-Specific Pretraining* refers pre-training a model on the same task for which a larger dataset is available and fine-tuning the so-obtained model on the target dataset, which is usually much smaller. In this case, we use the TweetEval model trained for the task of sentiment analysis on a large English corpus, which we fine-tune on the Dravidian code-mixed datasets. *Cross-Lingual Transfer* is commonly referred to the phenomenon of leveraging features and contextual information learnt from a different set of languages for a task with a new target language. Leveraging cross-lingual transfer is one of the main reasons behind training multilingual BERT models, where we expect multilingual BERT models to perform better on an unknown language when compared to an English BERT model.

### 5.1 Monolingual Results

We first present Monolingual Sentiment Classification Results for Tamil-English and Malayalam-English datasets, as shown in Table 2 and Table 3 respectively. The baseline model for Malayalam-Engish is based on mBERT while the baseline

[1] https://scikit-learn.org/stable/modules/generated/sklearn.metrics.classification_report.html

| Train Lang | Test Lang: Tamil | | | Test Lang: Malayalam | | | Test Lang: Hinglish | | |
|---|---|---|---|---|---|---|---|---|---|
| | mBERT | xlm-r | TE | mBERT | xlm-r | TE | mBERT | xlm-r | TE |
| *English* | - | - | 0.197 | - | - | 0.345 | - | - | .506 |
| *Hinglish* | 0.389 | 0.393 | 0.403 | 0.423 | 0.413 | **0.473** | - | - | - |
| *Tamil* | - | - | - | 0.389 | 0.523 | 0.427 | 0.379 | 0.321 | 0.432 |
| *Malayalam* | 0.562 | 0.504 | **0.621** | - | - | - | 0.376 | 0.321 | **0.538** |

Table 4: Zero-shot prediction results for different models trained on the *Train Language*. Here we only report the weighted average F1 scores. We use '-' to represent cells that are Not Applicable to cross-lingual transfer. TE stands for the model built on top of the TweetEval sentiment classification model. xlm-r refers to the XLM-RoBERTa model.

model for Tamil-English was a Random Forest classifier as presented in (Chakravarthi et al., 2020c). The Baseline results were trained for a five-way classification problem, hence the weighted average scores have been re-weighted so that they correspond to a three-way classification problem. We also train an English BERT model to act as a baseline for understanding the effects of task-specific pre-training and cross lingual transfer.

We can see that the TweetEval Model improves on the Baseline results. The improvement is quite significant for Tamil-English. The unusually high improvement in the Tamil-English dataset can be due to the fact that the two models are trained for two different problems. The Baseline results are for a five-way classification problem where the F1 scores are re-weighted to only include three classes - positive, negative and neutral. Our models are trained specifically for a three-class classification problem. Our results can provide baselines for future work on sentiment analysis for the Dravidian datasets, which is usually studied as a three-class classification problem. The TweetEval model also performs the best out of all the models tested. We see that the multilingual BERT models perform better than the English BERT models, although the improvement is not very drastic. XLM-RoBERTa consistently performs better than mBERT.

The pre-trained mBERT and XLM-RoBERTa models are trained on multiple languages and in multiple scripts. We expect these models to leverage cross-lingual transfer and perform better than the English BERT model in the code-switched domain. Although we do see improvement in performance by multilingual BERT models over the English BERT models, the improvements are not very drastic. On the other hand, we see a consistently larger improvement due to task-specific pre-training when fine-tuning the TweetEval model on the Dravidian language datasets. We hypothesize two possible reasons for cross-lingual transfer being less effective for the Dravidian datasets. The first is that even though the multilingual BERT models were trained on multiple languages, they were trained in languages in their original scripts. The datasets we are considering contain Malayalam and Tamil in Romanized form. Due to this, the multilingual BERT models do not have representations and contexts of Malayalam and Tamil tokens in Romanized form. Thus the multilingual BERT model has to learn the representation of these new tokens just as an English BERT model would. The second reason is that that although the multilingual BERT models were trained on multiple languages, they were not trained on a code-switched dataset.

### 5.2 Cross-Lingual Transfer

In this section, we look at the zero-shot transfer between the different sets of languages for the above used models for sentiment analysis. The results are shown in Table 4. The first column of Table 4 refers to the language the given models were trained on. For Hindi-English (Hinglish), we used the Hinglish Sentimix dataset (Patwa et al., 2020).

We first look at the zero shot transfer of English language for Tamil-English, Malayalam-English and Hinglish datasets (refering to the entire first row of Table 4). This is same as looking at the zero-shot performance of the TweetEval model since it was trained on an English corpus. We see that an English sentiment analysis model has the best zero-shot performance for the Hinglish dataset. We hypothesize that this is because the TweetEval model is an in-domain model for the Hinglish dataset (Patwa et al., 2020) as the Hinglish dataset is also a Twitter corpus. The Malaylam and Tamil datasets are out of domain since they are made from Youtube comments.

We can also see that the best zero-shot transfer

| Model | Precision | Recall | F1 |
|---|---|---|---|
| XLM-RoBERTa | 0.76 | 0.76 | 0.76 |
| TweetEval | 0.77 | 0.77 | 0.77 |
| TweetEval + Hinglish | **0.78** | **0.78** | **0.78** |

Table 5: Comparison between performance of XLM-RoBERTa, TweetEval and TweetEval model pretrained on Hinglish data for the Malayalam-English dataset.

| Model | Precision | Recall | F1 |
|---|---|---|---|
| XLM-RoBERTa | 0.75 | 0.78 | 0.76 |
| TweetEval | 0.76 | 0.79 | 0.76 |
| TweetEval + Hinglish | **0.76** | **0.79** | **0.77** |

Table 6: Comparison between performance of XLM-RoBERTa, TweetEval and TweetEval model pretrained on Hinglish data for the Tamil-English dataset.

results are obtained when the TweetEval model is fine-tuned on a linguistically closer language than English for each of the three datasets. For example, the best zero-shot results on the Tamil dataset is achieved when we fine-tune the TweetEval model on Malayalam. Similarly, the best zero-shot results for Tamil are achieved when we fine-tune the TweetEval model on Hinglish. Finally, the best zero-shot results for the Hinglish dataset are achieved when we fine-tune the TweetEval model on Malayalam. These results show that task-specific pre-training is more effective for zero-shot performance and hint at the superiority of task-specific pre-training over cross-lingual transfer.

In the next experiment, we try to leverage cross-lingual transfer along with task-specific pre-training. To do this, we first fine-tune the TweetEval model on the Hinglish dataset. We expect this fine-tuned model to begin to learn code-switching and recognizing new tokens in Hinglish which are not a part of its vocabulary. To make sure that we don't let the model overfit on the Hinglish dataset, we only fine-tune the model on the Hinglish dataset for 1 epoch. Then we fine-tune this model on the target datasets - Tamil-English and Malayalam-English. The results for this experiment are shown in Table 5 and Table 6. Though the combined models show improvements for both datasets, the improvements are not statistically significant. Rigorous experiments to explore this idea will be part of our future work.

## 6 Conclusion

In this paper we present various experiments to compare the effects of task-specific pre-training and cross-lingual transfer on performance of sentiment classification models for code-switched data. To do so, we check the performance of four BERT models on two code-switched languages - Malaylam-English and Tamil English. We find that task-specific pre-training is superior to cross-lingual transfer for our chosen code-switched datasets.

The results presented in this paper for four different BERT models can be used as baselines for future work on sentiment analysis for the chosen datasets. We also present first results for the TweetEval (Barbieri et al., 2020) sentiment classification model for code-switched data.

## References

Francesco Barbieri, Jose Camacho-Collados, Leonardo Neves, and Luis Espinosa-Anke. 2020. Tweeteval: Unified benchmark and comparative evaluation for tweet classification. *arXiv preprint arXiv:2010.12421*.

Bharathi Raja Chakravarthi, Navya Jose, Shardul Suryawanshi, Elizabeth Sherly, and John Philip McCrae. 2020a. A sentiment analysis dataset for code-mixed Malayalam-English. In *Proceedings of the 1st Joint Workshop on Spoken Language Technologies for Under-resourced languages (SLTU) and Collaboration and Computing for Under-Resourced Languages (CCURL)*, pages 177–184, Marseille, France. European Language Resources association.

Bharathi Raja Chakravarthi and Vigneshwaran Muralidaran. 2021. Findings of the shared task on Hope Speech Detection for Equality, Diversity, and Inclusion. In *Proceedings of the First Workshop on Language Technology for Equality, Diversity and Inclusion*. Association for Computational Linguistics.

Bharathi Raja Chakravarthi, Vigneshwaran Muralidaran, Ruba Priyadharshini, and John Philip McCrae. 2020b. Corpus creation for sentiment analysis in code-mixed Tamil-English text. In *Proceedings of the 1st Joint Workshop on Spoken Language Technologies for Under-resourced languages (SLTU) and Collaboration and Computing for Under-Resourced Languages (CCURL)*, pages 202–210, Marseille, France. European Language Resources association.

Bharathi Raja Chakravarthi, Ruba Priyadharshini, Shubhanker Banerjee, Richard Saldhana, John Philip McCrae, Anand Kumar M, Parameswari Krishnamurthy, and Melvin Johnson. 2021a. Findings of the shared task on Machine Translation in Dravidian languages. In *Proceedings of the First Workshop on Speech and Language Technologies for Dravidian Languages*. Association for Computational Linguistics.

Bharathi Raja Chakravarthi, Ruba Priyadharshini, Navya Jose, Anand Kumar M, Thomas Mandl, Prasanna Kumar Kumaresan, Rahul Ponnusamy, Hariharan V, Elizabeth Sherly, and John Philip McCrae. 2021b. Findings of the shared task on Offensive Language Identification in Tamil, Malayalam, and Kannada. In *Proceedings of the First Workshop on Speech and Language Technologies for Dravidian Languages*. Association for Computational Linguistics.

Bharathi Raja Chakravarthi, Ruba Priyadharshini, Vigneshwaran Muralidaran, Shardul Suryawanshi, Navya Jose, Elizabeth Sherly, and John P. McCrae. 2020c. Overview of the Track on Sentiment Analysis for Dravidian Languages in Code-Mixed Text. In *Forum for Information Retrieval Evaluation*, FIRE 2020, page 21–24, New York, NY, USA. Association for Computing Machinery.

Alexis Conneau, Kartikay Khandelwal, Naman Goyal, Vishrav Chaudhary, Guillaume Wenzek, Francisco Guzmán, Edouard Grave, Myle Ott, Luke Zettlemoyer, and Veselin Stoyanov. 2019. Unsupervised cross-lingual representation learning at scale. *arXiv preprint arXiv:1911.02116*.

Jacob Devlin, Ming-Wei Chang, Kenton Lee, and Kristina Toutanova. 2018. Bert: Pre-training of deep bidirectional transformers for language understanding. *arXiv preprint arXiv:1810.04805*.

Nikhil Kumar Ghanghor, Parameswari Krishnamurthy, Sajeetha Thavareesan, Ruba Priyadharshini, and Bharathi Raja Chakravarthi. 2021a. IIITK@DravidianLangTech-EACL2021: Offensive Language Identification and Meme Classification in Tamil, Malayalam and Kannada. In *Proceedings of the First Workshop on Speech and Language Technologies for Dravidian Languages*, Online. Association for Computational Linguistics.

Nikhil Kumar Ghanghor, Rahul Ponnusamy, Prasanna Kumar Kumaresan, Ruba Priyadharshini, Sajeetha Thavareesan, and Bharathi Raja Chakravarthi. 2021b. IIITK@LT-EDI-EACL2021: Hope Speech Detection for Equality, Diversity, and Inclusion in Tamil, Malayalam and English. In *Proceedings of the First Workshop on Language Technology for Equality, Diversity and Inclusion*, Online.

Siddhanth U Hegde, Adeep Hande, Ruba Priyadharshini, Sajeetha Thavareesan, and Bharathi Raja Chakravarthi. 2021. UVCE-IIITT@DravidianLangTech-EACL2021: Tamil Troll Meme Classification: You need to Pay more Attention. In *Proceedings of the First Workshop on Speech and Language Technologies for Dravidian Languages*. Association for Computational Linguistics.

Sai Muralidhar Jayanthi and Akshat Gupta. 2021. Sj_aj@ dravidianlangtech-eacl2021: Task-adaptive pre-training of multilingual bert models for offensive language identification. *arXiv preprint arXiv:2102.01051*.

Navya Jose, Bharathi Raja Chakravarthi, Shardul Suryawanshi, Elizabeth Sherly, and John P. McCrae. 2020. A Survey of Current Datasets for Code-Switching Research. In *2020 6th International Conference on Advanced Computing and Communication Systems (ICACCS)*, pages 136–141.

Zhu Nanli, Zou Ping, Li Weiguo, and Cheng Meng. 2012. Sentiment analysis: A literature review. In *2012 International Symposium on Management of Technology (ISMOT)*, pages 572–576. IEEE.

Braja Gopal Patra, Dipankar Das, and Amitava Das. 2018. Sentiment analysis of code-mixed indian languages: An overview of sail_code-mixed shared task@ icon-2017. *arXiv preprint arXiv:1803.06745*.

Parth Patwa, Gustavo Aguilar, Sudipta Kar, Suraj Pandey, Srinivas PYKL, Björn Gambäck, Tanmoy Chakraborty, Thamar Solorio, and Amitava Das. 2020. Semeval-2020 task 9: Overview of sentiment analysis of code-mixed tweets. *arXiv e-prints*, pages arXiv–2008.

Ruba Priyadharshini, Bharathi Raja Chakravarthi, Mani Vegupatti, and John P. McCrae. 2020. Named Entity Recognition for Code-Mixed Indian Corpus using Meta Embedding. In *2020 6th International Conference on Advanced Computing and Communication Systems (ICACCS)*, pages 68–72.

Karthik Puranik, Adeep Hande, Ruba Priyadharshini, Sajeetha Thavareesan, and Bharathi Raja Chakravarthi. 2021. IIITT@LT-EDI-EACL2021-Hope Speech Detection: There is always hope in Transformers. In *Proceedings of the First Workshop on Language Technology for Equality, Diversity and Inclusion*. Association for Computational Linguistics.

Sunayana Sitaram, Khyathi Raghavi Chandu, Sai Krishna Rallabandi, and Alan W Black. 2019. A survey of code-switched speech and language processing. *arXiv preprint arXiv:1904.00784*.

Shardul Suryawanshi and Bharathi Raja Chakravarthi. 2021. Findings of the shared task on Troll Meme Classification in Tamil. In *Proceedings of the First Workshop on Speech and Language Technologies for Dravidian Languages*. Association for Computational Linguistics.

Sajeetha Thavareesan and Sinnathamby Mahesan. 2019. Sentiment Analysis in Tamil Texts: A Study on Machine Learning Techniques and Feature Representation. In *2019 14th Conference on Industrial and Information Systems (ICIIS)*, pages 320–325.

Sajeetha Thavareesan and Sinnathamby Mahesan. 2020a. Sentiment Lexicon Expansion using Word2vec and fastText for Sentiment Prediction in Tamil texts. In *2020 Moratuwa Engineering Research Conference (MERCon)*, pages 272–276.

Sajeetha Thavareesan and Sinnathamby Mahesan. 2020b. Word embedding-based Part of Speech tagging in Tamil texts. In *2020 IEEE 15th International Conference on Industrial and Information Systems (ICIIS)*, pages 478–482.

Konthala Yasaswini, Karthik Puranik, Adeep Hande, Ruba Priyadharshini, Sajeetha Thavareesan, and Bharathi Raja Chakravarthi. 2021. IIITT@DravidianLangTech-EACL2021: Transfer Learning for Offensive Language Detection in Dravidian Languages. In *Proceedings of the First Workshop on Speech and Language Technologies for Dravidian Languages*. Association for Computational Linguistics.

Yukun Zhu, Ryan Kiros, Rich Zemel, Ruslan Salakhutdinov, Raquel Urtasun, Antonio Torralba, and Sanja Fidler. 2015. Aligning books and movies: Towards story-like visual explanations by watching movies and reading books. In *Proceedings of the IEEE international conference on computer vision*, pages 19–27.

# Analysis of Uvama Urubugal in Tamil Sangam Literatures

**Subalalitha C.N**
Department of Computer Science and Engineering
SRM Institute of Science and Technology
Chengalpatu District, Tamil Nadu,India
subalaln@srmist.edu.in

## Abstract

Uvama urubugal in Tamil are used to explain a particular context by citing another equivalent context. This is referred to as "Uvamaiyani" in Tamil Grammar rules as stated in Tholkappiam. The uvama urubu is called as simile in English. Similes bring out many beautiful poetic contexts. Automatic extraction of such similes can help to build better Natural Language Generation applications such as, story generation systems and lyric suggestion systems. This paper attempts to automatically extract the uvama urubugal from Tamil Sangam Literatures. Natrinai and Mullai Pāṭu have been used for the analysis.There are 12 uvama urubugal in Tamil as per Nanool and this paper has attempted to analyze the usage of these 12 uvama urubugal in Sangam Literatures and compares their usage distribution in the Tamil film songs data set comprising of 4215 songs. It was found that only two uvama urubugal were used in the current-day Tamil film songs. This comparison was done to reveal the diminishing usage of these beautiful uvama urubugal by the current generation and the urge to use them again.

## 1 Introduction

Similes bring out different perception to a context and they add beauty to a text. In Tamil Language, similes are termed as uvamai and follows the grammar rules called, "Uvamayani". The "uvama urubugal" are those words that are used to frame the simile. There are 12 uvama urubugal in Tamil. The Tamil uvama urubugal and their respective English Transliteration is given in Table 1. The rest of this paper makes use of the English transliteration of uvama urubugal.

| S.No | Uvama Urubu (Tamil) | Uvama Urubu (English Transliteration |
|---|---|---|
| 1 | போல | Pōla |
| 2 | புரைய | puraiya |
| 3 | ஒப்ப | oppa |
| 4 | உறழ | urala |
| 5 | மான | māṉa |
| 6 | கடுப்ப | katuppa |
| 7 | இயைய | iayaiya |
| 8 | ஏய்ப்ப | ēyppa |
| 9 | நேர் | nēr |
| 10 | நிகர் | nigar |
| 11 | அன்ன | anna |
| 12 | இன்ன | inna |

Table 1: English Transliteration of Tamil Uvama Urubugal

The uvama urubu (singular form of uvama urubugal) Pōla is widely being used by the current generation . This paper attempts to dig and explore the usage and the distribution of these categories in Sangam literatures and compares with the Tamil film songs to show the decreasing usage of uvama urubugal.

Tamil language is one of the ancient languages in the world and the epigraphic attestations of Tamil have been written from the 6th century BC (Southworth, 2004) (Jesudasan, 2019) . Since then, Tamil language has transformed a lot in terms of its written form and speech form. These transformations have also reflected the beauty of the language followed during every time period through the word usages. This paper focuses on the language usage followed in Sangam literature era that spanned from 600



*Proceedings of the First Workshop on Speech and Language Technologies for Dravidian Languages*, pages 80–84
April 20, 2021 ©2021 Association for Computational Linguistics

BCE to 300 CE (Singh, 2008).

This paper tries to understand the simile usage in the two Sangam literatures namely, Mullai Pāṭu and Natrinai and has compared with 4215 Tamil film songs dataset (Siva Subramanian, 2020). The aim of this experiment is to increase the usage of these similes by the current Tamil generation. Also, this paper lays a foundation to explore more on applications such as, Automatic Lyric generation system and Automatic story generation system that can be built on top of an automatic simile detection system.The word, "Sangam Literature" used in the rest of the paper denotes only Natrinai and MullaiPāṭu.

The contribution of this paper is two-fold.

1. Analysing the usage distribution of twelve types of similes in two Sangam Literatures namely, Natrinai and Mullai Pāṭu.

2. Comparison of the simile usage in 4215 Tamil film songs dataset with the Sangam Literature.

Three types of data sets have been used for the analysis of uvama urubugal namely, 400 Natrinai songs, 103 lines of Mullai Pāṭu and 4215 Tamil film songs(Siva Subramanian, 2020). https://www.kaggle.com/sivaskvs/tamil-songs-lyrics-dataset.

The rest of the paper is organized as follows. Section 2 describes the Literature Survey, Section 3 describes the experimental set up that extracts and analyses the uvama urubugal and section 4 describes the conclusion and future work.

## 2 Literature Survey

This section focuses on three dimensions of the state-of -the art works namely, existing works on simile, works on Sangam Literature, and works on lyric generation. Since the paper is about type of similes, the existing works that have focused on simile analysis in other languages are discussed. Furthermore, the work that are done pertinent to Sangam Literature are also discussed. The automatic simile detection can lead to building lyric generation system and hence the works done in Tamil Lyric generation system are discussed.

(Manjusha and Raseek, 2018) have attempted to classify the similes using Convolution Neural Networks (CNN) and Machine Learning algorithms for English language.

(Chakrabarty et al., 2020) have attempted to generate similes using pretrained model BART which is a sequence-to-sequence models for English language.

(Zeng et al., 2020) have attempted to recognize similes for English language using BERT models.

The paper currently identifies the types of simile (Uvama urubugal) in Sangam literature. Deep learning models must be used as the extension of this work when the similes and their equivalent explanations are automatically extracted using the types of uvama urubugal. This kind of a deep learning-based classification can be used as the foundation for building automatic lyric generation system.

(Sridhar et al., 2018) have attempted to generate lyric in Tamil based on given tune and situation. These kinds of works could be improved if similes in Tamil are given much importance.

(Subalalitha, 2019) has attempted to extract information from Kurunthogai which is also a Sangam literature poem. In this work, the information such as flora, fauna, food, the vessels, and the water bodies mentioned in Kurunthogai are automatically extracted. The sangam literature depicts the life of the Tamils lived during the Sangam era portraying their culture and the five types of landscapes namely, kurunji, mullai, marutham, neithal and palai where they lived. These landscapes represent the mountains, sea, forest, agricultural land and desert encompassing the information about people lived in such different landscapes. This is the reason why in this paper, the analysis of types of simile used by Tamils is done on Sangam Literatures.

## 3 Experimental Set-up for Analysing Uvama Urubugal

### 3.1 Data set

Three types of data sets have been used for the analysis of uvama urubugal namely, 400 Natrinai songs, 103 lines of Mullai Pāṭu and 4215 Tamil film songs(Siva Subramanian, 2020). https://www.kaggle.com/sivaskvs/tamil-songs-lyrics-dataset.

### 3.2 The Experiment

The Natrinai and Mullai Pāṭu songs are scraped from the web page https://sangamtranslationsbyvaidehi.com/. This web page consists of all Sangam Literature poems in Tamil, their Translations, their explanation in Tamil and English. The experiment consists of Pre-processing, Uvama Urubu Classification and analysis. Pre-processing involves removing the HTML tags and separating out only the Natrinai and Mullai Pāṭu songs in Tamil . In Uvama Urubu Classification, the Sangam literature songs and Tamil film songs are checked for all 12 types of uvama urubugal and grouped under their appropriate classes. If the uvama urubu is a free morpheme then an exact match of it is looked for. If the uvama urubu is a bound morpheme, a partial match is found. Human judgement is used as the evaluation metric to check the correctness which is done by six domain experts .

Each uvama urubu has it's own peculiarity in usage. These peculiarities are analysed and recorded here.

Fig 1 shows the experimental set up for detecting the uvama urubugal.

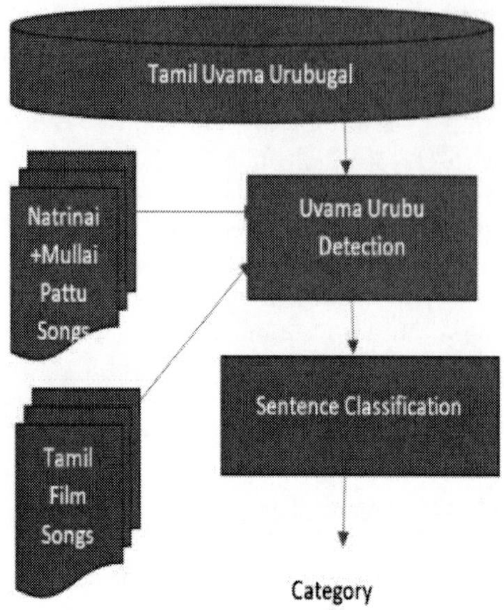


Fig 1: Uvama Urubu Classification

It was observed that the uvama urubu Pōla has been used so frequently compared to the other uvama urubugal both in Sangam literature and Tamil film songs. Tamil film songs had only Pōla and māṉa. The interesting fact is that māṉa was not found in Sangam literature as per the experiment. While observing the uvama urubu puraiya, it was found both as a free morpheme and a bound morpheme attached along with a suffix யும் (yum). The uvama urubu oppa was found along with the bound morpheme இன் (ஒப்பின் ) .The uvama urubu uṟaḻa was not identified by the experiment. The uvama urubu kaṭuppa has found to have been used relatively frequent and it has been used as a free morpheme. The uvama urubu iyaiya has occurred only once in Sangam literature as per the experiment. The uvama urubu ēyppa was found as a free morpheme and was found in least counts. nēr was found as a free morpheme. The uvama urubu,nikar was found as nikarpa attaching itself with a bound morpheme and was only found only twice. The uvama urubu aṉṉa is also a frequently used like pōla), and is used as a free morpheme. The uvama urubu iṉṉa was not found by the experiment.

Table 2 shows the distribution of the uvama

urubu in Sangam literature and Tamil film songs.

| S.No | uvama urubu | Count in Sangam Literature | Count in Tamil Film songs |
|---|---|---|---|
| 1 | போல(Pōla) | 102 | 32 |
| 2 | புரைய(puraiya) | 10 | 0 |
| 3 | ஒப்ப (oppa) | 6 | 0 |
| 4 | உறழ (uṟaḻa), | 0 | 0 |
| 5 | மான((māṉa) | 0 | 2 |
| 6 | கடுப்ப (kaṭuppa) | 16 | 0 |
| 7 | இயைய(iyaiya) | 1 | 0 |
| 8 | ஏய்ப்ப (ēyppa) | 3 | 0 |
| 9 | நேர்(nēr) | 13 | 0 |
| 10 | நிகர்(nikar) | 2 | 0 |
| 11 | அன்ன( aṉṉa) | 56 | 0 |
| 12 | இன்ன( inna) | 2 | 0 |

Table 2:Uvama Urubugal Count Comparison

Fig 2 shows the graph visualization of the comparison of uvama urubugal count in sangam literature and Tamil film songs.

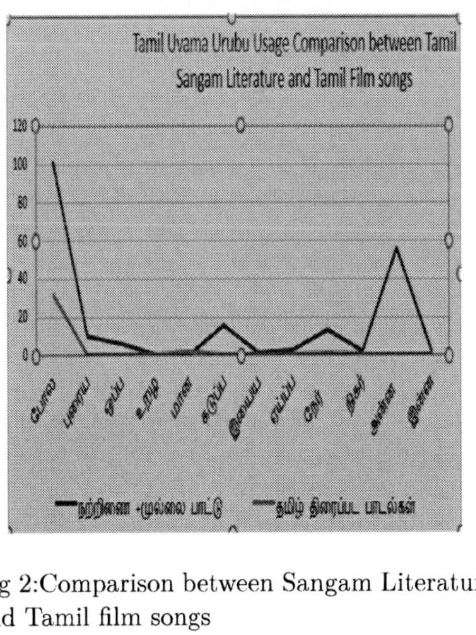


Fig 2:Comparison between Sangam Literature and Tamil film songs

The uvama urubu count obtained by the experiment from Natrinai songs and Mullai Pāṭu is not the exact count of uvama urubugal and needs to be validated by the Tamil experts. However, the uvama urubugal identified by the experiment are correct as per the human expert judgements. It was observed that mullai Pāṭu did not contribute towards the count and had only one uvama urubu as it is the shortest Sangam literature song containing 103 lines. The calculation of recall can only reveal the exact distribution of all uvama urubugal in the sangam literature songs considered. Apart from the bound morphemes identified by the experiment discussed in this paper many other variants of the uvama urubugal need to be explored by conducting the experiment with all Sangam literature songs. The experiment also revealed that the usage of similes has drastically reduced and should be used again to renovate the beauty of the language.

## 4 Conclusion and Future work

Similes capture the different yet beautiful dimensions of the language. Uvama urubu in Tamil is used to express the similes. Tamil language has seen many transformations in terms of it's word usage both in text and speech forms since 2nd century BC. There are 12 uvama urupugal in Tamil language and currently Pōla and māṉa are only used. As this is an initial experiment it is tested only with Natrinai and Mullai Pāṭu. It has to be tested with rest of the Sangam songs to get a wider view.

This work has many directions in which it can be extended. The experiment discussed can be viewed as a multi-classification problem and can be implemented using Machine learning and deep learning algorithms to automatically classify the similes and their equivalent contexts. The contextual features must be identified for each uvama urubu and the model needs to be trained with many Tamil literature texts. The extraction of these similes and their contexts can throw a lot of light in creative usage of Tamil language mainly in Natural language generation-based applications such as lyric generation and story generation.

## References

Tuhin Chakrabarty, Smaranda Muresan, and Nanyun Peng. 2020. Generating similes< effortlessly> like a pro: A style transfer approach for simile generation. *arXiv preprint arXiv:2009.08942*.

Dennis S. Jesudasan. 2019. Keezhadi excavations: Sangam era older than previously thought, finds study. *The Hindu*.

PD Manjusha and C Raseek. 2018. Convolutional neural network based simile classification system. In *2018 International Conference on Emerging Trends and Innovations In Engineering And Technological Research (ICETIETR)*, pages 1–5. IEEE.

Upinder Singh. 2008. *A history of ancient and early medieval India: from the Stone Age to the 12th century*. Pearson Education India.

Franklin Southworth. 2004. *Linguistic archaeology of south Asia*. Routledge.

Rajeswari Sridhar, Subasree Venkatsubhramaniyen, and S Subha Rashmi. 2018. Automatic singable tamil lyric generation for a situation and tune based on causal effect. In *2018 International Conference on Advances in Computing, Communications and Informatics (ICACCI)*, pages 1152–1159. IEEE.

CN Subalalitha. 2019. Information extraction framework for kurunthogai. *Sādhanā*, 44(7):1–6.

Jiali Zeng, Linfeng Song, Jinsong Su, Jun Xie, Wei Song, and Jiebo Luo. 2020. Neural simile recognition with cyclic multitask learning and local attention. In *Proceedings of the AAAI Conference on Artificial Intelligence*, volume 34, pages 9515–9522.

# Task-Oriented Dialog Systems for Dravidian Languages

**Tushar Kanakagiri*** **Karthik Radhakrishnan***
Language Technologies Institute
Carnegie Mellon University
{kradhak2, tkanakag}@cs.cmu.edu

## Abstract

Task-oriented dialog systems help a user achieve a particular goal by parsing user requests to execute a particular action. These systems typically require copious amounts of training data to effectively understand the user intent and its corresponding slots. Acquiring large training corpora requires significant manual effort in annotation, rendering its construction infeasible for low-resource languages. In this paper, we present a two step approach for automatically constructing task-oriented dialogue data in such languages by making use of annotated data from high resource languages. First, we use a machine translation (MT) system to translate the utterance and slot information to the target language. Second, we use token prefix matching and mBERT based semantic matching to align the slot tokens to the corresponding tokens in the utterance. We hand-curate a new test dataset in two low-resource Dravidian languages and show the significance and impact of our training dataset construction using a state-of-the-art mBERT model - achieving a Slot $F_1$ of 81.51 (Kannada) and 78.82 (Tamil) on our test sets.

## 1 Introduction

With the surge in popularity of digital assistants (Google, Siri, Alexa) task-oriented dialog (TOD) systems have become commonplace in NLP research today. TOD systems are designed to complete a particular user goal by understanding requests from users and providing relevant information (Liu and Lane, 2018). They typically consist of four major components - Natural Language Understanding (Chen et al., 2016), Dialog State Tracking (Rastogi et al., 2020; Campagna et al., 2020), Dialog Policy Learning (Takanobu et al., 2019; Li et al., 2020), and Response Generation (Kummerfeld et al., 2019; Galley et al., 2019; Kale and Rastogi, 2020). In this work, we focus on NLU and its two subtasks - Intent Detection and Slot Filling. Intent Detection is typically cast as a sequence classification problem where the task is to classify the purpose or goal that underlies a user utterance into one of several predefined classes called intents (ex. CHECK-SUNRISE, SET-ALARM). The brevity and succinctness of the utterances coupled with the requirements to scale to different domains pose challenges to Intent Detection.

| What's | temperature | in | New | York |
|---|---|---|---|---|
| O | B-weather | O | B-Loc | I-Loc |
| Intent : weather/find | | | | |

Table 1: Example of an utterance along with its slot in BIO (Beginning, Inside, Outside) notation and intent label.

Slot Filling involves identifying the intent arguments and is typically cast as a sequence labelling problem using the BIO notation. (see table 1 for an example). Prior research on the two tasks have mainly focused on English, reporting excellent performance owing to the availability of high quality and large amounts of annotated data (Schuster et al., 2018; Wu et al., 2020). But such performance has not been achieved in low-resource languages due to lack of such data which can be expensive to construct.

In this work, we present a simple but effective method to automatically create annotated training data for slot filling and intent detection in low resource languages making

*Equal contribution



*Proceedings of the First Workshop on Speech and Language Technologies for Dravidian Languages*, pages 85–93
April 20, 2021 ©2021 Association for Computational Linguistics

use of available English data. First, we independently translate utterances and annotated slots in English to the target language. Second, to align the slots with the utterance in the generated translation, we make use of morphology and semantics of the target language (§3). We conduct experiments on two Dravidian languages such as Tamil(TAM) and Kannada(KAN) and evaluate our methods on hand-annotated test sets of 600 utterances across the two languages. Tamil and Kannada belongs to south Dravidian (Tamil-Kannada) languages (Thavareesan and Mahesan, 2019, 2020a,b). By training using state-of-the-art Multilingual BERT : mBERT (Devlin et al., 2018) model for slot filling and intent detection, we show in §6 that our simple alignment heuristics outperform prior approaches relying on existing word alignment methods[1].

## 2 Related Work

**TOD Systems** - In the recent years, there has been a lot of work on building TOD systems broadly around two themes - Building out each component of the system independently (Chen et al., 2016; Campagna et al., 2020; Takanobu et al., 2019; Kummerfeld et al., 2019) and end-to-end TOD systems (Hosseini-Asl et al., 2020; Ham et al., 2020; Liang et al., 2020). Though end-to-end systems show better generalization, they usually require larger amounts of training data and may not be very feasible for low-resource settings. In this work, we primarily tackle the NLU component which performs Intent detection and Slot identification.

Since these tasks are framed as sequence classification and tagging tasks, sentence encoder models have been used to tackle them. Prior works have utilized Recurrent Neural Networks (Liu and Lane, 2016; Goo et al., 2018; E et al., 2019) and more recently have used BERT (Chen et al., 2019).

**Multilingual TOD** - Though there currently exist multiple large-scale datasets for TOD (Byrne et al., 2019; Budzianowski et al., 2018; Hemphill et al., 1990), they are monolingual English Corpora. Schuster et al. (2018) released the Facebook TOD dataset which contains utterances from three languages - English, Spanish, Thai geared towards cross-lingual transfer of dialog. On this dataset, there have been works on zero and few-shot transfer using Latent Variable Transfer (Liu et al., 2019), Mixed Language Training (Liu et al., 2020) but they don't display consistent gains over augmentation with MT+Word alignment data.

On Indian languages, there have been works towards Indic and Code-Switched TOD systems (Jayarao and Srivastava, 2018; Banerjee et al., 2018; Mandl et al., 2020) but these datasets are manually constructed and are smaller in size. Furthermore, they're primarily for Hindi and there currently exists no dataset for languages like Kannada, Telugu, etc.

**Auto-construction of datasets** - Given the cost and difficulty in acquiring annotators, prior works have employed methods to create synthetic training data. Gupta et al. (2020) use Google Translate to create synthetic utterances in Indic languages towards the task of spoken intent detection but do not tackle the slot filling task. More recently López de Lacalle et al. (2020) employed a Seq2Seq translation and word alignment to project the Spanish slot tags to Basque. However, we show that given the flexible word ordering and rich morphology, word alignment systems do not work particularly well for Dravidian languages. Furthermore, since Dravidian languages do not have large open-source corpora to learn MT and alignment systems reliably, we utilize Google Translate API, morphology and semantics based heuristic slot aligner which does not require any parallel data.

## 3 Dataset Construction

The training dataset for the low-resource languages is constructed from the Facebook Multilingual Task-Oriented Dialog dataset (Schuster et al., 2018) which contains utterances in English, Spanish and Thai tagged with the corresponding intent and slot labels by hand.

### 3.1 Auto-construction from English data

Our dataset construction consists of two steps - Translation and slot assignment. The translation phase converts the English utterances

[1]Code and data available at `https://github.com/karthikradhakrishnan96/TOD-Dravidian`

to their target language equivalents and the slot assignment phase transfers slot labels from the English phrases to their target language equivalents. As seen in Figure 1, words often get translated to multiple words/don't have an equivalent in the translated language ('the' in the sentence is folded into 'groomer' in the target language), making the slot assignment problem non-trivial.

For the translation phase, we experiment with two methods - Google Translate and a transformer based Seq2Seq model.

Previous works have tackled slot transfer using Word Alignment (López de Lacalle et al., 2020; Schuster et al., 2018) by first predicting the word alignment between the translations and then copying over the labels from the source language words to their corresponding target language equivalents. This maximises sentence level alignment probabilities and is usually learned using a parallel sentence corpora. Furthermore, owing to the rich morphology and flexible word-ordering of Dravidian languages, these models typically have high alignment error rates. To transfer the slot spans from English to our target language, we only require the alignments of the slot spans and not the entire utterance. We tackle this by translating the annotated English spans to our target language and using various heuristics to align the slots to the utterance.

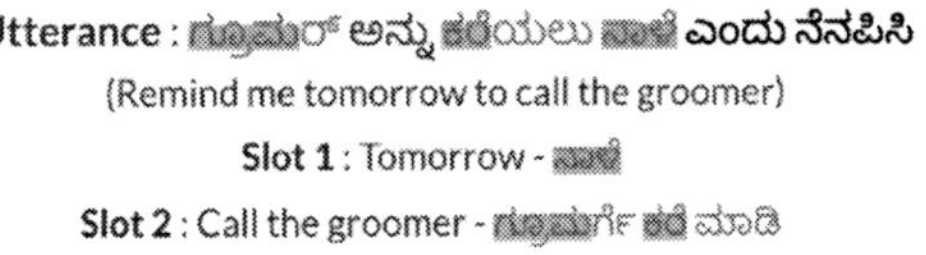


Figure 1: Our prefix matching and span expansion technique. Highlighted text shows the matching prefix of tokens from slots and utterances. We can observe how span expansion helps label the ಅನ್ನು token correctly and obtain a contiguous span and account for noise in our alignment technique.

We use a simple word match as our baseline, where we identify words from utterances that match words from the annotated slots. This baseline achieves a poor Slot $F_1$ score owing to the variation in translation of certain words when translated independently and as part of a sentence. This can be attributed to the morphologically rich nature of Indian languages, where the context of the inflection can lead to different suffixes during translation for each word. To tackle this, as seen in Figure 1, we use a technique that matches a word from the annotated slot to a word from the utterance that has the maximum prefix overlap. This helps account for a wide variety of variations and greatly helps in the automatic construction of the low-resource dataset.

Finally, we apply a span expansion technique where we assign the labels of the aligned slot tokens to those intra-span tokens that did not align with any slot. This helps us obtain a contiguous span which is a requirement of sequence tagging models. Additionally, this also helps account for errors in our alignment approach when certain intra-span tokens do not get aligned with any utterance token.

### 3.2 Including Semantic Matching

Upon analyzing the unmatched words from our aligner, we noticed that the words get translated differently when used in a complete sentence and when used individually. These variations could be due to transliteration (Word gets transliterated when used in slot phrase but translated when used in the utterance), synonyms (Phrase and utterance translations are synonyms) etc. Since the words are completely different, the prefix matching does not find any matching candidates. We use mBERT to obtain word embedding in-phrase and word embeddings in-utterance and cosine similarity to find the closest matching word to align to.

### 3.3 Manual tagging for test set

To quantitatively evaluate the quality of our automatically constructed training data, we require a gold test set in the target low-resource language. As this is unavailable for many Dravidian languages, we manually tag a test set for two of them (Kannada and Tamil), to obtain the gold alignments in the low-resource languages between annotated slots and the utterances. We first translate utterances to the low-resource language using Google Translate. Next, we remove examples that contain incorrect utterance translations. We finally obtain a sample of 300 examples for

| Ex. 1 | அடுத்த வாரம் வெப்பநிலை என்ன? (What is the temperature next week?) |
|---|---|
| Slots | B-DT I-DT B-WN O |
| Ex. 2 | Necesitaré un suéter en Denver mañana? (WillIneed a sweater in Denver tomorrow?) |
| Slots | O O B-WA O B-LOC B-DT |
| Ex. 3 | ಸಾಂತಾ ಬರಾಬರಾದಲ್ಲಿ ಈ ವಾರಾಂತ್ಯದಲ್ಲಿ ತಾಪಮಾನ ಹೇಗಿರುತ್ತದೆ (Santa **Barbara this** weekend temperature what) |
| Slots | B-LOC **B-LOC I-DT** I-DT B-WN |
| Ex. 4 | Necesito un informe *meteorológico* para el viernes (needed a report weather for Friday) |
| Slots | O O B-WN *I-WN* B-DT I-DT I-DT |

Table 2: Some qualitative examples from our dataset (With word-by-word ENG translations) and predictions by our mBERT model. (DT - DateTime, WN - Weather Noun, LOC - Location, WA - Weather Attribute)

each language. For each language and each example, the utterance tokens corresponding to the slots are tagged, by two graduate students who are native speakers of the language (We obtain an inter-annotator Cohen Kappa score of 0.9303 for KAN and 0.9606 for TAM).

To aid with annotation, we make use of Doccano (Nakayama et al., 2018) to help provide the annotators an easy to use interface (Figure 3).

## 4 Model

We learn the intent and slot filling tasks jointly with BERT (Devlin et al., 2018), more specifically, the multilingual variant - mBERT which is pre-trained on 104 languages. We pass the [CLS] vector representations onto a Multi-Layer perceptron to classify the intent onto one of the predefined intent classes. We pass the token representations produced by the mBERT model onto another Multi-Layer perceptron to identify the slots. In the case of a word consisting of multiple tokens, we only use the first sub-word token and ignore the others during training and test. Figure 2 shows the architecture of our system. Since mBERT is pre-trained across many languages, we follow the same architecture for our zero-shot and few-shot experiments.

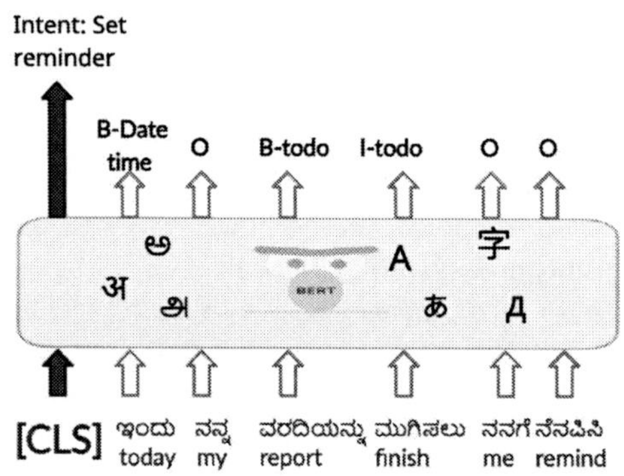


Figure 2: Model Architecture showcasing a KAN utterance passed to mBERT model. (word-by-word ENG translations are included for readability). Sub-word tokens omitted for brevity. Slot labels and intent are predicted from word and [CLS] representations respectively

## 5 Experiment Setup

We use the BASE model of BERT and mBERT in all our experiments with a batch size of 64 and a learning rate of 1e-5 with Adam (Kingma and Ba, 2014) optimizer. On zero and few shot transfer experiments, the model is trained for about 10 epochs before evaluation/fine-tuning on few shot data.

## 6 Analysis and Discussion of Results

### 6.1 Qualitative examples

Table 2 shows some qualitative examples from our dataset and the predictions made by our model. The first two examples demonstrate successful predictions on TAM and ES when trained on 5K auto-tagged examples. The third example demonstrates an error due to local normalization during optimization. Since we don't explicitly model that B-LOC (Beginning Location) does not occur immediately after a B-LOC and that I-LOC is more probable, the model predicts B-LOC for both slots. Utilising global normalization over BERT (CRF) could help resolve this issue.

The fourth example showcases the efficacy of using mBERT during alignment. On our training set, we noticed that the word 'weather' gets translated into 'meteorológico' when used in a sentence but gets translated to 'clima' when used individually. Since these words have no common prefix, the words are not usually tagged by our aligner. But when mBERT is used, since these terms are very close semantically, the slots are assigned correctly, subsequently resulting in better predictions.

### 6.2 Effect of Dataset construction heuristic

Without any models, we first evaluated the efficacy of our dataset tagger by autotagging and manually tagging the 300 test examples and comparing the slot $F_1$ between them. On our hand-annotated set of 300 examples, we show that the slot $F_1$ obtained by our tagging method (§3) outperforms simple word match and existing word alignment baselines in Table 3.

| Method | Lang | Slot F1 |
|---|---|---|
| Word Alignment | TAM | 31.17 |
| Translate+Overlap | TAM | 46.82 |
| Ours | TAM | 80.70 |
| Ours | KAN | 80.76 |

Table 3: Performance of different slot alignment methods

### 6.3 Effect of number of training samples

We conduct experiments with varying amounts of data to show the effect of training data size in Table 4. We can see that even with 300 examples from our auto-tagged dataset, the model is able to achieve significant boost as compared to the zero shot setting of training on ENG and testing on KAN. Initial training on ENG followed by a few shot adaptation on KAN provides an even higher boost in slot performance. Upon varying the number of training samples to 10K and 20K for KAN, we see some minor improvement for 10K for the slot but see a 1.5 F1 boost when using 20K auto-annotated samples.

Given that KAN and TAM are more closely related, we can see that the zero shot transfer from KAN to TAM achieves 62.22 & 46.16, outperforming the transfer from ENG to TAM. We also experimented with training a single model jointly on KAN and TAM but observed similar but slightly reduced performance as compared to using 5K examples from just one language (Rows 8, 13 and 6,14) which could be due to interference when optimizing for multiple languages. We also observe that using 300 examples of KAN and 5K of TAM achieves better performance on the TAM further corroborating the hypothesis that larger number of related language datapoints cause interference, leading to lower scores.

| Train | Test | Intent | Slot |
|---|---|---|---|
| ENG-30K | KAN | 51.96 | 21.46 |
| KAN-300 | KAN | 86.27 | 62.24 |
| ENG-30K, KAN-300 | KAN | 81.04 | 65.82 |
| ENG-30K | TAM | 30.50 | 27.81 |
| TAM-300 | TAM | 82.07 | 59.67 |
| TAM-5K | TAM | 93.08 | 78.68 |
| ENG-30K, TAM-300 | TAM | 79.55 | 65.01 |
| KAN-5K | KAN | 93.13 | 79.87 |
| KAN-10K | KAN | 91.80 | 79.95 |
| KAN-20K | KAN | 93.79 | 81.51 |
| KAN-5K | TAM | 62.22 | 46.16 |
| TAM-5K | KAN | 59.47 | 37.24 |
| KAN-5K, TAM-5K | KAN | 93.46 | 79.75 |
| TAM-5K, KAN-5K | TAM | 92.76 | 78.21 |
| KAN-300, TAM-5K | TAM | 93.71 | 78.82 |

Table 4: Zero and Few shot transfer performance

### 6.4 Effect of the MT system

Given the key role of the MT system in the dataset construction, we compare the performance of two approaches - Google Translate and our own Seq2Seq Transformer MT system. On the EnTam corpus (Ramasamy et al., 2012), our MT system achieved a BLEU score of 10.89 (the best reported score on this dataset is 9.39 (Kumar and Singh, 2019)). The low performance of the mBERT model could be attributed to the low quality of the translations for the training dataset resulting from domain gap in the MT system. Since the EnTam corpus contains articles on Cinema, News, and Bible, it doesn't translate TOD utterances accurately (We examined frequent words in our training corpus - Remind, Alarm, etc and observed that these words didn't exist or were very infrequent in the EnTam corpus) Furthermore, owing to the differences in style (EnTam contains statements while TOD contains questions) we observed that some translations had changes in their meanings. We hence observe that 300 high quality training examples lead to similar performance as compared to 25K noisy training examples (Table 5)

| MT System | Lang | Intent | Slot |
|---|---|---|---|
| TAM-300-Google MT | TAM | 82.07 | 59.67 |
| TAM-5K-Google MT | TAM | 93.08 | 78.68 |
| TAM-5K-Seq2Seq | TAM | 80.50 | 51.32 |
| TAM-25K-Seq2Seq | TAM | 81.76 | 56.56 |

Table 5: Performance of different MT systems

### 6.5 Effect of Semantic Matching

We now present results when mBERT based semantic matching is included in the aligner in Table 6. We noticed a small increase in F1 score for KAN but a small drop for TAM. This could be attributed to two reasons: 1) Our alignment heuristic already tags spans accurately and the inclusion of mBERT only provides minor improvements and 2) Languages like KAN and TAM are underrepresented in the mBERT training set leading to lower performance on these languages.

On a non-Dravidian language Spanish, we notice a larger boost in performance (6 F1), indicating the strength of the mBERT representations for ES. We present a more detailed analysis of the performance on ES in the next section.

### 6.6 Performance on non-Dravidian Languages

Though our aligner was designed for Dravidian languages, there are languages in other families which also exhibit suffix-based morphology. We evaluate the performance of our system on Spanish by auto-creating the training data from ENG using our method and evaluating on the hand-annotated ES data provided in the Facebook dataset.

| Lang | Slot F1 | +mBERT |
|---|---|---|
| KAN-5K | 79.87 | 80.63 |
| KAN-20K | 81.51 | 82.01 |
| TAM-5K | 78.68 | 76.24 |
| ES-5K | 71.85 | 77.66 |

Table 6: Performance difference due to the inclusion of mBERT

We can see from Table 7 that our auto-created dataset of 5K examples performs only 12 $F_1$ worse than training on the entire hand-annotated ES dataset (Consisting of 3.6K examples) further showcasing the quality of training examples produced by our method.

| Train | Intent | Slot F1 |
|---|---|---|
| ES-5K-auto | 97.63 | 71.85 |
| ES-5k-mBERT | 97.13 | 77.66 |
| ES-20K-mBERT | 97.46 | 79.47 |
| ES-FB | 98.78 | 89.39 |

Table 7: Performance on a Romance language ES

## 7 Conclusion & Future Work

In this work, we demonstrated techniques to project training data from high resource languages to low-resource settings, thus efficiently obtaining large scale synthetic data for training TOD systems. We also showcased the efficacy of the dataset creation on a manually curated test set on KAN and TAM.

In the future, we hope to add more Dravidian languages - Telugu and Malayalam. We also hope to utilize social media data from these languages to generate code-switched/more natural utterances.

## References

Suman Banerjee, Nikita Moghe, Siddhartha Arora, and Mitesh M Khapra. 2018. A dataset for building code-mixed goal oriented conversation systems. *arXiv preprint arXiv:1806.05997*.

Paweł Budzianowski, Tsung-Hsien Wen, Bo-Hsiang Tseng, Iñigo Casanueva, Ultes Stefan, Ramadan Osman, and Milica Gašić. 2018. Multiwoz - a large-scale multi-domain wizard-of-oz dataset for task-oriented dialogue modelling. In *Proceedings of the 2018 Conference on Empirical Methods in Natural Language Processing (EMNLP)*.

Bill Byrne, Karthik Krishnamoorthi, Chinnadhurai Sankar, Arvind Neelakantan, Daniel Duckworth, Semih Yavuz, Ben Goodrich, Amit Dubey, Kyu-Young Kim, and Andy Cedilnik. 2019. Taskmaster-1: Toward a realistic and diverse dialog dataset.

Giovanni Campagna, Agata Foryciarz, Mehrad Moradshahi, and Monica Lam. 2020. Zero-shot transfer learning with synthesized data for multi-domain dialogue state tracking. In *Proceedings of the 58th Annual Meeting of the Association for Computational Linguistics*, pages 122–132, Online. Association for Computational Linguistics.

Qian Chen, Zhu Zhuo, and Wen Wang. 2019. Bert for joint intent classification and slot filling. *arXiv preprint arXiv:1902.10909*.

Yun-Nung Chen, Dilek Hakkani-Tür, Jianfeng Gao, and Li Deng. 2016. End-to-end memory networks with knowledge carryover for multi-turn spoken language understanding.

Jacob Devlin, Ming-Wei Chang, Kenton Lee, and Kristina Toutanova. 2018. Bert: Pre-training of deep bidirectional transformers for language understanding. *arXiv preprint arXiv:1810.04805*.

Haihong E, Peiqing Niu, Zhongfu Chen, and Meina Song. 2019. A novel bi-directional interrelated model for joint intent detection and slot filling. In *Proceedings of the 57th Annual Meeting of the Association for Computational Linguistics*, pages 5467–5471, Florence, Italy. Association for Computational Linguistics.

Michel Galley, Chris Brockett, Xiang Gao, Jianfeng Gao, and B. Dolan. 2019. Grounded response generation task at dstc7.

Chih-Wen Goo, Guang Gao, Yun-Kai Hsu, Chih-Li Huo, Tsung-Chieh Chen, Keng-Wei Hsu, and Yun-Nung Chen. 2018. Slot-gated modeling for joint slot filling and intent prediction. In *Proceedings of the 2018 Conference of the North American Chapter of the Association for Computational Linguistics: Human Language Technologies, Volume 2 (Short Papers)*, pages 753–757, New Orleans, Louisiana. Association for Computational Linguistics.

Akshat Gupta, Xinjian Li, Sai Krishna Rallabandi, and Alan W Black. 2020. Acoustics based intent recognition using discovered phonetic units for low resource languages. *arXiv preprint arXiv:2011.03646*.

Donghoon Ham, Jeong-Gwan Lee, Youngsoo Jang, and Kee-Eung Kim. 2020. End-to-end neural pipeline for goal-oriented dialogue systems using GPT-2. In *Proceedings of the 58th Annual Meeting of the Association for Computational Linguistics*, pages 583–592, Online. Association for Computational Linguistics.

Charles T. Hemphill, John J. Godfrey, and George R. Doddington. 1990. The ATIS spoken language systems pilot corpus. In *Speech and Natural Language: Proceedings of a Workshop Held at Hidden Valley, Pennsylvania, June 24-27,1990*.

Ehsan Hosseini-Asl, Bryan McCann, Chien-Sheng Wu, Semih Yavuz, and Richard Socher. 2020. A simple language model for task-oriented dialogue. *arXiv preprint arXiv:2005.00796*.

Pratik Jayarao and Aman Srivastava. 2018. Intent detection for code-mix utterances in task oriented dialogue systems. In *2018 International Conference on Electrical, Electronics, Communication, Computer, and Optimization Techniques (ICEECCOT)*, pages 583–587. IEEE.

Mihir Kale and Abhinav Rastogi. 2020. Template guided text generation for task-oriented dialogue. In *Proceedings of the 2020 Conference on Empirical Methods in Natural Language Processing (EMNLP)*, pages 6505–6520, Online. Association for Computational Linguistics.

Diederik P Kingma and Jimmy Ba. 2014. Adam: A method for stochastic optimization. *arXiv preprint arXiv:1412.6980*.

Amit Kumar and Anil Kumar Singh. 2019. NLPRL at WAT2019: Transformer-based Tamil – English indic task neural machine translation system. In *Proceedings of the 6th Workshop on Asian Translation*, pages 171–174, Hong Kong, China. Association for Computational Linguistics.

Jonathan K. Kummerfeld, Sai R. Gouravajhala, Joseph Peper, Vignesh Athreya, Chulaka Gunasekara, Jatin Ganhotra, Siva Sankalp Patel, Lazaros Polymenakos, and Walter S. Lasecki. 2019. A large-scale corpus for conversation disentanglement. In *Proceedings of the 57th Annual Meeting of the Association for Computational Linguistics (Volume 1: Long Papers)*.

Maddalen López de Lacalle, Xabier Saralegi, and Iñaki San Vicente. 2020. Building a task-oriented dialog system for languages with no training data: the case for Basque. In *Proceedings of the 12th Language Resources and Evaluation Conference*, pages 2796–2802, Marseille,

France. European Language Resources Association.

Ziming Li, Sungjin Lee, Baolin Peng, Jinchao Li, Julia Kiseleva, Maarten de Rijke, Shahin Shayandeh, and Jianfeng Gao. 2020. Guided dialogue policy learning without adversarial learning in the loop. In *Findings of the Association for Computational Linguistics: EMNLP 2020*, pages 2308–2317, Online. Association for Computational Linguistics.

Weixin Liang, Youzhi Tian, Chengcai Chen, and Zhou Yu. 2020. Moss: End-to-end dialog system framework with modular supervision. In *AAAI*, pages 8327–8335.

Bing Liu and Ian Lane. 2016. Attention-based recurrent neural network models for joint intent detection and slot filling. *arXiv preprint arXiv:1609.01454*.

Bing Liu and Ian Lane. 2018. End-to-end learning of task-oriented dialogs. In *Proceedings of the 2018 Conference of the North American Chapter of the Association for Computational Linguistics: Student Research Workshop*, pages 67–73.

Zihan Liu, Jamin Shin, Yan Xu, Genta Indra Winata, Peng Xu, Andrea Madotto, and Pascale Fung. 2019. Zero-shot cross-lingual dialogue systems with transferable latent variables. *arXiv preprint arXiv:1911.04081*.

Zihan Liu, Genta Indra Winata, Zhaojiang Lin, Peng Xu, and Pascale Fung. 2020. Attention-informed mixed-language training for zero-shot cross-lingual task-oriented dialogue systems. *Proceedings of the AAAI Conference on Artificial Intelligence*, 34(05):8433–8440.

Thomas Mandl, Sandip Modha, Anand Kumar M, and Bharathi Raja Chakravarthi. 2020. Overview of the HASOC Track at FIRE 2020: Hate Speech and Offensive Language Identification in Tamil, Malayalam, Hindi, English and German. In *Forum for Information Retrieval Evaluation*, FIRE 2020, page 29–32, New York, NY, USA. Association for Computing Machinery.

Hiroki Nakayama, Takahiro Kubo, Junya Kamura, Yasufumi Taniguchi, and Xu Liang. 2018. doccano: Text annotation tool for human. Software available from https://github.com/doccano/doccano.

Loganathan Ramasamy, Ondřej Bojar, and Zdeněk Žabokrtský. 2012. Morphological processing for english-tamil statistical machine translation. In *Proceedings of the Workshop on Machine Translation and Parsing in Indian Languages*, pages 113–122.

Abhinav Rastogi, Xiaoxue Zang, Srinivas Sunkara, Raghav Gupta, and Pranav Khaitan. 2020. Schema-guided dialogue state tracking task at dstc8. *arXiv preprint arXiv:2002.01359*.

Sebastian Schuster, Sonal Gupta, Rushin Shah, and Mike Lewis. 2018. Cross-lingual transfer learning for multilingual task oriented dialog. *arXiv preprint arXiv:1810.13327*.

Ryuichi Takanobu, Hanlin Zhu, and Minlie Huang. 2019. Guided dialog policy learning: Reward estimation for multi-domain task-oriented dialog. In *Proceedings of the 2019 Conference on Empirical Methods in Natural Language Processing and the 9th International Joint Conference on Natural Language Processing (EMNLP-IJCNLP)*, pages 100–110, Hong Kong, China. Association for Computational Linguistics.

Sajeetha Thavareesan and Sinnathamby Mahesan. 2019. Sentiment Analysis in Tamil Texts: A Study on Machine Learning Techniques and Feature Representation. In *2019 14th Conference on Industrial and Information Systems (ICIIS)*, pages 320–325.

Sajeetha Thavareesan and Sinnathamby Mahesan. 2020a. Sentiment Lexicon Expansion using Word2vec and fastText for Sentiment Prediction in Tamil texts. In *2020 Moratuwa Engineering Research Conference (MERCon)*, pages 272–276.

Sajeetha Thavareesan and Sinnathamby Mahesan. 2020b. Word embedding-based Part of Speech tagging in Tamil texts. In *2020 IEEE 15th International Conference on Industrial and Information Systems (ICIIS)*, pages 478–482.

Chien-Sheng Wu, Steven Hoi, Richard Socher, and Caiming Xiong. 2020. Tod-bert: Pre-trained natural language understanding for task-oriented dialogues. *arXiv preprint arXiv:2004.06871*.

# Appendix

## A Annotation Tool

Figure 3: Annotation User Interface for manual creation of test dataset. The slot spans in English are shown in the right and the annotators were required to mark the corresponding slots in the low-resource language utterance on the left

# A Survey on Paralinguistics in Tamil Speech Processing

**Anosha Ignatius and Uthayasanker Thayasivam**
University of Moratuwa
Sri Lanka
anoshai@uom.lk, rtuthaya@cse.mrt.ac.lk

## Abstract

Speech carries not only the semantic content but also the paralinguistic information which captures the speaking style. Speaker traits and emotional states affect how words are being spoken. The research on paralinguistic information is an emerging field in speech and language processing and it has many potential applications including speech recognition, speaker identification and verification, emotion recognition and accent recognition. Among them, there is a significant interest in emotion recognition from speech. A detailed study of paralinguistic information present in speech signal and an overview of research work related to speech emotion for Tamil Language is presented in this paper.

## 1 Introduction

The field of Paralinguistics deals with how something is being spoken and is limited to non-verbal aspects of speech. It covers the manner of speaking and information characterizing speaker traits and states. Paralinguistic content present in the speech signal provides information which is mainly grouped into short-term traits and long-term traits. Short-term traits include speaking style, voice quality, and emotional states while long-term traits include biological trait primitives such as height, weight, age and gender, ethnicity, culture, and personality. Health state, intoxication, mood, and sleepiness are categorized as medium term traits between short term and permanent traits. (Schuller and Batliner, 2014)

The research on paralinguistics is beneficial in a wide range of speech processing applications. Performance of automatic speech recognition (ASR) is affected by variability in the speaking style due to speaker traits emotions. Analyzing the paralinguistic information in the speech help to compensate for the speaker variability through normalization techniques (Anosha and Uthayasanker, 2020). In addition to this, several paralinguistic tasks including speaker recognition, accent recognition, and emotion recognition have been investigated over the past years. Interest in paralinguistics has significantly grown in the past years and Interspeech conference hosts a computational paralinguistics challenge ComParE since 2009 with different sets of tasks each year. The most popular paralinguistic task is speech emotion recognition. Emotion detection can help in making the human computer interface adapt to user's emotional condition, thus improving the user satisfaction. Study of paralinguistics can also be applied in diagnosing and monitoring the disease progression in diseases like neurodegenerative disorders which show speech impairment as one of the early signs.

Selecting appropriate feature extraction techniques is important for discriminating between classes in paralinguistic tasks. Then most common features that capture paralinguistic information are low-level descriptors (LLD) (Schuller et al., 2013) which include mel frequency cepstral coefficients (MFCC), energy, pitch frequency, loudness, zero crossing rate, harmonicity, jitter, shimmer etc. Recent research works use deep neural networks (DNNs) to learn high-level acoustic features from utterance-level LLD or directly from raw speech signal. DNNs have shown significant performance in a variety of applications ranging from speech recognition to speaker identification and verification.

This paper presents the background of paralinguistics and focuses on the research work related to speech based emotion recognition for Tamil language. Tamil is a Dravidian language natively spoken by South Asia's Tamil people. Tamil is the official language of two sovereign states, Singapore and Sri Lanka, as well as the Indian province of Tamil Nadu and Puducherry (Chakravarthi et al.,



*Proceedings of the First Workshop on Speech and Language Technologies for Dravidian Languages*, pages 94–99
April 20, 2021 

2018, 2019; Chakravarthi, 2020). With a history stretching back to 600 BCE, the Tamil language is one of the world's longest-surviving classical languages. Poetry dominates Tamil literature, especially Sangam literature, which consists of poems written between 600 BCE and 300 CE. The Tamil language accounts for more than 55 percent of the epigraphical inscriptions discovered by the Archaeological Survey of India (approximately 55,000) (Caldwell, 1875). The rest of the paper is organized as follows: Section II describes in detail about paralinguistic information in speech and explores various acoustic features extracted from the speech signal. Section III discusses speech emotion recognition and presents a survey of research work done for Tamil language. The paper is concluded in Section IV, with discussions in this research area.

## 2 Background

Speech signal carries two types of information: linguistic information which conveys the spoken content and paralinguistic information that covers the speaker attributes. Paralinguistic information can be categorized into three types as shown in Figure 1. The following sections discuss about paralinguistic features, its applications and acoustic features that represent them.

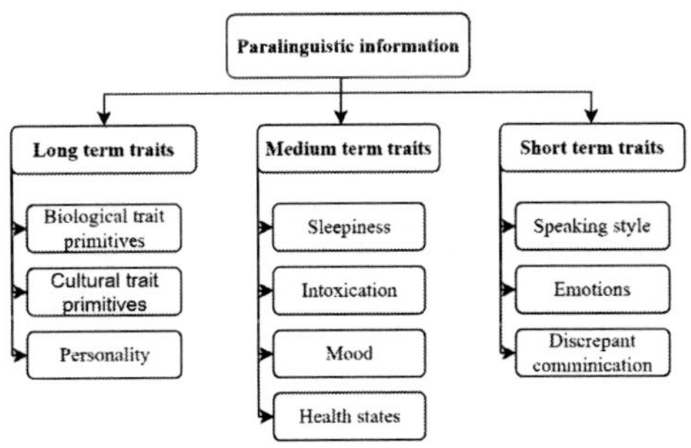


Figure 1: Types of paralinguistic information

### 2.1 Paralinguistic information in speech

Mainly paralinguistics deal with age, gender, personality, emotion, deviant speech, and discrepant communication. Biological trait primitives such as age and gender are designed by nature. Male and female voices differ due to physiological differences. In addition to this, age and cultural factors contribute to variations in speech. Cultural background determines the native language and regional dialect. Both the biological trait primitives and cultural trait primitives heavily influence the speech.

Deviant Speech is normally a long-term condition caused by disorders such as autism spectrum disorder (ASD), Alzheimer's disease, Parkinson's disease and motor neuron disease. Medium term states such as sleepiness and intoxication by alcohol consumption can also affect the normal speech. However, it returns to normal state quite soon. In the case of discrepant speech, speaker intentionally chooses to use deviant speech, deceptive speech, irony, or sarcasm. Detection of deceptive speech could be beneficial in therapeutic scenarios and forensic scenarios.

In speaker recognition, combined traits of a speaker are considered. Speaker recognition assigns a given speech segment to a particular speaker. Thus, speech features are used to find biological traits, thereby identifying the speaker. The typical application of speaker characteristics in forensics is speaker identification. The other field of speaker recognition is speaker verification, used in access control systems. The system has to verify that the given speech segment belongs to a speaker within a group of people who are allowed access.

The current emotional state of the speaker influences the tone, volume, and speech rate. Each emotion can be characterized by a unique acoustic pattern. Several studies on speech emotion recognition have been carried out over the time. Prosodic features such as pitch, duration, and quality are found to be important in emotion recognition. The way emotions are expressed depends on the personality of the speaker. Also, some aspects of emotions vary with language and culture. Therefore, it is challenging to develop emotion recognition systems across cultures.

### 2.2 Acoustic features representing paralinguistic information

Speech is a time varying signal and it is analyzed frame by frame. The most common features representing the speech signal are referred to as LLDs. Typical LLDs cover intensity, intonation, linear prediction cepstral coefficients (LPCCs), perceptual linear prediction (PLP), mel frequency cepstral coefficients (MFCCs), gammatone frequecny cepstral coefficients (GFCCs) formants, harmonicity, vocal cord perturbation etc. Breakdown of these features into three types namely prosodic, spectral, and voice quality features is shown in Table 1. These features are generally augmented by other descriptors computed from the raw LLDs such as delta coefficients or regression coefficients.

MFCCs are the most widely used feature extraction technique in speech processing applications. MFCCs are computed as follows. Windowed speech signal transformed to frequency domain using discrete Fourier transform, mel filter bank is applied to the magnitude transform and discrete cosine transform is computed on the logs of powers at each mel frequencies.

Formants are resonant frequencies of the vocal tract. They vary according to the spoken content. In particular, the lower resonance frequencies of the vocal tract, that is, the first two formants are well correlated with the phonetic content while the higher formants describe speaker characteristics. Formants are mostly computed from LPCs. Fundamental frequency and formant frequencies are most important speech parameters and its detection has a significant influence in recognizing emotion from speech (Belean, 2013).

Vocal cord perturbation measures such as jitter and shimmer describe the quality of the voice. Jitter is the fluctuation in the length of the fundamental period from one cycle to the next and shimmer is the variation of the waveform amplitude from one cycle to the next. As they describe the pathological characteristics of voice, jitter, and shimmer measures are helpful in determining speaker age or voice pathology (Teixeira and Gonçalves, 2016).

Derived features can be computed from the LLDs and they could be combinations of the above-mentioned features. The most popular ones that capture the temporal information are the first and second order derivatives referred to as delta, delta-delta coefficients respectively.

| Feature Type | Feature |
|---|---|
| Prosodic | Pitch |
| | Duration |
| | Energy |
| Spectral | MFCC |
| | GFCC |
| | LPCC |
| | PLP |
| | Formants |
| Voice quality | Jitter |
| | Shimmer |
| | Harmonics to noise ratio |
| | Normalized amplitude quotient |
| | Quasi open quotient |

Table 1: Acoustic features

## 3 Speech Emotion Recognition for Tamil Language

Emotion recognition from speech is one of the major topics in the field of computational paralinguistics. It helps to understand the emotional condition and actual intentions of the speakers which would be beneficial in improving the speech based applications such as automatic speech recognition (Jose et al., 2012; Madhavaraj and Ramakrishnan, 2017; Lokesh et al., 2019) and spoken intent recognition (Yohan et al., 2019b,a). It can be used to enhance the human computer interaction and to identify the emotional state of the user in call centers. Several research studies have worked on developing speech emotion recognition systems using DNNs. Emotion expression varies across cultures and every emotion is expressed somewhat differently by each culture. Thus, there is a need to build and evaluate a Tamil emotional speech corpus to observe the representation of different emotions in Tamil speech. Some of the available Tamil speech datasets include mozilla common voice (Ardila et al., 2020), Open SLR - Tamil (He et al., 2020), Microsoft Speech Corpus (Indian languages) - Tamil (mic), and Tamil Speech Intent Dataset - UoM (Buddhika et al., 2018). However, there is no standard database available for Tamil emotional speech.

Emotional speech corpora can consist of three types of emotional speech: acted emotions which is simulated by actors, spontaneous emotions from real life situations, and elicited emotions stimulated through emotional movies, stories and games. It is desired to have good quality speech recordings of diverse set of emotions collected from a large group of speakers. Though spontaneous emotions are preferred, it is difficult to acquire. Therefore, most of the available speech corpora contain acted emotional speech.

Joe (2014) built a Tamil emotional speech corpus with speech data consisting of five emotions Happy, Sad, Anger, Fear, and Neutral. Speech recordings were collected from acted emotional speech in Tamil audio plays. Support vector machine (SVM)-based emotion recognition system was used to perform classification with MFCCs as input features. This corpus was extended in (Vasuki et al., 2020) and another emotion corpus was developed separately for children using the samples collected from Tamil movies. Having an emotion corpus consisting of utterances of both the adults and children could help in investigating the influence of age in emotion expression.

In (Renjith and Manju, 2017), an acoustic feature-based emotion recognition system is presented. The database used in this work is Amritaemo (Poorna et al., 2015) which consists of speech recordings in Tamil and Telugu languages with three emotions: anger, happiness, and sadness. K-Nearest Neighbor (KNN) and Artificial Neural Network (ANN) were used to classify emotions based on two features namely Linear Predictive Cepstral Coefficients (LPCCs) and Hurst Parameter. Hurst parameter is the decaying rate of the autocorrelation coefficient function of the speech signal. The experimental results showed that when individual features were considered, for both the languages Hurst parameter achieved higher accuracy, precision, and recall when compared to LPCCs while the combination of these features resulted in a better performance.

Murali et al. (2018) proposed a Gaussian Mixture Model (GMM) – Deep Belief Network (DBN) system for emotion recognition. It models GMM for each emotion independently using MFCC features extracted from the speech signal. The minimum distance between the distribution of features for each utterance with respect to each emotion model is derived as Bag of acoustic features and it is fed to DBN as the feature vector. The proposed system was evaluated on Berlin emotional speech corpus (Burkhardt et al., 2005) as well the emotional database for Tamil language. The database used in this work consists of four emotions namely anger, happy, sad, and neutral state for three languages Tamil, English, and Malayalam.

Ram and Ponnusamy (2018) developed a speech corpus to evaluate the Tamil speech emotion recognition of children with autism spectrum disorder. In addition, emotional speech recordings for Tamil and Telugu language were collected from movies and Berlin emotional speech corpus was used as well for training. The selected emotion classes were anger, neutral, happiness, sadness, and fear. MFCC, pitch frequency, and energy were used as the set of features fed to the SVM based classifier.

An emotion recognition system using weighted features is proposed in (Poorna et al., 2018). A speech dataset consisting of audio recordings expressing five emotions namely anger, surprise, disgust, sadness, and happiness was created for three South Indian languages Tamil, Telugu, and Malayalam. Mean and variance of energy contour, first five formant frequencies, and Linear predictive coding (LPC) coefficients were chosen as the speech features and classification was performed using KNN, SVM, and ANN. Classification performance using normal features and weighted features were compared and a significant increase in recognition accuracy was observed with weighted features. ANN achieved the best accuracy among the considered classifier models. The results indicated that the weight factors are language dependent for the input features.

The paper (Rajan et al., 2019) presents a multilingual emotional speech corpus TaMaR-EmoDB developed for Tamil, Malayalam, and Ravula. The corpus contains short speech utterances in five emotions: anger, anxiety, happiness, sadness, and neutral state. The corpus was built using simulated speech utterances where the subjects were asked to read a sentence, expressing a given emotion. It was evaluated using a DNN-based classifier and the classification was performed using the fusion of MFCCs and prosodic features such as short-time energy, zero crossing rate, and standard deviation, skewness, and kurtosis of pitch. Sowmya and Rajeswari (2020) created a speech dataset for Tamil language and built a classifier to predict emotions with MFCC and energy as the input features. The database consists of four emotions anger, sad, neutral, and happiness. KNN, SVM, and ANN were used for emotion classification where SVM and ANN achieved higher accuracy.

## 4 Conclusion

The presented study discussed about the paralinguistic information present in speech signal and its relevance in many speech processing applications. The Low-level descriptors characterize the underlying paralinguistic content and they can be used as input features to DNN based models. High level speech representations can be extracted directly from raw speech signal as well using DNNs. These models have shown significant performance in many paralinguistic tasks. Paralinguistic information can also be applied in improving speech recognition systems using normalization techniques. The most popular paralinguistic task, emotion recognition is challenging when applied across different languages and cultures since aspects of emotion expression are language and culture specific.

Therefore, a proper emotional speech database is required to build effective emotion detection models for Tamil language. Several research studies have created speech databases for Tamil language and evaluated them using SVM or DNN based classifiers which reported good performance. However, further improvements are still needed and a standard Tamil emotional speech database needs to be built with a diverse set of emotions and a large number of speakers.

## Acknowledgment

This research was supported by Accelerating Higher Education Expansion and Development (AHEAD) Operation of the Ministry of Education, Sri Lanka funded by the World Bank.

## References

Interspeech (2018) Low resource speech recognition challenge for Indian Languages.

I. Anosha and T. Uthayasanker. 2020. In *Tamil Internet Conference*.

R. Ardila, M. Branson, K.Davis, M. Henretty, M. Kohler, J. Meyer, R. Morais, L. Saunders, F.M. Tyers, and G. Weber. 2020. Common voice: A massively-multilingual speech corpus. In *Proceedings of the 12th Conference on Language Resources and Evaluation (LREC 2020)*, pages 4211–4215.

Bogdan Belean. 2013. Comparison of formant detection methods used in speech processing applications. *AIP Conference Proceedings*, 1565:85–89.

D. Buddhika, R. Liyadipita, S. Nadeeshan, H. Witharana, S. Jayasena, and U. Thayasivam. 2018. Voicer: A crowd sourcing tool for speech data collection. In *2018 18th International Conference on Advances in ICT for Emerging Regions (ICTer)*, pages 174–181.

F. Burkhardt, A. Paeschke, M. Rolfes, W. Sendlmeier, and B. Weiss. 2005. A database of german emotional speech. volume 5, pages 1517–1520.

Robert Caldwell. 1875. *A comparative grammar of the Dravidian or South-Indian family of languages.* Trübner.

Bharathi Raja Chakravarthi. 2020. *Leveraging orthographic information to improve machine translation of under-resourced languages*. Ph.D. thesis, NUI Galway.

Bharathi Raja Chakravarthi, Mihael Arcan, and John P. McCrae. 2018. Improving wordnets for under-resourced languages using machine translation. In *Proceedings of the 9th Global Wordnet Conference*, pages 77–86, Nanyang Technological University (NTU), Singapore. Global Wordnet Association.

Bharathi Raja Chakravarthi, Mihael Arcan, and John P. McCrae. 2019. WordNet gloss translation for under-resourced languages using multilingual neural machine translation. In *Proceedings of the Second Workshop on Multilingualism at the Intersection of Knowledge Bases and Machine Translation*, pages 1–7, Dublin, Ireland. European Association for Machine Translation.

Fei He, Shan-Hui Cathy Chu, Oddur Kjartansson, Clara Rivera, Anna Katanova, Alexander Gutkin, Isin Demirsahin, Cibu Johny, Martin Jansche, Supheakmungkol Sarin, and Knot Pipatsrisawat. 2020. Open-source Multi-speaker Speech Corpora for Building Gujarati, Kannada, Malayalam, Marathi, Tamil and Telugu Speech Synthesis Systems. In *Proceedings of The 12th Language Resources and Evaluation Conference (LREC)*, pages 6494–6503, Marseille, France. European Language Resources Association (ELRA).

C. V. Joe. 2014. Developing tamil emotional speech corpus and evaluating using svm. In *2014 International Conference on Science Engineering and Management Research (ICSEMR)*, pages 1–6.

J. Melvin Jose, N. T. Vu, and T. Schultz. 2012. Initial experiments with tamil lvcsr.

S. Lokesh, Priyan Malarvizhi Kumar, M. Ramya Devi, P. Parthasarathy, and C. Gokulnath. 2019. An automatic tamil speech recognition system by using bidirectional recurrent neural network with self-organizing map. *Neural Computing and Applications*, 31.

A. Madhavaraj and A.G. Ramakrishnan. 2017. Design and development of a large vocabulary, continuous speech recognition system for tamil. In *2017 14th IEEE India Council International Conference (INDICON)*, pages 1–5.

Murali, Srikanth, Pravena, and Govind. 2018. Tamil speech emotion recognition using deep belief network(dbn). In *Advances in Signal Processing and Intelligent Recognition Systems*, pages 328–336.

S.S. Poorna, K. Anuraj, and G. Nair. 2018. A Weight Based Approach for Emotion Recognition from Speech: An Analysis Using South Indian Languages. In *Second International Conference, ICSCS*, pages 14–24.

S.S. Poorna, C. Jeevitha, S. Nair, S. Santhosh, and G.J. Nair. 2015. Emotion recognition using multi-parameter speech feature classification. In *2015 International Conference on Computers, Communications, and Systems (ICCCS)*, pages 217–222.

Rajeev Rajan, U.G. Haritha, A.C. Sujitha, and T.M. Rejisha. 2019. Design and Development of a Multi-Lingual Speech Corpora (TaMaR-EmoDB) for Emotion Analysis. In *INTERSPEECH*, pages 3267–3271.

C. Sunitha Ram and R. Ponnusamy. 2018. Toward design and enhancement of emotion recognition system through speech signals of autism spectrum disorder children for tamil language using multi-support vector machine. In *Proceedings of International Conference on Computational Intelligence and Data Engineering*, pages 145–158.

S. Renjith and K.G. Manju. 2017. Speech based emotion recognition in tamil and telugu using lpcc and hurst parameters — a comparitive study using knn and ann classifiers. In *2017 International Conference on Circuit ,Power and Computing Technologies (ICCPCT)*, pages 1–6.

Björn Schuller, Stefan Steidl, Anton Batliner, Felix Burkhardt, Laurence Devillers, Christian Müller, and Shrikanth Narayan. 2013. Paralinguistics in speech and language - state-of-the-art and the challenge. *Computer Speech and Language, Special Issue on Paralinguistics in Naturalistic Speech and Language*.

Björn W. Schuller and Anton M. Batliner. 2014. *Computational Paralinguistics: Emotion, Affect and Personality in Speech and Language Processing*.

V. Sowmya and A. Rajeswari. 2020. Speech emotion recognition for tamil language speakers. In *Advances in Intelligent Systems and Computing, Machine Intelligence and Signal Processing. MISP*, pages 125–136.

João Paulo Teixeira and André Gonçalves. 2016. Algorithm for jitter and shimmer measurement in pathologic voices. *Procedia Computer Science*, 100:271 – 279.

P. Vasuki, B. Sambavi, and Vijesh Joe. 2020. Construction and evaluation of tamil speech emotion corpus. *National Academy Science Letters*, 43.

K. Yohan, T. Uthayasanker, and R. Surangika. 2019a. Sinhala and tamil speech intent identification from english phoneme based asr. *2019 International Conference on Asian Language Processing (IALP)*, pages 234–239.

K. Yohan, T. Uthayasanker, and R. Surangika. 2019b. Transfer learning based free-form speech command classification for low-resource languages. In *Proceedings of the 57th Annual Meeting of the Association for Computational Linguistics: Student Research Workshop*, pages 288–294, Florence, Italy. Association for Computational Linguistics.

# Is this Enough? An evaluation of the Malayalam Wordnet

**Nandu Chandran Nair, Maria-Chiara Giangregorio, Fausto Giunchiglia**
University of Trento
nandu.chandrannair@unitn.it,mariegiangregorio@protonmail.com
fausto.giunchiglia@unitn.it

## Abstract

The quality of a product is the degree to which a product meets the Customer's expectations, which must also be valid in the case of lexical-semantic resources. Conducting a periodic evaluation of resources is essential to ensure that they meet a native speaker's expectations and are free from errors. This paper defines the possible errors that a lexical-semantic resource can contain, how they may impact downstream applications and explains the steps applied to evaluate and quantify the quality of Malayalam WordNet. Malayalam is one of the classical languages of India. We propose an approach allowing to subset the part of the WordNet tied to the lowest quality scores. We aim to work on this subset in a crowdsourcing context to improve the quality of the resource.

## 1 Introduction

Internet is composed of machine-readable lexical or lexical semantic resources (Herring, 2008). However, only a small percentage of languages have these resources developed in full scale (Herring, 2008). Hence the majority of languages are classified as under-resourced (Besacier et al., 2014). In our study, we consider a language to be under-resourced if it has the following characteristics: lack of computer-readable resources, lack of linguist experts, and limited usage on the internet (Krauwer, 2003). The different large scale availability of language resources results in a digital language divide (Warschauer, 2002). Figure 1 shows the visual representation of the study's findings on language-wise Internet users in 2021 and was conducted by KPMG India. We notice that usage of Hindi is greater than Malayalam. Bringing more languages online may ultimately be an exercise in cultural preservation, rather than utility. The probability of retrieving a relevant result using an under-resourced language is comparatively lower than with languages falling in the opposite category (Wheeler and Dillahunt, 2018). To diminish the divide, we either need new methodologies that allow for the creation of language resources or the creation of a platform supporting the continuous development of such resources (Chakravarthi et al., 2018, 2019, 2020a; Chakravarthi, 2020).

A person communicates their need for knowledge through words with a precise meaning, however from a machine point of view meaning( as well as specific acceptations) do not automatically come in conjunction with the word. Lexical-semantic resources come into play to bridge this gap, associating meanings to words. The most commonly used lexical-semantic resource is the Princeton WordNet(PWN) (Miller, 1998). PWN is a lexical database for English that is organized around synsets. The popularity of PWN has spread in the language community and has lead to the generation of similar resources. One such attempt was made in India, a Country both rich in culture and languages. IndoWordNet(IWN) is first multilingual WordNet for Indian languages developed through the joint efforts of different reputed universities across the country. IWN developed intending to sketch India's cultures in length and breadth by including 18 languages out of 22 official languages (Dash et al., 2017). All the languages in the IWN does not have the same synset IDs as PWN. For each synset in IWN, there is a corresponding synset in English that represent the same concept. In the paper, (Nair et al., 2019) authors extended this idea to align the IWN with PWN with the help of a large-scale multilingual resource called the Universal Knowledge Core(UKC) (Tawfik et al., 2014). The



*Proceedings of the First Workshop on Speech and Language Technologies for Dravidian Languages*, pages 100–108
April 20, 2021 

UKC has a similar structure of PWN and is designed as a multilayered ontology that has a language-independent semantic layer called the Concept Core (CC) and a language-specific lexico-semantic layer called the Language Core (LC). Hence, in the UKC, the meaning of the words are represented not only by the synsets but also using lexical concepts (Giunchiglia et al., 2018). Many works have been conducted under the UKC. Recent one is (Bella et al., 2020), where authors explores the unique grammatical properties of natural language text and perform experiments on tokenisation, part of speech tagging and named entity recognition over real-world structured data. Another important one is (Batsuren et al., 2019), which introduces a large-scale lexical database that provides words of common origin and meaning across languages.

Before enriching an existing resource, ensuring the quality and finding hidden errors is recommended in order to avoid producing a low-quality extensive resource. Inadequate quality resources are not suitable to train artificial intelligence tools (Chakravarthi et al., 2020b). One of the methods to ensure the quality of a resource is getting it validated using linguistic experts. Hiring linguists are expensive, or for some languages it is difficult. And another drawback is that contribution from one expert could be biased (Bonvillain, 2019). Hence we need faster and cheaper ways to estimate the quality of a WordNet. Also, the main question here is what are the factors that define the quality of a WordNet. As per the literature, a WordNet development team usually does structural check and whether the WordNet can perform applications like information retrieval (Baeza-Yates et al., 2015) and question-answering (Moldovan and Rus, 2001).

In this paper, we classify possible errors that affect the quality of the WordNet: schema errors and semantic errors. We list five schema errors from the IWN. We estimate semantic error by computing cosine similarity(Rahutomo et al., 2012) between two WordNets and within the WordNet using a pre-trained machine learning model(Zhou, 2016) for Indian languages. Using our approach, we generate a candidate set of synsets with very high semantic error that will be verified by native speakers in a crowdsourcing application(Brabham, 2013).

Figure 1: Language wise Internet users based on the study conducted by KPMG

This paper is structured as follows: Section 2 covers details about the language Malayalam and Malayam Wordnet (MWN), section 3 defines the quality of the WordNet and lists out the possible errors in WordNet, section 4 covers the procedure we used to find and establish the quality of the MWN, section 5 lists results and finally section 6 provides conclusions and direction for further work.

## 2 Malayalam Language

Malayalam(Asher, 2013) is a Dravidian language spoken in the Indian state of Kerala and union territories of Lakshadweep and Puducherry. Malayalam evolved from Tamil language after 16 century CE by Father of Malayalam Thunchaththu Ramanujan Ezhuthachan. In the early 21st century, Malayalam was spoken by around 38 million people all over the world (Asher, 2013). In the past, media like television, newspaper, short stories, novels, etc. helped with the diffusion and prospering of Malayalam language and literature(Palakeel, 1996). Nowadays smartphones, laptops, and Internet usage have become an important part of people's lives. The use of Malayalam language through these platforms has helped people to communicate, learn and express. Introduction of 'Unicode' technology in the Malayalam language helped correct spelling mistakes, grammatical errors, etc (Sooraj et al., 2018) (Santhosh et al., 2002), which was initially possible only in the English language. The stories and articles were in the regional language, though they used English words for different technical terms(Sasidharan et al., 2009). For example, the Malayalam word for mobile phones is "ദൂരഭാഷണശ്രവണസഹായി" (Dhoora bashana sravana sahayi), which was never used in any of the articles/blogs/news videos. The word 'Switch' in Malayalam was "വൈദ്യുത ആഗമന നിയന്ത്രണ യന്ത്രം" (Vaidhyutha agamana niyanthrana yanthram). But due to its complexity, these words were never used. The Malayalam language lost lots of words due to this reason(Prasanth, 2016). The Malayalam vocabulary is rich in terms from specific domains, with the notable example of terms reflecting family relations(George, 1972). In Kerala, where Malayalam is mother tongue, family relations are essential and there are particular names for each type of relation. A notable example of this richness is represented by the English word *cousin*: "the child of your aunt or uncle". In Malayalam the term used to denote a *cousin* will change depending on age, gender, whether the relation is from the paternal or maternal side. Sometimes the background of the family is also a factor influencing the selection of a different term. There is no such thing as a direct translation of the word *cousin* in Malayalam.

The Indian University, Amrita Vishwa Vidyapeetham, took part in the development of MWN (Rajendran and Soman, 2017) in 2011 as part of the project entitled "Development of Dravidian wordnet: an integrated wordnet for Telugu, Tamil, Kannada and Malayalam" which later integrated into IWN along with other Indian languages. The development of MWN is motivated by PWN. The initial idea of PWN was to aid the search in dictionaries, conceptually rather than alphabetically. Based on inspiration coming from current psycholinguistics (Foss, 1972) theories of human memory and its working, PWN organizes English *nouns*, *verbs*,*adverbs*, and *adjectives* into *synonym* sets or *synset*, each representing one underlying lexical concept. Synonyms are defined as words holding the same meaning in the same language (Miller, 1998). A set of synonymous words is called synset. For instance, "head" and "caput" are the synsets with the meaning "the front or the upper part of the body of animals bearing the face and brains". In PWN, synsets are associated with a *gloss*. A Gloss defines the meaning of a synset, the concept associated with the synset. MWN uses the same structure and lists the following entries for each concept: synset ID, synsets, gloss and example sentence. Synset ids used in MWN are different from PWN as the expand approach was used to develop MWN. In the expand approach, Hindi synsets are translated into Malayalam, this ensures concepts which are culturally relevant to India are retained as part of MWN. In our study, we are using source files of MWN we received from Amrita Vishwa Vidyapeetham. There are 30139 synsets available in MWN. In which, 20071 synsets are nouns, 3311 synsets are verbs, 501 synsets are adverbs, and 6256 synsets are adjectives.

## 3 Defining Quality

Within the translation industry, three terms are used somewhat interchangeably to refer to quality-related initiatives: quality assessment(House, 2014), quality assurance(Vîlceanu, 2017) and quality control(Ibba and Söll, 1999).

- Quality assessment or quality evaluation is the measurement of the extent to which a product complies with quality specifications(Lommel et al., 2014).

- Quality assurance refers to ways of preventing mistakes or defects in manufactured products and avoiding problems when delivering solutions or services to customers. Quality assurance relies on continual assessment of quality(Lommel et al., 2014).

- Quality control is the process of checking whether manufactured products meet stated quality specifications. While quality assurance relates to how a process is performed or how a product is made, quality control is tied more to the inspection aspect of quality management(Lommel et al., 2014).

Based on the definition, quality control requires specifications(Gouadec, 2010) which can then be used to assess whether a resource meets quality thresholds. In our work, we are performing quality control of the MWN. We are defining the minimum specifications in order to evaluate the WordNet and assess whether it is a good quality resource.

Multidimensional Quality Metrics (MQM)(Lommel et al., 2014) provides a framework for describing and defining quality metrics used to assess the quality of translated texts and to identify specific issues in those texts. The scope of this framework is limited to quality assessment of translated content. It does not apply to the evaluation of the translation process or projects. MQM defines the quality as adherence of the text to appropriate specifications. As per MQM, specifications are a description of requirements for the translation. In our work, we have been inspired to adapt ideas used as part of MQM for defining quality specifications of the WordNet. In MQM, a target document quality score is defined as

$$TQ = 100 - TP + SP$$

TQ being the quality score, TP the penalties for target content, and SP the penalty tied to source content. We then define a resource as being of good quality if the resource is free from errors.

We define two categories of errors in WordNet: schema errors and semantic errors.

### 3.1 Schema Errors

Schema errors occur when there is a problem with the file's structure or order, or an invalid character is included. There are five observed schema errors. They are:

- Category A: Empty gloss and/or synset and/or example sentence
- Category B: Poorly defined gloss
- Category C: Unknown characters in the fields
- Category D: Poorly defined part of speech
- Category E: Duplicate gloss

We consider a record as having unique synset id, gloss, example sentence and synset. Category A is the number of records with empty gloss and/or empty example sentence and/or empty synset(Figure 2). In some WordNets, example sentences are optional, so we will do a manual check in the beginning to verify metadata. Category B represents the number of records having a poorly defined gloss (Figure 3). Poorly defined glosses are very general, and computing this value is a bit challenging. Hence, we consider the number of records that have the same gloss as the corresponding synset. Category C is the number of records that have unknown characters in any of the fields (Figure 4). Category D is very rare but possible, including records that have poorly defined parts of speech (Figure 5). Four parts of speech are included in MWN: noun, adjective, verb and adverb. Due to errors during the development phase, these values may have spelling mistakes. This eventually affects the quality of the WordNet. Category E includes the number of records having the same gloss (Figure 6). For these records, synset id, example sentence and synsets are different, gloss is the same.

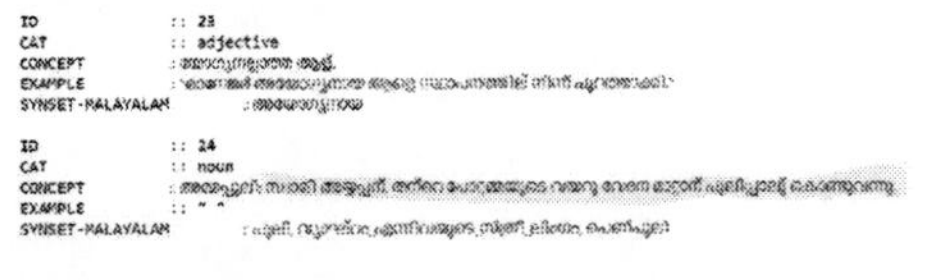


Figure 2: Example for Empty example sentence

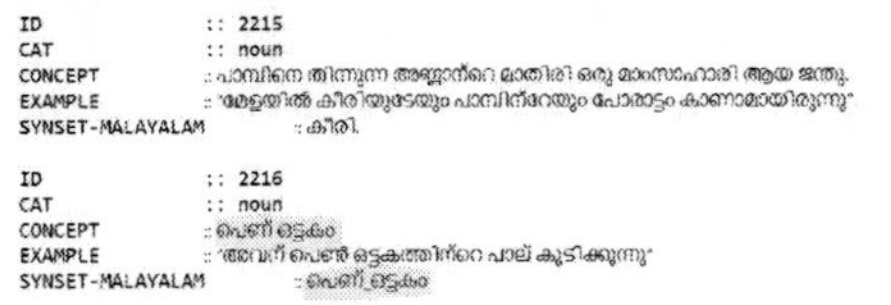


Figure 3: Example for poorly defined gloss

### 3.2 Semantic Errors

Meanings can be represented in many languages if the corresponding concept is available across all languages that are taken into account (Mercer, 2002). Meaning is defined as what is meant by a word, text, concept, or action. For example, the word "rain" means "water falling in drops from vapor condensed in the atmosphere" and the same meaning is represented in Italian as "pioggia", in Dutch as "regen". It is also worth keeping in mind that the word "rain" has two additional possible meanings, available depending on the context the word is used in.

Semantic errors are estimated when comparing across WordNets; checking how good conceptual alignment between the languages

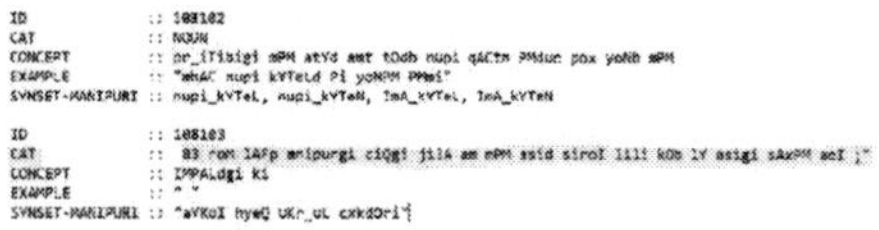

Figure 4: Example for poorly defined pos

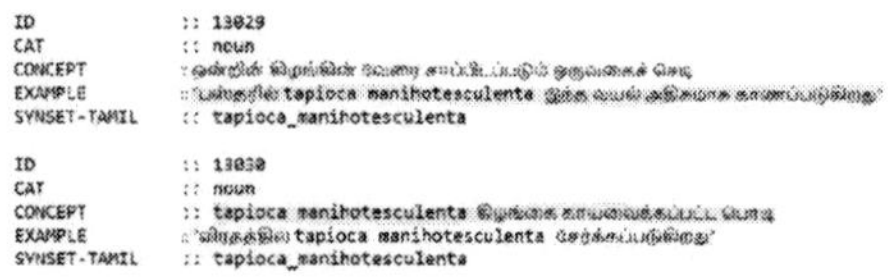

Figure 5: Example for unknown characters in gloss

is. In our work, we are using PWN and HWN to find the semantic error in MWN. Semantic errors are caused by factors like cultural differences, linguistic differences, and mistakes made by humans.

Figure 7 listing out some examples from these category and we have taken these values from IWN. Figures 7a, 7c, 7d and 7e are synsets specific to the language and culture. Finding out this candidate set could help the researchers to understand the diversity and similarity (Giunchiglia et al., 2017) across languages.

## 4 Evaluating MWN

In this section, we evaluate schema errors and semantic errors for the MWN. We estimated the schema errors of the resource as listed in the table 1. There are three categories of schema errors presented in the MWN; category A, B and E. 181 records have empty example sentence, 1789 records have empty synsets and 2374 records have poorly defined glosses. And then we found 925 records with duplicate gloss.

We sampled synsets common to English,

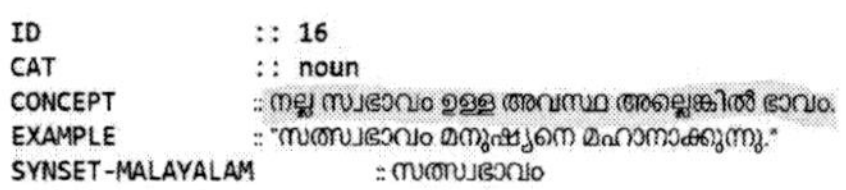


(a) For synset id 16

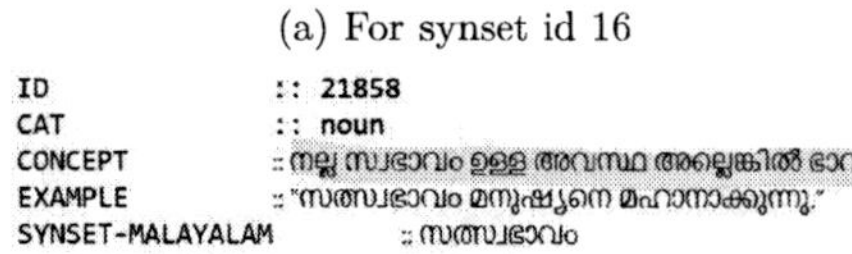


(b) For synset id 21858

Figure 6: Example for duplicate gloss

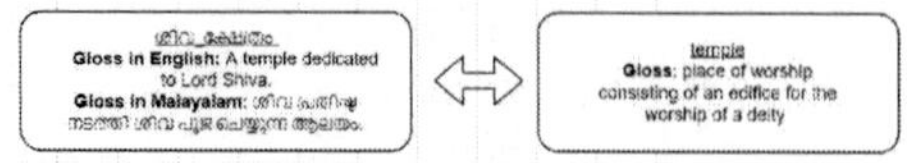

(a) Synset "temple" vs "ശിവ _ക്ഷേത്രം"(shiva_kshetram)

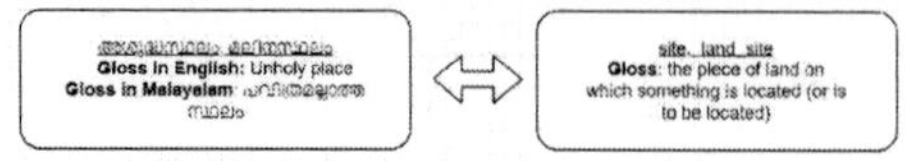

(b) Synset "site" vs "അശുദ്ധസ്ഥലം"(ashudhasthalam)

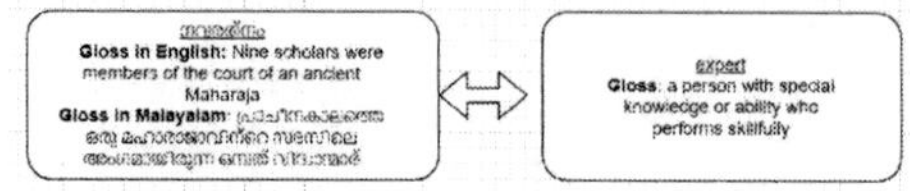

(c) Synset "expert" vs "നവരത്നം" (navarathnam)

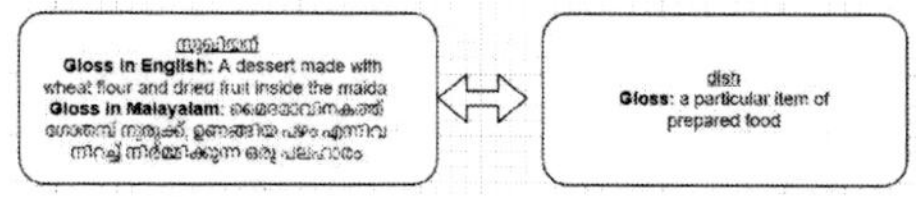

(d) Synset "dish" vs "സുഖിയൻ"(sukhiyan)

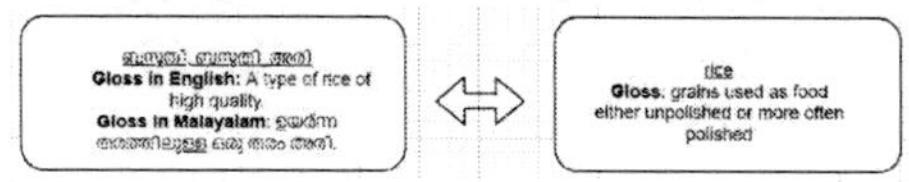

(e) Synset "rice" vs "ബസ്മതി _അരി"(basmati _ari)

Figure 7: Examples for semantic errors

Hindi and Malayalam WordNets; this yielded 18938 synsets. We then computed cosine similarity in order to identify synsets tied to poor semantic alignment and through this be able to identify semantic errors. We propose a cosine similarity score based classification parsed into three classes: low alignment for scores lower than 0.4; moderate for scores between 0.4 and 0.7; strong for scores greater than 0.7. We have used the threshold of minimum 0.4 inspired by the work by (Khodak et al., 2017). In (Khodak et al., 2017) authors automatically generate WordNet data by using a machine-readable dictionary. Based on our classification, we will consider the sets of synsets having cosine similarity scores below 0.4 as requiring attention.

We used two approaches to measure semantic errors: we computed cosine similarity(semantic alignment) between two languages; we then calculated semantic alignment within the language. Algorithm 1 shows the steps followed in computing the semantic similarity between English gloss and Malayalam gloss. We have used the same steps to calculate the semantic similarity between English word sense and Malayalam word sense. And repeat the above steps also for language Hindi. Algorithm 2

| Type of schema error | No.synsetids |
|---|---|
| Empty example sentence | 181 |
| Empty synsets | 1789 |
| Poorly defined gloss | 2374 |
| Duplicate gloss | 925 |

Table 1: Schema errors in Malayalam lexical-semantic resource

shows the steps followed in computing the semantic similarity between a word sense in the synset and the gloss of MWN.

A pre-trained machine learning model was used in order to compute semantic alignment and cosine similarity. There are a number of pre-trained models available for similarity checking. Multilingual BERT(mBERT)(Pires et al., 2019), XLM-RoBERTa(Conneau et al., 2019) and Sentence transformers(Reimers and Gurevych, 2019) are only few of them. Multilingual BERT(mBERT) and XLM-RoBERTa have been known to produce less than ideal sentence representations when deployed out-of-box. They would additionally pose the problem of coming with non- aligned vector spaces across languages. As a result, sentences with the same semantic content, expressed with different languages, would be mapped to different vector spaces. As part of our work we used sentence transformers: a Python framework for state of the art sentence and text embeddings that can be used to compute sentence/text embeddings for more than 100 languages. These embeddings can be compared through cosine similarity, allowing for the identification of sentences with similar meaning. The framework is based on PyTorch(Paszke et al., 2019), Transformers and offers a large collection of pre-trained models tuned for various tasks. We have used the pre-trained multilingual model *stsb-xlm-r-multilingual* and aligned vector spaces allowing for similar inputs across languages to be mapped close within the same vector space. XLM-R supports 100 languages including 13 Indian languages, and is as such able to handle linguistic inputs without the need to specify what the input language is upfront. The model produces similar embeddings as the bert-base-nli-stsb-mean-token model.

**Algorithm 1:** Semantic similarity between English and Malayalam

**Input:** A CSV file contains gloss and seed term of synset for languages English and Malayalam
**Output:** A CSV file contains id and semantic similarity score between English and Malayalam
**Data:** Common concepts in English and Malayalam languages
**foreach** *row in CSV file* **do**
    Compute embeddings of the English and Malayalam gloss
    Calculate cosine-similarity between the embeddings
    Write the id and semantic similarity score into a CSV file

**Algorithm 2:** Semantic similarity between Malayalam gloss and each word in the synset

**Input:** A CSV file contains gloss and a word for Malayalam language
**Output:** A CSV file contains id and semantic similarity score of Malayalam gloss and word
**Data:** Common concepts in English and Malayalam languages
**foreach** *row in CSV file* **do**
    Compute embeddings of the Malayalam gloss and word
    Calculate cosine-similarity between the embeddings
    Write the id and semantic similarity score into a CSV file

## 5 Results

There are 30139 Synsets available in the Malayalam language. Using our approach, we estimated that 14% of the Synsets have schema errors.

| | Gloss | | Word sense | |
|---|---|---|---|---|
| | Eng-Mal | Hin-Mal | Eng-Mal | Hin-Mal |
| Low(less than 0.4) | 30% | 4% | 17% | 2% |
| Moderate(0.4-0.7) | 55% | 35% | 59% | 28% |
| High(grater than 0.7) | 15% | 61% | 24% | 70% |

Figure 8: Summary of the similarity agreement of MWN between PWN and HWN

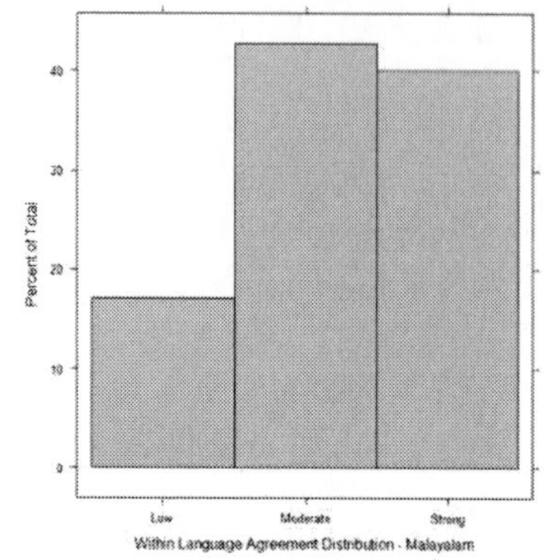


Figure 9: Distribution of similarity agreement within MWN

Figure 8 summarizes cosine similarity score distribution. 30% of gloss-wise similarity scores for PWN-MWN synsets fall in the low alignment category, the score goes down to 17% if looking at word sense level alignment for PWN-MWN entries. Interestingly, when looking at HWN-MWN data, synsets falling into the low alignment category decrease to 4% when looking at gloss-wise alignment; 2% when looking at word sense-wise alignment. Looking at within language data, reflects that 20% of MWN word senses are tied to low scores(below 0.4). Figure 9 shows the distribution of similarity agreement within the Malayalam language and Figure 10 shows the similarity distribution of Malayalam language between English and Hindi.

Computing semantic similarity within the language helps us understand and isolate poorly aligned word senses and better word senses. Results aligned how Malayalam language entries are more semantically aligned with Hindi than English, which is expected.

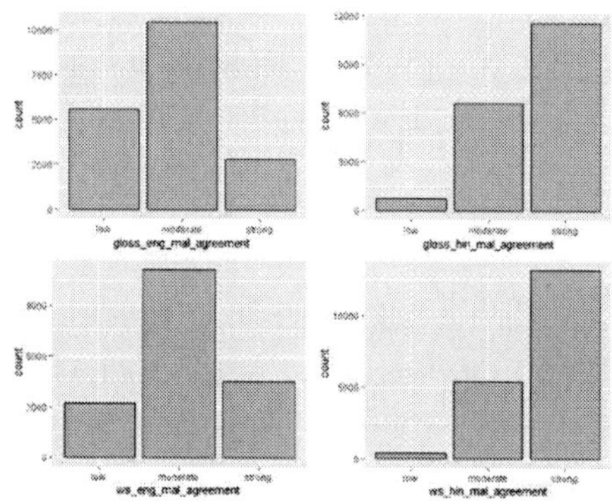


Figure 10: Distribution of similarity of MWN between PWN and HWN

## 6 Conclusion and Future work

This paper proposes specifications to be considered for a good quality lexical-semantic resource. We believe a resource without schema and semantic errors to be a useful resource. We defined schema errors and semantic errors for WordNet and estimated the presence of both for MWN. 14% of the Malayalam resource has schema errors. An average of 23.5% meanings representing the same concepts across English and Malayalam are tied to low similarity scores( poor semantic alignment). Only 3% of meanings representing the same concepts across Hindi and Malayalam have low similarity scores. Our approach concluded that when looking at within language data, 20% of MWN word senses are poorly aligned with their gloss. With this finding, we can classify MWN into two parts: Synsets requiring human revision and Synsets that can be readily shared with the world. We will be using MWN as part of a web application that supports end- Users in finding translations.

We are not taking these values as the final deciding factor. We will be using this low score synsets as a candidate set for our crowdsourcing application. This application will have different tasks like define gloss, provide Synset, validate the gloss, and so on.

## References


Ronald Asher. 2013. *Malayalam*. Routledge.

Ricardo Baeza-Yates, Luz Rello, and Julia Dembowski. 2015. CASSA: A context-aware synonym simplification algorithm. In *Proceedings of the 2015 Conference of the North American Chapter of the Association for Computational Linguistics: Human Language Technologies*, pages 1380–1385, Denver, Colorado. Association for Computational Linguistics.

Khuyagbaatar Batsuren, Gábor Bella, and Fausto Giunchiglia. 2019. Cognet: A large-scale cognate database. In *Proceedings of the 57th Annual Meeting of the Association for Computational Linguistics*, pages 3136–3145.

Gábor Bella, Linda Gremes, and Fausto Giunchiglia. 2020. Exploring the language of data. In *Proceedings of the 28th International Conference on Computational Linguistics*, pages 6638–6648, Barcelona, Spain (Online). International Committee on Computational Linguistics.

Laurent Besacier, Etienne Barnard, Alexey Karpov, and Tanja Schultz. 2014. Automatic speech recognition for under-resourced languages: A survey. *Speech Communication*, 56:85–100.

Nancy Bonvillain. 2019. *Language, culture, and communication: The meaning of messages*. Rowman & Littlefield.

Daren C Brabham. 2013. *Crowdsourcing*. Mit Press.

Bharathi Raja Chakravarthi. 2020. *Leveraging orthographic information to improve machine translation of under-resourced languages*. Ph.D. thesis, NUI Galway.

Bharathi Raja Chakravarthi, Mihael Arcan, and John P McCrae. 2018. Improving wordnets for under-resourced languages using machine translation. In *Proceedings of the 9th Global WordNet Conference (GWC 2018)*, page 78.

Bharathi Raja Chakravarthi, Mihael Arcan, and John P. McCrae. 2019. WordNet gloss translation for under-resourced languages using multilingual neural machine translation. In *Proceedings of the Second Workshop on Multilingualism at the Intersection of Knowledge Bases and Machine Translation*, pages 1–7, Dublin, Ireland. European Association for Machine Translation.

Bharathi Raja Chakravarthi, Navaneethan Rajasekaran, Mihael Arcan, Kevin McGuinness, Noel E. O'Connor, and John P. McCrae. 2020a. Bilingual lexicon induction across orthographically-distinct under-resourced Dravidian languages. In *Proceedings of the 7th Workshop on NLP for Similar Languages, Varieties and Dialects*, pages 57–69, Barcelona, Spain (Online). International Committee on Computational Linguistics (ICCL).

Bharathi Raja Chakravarthi, Priya Rani, Mihael Arcan, and John P McCrae. 2020b. A survey of orthographic information in machine translation. *arXiv preprint arXiv:2008.01391*.

Alexis Conneau, Kartikay Khandelwal, Naman Goyal, Vishrav Chaudhary, Guillaume Wenzek, Francisco Guzmán, Edouard Grave, Myle Ott, Luke Zettlemoyer, and Veselin Stoyanov. 2019. Unsupervised cross-lingual representation learning at scale. *arXiv preprint arXiv:1911.02116*.

Niladri Sekhar Dash, Pushpak Bhattacharyya, and Jyoti D Pawar. 2017. *The WordNet in Indian Languages*. Springer.

Donald Foss. 1972. Psycholinguistics. *Psyccritiques*, 17(12).

Karimpumannil Mathai George. 1972. *Western influence on Malayalam language and literature*. Sahitya Akademi.

Fausto Giunchiglia, Khuyagbaatar Batsuren, and Gabor Bella. 2017. Understanding and exploiting language diversity. In *IJCAI*, pages 4009–4017.

Fausto Giunchiglia, Khuyagbaatar Batsuren, and Abed Alhakim Freihat. 2018. One world–seven thousand languages. In *Proceedings 19th International Conference on Computational Linguistics and Intelligent Text Processing, CiCling2018, 18-24 March 2018*.

Daniel Gouadec. 2010. Quality in translation. *Handbook of translation studies*, 1:270–275.

Susan C Herring. 2008. Language and the internet. *The International Encyclopedia of Communication*.

Juliane House. 2014. Translation quality assessment: Past and present. In *Translation: A multidisciplinary approach*, pages 241–264. Springer.

Michael Ibba and Dieter Söll. 1999. Quality control mechanisms during translation. *Science*, 286(5446):1893–1897.

Mikhail Khodak, Andrej Risteski, Christiane Fellbaum, and Sanjeev Arora. 2017. Automated WordNet construction using word embeddings. In *Proceedings of the 1st Workshop on Sense, Concept and Entity Representations and their Applications*, pages 12–23, Valencia, Spain. Association for Computational Linguistics.

Steven Krauwer. 2003. The basic language resource kit (blark) as the first milestone for the language resources roadmap. *Proceedings of SPECOM 2003*, pages 8–15.

Arle Lommel, Hans Uszkoreit, and Aljoscha Burchardt. 2014. Multidimensional quality metrics (mqm): A framework for declaring and describing translation quality metrics. *Tradumàtica*, (12):0455–463.

Neil Mercer. 2002. *Words and minds: How we use language to think together.* Routledge.

George A Miller. 1998. *WordNet: An electronic lexical database.* MIT press.

Dan Moldovan and Vasile Rus. 2001. Logic form transformation of WordNet and its applicability to question answering. In *Proceedings of the 39th Annual Meeting of the Association for Computational Linguistics*, pages 402–409, Toulouse, France. Association for Computational Linguistics.

Nandu Chandran Nair, Rajendran Sankara Velayuthan, and Khuyagbaatar Batsuren. 2019. Aligning the indowordnet with the princeton wordnet. In *Proceedings of the 3rd International Conference on Natural Language and Speech Processing*, pages 9–16.

Thomas Palakeel. 1996. Twentieth century malayalam literature. *Handbook of Twentieth-century Literatures of India*, pages 180–200.

Adam Paszke, Sam Gross, Francisco Massa, Adam Lerer, James Bradbury, Gregory Chanan, Trevor Killeen, Zeming Lin, Natalia Gimelshein, Luca Antiga, et al. 2019. Pytorch: An imperative style, high-performance deep learning library. In *Advances in neural information processing systems*, pages 8026–8037.

Telmo Pires, Eva Schlinger, and Dan Garrette. 2019. How multilingual is multilingual bert? *arXiv preprint arXiv:1906.01502.*

RI Prasanth. 2016. Lost word is lost world-a study of malayalam. *Language in India*, 16(6).

Faisal Rahutomo, Teruaki Kitasuka, and Masayoshi Aritsugi. 2012. Semantic cosine similarity. In *The 7th International Student Conference on Advanced Science and Technology ICAST*, volume 4.

S Rajendran and KP Soman. 2017. Malayalam wordnet. In *The WordNet in Indian Languages*, pages 119–145. Springer.

Nils Reimers and Iryna Gurevych. 2019. Sentence-bert: Sentence embeddings using siamese bert-networks. *arXiv preprint arXiv:1908.10084.*

T Santhosh, KG Varghese, R Sulochana, and R Kumar. 2002. Malayalam spell checker. In *Proceedings of the International Conference on Universal Knowledge and Language-2002.*

Sumaja Sasidharan, R Loganathan, and KP Soman. 2009. English to malayalam transliteration using sequence labeling approach. *International Journal of Recent Trends in Engineering*, 1(2):170.

S Sooraj, K Manjusha, M Anand Kumar, and KP Soman. 2018. Deep learning based spell checker for malayalam language. *Journal of Intelligent & Fuzzy Systems*, 34(3):1427–1434.

Ahmed Tawfik, Fausto Giunchiglia, and Vincenzo Maltese. 2014. A collaborative platform for multilingual ontology development. *World Academy of Science, Engineering and Technology*, 8(12):1.

Titela Vîlceanu. 2017. Quality assurance in translation. a process-oriented approach. *Romanian Journal of English Studies*, 14(1):141–146.

Mark Warschauer. 2002. Reconceptualizing the digital divide. *First monday*, 7(7).

Earnest Wheeler and Tawanna R Dillahunt. 2018. Navigating the job search as a low-resourced job seeker. In *Proceedings of the 2018 CHI Conference on Human Factors in Computing Systems*, page 48. ACM.

Zhi-Hua Zhou. 2016. Learnware: on the future of machine learning. *Frontiers Comput. Sci.*, 10(4):589–590.

# LA-SACo: A Study of Learning Approaches for Sentiments Analysis in Code-Mixing Texts

**F. Balouchzahi**
Department of Computer Science,
Mangalore University,
Mangalore - 574199, India
frs_b@yahoo.com

**H. L. Shashirekha**
Department of Computer Science,
Mangalore University,
Mangalore - 574199, India
hlsrekha@gmail.com

## Abstract

Sentiments are usually written using a combination of languages such as English which is resource rich and regional languages such as Tamil, Kannada, Malayalam, etc. which are resource poor. However, due to technical constraints, many users prefer to pen their opinions in Roman script rather than using their native scripts. These kinds of texts written in two or more languages using a common language script or different language scripts are called code-mixing texts. Code-mixed texts are increasing day-by-day with the increase in the number of users depending on various online platforms. Analyzing such texts pose a real challenge for the researchers. In view of the challenges posed by the code-mixed texts, this paper describes three proposed models namely, SACo-Ensemble, SACo-Keras, and SACo-ULMFiT using Machine Learning (ML), Deep Learning (DL), and Transfer Learning (TL) approaches respectively for the task of sentiments analysis in Tamil-English and Malayalam-English code-mixed texts. The results illustrate that SACo-Ensemble with weighted F1-scores of 0.62 and 0.72 on Tamil-English and Malayalam-English language pairs respectively outperformed other proposed models.

## 1 Introduction

Feelings, opinions, or reviews of customers in online shops or social media such as YouTube, Facebook, WhatsApp, Instagram, Twitter, etc. are called sentiments. Feedback or opinion about whatever is available on the internet can also be seen as sentiments (Thavareesan and Mahesan, 2019, 2020a,b). Increase in the number of people using social media and online platforms have given rise to increasing amount of text data in general and sentiments or opinions in particular. Sentiments or reviews posted by users affect the popularity of a post, and video in social media or a product in online shops (Chakravarthi and Muralidaran, 2021; Chakravarthi et al., 2021; Suryawanshi and Chakravarthi, 2021). For example, positive sentiments could be a reason for making a post/product popular whereas negative reviews could go to the extent of rejecting or discarding a particular post/product. The sentiments extracted from users' posts and customers feedbacks tend to be valuable information not only for a particular user to be encouraged to watch a movie or buy a product but also for many social media companies and online shops or even movie makers, automakers etc. to improve their weaknesses and strengths. For instance, the negative feedbacks and sentiments gained from users about confusion in the new policy of WhatsApp about sharing data and location, and business messaging has substantially reduced the popularity of this platform[1]. Hence, Sentiment Analysis (SA), the task of automatically analyzing these sentiments or reviews posted by the users for the proper identification and classification of sentiments is becoming crucial these days (Balouchzahi and Shashirekha, 2020a).

Researchers motivated to explore SA have developed many tools and techniques to analyze sentiments written in rich resource languages such as English, Spanish, etc. But, most of the people would like to express opinions in their native language in native script or other language script due to freedom to use any language and any script in online platforms (Chakravarthi et al., 2018). For example, South Indian people may use Dravidian languages (Telugu, Tamil, Malayalam, and Kannada) to post their sentiments (Chakravarthi et al., 2020b). In the 2nd century BCE, the Dravidian languages were first attested to as a Tamili [2] script inscribed

[1]https://indianexpress.com/article/technology/tech-news-technology/whatsapp-privacy-policy-update-delay-backlash-7149456/

[2]also called Damili or Tamil-Bhrami



*Proceedings of the First Workshop on Speech and Language Technologies for Dravidian Languages*, pages 109–118
April 20, 2021 

on the cave walls of Tamil Nadu's Madurai and Tirunelveli districts. Telugu, Tamil, Kannada, and Malayalam are the Dravidian languages with the most speakers (in descending order of number of speakers), of which Tamil have long literary traditions from 600 BCE. Over 55% of the epigraphical engravings (around 55,000) found by the Archeological Survey of India are in the Tamil language. However due to technical constraints and difficulty in using Indian languages scripts users usually use Roman script instead of their native scripts along with English words (Balouchzahi and Shashirekha, 2020a; Chakravarthi, 2020b). Mixing two or more languages in a text using a common language script or different languages scripts is called Code-Mixing and code-mixed texts are increasing with the popularity of social media and online shopping (Ansari and Govilkar, 2018; Chakravarthi, 2020a).

SA task is more challenging with code-mixed texts since the sentiments or reviews written in words of different languages increases the complexity of analyzing such texts due to code-mixing at various levels such as words, phrases, and sentences (Lal et al., 2019; Priyadharshini et al., 2020; Jose et al., 2020). Further, as there are no rules governing the formation of code-mixed texts such texts usually contain incomplete and incorrect sentences, short forms of words and words with repetitive letters, e.g. hellooooo, aaaaaa, soooorrryyyy (Puranik et al., 2021; Hegde et al., 2021; Yasaswini et al., 2021; Ghanghor et al., 2021b,a). These complexities give rise to building new features structures such as combined vocabulary and grammar of different languages which cannot be handled by conventional SA models as they fail to capture the meaning of the sentences in code-mixed text (Choudhary et al., 2018).

In view of the complexities and challenges of code-mixed texts, this paper describes the three proposed SA models namely, SACo-Ensemble, SACo-Keras, and SACo-ULMFiT using Machine Learning (ML), Deep Learning (DL), and Transfer Learning (TL) approaches respectively for the task of SA in Tamil-English (Ta-En) and Malayalam-English (Ma-En) code-mixed texts. While SACo-Ensemble and SACo-Keras models utilize a set of features comprised of char sequences, BytePair Encoded words, and syntactic ngrams, SACo-ULMFiT model uses the knowledge obtained from a source model called Language Model in training the sentiment analysis classifier as target model.

## 2 Related Work

Several datasets, tools, and techniques have been developed to deal with code-mixed data of different language pairs for various tasks including SA, language identification, POS tagging, NER, etc. Some of recent ones are given below: The objective of shared task "Sentiment Analysis of Dravidian Languages in Code-Mixed Text"[3] (Chakravarthi et al., 2020c) was to develop and test SA models for Ta-En and Ma-En code-mixed datasets created by (Chakravarthi et al., 2020b) (Chakravarthi et al., 2020a). This task received 32 and 38 submissions for Ta-En and Ma-En respectively and a given sentiment was categorized into one of five categories, namely, Positive, Negative, Unknown_state, Mixed-Feelings, and Other_languages. Overall results based on weighted F1-score illustrates that there was very tough and close competition among the participating teams. Differences between the weighted F1-score of first and fourth rank of Ta-En task and first and sixth rank of Ma-En task (our team MUCS) (Balouchzahi and Shashirekha, 2020a) are only 0.03 and 0.05 respectively. Therefore, two top submissions along with our SACo model (Balouchzahi and Shashirekha, 2020a) are used for comparison in this study and the same are described below: (Sun and Zhou, 2020) presents a XLM-Roberta model for SA which uses extracted output of top hidden layers and feed them to concatenated Convolution Neural Networks (CNN). This model which is able to extract the semantic information from texts obtained first ranks for both Ta-En and Ma-En code-mixed texts with a weighted F1-score of 0.65 and 0.74 for Ta-En and Ma-En code-mixed texts respectively.

(Ou and Li, 2020) have used XLM-Roberta pre-trained multi-language models and K-folding method to ensemble them for solving the SA problem of multilingual code-mixed texts. They obtained 0.63 and 0.74 weighted F1-score and third and first ranks on Ta-En and Ma-En code-mixed texts respectively.

(Balouchzahi and Shashirekha, 2020a) proposed SACo-HVC, a hybrid model that ensembles the DL and ML models for SA of code-mixed texts. They train a Multi-Layer Perceptron (MLP) classifier with a combination of traditional char and word n-grams, Multinomial Naïve Bayes (MNB) classifier on Skipgram word vector generated from

[3] https://dravidian-codemix.github.io/2020/index.html

the training set, and also BiLSTM networks on subWords embedding generated from the training set. Using majority voting of predictions they obtained 0.62 and 0.68 weighted F1-score and forth and sixth ranks on Ta-En and Ma-En respectively.

## 3 Methodology

Using three different learning approaches, we propose three models namely, SACo-Ensemble - a ML approach, SACo-Keras - a DL approach and SACo-ULMFiT – a TL approach for the SA of Ta-En and Ma-En code-mixed texts. The first two models are trained on vectors generated using Count Vectorizer[4] from a feature set of char sequences, Byte-Pair Encoding (BPEmb) (Heinzerling and Strube, 2017) encoded words and syntactic n-grams. Subsection 3.1 gives details of feature engineering module for ML and DL approaches. Details of the proposed models are presented in Section 3.2.

### 3.1 Feature Engineering Module

The feature engineering module is responsible to prepare features for the proposed ML and DL approaches. This module will receive dataset as input and preprocess it by converting emojis to corresponding text (using emoji library[5]), removing punctuations, words of length less than 2, unwanted characters (such as !()-[];:",¡¿./?$=% +@*_ ', etc.) and converting the text to lowercase. Then the following features are extracted from the remaining text:

- **Char sequences:** of length 2 to 6 are extracted from every sentence using everygrams function from NLTK library. For example, given a sentence "yuvanvera level ya" in Ta-En code-mixed text, "yu, uv, va, an, n_, _v, ve, er, ra, a_, _l, le, ev, ve, el, l_, _y, ya, yuv, uva, van, an_, _ve, ver, era, ra_, _le, lev, eve, vel, el_, _ya, yuva, uvan, van_, _ver, vera, era_, _lev, leve, evel, vel_, yuvan, uvan_, _vera, vera_, _leve, level, evel_, yuvan_, _vera_, _level, level_" will be generated as features.

- **BPEmb subWords:** is a collection of pre-trained subWords embeddings for 275 languages trained on Wikipedia texts in their own scripts. In this work, a embedding of vocabulary size 10,000 is chosen for English language to encode code-mixing text and extract subWords from sentences. For example, given a sentence "Indiayale friend" in Ma-En code-mixed text, the encoded features will be "India, yale, friend". It can be observed that exact English words and the affixes are extracted which will otherwise have a different meaning in Malayalam.

- **Syntactic n-grams:** Inspired by (Sidorov et al., 2013) instead of traditional n-grams, syntactic n-grams (sn-grams) are used as features. sn-grams are constructed by following paths in syntactic trees that enables n-grams to bring syntactic knowledge into ML methods. The difference between sn-grams and traditional n-grams comes in the way of following syntactic relations in syntactic trees by neighbors, whereas traditional n-grams concepts is based on the words presence in a text and are taken from surface strings (Posadas-Durán et al., 2015). Bi and Tri sn-grams are extracted from texts using SNgramExtractor[6] library and the generated sn-grams are attached to feature set. For example, for the sentence 'Economic news have little effect on financial markets' in English, the sn-grams are:

  **Bi-sn-grams:** news_Economic, have_news, effect_little, have_effect, effect_on, markets_financial, on_markets, have_.

  **Tri-sn-grams:** effect_on_markets, on_markets_financial.

The combination of above mentioned features are transformed to vectors using CountVectorizer library. Graphical representation of feature engineering module for SACo-Ensemble and SACo-Keras is given in Figure 1.

### 3.2 Learning Approaches

The proposed models are described below:

#### 3.2.1 SACo-Ensemble:

Three sklearn classifiers, namely, Multi-Layer Perceptron (MLP), eXtreme Gradient Boosting (XGB) and Logistic Regression (LR) are ensembled based on hard majority voting as shown in Figure 2. This model has been trained on count vectors of extracted feature set that consists of char sequences, BPEmb subWords and Syntactic n-grams.

[4]https://scikit-learn.org/stable/

[5]https://pypi.org/project/emoji/

[6]https://pypi.org/project/SNgramExtractor

Details about the three sklearn classifiers used are given below:

- MLP is a feed-forward Artificial Neural Network (ANN) that consists of at least three layers: an input layer, a hidden layer and an output layer and it is based on a supervised learning technique called back propagation for training. An MLP also can be considered as one of the most traditional types of DL architectures where every element of a previous layer is connected to every element of the next layer. In proposed model, the parameters for MLP, namely, hidden layer sizes, maximum iteration, activation, solver and random state have been set to (150, 100, 50), 300, Relu, Adam and 1 respectively.

- XGB which uses a gradient boosting framework is a decision-tree-based ML algorithm (Chen and Guestrin, 2016) designed to be highly efficient, flexible and portable. It combines hundreds of simple trees to build a more accurate model in such way that in every iteration a new tree for the model will be generated (Zhang and Zhan, 2017). Execution speed and model performance are the two main advantages of XGB classifier[7]. In this study, following configuration has been used for XGB classifier: max_depth is set to 20, and n_estimators, learning rate, colsample_bytree, gamma, reg_alpha, and objective are set to 80, 0.1, 0.7, 0.01, 4, 'multi:softmax' respectively.

- LR is a method primarily used for binary classification problems. However, in the multi-class case, the one-vs-rest (OvR) scheme will be used in training the model. LR classifier has been used with default parameters.

#### 3.2.2 SACo-Keras:

A simple architecture of Keras[8] sequential model has been used to build a Neural Network (NN). Similar to SACo-Ensemble model, feature vectors obtained from feature engineering module are used to train a Keras dense neural network architecture available at

`https://www.kaggle.com/ismu94/tf-idf-deep-neural-net`

[7]https://machinelearningmastery.com/gentle-introduction-xgboost-applied-machine-learning

[8]https://keras.io/

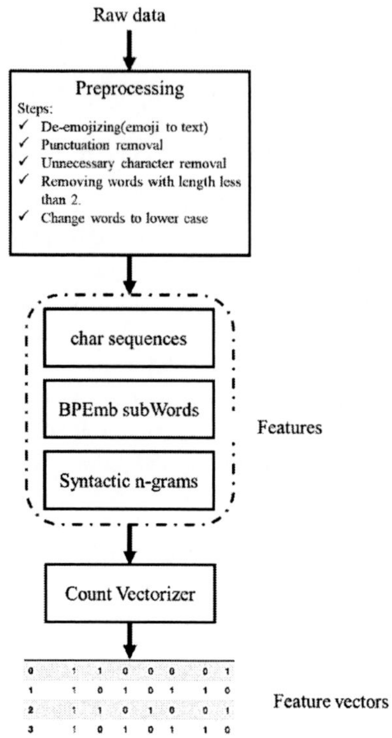


Figure 1: Feature engineering module for SACo-Ensemble and SACo-Keras

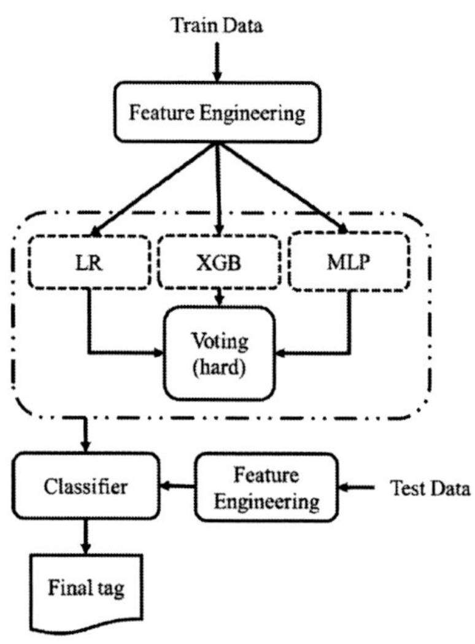


Figure 2: Architecture of SACo-Ensemble model

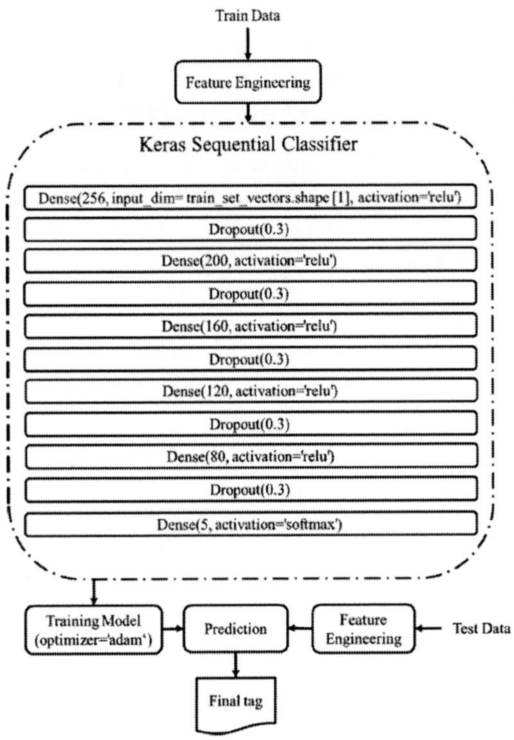


Figure 3: Overview of NN layers in SACo-Keras Model

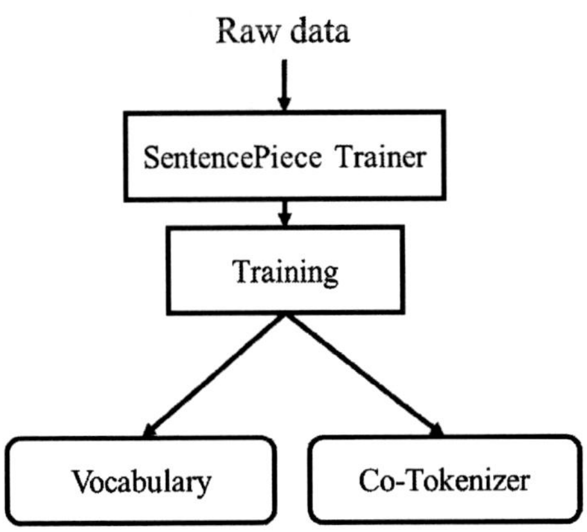


Figure 4: Steps for training CoTokenizer

SACo-Keras model has been trained for 40 epochs with batch size of 128. Figure 3 gives the details of SACo-Keras model with all NN layers and configurations.

### 3.2.3 SACo-ULMFiT:

This model is based on TL approach where the knowledge obtained from source model (a universal language model in this case) will be transferred to a target model (SA model) affecting the performance of target model (Balouchzahi and Shashirekha, 2020b) (S. Faltl, 2019). ULMFiT model architecture inspired by (Howard and Ruder, 2018) consists of training Language Model (LM) that is a probability distribution over word sequences in a language and then transferring the obtained weights and fine tuning them using texts from training set for SA model.

Fine tuning is the procedure of producing weights for words that are present in training set but are missing in LM due to difference in domains of texts used in training LM and training set for the given task. As these missing words usually are important features, fine tuning the knowledge obtained from pre-trained LM enhances the performance of model.

Training SACo-ULMFiT model includes three major steps, namely, (i) training code-mixed tokenizer and universal language model from raw texts, (ii) transferring the obtained language model and knowledge to final SA model and fine tuning the language model using training set and (iii) training the final SA model for predicting the labels of test set.

The raw text from Dakshina[9] dataset (Roark et al., 2020) along with Ta-En and Ma-En code-mixed datasets (Chakravarthi et al., 2020b) (Chakravarthi et al., 2020a) are used to train code-mixed tokenizer called as Co-Tokenizer (called Co-Tokenizer because it learns from code-mixed raw data and will tokenize texts based on their code-mixing form) which is then used for training code-mixed language models and SA models for Ta-En and Ma-En tasks. The steps for training tokenizer are shown in Figure 4 and the SACo-ULMFiT model architecture for SA of code mixed texts is shown in Figure 5. The text.models tools from Fastai[10] library are used to build both LM and SA models. This tool implements an encoder for an ASGD Weight-Dropped LSTM (AWD-LSTM)

[9]https://github.com/google-research-datasets/dakshina
[10]https://nlp.fast.ai/

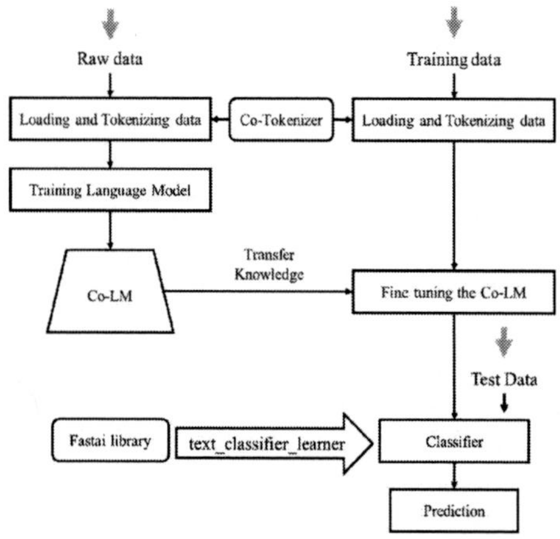


Figure 5: SACo-ULMFiT model architecture

that consists of a word embedding of size 400, 3 hidden layers and 1150 hidden activations per layer that is plugged in with a decoder and classifying layers to create a text classifier (Merity et al., 2017). The preprocessing steps used in this model are the same as that of earlier models.

# 4 Experimental Results

## 4.1 Datasets

Datasets used in this study includes unannotated texts from Dakshina dataset which is a collection of text in both Roman and native scripts for 12 South Asian languages such as Malayalam, Tamil, Kannada, etc. (Roark et al., 2020) and labeled datasets for code-mixed SA task in Ma-En and Ta-En (Chakravarthi et al., 2020b) (Chakravarthi et al., 2020a) distributed into 5 classes namely, Positive, Negative, Mixed-Feelings, unknown_state, and other_languages. Since training an efficient LM requires a large amount of data, both Romanized Malayalam data (Ma-Co raw) from Dakshina dataset and the above mentioned code-mixed Ma-En datasets are combined for Malayalam Code-mixing LM (Co-LM). Similarly, Romanized Tamil data (Ta-Co raw) from Dakshina dataset is combined with the above mentioned code-mixed Ta-En dataset for training Tamil Co-LM. Details of the datasets used in this work are given in Table 1 and statistics of the labeled datasets is given in Table 2.

Statistics of the datasets given in Table 1[11] illustrate that Ta-En texts are more than Ma-En texts in both annotated and unannotated case. Further, since unannotated data are used in training Co-LMs, it is expected that less number of unannotated data will affect the efficiency of obtained LM and knowledge which in turn will affect the performance of target SA in SACo-ULMFiT model.

[11] **TaCo**: texts from combination of Ta-En with Romanized Tamil (Dakshina) datasets
**MaCo**: texts from combination of Ma-En with Romanized Malayalam (Dakshina) datasets

| Dataset | Type | No. Sentences |
|---|---|---|
| TaCo raw | unannotated | 41454 |
| MaCo raw | unannotated | 16739 |
| Malayalam-English | annotated | 6739 |
| Tamil-English | annotated | 15744 |

Table 1: Datasets used in this work

| Labels | Malayalam-English | | Tamil-English | |
|---|---|---|---|---|
| | Training | Test | Training | Test |
| Positive | 2246 | 565 | 8484 | 2075 |
| Negative | 600 | 138 | 1613 | 424 |
| Mixed-Feelings | 333 | 70 | 1424 | 377 |
| Unknown-state | 1505 | 398 | 677 | 173 |
| Other-languages | 707 | 177 | 397 | 100 |

Table 2: Statistics of labeled datasets

The distribution of labels in annotated datasets given in Figure 6 illustrates that both the labeled datasets are imbalanced. However, as the percentage of imbalance sounds to be less in Ma-En dataset, it is expected that proposed model performs better for this dataset compared to Ta-En dataset.

### 4.1.1 Results

The proposed models are compared with the top 2 ranked models namely, SRJ (Sun and Zhou, 2020) and YNU (Ou and Li, 2020) along with our model SACo-HVC (4$^{th}$ rank in Tamil and 6$^{th}$ rank in

| Model | Mal-En | | | Ta-En | | |
|---|---|---|---|---|---|---|
| | P | R | F1 | P | R | F1 |
| SRJ | 0.74 | 0.75 | 0.74 | 0.64 | 0.67 | 0.65 |
| YNU | 0.74 | 0.74 | 0.74 | 0.61 | 0.67 | 0.63 |
| SACo-HVC | 0.68 | 0.68 | 0.68 | 0.60 | 0.66 | 0.62 |
| SACo-Ensemble | 0.72 | 0.72 | 0.72 | 0.60 | 0.66 | 0.62 |
| SACo-Keras | 0.70 | 0.70 | 0.70 | 0.61 | 0.65 | 0.62 |
| SACo-ULMFiT | 0.65 | 0.66 | 0.65 | 0.52 | 0.62 | 0.60 |

Table 3: Results of the SA models

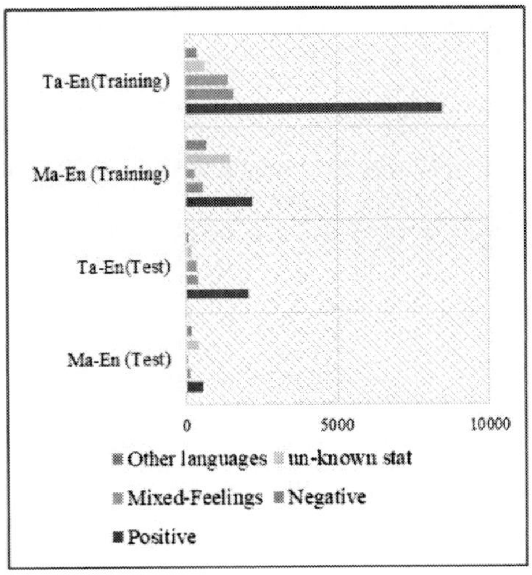


Figure 6: Label distribution in annotated datasets

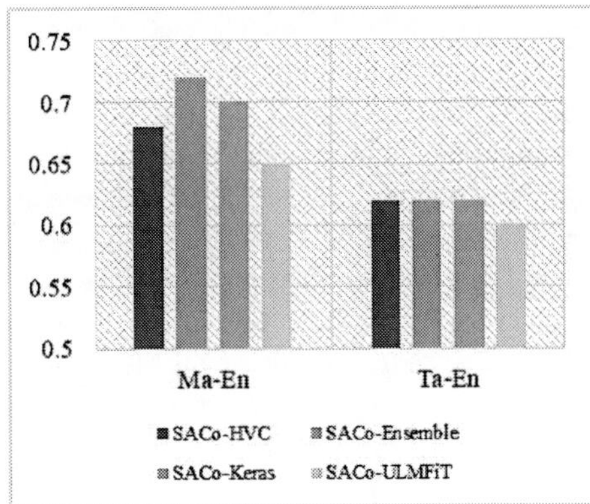


Figure 7: Comparison of our models

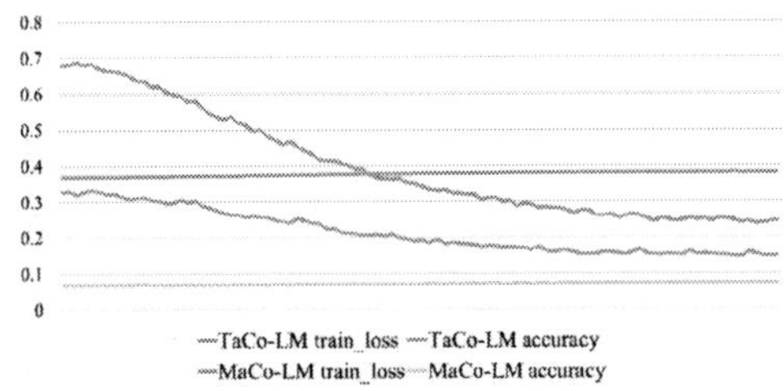


Figure 8: History of training Co-LMs: X and Y axes represent epochs and training accuracy respectively

Malayalam) (Balouchzahi and Shashirekha, 2020a) submitted to "Sentiment Analysis of Dravidian Languages in Code-Mixed Text [12]" shared task in FIRE 2020 and described in (Chakravarthi et al., 2020c). Results obtained in terms of weighted Precision, Recall, and F1-score using Sklearn.metrics library are shown in Table 3. As the results of the proposed models illustrate reasonable performance compared with the top 2 ranked models they still need to be improved.

Comparison of the proposed models and SACo-HVC in terms of weighted F1-score is shown in Figure 7. It can be observed that there is no much improvement in results obtained by new models compared to SACo-HVC for Ta-En dataset. However, SACo-Ensemble and SACo-Keras outperformed the previous SACo-HVC model for Ma-En dataset as the percentage of imbalance is less compared to Ta-En dataset. SACo-ULMFiT model was expected to outperform for Ta-En dataset compared to Ma-En due to large dataset in training LM step, but results show that SACo-ULMFiT for Ma-En dataset obtained better results. Figure 8 presents the history of training each Co-LM for 100 epochs. It illustrates that small number of raw texts for Ma-En Co-LM resulted in less efficient LM model compared to that of Ta-En Co-LM.

[12]https://dravidian-codemix.github.io/2020/index.html

## 5 Conclusion and Future Work

This paper describes the three proposed models, namely, SACo-Ensemble, SACo-Keras, and SACo-ULMFiT based on ML, DL and TL for the task of SA for Ta-En and Ma-En code-mixed texts. Ta-En and Ma-En datasets are used to train and evaluate the proposed models. Further, Romanized Tamil and Malayalam unannotated datasets from Dakshina dataset are used to train the code-mixed LMs. The results obtained using proposed models are compared with our previous model, SACo-HVC and with the top 2 ranked models of "Sentiment Analysis for Dravidian Languages in Code-Mixed Text" shared task in FIRE 2020.

The results illustrate that SACo-Ensemble and SACo-Keras models have shown reasonable performance while SACo-ULMFiT exhibited an average performance. Analysis of the results shows that SACo-Ensemble model based on ML approach using a feature set of char sequences, BPEmb sub-Words, and Syntactic n-grams outperformed the other two proposed models for both datasets. However, the comparison of the proposed models with top 2 ranked models illustrates only a reasonable performance. A DL based SACo-Keras model fed with the same feature set as that of SACo-Ensemble model achieved results with very less difference compared to SACo-Ensemble model. This illustrates that there is no much difference between the performances of ML and DL approaches. The SACo-ULMFiT model based TL approach did not perform well which could be due to insufficient unannotated texts for training LMs. As future work, we will collect more raw texts from YouTube and Twitter to build a rich code mixed LM that hopefully will improve the performance of SACo-ULMFiT. Further, we plan to explore different feature sets and feature selection models to improve the performance of our proposed models.

## References


Mohammed Arshad Ansari and Sharvari Govilkar. 2018. Sentiment analysis of mixed code for the transliterated Hindi and Marathi texts. *International Journal on Natural Language Computing (IJNLC) Vol*, 7.

F. Balouchzahi and H.L. Shashirekha. 2020a. MUCS@Dravidian-CodeMix-FIRE2020: SACO-Sentiments Analysis for CodeMix Text. In *Forum for Information Retrieval Evaluation*. CEUR Workshop Proceedings.

Fazlourrahman Balouchzahi and HL Shashirekha. 2020b. Puner-parsi ulmfit for named-entity recognition in persian texts. Technical report, EasyChair.

Bharathi Raja Chakravarthi. 2020a. HopeEDI: A multilingual hope speech detection dataset for equality, diversity, and inclusion. In *Proceedings of the Third Workshop on Computational Modeling of People's Opinions, Personality, and Emotion's in Social Media*, pages 41–53, Barcelona, Spain (Online). Association for Computational Linguistics.

Bharathi Raja Chakravarthi. 2020b. *Leveraging orthographic information to improve machine translation of under-resourced languages*. Ph.D. thesis, NUI Galway.

Bharathi Raja Chakravarthi, Mihael Arcan, and John P. McCrae. 2018. Improving wordnets for under-resourced languages using machine translation. In *Proceedings of the 9th Global Wordnet Conference*, pages 77–86, Nanyang Technological University (NTU), Singapore. Global Wordnet Association.

Bharathi Raja Chakravarthi, Navya Jose, Shardul Suryawanshi, Elizabeth Sherly, and John Philip McCrae. 2020a. A sentiment analysis dataset for code-mixed Malayalam-English. In *Proceedings of the 1st Joint Workshop on Spoken Language Technologies for Under-resourced languages (SLTU) and Collaboration and Computing for Under-Resourced Languages (CCURL)*, pages 177–184, Marseille, France. European Language Resources association.

Bharathi Raja Chakravarthi and Vigneshwaran Muralidaran. 2021. Findings of the shared task on Hope Speech Detection for Equality, Diversity, and Inclusion. In *Proceedings of the First Workshop on Language Technology for Equality, Diversity and Inclusion*. Association for Computational Linguistics.

Bharathi Raja Chakravarthi, Vigneshwaran Muralidaran, Ruba Priyadharshini, and John Philip McCrae. 2020b. Corpus creation for sentiment analysis in code-mixed Tamil-English text. In *Proceedings of the 1st Joint Workshop on Spoken Language Technologies for Under-resourced languages (SLTU) and Collaboration and Computing for Under-Resourced Languages (CCURL)*, pages 202–210, Marseille, France. European Language Resources association.

Bharathi Raja Chakravarthi, Ruba Priyadharshini, Navya Jose, Anand Kumar M, Thomas Mandl, Prasanna Kumar Kumaresan, Rahul Ponnusamy, Hariharan V, Elizabeth Sherly, and John Philip McCrae. 2021. Findings of the shared task on Offensive Language Identification in Tamil, Malayalam, and Kannada. In *Proceedings of the First Workshop on Speech and Language Technologies for Dravidian Languages*. Association for Computational Linguistics.

Bharathi Raja Chakravarthi, Ruba Priyadharshini, Vigneshwaran Muralidaran, Shardul Suryawanshi, Navya Jose, Elizabeth Sherly, and John P. McCrae. 2020c. Overview of the Track on Sentiment Analysis for Dravidian Languages in Code-Mixed Text. In *Forum for Information Retrieval Evaluation*, FIRE 2020, page 21–24, New York, NY, USA. Association for Computing Machinery.

Tianqi Chen and Carlos Guestrin. 2016. Xgboost: A scalable tree boosting system. In *Proceedings of the 22nd acm sigkdd international conference on knowledge discovery and data mining*, pages 785–794.

Nurendra Choudhary, Rajat Singh, Ishita Bindlish, and Manish Shrivastava. 2018. Sentiment analysis of code-mixed languages leveraging resource rich languages. *arXiv preprint arXiv:1804.00806*.

Nikhil Kumar Ghanghor, Parameswari Krishnamurthy, Sajeetha Thavareesan, Ruba Priyadharshini, and Bharathi Raja Chakravarthi. 2021a. IIITK@DravidianLangTech-EACL2021: Offensive Language Identification and Meme Classification in Tamil, Malayalam and Kannada. In *Proceedings of the First Workshop on Speech and Language Technologies for Dravidian Languages*, Online. Association for Computational Linguistics.

Nikhil Kumar Ghanghor, Rahul Ponnusamy, Prasanna Kumar Kumaresan, Ruba Priyadharshini, Sajeetha Thavareesan, and Bharathi Raja Chakravarthi. 2021b. IIITK@LT-EDI-EACL2021:

Hope Speech Detection for Equality, Diversity, and Inclusion in Tamil, Malayalam and English. In *Proceedings of the First Workshop on Language Technology for Equality, Diversity and Inclusion*, Online.

Siddhanth U Hegde, Adeep Hande, Ruba Priyadharshini, Sajeetha Thavareesan, and Bharathi Raja Chakravarthi. 2021. UVCE-IIITT@DravidianLangTech-EACL2021: Tamil Troll Meme Classification: You need to Pay more Attention. In *Proceedings of the First Workshop on Speech and Language Technologies for Dravidian Languages*. Association for Computational Linguistics.

Benjamin Heinzerling and Michael Strube. 2017. Bpemb: Tokenization-free pre-trained subword embeddings in 275 languages. *arXiv preprint arXiv:1710.02187*.

Jeremy Howard and Sebastian Ruder. 2018. Universal language model fine-tuning for text classification. *arXiv preprint arXiv:1801.06146*.

Navya Jose, Bharathi Raja Chakravarthi, Shardul Suryawanshi, Elizabeth Sherly, and John P. McCrae. 2020. A Survey of Current Datasets for Code-Switching Research. In *2020 6th International Conference on Advanced Computing and Communication Systems (ICACCS)*, pages 136–141.

Yash Kumar Lal, Vaibhav Kumar, Mrinal Dhar, Manish Shrivastava, and Philipp Koehn. 2019. De-mixing sentiment from code-mixed text. In *Proceedings of the 57th Annual Meeting of the Association for Computational Linguistics: Student Research Workshop*, pages 371–377.

Stephen Merity, Nitish Shirish Keskar, and Richard Socher. 2017. Regularizing and optimizing LSTM language models. *arXiv preprint arXiv:1708.02182*.

X. Ou and H. Li. 2020. YNU@Dravidian-CodeMix-FIRE2020: XLM-RoBERTa for Multi-language Sentiment Analysis. In *Forum for Information Retrieval Evaluation*. CEUR Workshop Proceedings.

Juan-Pablo Posadas-Durán, Ilia Markov, Helena Gómez-Adorno, Grigori Sidorov, Ildar Batyrshin, Alexander Gelbukh, and Obdulia Pichardo-Lagunas. 2015. Syntactic n-grams as features for the author profiling task. *Working Notes Papers of the CLEF*.

Ruba Priyadharshini, Bharathi Raja Chakravarthi, Mani Vegupatti, and John P. McCrae. 2020. Named Entity Recognition for Code-Mixed Indian Corpus using Meta Embedding. In *2020 6th International Conference on Advanced Computing and Communication Systems (ICACCS)*, pages 68–72.

Karthik Puranik, Adeep Hande, Ruba Priyadharshini, Sajeetha Thavareesan, and Bharathi Raja Chakravarthi. 2021. IIITT@LT-EDI-EACL2021-Hope Speech Detection: There is always hope in Transformers. In *Proceedings of the First Workshop on Language Technology for Equality, Diversity and Inclusion*. Association for Computational Linguistics.

Brian Roark, Lawrence Wolf-Sonkin, Christo Kirov, Sabrina J Mielke, Cibu Johny, Isin Demirsahin, and Keith Hall. 2020. Processing south asian languages written in the latin script: the dakshina dataset. *arXiv preprint arXiv:2007.01176*.

C. Hackober S. Faltl, M. Schimpke. 2019. *ULMFiT: State-of-the-art in text analysis*. `https://humboldt-wi.github.io/blog/research/information_systems_1819/group4_ulmfit/`.

Grigori Sidorov, Francisco Velasquez, Efstathios Stamatatos, Alexander Gelbukh, and Liliana Chanona-Hernández. 2013. Syntactic dependency-based n-grams: More evidence of usefulness in classification. In *International Conference on Intelligent Text Processing and Computational Linguistics*, pages 13–24. Springer.

R. Sun and X. Zhou. 2020. SRJ @ Dravidian-CodeMix-FIRE2020:Automatic Classification and Identification Sentiment in Code-mixed Text. In *Forum for Information Retrieval Evaluation*. CEUR Workshop Proceedings.

Shardul Suryawanshi and Bharathi Raja Chakravarthi. 2021. Findings of the shared task on Troll Meme Classification in Tamil. In *Proceedings of the First Workshop on Speech and Language Technologies for Dravidian Languages*. Association for Computational Linguistics.

Sajeetha Thavareesan and Sinnathamby Mahesan. 2019. Sentiment Analysis in Tamil Texts: A Study on Machine Learning Techniques and Feature Representation. In *2019 14th Conference on Industrial and Information Systems (ICIIS)*, pages 320–325.

Sajeetha Thavareesan and Sinnathamby Mahesan. 2020a. Sentiment Lexicon Expansion using Word2vec and fastText for Sentiment Prediction in Tamil texts. In *2020 Moratuwa Engineering Research Conference (MERCon)*, pages 272–276.

Sajeetha Thavareesan and Sinnathamby Mahesan. 2020b. Word embedding-based Part of Speech tagging in Tamil texts. In *2020 IEEE 15th International Conference on Industrial and Information Systems (ICIIS)*, pages 478–482.

Konthala Yasaswini, Karthik Puranik, Adeep Hande, Ruba Priyadharshini, Sajeetha Thavareesan, and Bharathi Raja Chakravarthi. 2021. IIITT@DravidianLangTech-EACL2021: Transfer Learning for Offensive Language Detection in Dravidian Languages. In *Proceedings of the First Workshop on Speech and Language Technologies for Dravidian Languages*. Association for Computational Linguistics.

Licheng Zhang and Cheng Zhan. 2017. Machine learning in rock facies classification: an application of xgboost. In *International Geophysical Conference, Qingdao, China, 17-20 April 2017*, pages 1371–1374. Society of Exploration Geophysicists and Chinese Petroleum Society.

# Findings of the Shared Task on Machine Translation in Dravidian languages

**Bharathi Raja Chakravarthi**[1], **Ruba Priyadharshini**[2]
**Shubhanker Banerjee**[1], **Richard Saldanha**[3], **John P. McCrae**[1],
**Anand Kumar M**[3], **Parameshwari Krishnamurthy**[4], **and Melvin Johnson**[5]
[1]National University of Ireland Galway, [2]Madurai Kamaraj University,
[3]National Institute of Technology Karnataka Surathkal, [4]University of Hyderabad,
[5]Google Research, USA
bharathi.raja@insight-centre.org

## Abstract

This paper presents an overview of the shared task on machine translation of Dravidian languages. We presented the shared task results at the EACL 2021 workshop on Speech and Language Technologies for Dravidian Languages. This paper describes the datasets used, the methodology used for the evaluation of participants, and the experiments' overall results. As a part of this shared task, we organized four sub-tasks corresponding to machine translation of the following language pairs: English to Tamil, English to Malayalam, English to Telugu and Tamil to Telugu which are available at https://competitions.codalab.org/competitions/27650. We provided the participants with training and development datasets to perform experiments, and the results were evaluated on unseen test data. In total, 46 research groups participated in the shared task and 7 experimental runs were submitted for evaluation. We used BLEU scores for assessment of the translations.

## 1 Introduction

In this paper, we present the results of the shared task on machine translation of Dravidian languages of the Workshop on Speech and Language Technologies for Dravidian Languages held at EACL 2021. The shared task features four sub-tasks: a translation task from English to Tamil, English to Telugu, English to Malayalam and Tamil to Telugu. They all closely related languages and are under-resourced now. They are mutually intelligible since speakers of Dravidian (Tamil) languages can readily understand each other without prior familiarity or special effort (Krishnamurti, 2016; Thavareesan and Mahesan, 2019).

The performance of our tasks was evaluated using automatic measures BLEU (Papineni et al., 2002). This shared task's primary objectives are to further state of the art in machine translation of low resource languages belonging to the Dravidian (Tamil) language family. The training data, development data and test data, and results are available publicly[1]. We hope the datasets released as a part of this task will contribute positively towards forwarding research in the machine translation of under-resourced languages.

## 2 Related Work

Machine translation of under resource languages is an open and an active research area. In this day and age when translation systems are increasingly being built upon neural network-based architectures (Bahdanau et al., 2014; Luong et al., 2015; Cho et al., 2014; Wu et al., 2016), the development of such systems for under-resourced languages is a challenging task due to the lack of availability of resources. Multilingual extensions to these architectures have been proposed (Firat et al., 2016; Ha et al.; Johnson et al., 2017) which have been shown to improve on low-resource languages. Recent studies have also extended this to a massively multilingual setting (Aharoni et al., 2019). Gu et al. (2018) demonstrated a transfer learning-based approach by utilizing shared lexical and sentence level representations across multiple source languages, thereby developing a system that performs well in low resource scenarios. Xia et al. (2019) propose a general framework for data augmentation in low-resource machine translation that not only uses target-side monolingual data but also pivots through a related high-resource language HRL.

Zoph et al. (2016)'s key idea is first to train a high-resource language pair (the parent model), then transfer some of the learned parameters to the low-resource pair (the child model) to initialize and constrain training. Kocmi and Bojar (2018)

[1]https://competitions.codalab.org/competitions/27650



*Proceedings of the First Workshop on Speech and Language Technologies for Dravidian Languages*, pages 119–125
April 20, 2021 

propose a transfer learning-based method, wherein they train a "parent" model with a high-resource language pair followed by which they train on a "child" model on a corpus of a low-resource language pair. It was observed that this model is better than the models trained on just the low-resource languages. Zoph et al. (2016) propose a transfer learning-based method, wherein they train a parent model trained on a high-resource language pair, followed by which they transfer some of parameters to a child model that they subsequently train on the low-resource language pair. Lakew et al. (2017) leverage the use of duality of translations generated by the system for zero-shot; these translations are used along with the parallel data to train the neural network. Ojha et al. (2020) show the results of the LoResMT 2020 shared task. This workshop was held along with AACL and reported good BLEU scores in case of the low-resource Bhojpuri-Hindi language pair. Koehn et al. (2019) focussed on the translation of the low resource language pairs Nepali-English and Sinhala-English. They reported the results of these translation tasks for statistical as well as phrase-based methods. Chakravarthi et al. (2019c) created a multimodal corpora for Dravidian languages. M (2013) developed a statistical machine translation system for English-Tamil using transfer based on computational linguistics. Kumar et al. (2014) proposed a factored statistical machine translation system for English to the Tamil language. Kumar et al. (2019) conducted the Machine Translation for Indian Languages shared task in 2017. As a part of this shared task, organizers have released the parallel corpora for English-Tamil and English-Malayalam.

For Dravidian language translation, Chakravarthi et al. (2018, 2019b, 2020a) created a machine translation to improve WordNet entries. Krishnamurthy (2019) demonstrate a transfer learning based translation system and a divergence index to calculate the success rate of the system. Chandramma et al. (2017) propose a multi-layer neural network based approach wherein they use n-grams extracting from connecting phrases of the phrase table for the task of machine translation on Kannada-Telugu language pair. Chakravarthi et al. (2019a, 2020b); Chakravarthi (2020) studied the utilisation of orthographic information to improve the machine translation for Dravidian languages.

## 3 Dravidian Languages

Tamil is an official language in Tamil Nadu, Puducherry, Sri Lanka and Singapore (Thavareesan and Mahesan, 2020a,b). Tamil was the first to be listed as a classical language of India, one of 22 scheduled languages in India's Constitution, and is one of the world's longest-surviving classical languages. In Jain Samavayanga Sutta (3rd-4th century BCE) and Pannavana Sutta, a script called Damili (Tamili) is listed as the seventeenth of eighteen scripts in India, an early mention of a script for writing the Tamil language (Salomon, 1998). Similarly, Lipisala Samdarshana Parivarta, the tenth chapter of the Lalitavistara Sutta (3rd century CE) a Sanskrit text, mentions Siddhartha (later Gautam Buddha) learning Dravida-script (Tamil Script) and Dakshinya-script (Southern Tamil Script) along with other sixty two scripts. Tamil was called Damil in Jain Prakrit, Dramil in Buddhist Pali, and Dravida in Sanskrit (Caldwell, 1875; Oberlies, 2011). The Tamil scripts are first attested in the 580 BCE as Tamili[2] script inscribed[3] on the pottery of Keezhadi, Sivagangai and Madurai district of Tamil Nadu, India (Sivanantham and Seran, 2019)[4] by Tamil Nadu State Department of Archaeology and Archaeological Survey of India. The writing systems of Tamili was explained in the old grammar text Tolkappiyam dates between 8000 BCE to 580BCE (Takahashi, 1995; Pillai, 1904; Swamy, 1975; Albert et al., 1985; Rajendran, 2004).

Malayalam was Tamil's west coast dialect until about the 15th-century CE (Blackburn, 2006). The dialect gradually developed into a different language in the 16th century (Sekhar, 1951) due to geographical separation by the steep Western Ghats from the main speech group. Ramacaritam ('Deeds of Rama') was the first literary work in Malayalam written in Malayalam, a combination Tamil and Sanskrit, using the Tamil Grantha script which was used in Tamil Nadu to write Sanskrit and foreign words (Andronov, 1996). Telugu existed in the earliest time in the form of inscriptions from 575 CE onwards. Telugu literary works split from Tamil by the first grammar of Telugu in the 13th century CE which was written by Atharvana Acharya, naming it the Trilinga Śabdānusāsana (or Trilinga Grammar). Similarly, Kannada also split from Tamil by 8th century CE. The Kappe Arab-

[2]also called Damili or Tamil-Brahmi

[3]Tamil-inscription

[4]Keeladi-Book-English-18-09-2019.pdf

| Team | Languages | BLEU |
|---|---|---|
| GX (Xie, 2021) | English-Telugu | 38.86 |
| IRLAB-DAIICT (Prajapati et al., 2021) | English-Telugu | 6.25 |
| MUCS Shared Task (Hegde et al., 2021) | English-Telugu | 0.29 |
| GX (Xie, 2021) | English-Tamil | 36.66 |
| Spartans | English-Tamil | 28.27 |
| IRLAB-DAIICT (Prajapati et al., 2021) | English-Tamil | 6.04 |
| MUCS Shared Task (Hegde et al., 2021) | English-Tamil | 1.66 |
| GX (Xie, 2021) | English-Malayalam | 19.84 |
| Spartans | English-Malayalam | 15.31 |
| IRLAB-DAIICT (Prajapati et al., 2021) | English-Malayalam | 8.43 |
| MUCS Shared Task (Hegde et al., 2021) | English-Malayalam | 0.48 |
| GX (Xie, 2021) | Tamil-Telugu | 35.29 |
| MUCS Shared Task (Hegde et al., 2021) | Tamil-Telugu | 0.43 |
| IRLAB-DAIICT (Prajapati et al., 2021) | Tamil-Telugu | 0.0 |

Table 1: Results of the participating systems in BLEU score.

hatta record of 700 CE is the oldest extant form of Kannada poetry in the Tripadi metre. It is based in part on Kavyadarsha, a Sanskrit text (Rawlinson, 1930; Hande et al., 2020). Dravidian is the name for the Tamil languages or Tamil people in Sanskrit, and all the current Dravidian languages were called a branch of Tamil in old Jain, Bhraminic, and Buddhist literature (Caldwell, 1875).

## 4 Task Description and Dataset

### 4.1 Task

The shared task was hosted on Codalab. Four translation sub-tasks were organized as a part of this task: English to Tamil, English to Malayalam, English to Telugu and Tamil to Telugu. Participants were given a choice to participate in the sub-tasks they wanted to. Training, development and test datasets of parallel sentences for each language pair were provided to all the participants. The task was to train/develop machine translation systems for the given languages. For evaluation, the participants translated the test data using the translation systems and the results were submitted to the organizers of the workshop. The submissions were evaluated by comparing them with the gold standard test set translations available, for which BLEU scores were used as the metric to rank the participants and subsequently the results were returned to the participants.

### 4.2 Dataset

The datasets were collected from the repository of Opensubtitles released in 2018 and available at Opus [5] and consisted of bilingual parallel corpora for each of the four language pairs. We created the training, development and test datasets in the following way: each of the bilingual corpora were divided into three sub-corpora according to the following criterion: the first 2,000 sentence pairs were compiled as the test corpora while the next 2,000 sentence pairs were used for the development set and the remaining data was compiled as the training dataset. The English-Malayalam training data had 382,868 sentence pairs, the one for English-Tamil had 28,417 sentence pairs, the English-Telugu training set had 23,222 sentence pairs whereas the Tamil-Telugu dataset had 17,155 sentence pairs.

## 5 System Description

A summary of the results of the shared task can be found in Tables 1. To evaluate the performance of the submitted systems, we calculated BLEU scores for each of these systems. We have listed out the short description of participants systems, for more details please refer their paper.

- Xie (2021) adopted two methods to improve the overall performance: (1) multilingual translation, they used a shared encoder-decoder multilingual translation model han-

[5] `http://opus.nlpl.eu/OpenSubtitles-v2018.php`

| Language Pairs | Team Name | Rank |
|---|---|---|
| English - Telugu | GX (Xie, 2021) | 1 |
| | IRLAB-DAIICT (Prajapati et al., 2021) | 2 |
| | MUCS Shared Task (Hegde et al., 2021) | 3 |
| English - Tamil | GX (Xie, 2021) | 1 |
| | Spartans | 2 |
| | IRLAB-DAIICT (Prajapati et al., 2021) | 3 |
| English - Malayalam | GX (Xie, 2021) | 1 |
| | Spartans | 2 |
| | IRLAB-DAIICT (Prajapati et al., 2021) | 3 |
| Tamil - Telugu | GX (Xie, 2021) | 1 |
| | MUCS Shared Task (Hegde et al., 2021) | 2 |
| | IRLAB-DAIICT (Prajapati et al., 2021) | 3 |

Table 2: System Ranks for each Translation Language Pair

dling multiple languages simultaneously to facilitate the translation performance of these languages; (2) backtranslation, they collected other open-source parallel and monolingual data and apply back- translation to benefit from the monolingual data. The experimental results show that they achieved good translation results in these Dravidian languages and rank first in the four translation directions on the ranklist.

- Prajapati et al. (2021) propose a neural machine translation model that tries to learn the parameters $\theta$ by maximizing the conditional probability $P(a|b;\theta)$ (a = target language, b = source language). The encoder learns a hidden representation for each input sentence which is further decoded by the decoder and translations are generated. They propose that the individual units in the encoder/decoder architecture can be GRUs or LSTMs alongside as self attention mechanism.

- Hegde et al. (2021) propose a sequence-to-sequence architecture based on a stacked LSTM model as the translation system. The proposed system has multiple layers in order to learn better representations and enhance the learnability of the model. A stacked LSTM model consists of multiple hidden LSTM layers. Stacking makes the model deeper and more accurate.

## 6 Results and Discussion

Based on the results reported for the test sets by the top 3 teams in each language translation subtask as shown in Table 1 the submitted systems are ranked for each translation language pair, as shown in Table 2.

Using the System descriptions along with information from Tables 1 and 2, the system rankings can be summarized as follows:

- In the English-Telugu translation, the system submitted by (Xie, 2021) is ranked number 1, with a BLEU score of 38.86, followed by (Prajapati et al., 2021) with a score of 6.25 and (Hegde et al., 2021) with a score of 0.29.

- For the English-Tamil and English-Malayalam translation, (Xie, 2021)'s is again ranked number 1 with BLEU scores of 36.66 and 19.84 respectively, followed by Spartans with scores of 28.27 and 15.31. (Hegde et al., 2021) is ranked number 3 with scores of 1.66 and 19.84 respectively.

- Finally, in the Tamil-Telugu translation, the system submitted by (Xie, 2021) is again ranked number 1, with a BLEU score of 35.29, followed by (Hegde et al., 2021) with a score of 0.43 and (Prajapati et al., 2021) with a score of 0.0.

The reason for the variation in results among language pair tasks is due the following reasons as reported in the System descriptions:

- In Xie (2021), the system does not give good scores due the variation in the test set for English - Malayalam when compared with the development set where the BLEU score for the checkpoint average is 25.87.

- Prajapati et al. (2021) report that the overall translation quality of the test set is not as good as that of the validation data due to the variation in data in terms of sentence complexity and length when compared to the validation data.
- The reason for lower BLEU scores on the test set is due to the complexity of translation due to the presence of special characters, morphological richness of the language pairs and also due to the test set sentences being longer in length, according to Hegde et al. (2021)

To summarize, the systems submitted by the teams have shown improvement when additional data corpora were used and when additional preprocessing steps and/or layers/mechanisms were added. The teams reported that the overall system scores for the test set are not good when compared to the validation set, due to the complexity of the test set in terms of longer length sentences and morphological richness in the language pairs.

## 7 Conclusion

This paper described the shared task of machine translation of Dravidian (Tamil) languages to be presented at the first workshop on Speech and Language Technologies for Dravidian Technologies and summarized the results of this workshop. The best performing systems submitted to this workshop achieved good performance in terms of BLEU scores inspite of the lack of data available for training. This is a promising result in that such similar techniques can be applied to other under resourced languages. We would like to conclude by saying that we hope to continue to conduct this workshop over the coming years, and therefore continue to contribute to the development of language technology for under-resourced Dravidian (Tamil) languages.

## Acknowledgments

This publication is the outcome of the research supported in part by a research grant from Science Foundation Ireland (SFI) under Grant Number SFI/12/RC/2289_P2 (Insight_2) and 13/RC/2106_P2 (ADAPT), co-funded by the European Regional Development Fund and Irish Research Council grant IRCLA/2017/129 (CARDAMOM-Comparative Deep Models of Language for Minority and Historical Languages).

## References

Roee Aharoni, Melvin Johnson, and Orhan Firat. 2019. Massively multilingual neural machine translation. In *Proceedings of the 2019 Conference of the North American Chapter of the Association for Computational Linguistics: Human Language Technologies, Volume 1 (Long and Short Papers)*, pages 3874–3884, Minneapolis, Minnesota. Association for Computational Linguistics.

Devasagayam Albert et al. 1985. *Tolkāppiyam Phonology and Morphology: An English Translation*, volume 115. International Institute of Tamil Studies.

Mikhail Sergeevich Andronov. 1996. *A grammar of the Malayalam language in historical treatment*, volume 1. Otto Harrassowitz Verlag.

Dzmitry Bahdanau, Kyunghyun Cho, and Yoshua Bengio. 2014. Neural machine translation by jointly learning to align and translate. *arXiv preprint arXiv:1409.0473*.

Stuart H Blackburn. 2006. *Print, folklore, and nationalism in colonial South India*. Orient Blackswan.

Robert Caldwell. 1875. *A comparative grammar of the Dravidian or South-Indian family of languages*. Trübner.

Bharathi Raja Chakravarthi. 2020. *Leveraging orthographic information to improve machine translation of under-resourced languages*. Ph.D. thesis, NUI Galway.

Bharathi Raja Chakravarthi, Mihael Arcan, and John P. McCrae. 2018. Improving Wordnets for Under-Resourced Languages Using Machine Translation. In *Proceedings of the 9th Global WordNet Conference*. The Global WordNet Conference 2018 Committee.

Bharathi Raja Chakravarthi, Mihael Arcan, and John P. McCrae. 2019a. Comparison of Different Orthographies for Machine Translation of Under-Resourced Dravidian Languages. In *2nd Conference on Language, Data and Knowledge (LDK 2019)*, volume 70 of *OpenAccess Series in Informatics (OASIcs)*, pages 6:1–6:14, Dagstuhl, Germany. Schloss Dagstuhl–Leibniz-Zentrum fuer Informatik.

Bharathi Raja Chakravarthi, Mihael Arcan, and John P. McCrae. 2019b. WordNet gloss translation for under-resourced languages using multilingual neural machine translation. In *Proceedings of the Second Workshop on Multilingualism at the Intersection of Knowledge Bases and Machine Translation*, pages 1–7, Dublin, Ireland. European Association for Machine Translation.

Bharathi Raja Chakravarthi, Ruba Priyadharshini, Bernardo Stearns, Arun Jayapal, Sridevy S, Mihael Arcan, Manel Zarrouk, and John P McCrae. 2019c. Multilingual multimodal machine translation for Dravidian languages utilizing phonetic transcription. In *Proceedings of the 2nd Workshop on*

*Technologies for MT of Low Resource Languages*, pages 56–63, Dublin, Ireland. European Association for Machine Translation.

Bharathi Raja Chakravarthi, Navaneethan Rajasekaran, Mihael Arcan, Kevin McGuinness, Noel E.O'Connor, and John P McCrae. 2020a. Bilingual lexicon induction across orthographically-distinct under-resourced Dravidian languages. In *Proceedings of the Seventh Workshop on NLP for Similar Languages, Varieties and Dialects*, Barcelona, Spain.

Bharathi Raja Chakravarthi, Priya Rani, Mihael Arcan, and John P McCrae. 2020b. A survey of orthographic information in machine translation. *arXiv e-prints*, pages arXiv–2008.

Chandramma, P. Kumar Pareek, K. Swathi, and P. Shetteppanavar. 2017. An efficient machine translation model for Dravidian language. In *2017 2nd IEEE International Conference on Recent Trends in Electronics, Information Communication Technology (RTEICT)*, pages 2101–2105.

Kyunghyun Cho, Bart van Merriënboer, Dzmitry Bahdanau, and Yoshua Bengio. 2014. On the properties of neural machine translation: Encoder–decoder approaches. In *Proceedings of SSST-8, Eighth Workshop on Syntax, Semantics and Structure in Statistical Translation*, pages 103–111, Doha, Qatar. Association for Computational Linguistics.

Orhan Firat, Baskaran Sankaran, Yaser Al-Onaizan, Fatos T Yarman Vural, and Kyunghyun Cho. 2016. Zero-resource translation with multi-lingual neural machine translation. In *Proceedings of the 2016 Conference on Empirical Methods in Natural Language Processing*, pages 268–277.

Jiatao Gu, Hany Hassan, Jacob Devlin, and Victor O.K. Li. 2018. Universal neural machine translation for extremely low resource languages. In *Proceedings of the 2018 Conference of the North American Chapter of the Association for Computational Linguistics: Human Language Technologies, Volume 1 (Long Papers)*, pages 344–354, New Orleans, Louisiana. Association for Computational Linguistics.

Thanh-Le Ha, Jan Niehues, and Alexander Waibel. Toward multilingual neural machine translation with universal encoder and decoder. *Institute for Anthropomatics and Robotics*, 2(10.12):16.

Adeep Hande, Ruba Priyadharshini, and Bharathi Raja Chakravarthi. 2020. KanCMD: Kannada CodeMixed dataset for sentiment analysis and offensive language detection. In *Proceedings of the Third Workshop on Computational Modeling of People's Opinions, Personality, and Emotion's in Social Media*, pages 54–63, Barcelona, Spain (Online). Association for Computational Linguistics.

Asha Hegde, Ibrahim Gashaw, and Shashirekha H.L. 2021. MUCS@ - Machine Translation for Dravidian Languages using Stacked Long Short Term Memory. In *Proceedings of the First Workshop on Speech and Language Technologies for Dravidian Languages*. Association for Computational Linguistics.

Melvin Johnson, Mike Schuster, Quoc V Le, Maxim Krikun, Yonghui Wu, Zhifeng Chen, Nikhil Thorat, Fernanda Viégas, Martin Wattenberg, Greg Corrado, et al. 2017. Google's multilingual neural machine translation system: Enabling zero-shot translation. *Transactions of the Association of Computational Linguistics*, 5(1):339–351.

Tom Kocmi and Ondrej Bojar. 2018. Trivial transfer learning for low-resource neural machine translation. *WMT 2018*, page 244.

Philipp Koehn, Francisco Guzmán, Vishrav Chaudhary, and Juan Pino. 2019. Findings of the WMT 2019 shared task on parallel corpus filtering for low-resource conditions. In *Proceedings of the Fourth Conference on Machine Translation (Volume 3: Shared Task Papers, Day 2)*, pages 54–72, Florence, Italy. Association for Computational Linguistics.

Parameswari Krishnamurthy. 2019. Development of Telugu-Tamil Transfer-Based Machine Translation System: An Improvization Using Divergence Index. *Journal of Intelligent Systems*, 28(3):493–504.

Bhadriraju Krishnamurti. 2016. Comparative Dravidian studies. *Current trends in linguistics*, page 309.

M Anand Kumar, V Dhanalakshmi, KP Soman, and S Rajendran. 2014. Factored Statistical Machine Translation System for English to Tamil Language. *Pertanika Journal of Social Sciences & Humanities*, 22(4).

M. Anand Kumar, B. Premjith, Shivkaran Singh, S. Rajendran, and K. P. Soman. 2019. An Overview of the Shared Task on Machine Translation in Indian Languages (MTIL) – 2017. *Journal of Intelligent Systems*, 28(3):455–464.

Surafel M Lakew, Quintino F Lotito, Matteo Negri, Marco Turchi, and Marcello Federico. 2017. Improving zero-shot translation of low-resource languages. In *14th International Workshop on Spoken Language Translation*.

Thang Luong, Hieu Pham, and Christopher D. Manning. 2015. Effective approaches to attention-based neural machine translation. In *Proceedings of the 2015 Conference on Empirical Methods in Natural Language Processing*, pages 1412–1421, Lisbon, Portugal. Association for Computational Linguistics.

Anand Kumar M. 2013. Morphology based prototype statistical machine translation system for English to Tamil language. *Unpublished PhD Thesis*.

Thomas Oberlies. 2011. *Pali: A Grammar of the Language of the Theravada Tipitaka. With a Concordance to Pischel's Grammatik der Prakrit-Sprachen*, volume 3. Walter de Gruyter.

Atul Kr. Ojha, Valentin Malykh, Alina Karakanta, and Chao-Hong Liu. 2020. Findings of the LoResMT 2020 shared task on zero-shot for low-resource languages. In *Proceedings of the 3rd Workshop on Technologies for MT of Low Resource Languages*, pages 33–37, Suzhou, China. Association for Computational Linguistics.

Kishore Papineni, Salim Roukos, Todd Ward, and Wei-Jing Zhu. 2002. Bleu: a method for automatic evaluation of machine translation. In *Proceedings of the 40th Annual Meeting of the Association for Computational Linguistics*, pages 311–318, Philadelphia, Pennsylvania, USA. Association for Computational Linguistics.

MS Purnalingam Pillai. 1904. *A Primer of Tamil Literature*. Ananda Press.

Raj Prajapati, Vedant Vijay Parikh, and Prasenjit Majumder. 2021. Neural Machine Translations for Dravidian Languages EACL 2021. In *Proceedings of the First Workshop on Speech and Language Technologies for Dravidian Languages*. Association for Computational Linguistics.

S Rajendran. 2004. Strategies in the formation of compound nouns in Tamil. *Languages Of India*, 4.

HG Rawlinson. 1930. THE KADAMBA KULA—A History of Ancient and Mediæval Karnataka.(Studies in Indian History of the Indian Historical Research Institute, St. Xavier's College, Bombay, No. 5).

Richard Salomon. 1998. *Indian epigraphy: a guide to the study of inscriptions in Sanskrit, Prakrit, and the other Indo-Aryan languages*. Oxford University Press on Demand.

A. C. Sekhar. 1951. [evolution of malayalam]. *Bulletin of the Deccan College Research Institute*, 12(1/2):1–216.

R Sivanantham and M Seran. 2019. Keeladi: An Urban Settlement of Sangam Age on the Banks of River Vaigai. *India: Department of Archaeology, Government of Tamil Nadu, Chennai*.

BGL Swamy. 1975. The Date of Tolkappiyam: A Retrospect. *Annals of Oriental Research (Madras), Silver Jubilee*, 292:317.

Takanobu Takahashi. 1995. *Tamil love poetry and poetics*, volume 9. Brill.

Sajeetha Thavareesan and Sinnathamby Mahesan. 2019. Sentiment Analysis in Tamil Texts: A Study on Machine Learning Techniques and Feature Representation. In *2019 14th Conference on Industrial and Information Systems (ICIIS)*, pages 320–325.

Sajeetha Thavareesan and Sinnathamby Mahesan. 2020a. Sentiment Lexicon Expansion using Word2vec and fastText for Sentiment Prediction in Tamil texts. In *2020 Moratuwa Engineering Research Conference (MERCon)*, pages 272–276.

Sajeetha Thavareesan and Sinnathamby Mahesan. 2020b. Word embedding-based Part of Speech tagging in Tamil texts. In *2020 IEEE 15th International Conference on Industrial and Information Systems (ICIIS)*, pages 478–482.

Yonghui Wu, Mike Schuster, Zhifeng Chen, Quoc V Le, Mohammad Norouzi, Wolfgang Macherey, Maxim Krikun, Yuan Cao, Qin Gao, Klaus Macherey, et al. 2016. Google's neural machine translation system: Bridging the gap between human and machine translation. *arXiv preprint arXiv:1609.08144*.

Mengzhou Xia, Xiang Kong, Antonios Anastasopoulos, and Graham Neubig. 2019. Generalized data augmentation for low-resource translation. In *Proceedings of the 57th Annual Meeting of the Association for Computational Linguistics*, pages 5786–5796.

Wanying Xie. 2021. GX@DravidianLangTech-EACL2021: Multilingual Neuron Machine Translation and Back-translation . In *Proceedings of the First Workshop on Speech and Language Technologies for Dravidian Languages*. Association for Computational Linguistics.

Barret Zoph, Deniz Yuret, Jonathan May, and Kevin Knight. 2016. Transfer learning for low-resource neural machine translation. In *Proceedings of the 2016 Conference on Empirical Methods in Natural Language Processing*, pages 1568–1575.

# Findings of the Shared Task on Troll Meme Classification in Tamil

**Shardul Suryawanshi** and **Bharathi Raja Chakravarthi**
Insight SFI Research Centre for Data Analytics,
Data Science Institute,
National University of Ireland Galway
Galway, Ireland

## Abstract

The internet has facilitated its user-base with a platform to communicate and express their views without any censorship. On the other hand, this freedom of expression or free speech can be abused by its user or a troll to demean an individual or a group. Demeaning people based on their gender, sexual orientation, religious believes or any other characteristics –trolling– could cause significant distress in the online community. Hence, the content posted by a troll needs to be identified and dealt with before causing any more damage. Amongst all the forms of troll content, memes are most prevalent due to their popularity and ability to propagate across cultures. A troll uses a meme to demean, attack or offend its targetted audience. In this shared task, we provide a resource (TamilMemes) that could be used to train a system capable of identifying a troll meme in the Tamil language. In our TamilMemes dataset, each meme has been categorized into either a "troll" or a "not_troll" class. Along with the meme images, we also provided the Latin transcripted text from memes. We received ten system submissions from the participants, which were evaluated using the weighted average F1-score. The system with the weighted average F1-score of 0.55 secured the first rank.

## 1 Introduction

We have seen a rise in the usage of memes on the internet. Memes could come in many forms and languages, but we emphasize on the image with text (IWT) memes (Du et al., 2020) in the Tamil language. IWT memes are inherently multimodal as their meaning is not understood when just the image or the text considered in isolation; hence, both image and text should be considered. These memes can propagate and mutate through cultures like the selfish gene (Dawkins, 2016). Propagation and mutation of memes ensure widespread on the internet; hence they could be weaponized by trolls (Mandl et al., 2020). Trolls are individuals or users on the internet who tend to attack or offend other individuals or groups in a demeaning manner (Tomaiuolo et al., 2020).

A meme used by troll –troll meme– could come in any languages, and since languages are representative of cultures, a meme in one language could represent a culture. In this shared task, we provide the TamilMemes dataset (Suryawanshi et al., 2020) that consists of 2,969 memes to the participants. Additionally, we also provided the text (caption) associated with each meme. The text has been transcripted in Latin by a native Tamil speaker, which was later evaluated and corrected by the expert.

Tamil (ISO 639-3: tam) is an official language in Tamil Nadu, Puducherry, Sri Lanka, Singapore and a recognised minority language in Malaysia and South Africa with a 75 million speaker base (Chakravarthi et al., 2018; Thavareesan and Mahesan, 2019, 2020a,b). Tamil inscription in pottery from Kodumanal and Porunthal [1] [2] was the oldest inscription in India dating to 580 BCE then Asoka inscription in Prakrit, Greek and Aramaic dating to 260 BCE (Mahadevan, 2002; Rajakumar and Bharathi, 2012). In Sanskrit, the oldest known inscriptions are from the 1st century CE, such as Dhana's Ayodhya Inscription and Ghosundi-Hathibada. The first book printed in India in an Indian language was Tampiran Vanakkam in Tamil on 1578 CE, a 16-page translation of the Portuguese "Doctrina Christam" (Balachandran, 2005). In the modern Tamil script, there are 12 vowels, 18 consonants and one special character, the āytam (Chakravarthi, 2020b). The vowels and consonants combine in order to form 216 compound characters, giving a total of 247 characters.

[1] Tamil inscriptions wiki

[2] Iron Age - Early Historic Transition in South Indian Appraisal



*Proceedings of the First Workshop on Speech and Language Technologies for Dravidian Languages*, pages 126–132
April 20, 2021 

However, Tamil is often transcribed in Latin Script by a multilingual speaker on social media platforms (Chakravarthi, 2020a). This behaviour could be attributed to the ease or comfort in scripting Tamil in Latin script (Chakravarthi et al., 2019; Hande et al., 2020). Also, these multilingual speakers tend to switch to another language such as English. This phenomenon, also known as code-mixing or code-switching is commonly observed amongst multilingual speakers (Jose et al., 2020; Priyadharshini et al., 2020). A great deal of work and resources (Chakravarthi et al., 2020a,c) has been created for Dravidian languages but the multimodal aspect of code-mixed content in the form of meme remains unexplored.

In recent years, we have seen a rise in awareness of tackling multimodal offensive (Sharma et al., 2020) or hate (Kiela et al., 2020) content in memes in the English language, but other under-resourced languages remain unexplored. Our "Troll Meme Classification in Tamil" task aims to promote research in multimodal troll meme classification in under-resourced Tamil language. Moreover, this task provides a unique opportunity to study the effect of code-switching or code-mixing in the English transcript of Tamil (Chakravarthi et al., 2020b) in association with the image from the meme.

## 2 Task Description

The goal of the "Troll Meme Classification in Tamil" shared task was to classify if a given meme is a "troll" or "not-troll" based on the image and text associated with the meme in the Tamil language. The text from the meme is written in either the Tamil grammar and English lexicon or English grammar and Tamil lexicon. However, for consistency, we transcripted the text in Latin.

Troll meme is a meme, which consists of offensive text and non-offensive images, offensive images with non-offensive text, sarcastically offensive text with non-offensive images, or sarcastic images with offensive text to provoke, distract and has digressive or off-topic content with intend to demean or offend particular people, group or race, otherwise, a not-troll meme (Suryawanshi et al., 2020). Figure 1 shows examples of a troll and not-troll meme from the TamilMeme dataset. Example 1 is a troll meme targeted towards the potato chip brand called "Lays". In this example, an image is harmless with just a picture of the potato chips

| Split | Troll | Not-troll | Total |
|---|---|---|---|
| Train | 1,282 | 1,018 | 2,300 |
| Test | 395 | 272 | 667 |
| Total | 1,677 | 1,290 | 2,967 |

Table 1: A class distribution in the training and test set of the TamilMemes dataset

packet, but the translation of the text is *"If you buy one packet air, then 5 chips free"* which is offensive for the brand. The translation of Example 2 would be *"Sorry my friend (girl)"*. This example does not contain any provoking or offensive image or text and hence, it is a not-troll meme.

Previously, we developed this TamilMemes dataset and treated the task of identifying a troll meme as an image classification problem. Since the text associated with the meme acts as a context of the image, we enhanced our TamilMemes dataset by providing the text as a separate modality for the shared task. We expected our participant to approach the task in a multimodal way.

(a) An example on troll meme from TamilMemes dataset

(b) An example on not-troll meme from TamilMemes dataset

Figure 1: Examples for a troll and not-troll meme from the TamilMemes dataset

| Rank | Team | Precision | Recall | F1-score |
|---|---|---|---|---|
| 1 | Codewithzichao (Li, 2021) | 0.57 | 0.60 | 0.55 |
| 2 | IIITK (Ghanghor et al., 2021) | 0.56 | 0.59 | 0.54 |
| 3 | NLP@CUET (Hossain et al., 2021) | 0.55 | 0.58 | 0.52 |
| 4 | SSNCSE_NLP (Silvia A and B, 2021) | 0.58 | 0.60 | 0.50 |
| 5 | Simon_work (Que et al., 2021) | 0.53 | 0.58 | 0.49 |
| 6 | TrollMeta (J and HS, 2021) | 0.45 | 0.41 | 0.48 |
| 7 | UVCE-IIITT (Hegde et al., 2021) | 0.60 | 0.60 | 0.46 |
| 8 | cean | 0.53 | 0.57 | 0.43 |
| 9 | HUB (Huang and Bai, 2021) | 0.50 | 0.54 | 0.40 |
| 10 | iiit_dwd (Mishra and Saumya, 2021) | 0.52 | 0.59 | 0.30 |

Table 2: The rank list with detailed report on Precision (P), Recall (R), F1-score (F1) of submissions for the "Troll Meme Classification in Tamil" task

## 3 Evaluation

Table 1 shows the class distribution in the training and test set for the TamilMemes dataset. We provided a training set of 2,500 memes (with the Latin scripted text) to the participants. Later, we evaluated all the systems on the held-out or test set of 667 memes. We considered a weighted average version of the F1-score as a primary evaluation metric by taking class imbalance into the account. The weighted average F1-score[3] is calculated by averaging the support-weighted mean F1 score per-class.

## 4 Methodology

In system submissions, we saw a variety of methodologies used by the participants which were as simple as Logistic Regression (Wright, 1995) and as complex as BERT (Devlin et al., 2018). By keeping multimodality in mind, most of the participants implemented a method that could leverage both text and image. Mostly, the image part has been processed using Convolutional Neural Network (CNN) such as ResNet152 (He et al., 2016) or the custom residual networks while the text has been processed RNN (LSTM (Hochreiter and Schmidhuber, 1997)), transformer (BERT, ROBERTA (Liu et al., 2019)). However, in one exceptional case, one participant has used a transformer for processing both modalities.

- Li (2021) utilized a transformer-based approach that leverages the pre-trained BERT and ResNet152 model to derive the text and image features. The novelty of the work comes from the implementation of multi-modal attention which considers the whole text caption in the context of the image by mapping both image and text features in the same semantic space. Their model achieved a 0.55 weighted average F1 score and ranked first in the shared task.
- Ghanghor et al. (2021) utilized a transformer-based approach to identify the troll and not-troll Tamil meme. The state of the art text classifier (BERT) and image (CNN) classifiers were used to extract useful attention features. Their system submission for Tamil troll meme classification achieved a 0.54 weighted average F1 score.
- Hossain et al. (2021) utilized a systematic text-based, image-based and multimodal approach to identify a troll meme. The paper laid out a detailed investigation into the problem presented in the shared task by capturing visual and textual features using CNN, VGG16 (Simonyan and Zisserman, 2014), Inception (Szegedy et al., 2017), m-BERT, XLM-RoBERTa, XLNet (Yang et al., 2019). Multimodal features were extracted by combining image (CNN, ResNet50, Inception) and text (BiLSTM) (Zhou et al., 2016) features using an early fusion technique. But the results showed that the text-based approach with XLNet achieved the highest weighted F1-score of 0.58, and enabled their system implementation to secure 3rd rank.
- Silvia A and B (2021) used traditional NLP approaches such as Multilayer perceptron (MLP (Haykin and Network, 2004)), Random forest

[3]Weighted average F-1 score is calculated with the help of the sklearn classification report utility

(RF) (Breiman, 2001) and K-nearest neighbour (KNN ) (Cunningham and Delany, 2020) on the text features derived from tf-idf, count vector and mBERT embeddings. The paper opts for a text-based approach over the multimodal approach and achieved a weighted average F1-score of 0.50.

- Que et al. (2021) used a text-based approach to deal with the multimodal issue of identifying troll memes. Here the author trains XLM-Roberta in combination with the custom CNN on the text modality and achieves a weighted average F1-score of 0.49.
- J and HS (2021) utilized ResNet-50 to identify if a given meme is a troll or not based on the visual features. However, no text modality has been used as a feature while training the system. Their system achieved a weighted average F1-score of 0.48 and ranked sixth.
- Hegde et al. (2021) utilized a transformer-based approach to identify the troll and not-troll Tamil meme. The state of the art text (mBERT) and image (Vision transformer) (Dosovitskiy et al., 2020) classifiers were used to extract useful attention features. They achieve a weighted average F1-score of 0.46 and ranked seventh.
- Huang and Bai (2021) used a BiGRU (Dey and Salem, 2017) and custom CNN to capture text and image features, which later are concatenated to form a multimodal representation of a meme. They ranked ninth with a weighted average F1-score of 0.40.
- Mishra and Saumya (2021) used a hybrid approach that combines text and image features using CNN and BiLSTM. Their proposed model obtained 10th rank in the shared task and reported a weighted F1-score of 0.30.

## 5 Results and Discussion

We have received 10 submissions for the shared task. Table 2 shows that the maximum weighted average F1-score could only reach 0.55, which is less. While the submissions claimed that the evaluation metric exceeded the validation set, the poor performance on the test set point towards overfitting. Overfitting is commonly seen when complex models with large numbers of parameters are trained on small datasets.

In this shared task, we provided 2,967 samples which might be less for the data-hungry models such as BERT and it's predecessor such as ROBERTa, XLM-RoBERTa. Moreover, due to the high dimensionality presented by the images, the traditional machine learning models such as logistic regression, Naive Bayes are not able to generalize. The poor performance of the traditional machine learning model shows that they are rather too simple to learn useful features from the high dimensional data presented in the form of image and text. Furthermore, the Tamil text (could be with or without code-mixed) from the meme is transcripted in the Latin script leaves little room for using pre-trained models (e.g. multilingual BERT) which are primarily trained in English or zero-shot transferred to other languages written in their native script. Hence, such multilingual models need to be finetuned on the more code-mixed, transliterated data. In the case of images, the visual features have been captured using a CNN pre-trained on the imagenet weights.

In the previous study, we observed that the visual features captured by such CNNs tend to be less useful for identifying a troll Tamil meme. The same effect has been observed in the system submitted to the shared task. Overall, we need a robust approach that takes into account all the aspects of this multimodal classification problem –lack of data, high dimensionality, low resource language processing and code-mixing.

## 6 Conclusion

In the "Troll Meme Classification in Tamil" shared task, we presented a unique multimodal classification problem by providing a newly improved TamilMeme dataset which now has Tamil text (in the form of transcripted Latin text) from memes. This task was not only a multimodal classification problem but also posed challenges such as natural language processing of low-resourced language, transcripted code-mixed text. The submissions received from the participants showed multiple ways to approach the problem and we hope that their contribution along with our enriched dataset will kindle the research in this less explored area.

## Acknowledgments

This publication is the outcome of the research supported in part by a research grant from Science Foundation Ireland (SFI) under

Grant Number SFI/12/RC/2289_P2 (Insight_2) and 13/RC/2106_P2 (ADAPT), co-funded by the European Regional Development Fund and Irish Research Council grant IRCLA/2017/129 (CARDAMOM-Comparative Deep Models of Language for Minority and Historical Languages).

## References

R Balachandran. 2005. Pioneers of Tamil Literature: Transition to Modernity. *Indian Literature*, 49(2 (226):179–184.

Leo Breiman. 2001. Random forests. *Machine learning*, 45(1):5–32.

Bharathi Raja Chakravarthi. 2020a. HopeEDI: A multilingual hope speech detection dataset for equality, diversity, and inclusion. In *Proceedings of the Third Workshop on Computational Modeling of People's Opinions, Personality, and Emotion's in Social Media*, pages 41–53, Barcelona, Spain (Online). Association for Computational Linguistics.

Bharathi Raja Chakravarthi. 2020b. *Leveraging orthographic information to improve machine translation of under-resourced languages*. Ph.D. thesis, NUI Galway.

Bharathi Raja Chakravarthi, Mihael Arcan, and John P. McCrae. 2018. Improving wordnets for under-resourced languages using machine translation. In *Proceedings of the 9th Global Wordnet Conference*, pages 77–86, Nanyang Technological University (NTU), Singapore. Global Wordnet Association.

Bharathi Raja Chakravarthi, Mihael Arcan, and John P. McCrae. 2019. WordNet gloss translation for under-resourced languages using multilingual neural machine translation. In *Proceedings of the Second Workshop on Multilingualism at the Intersection of Knowledge Bases and Machine Translation*, pages 1–7, Dublin, Ireland. European Association for Machine Translation.

Bharathi Raja Chakravarthi, Navya Jose, Shardul Suryawanshi, Elizabeth Sherly, and John Philip McCrae. 2020a. A sentiment analysis dataset for code-mixed malayalam-english. In *Proceedings of the 1st Joint Workshop on Spoken Language Technologies for Under-resourced languages (SLTU) and Collaboration and Computing for Under-Resourced Languages (CCURL)*, pages 177–184.

Bharathi Raja Chakravarthi, M Anand Kumar, John Philip McCrae, Premjith B, Soman KP, and Thomas Mandl. 2020b. Overview of the track on HASOC-Offensive Language Identification-DravidianCodeMix. In *Working Notes of the Forum for Information Retrieval Evaluation (FIRE 2020). CEUR Workshop Proceedings. In: CEUR-WS. org, Hyderabad, India.*

Bharathi Raja Chakravarthi, Vigneshwaran Muralidaran, Ruba Priyadharshini, and John Philip McCrae. 2020c. Corpus creation for sentiment analysis in code-mixed Tamil-English text. In *Proceedings of the 1st Joint Workshop on Spoken Language Technologies for Under-resourced languages (SLTU) and Collaboration and Computing for Under-Resourced Languages (CCURL)*, pages 202–210, Marseille, France. European Language Resources association.

Padraig Cunningham and Sarah Jane Delany. 2020. k-nearest neighbour classifiers–. *arXiv preprint arXiv:2004.04523*.

Richard Dawkins. 2016. *The selfish gene*. Oxford university press.

Jacob Devlin, Ming-Wei Chang, Kenton Lee, and Kristina Toutanova. 2018. Bert: Pre-training of deep bidirectional transformers for language understanding. *arXiv preprint arXiv:1810.04805*.

R. Dey and F. M. Salem. 2017. Gate-variants of gated recurrent unit (gru) neural networks. In *2017 IEEE 60th International Midwest Symposium on Circuits and Systems (MWSCAS)*, pages 1597–1600.

Alexey Dosovitskiy, Lucas Beyer, Alexander Kolesnikov, Dirk Weissenborn, Xiaohua Zhai, Thomas Unterthiner, Mostafa Dehghani, Matthias Minderer, Georg Heigold, Sylvain Gelly, et al. 2020. An image is worth 16x16 words: Transformers for image recognition at scale. *arXiv preprint arXiv:2010.11929*.

Yuhao Du, Muhammad Aamir Masood, and Kenneth Joseph. 2020. Understanding visual memes: An empirical analysis of text superimposed on memes shared on twitter. In *Proceedings of the International AAAI Conference on Web and Social Media*, volume 14, pages 153–164.

Nikhil Ghanghor, Bharathi Raja Chakravarthi, Ruba Priyadharshini, Sajeetha Thavareesan, and Parameswari Krishnamurthy. 2021. IIITK@DravidianLangtech-EACL2021: Offensive Language Identification and Meme Classification in Tamil, Malayalam and Kannada. In *Proceedings of the First Workshop on Speech and Language Technologies for Dravidian Languages*. Association for Computational Linguistics.

Adeep Hande, Ruba Priyadharshini, and Bharathi Raja Chakravarthi. 2020. KanCMD: Kannada CodeMixed dataset for sentiment analysis and offensive language detection. In *Proceedings of the Third Workshop on Computational Modeling of People's Opinions, Personality, and Emotion's in Social Media*, pages 54–63, Barcelona, Spain (Online). Association for Computational Linguistics.

Simon Haykin and N Network. 2004. A comprehensive foundation. *Neural networks*, 2(2004):41.

Kaiming He, Xiangyu Zhang, Shaoqing Ren, and Jian Sun. 2016. Deep residual learning for image recognition. In *Proceedings of the IEEE conference on computer vision and pattern recognition*, pages 770–778.

Siddhanth U Hegde, Adeep Hande, Ruba Priyadharshini, Sajeetha Thavareesan, and Bharathi Raja Chakravarthi. 2021. Uvce-iiitt@DravidianLangTech-EACL2021: Tamil Troll Meme Classification: You need to Pay more Attention. In *Proceedings of the First Workshop on Speech and Language Technologies for Dravidian Languages*. Association for Computational Linguistics.

Sepp Hochreiter and Jürgen Schmidhuber. 1997. Long short-term memory. *Neural computation*, 9(8):1735–1780.

Eftekhar Hossain, Omar Sharif, and Mohammed Moshiul Hoque. 2021. NLP-CUET@DravidianLangtech-EACL2021: Investigating Visual and Textual Features to Identify Trolls from Multimodal Social Media Memes. In *Proceedings of the First Workshop on Speech and Language Technologies for Dravidian Languages*. Association for Computational Linguistics.

Bo Huang and Yang Bai. 2021. HUB@DravidianLangTech-EACL2021: Meme Classification for Tamil Text-Image Fusion. In *Proceedings of the First Workshop on Speech and Language Technologies for Dravidian Languages*. Association for Computational Linguistics.

Manoj Balaji J and Chinmaya HS. 2021. Troll-meta@DravidianLangtech-EACL2021: Meme classification using deep learning. In *Proceedings of the First Workshop on Speech and Language Technologies for Dravidian Languages*. Association for Computational Linguistics.

Navya Jose, Bharathi Raja Chakravarthi, Shardul Suryawanshi, Elizabeth Sherly, and John P. McCrae. 2020. A Survey of Current Datasets for Code-Switching Research. In *2020 6th International Conference on Advanced Computing and Communication Systems (ICACCS)*, pages 136–141.

Douwe Kiela, Hamed Firooz, Aravind Mohan, Vedanuj Goswami, Amanpreet Singh, Pratik Ringshia, and Davide Testuggine. 2020. The hateful memes challenge: Detecting hate speech in multimodal memes. *arXiv preprint arXiv:2005.04790*.

Zichao Li. 2021. Codewithzichao@DravidianLangtech-EACL2021: Exploring Multimodal Transformers for Meme Classification in Tamil Language. In *Proceedings of the First Workshop on Speech and Language Technologies for Dravidian Languages*. Association for Computational Linguistics.

Yinhan Liu, Myle Ott, Naman Goyal, Jingfei Du, Mandar Joshi, Danqi Chen, Omer Levy, Mike Lewis, Luke Zettlemoyer, and Veselin Stoyanov. 2019. Roberta: A robustly optimized bert pretraining approach. *arXiv preprint arXiv:1907.11692*.

Iravatham Mahadevan. 2002. Aryan or dravidian or neither? a study of recent attempts to decipher the indus script (1995-2000). *Electronic Journal of Vedic Studies*, 8(1):1–19.

Thomas Mandl, Sandip Modha, Anand Kumar M, and Bharathi Raja Chakravarthi. 2020. Overview of the HASOC Track at FIRE 2020: Hate Speech and Offensive Language Identification in Tamil, Malayalam, Hindi, English and German. In *Forum for Information Retrieval Evaluation*, FIRE 2020, page 29–32, New York, NY, USA. Association for Computing Machinery.

Ankit Kumar Mishra and Sunil Saumya. 2021. IIIT_DWD@DravidianLangtech-EACL2021: Identifying Tamil troll meme using a hybrid deep learning approach. In *Proceedings of the First Workshop on Speech and Language Technologies for Dravidian Languages*. Association for Computational Linguistics.

Ruba Priyadharshini, Bharathi Raja Chakravarthi, Mani Vegupatti, and John P. McCrae. 2020. Named Entity Recognition for Code-Mixed Indian Corpus using Meta Embedding. In *2020 6th International Conference on Advanced Computing and Communication Systems (ICACCS)*, pages 68–72.

Qinyu Que, Yuanchi Qu, and Suidong Qu. 2021. Simon@DravidianLangtech-EACL2021: Meme Classification for Tamil with BERT. In *Proceedings of the First Workshop on Speech and Language Technologies for Dravidian Languages*. Association for Computational Linguistics.

S Rajakumar and V Subbiah Bharathi. 2012. Eighth century tamil consonants recognition from stone inscriptions. In *2012 International Conference on Recent Trends in Information Technology*, pages 40–43. IEEE.

Chhavi Sharma, William Paka, Scott, Deepesh Bhageria, Amitava Das, Soujanya Poria, Tanmoy Chakraborty, and Björn Gambäck. 2020. Task Report: Memotion Analysis 1.0 @SemEval 2020: The Visuo-Lingual Metaphor! In *Proceedings of the 14th International Workshop on Semantic Evaluation (SemEval-2020)*, Barcelona, Spain. Association for Computational Linguistics.

Agnusimmaculate Silvia A and Bharathi B. 2021. SSNCSE NLP@DravidianLangtech-EACL2021: Meme classification for Tamil using machine learning approach. In *Proceedings of the First Workshop on Speech and Language Technologies for Dravidian Languages*. Association for Computational Linguistics.

Karen Simonyan and Andrew Zisserman. 2014. Very deep convolutional networks for large-scale image recognition. *arXiv preprint arXiv:1409.1556*.

Shardul Suryawanshi, Bharathi Raja Chakravarthi, Pranav Verma, Mihael Arcan, John Philip McCrae, and Paul Buitelaar. 2020. A dataset for troll classification of TamilMemes. In *Proceedings of the WILDRE5– 5th Workshop on Indian Language Data: Resources and Evaluation*, pages 7–13, Marseille, France. European Language Resources Association (ELRA).

Christian Szegedy, Sergey Ioffe, Vincent Vanhoucke, and Alexander Alemi. 2017. Inception-v4, inception-resnet and the impact of residual connections on learning. In *Proceedings of the AAAI Conference on Artificial Intelligence*, volume 31.

Sajeetha Thavareesan and Sinnathamby Mahesan. 2019. Sentiment Analysis in Tamil Texts: A Study on Machine Learning Techniques and Feature Representation. In *2019 14th Conference on Industrial and Information Systems (ICIIS)*, pages 320–325.

Sajeetha Thavareesan and Sinnathamby Mahesan. 2020a. Sentiment Lexicon Expansion using Word2vec and fastText for Sentiment Prediction in Tamil texts. In *2020 Moratuwa Engineering Research Conference (MERCon)*, pages 272–276.

Sajeetha Thavareesan and Sinnathamby Mahesan. 2020b. Word embedding-based Part of Speech tagging in Tamil texts. In *2020 IEEE 15th International Conference on Industrial and Information Systems (ICIIS)*, pages 478–482.

Michele Tomaiuolo, Gianfranco Lombardo, Monica Mordonini, Stefano Cagnoni, and Agostino Poggi. 2020. A survey on troll detection. *Future Internet*, 12(2):31.

Raymond E Wright. 1995. Logistic regression.

Zhilin Yang, Zihang Dai, Yiming Yang, Jaime Carbonell, Ruslan Salakhutdinov, and Quoc V Le. 2019. Xlnet: Generalized autoregressive pretraining for language understanding. *arXiv preprint arXiv:1906.08237*.

Peng Zhou, Wei Shi, Jun Tian, Zhenyu Qi, Bingchen Li, Hongwei Hao, and Bo Xu. 2016. Attention-based bidirectional long short-term memory networks for relation classification. In *Proceedings of the 54th annual meeting of the association for computational linguistics (volume 2: Short papers)*, pages 207–212.

# Findings of the Shared Task on Offensive Language Identification in Tamil, Malayalam, and Kannada

**Bharathi Raja Chakravarthi**[1], **Ruba Priyadharshini**[2], **Navya Jose**[3]
**Anand Kumar M** [4], **Thomas Mandl** [5], **Prasanna Kumar Kumaresan**[3],
**Rahul Ponnusamy**[3], **Hariharan R L** [4], **John Philip McCrae** [1] **and Elizabeth Sherly**[3]
[1]National University of Ireland Galway, [2]Madurai Kamaraj University,
[3]Indian Institute of Information Technology and Management-Kerala,
[4]National Institute of Technology Karnataka Surathkal,
[5]University of Hildesheim Germany
bharathi.raja@insight-centre.org

## Abstract

Detecting offensive language in social media in local languages is critical for moderating user-generated content. Thus, the field of offensive language identification for under-resourced languages like Tamil, Malayalam and Kannada is of essential importance. As user-generated content is often code-mixed and not well studied for under-resourced languages, it is imperative to create resources and conduct benchmark studies to encourage research in under-resourced Dravidian languages. We created a shared task on offensive language detection in Dravidian languages. We summarize the dataset for this challenge which are openly available at `https://competitions.codalab.org/competitions/27654`, and present an overview of the methods and the results of the competing systems.

## 1 Introduction

The dawn of social media helped to bridge the gap between the borders and paved the way for the people to communicate or express their opinions more easily than any other time in human history (Edosomwan et al., 2011). But with this advent of social media, the platforms like YouTube, Facebook, and Twitter not only helped information sharing and networking but also became the place that target, defame and marginalize people merely on the basis of their physical appearance, religion or sexual orientation (Keipi et al., 2016; Benikova et al., 2018; Pamungkas et al., 2020). Social media has moulded itself into its specialised tool with which the people are verbally threatened and cornered not for what they have done but for who they are (Maitra and McGowan, 2012; Patton et al., 2013). Undoubtedly, the infiltration depth and width of this 'digital wonder' equipped the erstwhile 'invisible and socially paralysed' communities to play cards, if not extravagantly noticeable (Barnidge et al., 2019).

Research in hate speech detection (Kumar et al., 2018) or offensive language detection (Zampieri et al., 2020; Mandl et al., 2020) using Natural Language Processing (NLP) has significantly improved in recent years. However, the work on under-resourced languages is still limited (Chakravarthi, 2020). For example, under-resourced languages such as Tamil, Malayalam, and Kannada lack tools and datasets (Chakravarthi et al., 2020a,c; Thavareesan and Mahesan, 2019, 2020a,b). Recently, shared sentiment analysis for Tamil and Malayalam by Chakravarthi et al. (2020d) and offensive language identification in Tamil and Malayalam by Chakravarthi et al. (2020b) paved the wave for more research on Dravidian languages. Tamil, Malayalam and Kannada belong to the Dravidian language family and are spoken by some 220 million people in the Indian subcontinent, Singapore and Sri Lanka (Krishnamurti, 2003). It is essential to create NLP systems such as hate speech detection or offensive language detection in local languages since most user-generated content is in such languages.

The Dravidian language family is reported as being approximately 4500 years old by Bayesian phylogenetic analysis of cognate-coded lexical data (Kolipakam et al., 2018). The Dravidian languages scripts are first attested in the 580 BCE as Tamili[1] script inscribed on the pottery of Keezhadi, Sivagangai and Madurai district of Tamil Nadu, India (Sivanantham and Seran, 2019)[2] by Tamil Nadu State Department of Archaeology and Archaeological Survey of India. The modern Dravidian languages have its own scripts evolved from Tamili scripts. The scripts are alpha-syllabic, belonging to a family of the abugida writing systems that are partially alphabetic and partially syllable-based

[1]also called Damili or Dramili or Tamil-Brahmi
[2]Keeladi-Book-English-18-09-2019.pdf



*Proceedings of the First Workshop on Speech and Language Technologies for Dravidian Languages*, pages 133–145
April 20, 2021 

(Albert et al., 1985; Rajendran, 2004). The writing system of Tamili was explained in the old grammar text Tolkappiyam which dates are various proposed between 9th century BCE to 6nd century BCE (Pillai, 1904; Swamy, 1975; Zvelebil, 1991; Takahashi, 1995) and in the Jaina work Samavayanga Sutta and Pannavana Sutta, these two Jain works date to 3rd-4th century BCE (Salomon, 1998).

Up until around the 15th-century CE, Malayalam was the west coast dialect of Tamil (Blackburn, 2006). Due to geographical isolation by the steep Western Ghats from the main speech community, the dialect eventually evolved into a distinct language by the 15th century (Sekhar, 1951). The first literary work in Malayalam was Ramacaritam ("Deeds of Rama") was written using Tamil Grantha script which was used to write Pali, Prakrit and foreign words in Tamil (Andronov, 1996). The first printed work in an Indian language and script was a Roman Catholic catechism translated by Henrique which is Thambiran Vanakkam (Doctrina Christam en Lingua Malauar Tamul in Portuguese) on 20 October 1,578 CE at Quilon, Venad (present day Kerala) (George, 1972). Similarly, Kannada also split from Tamil by 9th century CE; for example, Taayviru is a term of Kannada origin and is found in a Tamil inscription from the 4th-century CE. The Kappe Arabhatta record of 700 CE is the oldest extant form of Kannada poetry in the Tripadi metre, it is based in part on Kavyadarsha (Rawlinson, 1930; Hande et al., 2020).

However, user-generated content is often adopted to Roman script for typing due to historical reason and modern computer keyboard layouts. Hence, the majority of user-generated data for these Dravidian languages are code-mixed (Priyadharshini et al., 2020; Jose et al., 2020). Due to the growth of social media platforms across the world and the possibility of writing content without any moderation, users write content in multilingual code-switching without grammatical restrictions and using non-native scripts (Chakravarthi et al., 2019). In linguistics, code-switching is switching between two or more language in the same utterance. This explosion of code-mixed user-generated content in the social media platforms aroused interest in NLP. In this paper, we dicuss about the offensive language identification shared task for Tamil, Malayalam and Kannada languages and the participant's submissions.

## 2 Task Description

Offensive language identification for Dravidian languages at different levels of complexity were developed following the work of (Zampieri et al., 2019). It was customized to our annotation method from three-level hierarchical annotation schema. A new category **Not in intended language** was added to include comments written in a language other than the Dravidian languages. Annotations decision for offensive language categories were split into six labels to simplify the annotation process.

- **Not Offensive**: Comment/post does not have offence, obscenity, swearing, or profanity.
- **Offensive Untargeted**: Comment/post have offence, obscenity, swearing, or profanity not directed towards any target. These are the comments/posts which have inadmissible language without targeting anyone.
- **Offensive Targeted Individual**: Comment/post have offence, obscenity, swearing, or profanity which targets an individual.
- **Offensive Targeted Group**: Comment/post have offence, obscenity, swearing, or profanity which targets a group or a community.
- **Offensive Targeted Other**: Comment/post have offence, obscenity, swearing, or profanity which does not belong to any of the previous two classes.
- **Not in indented language**: If the comment is not in the intended language. For example, in the Malayalam task, if the sentence does not contain Malayalam written in Malayalam script or Latin script, then it is not Malayalam.

Sample of not-offensive comments in our dataset provided for the participants is given below with the corresponding English glosses..

- Tamil-English: *Paka thana poro movie la Enna irukunu baki ellam*

  English: "You will see what is the movie"

Sample offensive language text from the dataset

- Tamil-English: *Ghibran p—a vitta ungalukku vera aale kedaika laya da.*

  English: "Dont you get anyone else other than Ghibran V—a"

| Language | Tamil | Malayalam | Kannada |
|---|---|---|---|
| Number of words | 511,734 | 202,134 | 65,702 |
| Vocabulary size | 94,772 | 40,729 | 20,796 |
| Number of comments | 43,919 | 20,010 | 7,772 |
| Number of sentences | 52,617 | 23,652 | 8,586 |
| Average number of words per sentence | 11 | 10 | 8 |
| Average number of sentences per comment | 1 | 1 | 1 |

Table 1: Corpus statistics for Offensive Language Identification

| Class | Tamil | Malayalam | Kannada |
|---|---|---|---|
| Not Offensive | 31,808 | 17,697 | 4,336 |
| Offensive Untargeted | 3,630 | 240 | 278 |
| Offensive Targeted Individual | 2,965 | 290 | 628 |
| Offensive Targeted Group | 3,140 | 176 | 418 |
| Offensive Targeted Others | 590 | - | 153 |
| Not in indented language | 1,786 | 1,607 | 1,898 |
| Total | 43,919 | 20,010 | 7,772 |

Table 2: Offensive language Identification Dataset Distribution.

This is an example of Offensive Targeted Individual. Mr. Ghibran is a popular music composer in Tamil films, and the author tries to insult him.

- Malayalam-English: *Verupikkal manju ullathu ozhichal baki ellam super aanu ee padam.*

  English: "Except the presence of disgusting Manju, everything is super in this movie"

This is an example of Offensive Targeted Individual. Mrs. Manju Warrier is a popular actress in South Indian films, and the author tries to discredit her by clearly mentioning that her presence is disgusting.

- Malayalam-English: *Nalla trailer nu okke keri dislike adikunne ethelum thanthayillathavanmar aayirikum. poyi chavinedey...*

  English: "Those who dislike any trailers will probably be assholes. Go to hell..."

This is an example of Offensive Untargeted comment. This text have inadmissible language without targeting anyone.

### 2.1 Dataset

Data was compiled from different film trailers of Tamil, Kannada, and Malayalam languages from YouTube comments in the year 2019. The *YouTube Comment Scraper tool*[3] was used to collect comments from YouTube social media. These comments were utilized to make the datasets for offensive language identification shared task. We collected comments that contain code-mixing at various levels of the text, with enough representation for each sentiment in all the three languages. *Langdetect library* [4] was used to detect different languages apart and eliminate the unintended languages. Our dataset contains different types of real-time code-mixing due to that fact that data was collected from social media. The dataset contains all forms of code-mixing ranging from purely monolingual texts in native languages to mixing of scripts, words, morphology, inter-sentential and intra-sentential switches.

Dataset statistics (number of words, vocabulary size, number of comments, number of sentences, and average number of words per sentences) are given in Table 1 and class-wise distribution is given in Table 2. From the Table 1 we can see that vocabulary size is very big for Tamil and Malayalam this is due to the code mixing and complex morphology of these languages. Table 2 shows that all languages have the not-offensive class in the majority. In the case of Tamil, 71% of the total comments are not offensive, while Malayalam has

[3]https://github.com/philbot9/youtube-remarkscraper

[4]https://pypi.org/venture/langdetect/

85% non-offensive comments. But there is no consistent trends observable amongst offensive classes across the languages.

### 2.2 Training Phase

In the first phase, data is released for training and or development of offensive language detection models. Participants were given training data and validation dataset for preliminary evaluations or tuning of hyper-parameters. They were also given the option to perform cross-validation on the training data. In total, 119 participant register for the task and downloaded the data.

### 2.3 Evaluation Phase

In the second phase, test sets for evaluation are released for all three languages. Each participating team submitted their generated prediction for evaluation. Predictions are submitted via Google form to the organizing committer to evaluate the systems. CodaLab is an established platform to organize shared-tasks. However, we faced issues with running evaluation, so we choose to evaluate manually. The metrics used for evaluation is the weighted average F1 score.

## 3 Systems

### 3.1 System Descriptions

- Dowlagar and Mamidi (2021) used a pretrained multilingual BERT transformer model with transliteration and class balancing loss for offensive content identification. They have ranked 2nd in Malayalam-English and 4th in Tamil-English languages.

- Li (2021) participated in all three of offensive language identification. They explored multilingual models based on XLM-RoBERTa and multilingual BERT trained on mixed data of three code-mixed languages. They solved the class-imbalance problem existed in the training data by class weights and class combination. Their model achieved a weighted average F1 scores of 0.75 (ranked 4th), 0.94 (ranked 4th) and 0.72 (ranked 3rd) on offensive language identification in code-mixed Tamil-English language, Malayalam-English language and Kannada-English language, respectively.

- Yasaswini et al. (2021) used various transfer learning-based models to classify a given post or comment in Tamil, Malayalam, and Kannada. They have fine-tuned transformer models to get better performance. The relatively high F1-scores of 0.9603, 0.7895 on Malayalam, Tamil were achieved by ULMFiT and 0.7277 on Kannada was achieved by DistilBERT models.

- Vasantharajan and Thayasivam (2021) participated in Tamil, Kannada, and Malayalam language using the BERT fine-tuning strategies. Their model got a 0.96 F1- score for Malayalam, 0.73 F1-score for Tamil, and 0.70 F1-score for Kannada. Moreover, in the view of multilingual models, this modal ranked 3rd and achieved favorable results and confirmed the model as the best among all systems submitted to these shared tasks in these three languages. They got 2nd, 5th, 6th ranks in the leader-board for the Malayalam, Kannada, and Tamil test set respectively.

- Huang and Bai (2021) used the multilingual BERT model to complete in all three languages. For all three language data sets, they combined the Tf-Idf algorithm and the multilingual BERT model's output and introduced the CNN block as a shared layer.

- Zhao (2021) proposed a system based on the multilingual model XLM-Roberta and DPCNN. The test results on the official test data set confirm the effectiveness of their system. They achieved a weighted average F1-score of Kannada, Malayalam, and Tami language of 0.69, 0.92, and 0.76, respectively, ranked 6th, 6th, and 3rd.

- Ghanghor et al. (2021) used multilingual-BERT-base for offensive language identification, their system achieved a weighted F1 scores of 0.75 for Tamil, 0.95 for Malayalam, and 0.71 for Kannada. and ranked 3rd, 3rd and 4th for Tamil, Malayalam and Kannada respectively.

- Chen and Kong (2021) used multilingual BERT and TextCNN for semantic extraction and text classification. The results are not be ideal. They ranked 5th,5th, and 9th for Tamil, Malayalam and Kannada respectively.

- Renjit and Idicula (2021) used language-agnostic BERT (Bidirectional Encoder Rep-

| Team-Name | Precision | Recall | F1 Score | Rank |
|---|---|---|---|---|
| hate-alert (Saha et al., 2021) | 0.78 | 0.78 | 0.78 | 1 |
| indicnlp@kgp (Kedia and Nandy, 2021) | 0.75 | 0.79 | 0.77 | 2 |
| ZYJ123 (Zhao, 2021) | 0.75 | 0.77 | 0.76 | 3 |
| ALI-B2B-AI | 0.75 | 0.78 | 0.76 | 3 |
| SJ-AJ (Jayanthi and Gupta, 2021) | 0.75 | 0.79 | 0.76 | 3 |
| No offense (Awatramani, 2021) | 0.75 | 0.78 | 0.76 | 3 |
| NLP@CUET (Sharif et al., 2021) | 0.75 | 0.78 | 0.76 | 3 |
| Codewithzichao (Li, 2021) | 0.74 | 0.77 | 0.75 | 4 |
| hub (Huang and Bai, 2021) | 0.73 | 0.78 | 0.75 | 4 |
| MUCS (Balouchzahi et al., 2021) | 0.74 | 0.77 | 0.75 | 4 |
| bitions (Tula et al., 2021) | 0.74 | 0.77 | 0.75 | 4 |
| IIITK (Ghanghor et al., 2021) | 0.74 | 0.77 | 0.75 | 4 |
| OFFLangOne (Dowlagar and Mamidi, 2021) | 0.74 | 0.75 | 0.75 | 4 |
| spartans | 0.74 | 0.78 | 0.75 | 4 |
| cs (Chen and Kong, 2021) | 0.74 | 0.75 | 0.74 | 5 |
| Zeus | 0.72 | 0.78 | 0.73 | 6 |
| hypers (Vasantharajan and Thayasivam, 2021) | 0.71 | 0.76 | 0.73 | 6 |
| SSNCSE-NLP (B and Silvia A, 2021) | 0.74 | 0.73 | 0.73 | 6 |
| JUNLP (Garain et al., 2021) | 0.71 | 0.74 | 0.72 | 7 |
| snehan-coursera | 0.7 | 0.73 | 0.71 | 8 |
| IIITT (Yasaswini et al., 2021) | 0.7 | 0.73 | 0.71 | 8 |
| IRNLP-DAIICT (Dave et al., 2021) | 0.72 | 0.77 | 0.71 | 8 |
| CUSATNLP (Renjit and Idicula, 2021) | 0.67 | 0.71 | 0.69 | 9 |
| e8ijs | 0.71 | 0.76 | 0.69 | 9 |
| KU-NLP | 0.66 | 0.75 | 0.67 | 10 |
| cognizyr | 0.68 | 0.74 | 0.66 | 11 |
| Agilna | 0.63 | 0.72 | 0.65 | 12 |
| DLRG | 0.57 | 0.74 | 0.64 | 13 |
| Amrita-CEN-NLP (K et al., 2021) | 0.64 | 0.62 | 0.62 | 14 |
| KBCNMUJAL | 0.75 | 0.56 | 0.62 | 14 |
| JudithJeyafreeda (Andrew, 2021) | 0.54 | 0.73 | 0.61 | 15 |

Table 3: Rank list based on F1-score along with other evaluation metrics (Precision and Recall) for Tamil language

| Team-Name | Precision | Recall | F1 Score | Rank |
|---|---|---|---|---|
| hate-alert (Saha et al., 2021) | 0.97 | 0.97 | 0.97 | 1 |
| MUCS (Balouchzahi et al., 2021) | 0.97 | 0.97 | 0.97 | 1 |
| indicnlp@kgp (Kedia and Nandy, 2021) | 0.97 | 0.97 | 0.97 | 1 |
| bitions (Tula et al., 2021) | 0.97 | 0.97 | 0.97 | 1 |
| hypers (Vasantharajan and Thayasivam, 2021) | 0.96 | 0.96 | 0.96 | 2 |
| ALI-B2B-AI | 0.96 | 0.97 | 0.96 | 2 |
| OFFLangOne (Dowlagar and Mamidi, 2021) | 0.96 | 0.96 | 0.96 | 2 |
| SJ-AJ (Jayanthi and Gupta, 2021) | 0.97 | 0.97 | 0.96 | 2 |
| CUSATNLP (Renjit and Idicula, 2021) | 0.95 | 0.95 | 0.95 | 3 |
| IIITK (Ghanghor et al., 2021) | 0.94 | 0.95 | 0.95 | 3 |
| SSNCSE-NLP (B and Silvia A, 2021) | 0.95 | 0.96 | 0.95 | 3 |
| IRNLP-DAIICT (Dave et al., 2021) | 0.96 | 0.96 | 0.95 | 3 |
| Codewithzichao (Li, 2021) | 0.93 | 0.94 | 0.94 | 4 |
| JudithJeyafreeda (Andrew, 2021) | 0.94 | 0.94 | 0.93 | 5 |
| cs (Chen and Kong, 2021) | 0.92 | 0.94 | 0.93 | 5 |
| Zeus | 0.92 | 0.95 | 0.93 | 5 |
| Maoqin (Yang, 2021) | 0.91 | 0.94 | 0.93 | 5 |
| NLP@CUET (Sharif et al., 2021) | 0.92 | 0.94 | 0.93 | 5 |
| ZYJ123 (Zhao, 2021) | 0.91 | 0.94 | 0.92 | 6 |
| hub (Huang and Bai, 2021) | 0.89 | 0.93 | 0.91 | 7 |
| No offense (Awatramani, 2021) | 0.9 | 0.93 | 0.91 | 7 |
| e8ijs | 0.89 | 0.92 | 0.9 | 8 |
| snehan-coursera | 0.9 | 0.89 | 0.89 | 9 |
| KU-NLP | 0.87 | 0.91 | 0.89 | 9 |
| KBCNMUJAL | 0.93 | 0.88 | 0.89 | 9 |
| IIITT (Yasaswini et al., 2021) | 0.84 | 0.87 | 0.86 | 10 |
| Agilna | 0.85 | 0.88 | 0.86 | 10 |
| Amrita-CEN-NLP (K et al., 2021) | 0.9 | 0.82 | 0.85 | 11 |
| professionals (Nair and Fernandes, 2021) | 0.89 | 0.84 | 0.85 | 11 |
| JUNLP (Garain et al., 2021) | 0.77 | 0.43 | 0.54 | 12 |

Table 4: Rank list based on F1-score along with other evaluation metrics (Precision and Recall) for Malayalam language

| Team-Name | Precision | Recall | F1 Score | Rank |
|---|---|---|---|---|
| SJ-AJ (Jayanthi and Gupta, 2021) | 0.73 | 0.78 | 0.75 | 1 |
| hate-alert (Saha et al., 2021) | 0.76 | 0.76 | 0.74 | 2 |
| indicnlp@kgp(Kedia and Nandy, 2021) | 0.71 | 0.74 | 0.72 | 3 |
| Codewithzichao (Li, 2021) | 0.7 | 0.75 | 0.72 | 3 |
| IIITK (Ghanghor et al., 2021) | 0.7 | 0.75 | 0.72 | 3 |
| e8ijs | 0.7 | 0.74 | 0.71 | 4 |
| NLP@CUET(Sharif et al., 2021) | 0.7 | 0.74 | 0.71 | 4 |
| ALI-B2B-AI | 0.7 | 0.73 | 0.71 | 4 |
| Zeus | 0.66 | 0.75 | 0.7 | 5 |
| hypers (Vasantharajan and Thayasivam, 2021) | 0.69 | 0.72 | 0.7 | 5 |
| bitions (Tula et al., 2021) | 0.69 | 0.72 | 0.7 | 5 |
| SSNCSE-NLP (B and Silvia A, 2021) | 0.71 | 0.74 | 0.7 | 5 |
| MUCS (Balouchzahi et al., 2021) | 0.68 | 0.72 | 0.69 | 6 |
| ZYJ123 (Zhao, 2021) | 0.65 | 0.74 | 0.69 | 6 |
| MUM | 0.69 | 0.71 | 0.69 | 6 |
| JUNLP (Garain et al., 2021) | 0.62 | 0.71 | 0.66 | 7 |
| OFFLangOne (Dowlagar and Mamidi, 2021) | 0.66 | 0.65 | 0.65 | 8 |
| cs (Chen and Kong, 2021) | 0.64 | 0.67 | 0.64 | 9 |
| hub (Huang and Bai, 2021) | 0.65 | 0.69 | 0.64 | 9 |
| No offense (Awatramani, 2021) | 0.62 | 0.7 | 0.64 | 9 |
| IRNLP-DAIICT (Dave et al., 2021) | 0.69 | 0.69 | 0.64 | 9 |
| JudithJeyafreeda (Andrew, 2021) | 0.66 | 0.67 | 0.63 | 10 |
| CUSATNLP (Renjit and Idicula, 2021) | 0.62 | 0.63 | 0.62 | 11 |
| Agilna | 0.58 | 0.65 | 0.59 | 12 |
| Amrita-CEN-NLP (K et al., 2021) | 0.65 | 0.54 | 0.58 | 13 |
| snehan-coursera | 0.56 | 0.61 | 0.54 | 14 |
| KBCNMUJAL | 0.72 | 0.48 | 0.52 | 15 |
| IIITT (Yasaswini et al., 2021) | 0.46 | 0.48 | 0.47 | 16 |
| Simon (Que et al., 2021) | 0.6 | 0.3 | 0.33 | 17 |

Table 5: Rank list based on F1-score along with other evaluation metrics (Precision and Recall) for Kannada language

resentation from Transformers) for sentence embedding and a Softmax classifier. The language-agnostic representation based classification helped obtain good performance for all the three languages, out of which results for the Malayalam language are good enough to obtain a third position among the participating teams.

- K et al. (2021) implemented three deep neural network architectures such as a hybrid network with a Convolutional layer, a Bidirectional Long Short- Term Memory network (Bi-LSTM) layer and a hidden layer, a network containing a Bi- LSTM and another with a Bidirectional Recurrent Neural Network (Bi-RNN). In addition to that, they incorporated a cost-sensitive learning approach to deal with the problem of class imbalance in the training data. Among the three models, the hybrid network exhibited better training performance, and they submitted the predictions based on the same.

- Sharif et al. (2021) employed two machine learning techniques (LR, SVM), three deep learning (LSTM, LSTM+Attention) techniques and three transformers (m-BERT, Indic-BERT, XLM-R) based methods. They showed that XLM-R outperforms other techniques in Tamil and Malayalam languages while m-BERT achieves the highest score in the Kannada language. Their proposed models gained a weighted F1 score of 0.76 (for Tamil), 0.93 (for Malayalam ), and 0.71 (for Kannada) with a rank of 3rd , 5th and 4th respectively.

- Dave et al. (2021) used TF-IDF character n-grams and pretrained MuRIL embeddings for text representation and Logistic Regression and Linear SVM for classification. Their best approach achieved ninth, third and eighth with weighted F1 score of 0.64, 0.95 and 0.71 in Kannada, Malayalam and Tamil on the test dataset respectively.

- Saha et al. (2021) presented an exhaustive exploration of different transformer models, also provided a genetic algorithm technique for ensembling different models. Their ensembled models trained separately for each language secured the first position in Tamil, the second position in Kannada, and the first position in Malayalam sub-tasks.

- Yang (2021) only participate in one of the language task- Malayalam. They used the transformer-based language model with BiGRU-Attention to complete this task. They ranked 5th in this task with a weighted average F1 score of 0.93 on the private leader board.

- Awatramani (2021) participated for Tamil language. They used mBERT-cased and XLM-RoBERTa. Their system was ranked 3 rd in the task leaderboard achieving an F1-score 0.76 for detecting offensive Tamil YouTube comments.

- Nair and Fernandes (2021) used Indic-BERT to generate word embeddings which is then fed into a 4-layer Multi Layer Perceptron (MLP) which does the multi-class classification task and achieve an F1 score of 0.85 for Malayalam language.

- Andrew (2021) did language-specific preprocessing before using several machine learning algorithms. For the Tamil language, they achieve a precision of 0.54, a recall of 0.73 and an F1-score of 0.61, a precision of 0.94, a recall of 0.94 and an F1-score of 0.93 for the Malayalam language and a precision of 0.66, a recall of 0.67 and an F1-score of 0.63 for the Kannada language.

- Que et al. (2021) used the XLM-Roberta model for pre-training for the Kannada language. They scored a very low score of 0.33 weighted

- Tula et al. (2021) proposed a multilingual ensemble based model from ULMFiT, DistilmBERT, and IndicBERT. Their model is able to handle both code-mixed data as well as instances where the script used is mixed (for instance, Tamil and Latin). They ranked number one for Malayalam dataset and ranked 4th and 5th for Tamil and Kannada, respectively.

- Jayanthi and Gupta (2021) system is an ensemble of mBERT and XLM-RoBERTa models which leverage task-adaptive pre-training of multilingual BERT models with a masked language modeling objective. They ranked 1st for Kannada, 2nd for Malayalam and 3rd for Tamil.

- B and Silvia A (2021) described an automatic offensive language identification from Dravidian languages with various machine learning algorithms. They achieved F1 scores of 0.95 for Malayalam, 0.7 for Kannada and 0.73 for task2-Tamil on the test-set.

- Garain et al. (2021) used IndicBERT and BERT architectures, to facilitate identification of offensive languages for Kannada-English, Malayalam-English, and Tamil-English code-mixed language pairs extracted from social media. F1 score for language pair Kannada-English as 0.62, 0.71, and 0.66, respectively, for language pair Malayalam-English as 0.77, 0.43, and 0.53, respectively, and for Tamil-English as 0.71, 0.74, and 0.72, respectively.

- Balouchzahi et al. (2021) Two models, namely, COOLI-ensemble and COOLI-Keras were trained with the char sequences extracted from the sentences combined with words as features. Out of the two proposed models, the COOLI-Ensemble model (best among our models) obtained the first rank for the Ma-En language pair with 0.97 weighted F1- and fourth and sixth rank with a 0.75 and a 0.69 weighted F1-score for Ta-En and Kn-En language pairs respectively.

- Kedia and Nandy (2021) leveraged existing state of the art approaches in text classification by incorporating additional data and transfer learning on pre-trained models. Their final submission is an ensemble of an AWD-LSTM based model along with 2 different transformer model architectures based on BERT and RoBERTa. They achieved weighted- average F1 scores of 0.97, 0.77, and 0.72 in the Malayalam-English, Tamil-English, and Kannada-English datasets ranking 1st, 2nd, and 3rd on the respective tasks.

| Language | Team-Name | Rank |
|---|---|---|
| Tamil | hate-alert | 1 |
| | indicnlp@kgp | 2 |
| | ZYJ123,ALI-B2B-AI, SJ-AJ,No offense, NLP@CUET | 3 |
| Malayalam | hate-alert, MUCS, indicnlp@kgp,bitions | 1 |
| | hypers, ALI-B2B-AI, OFFLangOne,SJ-AJ | 2 |
| | CUSATNLP, IIITK, SSNCSE-NLP, IRNLP-DAIICT | 3 |
| Kannada | SJ-AJ | 1 |
| | hate-alert | 2 |
| | indicnlp@kgp, Codewithzichao, IIITK | 3 |

Table 6: Overall Results with Top Three Ranks

## 4 Results and Discussion

The offensive language identification shared task was organized for three languages Tamil, Malayalam, and Kannada. Many participants connecting to all three languages had submitted their solutions as described in the previous section. Here in this section, we'll be highlighting the results of all three languages, which have ranked top positions on the leaderboard. Table 6 shows the overall results and teams which are placed in the top three positions.

The team hate-alert (Saha et al. (2021)) came at the first position in Tamil and Malayalam languages and second in Kannada as well, and the team indicnlp@kgp (Kedia and Nandy (2021)) came second in Tamil, first in Malayalam, and third in Kannada. The team SJ-AJ (Jayanthi and Gupta (2021)) came at the first position in Kannada and third and second in Tamil and Malayalam respectively.As per the F1-scores apart from Malayalam, the other two languages got scores around 0.75, whereas 0.97 was the former's score. As the vocabulary size of Malayalam is more, it has produced better results compared to Tamil (which is having the maximum), and Kannada, where vocabulary is less but has got similar results to that of Tamil.

## 5 Conclusion

We presented the results of the first shared task on Offensive Language Identification in Tamil, Malayalam, and Kannada relying on a thoroughly annotated data set based on human judgements. The task setup provided an opportunity to test model in multilingual scenarios along with code-mixing phenomenon. However, several teams reach high performance in all three languages. We found out that the type of embedding strongly influence the results. We hope this task and dataset will intrigue and facilitate further research on under-resourced Dravidian languages.

## Acknowledgments

This publication is the outcome of the research supported in part by a research grant from Science Foundation Ireland (SFI) under Grant Number SFI/12/RC/2289_P2 (Insight_2) and 13/RC/2106_P2 (ADAPT), co-funded by the European Regional Development Fund and Irish Research Council grant IRCLA/2017/129 (CARDAMOM-Comparative Deep Models of Language for Minority and Historical Languages).

## References

Devasagayam Albert et al. 1985. *Tolkāppiyam Phonology and Morphology: An English Translation*, volume 115. International Institute of Tamil Studies.

JudithJeyafreeda Andrew. 2021. JudithJeyafreedaAndrew@DravidianLangTech-EACL2021:Offensive language detection for Dravidian Code-mixed YouTube comments. In *Proceedings of the First Workshop on Speech and Language Technologies for Dravidian Languages*. Association for Computational Linguistics.

Mikhail Sergeevich Andronov. 1996. *A grammar of the Malayalam language in historical treatment*, volume 1. Otto Harrassowitz Verlag.

Vasudev Awatramani. 2021. No Offense@DravidianLangTech-EACL2021: Offensive Tamil Identification and beyond the performance . In *Proceedings of the First Workshop on Speech and Language Technologies for Dravidian Languages*. Association for Computational Linguistics.

Bharathi B and Agnusimmaculate Silvia A. 2021. SSNCSE NLP@DravidianLangTech-EACL2021: Offensive Language Identification on Multilingual Code Mixing Text. In *Proceedings of the First Workshop on Speech and Language Technologies for Dravidian Languages*. Association for Computational Linguistics.

Fazlourrahman Balouchzahi, Aparna B K, and H L Shashirekha. 2021. MUCS@DravidianLangTech-EACL2021:COOLI-Code-Mixing Offensive Language Identification. In *Proceedings of the First Workshop on Speech and Language Technologies for Dravidian Languages*. Association for Computational Linguistics.

Matthew Barnidge, Bumsoo Kim, Lindsey A. Sherrill, Žiga Luknar, and Jiehua Zhang. 2019. Perceived exposure to and avoidance of hate speech in various communication settings. *Telematics and Informatics*, 44:101263.

Darina Benikova, Michael Wojatzki, and Torsten Zesch. 2018. What Does This Imply? Examining the Impact of Implicitness on the Perception of Hate Speech. In *Language Technologies for the Challenges of the Digital Age*, pages 171–179, Cham. Springer International Publishing.

Stuart H Blackburn. 2006. *Print, folklore, and nationalism in colonial South India*. Orient Blackswan.

Bharathi Raja Chakravarthi. 2020. *Leveraging orthographic information to improve machine translation of under-resourced languages*. Ph.D. thesis, NUI Galway.

Bharathi Raja Chakravarthi, Mihael Arcan, and John P. McCrae. 2019. Comparison of Different Orthographies for Machine Translation of Under-Resourced Dravidian Languages. In *2nd Conference on Language, Data and Knowledge (LDK 2019)*, volume 70 of *OpenAccess Series in Informatics (OASIcs)*, pages 6:1–6:14, Dagstuhl, Germany. Schloss Dagstuhl–Leibniz-Zentrum fuer Informatik.

Bharathi Raja Chakravarthi, Navya Jose, Shardul Suryawanshi, Elizabeth Sherly, and John Philip McCrae. 2020a. A sentiment analysis dataset for code-mixed Malayalam-English. In *Proceedings of the 1st Joint Workshop on Spoken Language Technologies for Under-resourced languages (SLTU) and Collaboration and Computing for Under-Resourced Languages (CCURL)*, pages 177–184, Marseille, France. European Language Resources association.

Bharathi Raja Chakravarthi, M Anand Kumar, John Philip McCrae, Premjith B, Soman KP, and Thomas Mandl. 2020b. Overview of the track on "HASOC-Offensive Language Identification-DravidianCodeMix". In *Proceedings of the 12th Forum for Information Retrieval Evaluation*, FIRE '20.

Bharathi Raja Chakravarthi, Vigneshwaran Muralidaran, Ruba Priyadharshini, and John Philip McCrae. 2020c. Corpus creation for sentiment analysis in code-mixed Tamil-English text. In *Proceedings of the 1st Joint Workshop on Spoken Language Technologies for Under-resourced languages (SLTU) and Collaboration and Computing for Under-Resourced Languages (CCURL)*, pages 202–210, Marseille, France. European Language Resources association.

Bharathi Raja Chakravarthi, Ruba Priyadharshini, Vigneshwaran Muralidaran, Shardul Suryawanshi, Navya Jose, Elizabeth Sherly, and John P. McCrae. 2020d. Overview of the track on sentiment analysis for dravidian languages in code-mixed text. In *Forum for Information Retrieval Evaluation*, FIRE

2020, page 21–24, New York, NY, USA. Association for Computing Machinery.

Shi Chen and Bing Kong. 2021. cs@DravidianLangTech-EACL2021: Offensive Language Identification Based On Multilingual BERT Model. In *Proceedings of the First Workshop on Speech and Language Technologies for Dravidian Languages*. Association for Computational Linguistics.

Bhargav Dave, Shripad Bhat, and Prasenjit Majumder. 2021. IRNLPDAIICT@DravidianLangTech-EACL2021:Offensive Language identification in Dravidian Languages using TF-IDF Char N-grams and MuRIL . In *Proceedings of the First Workshop on Speech and Language Technologies for Dravidian Languages*. Association for Computational Linguistics.

Suman Dowlagar and Radhika Mamidi. 2021. OFFLangOne@DravidianLangTech-EACL2021: Transformers with the Class Balanced Loss for Offensive Language Identification in Dravidian Code-Mixed text . In *Proceedings of the First Workshop on Speech and Language Technologies for Dravidian Languages*. Association for Computational Linguistics.

Simeon Edosomwan, Sitalaskshmi Kalangot Prakasan, Doriane Kouame, Jonelle Watson, and Tom Seymour. 2011. The history of social media and its impact on business. *Journal of Applied Management and entrepreneurship*, 16(3):79–91.

Avishek Garain, Atanu Mandal, and Sudip Kumar Naskar. 2021. JUNLP@DravidianLangTech-EACL2021: Offensive Language Identification in Dravidian Langauges . In *Proceedings of the First Workshop on Speech and Language Technologies for Dravidian Languages*. Association for Computational Linguistics.

Karimpumannil Mathai George. 1972. *Western influence on Malayalam language and literature*. Sahitya Akademi.

Nikhil Ghanghor, Bharathi Raja Chakravarthi, Ruba Priyadharshini, Sajeetha Thavareesan, and Parameswari Krishnamurthy. 2021. IIITK@DravidianLangTech-EACL2021: Offensive Language Identification and Meme Classification in Tamil, Malayalam and Kannada . In *Proceedings of the First Workshop on Speech and Language Technologies for Dravidian Languages*. Association for Computational Linguistics.

Adeep Hande, Ruba Priyadharshini, and Bharathi Raja Chakravarthi. 2020. KanCMD: Kannada CodeMixed dataset for sentiment analysis and offensive language detection. In *Proceedings of the Third Workshop on Computational Modeling of People's Opinions, Personality, and Emotion's in Social Media*, pages 54–63, Barcelona, Spain (Online). Association for Computational Linguistics.

Bo Huang and Yang Bai. 2021. HUB@DravidianLangTech-EACL2021: Identify and Classify Offensive Text in Multilingual Code Mixing in Social Media. In *Proceedings of the First Workshop on Speech and Language Technologies for Dravidian Languages*. Association for Computational Linguistics.

Sai Muralidhar Jayanthi and Akshat Gupta. 2021. SJAJ@DravidianLangTech-EACL2021: Task-Adaptive Pre-Training of Multilingual BERT models for Offensive Language Identification. In *Proceedings of the First Workshop on Speech and Language Technologies for Dravidian Languages*. Association for Computational Linguistics.

Navya Jose, Bharathi Raja Chakravarthi, Shardul Suryawanshi, Elizabeth Sherly, and John P. McCrae. 2020. A Survey of Current Datasets for Code-Switching Research. In *2020 6th International Conference on Advanced Computing and Communication Systems (ICACCS)*.

Sreelakshmi K, Premjith B, and Soman KP. 2021. AmritaCENNLP@DravidianLangTech-EACL2021: Deep Learning-based Offensive Language Identification in Malayalam, Tamil and Kannada . In *Proceedings of the First Workshop on Speech and Language Technologies for Dravidian Languages*. Association for Computational Linguistics.

Kushal Kedia and Abhilash Nandy. 2021. indicnlp@kgp@DravidianLangTech-EACL2021: Offensive Language Identification in Dravidian Languages . In *Proceedings of the First Workshop on Speech and Language Technologies for Dravidian Languages*. Association for Computational Linguistics.

Teo Keipi, Matti Näsi, Atte Oksanen, and Pekka Räsänen. 2016. *Online hate and harmful content: Cross-national perspectives*. Taylor & Francis.

Vishnupriya Kolipakam, Fiona M Jordan, Michael Dunn, Simon J Greenhill, Remco Bouckaert, Russell D Gray, and Annemarie Verkerk. 2018. A bayesian phylogenetic study of the dravidian language family. *Royal Society open science*, 5(3):171504.

Bhadriraju Krishnamurti. 2003. *The Dravidian languages*. Cambridge University Press.

Ritesh Kumar, Atul Kr. Ojha, Shervin Malmasi, and Marcos Zampieri. 2018. Benchmarking aggression identification in social media. In *Proceedings of the First Workshop on Trolling, Aggression and Cyberbullying (TRAC-2018)*, pages 1–11, Santa Fe, New Mexico, USA. Association for Computational Linguistics.

Zichao Li. 2021. Codewithzichao@DravidianLangTech-EACL2021: Exploring Multilingual Transformers for Offensive Language Identification on Code Mixing Text . In *Proceedings of the First Workshop on Speech and Language Technologies for Dravidian Languages*. Association for Computational Linguistics.

Ishani Maitra and Mary Kate McGowan. 2012. *Speech and harm: Controversies over free speech*. Oxford University Press on Demand.

Thomas Mandl, Sandip Modha, Anand Kumar M, and Bharathi Raja Chakravarthi. 2020. Overview of the HASOC Track at FIRE 2020: Hate Speech and Offensive Language Identification in Tamil, Malayalam, Hindi, English and German. In *Forum for Information Retrieval Evaluation*, FIRE 2020, page 29–32, New York, NY, USA. Association for Computing Machinery.

Srinath Nair and Dolton Fernandes. 2021. professionals@DravidianLangTech-EACL2021. In *Proceedings of the First Workshop on Speech and Language Technologies for Dravidian Languages*. Association for Computational Linguistics.

Endang Wahyu Pamungkas, Valerio Basile, and Viviana Patti. 2020. Do You Really Want to Hurt Me? Predicting Abusive Swearing in Social Media. In *Proceedings of the 12th Language Resources and Evaluation Conference*, pages 6237–6246, Marseille, France. European Language Resources Association.

Desmond Upton Patton, Robert D. Eschmann, and Dirk A. Butler. 2013. Internet banging: New trends in social media, gang violence, masculinity and hip hop. *Computers in Human Behavior*, 29(5):A54 – A59.

MS Purnalingam Pillai. 1904. *A Primer of Tamil Literature*. Ananda Press.

Ruba Priyadharshini, Bharathi Raja Chakravarthi, Mani Vegupatti, and John P. McCrae. 2020. Named entity recognition for code-mixed Indian corpus using meta embedding. In *2020 6th International Conference on Advanced Computing and Communication Systems (ICACCS)*.

Qinyu Que, Gang Wang, and Shuangjun Jia. 2021. Simon @ DravidianLangTech-EACL2021: Detecting Offensive Content in Kannada Language . In *Proceedings of the First Workshop on Speech and Language Technologies for Dravidian Languages*. Association for Computational Linguistics.

S Rajendran. 2004. Strategies in the formation of compound nouns in tamil. *Languages Of India*, 4.

HG Rawlinson. 1930. The kadamba kula—a history of ancient and mediæval karnataka.(studies in indian history of the indian historical research institute, st. xavier's college, bombay, no. 5).

Sara Renjit and Sumam Mary Idicula. 2021. CUSATNLP@DravidianLangTech-EACL2021:Language Agnostic Classification of Offensive Content in Tweets. In *Proceedings of the First Workshop on Speech and Language Technologies for Dravidian Languages*. Association for Computational Linguistics.

Debjoy Saha, Naman Paharia, Debajit Chakraborty, Punyajoy Saha, and Animesh Mukherjee. 2021. Hate-Alert@DravidianLangTech-EACL2021: Ensembling strategies for Transformer-based Offensive language Detection . In *Proceedings of the First Workshop on Speech and Language Technologies for Dravidian Languages*. Association for Computational Linguistics.

Richard Salomon. 1998. *Indian epigraphy: a guide to the study of inscriptions in Sanskrit, Prakrit, and the other Indo-Aryan languages*. Oxford University Press on Demand.

A. C. Sekhar. 1951. [Evolution of Malayalam]. *Bulletin of the Deccan College Research Institute*, 12(1/2):1–216.

Omar Sharif, Eftekhar Hossain, and Mohammed Moshiul Hoque. 2021. NLP-CUET@DravidianLangTech-EACL2021: Offensive Language Detection from Multilingual Code-Mixed Text using Transformers. In *Proceedings of the First Workshop on Speech and Language Technologies for Dravidian Languages*. Association for Computational Linguistics.

R Sivanantham and M Seran. 2019. Keeladi: An Urban Settlement of Sangam Age on the Banks of River Vaigai. *India: Department of Archaeology, Government of Tamil Nadu, Chennai*.

BGL Swamy. 1975. The Date of Tolkappiyam: A Retrospect. *Annals of Oriental Research (Madras), Silver Jubilee*, 292:317.

Takanobu Takahashi. 1995. *Tamil love poetry and poetics*, volume 9. Brill.

Sajeetha Thavareesan and Sinnathamby Mahesan. 2019. Sentiment Analysis in Tamil Texts: A Study on Machine Learning Techniques and Feature Representation. In *2019 14th Conference on Industrial and Information Systems (ICIIS)*, pages 320–325.

Sajeetha Thavareesan and Sinnathamby Mahesan. 2020a. Sentiment Lexicon Expansion using Word2vec and fastText for Sentiment Prediction in Tamil texts. In *2020 Moratuwa Engineering Research Conference (MERCon)*, pages 272–276.

Sajeetha Thavareesan and Sinnathamby Mahesan. 2020b. Word embedding-based Part of Speech tagging in Tamil texts. In *2020 IEEE 15th International Conference on Industrial and Information Systems (ICIIS)*, pages 478–482.

Debapriya Tula, Prathyush Potluri, Shreyas MS, Sumanth Doddapaneni, Pranjal Sahu, Rohan Sukumaran, and Parth Patwa. 2021. Bitions@DravidianLangTech-EACL2021: Ensemble of Multilingual Language Models with

Pseudo Labeling for Offense Detection in Dravidian Languages. In *Proceedings of the First Workshop on Speech and Language Technologies for Dravidian Languages*. Association for Computational Linguistics.

Charangan Vasantharajan and Uthayasanker Thayasivam. 2021. Hypers@DravidianLangTech-EACL2021: Offensive language identification in Dravidian code-mixed YouTube Comments and Posts. In *Proceedings of the First Workshop on Speech and Language Technologies for Dravidian Languages*. Association for Computational Linguistics.

Maoqin Yang. 2021. Maoqin @ DravidianLangTech-EACL2021: The Application of Transformer-Based Model . In *Proceedings of the First Workshop on Speech and Language Technologies for Dravidian Languages*. Association for Computational Linguistics.

Konthala Yasaswini, Karthik Puranik, Adeep Hande, Ruba Priyadharshini, Sajeetha Thavareesan, and Bharathi Raja Chakravarthi. 2021. IIITT@DravidianLangTech-EACL2021: Transfer Learning for Offensive Language Detection in Dravidian Languages . In *Proceedings of the First Workshop on Speech and Language Technologies for Dravidian Languages*. Association for Computational Linguistics.

Marcos Zampieri, Shervin Malmasi, Preslav Nakov, Sara Rosenthal, Noura Farra, and Ritesh Kumar. 2019. Predicting the type and target of offensive posts in social media. In *Proceedings of the 2019 Conference of the North American Chapter of the Association for Computational Linguistics: Human Language Technologies, Volume 1 (Long and Short Papers)*, pages 1415–1420, Minneapolis, Minnesota. Association for Computational Linguistics.

Marcos Zampieri, Preslav Nakov, Sara Rosenthal, Pepa Atanasova, Georgi Karadzhov, Hamdy Mubarak, Leon Derczynski, Zeses Pitenis, and Çağrı Çöltekin. 2020. SemEval-2020 task 12: Multilingual offensive language identification in social media (OffensEval 2020). In *Proceedings of the Fourteenth Workshop on Semantic Evaluation*, pages 1425–1447, Barcelona (online). International Committee for Computational Linguistics.

Yingjia Zhao. 2021. ZYJ123@DravidianLangTech-EACL2021: Offensive Language Identification based on XLM-RoBERTa with DPCNN. In *Proceedings of the First Workshop on Speech and Language Technologies for Dravidian Languages*. Association for Computational Linguistics.

Kamil V Zvelebil. 1991. Comments on the Tolkappiyam Theory of Literature. *Archív Orientální*, 59:345–359.

# GX@DravidianLangTech-EACL2021: Multilingual Neural Machine Translation and Back-Translation

**Wanying Xie**
Beijing Language and Culture University, China
xiewanying07@gmail.com

## Abstract

In this paper, we describe the GX system in the EACL2021 shared task on machine translation in Dravidian languages. Given the low amount of parallel training data, We adopt two methods to improve the overall performance: (1) *multilingual translation*, we use a shared encoder-decoder multilingual translation model handling multiple languages simultaneously to facilitate the translation performance of these languages; (2) *back-translation*, we collected other open-source parallel and monolingual data and apply back-translation to benefit from the monolingual data. The experimental results show that we can achieve good translation results in these Dravidian languages and rank first in the four translation directions on the ranklist.

## 1 Introduction

In recent years, encoder-decoder based on neural machine translation (NMT) has become the mainstream paradigm in the field of machine translation (Kalchbrenner and Blunsom, 2013; Sutskever et al., 2014; Bahdanau et al., 2015; Gehring et al., 2017). The Transformer model (Vaswani et al., 2017), which is completely based on self-attention mechanism, is the best model architecture for translation performance. However, these data-driven neural machine translation depends heavily on large-scale annotated parallel data, the translation performance of low-resource languages remains a concern (Zoph et al., 2016). One such language family is the Dravidian family of languages, which are under-resourced in speech and natural language processing (Chakravarthi et al., 2021). The Dravidian languages are first attested in the 6th century BCE as Tamili [1] script inscribed on the cave walls and pottery in the Madurai and Tirunelveli districts of Tamil Nadu. The Dravidian languages with the most speakers are Tamil, Kannada and Malayalam, of which Tamil have long literary traditions from 600 BCE.

In this paper, we adopt two approaches to get a reliable translation for improving access to and production of information for monolingual speakers of Dravidian languages. The first approach is multilingual translation. Compared with translating from a resource-poor language to English, translating from English to a resource-poor language is much more difficult. Translating from a resource-poor language to English, can apply transfer learning to make use of large parallel corpora between English and other languages (Zoph et al., 2016; Chakravarthi, 2020). However, the situation of translating from English to a resource-poor language is tough because there is little parallel data for the target language and other languages.

In the case of low resources, the multilingual translation method is often better than the performance of individual language pair, because too little data makes it difficult for the model to converge to the best (Dong et al., 2015; Tan et al., 2019; Chakravarthi et al., 2019b,a). The other approach is back-translation.Data augmentation methods can help alleviate this resource shortage by increasing the amount of data. Back-translation is a typical method of data augmentation that can enrich training data with monolingual data. These work are often based on automatically creating pseudo-parallel sentences through back-translation (Irvine and Callison-Burch, 2013; Sennrich et al., 2016a; Feldman and Coto-Solano, 2020).

For the EACL2021 shared task on machine translation in Dravidian languages, we present our results on the four language pairs: English-Tamil, English-Malayalam, English-Telugu, and Tamil-Telugu. Overall, the four language pairs can be divided into two subtasks: *between English and Dravidian languages* and *between Dravidian Lan-*

[1] also called Damili or Tamil Bhrami



*Proceedings of the First Workshop on Speech and Language Technologies for Dravidian Languages*, pages 146–153
April 20, 2021 

*guages*. To get better performance, we implement a translation system for each subtask. Since the systems are not constrained using exclusive data provided by the task's organization, we collect other open-source monolingual data of Tamil, Malayalam, and Telugu. We use back-translation to create pseudo-parallel sentences. Based on official and pseudo-parallel data, we train multilingual models to perform the translation task.

## 2 Background

We briefly describe neural machine translation model here. Given the source sentence $\mathbf{x} = (x_1, \ldots, x_I)$ and the corresponding target sentence $\mathbf{y} = (y_1, \ldots, y_J)$, a standard NMT model directly optimizes the conditional probability:

$$P(\mathbf{y} \mid \mathbf{x}; \theta) = \prod_{j=1}^{J} P\left(y_j \mid \mathbf{y}_{<j}, \mathbf{x}; \theta\right) \quad (1)$$

where $\theta$ is the set of the model parameters and $\mathbf{y}_{<j}$ denotes the partial translation. The architecture of machine translation model is the neural network based encoder-decoder framework (Sutskever et al., 2014). The input sentence $\mathbf{x}$ will be first converted to a sequence of vectors and fed into the encoder. Then the Encoder generates a context vector which is an accumulation of the hidden state information related to each source language word. The decoder decodes the target language words from this context vector. Typically, this framework can be implemented as recurrent neural network (RNN) (Bahdanau et al., 2015), convolutional neural network (CNN) (Gehring et al., 2017) and Transformer (Vaswani et al., 2017). The parameters of the NMT model are trained to maximize the likelihood of a set of training examples $L = \{[\mathbf{x}^m, \mathbf{y}^m]\}_{m=1}^{M}$:

$$\mathcal{L}(\theta) = \arg\max_{\theta} \sum_{m=1}^{M} \log P\left(\mathbf{y}^m \mid \mathbf{x}^m; \theta\right) \quad (2)$$

where $M$ is the amount of training samples.

## 3 Data Preparation

The data of Dravidian languages provided by the organizers are scarce, with only tens or hundreds of thousands of parallel sentences per language pair, which is shown in Table 1. In general, it is difficult to train a well-performing translation model with such a small amount of data, because it is difficult for the model to learn enough translation knowledge and ability.

| **Official** | En-Ta | En-Te | En-Ml | Ta-Te |
|---|---|---|---|---|
| Release | 28417 | 23222 | 382868 | 17155 |

Table 1: Statistics of the official published data for each language pair.

| **Parallel** | En-Ta | En-Te | En-Ml |
|---|---|---|---|
| Wiki Titles v2 | 102142 | - | - |
| PMIndia v1 | 33669 | 40283 | 33669 |
| Tanzil v1 | 93540 | - | 187081 |
| NLPC_UOM | 8949 | - | - |
| UFAL EnTam | 166871 | - | - |
| **Monolingual** | Ta | Te | Ml |
| PMIndia v1 | 97216 | 118274 | 88244 |

Table 2: Statistics of other open source datasets, including paraller and monolingual data.

In this work, all proposed systems are allowed to use data other than those provided by the task organizer. Therefore, We use other open-source datasets, including Wiki Titles v2[2], PMIndia v1[3], Tanzil v1 (Tiedemann, 2012), The NLPC_UOM En-Ta corpus and glossary (v1.0.3) (Fernando et al., 2020) and The UFAL EnTam corpus (Ramasamy et al., 2012). As monolingual data, we use the data of PMIndia v1. See Table 2 for statistics imformation.

Sentences of English were tokenized by the Moses scripts[4]. All non-English data were tokenized by the Indic NLP Library tool (Kunchukuttan, 2020), which is a library to provide a general solution to very commonly required toolsets for Indian language text. Then, all sentences further segmented into subword symbols using Byte-Pair Encoding (BPE) rules (Sennrich et al., 2016b) with 40K merge operations for all languages jointly.

## 4 System Description

In this section, we will describe our translation system with the adapted methods in detail for different categories of translation direction, including *between English and Dravidian languages* and *between Dravidian Languages*.

[2]http://data.statmt.org/wikititles/v2/

[3]http://data.statmt.org/pmindia/

[4]http://www.statmt.org/moses/

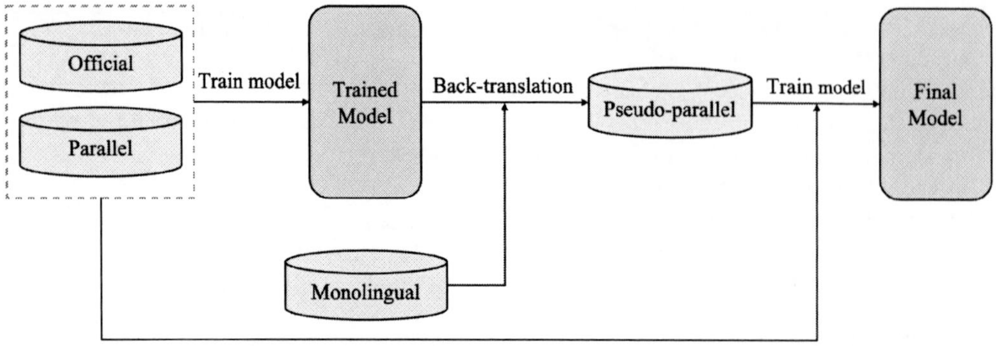


Figure 1: The whole training process of the proposed system. The orange data represents official data shown in Table 1, which is released by the organizers. The blue datasets represent other open-source data shown in Table 2. The green data represents pseudo-parallel data which is generated by applying back-translation on monolingual data.

### 4.1 Between English and Dravidian Languages

In this part, there are three language pairs: English-Tamil, English-Malayalam, and English-Telugu. There is a one-to-three multilingual neural machine translation model for these three language pairs.

As shown in Figure 1, we first train a Three-to-En multilingual neural machine translation model by the sum of the data of the organizer and we collected (that is, the sum data of Official data in Table 1 and Parallel data in Tabel 2). With this well-trained translation model, we adapt back-translation method on the monolingual data of Tamil, Malayalam, and Telugu (that is, Monolingual data in Tabel 2) to generate pseudo-parallel sentences. Finally, we train an English-to-Three multilingual translation model based on the sum of the real and pseudo parallel corpora as our final model.

### 4.2 Between Dravidian Languages

Tamil-Telugu is the most difficult one because this language pair has very little parallel and monolingual data. There is a four-to-four multilingual neural machine translation model for this language pair.

It has been shown that it is helpful to improve the overall performance when similar languages or languages in the same language family are trained together (Tan et al., 2019). Therefore, to facilitate this low resource translation language pair, we combine all the bilingual corpora to train a multilingual model. As shown in Figure 1, first, on the parallel data released by the organizer and we collected (that is, the sum data of Official data in Table 1 and Parallel data in Tabel 2), we train a four-to-four multilingual neural machine translation model with eight directions of English↔Tamil, English↔Malayalam, English↔Telugu and Tamil↔Telugu. Then, pseudo-parallel sentences were generated by this multilingual on monolingual data of Telugu. Finally, we train a multilingual translation model of these eight directions based on the sum of all languages data as our final model.

## 5 Experiments

We first introduce the training details and empirically evaluate the systems in two scenarios.

### 5.1 Training Details

We implemented all proposed systems on the advanced Transformer (Vaswani et al., 2017) model using the open-source toolkit *Fairseq-py* (Ott et al., 2019), which consists of 6 stacked encoder/decoder layers with the layer size being 512 and 4 heads in each attention layer and feedforward network size being 1024. All the models were trained on 4 GeForce RTX 3090, with 24GB memory, where each was allocated with a batch size of 2,000 tokens for these two scenarios. We trained the model with dropout = 0.3 and using Adam optimizer (Kingma and Ba, 2015) with $\beta_1 = 0.9$, $\beta_2 = 0.98$, and $\epsilon = 10^{-9}$. For evaluation, we average the last 5 checkpoints saved and use beam search with a beam size of 5 and length penalty $\alpha = 0.6$. The translation quality of development sets was evaluated using the multi-bleu.pl scipt (Papineni et al., 2002) based on n-gram matching with n up to 4.

| Systems | En-Ta | Δ | En-Te | Δ | En-Ml | Δ | Ta-Te | Δ |
|---|---|---|---|---|---|---|---|---|
| Individual | 32.92 | - | 34.62 | - | 24.82 | - | 28.63 | - |
| Multilingual | 47.97 | 15.05 | 40.39 | 5.77 | 25.01 | 0.19 | 54.97 | 26.34 |
| +Monolingual | 50.51 | 2.53 | 45.35 | 4.96 | 25.85 | 0.84 | 58.23 | 3.26 |
| +Checkpoint Avg | 50.70 | 0.21 | 45.65 | 0.30 | 25.87 | 0.02 | 58.27 | 0.04 |

Table 3: Results of development sets measured in BLEU on the Dravidian languages Translation task. Δ means the difference between the current result and the previous row. Individual means an separate NMT model for each language pair without any other approaches. Multilingual means Multi-NMT models for the two tasks without other approaches.

## 5.2 Systems

The specific meanings of each system in the experiment are as follows:

**Individual** A NMT model is trained for each language pair. Therefore, there are 4 different models for the translation directions.

**Multilingual** (Johnson et al., 2017) Handling multiple languages in a single transformer model which contains one encoder and one decoder with a special language indicator added to the input sentence.

**+Monolingual** Add the monolingual data on the Multilingual system. It is the back-translation method, which are introduced in Section 4.

**+Checkpoint Avg** On the basis of +Monolingual system, we average the last 5 checkpoints to get the final model.

## 5.3 Results

In this section we will introduce the results of development sets and test sets.

**Development Sets** The development sets results of the four directions are reported in Table 3. We will discuss the two parts of the results separately.

Between English and Dravidian Languages, there is a huge boost between multilingual and individual, which up to 15.05 in En→Ta. This also proves that it is difficult to achieve good results that train an individual translation model only on low-resource language pairs. While multilingual neural machine translation, especially training on multiple similar languages, will greatly improve the translation performance of low-resource language pairs. Moreover, the addition of pseudo-parallel corpus generated by monolingual data can also bring improvement, but the improvement is relatively weak. This may be because the monolingual data is not enough, and the parallel sentence requirements of training excellent models still cannot be met. Besides, checkpoint average also improves the translation performance but the increase is very low. It is worth noting that the En→Ml is not highly promoted by our method. This may be because the parallel sentences are more than other languages so that it is difficult to gain knowledge from multilingual translation and other approaches to improve.

| Systems | En-Ta | En-Te | En-Ml | Ta-Te |
|---|---|---|---|---|
| Ours | 36.66 | 38.86 | 19.84 | 35.29 |

Table 4: Results of test sets measured in BLEU on the Dravidian languages translation task.

Between Dravidian Languages, the translation performance of Ta→Te benefit a lot from multilingual translation. That is because individual baseline trained on extremely low resources hard to get a good performance and the directions training samples of Ta→En and En→Te may boost the performance of Ta→Te when training a multilingual neural machine translation model. At the same time, other approaches such as back-translation and checkpoint average also improve the overall translation quality.

**Test Sets** We evaluate the test set using the model that works best on the validation set, the final model that **+Checkpoint Avg** produced. The results are shown in Table 4. Surprisingly, all systems score low on the test sets, presumably because the validation set was easy and the test set was hard. In the ranklist given by the organizer, our system ranks first in all four translation directions, but our system did not perform particularly well. Other competitors' systems also struggled to perform well, which shows that Dravidian languages translation is a difficult task. To obtain a satisfactory translation result, we still have a lot of effort to do.

## 6 Related Work

There are several ways focusing on low-resource translation, including: (a) learning knowledge from high-resource pairs to promotes low-resource translation, such as transfer learning, transferring proper parameters (Zoph et al., 2016; Gu et al., 2018b), lexical knowledge(Nguyen and Chiang, 2017; Lakew et al., 2018) and syntactic knowledge (Gu et al., 2018a; Murthy et al., 2019) from high-resource language, and multilingual translation, including sharing encoders (Dong et al., 2015), sharing decoders (Zoph et al., 2016), sharing sublayers (Firat et al., 2016) and an universal Multi-NMT model with a target language token to indicate the translation direction (Ha et al., 2016; Johnson et al., 2017); (b) data augmentation in NMT, such as back-translation (BT) translates target-language monolingual text to create synthetic parallel sentences (Irvine and Callison-Burch, 2013; Sennrich et al., 2016a) and adding an auxiliary auto-encoding task on monolingual data (Cheng et al., 2016; Currey et al., 2017).

Also, Indian languages have been studied in recent years (Tennage et al., 2017; Chakravarthi et al., 2018; Kumar and Singh, 2019; Barrault et al., 2020). Choudhary et al. (2018) show that subword units mehtod is helpful when translation Tamil language. Escolano et al. (2020) adopt a multilingual adaptation method to benefit from the positive transfer from high resource languages in English and Tamil translation. Bao et al. (2020) explore pre-training and iterative back translation for low-resource English-Tamil. Chen et al. (2020) explore self-supervised model pretraining, multilingual models, data augmentation, and reranking techniques to solve the low resource problem.

## 7 Conclusion

In this paper, we describe the GX system in the Dravidian translation task of EACL2021. We use two main methods, multilingual translation and back-translation, to enable the model to benefit from multiple languages joint learning and monolingual data. Experimental results show that the system can successfully introduce multilingual neural machine translation and back-translation on monolingual data and improve the performance of the system.

## Acknowledgments

We would like to thank the anonymous reviewers for their insightful comments. We thank Shuhao Gu for his helpful suggestions and inspiration.

## References

Dzmitry Bahdanau, Kyunghyun Cho, and Yoshua Bengio. 2015. Neural machine translation by jointly learning to align and translate. In *3rd International Conference on Learning Representations, ICLR 2015, San Diego, CA, USA, May 7-9, 2015, Conference Track Proceedings*.

Calvin Bao, Yow-Ting Shiue, Chujun Song, Jie Li, and Marine Carpuat. 2020. The university of maryland's submissions to the WMT20 chat translation task: Searching for more data to adapt discourse-aware neural machine translation. In *Proceedings of the Fifth Conference on Machine Translation, WMT@EMNLP 2020, Online, November 19-20, 2020*, pages 456–461. Association for Computational Linguistics.

Loïc Barrault, Magdalena Biesialska, Ondrej Bojar, Marta R. Costa-jussà, Christian Federmann, Yvette Graham, Roman Grundkiewicz, Barry Haddow, Matthias Huck, Eric Joanis, Tom Kocmi, Philipp Koehn, Chi-kiu Lo, Nikola Ljubesic, Christof Monz, Makoto Morishita, Masaaki Nagata, Toshiaki Nakazawa, Santanu Pal, Matt Post, and Marcos Zampieri. 2020. Findings of the 2020 conference on machine translation (WMT20). In *Proceedings of the Fifth Conference on Machine Translation, WMT@EMNLP 2020, Online, November 19-20, 2020*, pages 1–55. Association for Computational Linguistics.

Bharathi Raja Chakravarthi. 2020. *Leveraging orthographic information to improve machine translation of under-resourced languages*. Ph.D. thesis, NUI Galway.

Bharathi Raja Chakravarthi, Mihael Arcan, and John P. McCrae. 2018. Improving wordnets for under-resourced languages using machine translation. In *Proceedings of the 9th Global Wordnet Conference*, pages 77–86, Nanyang Technological University (NTU), Singapore. Global Wordnet Association.

Bharathi Raja Chakravarthi, Mihael Arcan, and John P. McCrae. 2019a. WordNet gloss translation for under-resourced languages using multilingual neural machine translation. In *Proceedings of the Second Workshop on Multilingualism at the Intersection of Knowledge Bases and Machine Translation*, pages 1–7, Dublin, Ireland. European Association for Machine Translation.

Bharathi Raja Chakravarthi, Ruba Priyadharshini, Shubhanker Banerjee, Richard Saldhana, John Philip McCrae, Anand Kumar M, Parameswari Krishnamurthy, and Melvin Johnson. 2021. Findings of the shared task on Machine Translation in Dravidian languages. In *Proceedings of the First Workshop on Speech and Language Technologies for Dravidian Languages*. Association for Computational Linguistics.

Bharathi Raja Chakravarthi, Ruba Priyadharshini, Bernardo Stearns, Arun Jayapal, Sridevy S, Mihael Arcan, Manel Zarrouk, and John P McCrae. 2019b. Multilingual multimodal machine translation for Dravidian languages utilizing phonetic transcription. In *Proceedings of the 2nd Workshop on Technologies for MT of Low Resource Languages*, pages 56–63, Dublin, Ireland. European Association for Machine Translation.

Peng-Jen Chen, Ann Lee, Changhan Wang, Naman Goyal, Angela Fan, Mary Williamson, and Jiatao Gu. 2020. Facebook ai's WMT20 news translation task submission. In *Proceedings of the Fifth Conference on Machine Translation, WMT@EMNLP 2020, Online, November 19-20, 2020*, pages 113–125. Association for Computational Linguistics.

Yong Cheng, Wei Xu, Zhongjun He, Wei He, Hua Wu, Maosong Sun, and Yang Liu. 2016. Semi-supervised learning for neural machine translation. In *Proceedings of the 54th Annual Meeting of the Association for Computational Linguistics, ACL 2016, August 7-12, 2016, Berlin, Germany, Volume 1: Long Papers*. The Association for Computer Linguistics.

Himanshu Choudhary, Aditya Kumar Pathak, Rajiv Ratan Saha, and Ponnurangam Kumaraguru. 2018. Neural machine translation for english-tamil. In *Proceedings of the Third Conference on Machine Translation: Shared Task Papers, WMT 2018, Belgium, Brussels, October 31 - November 1, 2018*, pages 770–775. Association for Computational Linguistics.

Anna Currey, Antonio Valerio Miceli Barone, and Kenneth Heafield. 2017. Copied monolingual data improves low-resource neural machine translation. In *Proceedings of the Second Conference on Machine Translation, WMT 2017, Copenhagen, Denmark, September 7-8, 2017*, pages 148–156. Association for Computational Linguistics.

Daxiang Dong, Hua Wu, Wei He, Dianhai Yu, and Haifeng Wang. 2015. Multi-task learning for multiple language translation. In *Proceedings of the 53rd Annual Meeting of the Association for Computational Linguistics and the 7th International Joint Conference on Natural Language Processing of the Asian Federation of Natural Language Processing, ACL 2015, July 26-31, 2015, Beijing, China, Volume 1: Long Papers*, pages 1723–1732.

Carlos Escolano, Marta R. Costa-jussà, and José A. R. Fonollosa. 2020. The TALP-UPC system description for WMT20 news translation task: Multilingual adaptation for low resource MT. In *Proceedings of the Fifth Conference on Machine Translation, WMT@EMNLP 2020, Online, November 19-20, 2020*, pages 134–138. Association for Computational Linguistics.

Isaac Feldman and Rolando Coto-Solano. 2020. Neural machine translation models with back-translation for the extremely low-resource indigenous language bribri. In *Proceedings of the 28th International Conference on Computational Linguistics, COLING 2020, Barcelona, Spain (Online), December 8-13, 2020*, pages 3965–3976. International Committee on Computational Linguistics.

Aloka Fernando, Surangika Ranathunga, and Gihan Dias. 2020. Data augmentation and terminology integration for domain-specific sinhala-english-tamil statistical machine translation. *CoRR*, abs/2011.02821.

Orhan Firat, Kyunghyun Cho, and Yoshua Bengio. 2016. Multi-way, multilingual neural machine translation with a shared attention mechanism. In *NAACL HLT 2016, The 2016 Conference of the North American Chapter of the Association for Computational Linguistics: Human Language Technologies, San Diego California, USA, June 12-17, 2016*, pages 866–875.

Jonas Gehring, Michael Auli, David Grangier, Denis Yarats, and Yann N. Dauphin. 2017. Convolutional sequence to sequence learning. In *Proceedings of the 34th International Conference on Machine Learning, ICML 2017, Sydney, NSW, Australia, 6-11 August 2017*, pages 1243–1252.

Jiatao Gu, Hany Hassan, Jacob Devlin, and Victor O. K. Li. 2018a. Universal neural machine translation for extremely low resource languages. In *Proceedings of the 2018 Conference of the North American Chapter of the Association for Computational Linguistics: Human Language Technologies, NAACL-HLT 2018, New Orleans, Louisiana, USA, June 1-6, 2018, Volume 1 (Long Papers)*, pages 344–354.

Jiatao Gu, Yong Wang, Yun Chen, Victor O. K. Li, and Kyunghyun Cho. 2018b. Meta-learning for low-resource neural machine translation. In *Proceedings of the 2018 Conference on Empirical Methods in Natural Language Processing, Brussels, Belgium, October 31 - November 4, 2018*, pages 3622–3631. Association for Computational Linguistics.

Thanh-Le Ha, Jan Niehues, and Alexander H. Waibel. 2016. Toward multilingual neural machine translation with universal encoder and decoder. *CoRR*, abs/1611.04798.

Ann Irvine and Chris Callison-Burch. 2013. Combining bilingual and comparable corpora for low resource machine translation. In *Proceedings of the Eighth Workshop on Statistical Machine Translation, WMT@ACL 2013, August 8-9, 2013, Sofia, Bulgaria*, pages 262–270. The Association for Computer Linguistics.

Melvin Johnson, Mike Schuster, Quoc V. Le, Maxim Krikun, Yonghui Wu, Zhifeng Chen, Nikhil Thorat, Fernanda B. Viégas, Martin Wattenberg, Greg Corrado, Macduff Hughes, and Jeffrey Dean. 2017. Google's multilingual neural machine translation system: Enabling zero-shot translation. *TACL*, 5:339–351.

Nal Kalchbrenner and Phil Blunsom. 2013. Recurrent continuous translation models. In *Proceedings of the 2013 Conference on Empirical Methods in Natural Language Processing, EMNLP 2013, 18-21 October 2013, Grand Hyatt Seattle, Seattle, Washington, USA, A meeting of SIGDAT, a Special Interest Group of the ACL*, pages 1700–1709.

Diederik P. Kingma and Jimmy Ba. 2015. Adam: A method for stochastic optimization. In *3rd International Conference on Learning Representations, ICLR 2015, San Diego, CA, USA, May 7-9, 2015, Conference Track Proceedings*.

Amit Kumar and Anil Kumar Singh. 2019. NLPRL at WAT2019: transformer-based tamil - english indic task neural machine translation system. In *Proceedings of the 6th Workshop on Asian Translation, WAT@EMNLP-IJCNLP 2019, Hong Kong, China, November 4, 2019*, pages 171–174. Association for Computational Linguistics.

Anoop Kunchukuttan. 2020. The IndicNLP Library. `https://github.com/anoopkunchukuttan/indic_nlp_library/blob/master/docs/indicnlp.pdf`.

Surafel Melaku Lakew, Aliia Erofeeva, Matteo Negri, Marcello Federico, and Marco Turchi. 2018. Transfer learning in multilingual neural machine translation with dynamic vocabulary. *CoRR*, abs/1811.01137.

V. Rudra Murthy, Anoop Kunchukuttan, and Pushpak Bhattacharyya. 2019. Addressing word-order divergence in multilingual neural machine translation for extremely low resource languages. In *Proceedings of the 2019 Conference of the North American Chapter of the Association for Computational Linguistics: Human Language Technologies, NAACL-HLT 2019, Minneapolis, MN, USA, June 2-7, 2019, Volume 1 (Long and Short Papers)*, pages 3868–3873. Association for Computational Linguistics.

Toan Q. Nguyen and David Chiang. 2017. Transfer learning across low-resource, related languages for neural machine translation. In *Proceedings of the Eighth International Joint Conference on Natural Language Processing (Volume 2: Short Papers)*, pages 296–301, Taipei, Taiwan. Asian Federation of Natural Language Processing.

Myle Ott, Sergey Edunov, Alexei Baevski, Angela Fan, Sam Gross, Nathan Ng, David Grangier, and Michael Auli. 2019. fairseq: A fast, extensible toolkit for sequence modeling. In *Proceedings of NAACL-HLT 2019: Demonstrations*.

Kishore Papineni, Salim Roukos, Todd Ward, and Wei-Jing Zhu. 2002. Bleu: a method for automatic evaluation of machine translation. In *Proceedings of the 40th Annual Meeting of the Association for Computational Linguistics, July 6-12, 2002, Philadelphia, PA, USA*, pages 311–318.

Loganathan Ramasamy, Ondřej Bojar, and Zdeněk Žabokrtský. 2012. Morphological processing for english-tamil statistical machine translation. In *Proceedings of the Workshop on Machine Translation and Parsing in Indian Languages (MTPIL-2012)*, pages 113–122.

Rico Sennrich, Barry Haddow, and Alexandra Birch. 2016a. Improving neural machine translation models with monolingual data. In *Proceedings of the 54th Annual Meeting of the Association for Computational Linguistics, ACL 2016, August 7-12, 2016, Berlin, Germany, Volume 1: Long Papers*. The Association for Computer Linguistics.

Rico Sennrich, Barry Haddow, and Alexandra Birch. 2016b. Neural machine translation of rare words with subword units. In *Proceedings of the 54th Annual Meeting of the Association for Computational Linguistics, ACL 2016, August 7-12, 2016, Berlin, Germany, Volume 1: Long Papers*.

Ilya Sutskever, Oriol Vinyals, and Quoc V. Le. 2014. Sequence to sequence learning with neural networks. In *Advances in Neural Information Processing Systems 27: Annual Conference on Neural Information Processing Systems 2014, December 8-13 2014, Montreal, Quebec, Canada*, pages 3104–3112.

Xu Tan, Jiale Chen, Di He, Yingce Xia, Tao Qin, and Tie-Yan Liu. 2019. Multilingual neural machine translation with language clustering. In *Proceedings of the 2019 Conference on Empirical Methods in Natural Language Processing and the 9th International Joint Conference on Natural Language Processing, EMNLP-IJCNLP 2019, Hong Kong, China, November 3-7, 2019*, pages 963–973.

Pasindu Tennage, Prabath Sandaruwan, Malith Thilakarathne, Achini Herath, Surangika Ranathunga, Sanath Jayasena, and Gihan Dias. 2017. Neural machine translation for sinhala and tamil languages. In *2017 International Conference on Asian Language Processing, IALP 2017, Singapore, December 5-7, 2017*, pages 189–192. IEEE.

Jörg Tiedemann. 2012. Parallel data, tools and interfaces in OPUS. In *Proceedings of the Eighth International Conference on Language Resources and Evaluation, LREC 2012, Istanbul, Turkey, May 23-25, 2012*, pages 2214–2218. European Language Resources Association (ELRA).

Ashish Vaswani, Noam Shazeer, Niki Parmar, Jakob Uszkoreit, Llion Jones, Aidan N. Gomez, Lukasz Kaiser, and Illia Polosukhin. 2017. Attention is all you need. In *Advances in Neural Information Processing Systems 30: Annual Conference on Neural Information Processing Systems 2017, 4-9 December 2017, Long Beach, CA, USA*, pages 5998–6008.

Barret Zoph, Deniz Yuret, Jonathan May, and Kevin Knight. 2016. Transfer learning for low-resource neural machine translation. In *Proceedings of the 2016 Conference on Empirical Methods in Natural*

*Language Processing, EMNLP 2016, Austin, Texas, USA, November 1-4, 2016*, pages 1568–1575. The Association for Computational Linguistics.

# OFFLangOne@DravidianLangTech-EACL2021: Transformers with the Class Balanced Loss for Offensive Language Identification in Dravidian Code-Mixed text.

**Suman Dowlagar**
LTRC
IIIT-Hyderabad
suman.dowlagar
@research.iiit.ac.in

**Radhika Mamidi**
LTRC
IIIT-Hyderabad
radhika.mamidi
@iiit.ac.in

## Abstract

The intensity of online abuse has increased in recent years. Automated tools are being developed to prevent the use of hate speech and offensive content. Most of the technologies use natural language and machine learning tools to identify offensive text. In a multilingual society, where code-mixing is a norm, the hate content would be delivered in a code-mixed form in social media, which makes offensive content identification, further challenging. In this work, we participated in the EACL task to detect offensive content in the code-mixed social media scenario. The methodology uses a transformer model with transliteration and class balancing loss for offensive content identification. In this task, our model has been ranked $2^{nd}$ in Malayalam-English and $4^{th}$ in Tamil-English code-mixed languages.

## 1 Introduction

Language is a social phenomenon. It is through language that day-to-day interactions and interpersonal relations are possible (Barnali et al., 2017). Languages keep on changing and adapting. In a multilingual scenario, the languages influence each other in certain ways. Normally, this interaction is reflected in language convergence, borrowing, and replacement. It also leads to the emergence of hybrid languages, such as pidgins, creoles, and other mixed languages. This form of language interaction is known as Language contact (Thomason, 2001). Language contact is considered to be an important phenomenon, especially in multilingual societies. In bilingual or multilingual communities, speakers use their native tongue and their second language in different domains. This form of alternation of two or more languages is called 'code-mixing' (CM) (Muysken et al., 2000).

With the increase in social media access, Offensive content and hateful material on the internet has increased in the recent past (Thavareesan and Mahesan, 2019, 2020a,b). The internet harbors a variety of hateful and offensive statements, and nowadays, social media is a hotbed of such conversations. Recently, countries across the world have already begun to address hate speech and offensive content and how it affects society's functioning (Chakravarthi, 2020). Research and technologies worldwide are utilizing natural language and machine learning tools to detect and curb the use of offensive content on social media.

In a multilingual society, code-mixing has become a norm. The hateful and offensive content is delivered in a code-mixed form (Jose et al., 2020; Priyadharshini et al., 2020). Automatic hate speech detection on code-mixed data has faced quite many challenges due to the non-standard variations in spelling and grammar (Bali et al., 2014). The typical hate-speech and offensive language tools developed for monolingual data will not work for code-mixed data. So there is a need for more research and analysis to be done to identify the offensive content in code-mixed social media data.

To encourage research on code-mixing and restrain the use of offensive texts on social media, the NLP community has organized several workshops such as Workshops on Computational Approaches to Linguistic Code-Switching, SentiMix (Patwa et al., 2020), Dravidian CodeMix (Chakravarthi et al., 2020d), HASOC Dravidian CodeMix [1] (Chakravarthi et al., 2020b; Mandl et al., 2020). Similarly, the European Association of Computational Linguistics 2021's DravidianLangTech (Chakravarthi et al., 2021) was also devoted to identifying offensive content on Kannada-English, Tamil-English, and Malayalam-English code-mixed languages. This task aims to classify the given code-mixed com-

[1] https://sites.google.com/view/dravidian-codemix-fire2020/overview



*Proceedings of the First Workshop on Speech and Language Technologies for Dravidian Languages*, pages 154–159
April 20, 2021 ©2021 Association for Computational Linguistics

ments into one of the six predefined categories: Not-offensive, offensive-untargeted, Offensive-Targeted-Insult-Individual, Offensive- Targeted-Insult-Group, Offensive-Targeted-Insult-Other, or Not-in-indented-language.

This paper presents a pre-trained BERT model with the class balanced loss for offensive content identification on the Dravidian code-mixed text.

The paper is organized as follows. Section 2 provides related work on offensive content identification on CM social media text. Section 3 provides information on the task and datasets. Section 4 describes the proposed work. Section 5 presents the experimental setup and the performance of the model. Section 6 concludes our work.

## 2 Related Work

This section describes the related work on hate speech detection and offensive content identification in the code-mixed scenario.

Bohra et al. (2018) created a dataset for hate speech detection from Hindi-English tweets. They collected around 4575 Hindi-English tweets and used traditional machine learning models with feature engineering for hateful and offensive content identification. Mandl et al. (2019) created a Hindi-English dataset for a hate speech and offensive content identification Task (HASOC), organized at FIRE 2019. It consists of 4665 Hindi-English annotated posts collected from social media sites. They used Twitter API for crawling an unbiased dataset. The top models used the Long Short Term Memory (LSTM) (Schmidhuber and Hochreiter, 1997) with attention mechanism, pre-trained Bidirectional encoder representations with transformers (BERT) (Devlin et al., 2018) models, and convolutional neural networks (CNN) for hate speech and offensive content identification. Kumar et al. (2018) created the dataset for an aggression detection task. The dataset was annotated for a comparison task by (Rani et al., 2020). This data set consists of 3367 posts and tweets collected from social media sites. The authors used traditional machine learning classification models for hate speech detection. A shared task called Dravidian Code-Mix (Chakravarthi et al., 2020b) was organized to identify the offensive language from comments/posts in code-mixed Dravidian Languages (Tamil-English and Malayalam-English) collected from social media. Each comment/post is annotated with the offensive language label at the comment/post level. The data set has been collected from YouTube comments and Tweets. The dataset contains 4000 annotated Youtube comments and 4952 annotated tweets for the Malayalam language, and 4940 annotated tweets for the Tamil language. The top models used deep learning models like LSTM, CNN, and BERT for hate speech and offensive content detection on the given Dravidian data.

## 3 Task and Dataset information

The goal of offensive language identification is to identify the offensive language content of the code-mixed dataset of comments/posts in Tamil-English (Chakravarthi et al., 2020c), Malayalam-English (Chakravarthi et al., 2020a), and Kannada-English (Hande et al., 2020) Dravidian languages collected from social media. Each comment or post is annotated with offensive, not-offensive, and not-in-intended-language labels. Where the offensive label is fine-grained into further categories. The description of each label is given below

- Offensive-targeted-individual: offensive text delivered to an individual or person
- Offensive-targeted-group: offensive text delivered to a group of people
- Offensive-targeted-other: offensive text delivered to topics such as films, elections, sports, and so on.
- Offensive-untargeted: the offensive text is delivered but without targeting any person or a topic.
- Not-in-indented-language: the given content is not in the intended language.
- Not-offensive: the post does not contain any offensive content

The dataset for offensive content identification into divided into train, development(dev), and test sets for the given languages.

The details of the dataset are given in table 1.

## 4 Our work

In this section, we start with pre-processing of code-mixed text. Later we describe the pre-trained multilingual BERT model with the class balanced loss for offensive content identification.

| Data | #train | #dev | #test | #total |
|---|---|---|---|---|
| **Kannada-English CM** | 6217 | 777 | 778 | 7772 |
| **Malayalam-English CM** | 16010 | 1999 | 2001 | 20010 |
| **Tamil-English CM** | 35138 | 4388 | 4392 | 43919 |

Table 1: Data Statistics

### 4.1 Pre-processing

The given code-mixed dataset depicts real-time scenarios of variations in the spelling, script changes, use of hashtags, mentions, and emoticons in the text and has imbalance problems. So pre-processing is necessary for such a dataset. During pre-processing,

- To resolve the ambiguities resulting from script change, we back-transliterated the script to the native language. As the data has Dravidian and English comments, we used the NLTK[2] English word corpus to detect if the word is in English or not. Later we back-transliterated the word to its native script. We applied linguistic rules not to transliterate the tweet/comment "not-Kannada/not-Tamil/not-Malayalam" as they are not in the intended language.
- We removed all the punctuations, URLs, mentions, unwanted numbers, and emoticons from the given dataset. We accepted repetitions of characters up to a length of 2 and removed others.

### 4.2 Our proposed model

In our approach, we have used multilingual pre-trained BERT with the class balanced loss on the transliterated data.

We have used multilingual pre-trained BERT (Devlin et al., 2018) in this work because it is a transformer-based self multi-headed attention model that is pre-trained on a huge collection of data and can be finetuned for our offensive content classification task. This kind of transfer learning is very successful when we want to learn a classifier from a small set of data by taking advantage of pre-trained embeddings.

BERT is a non-regressive model that reads the whole string of terms present in the text in a single stretch. BERT analyzes the meaning of a term depending on its context given on both sides. As they are pre-trained on a large corpus, the semantic and syntactic information is well modeled and can be directly finetuned for a specific task.

The transformer part in the BERT works like an attention mechanism capable of learning the contextual relationships between the terms in a sentence. The basic form of transformer consists of an encoder and a decoder. The encoder part reads the text as the input, and the decoder part gives the corresponding predictions.

### 4.3 Class balanced loss to handle dataset imbalance

While handling an imbalanced dataset (one with most of the samples belonging to very few of the classes and many other classes with very few instances), loss calculation can be tricky. The most common approach to balance the loss is assigning weights to the loss. The weights are calculated as the inverse of the number of class instances or inverse of the square root of the number of class instances. This form of weighing scheme creates the problem by shifting focus entirely to the classes with very few instances.

To handle the shift, the authors Cui et al. (2019) proposed a Class-Balanced Loss based on Effective Number of Samples. A framework to measure data overlap by associating each sample to a small neighboring region rather than a single point. The effective number of samples is defined as the volume of samples and can be calculated by a simple formula $(1-b^n)/(1-b)$, where n is the number of samples and b is a hyper-parameter, and it takes values between [0,1]. The authors designed a re-weighting scheme that uses sufficient samples for each class to re-balance the loss, thereby yielding a class-balanced loss.

$$\mathrm{CB}(\mathbf{p}, y) = \frac{1}{E_{n_y}} \mathcal{L}(\mathbf{p}, y) = \frac{1-\beta}{1-\beta^{n_y}} \mathcal{L}(\mathbf{p}, y) \tag{1}$$

Here, $\mathcal{L}(\mathbf{p}, y)$ can be any loss function.$n_y$ is the number of estimated samples for each labels $y$.

[2] `https://www.nltk.org/`

| Malayalam-English CM data | Accuracy | macro-F1 | Weighted-F1 |
|---|---|---|---|
| **SVM** | 0.96 | 0.78 | **0.96** |
| **mBERT** | 0.68 | 0.38 | 0.70 |
| **mBERT 'balanced'** | 0.68 | 0.38 | 0.70 |
| **mBERT 'transliterated'** | 0.96 | 0.78 | **0.96** |
| **Our approach** | **0.97** | **0.80** | **0.96** |

Table 2: Classification metrics for Malayalam-English CM data

| Tamil-English CM data | Accuracy | macro-F1 | Weighted-F1 |
|---|---|---|---|
| **SVM** | 0.77 | 0.43 | **0.80** |
| **mBERT** | 0.76 | 0.45 | 0.78 |
| **mBERT 'balanced'** | 0.76 | 0.46 | 0.78 |
| **mBERT 'transliterated'** | **0.78** | 0.47 | **0.80** |
| **Our approach** | **0.78** | **0.48** | **0.80** |

Table 3: Classification metrics for Tamil-English CM data

| Kannada-English CM data | Accuracy | macro-F1 | Weighted-F1 |
|---|---|---|---|
| **SVM** | 0.70 | 0.43 | 0.73 |
| **mBERT** | **0.74** | 0.44 | **0.77** |
| **mBERT 'balanced'** | **0.74** | **0.45** | **0.77** |
| **mBERT 'transliterated'** | 0.66 | 0.42 | 0.64 |
| **Our approach** | 0.66 | 0.43 | 0.65 |

Table 4: Classification metrics for Kannada-English CM data

## 5 Experiments

The section presents the baselines, hyper-parameter settings, and analysis of observed results.

The baselines used for the proposed work is:

1. **SVM with TF-IDF** Term frequency and inverse document frequency-based vectorization is used to represent the text data, and the support vector machine is used to classify the data.

2. **Pre-trained multilingual BERT (mBERT)** A pre-trained multilingual BERT model with a feed-forward network for classification.

3. **mBERT with class balanced loss (mBERT "balanced")** A pre-trained multilingual BERT model with a feed-forward network and class balanced loss is used for classification.

4. **mBERT with transliteration (mBERT "transliterated")** A pre-trained multilingual BERT model with a feed-forward network with transliterated data is used for classification

### 5.1 Hyperparameters and libraries used

During pre-processing, we have used a deep transliteration tool known as ai4bharat-transliteration[3] library. We have used SVM with TF-IDF vectorization from the scikit-learn library (Pedregosa et al., 2011). The default parameters are used to train the SVM for multi-class classification. The multilingual pre-trained BERT is obtained from huggingface transformers library (Wolf et al., 2019) and is finetuned for this sentence classification task. The optimizer used is weighted Adam with the learning rate of 2e-5 and epsilon value equal to 1e-8. The loss function used is a cross-entropy loss. The number of epochs used for training the model is 30.

### 5.2 Results and Analysis

Tables 2, 3 and 4 presents the f1-score and accuracy of the models on the Dravidian code-mixed datasets.

From the above results, for Malayalam and Tamil datasets, it is clear that our approach of the multilingual pre-trained BERT model with the class

[3]https://pypi.org/project/ai4bharat-transliteration/

balanced loss and transliteration works best for the given datasets. It is due to the effectiveness of the pre-processing and class balanced loss. Removing URLs, punctuations and emojis features helped the BERT model to focus on the relevant information. As the script is associated with the embeddings, back-transliteration helped the BERT model distinguish between the native script and English words that improved the model's accuracy. The class balanced loss statistically estimated the weightage of each label and helped the model not to favour the label with maximum instances.

Our approach for Kannada-English CM dataset didn't give best results. It might be due to the problems given below,

1. The transliteration tool didn't function well for the Kannada data.

2. There were more English words in the data, with small spelling variations or abbreviations, that are not detected by the NLTK corpus and transliterated to Malayalam script.

### 5.3 Conclusion

We used pre-trained multilingual bi-directional encoder representations using transformers (BERT) for offensive content identification given the Kannada-English, Malayalam-English, and Tamil-English code-mixed datasets. We compared the BERT with traditional machine learning classification methods with and without class balanced loss. The results showed that using the back-transliteration helped the module to obtain the nativeness of script and class balanced loss handled the problem of imbalanced data. During back-transliteration, we observed that the data has many spelling variations for the same word. So the back-transliteration had many instances of the same word with small variations. In the future, we wish to normalize these transliterations based on the context, such models, if developed, will help in handling the code-mixed real-time data better. It would also be an interesting study to analyze the effects of different loss functions in our model on given imbalanced data.

## References


Kalika Bali, Jatin Sharma, Monojit Choudhury, and Yogarshi Vyas. 2014. "I am borrowing ya mixing?" An Analysis of English-Hindi Code Mixing in Facebook. In *Proceedings of the First Workshop on Computational Approaches to Code Switching*, pages 116–126.

Chetia Barnali et al. 2017. Code-Switching and Mixing in Communication- A Study on Language Contact in Indian Media. In *The Future of Ethics, Education and Research*, pages 110–123. Scientia Moralitas Research Institute.

Aditya Bohra, Deepanshu Vijay, Vinay Singh, Syed Sarfaraz Akhtar, and Manish Shrivastava. 2018. A dataset of Hindi-English code-mixed social media text for hate speech detection. In *Proceedings of the second workshop on computational modeling of people's opinions, personality, and emotions in social media*, pages 36–41.

Bharathi Raja Chakravarthi. 2020. HopeEDI: A multilingual hope speech detection dataset for equality, diversity, and inclusion. In *Proceedings of the Third Workshop on Computational Modeling of People's Opinions, Personality, and Emotion's in Social Media*, pages 41–53, Barcelona, Spain (Online). Association for Computational Linguistics.

Bharathi Raja Chakravarthi, Navya Jose, Shardul Suryawanshi, Elizabeth Sherly, and John Philip McCrae. 2020a. A sentiment analysis dataset for code-mixed Malayalam-English. In *Proceedings of the 1st Joint Workshop on Spoken Language Technologies for Under-resourced languages (SLTU) and Collaboration and Computing for Under-Resourced Languages (CCURL)*, pages 177–184, Marseille, France. European Language Resources association.

Bharathi Raja Chakravarthi, M Anand Kumar, John Philip McCrae, Premjith B, Soman KP, and Thomas Mandl. 2020b. Overview of the track on HASOC-Offensive Language Identification-DravidianCodeMix. In *Working Notes of the Forum for Information Retrieval Evaluation (FIRE 2020). CEUR Workshop Proceedings. In: CEUR-WS. org, Hyderabad, India.*

Bharathi Raja Chakravarthi, Vigneshwaran Muralidaran, Ruba Priyadharshini, and John Philip McCrae. 2020c. Corpus creation for sentiment analysis in code-mixed Tamil-English text. In *Proceedings of the 1st Joint Workshop on Spoken Language Technologies for Under-resourced languages (SLTU) and Collaboration and Computing for Under-Resourced Languages (CCURL)*, pages 202–210, Marseille, France. European Language Resources association.

Bharathi Raja Chakravarthi, Ruba Priyadharshini, Navya Jose, Anand Kumar M, Thomas Mandl, Prasanna Kumar Kumaresan, Rahul Ponnusamy, Hariharan V, Elizabeth Sherly, and John Philip McCrae. 2021. Findings of the shared task on Offensive Language Identification in Tamil, Malayalam, and Kannada. In *Proceedings of the First Workshop on Speech and Language Technologies for Dravidian Languages*. Association for Computational Linguistics.

Bharathi Raja Chakravarthi, Ruba Priyadharshini, Vigneshwaran Muralidaran, Shardul Suryawanshi, Navya Jose, Elizabeth Sherly, and John P. McCrae. 2020d. Overview of the Track on Sentiment Analysis for Dravidian Languages in Code-Mixed Text. In *Forum for Information Retrieval Evaluation*, FIRE 2020, page 21–24, New York, NY, USA. Association for Computing Machinery.

Yin Cui, Menglin Jia, Tsung-Yi Lin, Yang Song, and Serge Belongie. 2019. Class-balanced loss based on effective number of samples. In *Proceedings of the IEEE Conference on Computer Vision and Pattern Recognition*, pages 9268–9277.

Jacob Devlin, Ming-Wei Chang, Kenton Lee, and Kristina Toutanova. 2018. Bert: Pre-training of deep bidirectional transformers for language understanding. *arXiv preprint arXiv:1810.04805*.

Adeep Hande, Ruba Priyadharshini, and Bharathi Raja Chakravarthi. 2020. KanCMD: Kannada CodeMixed dataset for sentiment analysis and offensive language detection. In *Proceedings of the Third Workshop on Computational Modeling of People's Opinions, Personality, and Emotion's in Social Media*, pages 54–63, Barcelona, Spain (Online). Association for Computational Linguistics.

Navya Jose, Bharathi Raja Chakravarthi, Shardul Suryawanshi, Elizabeth Sherly, and John P. McCrae. 2020. A Survey of Current Datasets for Code-Switching Research. In *2020 6th International Conference on Advanced Computing and Communication Systems (ICACCS)*, pages 136–141.

Ritesh Kumar, Aishwarya N Reganti, Akshit Bhatia, and Tushar Maheshwari. 2018. Aggression-annotated corpus of Hindi-English code-mixed data. *arXiv preprint arXiv:1803.09402*.

Thomas Mandl, Sandip Modha, Anand Kumar M, and Bharathi Raja Chakravarthi. 2020. Overview of the HASOC Track at FIRE 2020: Hate Speech and Offensive Language Identification in Tamil, Malayalam, Hindi, English and German. In *Forum for Information Retrieval Evaluation*, FIRE 2020, page 29–32, New York, NY, USA. Association for Computing Machinery.

Thomas Mandl, Sandip Modha, Prasenjit Majumder, Daksh Patel, Mohana Dave, Chintak Mandlia, and Aditya Patel. 2019. Overview of the HASOC track at FIRE 2019: Hate speech and offensive content identification in Indo-European languages. In *Proceedings of the 11th Forum for Information Retrieval Evaluation*, pages 14–17.

Pieter Muysken, Pieter Cornelis Muysken, et al. 2000. *Bilingual speech: A typology of code-mixing*. Cambridge University Press.

Parth Patwa, Gustavo Aguilar, Sudipta Kar, Suraj Pandey, Srinivas PYKL, Björn Gambäck, Tanmoy Chakraborty, Thamar Solorio, and Amitava Das. 2020. Semeval-2020 task 9: Overview of sentiment analysis of code-mixed tweets. *arXiv e-prints*, pages arXiv–2008.

F. Pedregosa, G. Varoquaux, A. Gramfort, V. Michel, B. Thirion, O. Grisel, M. Blondel, P. Prettenhofer, R. Weiss, V. Dubourg, J. Vanderplas, A. Passos, D. Cournapeau, M. Brucher, M. Perrot, and E. Duchesnay. 2011. Scikit-learn: Machine learning in Python. *Journal of Machine Learning Research*, 12:2825–2830.

Ruba Priyadharshini, Bharathi Raja Chakravarthi, Mani Vegupatti, and John P. McCrae. 2020. Named Entity Recognition for Code-Mixed Indian Corpus using Meta Embedding. In *2020 6th International Conference on Advanced Computing and Communication Systems (ICACCS)*, pages 68–72.

Priya Rani, Shardul Suryawanshi, Koustava Goswami, Bharathi Raja Chakravarthi, Theodorus Fransen, and John Philip McCrae. 2020. A comparative study of different state-of-the-art hate speech detection methods in hindi-english code-mixed data. In *Proceedings of the Second Workshop on Trolling, Aggression and Cyberbullying*, pages 42–48.

Jürgen Schmidhuber and Sepp Hochreiter. 1997. Long short-term memory. *Neural Comput*, 9(8):1735–1780.

Sajeetha Thavareesan and Sinnathamby Mahesan. 2019. Sentiment Analysis in Tamil Texts: A Study on Machine Learning Techniques and Feature Representation. In *2019 14th Conference on Industrial and Information Systems (ICIIS)*, pages 320–325.

Sajeetha Thavareesan and Sinnathamby Mahesan. 2020a. Sentiment Lexicon Expansion using Word2vec and fastText for Sentiment Prediction in Tamil texts. In *2020 Moratuwa Engineering Research Conference (MERCon)*, pages 272–276.

Sajeetha Thavareesan and Sinnathamby Mahesan. 2020b. Word embedding-based Part of Speech tagging in Tamil texts. In *2020 IEEE 15th International Conference on Industrial and Information Systems (ICIIS)*, pages 478–482.

Salah G Thomason. 2001. *Language contact*. Citeseer.

Thomas Wolf, Lysandre Debut, Victor Sanh, Julien Chaumond, Clement Delangue, Anthony Moi, Pierric Cistac, Tim Rault, Rémi Louf, Morgan Funtowicz, et al. 2019. Huggingface's transformers: State-of-the-art natural language processing. *ArXiv*, pages arXiv–1910.

# Simon @ DravidianLangTech-EACL2021: Detecting Offensive Content in Kannada Language

**Qinyu Que**
School of Information Science and Engineering,
Yunnan University, Yunnan, P.R. China
1309487642@qq.com

## Abstract

This article introduces the system for the shared task of Offensive Language Identification in Dravidian Languages-EACL 2021. The world's information technology develops at a high speed. People are used to expressing their views and opinions on social media. This leads to a lot of offensive language on social media. As people become more dependent on social media, the detection of offensive language becomes more and more necessary. This shared task is in three languages: Tamil, Malayalam, and Kannada. Our team takes part in the Kannada language task. To accomplish the task, we use the XLM-Roberta model for pre-training. But the capabilities of the XLM-Roberta model do not satisfy us in terms of statement information collection. So we made some tweaks to the output of this model. In this paper, we describe the models and experiments for accomplishing the task of the Kannada language.

## 1 Introduction

The network platform builds a brand new living and cultural space and promotes communication among netizens. This leads to an exponential growth of information and speech in cyberspace. The popularity of the Internet facilitates the spread of offensive remarks, and also brings some negative social effects (Chakravarthi et al., 2020c). The people who communicate on the Internet come from different countries (Thavareesan and Mahesan, 2019, 2020a,b). Due to the differences in history and culture of different countries, people in different regions have great differences in their understanding of Offensive speech (Mandl et al., 2020). So it's easy for people to inadvertently make offensive remarks about other people. Offensive language is not a recent phenomenon, but its impact is growing because of its rapid spread on social media. A large amount of offensive language on the Internet can cause serious social problems. Therefore, detection of offensive content is very necessary. This is not only conducive to purifying the network environment but also conducive to promoting the positive development of society (Chakravarthi, 2020a; Chakravarthi and Muralidaran, 2021).

Kannada is a Dravidian language spoken mainly by Karnataka residents in India's south western region (Chakravarthi, 2020b). After AD 600, Kannada developed from the old Tamil script. Tamil has the most ancient Indian non-Sanskritic literature of Indian languages. The Kappe Arabhatta record from AD 700 is the oldest extant record of Kannada poetry in Tripadi meter. The data set used in the experiment is provided by the competition organization(Chakravarthi et al., 2021, 2020a,b; Hande et al., 2020). The data was collected from various social media platforms. In the following content, we introduce recent relevant work, the models we use, our experimental processes, and results.

## 2 Related Work

Online social media is now one of the main channels of communication. But the growth of offensive content is troubling users and the companies that run social media. The need to identify offensive content has increased dramatically. The purpose of the identification of offensive content is to reduce offensive content in social media and thus improve users' communication experience on social media. Some scholars have done a lot of work on the classification of offensive language. Offensive language attacks people for a variety of reasons. People can be targeted with offensive language because of their gender, skin color, or nationality(Reddy and Vasu, 2002; Gatehouse et al., 2017; Erjavec and Kovali, 2012). In the field of detecting offen-



*Proceedings of the First Workshop on Speech and Language Technologies for Dravidian Languages*, pages 160–163
April 20, 2021 ©2021 Association for Computational Linguistics

| Label | Train set | validation set |
|---|---|---|
| N_o | 57.01% | 54.38% |
| O_T_I_O | 1.98% | 2.06% |
| O_T_I_I | 7.83% | 8.49% |
| O_T_I_G | 5.29% | 5.79% |
| n_K | 24.48% | 24.58% |
| O_U | 3.41% | 4.25% |

Table 1: Label distribution of Kannada language subtask

sive language, many tasks related to it have been completed by scholars. These tasks include the detection of bullying language(Van Hee et al., 2015) and hate language(Davidson et al., 2017) on social platforms. People use various methods to achieve the classification of text. LSTM(Surhone et al., 2010) was proposed by Hochreiter et al. LSTM plays a great role in the field of natural language processing.

## 3 Methodology and Corpus

### 3.1 Data Description

In the Kannada language subtask, the data set contains six tags:

- Not_offensive(N_o): This tag indicates that the comment is Not offensive.
- Offensive_Targeted_Insult_Other(O_T_I_O): This tag indicates that a comment is an offensive text which is neither targetted towards an individual or group.
- Offensive_Targeted_Insult_Individual(O_T_I_I): This tag indicates that a comment is offensive to a person.
- Offensive_Targeted_Insult_Group(O_T_I_G): This tag indicates that a comment is offensive to a group.
- not_Kannada(n_K): This tag indicates that this comment is not in the Kannada language. Item Offensive_Untargetede(O_U): The tag indicates that the comment is offensive, but does not have a specific target.

We can see that this is a six-category classification task. The data set for this task is classified in a very detailed way. This also makes Classification difficult. Table 1 gives the details of the data set.

### 3.2 Data Preparation

Before training the data set, we preprocessed the text. The main purpose of preprocessing is to standardize the text collected from social media and reduce unnecessary words in the text. Here's what we do to the text:

- Removing punctuation marks and special characters
- Removing the URL
- Removing the emoticons

### 3.3 Model Description

In the experiment, we used XLM-Roberta(Conneau et al., 2020) as our preprocessing model. XLM-Roberta was released by Facebook in 2019. XLM-Roberta is an improvement based on BERT(Devlin et al., 2019). The researchers found that Bert was undertrained. So they made these improvements to XLM-Roberta on the basis of Bert: training the sequence with relatively large length, deleting the prediction for the next sentence, using dynamic changes in the masking model of training data, and increasing the training capacity of the model. XLM-Roberta is a multilingual model capable of handling text in 100 different languages. In the experiment, we are not satisfied with the statement information collection ability of the XLM-Roberta model. So our team came up with the model shown in Figure 1. This model mainly combines the last three hidden layers' outputs of XLM-Roberta with LSTM. We input the last three hidden layers of XLM-Roberta into the LSTM to get the output of the LSTM. Finally, the output of LSTM and the Pooler output of XLM-Roberta(P_O) are connected together and put into the classifier.

## 4 Experiment and Results

We combined the training set and validation set provided by the contest organizer, and then used Stratified K-fold Cross Validation to get the new training set and validation set. Cross-validation divides the data set multiple times. The common method of randomly dividing the data set will make the result have a contingency. Cross-validation reduces the chance that comes with a random partition. The model can complete the training of various types of data so as to improve the generalization ability of the model. The scale relationship of the Label in each layer of data is saved.

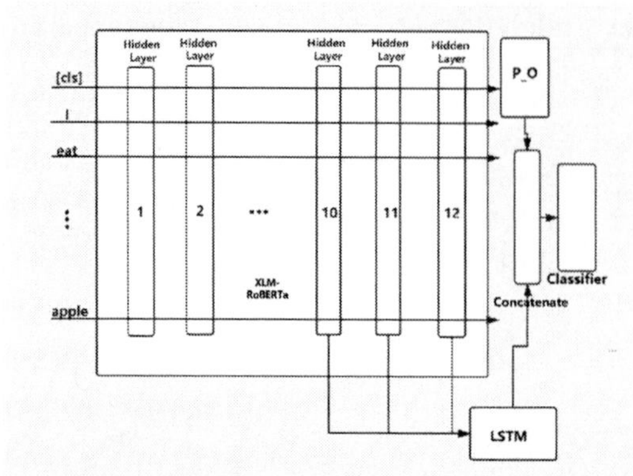


Figure 1: Model description: custom XLM-Roberta architecture that acts as a feature extractor to provide useful information from the given text to LSTM.

| Hyper-parameter | Value |
|---|---:|
| dropout | 0.5 |
| learning rate | 2e-5 |
| epoch | 4 |
| per gpu train batch size | 32 |
| gradient accumulation steps | 8 |

Table 2: The hyper-parameters

We used XLM-Roberta-Base[1] as our preprocessing model. In the experiment, the hyper-parameters we used are shown in Table 2. The task was evaluated by following the Macro Average F1 of ScikitLearn. In the Kannada language sub-task, our final F1-score in the official test set is 0.33.

## 5 Conclusion

Our ranking in this task is not ideal, and our test scores are not satisfactory. We think there are the following reasons: First, our team did not set the hyperparameters reasonably in the experiment, for example, the value setting of the epoch was small. Second, the classification task has a large number of categories, and the nature of the tags is very similar. That makes the task more difficult. Third, the data set is imbalanced. In the future, we will improve our model to accommodate the data imbalance.

## References


Bharathi Raja Chakravarthi. 2020a. HopeEDI: A multilingual hope speech detection dataset for equality, diversity, and inclusion. In *Proceedings of the Third Workshop on Computational Modeling of People's Opinions, Personality, and Emotion's in Social Media*, pages 41–53, Barcelona, Spain (Online). Association for Computational Linguistics.

Bharathi Raja Chakravarthi. 2020b. *Leveraging orthographic information to improve machine translation of under-resourced languages*. Ph.D. thesis, NUI Galway.

Bharathi Raja Chakravarthi, Navya Jose, Shardul Suryawanshi, Elizabeth Sherly, and John Philip McCrae. 2020a. A sentiment analysis dataset for code-mixed Malayalam-English. In *Proceedings of the 1st Joint Workshop on Spoken Language Technologies for Under-resourced languages (SLTU) and Collaboration and Computing for Under-Resourced Languages (CCURL)*, pages 177–184, Marseille, France. European Language Resources association.

Bharathi Raja Chakravarthi and Vigneshwaran Muralidaran. 2021. Findings of the shared task on Hope Speech Detection for Equality, Diversity, and Inclusion. In *Proceedings of the First Workshop on Language Technology for Equality, Diversity and Inclusion*. Association for Computational Linguistics.

Bharathi Raja Chakravarthi, Vigneshwaran Muralidaran, Ruba Priyadharshini, and John Philip McCrae. 2020b. Corpus creation for sentiment analysis in code-mixed Tamil-English text. In *Proceedings of the 1st Joint Workshop on Spoken Language Technologies for Under-resourced languages (SLTU) and Collaboration and Computing for Under-Resourced Languages (CCURL)*, pages 202–210, Marseille, France. European Language Resources association.

Bharathi Raja Chakravarthi, Ruba Priyadharshini, Navya Jose, Anand Kumar M, Thomas Mandl, Prasanna Kumar Kumaresan, Rahul Ponnusamy, Hariharan V, Elizabeth Sherly, and John Philip McCrae. 2021. Findings of the shared task on Offensive Language Identification in Tamil, Malayalam, and Kannada. In *Proceedings of the First Workshop*


[1]https://huggingface.co/xlm-roberta-base

*on Speech and Language Technologies for Dravidian Languages*. Association for Computational Linguistics.

Bharathi Raja Chakravarthi, Ruba Priyadharshini, Vigneshwaran Muralidaran, Shardul Suryawanshi, Navya Jose, Elizabeth Sherly, and John P. McCrae. 2020c. Overview of the Track on Sentiment Analysis for Dravidian Languages in Code-Mixed Text. In *Forum for Information Retrieval Evaluation*, FIRE 2020, page 21–24, New York, NY, USA. Association for Computing Machinery.

Alexis Conneau, Kartikay Khandelwal, Naman Goyal, Vishrav Chaudhary, and Veselin Stoyanov. 2020. Unsupervised cross-lingual representation learning at scale. In *Proceedings of the 58th Annual Meeting of the Association for Computational Linguistics*.

Thomas Davidson, Dana Warmsley, Michael Macy, and Ingmar Weber. 2017. Automated hate speech detection and the problem of offensive language.

Jacob Devlin, Ming-Wei Chang, Kenton Lee, and Kristina Toutanova. 2019. BERT: Pre-training of deep bidirectional transformers for language understanding. In *Proceedings of the 2019 Conference of the North American Chapter of the Association for Computational Linguistics: Human Language Technologies, Volume 1 (Long and Short Papers)*, pages 4171–4186, Minneapolis, Minnesota. Association for Computational Linguistics.

Karmen Erjavec and Melita Poler Kovali. 2012. "you don't understand, this is a new war!" analysis of hate speech in news web sites' comments. *Mass Communication Society*, 15(6):899–920.

Cally Gatehouse, Matthew Wood, Jo Briggs, James Pickles, and Shaun Lawson. 2017. Troubling vulnerability: Designing with lgbt young people's ambivalence towards hate crime reporting. In *Conference on Human Factors in Computing Systems*.

Adeep Hande, Ruba Priyadharshini, and Bharathi Raja Chakravarthi. 2020. KanCMD: Kannada CodeMixed dataset for sentiment analysis and offensive language detection. In *Proceedings of the Third Workshop on Computational Modeling of People's Opinions, Personality, and Emotion's in Social Media*, pages 54–63, Barcelona, Spain (Online). Association for Computational Linguistics.

Thomas Mandl, Sandip Modha, Anand Kumar M, and Bharathi Raja Chakravarthi. 2020. Overview of the HASOC Track at FIRE 2020: Hate Speech and Offensive Language Identification in Tamil, Malayalam, Hindi, English and German. In *Forum for Information Retrieval Evaluation*, FIRE 2020, page 29–32, New York, NY, USA. Association for Computing Machinery.

Reddy and Vasu. 2002. Perverts and sodomites: homophobia as hate speech in africa. *Southern African Linguistics Applied Language Studies*, 20(3):163–175.

Lambert M. Surhone, Mariam T. Tennoe, and Susan F. Henssonow. 2010. Long short term memory. *Betascript Publishing*.

Sajeetha Thavareesan and Sinnathamby Mahesan. 2019. Sentiment Analysis in Tamil Texts: A Study on Machine Learning Techniques and Feature Representation. In *2019 14th Conference on Industrial and Information Systems (ICIIS)*, pages 320–325.

Sajeetha Thavareesan and Sinnathamby Mahesan. 2020a. Sentiment Lexicon Expansion using Word2vec and fastText for Sentiment Prediction in Tamil texts. In *2020 Moratuwa Engineering Research Conference (MERCon)*, pages 272–276.

Sajeetha Thavareesan and Sinnathamby Mahesan. 2020b. Word embedding-based Part of Speech tagging in Tamil texts. In *2020 IEEE 15th International Conference on Industrial and Information Systems (ICIIS)*, pages 478–482.

Cynthia Van Hee, Ben Verhoeven, Els Lefever, Guy De Pauw, Walter Daelemans, and Veronique Hoste. 2015. Guidelines for the fine-grained analysis of cyberbullying, version 1.0.

# Codewithzichao@DravidianLangTech-EACL2021: Exploring Multilingual Transformers for Offensive Language Identification on Code Mixing Text

**Zichao Li**
School of Software and Microelectronics, Peking University, China
lizichao@pku.edu.cn

## Abstract

This paper describes our solution submitted to shared task on Offensive Language Identification in Dravidian Languages. We participated in all three of offensive language identification. In order to address the task, we explored multilingual models based on XLM-RoBERTa and multilingual BERT trained on mixed data of three code-mixed languages. Besides, we solved the class-imbalance problem existed in training data by class combination, class weights and focal loss. Our model achieved weighted average F1 scores of 0.75 (ranked 4th), 0.94 (ranked 4th) and 0.72 (ranked 3rd) in Tamil-English task, Malayalam-English task and Kannada-English task, respectively.

## 1 Introduction

Offensive language identification is a research field that has received increasing attention in recent years. Especially with the rise of social media platforms, it is essential to identify offensive language on code-mixed social media texts. It is a challenging task to identify offensive language on social media texts. Additionally, a lot of work has been done for offensive language identification in languages like English, Greek or Spanish (Zampieri et al., 2019; Pitenis et al., 2020; Ranasinghe and Zampieri, 2020), but little work has been done for offensive language identification of code-mixed text in Dravidian languages.

Shared task on Offensive Language Identification in Dravidian Languages (Tamil-English, Malayalam-English and Kannada-English) has changed this situation. The goal of this shared task is to identify offensive language on code-mixed text in Dravidian languages. The code-mixed text is collected from social media platforms. It is a comment or post level multilingual classification task that given a comment or post in code-mixed Tamil-English language, Malayalam-English language and Kannada-English language, systems have to classify it into Not-offensive, offensive-untargeted, offensive-targeted-individual, offensive-targeted-group, offensive-targeted-other, or Not-in-indented-language.

In this paper, we explore multilingual transformers on code-mixed text for offensive language identification in Dravidian languages. Inspired by the conclusion that lexical overlap among different languages can be helpful to improve the performance of the model in a single language given in (Pires et al., 2019), we combine the training data of three languages and trained our multilingual model on the mixed data. Besides, we solve the class-imbalance problem existed in training data by class combination, class weights and focal loss. Finally, we use adversarial training to further improve performance of our model. With these approaches, we achieved 4th Rank in Tamil-English, Malayalam-English task and 3rd Rank in Kannada-English task.

## 2 Data

We used the data provided by the organizers of shared task on Offensive Language Identification in Dravidian Languages (Chakravarthi et al., 2021, 2020b; Hande et al., 2020; Chakravarthi et al., 2020a), which have been annotated well at comment or post level. The numbers of Tamil, Malayalam and Kannada training data are 35139, 16010 and 6217, respectively. The statistics of data are shown in Table 1, Table 2 and Table 3.

There are four methods used to preprocess the data as follow:

- **Data combination:** Inspired by the conclusion that lexical overlap among different languages can be helpful to improve the performance of the model in a single language given in multilingual BERT, we combined the train-



*Proceedings of the First Workshop on Speech and Language Technologies for Dravidian Languages*, pages 164–168
April 20, 2021 

| Class | Train | Dev | Test |
|---|---|---|---|
| Not-offensive | 25425 | 3193 | 3190 |
| Offensive-Untargetede | 2906 | 356 | 368 |
| Offensive_Targeted_Insult_Individual | 2343 | 307 | 315 |
| Offensive_Targeted_Insult_Group | 2557 | 295 | 288 |
| Offensive_Targeted_Insult_Other | 454 | 65 | 71 |
| not_Tamil | 1454 | 172 | 160 |
| Count | 35139 | 4388 | 4392 |

Table 1: Statistics of Tamil-English language dataset.

| Class | Train | Dev | Test |
|---|---|---|---|
| Not-offensive | 14153 | 1779 | 1765 |
| Offensive-Untargetede | 191 | 20 | 29 |
| Offensive_Targeted_Insult_Individual | 239 | 24 | 27 |
| Offensive_Targeted_Insult_Group | 140 | 13 | 23 |
| Offensive_Targeted_Insult_Other | 0 | 0 | 0 |
| not_Malayalam | 1287 | 163 | 157 |
| Count | 16010 | 1999 | 2001 |

Table 2: Statistics of Malayalam-English language dataset.

ing data of the three languages and trained our model on the mixed data.

- **Noise removal:** Emojis and extra blanks in the code-mixed data are removed in advance. The experimental results show that removing these noise can improve the performance of our model.

- **Class combination:** We combined classes named not Tamil, not Malayalam and not Kannada which have few numbers into one class named Not in indented language, which is one of the ways to alleviate the class-imbalance problem. Finally there are 6 classes in training data.

- **Tokenization:** Texts are tokenized using the sentencepiece toolkit[1] and converted to the corresponding IDs through the vocabulary of XLM-RoBERTa (Conneau et al., 2020).

## 3 System

In this section, we first present our model for offensive language identification task, and then introduce the solution which is used to solve the class-imbalance problem and improve the robustness and generalization of our model.

[1]https://github.com/google/sentencepiece

### 3.1 Model Architecture

Our model is mainly divided into three layers: encoding layer, pooling layer and prediction layer.

#### 3.1.1 Encoding Layer

Given a sentence $X = \{x_1, x_2, ..., x_n\}$, which $x_i \in R^d$ and $n$ is the length of a sentence, they are fed into an encoder to obtain the contextual representation for each word of the sentence:

$$[h_1, h_2, ..., h_n] = Encoder([x_1, x_2, ..., x_n]), \quad (1)$$

where the $Encoder$ can be XLM-RoBERTa or multilingual BERT.

#### 3.1.2 Pooling Layer

Inspired by (Reimers and Gurevych, 2019), we use the average-over-time pooling $G \in R^d$ of the output of the last layer of the pre-trained model as the sentence embedding instead of the [CLS] embedding:

$$G = AvgPool([h_1, h_2, ..., h_n]). \quad (2)$$

#### 3.1.3 Prediction Layer

To classify each sentence, we put representation of each sentence into the softmax layer:

$$P(y_i|X) = softmax(W_G G + b). \quad (3)$$

| Class | Train | Dev | Test |
|---|---|---|---|
| Not-offensive | 3544 | 426 | 427 |
| Offensive-Untargetede | 212 | 33 | 33 |
| Offensive_Targeted_Insult_Individual | 487 | 66 | 75 |
| Offensive_Targeted_Insult_Group | 329 | 45 | 44 |
| Offensive_Targeted_Insult_Other | 123 | 16 | 14 |
| not_Kannada | 1522 | 191 | 185 |
| Count | 6217 | 777 | 778 |

Table 3: Statistics of Kannada-English language dataset.

| Language | Model | Precision | Recall | F1-score | Rank |
|---|---|---|---|---|---|
| Tamil | Multilingual-BERT | 0.74 | 0.75 | 0.74 | |
| | XLM-RoBERTa | 0.73 | 0.75 | 0.74 | |
| | **Our submission (Ensemble)** | **0.74** | **0.77** | **0.75** | 4 |
| Malayalam | Multilingual-BERT | 0.92 | 0.93 | 0.92 | |
| | XLM-RoBERTa | 0.93 | 0.94 | 0.93 | |
| | **Our submission (Ensemble)** | **0.93** | **0.94** | **0.94** | 4 |
| Kannada | Multilingual-BERT | 0.65 | 0.70 | 0.67 | |
| | XLM-RoBERTa | 0.70 | 0.74 | 0.71 | |
| | **Our submission (Ensemble)** | **0.70** | **0.75** | **0.72** | 3 |

Table 4: Official results and ablations of our model for Tamil, Malayalam and Kannada languages on the test datasets.

### 3.2 Class-Imbalance Problem

As mentioned in the second section, there is a serious class-imbalance problem in the training data. We have taken three ways to solve this problem as follow:

- **Class combination:** We combine the three classes named not-Tamil, not-Malayalam, and not-Kannada into one class named Not-in-indented-language, which helps to alleviate the class-imbalance problem.
- **Adjustment to class weights:** We count the frequency of each class: $P = \{p_i\}_{i=1}^{6}$, and then use the reciprocal of the log of frequency as class weights: $W = \{\frac{1}{log(p_i)}\}_{i=1}^{6}$. This can reduce the loss of classes which have large numbers and increase the loss of classes which have few numbers, so that the model can pay more attention to the classes which have few numbers (King and Zeng, 2001).
- **Focal loss:** Proposed by (Lin et al., 2017), focal loss has been proved to be able to deal with the class-imbalance problem. Experimental results prove that it can improve the performance of our model.

| Hyper-parameters | Value |
|---|---|
| Batch size | 8 |
| Dropout rate | 0.2 |
| Gradient clipping | 0.25 |
| Epoch | 80 |
| Learning rate | 2e-5 |

Table 5: Hyper-parameters of our model.

### 3.3 Adversarial Training

Adversarial training is an important way to enhance the robustness and generalization of neural networks. We adopt FGM (Goodfellow et al., 2015) method to interfere with the embedding layer, so as to further improve the performance of our model.

## 4 Experiment and Results

### 4.1 Experimental Settings

We use Pytorch (Paszke et al., 2017) and HuggingFace's transformers (Wolf et al., 2020) to implement our model. We use XLM-RoBERTa and multilingual BERT as encoders for text and combine XLM-RoBERTa and multilingual BERT model with the highest weighted average F1 score on the development dataset. We apply dropout with a

80% keep probability. We optimize the loss using AdamW (Loshchilov and Hutter, 2019) optimizer with a learning rate at 2e-5. We use mixed precision training based on Apex library[2]. We list all hyper-parameters in Table 5. We conduct the experiments on NVIDIA Tesla T4 GPUs. Our code is available at Github[3].

### 4.2 Results and Ablations

All teams were ranked by the weighted average F1 score. Table 4 shows results of our ensemble model on all three of languages. Our model achieved 0.75 weighted average F1 score (ranked 4th) in Tamil-English task, 0.94 weighted average F1 score (ranked 4th) in Malayalam-English task and 0.72 weighted average F1 score (ranked 3rd) in Kannada-English task.

In addition, the ablation results are also shown in Table 4. The results of the ensemble model on the test dataset of three languages are improved. The weighted average F1 score of the ensemble model on the test data is 0.01 higher than that of multilingual BERT and XLM-RoBERTa in Tamil-English task. The weighted average weighted average F1 score of the ensemble model on the test data is 0.02 higher than that of multilingual BERT and 0.01 higher than that of XLM-RoBERTa in Malayalam-English task. The result of the ensemble model on the test data is 0.05 higher than that of multilingual BERT and 0.01 higher than that of XLM-RoBERTa in Kannada-English task.

## 5 Conclusion

This paper describes our solution submitted to shared task on Offensive Language Identification in Dravidian Languages (Tamil-English, Malayalam-English, and Kannada-English). First of all, we use multilingual models trained on mixed data of three code-mixed languages to obtain better performance in all three of code-mixed languages. Secondly, we use class combination, class weights and focal loss to solve the class-imbalance problem existed in training data. Finally, we use adversarial training to further improve the performance of our model. We achieved 4th Rank in Tamil-English, Malayalam-English task and 3rd Rank in Kannada-English task. In future research, we will further consider the differences among different languages to further improve performance of our model.

[2]https://github.com/NVIDIA/apex

[3]https://github.com/codewithzichao/Multilingual-Transformers

## References


Bharathi Raja Chakravarthi, Navya Jose, Shardul Suryawanshi, Elizabeth Sherly, and John Philip McCrae. 2020a. A sentiment analysis dataset for code-mixed Malayalam-English. In *Proceedings of the 1st Joint Workshop on Spoken Language Technologies for Under-resourced languages (SLTU) and Collaboration and Computing for Under-Resourced Languages (CCURL)*, pages 177–184, Marseille, France.

Bharathi Raja Chakravarthi, Vigneshwaran Muralidaran, Ruba Priyadharshini, and John Philip McCrae. 2020b. Corpus creation for sentiment analysis in code-mixed Tamil-English text. In *Proceedings of the 1st Joint Workshop on Spoken Language Technologies for Under-resourced languages (SLTU) and Collaboration and Computing for Under-Resourced Languages (CCURL)*, pages 202–210, Marseille, France.

Bharathi Raja Chakravarthi, Ruba Priyadharshini, Navya Jose, Anand Kumar M, Thomas Mandl, Prasanna Kumar Kumaresan, Rahul Ponnusamy, Hariharan V, Elizabeth Sherly, and John Philip McCrae. 2021. Findings of the shared task on Offensive Language Identification in Tamil, Malayalam, and Kannada. In *Proceedings of the First Workshop on Speech and Language Technologies for Dravidian Languages*.

Alexis Conneau, Kartikay Khandelwal, Naman Goyal, Vishrav Chaudhary, Guillaume Wenzek, Francisco Guzmán, Edouard Grave, Myle Ott, Luke Zettlemoyer, and Veselin Stoyanov. 2020. Unsupervised cross-lingual representation learning at scale. In *Proceedings of the 58th Annual Meeting of the Association for Computational Linguistics*, pages 8440–8451, Online.

Ian J. Goodfellow, Jonathon Shlens, and Christian Szegedy. 2015. Explaining and harnessing adversarial examples. *CoRR*, abs/1412.6572.

Adeep Hande, Ruba Priyadharshini, and Bharathi Raja Chakravarthi. 2020. KanCMD: Kannada CodeMixed dataset for sentiment analysis and offensive language detection. In *Proceedings of the Third Workshop on Computational Modeling of People's Opinions, Personality, and Emotion's in Social Media*, pages 54–63, Barcelona, Spain (Online).

Gary King and Langche Zeng. 2001. Logistic regression in rare events data. *Political Analysis*, 9(2):137–163.

Tsung-Yi Lin, Priya Goyal, Ross Girshick, Kaiming He, and Piotr Dollar. 2017. Focal loss for dense object detection. In *Proceedings of the IEEE International Conference on Computer Vision (ICCV)*.

I. Loshchilov and F. Hutter. 2019. Decoupled weight decay regularization. In *ICLR*.

Adam Paszke, S. Gross, Soumith Chintala, G. Chanan, E. Yang, Zachary Devito, Zeming Lin, Alban Desmaison, L. Antiga, and A. Lerer. 2017. Automatic differentiation in pytorch. In *NIPS-W*.

Telmo Pires, Eva Schlinger, and Dan Garrette. 2019. How multilingual is multilingual BERT? In *Proceedings of the 57th Annual Meeting of the Association for Computational Linguistics*, pages 4996–5001, Florence, Italy. Association for Computational Linguistics.

Zesis Pitenis, Marcos Zampieri, and Tharindu Ranasinghe. 2020. Offensive language identification in Greek. In *Proceedings of the 12th Language Resources and Evaluation Conference*, pages 5113–5119, Marseille, France.

Tharindu Ranasinghe and Marcos Zampieri. 2020. Multilingual offensive language identification with cross-lingual embeddings. In *Proceedings of the 2020 Conference on Empirical Methods in Natural Language Processing (EMNLP)*, pages 5838–5844, Online.

Nils Reimers and Iryna Gurevych. 2019. Sentence-BERT: Sentence embeddings using Siamese BERT-networks. In *Proceedings of the 2019 Conference on Empirical Methods in Natural Language Processing and the 9th International Joint Conference on Natural Language Processing (EMNLP-IJCNLP)*, pages 3982–3992, Hong Kong, China.

Thomas Wolf, Lysandre Debut, Victor Sanh, Julien Chaumond, Clement Delangue, Anthony Moi, Pierric Cistac, Tim Rault, Rémi Louf, Morgan Funtowicz, Joe Davison, Sam Shleifer, Patrick von Platen, Clara Ma, Yacine Jernite, Julien Plu, Canwen Xu, Teven Le Scao, Sylvain Gugger, Mariama Drame, Quentin Lhoest, and Alexander M. Rush. 2020. Transformers: State-of-the-art natural language processing. In *Proceedings of the 2020 Conference on Empirical Methods in Natural Language Processing: System Demonstrations*, pages 38–45, Online.

Marcos Zampieri, Shervin Malmasi, Preslav Nakov, Sara Rosenthal, Noura Farra, and Ritesh Kumar. 2019. Predicting the type and target of offensive posts in social media. In *Proceedings of the 2019 Conference of the North American Chapter of the Association for Computational Linguistics: Human Language Technologies, Volume 1 (Long and Short Papers)*, pages 1415–1420, Minneapolis, Minnesota. Association for Computational Linguistics.

# JudithJeyafreedaAndrew@DravidianLangTech-EACL2021:Offensive language detection for Dravidian Code-mixed YouTube comments

**Judith Jeyafreeda Andrew**
Normandie Univ, UNICAEN, ENSICAEN, CNRS, GREYC, 14000 Caen, France
judithjeyafreeda@gmail.com

## Abstract

Messaging online has become one of the major ways of communication. At this level, there are cases of online/digital bullying. These include rants, taunts, and offensive phrases. Thus the identification of offensive language on the internet is a very essential task. In this paper, the task of offensive language detection on YouTube comments from the Dravidian languages of Tamil, Malayalam and Kannada are seen upon as a mutliclass classification problem. After being subjected to language specific pre-processing, several Machine Learning algorithms have been trained for the task at hand. The paper presents the accuracy results on the development datasets for all Machine Learning models that have been used and finally presents the weighted average scores for the test set when using the best performing Machine Learning model.

## 1 Introduction

With the growing freedom on the internet, facing digital bullying has become a daily phenomenon. Offensive languages can be found everywhere including comments on social media. These text are more often targeted to an individual or to a group. The task presented in this paper is to identify offensive language in YouTube comments and classify them in different categories. The comments are in code-mixed Dravidian languages of Tamil, Malayalam and Kannada. Tamil is a Dravidian language natively spoken by South Asia's Tamil people (Chakravarthi, 2020b). For over 2600 years, Tamil literature has been recorded. Sangam literature, the oldest period of Tamil literature, is dated from ca. 600 BC-300 AD. Among the Dravidian languages, Tamil has the oldest existing literature. Over 55 percent of the epigraphic inscriptions discovered by the Archaeological Survey of India (about 55,000) are in the Tamil language. Malayalam is Tamil's nearest major relative; the two started diverging around the 16th century AD.

Code-Mixing is mixing of two or more language in the same utterance. Many user generated in India are code-mixed (Chakravarthi et al., 2018; Chakravarthi, 2020a). Most of the comments contain multiple types of offensive contents. For this purpose a Multiclass classification method has been adapted to the task. Multiclass text classification is a process of classifying an instance into one of the multiple classes possible. In a multi class classification problem, an instance can belong only to one class. Several Machine Learning algorithms have been well established for Multiclass classification (Thavareesan and Mahesan, 2019, 2020a,b). However, not all of them suit the task at hand. It also has to be noted that Machine Learning algorithms has to be tuned to fit the Dravidian Languages under consideration (Tamil, Malayalam and Kannada). Thus several pre-processing techniques have been proposed for Dravidian Languages and Machine Learning algorithms have been fine tuned to suit the task (Ghanghor et al., 2021b,a; Puranik et al., 2021; Hegde et al., 2021; Yasaswini et al., 2021).

## 2 Related Work

Offensive Language Detection is one of the interesting topics where a lot of research has already been done. However, they have all been language specific. (Yin et al., 2009) has used a supervised learning approach with the context, sentiment and contextual features of the document for identifying harassment on the web. (Dadvar et al., 2013) also use supervised learning techniques with three important features: content-based features, cyberbullying features and user-based features. The content-based are based on the content of the text, the cyberbullying features aim to identify frequently bullied groups such as minority races, religion or physi-



*Proceedings of the First Workshop on Speech and Language Technologies for Dravidian Languages*, pages 169–174
April 20, 2021 ©2021 Association for Computational Linguistics

cal features, the user-based features exploits the user identity. (Razavi et al., 2010) uses pattern recognition and machine learning methods for offensive language detection. This method extracts features in different conceptual levels and applies a multilevel classification on them. (Spertus, 1997) presents Smokey, which is a system built for automatic recognition of hostile messages. (ming Xu et al.) uses a combination of Text categorization, Role labelling, sentiment analysis and topic modelling for identifying bullying on social media data. (Dinakar et al., 2012) uses common sense reasoning to identify and mitigate cyberbullying. . For this purpose, it uses a common sense knowledge base is used, which permits recognition over a broad spectrum of topics in everyday life. (Dinakar et al., 2012) concentrates on a more narrow range of subject matter associated with bullying like appearance,intelligence, racial and ethnic slurs, social acceptance, and rejection and constructs BullySpace, which is a commonsense knowledge base that encodes particular knowledge about bullying situations.

In this paper, the task of offensive language is approached as a Multiclass classification problem. (Pranckevičius and Marcinkevičius, 2017) compares various machine learning algorithms - Naïve Bayes, Random Forest, Decision Tree, Logistic Regression and support vector machines for the classification of text reviews. The findings indicate that the Logistic Regression for multi-class classification for product reviews is the best method in terms of accuracy. It should also be noted that the overall classification accuracy in combination with uni/bi/tri-gram models increases the average of classification accuracy.

With respect to research works done on Dravidian languages, particularly Dravidian code mixed text, a shared task has been proposed for the task of sentiment analysis of YouTube comments in Dravidian code-mixed text (Mandl et al., 2020). (Chakravarthi, 2020b) presents an improvement of word sense translation for under-resourced languages. It focuses on cleaning the noisy corpus in the form of code-mixed content at word-level based on orthographic information which results in improvement of Dravidian languages. It also proposes to alleviate the problem of different scripts by transcribing the native script into a common representation such as the Latin script or the International Phonetic Alphabet (IPA). (Jeyafreeda, 2020) proposed a Multiclass Classification method, where several Machine Learning algorithms have been adapted to the task of sentiment analysis and based on the accuracy of the algorithms on the development set the best suited technique is chosen for the language and the task. The languages involved are the Dravidian languages of Tamil and Malayalam. The Tamil language performed well with the Naive Bayes algorithm while the Malayalam language performed well with the Logistic Regression technique.

## 3 Data

The data for the shared task of offensive language detection in Dravidian Code-mixed languages (Chakravarthi et al., 2021) is a collection of YouTube comments. The languages used are Tamil, Malayalam and Kannada. The Tamil code-mixed YouTube comments are obtained from (Chakravarthi et al., 2020b). The Malayalam code-mixed YouTube comments are obtained from (Chakravarthi et al., 2020a). The Kannada code-mixed YouTube comments are obtained from (Hande et al., 2020). The classes are "Not-offensive", "offensive-untargeted", "offensive-targeted-individual", "offensive-targeted-group", "offensive-targeted-other", or "Not-in-indented-language". The data set for the Tamil code-mixed YouTube comments has 35,139 instances in the train set, 4,388 instances in the dev set and 4,392 instances in the test set. The data set for the Malayalam code-mixed YouTube comments has 16,010 instances in the train set, 1,999 instances in the dev set and 2,001 instances in the test set. The data set for the Kannada code-mixed YouTube comments has 6216 instances in the train set, 776 instances in the dev set and 778 instances in the test set.

## 4 Pre-processing

The Dravidian languages used needs some pre-processing in order to be able to adapt to machine learning algorithms. The pre-processing used in this paper are as follows:

- Firstly, the words in the script of the Dravidian languages of Tamil, Malayalam and Kannada are replaced by latin text (International Phonetic Alphabet (IPA)).
- Secondly, the emojis are replaced by the words that the emoji represents like happy, sad etc.

- Thirdly, removing stop words and punctuation. For this purpose, python packages for language specific stop words. The $advertools$ and $stopwordsiso$ are used for language specific stopwords.

For the purpose of training a supervised classifier, each YouTube comment in the dataset is represented by a numerical feature vector. One common approach for extracting features from text is to use the bag of words model. In this model, the frequency of the words is taken into consideration, but the order in which they occur is ignored. The Term Frequency, Inverse Document Frequency (tf-idf) measure is calculated for each term in the dataset (individually for Tamil, Malayalam and Kannada).

## 5 Machine Learning

### 5.1 Naïve Bayes

Naïve Bayes is a fairly simple yet powerful for classification. The Naïve Bayes uses conditional probabilities given by the equation 1.

$$P(h|d) = (P(d|h) * P(h))/P(d) \tag{1}$$

Where,

- P(h/d) is the probability of hypothesis h given the data d. This is called the posterior probability.
- P(d/h) is the probability of data d given that the hypothesis h was true.
- P(h) is the probability of hypothesis h being true (regardless of the data). This is called the prior probability of h.
- P(d) is the probability of the data (regardless of the hypothesis).

### 5.2 Support Vector Machines (SVM)

SVMs are very good classification algorithm. The idea is to identify hyper-planes that will separate the various features. A linear SVM is used in this paper. The classification decision is thus performed as follows:

$$f(x) = sign(W^*.x + b^*) \tag{2}$$

where x represents the input feature, W represents the model weight and b represents the bias. For the multi-class classification problem, a one-vs-rest (also known as one-vs-all) approach is used. It involves splitting the dataset into multiple binary classification problems. Thus a binary classification boundary is constructed to train each binary SVMs and the one with the highest confidence is used to solve the multi-class classification problem.

### 5.3 $K$ Nearest Neighbor(KNN)

As the name suggests, the "neighbor" plays a very important role. This algorithm calculates the distance between the new data point and the other data points. The data points with the shortest distances are selected and the new data variable is then assigned to the class with the most number of close neighbors. $K$ refers to a the number of data points with which the comparisons of distance is performed.

### 5.4 Decision Trees and Random Forests

A decision tree is the diagrammatic representation of classification. Decision trees are made through a flow-chart like structure whose:

- Internal node symbolizes an attribute
- Each branch symbolizes the outcome of the test
- Each leaf node symbolizes a class label
- The paths from the root to leaf symbolizes classification rules

Random Forest is a collection of large number of individual decision trees. Every decision tree predicts a class. Following this, each decision tree predicts a class. A vote is performed on all predicted results. The class with the maximum vote is decided on to be the output class. For the training process, the random subspace method is used (i.e) if one or a few features are very strong predictors for the target output, these features will be selected in many of the decision trees. This makes the features more correlated.

### 5.5 Logistic Regression

The well established multi-class logistic regression model is implemented for the task at hand (LR, 2017). The model of logistic regression for a multi-class classification problem forces the output layer to have discrete probability distributions over the possible $k$ classes. This is accomplished by using the softmax function. Given the input vector(z), the

| Model | Parameters |
|---|---|
| SVM | classifier=SVC; C=[0.001, 0.01, 0.1, 1, 10]; cv=3; n_jobs=4 |
| KNN | n_neighbors= [3,5,7,9];weights=['uniform', 'distance'] |
| Logistic Regression | multi_class='auto'; solver='newton-cg' |
| Naïve Bayes | alpha=0.7 |
| Decision Trees | max_depth=800; min_samples_split=5 |
| Random Forest Classifier | max_depth=800; min_samples_split=5 |

Table 1: Implementation details for the various machine learning models

| Model | Accuracy | Language |
|---|---|---|
| SVM | 0.67 | Tamil |
| KNN | 0.60 | Tamil |
| Logistic Regression | 0.67 | Tamil |
| Naïve Bayes | 0.01 | Tamil |
| Decision Tree | 0.51 | Tamil |
| Random Forest Classifier | 0.66 | Tamil |
| SVM | 0.94 | Malayalam |
| KNN | 0.92 | Malayalam |
| Logistic Regression | 0.93 | Malayalam |
| Naïve Bayes | 0.89 | Malayalam |
| Decision Tree | 0.92 | Malayalam |
| Random Forest Classifier | 0.93 | Malayalam |
| SVM | 0.64 | Kannada |
| KNN | 0.61 | Kannada |
| Logistic Regression | 0.62 | Kannada |
| Naïve Bayes | 0.59 | Kannada |
| Decision Tree | 0.60 | Kannada |
| Random Forest Classifier | 0.63 | Kannada |

Table 2: Accuracy of the different models.

softmax function works as follows:

$$softmax(z) = \frac{e^z}{\sum_{i=1}^{k} e^{z_i}} \quad (3)$$

At this point, there are $k$ outputs and thus there is a necessity to impose weights connecting each input to each output. The model thus is as follows:

$$\hat{y} = softmax(xW + b) \quad (4)$$

where, W is the weight matrix between the input and output, x being the input and b is the bias.

## 6 Implementation

The sklearn[1] package in Python is used for the feature extraction and model training. The models of logistic regression, linear support vector classification, multinomialNB, KNN, Decision Trees and random Forest provided by the sklearn toolkit are used for the training of the machine learning models discussed in section 5. The implementation details for these models are shown in table 1.

Every model described in section 5 is trained using the training sets for the three Dravidian Languages of Tamil, Malayalam and Kannada. The accuracy of each model for the three languages are calculated. The accuracy of the model is calculated using the development set. The accuracy of each model for the different languages are presented in table 2.

As seen from table 2, all models are quite closer to each other in terms of accuracy. However, the highest accurate model to use for the task of offensive language detection of YouTube comments in all three Dravidian languages(Tamil, Malayalam and Kannada) is the Support Vector Machine(SVM) classifier. From table 2, the Logistic Regression model for the Dravidian language of Tamil has the same accuracy as the SVM classifier. As the SVM classifier has the highest accuracy for the Malayalam and Kannada language, SVM classifier is still used for the Tamil language as well.

## 7 Results and Conclusions

The weighted averages for the precision, recall and F-score for the task at hand is shown in table 3. A precision of 0.54, a recall of 0.73 and a F1-score of 0.61 is achieved by the method presented in this paper for the Tamil language. A precision of 0.94, a recall of 0.94 and a F1-score of 0.93 is achieved by the method presented in this paper for the Malayalam language. A precision of 0.66, a recall of 0.67 and a F1-score of 0.63 is achieved by the method presented in this paper for the Kannada language. The same model, SVM, has been used for the offensive language detection for all three Dravidian languages of Tamil, Malayalam and Kannada. The Malayalam language has the highest value of Precision and Recall. On the other hand, Tamil language

[1] https://sklearn.org/

| Language | Precision | Recall | F1-score | Algorithm |
|---|---|---|---|---|
| Kannada | 0.66 | 0.67 | 0.63 | SVM |
| Tamil | 0.54 | 0.73 | 0.61 | SVM |
| Malayalam | 0.94 | 0.94 | 0.93 | SVM |

Table 3: Results.

has the lowest Precision value but the Recall value for the Tamil language is still high. The size of training data for the Tamil language is much higher than that of the other languages (Malayalam and Kannada). The lower precision and recall values for the Tamil language could be the result of over fitting.

Future directions of research would include using deep learning methods for the task at hand.

## References


2017. Multiclass logistic regression from scratch.

Bharathi Raja Chakravarthi. 2020a. HopeEDI: A multilingual hope speech detection dataset for equality, diversity, and inclusion. In *Proceedings of the Third Workshop on Computational Modeling of People's Opinions, Personality, and Emotion's in Social Media*, pages 41–53, Barcelona, Spain (Online). Association for Computational Linguistics.

Bharathi Raja Chakravarthi. 2020b. *Leveraging orthographic information to improve machine translation of under-resourced languages*. Ph.D. thesis, NUI Galway.

Bharathi Raja Chakravarthi, Mihael Arcan, and John P. McCrae. 2018. Improving wordnets for under-resourced languages using machine translation. In *Proceedings of the 9th Global Wordnet Conference*, pages 77–86, Nanyang Technological University (NTU), Singapore. Global Wordnet Association.

Bharathi Raja Chakravarthi, Navya Jose, Shardul Suryawanshi, Elizabeth Sherly, and John Philip McCrae. 2020a. A sentiment analysis dataset for code-mixed Malayalam-English. In *Proceedings of the 1st Joint Workshop on Spoken Language Technologies for Under-resourced languages (SLTU) and Collaboration and Computing for Under-Resourced Languages (CCURL)*, pages 177–184, Marseille, France. European Language Resources association.

Bharathi Raja Chakravarthi, Vigneshwaran Muralidaran, Ruba Priyadharshini, and John Philip McCrae. 2020b. Corpus creation for sentiment analysis in code-mixed Tamil-English text. In *Proceedings of the 1st Joint Workshop on Spoken Language Technologies for Under-resourced languages (SLTU) and Collaboration and Computing for Under-Resourced Languages (CCURL)*, pages 202–210, Marseille, France. European Language Resources association.

Bharathi Raja Chakravarthi, Ruba Priyadharshini, Navya Jose, Anand Kumar M, Thomas Mandl, Prasanna Kumar Kumaresan, Rahul Ponnusamy, Hariharan V, Elizabeth Sherly, and John Philip McCrae. 2021. Findings of the shared task on Offensive Language Identification in Tamil, Malayalam, and Kannada. In *Proceedings of the First Workshop on Speech and Language Technologies for Dravidian Languages*. Association for Computational Linguistics.

Maral Dadvar, Dolf Trieschnigg, Roeland Ordelman, and Franciska de Jong. 2013. Improving cyberbullying detection with user context. pages pp 693–696.

Karthik Dinakar, Birago Jones, Catherine Havasi, Henry Lieberman, and Rosalind Picard. 2012. Common sense reasoning for detection, prevention, and mitigation of cyberbullying. *ACM Trans. Interact. Intell. Syst.*, 2(3).

Nikhil Kumar Ghanghor, Parameswari Krishnamurthy, Sajeetha Thavareesan, Ruba Priyadharshini, and Bharathi Raja Chakravarthi. 2021a. IIITK@DravidianLangTech-EACL2021: Offensive Language Identification and Meme Classification in Tamil, Malayalam and Kannada. In *Proceedings of the First Workshop on Speech and Language Technologies for Dravidian Languages*, Online. Association for Computational Linguistics.

Nikhil Kumar Ghanghor, Rahul Ponnusamy, Prasanna Kumar Kumaresan, Ruba Priyadharshini, Sajeetha Thavareesan, and Bharathi Raja Chakravarthi. 2021b. IIITK@LT-EDI-EACL2021: Hope Speech Detection for Equality, Diversity, and Inclusion in Tamil, Malayalam and English. In *Proceedings of the First Workshop on Language Technology for Equality, Diversity and Inclusion*, Online.

Adeep Hande, Ruba Priyadharshini, and Bharathi Raja Chakravarthi. 2020. KanCMD: Kannada CodeMixed dataset for sentiment analysis and offensive language detection. In *Proceedings of the Third Workshop on Computational Modeling of People's Opinions, Personality, and Emotion's in Social Media*, pages 54–63, Barcelona, Spain (Online). Association for Computational Linguistics.

Siddhanth U Hegde, Adeep Hande, Ruba Priyadharshini, Sajeetha Thavareesan, and Bharathi Raja Chakravarthi. 2021. UVCE-IIITT@DravidianLangTech-EACL2021: Tamil Troll Meme Classification: You need to Pay more Attention. In *Proceedings of the First Workshop on Speech and Language Technologies for Dravidian Languages*. Association for Computational Linguistics.

Judith Jeyafreeda. 2020. JudithJeyafreeda@Dravidian-CodeMix-FIRE2020:Sentiment Analysis of YouTube Comments for Dravidian Languages.

Thomas Mandl, Sandip Modha, Anand Kumar M, and Bharathi Raja Chakravarthi. 2020. Overview of the

HASOC Track at FIRE 2020: Hate Speech and Offensive Language Identification in Tamil, Malayalam, Hindi, English and German. In *Forum for Information Retrieval Evaluation*, FIRE 2020, page 29–32, New York, NY, USA. Association for Computing Machinery.

Tomas Pranckevičius and Virginijus Marcinkevičius. 2017. Comparison of naive bayes, random forest, decision tree, support vector machines, and logistic regression classifiers for text reviews classification. *Baltic Journal of Modern Computing*, 5(2):221.

Karthik Puranik, Adeep Hande, Ruba Priyadharshini, Sajeetha Thavareesan, and Bharathi Raja Chakravarthi. 2021. IIITT@LT-EDI-EACL2021-Hope Speech Detection: There is always hope in Transformers. In *Proceedings of the First Workshop on Language Technology for Equality, Diversity and Inclusion*. Association for Computational Linguistics.

Amir H. Razavi, Diana Inkpen, Sasha Uritsky, and Stan Matwin. 2010. Offensive language detection using multi-level classification. In *Advances in Artificial Intelligence*, pages 16–27, Berlin, Heidelberg. Springer Berlin Heidelberg.

Ellen Spertus. 1997. Smokey: Automatic recognition of hostile messages. In *Aaai/iaai*, pages 1058–1065.

Sajeetha Thavareesan and Sinnathamby Mahesan. 2019. Sentiment Analysis in Tamil Texts: A Study on Machine Learning Techniques and Feature Representation. In *2019 14th Conference on Industrial and Information Systems (ICIIS)*, pages 320–325.

Sajeetha Thavareesan and Sinnathamby Mahesan. 2020a. Sentiment Lexicon Expansion using Word2vec and fastText for Sentiment Prediction in Tamil texts. In *2020 Moratuwa Engineering Research Conference (MERCon)*, pages 272–276.

Sajeetha Thavareesan and Sinnathamby Mahesan. 2020b. Word embedding-based Part of Speech tagging in Tamil texts. In *2020 IEEE 15th International Conference on Industrial and Information Systems (ICIIS)*, pages 478–482.

Jun ming Xu, Kwang sung Jun, Xiaojin Zhu, and Amy Bellmore. Learning from bullying traces in social media.

Konthala Yasaswini, Karthik Puranik, Adeep Hande, Ruba Priyadharshini, Sajeetha Thavareesan, and Bharathi Raja Chakravarthi. 2021. IIITT@DravidianLangTech-EACL2021: Transfer Learning for Offensive Language Detection in Dravidian Languages. In *Proceedings of the First Workshop on Speech and Language Technologies for Dravidian Languages*. Association for Computational Linguistics.

Dawei Yin, Zhenzhen Xue, Liangjie Hong, Brian Davison, April Edwards, and Lynne Edwards. 2009. Detection of harassment on web 2.0.

# professionals@DravidianLangTech-EACL2021: Malayalam Offensive Language Identification - A Minimalistic Approach

**Srinath Nair***
International Institute of Information Technology, Hyderabad
srinath.nair@research.iiit.ac.in

**Dolton Fernandes***
International Institute of Information Technology, Hyderabad
dolton.fernandes@research.iiit.ac.in

## Abstract

This paper is a description of the system that was designed by team "professionals" for the task Offensive Language Identification in Dravidian Languages-EACL 2021. Our system Dravidian Offensive Language Identifier Classifier (DrOLIC) uses Indic-BERT to generate word embeddings which is then fed into a 4-layer Multi Layer Perceptron (MLP) which does the multi-class classification task. The system helped us achieve an F1 score of 85% in the shared task for the Malayalam language.[1]

## 1 Introduction

Offensive language identification is a very popular multi-class classification research problem in NLP. A proper solution to the research problem could give the world ways and means to identify and restrict offensive content on the internet, especially on public platforms and social media. The rising demand for a system to identify offensive language on social media and in multiple languages is a testimony to the relevance of the Offensive Language Identification in Dravidian Languages task (Chakravarthi et al., 2021).

Dravidian languages are spoken in South Asia, especially in the Indian subcontinent and are a family of multiple languages including Tamil, Malayalam and Kannada, and more. Research on NLP in Indian languages was largely focused on Hindi which is spoken by a large section of people in India. Dravidian languages have now recently started getting attention from the research community which is viewed as a positive change.

In this work, we propose Dravidian Offensive Language Identifier Classifier (*DrOLIC*), a 4-layered Multi Layer Perceptron (MLP) to do the multi-class classification task of identifying offensive language for the Malayalam language. The reason for choosing a simple MLP over more complex neural networks was because of the simplicity that we see in an MLP. Our initial experimentation with MLP gave us pretty good results which were much better than what we were initially expecting out of a simple system like a Multi Layer Perceptron. This made us want to stick to the system and explore how well it would perform under different conditions.

## 2 Related Work

A lot of work has been put into identification of offensive language task in recent years with an aim to enable machines and platforms to automatically filter content, especially in social media platforms. SemEval Task-6 (Zampieri et al., 2019) is a notable shared task done in this direction where participants identified and categorized offensive language in social media. The dataset contained over 14,000 tweets in English and was divided into three sub-tasks. The sub-task A required participants to identify offensive language while sub-task B was an automatic categorization and sub-task C required participants to identify the offense target. The top teams experimented extensively with LSTM (Hochreiter and Schmidhuber, 1997), pre-trained BERT (Devlin et al., 2018) models, pre-trained GloVe vectors (Pennington et al., 2014) to achieve the results.

With the evolution of technology it has been made possible to prepare and circulate content in different languages and recent years have seen a lot of importance being given to Indian languages. The availability of content in Indian languages brought in a need to expand the task of offensive language identification into Indian languages. This resulted in much work being done in the domain, but we can

*Indicates equal contribution

[1]Link to code: https://github.com/snath99920/Professionals-EACL-2021



*Proceedings of the First Workshop on Speech and Language Technologies for Dravidian Languages*, pages 175–179
April 20, 2021 ©2021 Association for Computational Linguistics

see most work clearly leaning towards Hindi and a few other languages spoken mostly in the Northern and Central parts of India. One such work does an interesting comparative study of offensive and aggressive language in Hindi, Bangla and English (Kumar et al., 2021). They have used SVM, BERT and its derivatives like ALBERT (Lan et al., 2019) and DistilBERT (Sanh et al., 2019) to develop the classifiers. The performance of the classifiers were judged based on F1 score where they managed to achieve an F1 score as high as 0.80 using BERT.

HASOC (Hate Speech and Offensive Content identification in Indo-European Languages) track at FIRE 2019 (Mandl et al., 2019) and Fire 2020 (Mandl et al., 2020) is another such interesting initiative. The HASOC dataset was prepared from publicly available posts from Twitter Facebook and allows the participants to develop supervised models. The limitation to this task again lies in the fact that the task and the dataset are specific to three languages: English, Hindi and German.

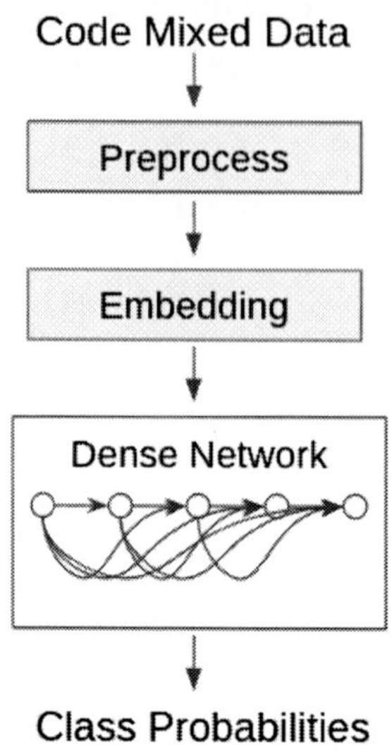


Figure 1: Overview of our method.

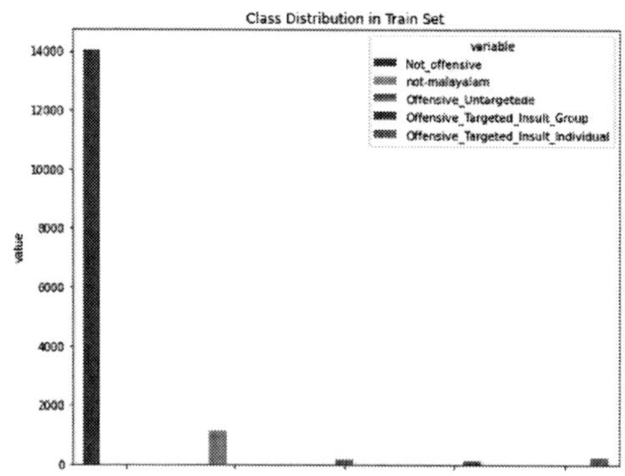


Figure 2: Visualization of train data.

## 3 System Description

We approach the problem as a multi-class classification of embeddings and for this we present the $DrOLIC$ architecture as depicted in figure 1. For every comment represented as an indic-BERT embedding, we pass it through a series of dense layers with ReLU activation to learn the representations. In order to make the layers do the learning more independently and avoid overfitting of the model, we introduce batch normalization and dropout layers respectively. To do the classification we introduce a dense softmax layer to output class probabilities.

## 4 Data and Experiments

### 4.1 Dataset

The data (Chakravarthi et al., 2021) (Chakravarthi et al., 2020a) (Chakravarthi et al., 2020b) (Hande et al., 2020) that was made available by the organizers of the task consisted of English-Malayalam code-mixed text. The data was prepared by collecting comments appearing on the trailers of various Malayalam movies on YouTube. The data was present in the form of a CSV file with the sentences belonging to the classes "Not offensive", "Offensive targeted insult group", "Offensive targeted insult individual", "Offensive untargeted" and "Not Malayalam". As one can see in figures 2, the training set has a noticeable class imbalance with most of the sentences belonging to the "Not offensive" class.

### 4.2 Data Preprocessing

The sentences in the dataset are code-mixed in Malayalam-English. We first transliterated the code-mixed sentences to English with the help of indic transliterator (Bhat et al., 2015). The sentences were then processed to remove hashtags, emojis and other unrecognised symbols. Now, out of these processed sentences, those whose length had significantly reduced (we kept the threshold as 4 words) were removed from the train and validation sets.

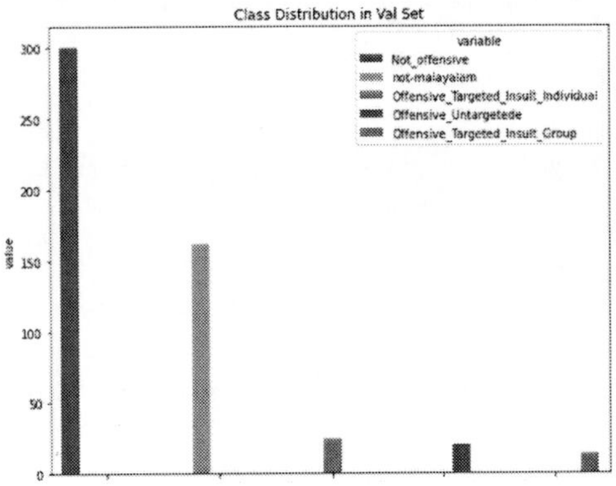


Figure 3: Visualization of validation data.

| layer | input size | output size | activation | parameters |
|---|---|---|---|---|
| $dense_1$ | 768 | 512 | $relu$ | 393728 |
| $BN_1$ | 512 | 512 | – | 2048 |
| $dense_2$ | 512 | 128 | $relu$ | 65664 |
| $BN_2$ | 128 | 128 | – | 512 |
| $dropout_1$ | 128 | 128 | – | 0 |
| $dense_3$ | 128 | 64 | $relu$ | 8256 |
| $BN_3$ | 64 | 64 | – | 256 |
| $dropout_2$ | 64 | 64 | – | 0 |
| $dense_4$ | 64 | 5 | $softmax$ | 325 |

Table 1: The detailed architecture of our model used for the multiclass classification of embeddings.

### 4.3 Generating Word Embeddings using Indic-BERT

IndicBERT (Kunchukuttan et al., 2020) (Kakwani et al., 2020), a multilingual NLU model that was pretrained on 12 Indian languages and evaluated on IndicGLUE. IndicBERT can be used for some of the most popularly spoken Dravidian languages including Malayalam, Tamil, Kannada, Telugu, etc. Notably, the model used here is ALBERT, a much more compact version of BERT with fewer parameters making it much more convenient to use.

For a comment X, we extract embeddings using indicBERT to get a 768 sized vector which is then used for training the MLP.

### 4.4 Model

We used a 4-layer Multi Layer Perceptron (MLP) to do the classification. The dimension and configuration of each layer of the model can be seen in table 1. We have 3 dense layers with ReLU activation followed by Batch Normalization layers to help the layers learn more independently. We add a dropout of 0.2 to two of the layers to reduce overfitting. At the end we have a dense layer with softmax activation to output the class probabilities. Our model has a total of 470,789 parameters out of which 469,381 are learnable.

### 4.5 Training

We first perform min-max scaling on the generated embedding vectors to not let any bias due to huge/small values propagate further into the network. The class labels are one hot encoded to make it suitable for the loss function. A random stratified split of 0.1 is done on the training data to get a validation set for our model. We don't use the original validation set provided for training in any way. It was only used to check our model's performance before submitting the final results.

As mentioned earlier, there was a huge class imbalance in the data provided. To not let this affect our model, we kept only 300 samples from the class with the highest samples in the validation set and transferred them to the the training set. The final training and validation set distribution are shown in figures 2 and 3 respectively.

The model is trained using Adam optimizer with a learning rate of $1e-5$ and a decay of $1e-4$ for 100 epochs. The learning rate was modified according to the following rule:

$$lr_i = \frac{initialLR}{1 + decay * i} \tag{1}$$

where $lr_i$ is the learning rate at the $i^{th}$ iteration, $initialLR$ is the initial learning rate, $decay$ is the decay factor and $i$ is the iteration number.

We use the categorical cross-entropy loss for evaluating how good our method is. The model computes categorical cross-entropy loss L between the predicted class probabilities and the correct class for the sample, as given below:

$$L(y, \bar{y}) = \sum y_i.log(\bar{y}_i) \tag{2}$$

where $y_i$ is the $i^{th}$ value in the model output $y$ and $\bar{y}_i$ is the $i^{th}$ value in the target $\bar{y}$.

### 4.6 Evaluation Metric

The organisers of the shared task used weighted average F1 score for getting an overall quality for the classification, so we used the same metric to seek a balance between precision and recall.

$$F1 = 2 * \frac{Precision * Recall}{Precision + Recall} \tag{3}$$

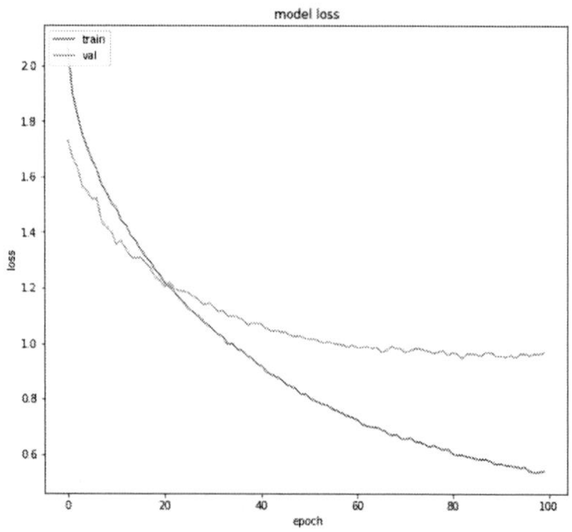


Figure 4: Loss

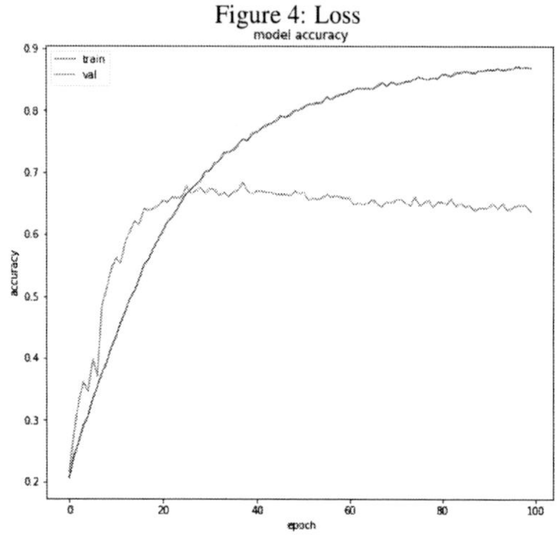


Figure 5: Accuracy

So the weighted F1 score is:

$$\tilde{F1} = \sum_{i=1}^{n} p_i x_i \tag{4}$$

where $p_i$ is the class probability for class i and n is the total number of classes.

## 5 Results and Analysis

The results of our method stands at 85% in the contest for the Malayalam language, but we have fine tuned our model since then and the latest results are reported here. The original test set was used for evaluation. The loss and accuracy curves for the training can be seen in figures 4 and 5 respectively. We noticed that MLP stops learning after some epochs, which is bound to happen because MLP's don't take care of vanishing gradients unlike for eg. LSTM.

| Sr. No. | Model | Precision | Recall | F1 |
|---|---|---|---|---|
| 1. | $MLP + Pr$ | 0.90 | 0.87 | 0.88 |
| 2. | $MLPw/oPr$ | 0.88 | 0.83 | 0.85 |

Table 2: The model descriptions and the results arranged in descending order of test F1 score. Here $Pr$ stands for preprocessing.

From table 2 we can see the importance of text processing. Without preprocessing we get a F1 score of 85%, but on preprocessing the text we get a F1 score of 88%.

## 6 Conclusion

This shared task is one of the first in the area of offensive language identification in Dravidian languages. With the advent of a need for localization of the internet by introducing content in multiple languages, this shared task is a positive step.

The most interesting aspect of our work lies in the fact that we have used a simple 4-layered MLP to train the multi-class classifier. While keeping the system, we managed to get an F1 score as high as 0.85 and achieve a shared $11^{th}$ position in the shared task. The sentences in the dataset were represented as IndicBERT embeddings. The use of IndicBERT gives us an added advantage by letting us use the same setup for around 12 popularly spoken Indian languages. To overcome the challenges of using a codemixed dataset, we transliterated the sentences into Malayalam before generating the IndicBERT embeddings. The system proposed by us can be further improved especially because, like we have mentioned earlier, this is a very simple setup. The first step that can be taken is replacing the MLP with an LSTM or an SVM which could give a significantly better result.

## 7 Acknowledgments

We would like to begin by thanking Dr. Radhika Mamidi from Language Technology Research Center (LTRC), IIIT Hyderabad for her support and guidance throughout the course of the shared task in both building the system and writing the paper for review. We would also like to thank the organizers of the Offensive Language Identification in Dravidian Languages for bringing us this opportunity. Lastly, we would like to thank the anonymous reviewers for their quality suggestions that helped us shape the paper better and for all their constructive feedback.

## References


Irshad Ahmad Bhat, Vandan Mujadia, Aniruddha Tammewar, Riyaz Ahmad Bhat, and Manish Shrivastava. 2015. Iiit-h system submission for fire2014 shared task on transliterated search. In *Proceedings of the Forum for Information Retrieval Evaluation*, FIRE '14, pages 48–53, New York, NY, USA. ACM.

Bharathi Raja Chakravarthi, Navya Jose, Shardul Suryawanshi, Elizabeth Sherly, and John Philip McCrae. 2020a. A sentiment analysis dataset for code-mixed Malayalam-English. In *Proceedings of the 1st Joint Workshop on Spoken Language Technologies for Under-resourced languages (SLTU) and Collaboration and Computing for Under-Resourced Languages (CCURL)*, pages 177–184, Marseille, France. European Language Resources association.

Bharathi Raja Chakravarthi, Vigneshwaran Muralidaran, Ruba Priyadharshini, and John Philip McCrae. 2020b. Corpus creation for sentiment analysis in code-mixed Tamil-English text. In *Proceedings of the 1st Joint Workshop on Spoken Language Technologies for Under-resourced languages (SLTU) and Collaboration and Computing for Under-Resourced Languages (CCURL)*, pages 202–210, Marseille, France. European Language Resources association.

Bharathi Raja Chakravarthi, Ruba Priyadharshini, Navya Jose, Anand Kumar M, Thomas Mandl, Prasanna Kumar Kumaresan, Rahul Ponnusamy, Hariharan V, Elizabeth Sherly, and John Philip McCrae. 2021. Findings of the shared task on Offensive Language Identification in Tamil, Malayalam, and Kannada. In *Proceedings of the First Workshop on Speech and Language Technologies for Dravidian Languages*. Association for Computational Linguistics.

Jacob Devlin, Ming-Wei Chang, Kenton Lee, and Kristina Toutanova. 2018. BERT: pre-training of deep bidirectional transformers for language understanding. *CoRR*, abs/1810.04805.

Adeep Hande, Ruba Priyadharshini, and Bharathi Raja Chakravarthi. 2020. KanCMD: Kannada CodeMixed dataset for sentiment analysis and offensive language detection. In *Proceedings of the Third Workshop on Computational Modeling of People's Opinions, Personality, and Emotion's in Social Media*, pages 54–63, Barcelona, Spain (Online). Association for Computational Linguistics.

Sepp Hochreiter and Jürgen Schmidhuber. 1997. Long short-term memory. *Neural computation*, 9:1735–80.

Divyanshu Kakwani, Anoop Kunchukuttan, Satish Golla, Gokul N.C., Avik Bhattacharyya, Mitesh M. Khapra, and Pratyush Kumar. 2020. IndicNLPSuite: Monolingual Corpora, Evaluation Benchmarks and Pre-trained Multilingual Language Models for Indian Languages. In *Findings of EMNLP*.

Ritesh Kumar, Bornini Lahiri, and Atul Kr. Ojha. 2021. Aggressive and offensive language identification in hindi, bangla, and english: A comparative study. *SN Computer Science*, 2(1):26.

Anoop Kunchukuttan, Divyanshu Kakwani, Satish Golla, Gokul N. C., Avik Bhattacharyya, Mitesh M. Khapra, and Pratyush Kumar. 2020. Ai4bharat-indicnlp corpus: Monolingual corpora and word embeddings for indic languages.

Zhenzhong Lan, Mingda Chen, Sebastian Goodman, Kevin Gimpel, Piyush Sharma, and Radu Soricut. 2019. ALBERT: A lite BERT for self-supervised learning of language representations. *CoRR*, abs/1909.11942.

Thomas Mandl, Sandip Modha, Anand Kumar M, and Bharathi Raja Chakravarthi. 2020. Overview of the hasoc track at fire 2020: Hate speech and offensive language identification in tamil, malayalam, hindi, english and german. In *Forum for Information Retrieval Evaluation*, FIRE 2020, page 29–32, New York, NY, USA. Association for Computing Machinery.

Thomas Mandl, Sandip Modha, Prasenjit Majumder, Daksh Patel, Mohana Dave, Chintak Mandlia, and Aditya Patel. 2019. Overview of the hasoc track at fire 2019: Hate speech and offensive content identification in indo-european languages. In *Proceedings of the 11th Forum for Information Retrieval Evaluation*, FIRE '19, page 14–17, New York, NY, USA. Association for Computing Machinery.

Jeffrey Pennington, Richard Socher, and Christopher Manning. 2014. Glove: Global vectors for word representation. In *Proceedings of the 2014 Conference on Empirical Methods in Natural Language Processing (EMNLP)*, pages 1532–1543, Doha, Qatar. Association for Computational Linguistics.

Victor Sanh, Lysandre Debut, Julien Chaumond, and Thomas Wolf. 2019. Distilbert, a distilled version of BERT: smaller, faster, cheaper and lighter. *CoRR*, abs/1910.01108.

Marcos Zampieri, Shervin Malmasi, Preslav Nakov, Sara Rosenthal, Noura Farra, and Ritesh Kumar. 2019. SemEval-2019 task 6: Identifying and categorizing offensive language in social media (OffensEval). In *Proceedings of the 13th International Workshop on Semantic Evaluation*, pages 75–86, Minneapolis, Minnesota, USA. Association for Computational Linguistics.

# UVCE-IIITT@DravidianLangTech-EACL2021: Tamil Troll Meme Classification: You need to Pay more Attention

**Siddhanth U Hegde**[1], **Adeep Hande**[2], **Ruba Priyadarshini**[3], **Sajeetha Thavareesan**[4], **Bharathi Raja Chakravarthi**[5]
[1] University Visvesvaraya College of Engineering, Bangalore University,
[2]Indian Institute of Information Technology Tiruchirappalli, Tamil Nadu,
[3]ULTRA Arts and Science College, India,[4]Eastern University, Sri Lanka
[5]National University of Ireland Galway
siddhanthhegde227@gmail.com

## Abstract

Tamil is a Dravidian language that is commonly used and spoken in the southern part of Asia. In the era of social media, memes have been a fun moment in the day-to-day life of people. Here, we try to analyze the true meaning of Tamil memes by categorizing them as troll and non-troll. We propose an ingenious model comprising of a transformer-transformer architecture that tries to attain state-of-the-art by using attention as its main component. The dataset consists of troll and non-troll images with their captions as text. The task is a binary classification task. The objective of the model is to pay more attention to the extracted features and to ignore the noise in both images and text.

## 1 Introduction

Over the past decade, memes have become a ubiquitous phenomenon over the internet. Memes can come in several formats such as images, video, etc. Memes can take a combined form of both text and images too. Due to its vast popularity, different people perceive memes distinctively. Recent studies have prompted the usage of memes as a mode of communication across social media platforms. The presence of text in images makes it harder to decode the sentiment or any other characteristic (Avvaru and Vobilisetty, 2020). Regardless of the type of the meme, they may be changed, recreated over social media networks, and tend to be used in contexts involving sensitive topics such as politics, casteism, etc, to add a sarcastic perspective (French, 2017; Nave et al., 2018). Due to its multimodality, conscientious analysis of memes can shed light on the societal factors, their implications on culture, and the values promoted by them (Milner, 2013). In addition to that, analyzing the intended emotion of a meme could help us acknowledge fake news, offensive content that is being propagated using the internet memes as a medium, thus helping in eradicating the spread of misinformation and hatred to the large user base in social media (Chakravarthi et al., 2020b,a). It is plausible that memes might become an integral part of most of the people, as it is used to understand racial and gender discourse on social media platforms such as Reddit (Milner, 2013; Ghanghor et al., 2021b,a). One of the approaches to overcome this is manually monitoring and moderating user-generated content. But due to the amount of data being generated on the internet every day, it would be ideal to develop automated systems to moderate them (Kumar et al., 2018; Yasaswini et al., 2021; Puranik et al., 2021; Chakravarthi et al., 2020c; Mandl et al., 2020).

Consider countries with huge populations such as India, several memes are directed towards targeted communities. To address these issues of identifying if a given meme is trolling a person's sentiments, a dataset for memes that were suspected to troll a particular community. We participate in the shared task on meme classification based on the troll classification of Tamil Memes (Suryawanshi et al., 2020). Tamil (ISO 639-3: tam) language is spoken in South Asia (Chakravarthi, 2020). The earliest inscription in India dated from 580 BCE was the Tamil inscription in pottery and then the Asoka inscription in Prakrit, Greek, and Aramaic dating from 260 BCE. The earliest known inscriptions in Sanskrit are from the inscriptions of the 1st century BCE. Tamil is the official language of Tamil Nadu, India, as well as of Singapore and Sri Lanka (Chakravarthi et al., 2018, 2019). The task primarily consists of identifying whether a meme is a *troll* or a *non-troll* (Suryawanshi and Chakravarthi, 2021). We use the images and captions that are provided to achieve the most efficient model to classify the memes. We use a combination of Vision Transform (ViT) (Dosovitskiy et al., 2021) and mBERT (Pires et al., 2019) over other pretrained models used for image classification as described in (Venkatesh et al., 2020, 2021).



*Proceedings of the First Workshop on Speech and Language Technologies for Dravidian Languages*, pages 180–186
April 20, 2021 ©2021 Association for Computational Linguistics

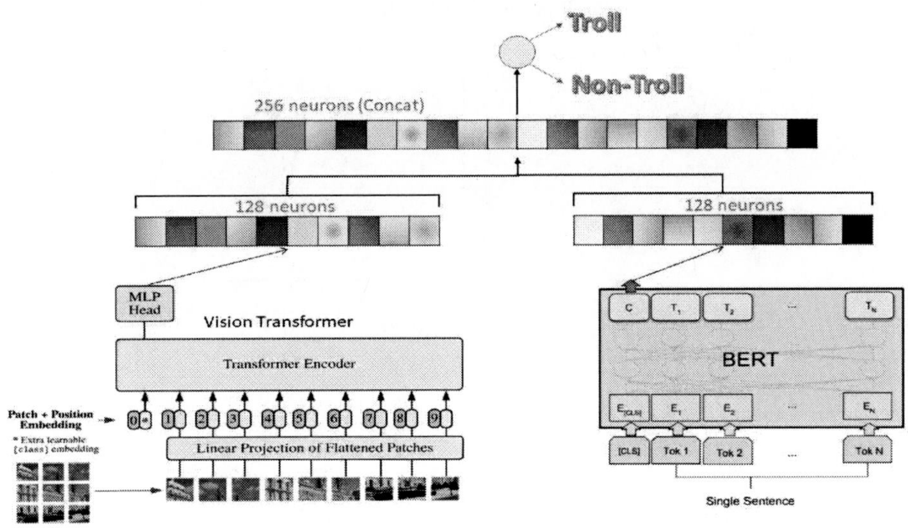


Figure 1: System Architecture (Dosovitskiy et al., 2021; Devlin et al., 2019)

## 2 Related Work

Internet memes have been a subject of interest for both Computer Vision and Natural Language Processing researchers. The type of memes that are being used illustrates the context of discussions on social media platforms. People are using memes to express themselves, and in the making, showcase their stance on a certain social issue, be it in acknowledgment or rejection of the issue (French, 2017; Boinepelli et al., 2020; Gal et al., 2016). There exist several reasons that suggest the spread of memes. Some of the reasons include novelty, simplicity, coherence. It also includes an emotional attachment, its ability to have different meanings, depending on how a person perceives it (Nave et al., 2018; Stephens, 2018; Chielens and Heylighen, 2002). Hu and Flaxman developed a multimodal sentiment analysis by developing a deep neural network that combines both visual analysis and text analysis to predict the emotional state of the user by using Tumblr posts.

## 3 Data

We use Troll Classification dataset of Tamil Memes (Suryawanshi et al., 2020). It consists of 2,699 memes, of which most of the images have text embedded within them. We are also provided with captions for all images. The distribution is shown is Table 1.

| Class | Train | Validation | Test |
|---|---|---|---|
| Troll | 1,154 | 128 | 395 |
| Non-Troll | 917 | 101 | 272 |
| total | 2,071 | 229 | 667 |

Table 1: Dataset Distribution

## 4 System Description

Multimodal deep learning is a robust and efficient way of addressing the main goals of artificial intelligence by integrating and combining multiple communicative modalities to obtain crucial results which usually improves the outcome of the single models trained. As deep learning models tend to extract features on their own, the objective can easily be achieved with the help of neural networks.

Given the images of Tamil Memes, along with the embedded text on the images, scrutiny of images and texts independently and then picking out relevant information for further process plays a climacteric role in our system. At the end of the training, the model has to output a single value stating the given meme is Troll or Non-Troll. The specialty of our model was to neither use the Convolutional Neural Networks (CNN) nor Recurrent Neural Networks (RNN). As the title of the paper points out, the model tries to gain more attention towards the salient portions of text and images. The proposed solution makes an effort to convey the importance of attention gain and its relation

| | Precision | Recall | F1-Score | Support |
|---|---|---|---|---|
| Non-Troll | 0.96 | 0.95 | 0.96 | 101 |
| Troll | 0.96 | 0.97 | 0.96 | 128 |
| Accuracy | | | 0.96 | 229 |
| Macro Avg | 0.96 | 0.96 | 0.96 | 229 |
| Weighted Avg | 0.96 | 0.96 | 0.96 | 229 |

Table 2: Classification report of ViT to images of validation set

| | Precision | Recall | F1-Score | Support |
|---|---|---|---|---|
| Non-Troll | 0.87 | 0.99 | 0.93 | 101 |
| Troll | 0.99 | 0.88 | 0.93 | 128 |
| Accuracy | | | 0.93 | 229 |
| Macro Avg | 0.93 | 0.94 | 0.93 | 229 |
| Weighted Avg | 0.94 | 0.93 | 0.93 | 229 |

Table 3: Classification report when memes are classified based on captions on validation set

to the performance of the model. The model is put forward to compute the classification is **Vision transformer** (Dosovitskiy et al., 2021) for images and **Bidirectional Encoder Representations from Transformers (BERT)** (Devlin et al., 2019) for captions of memes. This corresponds to a *transformer-transformer* architecture as shown in Fig 1.

### 4.1 Vision Transformer (ViT)

The architecture of the ViT is analogous to the transformer used for Natural Language Processing (NLP) tasks. NLP transformers use self-attention which is a highly cost-inefficient approach in regard to images. Admitting this, the technique applied here was Global Attention. Keeping the analogy of sentences, instead of 1D token embeddings as input, ViT receives a sequence of flattened 2D patches. If H, W is the height and width of the image and (P, P) is the resolution of each patch, $N = HW/P^2$ is the effective sequence length for the transformer (Dosovitskiy et al., 2021). Then the patches are projected linearly and then multiplied with an embedding matrix to eventually form patched embeddings. This along with position embeddings are sent through the transformer. Similar to BERT's [CLS] token, a token is prepended along with the patched embeddings. The transformer consists of an encoder block which consists of alternating layers of multiheaded self-attention blocks to generate attention for specific regions of the images. Layer normalization and residual connections are made comparable to the original NLP transformer.

### 4.2 BERT

The success of fine-tuning a pretrained model in computer-vision prompted researchers to do the same in Natural Language Processing. Therefore it was the objective of the researchers to develop a model which can be fine-tuned for NLP related works. **B**idirectional **E**ncoder **R**epresentations from **T**ransformers **(BERT)** (Devlin et al., 2019) is a language representation model which was trained on Wikipedia corpus. The training phase had two tasks. First was Masked Language Modelling(MLM), where the sentence had random masks in them and the model has to predict the masked word. The second task Next Sentence Prediction(NSP), where the model has to predict whether the second sentence is the continuation of the first one.

The input to the transformer is the sum of the token segmentation and positional embeddings. As the name suggests, the model is jointly conditioned on both left and right contexts to extract meaning. BERT is comparable to the transformer encoder block of (Vaswani et al., 2017). The NSP task matches the classification task for the objective of the model. During NSP, two sentence separated by [SEP] and [CLS] token are fed in and the output of the [CLS] token is pondered upon to determine the required class. Here, the input is only a single sentence with tokens and the model is fine-tuned as necessary. For this system, *bert-base-multilingual-cased* (L=12, H=768, A=12, Total Parameters=179M) was used. This model is pretrained on largest available Wikipedia dumps

|  | Precision | Recall | F1-Score | Support |
|---|---|---|---|---|
| Non-Troll | 0.60 | 0.03 | 0.06 | 272 |
| Troll | 0.60 | 0.98 | 0.74 | 395 |
| Accuracy |  |  | 0.60 | 667 |
| macro Avg | 0.60 | 0.51 | 0.40 | 667 |
| Weighted Avg | 0.60 | 0.60 | 0.47 | 667 |

Table 4: Classification report of our system on the test set

of the top 104 different languages, with the largest MLM objective, also making the model case sensitive (Pires et al., 2019).

## 5 Experiments

All suitable models were implemented using PyTorch version 1.5.0 in a google colaboratory environment. The early stages of this model include preprocessing of images. The dataset had pictures with various resolutions and had to be made equal. The images were resized to 256 X 256 pixels. Most of the images had texts on the top and bottom of the images. Texts in the images were considered as noise for classification, which resulted in performing a center crop for all images. The border of the portions was removed and images of size 224 X 224 were produced. Finally, the images were ready as the input to the transformer by normalizing the RGB channels with mean 0.485, 0.456, 0.406, and standard deviation 0.229, 0.224, 0.225 respectively. No augmentations were made to preserve the meaning of the images. The transformer was originally trained on the ImageNet dataset and had achieved remarkable results. The trained weights are transferred to this downstream task. The base version of ViT is fine-tuned which had default hyperparameters of 16 patches, an embed dimension of 768, 12 layers, 12 attention heads, and a dropout rate of 0.1. The head of the vision transformer, which outputs 1000 classes, is now replaced by a linear layer of 128 neurons. The texts were also preprocessed by removing stopwords, special characters, and punctuation. Texts need to be tokenized before feeding into the BERT configuration. After inserting it into the transformer, the resulting pooled output from the multilingual BERT model is also passed through a linear layer of 128 neurons.

The two layers obtained from the transformers are merged together to form a single layer with 256 neurons. This is passed through the ReLu activation function and a dropout to obtain one final neuron which determines the class as Troll or Non-Troll. A learning rate of $2e-5$ was used with a batch size of 16. The maximum length of the captions was truncated to 128 as memes usually do not contain very long sentences. The training was done for 4 epochs and with a linear schedule with warmup. To our surprise, the model learned very rapidly and achieved well progress on the validation set which mimicked the train set. It was also observed that merging the outputs of two different domain models did not harm the training, moreover, it helped in getting better results.

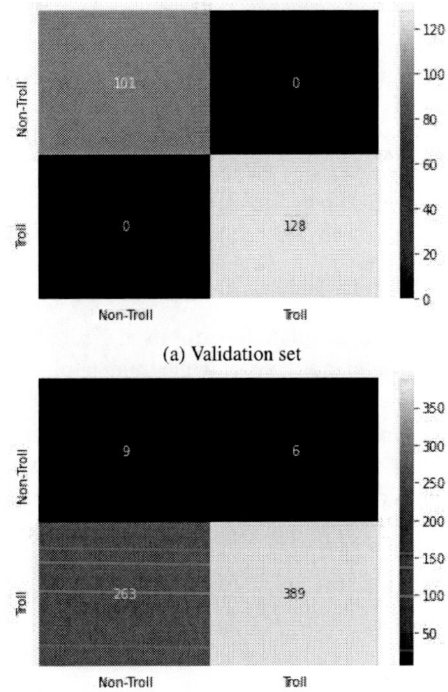


(a) Validation set

(b) Test set

Figure 2: Confusion Matrix

## 6 Results

We achieve an overall F1-score of 0.96 when we use images for classification using ViT as shown in 2. It is to be noted that using mBERT to classify memes solely based on the captions achieves 0.93 as F1-score as shown in Table 3. While we achieve such good results in comparison to the baseline scores of 0.59 mentioned in the dataset paper, we feel that if both of representations of ViT and mBERT were concatenated and then fed into a linear layer, the model would learn better. We find that the model achieves a perfect 1.00 weighted F1-score on the validation set. We believe that pre-processing of the images was a major factor for achieving a great F1-score on validation set. This argument is supported by our system's poor performance on the test set, as the test set was not coherent with the training data in terms of the positioning of texts on the images as shown in Table 4. The confusion matrix on validation and test set are as shown in Figures 2(a) and 2(b) respectively.

## 7 Conclusions

The proposed solution performs at greater heights on the validation and set in the training phase. The validation set mimics the train set as the memes are split looking at the distribution of the classes. The dataset is very small and augmenting it will not help for the optimal results. The algorithm overfits the train set undoubtedly. The reason behind the poor performance is due to the change in the distribution. The memes in the test set had multiple images which were difficult for the ViT to capture features. The model scored a F1 score of 0.46 on the test set and 1.0 on the validation set. Vast difference can be observed due to high bias. Here, in this paper, we have tried to come up with this innovation of transformer-transformer architecture which can achieve extreme results. In the future, we will be performing a wonderful task of having more transformers in parallel computation and syncing them makes an immense difference in this era of deep learning.

.

## References


Adithya Avvaru and Sanath Vobilisetty. 2020. BERT at SemEval-2020 task 8: Using BERT to analyse meme emotions. In *Proceedings of the Fourteenth Workshop on Semantic Evaluation*, pages 1094–1099, Barcelona (online). International Committee for Computational Linguistics.

Sravani Boinepelli, Manish Shrivastava, and Vasudeva Varma. 2020. SIS@IIITH at SemEval-2020 task 8: An overview of simple text classification methods for meme analysis. In *Proceedings of the Fourteenth Workshop on Semantic Evaluation*, pages 1190–1194, Barcelona (online). International Committee for Computational Linguistics.

Bharathi Raja Chakravarthi. 2020. *Leveraging orthographic information to improve machine translation of under-resourced languages*. Ph.D. thesis, NUI Galway.

Bharathi Raja Chakravarthi, Mihael Arcan, and John P. McCrae. 2018. Improving wordnets for under-resourced languages using machine translation. In *Proceedings of the 9th Global Wordnet Conference*, pages 77–86, Nanyang Technological University (NTU), Singapore. Global Wordnet Association.

Bharathi Raja Chakravarthi, Mihael Arcan, and John P. McCrae. 2019. WordNet gloss translation for under-resourced languages using multilingual neural machine translation. In *Proceedings of the Second Workshop on Multilingualism at the Intersection of Knowledge Bases and Machine Translation*, pages 1–7, Dublin, Ireland. European Association for Machine Translation.

Bharathi Raja Chakravarthi, Navya Jose, Shardul Suryawanshi, Elizabeth Sherly, and John Philip McCrae. 2020a. A sentiment analysis dataset for code-mixed Malayalam-English. In *Proceedings of the 1st Joint Workshop on Spoken Language Technologies for Under-resourced languages (SLTU) and Collaboration and Computing for Under-Resourced Languages (CCURL)*, pages 177–184, Marseille, France. European Language Resources association.

Bharathi Raja Chakravarthi, Vigneshwaran Muralidaran, Ruba Priyadharshini, and John Philip McCrae. 2020b. Corpus creation for sentiment analysis in code-mixed Tamil-English text. In *Proceedings of the 1st Joint Workshop on Spoken Language Technologies for Under-resourced languages (SLTU) and Collaboration and Computing for Under-Resourced Languages (CCURL)*, pages 202–210, Marseille, France. European Language Resources association.

Bharathi Raja Chakravarthi, Ruba Priyadharshini, Vigneshwaran Muralidaran, Shardul Suryawanshi, Navya Jose, Elizabeth Sherly, and John P. McCrae. 2020c. Overview of the Track on Sentiment Analysis for Dravidian Languages in Code-Mixed Text. In *Forum for Information Retrieval Evaluation*, FIRE 2020, page 21–24, New York, NY, USA. Association for Computing Machinery.

Klaas Chielens and F. Heylighen. 2002. Operationalization of meme selection criteria : Methodologies to empirically test memetic predictions.

Jacob Devlin, Ming-Wei Chang, Kenton Lee, and Kristina Toutanova. 2019. BERT: Pre-training of deep bidirectional transformers for language understanding. In *Proceedings of the 2019 Conference of the North American Chapter of the Association for Computational Linguistics: Human Language*

*Technologies, Volume 1 (Long and Short Papers)*, pages 4171–4186, Minneapolis, Minnesota. Association for Computational Linguistics.

Alexey Dosovitskiy, Lucas Beyer, Alexander Kolesnikov, Dirk Weissenborn, Xiaohua Zhai, Thomas Unterthiner, Mostafa Dehghani, Matthias Minderer, Georg Heigold, Sylvain Gelly, Jakob Uszkoreit, and Neil Houlsby. 2021. An image is worth 16x16 words: Transformers for image recognition at scale. In *International Conference on Learning Representations*.

J. H. French. 2017. Image-based memes as sentiment predictors. In *2017 International Conference on Information Society (i-Society)*, pages 80–85.

Noam Gal, Limor Shifman, and Zohar Kampf. 2016. "it gets better": Internet memes and the construction of collective identity. *New Media & Society*, 18:1698 – 1714.

Nikhil Kumar Ghanghor, Parameswari Krishnamurthy, Sajeetha Thavareesan, Ruba Priyadharshini, and Bharathi Raja Chakravarthi. 2021a. IIITK@DravidianLangTech-EACL2021: Offensive Language Identification and Meme Classification in Tamil, Malayalam and Kannada. In *Proceedings of the First Workshop on Speech and Language Technologies for Dravidian Languages*, Online. Association for Computational Linguistics.

Nikhil Kumar Ghanghor, Rahul Ponnusamy, Prasanna Kumar Kumaresan, Ruba Priyadharshini, Sajeetha Thavareesan, and Bharathi Raja Chakravarthi. 2021b. IIITK@LT-EDI-EACL2021: Hope Speech Detection for Equality, Diversity, and Inclusion in Tamil, Malayalam and English. In *Proceedings of the First Workshop on Language Technology for Equality, Diversity and Inclusion*, Online. Association for Computational Linguistics.

Anthony Hu and Seth Flaxman. 2018. Multimodal sentiment analysis to explore the structure of emotions. *Proceedings of the 24th ACM SIGKDD International Conference on Knowledge Discovery & Data Mining*.

Ritesh Kumar, Atul Kr. Ojha, Shervin Malmasi, and Marcos Zampieri. 2018. Benchmarking aggression identification in social media. In *Proceedings of the First Workshop on Trolling, Aggression and Cyberbullying (TRAC-2018)*, pages 1–11, Santa Fe, New Mexico, USA. Association for Computational Linguistics.

Thomas Mandl, Sandip Modha, Anand Kumar M, and Bharathi Raja Chakravarthi. 2020. Overview of the HASOC Track at FIRE 2020: Hate Speech and Offensive Language Identification in Tamil, Malayalam, Hindi, English and German. In *Forum for Information Retrieval Evaluation*, FIRE 2020, page 29–32, New York, NY, USA. Association for Computing Machinery.

R. M. Milner. 2013. Fcj-156 hacking the social: Internet memes, identity antagonism, and the logic of lulz. *The Fibreculture Journal*, pages 61–91.

Nir Noon Nave, Limor Shifman, and Keren Tenenboim-Weinblatt. 2018. Talking it personally: Features of successful political posts on facebook. *Social Media + Society*, 4.

Telmo Pires, Eva Schlinger, and Dan Garrette. 2019. How multilingual is multilingual BERT? In *Proceedings of the 57th Annual Meeting of the Association for Computational Linguistics*, pages 4996–5001, Florence, Italy. Association for Computational Linguistics.

Karthik Puranik, Adeep Hande, Ruba Priyadharshini, Sajeetha Thavareesan, and Bharathi Raja Chakravarthi. 2021. IIITT@LT-EDI-EACL2021-Hope Speech Detection: There is always hope in Transformers. In *Proceedings of the First Workshop on Language Technology for Equality, Diversity and Inclusion*. Association for Computational Linguistics.

Niall P Stephens. 2018. Ryan m. milner, the world made meme: Public conversations and participatory media. *International Journal of Communication*, 12:4.

Shardul Suryawanshi and Bharathi Raja Chakravarthi. 2021. Findings of the shared task on Troll Meme Classification in Tamil. In *Proceedings of the First Workshop on Speech and Language Technologies for Dravidian Languages*. Association for Computational Linguistics.

Shardul Suryawanshi, Bharathi Raja Chakravarthi, Pranav Verma, Mihael Arcan, John Philip McCrae, and Paul Buitelaar. 2020. A dataset for troll classification of TamilMemes. In *Proceedings of the WILDRE5– 5th Workshop on Indian Language Data: Resources and Evaluation*, pages 7–13, Marseille, France. European Language Resources Association (ELRA).

Ashish Vaswani, Noam Shazeer, Niki Parmar, Jakob Uszkoreit, Llion Jones, Aidan N Gomez, Ł ukasz Kaiser, and Illia Polosukhin. 2017. Attention is all you need. In *Advances in Neural Information Processing Systems*, volume 30. Curran Associates, Inc.

Venkatesh, Y Nagaraju, S SahanaT, S Swetha, and Siddhanth U Hegde. 2020. Transfer learning based convolutional neural network model for classification of mango leaves infected by anthracnose. *2020 IEEE International Conference for Innovation in Technology (INOCON)*, pages 1–7.

Venkatesh, Nagaraju Yallappa, Siddhanth Udayashankar Hegde, and Sangeetha Raj Stalin. 2021. Fine-tuned mobilenet classifier for classification of strawberry and cherry fruit types. *Journal of Computer Science*, 17(1):44–54.

Konthala Yasaswini, Karthik Puranik, Adeep Hande, Ruba Priyadharshini, Sajeetha Thavareesan, and Bharathi Raja Chakravarthi. 2021. IIITT@DravidianLangTech-EACL2021: Transfer Learning for Offensive Language Detection in Dravidian Languages. In *Proceedings of the First Workshop on Speech and Language Technologies for Dravidian Languages*. Association for Computational Linguistics.

# IIITT@DravidianLangTech-EACL2021: Transfer Learning for Offensive Language Detection in Dravidian Languages

**Konthala Yasaswini**[1], **Karthik Puranik**[1], **Adeep Hande**[1],
**Ruba Priyadarshini**[2], **Sajeetha Thavareesan**[3], **Bharathi Raja Chakravarthi**[4]
[1]Indian Institute of Information Technology Tiruchirappalli, Tamil Nadu,
[2]ULTRA Arts and Science College, Tamil Nadu, India,
[3]Eastern University, Sri Lanka, [4]National University of Ireland Galway
konthalay18c@iiitt.ac.in

## Abstract

This paper demonstrates our work for the shared task on Offensive Language Identification in Dravidian Languages-EACL 2021. Offensive language detection in the various social media platforms was identified previously. However, with the increase in the diversity of users, there is a need to identify the offensive language in multilingual posts which are largely code-mixed or written in a non-native script. We approach this challenge with various transfer learning-based models to classify a given post or comment in Dravidian languages (Malayalam, Tamil and Kannada) into 6 categories. The source codes for our systems are published [1].

## 1 Introduction

Over the past decade, there has been a tremendous increase in the user-generated content on social media platforms such as Twitter, YouTube, and Instagram (Wiedemann et al., 2020). They provide a common space for discussion and interactions, for users to connect with each other, express their opinions, and share their knowledge. Users may use offensive posts/comments which may be directed towards an individual or community(Chowdhury et al., 2020) which is one of the common problems in the online social media platforms (Nogueira dos Santos et al., 2018). They act as catalysts for leaving offensive content which could have a harmful and detrimental effect on users' mental health. The automatic detection of such malevolent comments/posts has become a crucial field of research in natural language processing in recent years(Wiedemann et al., 2019).

Tamil (ISO 639-1: ta), Malayalam (ISO 639-1: ml), and Kannada (ISO 639-3:kan) belong to the Dravidian languages, spoken mainly in India (Chakravarthi et al., 2019). The earliest inscription in India dated to 580 BCE was the Tamil inscription in pottery. A Tamil prayer book in ancient Tamil script called *Thambiran Vanakkam*, was written by Portuguese Christian missionaries in 1578, thereby rendering Tamil the first Indian language to be printed and published. One of the first dictionaries written in the Indian language was the Tamil Lexicon, published by the University of Madras. Tamil, Malayalam, and Kannada has its own script however users in the social media use the Latin script generating code-mixing (Chakravarthi et al., 2020c; Mandl et al., 2020). Code-mixing refers to the coupling of two or more languages in a single sentence (Priyadharshini et al., 2020). It is a quite common phenomenon observed in multilingual societies throughout the world (Chakravarthi, 2020; Bali et al., 2014; Jose et al., 2020). It is widely considered as a default mode of communication in countries like India and Mexico (Parshad et al., 2014; Pratapa et al., 2018; Chakravarthi et al., 2018). Code-mixed sentence maintains the fundamental grammar and script of the languages it is comprised of (Lal et al., 2019).

This paper is a description of our submission to the shared task for Offensive Language Detection (Chakravarthi et al., 2021). The task is to identify offensive content in the code-mixed comments/posts in the Dravidian languages collected from social media and classify it into Not Offensive, Offensive Untargeted, Offensive Targeted Insult Individual, Offensive Targeted Insult Group, Offensive Targeted Insult Other and Not in-indented-language.

The rest of the paper is organized as follows, Section 2 represents previous work on Offensive Language Detection in Dravidian Languages. Section 3 entails a detailed analysis of the datasets for Tamil, Malayalam, and Kannada. Section 4 presents a description of the models used for our purpose, while Section 5 explains the experiment setup for the models. Section 6 analyzes our re-

[1]https://github.com/adeepH/DravidianLangTech-OLD



*Proceedings of the First Workshop on Speech and Language Technologies for Dravidian Languages*, pages 187–194
April 20, 2021 ©2021 Association for Computational Linguistics

sults achieved, and Section 7 presents the future direction for our work.

## 2 Related Work

The extensive use of offensive content on social media platforms is disastrous to an advancing society as it serves to promote violence, chaos, abuse, and verbal hostility and extremely affects individuals at distinct levels. Research in offensive language detection has been evolving rapidly over the past few years. Fortuna and Nunes (2018) gives an outline of the current state-of-the-art in offensive language detection and related tasks like hate speech detection. Davidson et al. (2017) introduced a publicly available dataset, notably for offensive language detection, by classifying tweets into hate speech, offensive but not hate speech, and neither. Several attributes like TF-IDF, n-grams, readability scores, and sentiment were used to build machine learning models such as logistic regression and Support Vector Machine in their work. A system combination of SVM and deep neural networks were developed by Hassan et al. (2020) for detecting abusive language which achieved F1-score of 90.51% on the test set.

Various experiments have been performed on code-mixed data. Kumar et al. (2018) developed numerous systems for detecting offensive language in Hindi and English which used data from Twitter and Facebook. Hindi-English Offensive Tweet (HEOT) dataset comprising of tweets in Hindi-English code mixed language classified into three classes; non-offensive, abusive, and hate-speech was introduced by Mathur et al. (2018). Their work utilized transfer learning wherein the model used Convolutional Neural Networks which was pre-trained on tweets in English followed by retraining on Hinglish tweets. Bohra et al. (2018) examined the problem of hate speech detection in code-mixed texts and presented a dataset of code-mixed Hindi-English comprising of tweets posted on Twitter. Hussein et al. (2020) presented a system, C-BiGRU, comprised of a convolutional neural network(CNN) along with a bidirectional recurrent neural network(RNN) to identify offensive speech on social media. An embedding model-based classifier to identify offensive language from Manglish dataset was developed in Renjit and Idicula (2020). Multimodal systems of Tamil troll memes were developed to classify memes that were deemed offensive towards other people (Suryawanshi et al., 2020; Hegde et al., 2021).

## 3 Dataset

The organizers provided us with Tamil-English (Chakravarthi et al., 2020b), Malayalam-English (Chakravarthi et al., 2020a) and Kannada-English (Hande et al., 2020) code-mixed text data derived from social media. The datasets comprised of all six types of code-mixed sentences : No-code-mixing, Inter-sentential Code-Mixing, Only Tamil/Kannada/Malayalam (written in Latin script), Code-switching at morphological level (written in both Latin and Tamil/Kannada/Malayalam script), Intra-sentential mix of English and Tamil/Kannada/Malayalam (written in Latin script only) and Inter-sentential and Intra-sentential mix (Hande et al., 2020). The training dataset consists of comments in six different classes:

- **Not-Offensive**: Comments which are not offensive, impolite, rude, or profane.
- **Offensive-Targeted-Insult-Individual**: offensive comments targeting an individual.
- **Offensive-Targeted-Insult-Group**: offensive comments targeting a group.
- **Offensive-Targeted-Insult-Other**: offensive comments targeting an issue, an organization, or an event other than the previous two categories.
- **Offensive-Untargeted**: offensive comments targeting no one.
- **Not-in-intended-language**: comments not in Tamil/Malayalam/Kannada.

| Label | Tamil | Malayalam | Kannada |
|---|---|---|---|
| NO | 25,425 | 14,153 | 3,544 |
| NIL | 1,454 | 1,287 | 1,522 |
| OTI | 2,343 | 239 | 487 |
| OTG | 2,557 | 140 | 329 |
| OTO | 454 | - | 123 |
| OU | 2,906 | 191 | 212 |
| **Total** | **35,139** | **16,010** | **6,217** |

Table 1: Class distribution for Training set in Tamil, Malayalam and Kannada. **NO**-Not offensive, **NIL**-Not in indented language, **OTI**-Offensive-Targeted-Insult-Individual, **OTG** - Offensive Targeted Insult Group, **OTO**- Offensive Targeted Insult Other, **OU**- Offensive Untargeted

Table 1 shows the class distribution in Tamil, Malayalam, and Kannada training datasets. The imbalance of the dataset depicts a realistic picture observed on social media platforms.

## 4 System Description

We use pre-trained transformer models for classifying offensive speech in Tamil, Kannada, and Malayalam. We do not perform text preprocessing techniques such as lemmatization, stemming, removing sinp words, etc, to preserve context to the users' intent. Since we use transformer models, it is observed that stop words receive a similar amount of attention as non-stop words, as transformer models are contextual models ( BERT, XLM-RoBERTa, etc).

### 4.1 CNN-BiLSTM

This is a hybrid of bidirectional LSTM and CNN architectures (Chiu and Nichols, 2016). The convolutional neural network extracts character features from each word. The Convolutional neural network extracts feature vector from character-level feature. For each word, these vectors are concatenated and fed to the BiLSTM network and then to the output layers. CNN-BiLSTM, along with Doc2Vec embedding achieved very high results for sequence classification tasks (Rhanoui et al., 2019), thus we use GLoVE embedding along with CNN BiLSTM.

### 4.2 mBERT

Multilingual models of BERT (mBERT) (Pires et al., 2019) are largely based on the architecture of BERT (Devlin et al., 2019). This model was pretrained using the same pretraining strategy that was employed to BERT, i.e, Masked Language Modeling (MLM) and Next Sentence Prediction (NSP). It was pretrained on the Wikipedia dump of top 104 languages. To account for the data imbalance due to the size of Wikipedia for a given language, exponentially smoothed weighting of data was performed during data creation and wordpiece vocabulary creation. This results in high resource languages being under-sampled, while low resourced languages being over-sampled.

### 4.3 XLM-RoBERTa

XLM-RoBERTa (Conneau et al., 2020) is a large multi-lingual language model, trained on 2.5TB of cleaned CommonCrawl data in 100 languages. It can be recognized as a union of XLM (Lample and Conneau, 2019) and RoBERTa (Liu et al., 2019). The training process involves sampling streams of text from different languages and masking some tokens, such that the model predicts the missing tokens. Using SentencePiece (Kudo and Richardson, 2018) with a unigram language model (Kudo, 2018) subword tokenization is directly applied on raw text data. Since there are no language embeddings used, this allows the model to better deal with code-switching. XLM-RoBERTa manifested remarkable performance in various multilingual NLP tasks.

### 4.4 DistilmBERT

DistilBERT (Sanh et al., 2020) follows the same architecture of that of BERT (Devlin et al., 2019), while reducing the number of layers by a factor of 2. DistilBERT follows a triple loss language modeling, which combines cosine distance loss with knowledge distillation for it (student) to learn from the larger pretrained natural language model (teacher) during pretraining. In spite being a 40% smaller model than BERT in terms of the number of parameters, DistilBERT is 60% faster than the latter, and retains 97% of language understanding capabilities to that of BERT. The main reason we use a cased pretrained multilingual DistilBERT model is due to the presence of code-mixed data in our corpus (These tend to be case sensitive language in the corpus).

### 4.5 ALBERT

Training models with hundreds of millions, if not billions of parameters is becoming increasingly difficult, mainly owing to GPU/TPU limitations. ALBERT (Lan et al., 2020) aimed to reproduce the natural language understanding capabilities of BERT (Devlin et al., 2019) by opting several parameter reduction techniques. ALBERT (A Lite BERT) achieves State of The Art (SoTA) results on GLUE, RACE and SQUAD datasets. ALBERT uses cross-layer parameter sharing and Sentence Order Prediction objective (SoP), while disregarding Next Sentence Prediction Loss (NSP) which was previously used in BERT.

### 4.6 ULMFiT

ULMFiT (Howard and Ruder, 2018) effectively presented a method to fine-tune neural networks for inductive transfer learning for performing NLP tasks. Language models are trained to adapt to various features of the target task. The quality of the base model determines the final performance after fine-tuning. The language model is pre-trained on a large corpus of language to adapt and capture the important aspects and features of the language. Fine-tuning is essential for small and medium-sized datasets.

The target task LM is then fine-tuned to fit the particular task well. Discriminative fine-tuning and slanted triangular learning rates are used for this process. Different layers are found to capture different information, thus, they require different learning rates.

$$\theta_t^l = \theta_{t-1}^l - \eta^l.\nabla_{\theta^l} J(\theta) \quad (1)$$

The weights for each layer l=1, 2, ..., L is the layer number, $\eta^1$ is the learning rate for the lth layer, L is the number of layers, $\theta_t^i$ is the weights of the lth layer at iteration t and $\Delta(\theta^1)[J(\theta)]$ is the gradient regarding the model's objective function

## 5 Experiment Setup

We describe the experiment setup for our experiments performed. All of our systems were trained on Google Colab (Bisong, 2019). All of our models' parameters are as stated in Table 2. The results on the test set are tabulated in Table 3. For developing systems with pretrained transformer-based models, we use huggingface's transformer library for easier implementation (Wolf et al., 2020).

| Parameter | Value |
|---|---|
| Number of LSTM units | 256 |
| Dropout | 0.3 |
| Activation Function | Softmax |
| Max Len | 128 |
| Batch Size | 32 |
| Optimizer | AdamW |
| Learning Rate | 2e-5 |
| Loss Function | cross-entropy |
| n(Epochs) | 5 |

Table 2: parameters for the models

### 5.1 CNN-BiLSTM

We implemented a CNN (Kim, 2014) followed by a Bidirectional LSTM layer. GloVe[2] embeddings of dimensions = 100 were used. The architecture of the model has a 1D convolutional layer followed by a dropout layer and then bidirectional LSTM layer. The embedding texts are then fed into the convolution layer. The dropout layer is used for regularization. The output of the convolutional layer is then passed into the bidirectional LSTM layer. Finally, it consists of a dense layer followed by the output layer. Stochastic Gradient Descent (SGD) was used as the optimizer with a learning rate = 0.01. Kullback leibler divergence (Kullback and Leibler, 1951) was used as the loss function.

### 5.2 mBERT

The pretrained BERT Multilingual model ***bert-base-multilingual-uncased*** having 12 layers, 768 hidden, 12 attention heads with 110M parameters[3] was used. The model was implemented using PyTorch. During the fine-tuning of the model, bidirectional LSTM layers were integrated into the model. From the transformer encoder, the BiLSTM layer can take the embeddings as the input which leads to the increase in the information being fed which results in the improvement of the context and precision (Fang et al., 2019; Puranik et al., 2021).

### 5.3 XLM-R

We use **XLM-RoBERTa-base**, a pretrained multilingual language model that has been trained on over 100 languages. This model has 12 Layers, 768 Hidden, 12 attention heads and 270M parameters. We fine-tune this model for sequence classification on Malayalam and Kannada. It is trained on 3.3 GB, 7.6 GB, and 12.2 GB of monolingual Kannada, Malayalam, and Tamil corpus, respectively(Conneau et al., 2020). This model is also pretrained on 300.8 GB of English corpus. This allows the model for effective cross-lingual transfer. As we are primarily dealing with code-mixed data, it is effective as it has been pretrained on other languages before hand.

### 5.4 DistilBERT

The DistilBERT (Sanh et al., 2020) is a transformer model trained by distilling BERT base. A pretrained DistilBERT, ***distilbert-base-multilingual-cased*** comprised of 6-layers, 768-hidden, 12-heads, and 134M parameters, was fine-tuned by implementing in PyTorch.

[2]`http://nlp.stanford.edu/data/glove.6B.zip`

[3]`https://github.com/google-research/bert`

| Model | Weighted F1-Score | | |
|---|---|---|---|
| | Malayalam | Tamil | Kannada |
| CNN-BiLSTM | 0.8367 | 0.6102 | 0.4857 |
| mBERT-cased + BiLSTM | 0.9282 | 0.7149 | 0.7029 |
| mBERT-uncased | 0.8338 | 0.6189 | 0.3936 |
| mBERT-cased | 0.8296 | 0.6078 | 0.3882 |
| XLM-R-base | 0.8645 | 0.6173 | 0.4748 |
| DistilmBERT-cased | 0.9432 | 0.7569 | **0.7277** |
| albert-base-v2 | 0.8268 | 0.6112 | 0.3890 |
| ULMFiT | **0.9603** | **0.7895** | 0.7000 |

Table 3: Weighted F1-scores of offensive language detection models on the datasets

### 5.5 ALBERT

The architecture of ALBERT is very similar to BERT and has a much smaller parameter size compared to BERT. We fine-tuned the pretrained ALBERT model, ***albert-base-v2*** which has 12 repeating layers, 128 embedding, 768-hidden, 12-heads and 12M parameters. The training environment is same as that of BERT.

### 5.6 ULMFiT

After preprocessing the tweets, a pretrained language model AWD-LSTM is fed to the data. AWD-LSTM language model has an embeddings size of 400 and 3 layers which consists of 1150 hidden activations per layer. It also has a BPTT batch size of 70. Adam optimizer with default values, $\beta_1 = 0.9$ and $\beta_2 = 0.99$ is employed. The start and end learning rates are set to *1e-8 and 1e-2* respectively, and it's then fine-tuned by adhering to the slanted triangular learning rates by freezing few of the layers and dropouts with a multiplier of 0.5 were applied.

## 6 Results and Analysis

We have experimented with various classifiers like Multilingual BERT, XLM-RoBERTa, distilBERT, ULMFiT, CNN. The evaluation metric of this task is weighted average F1-score . This is done to account for the class imbalance in the dataset. The results of the experiments performed using different models on the test datasets of Malayalam, Tamil and Kannada are shown in Table 3.

We have trained BERT-BiLSTM, XLM-RoBERTa, CNN-BiLSTM and ULMFiT models on the training datasets of Malayalam, Tamil and Kannada. Among the mentioned models, CNN-BiLSTM gave a good F1-score of 0.8444 on Malayalam development set. For Tamil and Kannada, this model showed rather poor performance with F1-scores of 0.6128 and 0.4827, respectively. ULMFiT and XLM-RoBERTa models gave almost similar F1-scores of 0.7034 and 0.7083 respectively on Tamil. We submitted BERT-BiLSTM model as it has obtained an F1-score of 0.7285 on Tamil development set. ULMFiT gave F1-scores of 0.9048 and 0.7077 on Malayalam and Kannada development set. For Malayalam and Kannada, XLM-RoBERTa model was submitted with F1-scores of 0.9113 and 0.7156 as the model has marginally outclassed ULMFiT and BERT-BiLSTM models.

Models like multilingual BERT, ALBERT, and XLM-RoBERTa gave similar and poor results on the three test datasets. One of the reasons for the poor performance of these models is the imbalance in the distribution of the classes. In the dataset, the majority of the texts belong to not-offensive while the other classes like not-in-indented language, offensive-targeted-insult-group, offensive-targeted-insult-other, offensive-untargeted have a small classification of texts. These models performed better on the majority class and poorly on the minority classes. XLM-RoBERTa gave better results on the validation set, but due to the class imbalances and the use of code-mixed and writing in non-native languages, it could have underperformed on the test set. It is observed that the CNN-BiLSTM model also performed poorly. In the CNN-BiLSTM model, the convolution layer was not capturing the correlations and patterns within the input. Moreover, the BiLSTM layer did not apprehend the dependencies within the attributes extracted by the CNN layer, which has led to the poor performance of the model. For the word embeddings, we used GloVe embedding which did not perform well on the CNN. Multilingual BERT-BiLSTM performed well on the test set, but did not perform well on the development set. Fine-tuning the transformer model DistilBERT has resulted in a good performance. ULMFiT model attained a better performance in predicting the minority classes as well. The major reasons for the better performance of ULMFiT over other models are due to its superior fine-tuning methods and learning rate scheduler.

## 7 Conclusion

In this paper, we have explored various transformer models for detecting offensive language in social media posts in Malayalam, Tamil and Kannada. We observed a class imbalance problem in the provided datasets of the task, which has a consequential impact on system performance. Different network architectures can show different results. Our work manifests that fine-tuning transformer models result in better performance. The relatively high F1-scores of 0.9603, 0.7895 on Malayalam, Tamil were achieved by ULMFiT and 0.7277 on Kannada was achieved by DistilmBERT model. For future work, we intend to explore pseudo-Labelling and class weighting for better performance of our models.

## References

Kalika Bali, Jatin Sharma, Monojit Choudhury, and Yogarshi Vyas. 2014. "I am borrowing ya mixing ?" an analysis of English-Hindi code mixing in Facebook. In *Proceedings of the First Workshop on Computational Approaches to Code Switching*, pages 116–126, Doha, Qatar. Association for Computational Linguistics.

Ekaba Bisong. 2019. *Google Colaboratory*, pages 59–64. Apress, Berkeley, CA.

Aditya Bohra, Deepanshu Vijay, Vinay Singh, Syed Sarfaraz Akhtar, and Manish Shrivastava. 2018. A dataset of Hindi-English code-mixed social media text for hate speech detection. In *Proceedings of the Second Workshop on Computational Modeling of People's Opinions, Personality, and Emotions in Social Media*, pages 36–41, New Orleans, Louisiana, USA. Association for Computational Linguistics.

Bharathi Raja Chakravarthi. 2020. HopeEDI: A multilingual hope speech detection dataset for equality, diversity, and inclusion. In *Proceedings of the Third Workshop on Computational Modeling of People's Opinions, Personality, and Emotion's in Social Media*, pages 41–53, Barcelona, Spain (Online). Association for Computational Linguistics.

Bharathi Raja Chakravarthi, Mihael Arcan, and John P. McCrae. 2018. Improving wordnets for under-resourced languages using machine translation. In *Proceedings of the 9th Global Wordnet Conference*, pages 77–86, Nanyang Technological University (NTU), Singapore. Global Wordnet Association.

Bharathi Raja Chakravarthi, Mihael Arcan, and John P. McCrae. 2019. WordNet gloss translation for under-resourced languages using multilingual neural machine translation. In *Proceedings of the Second Workshop on Multilingualism at the Intersection of Knowledge Bases and Machine Translation*, pages 1–7, Dublin, Ireland. European Association for Machine Translation.

Bharathi Raja Chakravarthi, Navya Jose, Shardul Suryawanshi, Elizabeth Sherly, and John Philip McCrae. 2020a. A sentiment analysis dataset for code-mixed Malayalam-English. In *Proceedings of the 1st Joint Workshop on Spoken Language Technologies for Under-resourced languages (SLTU) and Collaboration and Computing for Under-Resourced Languages (CCURL)*, pages 177–184, Marseille, France. European Language Resources association.

Bharathi Raja Chakravarthi, Vigneshwaran Muralidaran, Ruba Priyadharshini, and John Philip McCrae. 2020b. Corpus creation for sentiment analysis in code-mixed Tamil-English text. In *Proceedings of the 1st Joint Workshop on Spoken Language Technologies for Under-resourced languages (SLTU) and Collaboration and Computing for Under-Resourced Languages (CCURL)*, pages 202–210, Marseille, France. European Language Resources association.

Bharathi Raja Chakravarthi, Ruba Priyadharshini, Navya Jose, Anand Kumar M, Thomas Mandl, Prasanna Kumar Kumaresan, Rahul Ponnusamy, Hariharan V, Elizabeth Sherly, and John Philip McCrae. 2021. Findings of the shared task on Offensive Language Identification in Tamil, Malayalam, and Kannada. In *Proceedings of the First Workshop on Speech and Language Technologies for Dravidian Languages*. Association for Computational Linguistics.

Bharathi Raja Chakravarthi, Ruba Priyadharshini, Vigneshwaran Muralidaran, Shardul Suryawanshi, Navya Jose, Elizabeth Sherly, and John P. McCrae. 2020c. Overview of the Track on Sentiment Analysis for Dravidian Languages in Code-Mixed Text. In *Forum for Information Retrieval Evaluation*, FIRE 2020, page 21–24, New York, NY, USA. Association for Computing Machinery.

Jason P.C. Chiu and Eric Nichols. 2016. Named entity recognition with bidirectional LSTM-CNNs. *Transactions of the Association for Computational Linguistics*, 4:357–370.

Shammur Absar Chowdhury, Hamdy Mubarak, Ahmed Abdelali, Soon-gyo Jung, Bernard J. Jansen, and Joni Salminen. 2020. A multi-platform Arabic news comment dataset for offensive language detection. In *Proceedings of the 12th Language Resources and Evaluation Conference*, pages 6203–6212, Marseille, France. European Language Resources Association.

Alexis Conneau, Kartikay Khandelwal, Naman Goyal, Vishrav Chaudhary, Guillaume Wenzek, Francisco Guzmán, Edouard Grave, Myle Ott, Luke Zettlemoyer, and Veselin Stoyanov. 2020. Unsupervised cross-lingual representation learning at scale.

Thomas Davidson, Dana Warmsley, Michael Macy, and Ingmar Weber. 2017. Automated hate speech detection and the problem of offensive language.

Jacob Devlin, Ming-Wei Chang, Kenton Lee, and Kristina Toutanova. 2019. BERT: Pre-training of deep bidirectional transformers for language understanding. In *Proceedings of the 2019 Conference of the North American Chapter of the Association for Computational Linguistics: Human Language Technologies, Volume 1 (Long and Short Papers)*, pages 4171–4186, Minneapolis, Minnesota. Association for Computational Linguistics.

M. Fang, H. Zhao, X. Song, X. Wang, and S. Huang. 2019. Using bidirectional LSTM with BERT for Chinese punctuation prediction. In *2019 IEEE International Conference on Signal, Information and Data Processing (ICSIDP)*, pages 1–5.

Paula Fortuna and Sérgio Nunes. 2018. A survey on automatic detection of hate speech in text. *ACM Comput. Surv.*, 51(4).

Adeep Hande, Ruba Priyadharshini, and Bharathi Raja Chakravarthi. 2020. KanCMD: Kannada CodeMixed dataset for sentiment analysis and offensive language detection. In *Proceedings of the Third Workshop on Computational Modeling of People's Opinions, Personality, and Emotion's in Social Media*, pages 54–63, Barcelona, Spain (Online). Association for Computational Linguistics.

Sabit Hassan, Younes Samih, Hamdy Mubarak, Ahmed Abdelali, Ammar Rashed, and Shammur Absar Chowdhury. 2020. ALT submission for OSACT shared task on offensive language detection. In *Proceedings of the 4th Workshop on Open-Source Arabic Corpora and Processing Tools, with a Shared Task on Offensive Language Detection*, pages 61–65, Marseille, France. European Language Resource Association.

Siddhanth U Hegde, Adeep Hande, Ruba Priyadharshini, Sajeetha Thavareesan, and Bharathi Raja Chakravarthi. 2021. UVCE-IIITT@DravidianLangTech-EACL2021: Tamil Troll Meme Classification: You need to Pay more Attention . In *Proceedings of the First Workshop on Speech and Language Technologies for Dravidian Languages*. Association for Computational Linguistics.

Jeremy Howard and Sebastian Ruder. 2018. Universal language model fine-tuning for text classification.

Omar Hussein, Hachem Sfar, Jelena Mitrović, and Michael Granitzer. 2020. NLP_Passau at SemEval-2020 task 12: Multilingual neural network for offensive language detection in English, Danish and Turkish. In *Proceedings of the Fourteenth Workshop on Semantic Evaluation*, pages 2090–2097, Barcelona (online). International Committee for Computational Linguistics.

Navya Jose, Bharathi Raja Chakravarthi, Shardul Suryawanshi, Elizabeth Sherly, and John P. McCrae. 2020. A Survey of Current Datasets for Code-Switching Research. In *2020 6th International Conference on Advanced Computing and Communication Systems (ICACCS)*, pages 136–141.

Yoon Kim. 2014. Convolutional neural networks for sentence classification.

Taku Kudo. 2018. Subword regularization: Improving neural network translation models with multiple subword candidates. In *Proceedings of the 56th Annual Meeting of the Association for Computational Linguistics (Volume 1: Long Papers)*, pages 66–75, Melbourne, Australia. Association for Computational Linguistics.

Taku Kudo and John Richardson. 2018. Sentencepiece: A simple and language independent subword tokenizer and detokenizer for neural text processing.

S. Kullback and R. A. Leibler. 1951. On Information and Sufficiency. *The Annals of Mathematical Statistics*, 22(1):79 – 86.

Ritesh Kumar, Atul Kr. Ojha, Shervin Malmasi, and Marcos Zampieri. 2018. Benchmarking aggression identification in social media. In *Proceedings of the First Workshop on Trolling, Aggression and Cyberbullying (TRAC-2018)*, pages 1–11, Santa Fe, New Mexico, USA. Association for Computational Linguistics.

Yash Kumar Lal, Vaibhav Kumar, Mrinal Dhar, Manish Shrivastava, and Philipp Koehn. 2019. De-mixing sentiment from code-mixed text. In *Proceedings of the 57th Annual Meeting of the Association for Computational Linguistics: Student Research Workshop*, pages 371–377, Florence, Italy. Association for Computational Linguistics.

Guillaume Lample and Alexis Conneau. 2019. Cross-lingual language model pretraining.

Zhenzhong Lan, Mingda Chen, Sebastian Goodman, Kevin Gimpel, Piyush Sharma, and Radu Soricut. 2020. ALBERT: A Lite BERT for Self-supervised Learning of Language Representations.

Yinhan Liu, Myle Ott, Naman Goyal, Jingfei Du, Mandar Joshi, Danqi Chen, Omer Levy, Mike Lewis, Luke Zettlemoyer, and Veselin Stoyanov. 2019. RoBERTa: A Robustly Optimized BERT Pretraining Approach.

Thomas Mandl, Sandip Modha, Anand Kumar M, and Bharathi Raja Chakravarthi. 2020. Overview of the HASOC Track at FIRE 2020: Hate Speech and Offensive Language Identification in Tamil, Malayalam, Hindi, English and German. In *Forum for Information Retrieval Evaluation*, FIRE 2020, page 29–32, New York, NY, USA. Association for Computing Machinery.

Puneet Mathur, Rajiv Shah, Ramit Sawhney, and Debanjan Mahata. 2018. Detecting offensive tweets in Hindi-English code-switched language. In *Proceedings of the Sixth International Workshop on Natural Language Processing for Social Media*, pages 18–26, Melbourne, Australia. Association for Computational Linguistics.

Rana D. Parshad, V. Chand, Neha Sinha, and Nitu Kumari. 2014. What is india speaking: The "hinglish" invasion. *ArXiv*, abs/1406.4824.

Telmo Pires, Eva Schlinger, and Dan Garrette. 2019. How multilingual is multilingual BERT? In *Proceedings of the 57th Annual Meeting of the Association for Computational Linguistics*, pages 4996–5001, Florence, Italy. Association for Computational Linguistics.

Adithya Pratapa, Gayatri Bhat, Monojit Choudhury, Sunayana Sitaram, Sandipan Dandapat, and Kalika Bali. 2018. Language modeling for code-mixing: The role of linguistic theory based synthetic data. In *Proceedings of the 56th Annual Meeting of the Association for Computational Linguistics (Volume 1: Long Papers)*, pages 1543–1553, Melbourne, Australia. Association for Computational Linguistics.

Ruba Priyadharshini, Bharathi Raja Chakravarthi, Mani Vegupatti, and John P. McCrae. 2020. Named Entity Recognition for Code-Mixed Indian Corpus using Meta Embedding. In *2020 6th International Conference on Advanced Computing and Communication Systems (ICACCS)*, pages 68–72.

Karthik Puranik, Adeep Hande, Ruba Priyadharshini, Sajeetha Thavareesan, and Bharathi Raja Chakravarthi. 2021. IIITT@LT-EDI-EACL2021-Hope Speech Detection: There is always hope in Transformers . In *Proceedings of the First Workshop on Language Technology for Equality, Diversity and Inclusion*. Association for Computational Linguistics.

Sara Renjit and Sumam Mary Idicula. 2020. CUSATNLP@HASOC-Dravidian-CodeMix-FIRE2020:Identifying Offensive Language from ManglishTweets.

Maryem Rhanoui, Mounia Mikram, Siham Yousfi, and Soukaina Barzali. 2019. A CNN-BiLSTM Model for Document-Level Sentiment Analysis. *Machine Learning and Knowledge Extraction*, 1(3):832–847.

Victor Sanh, Lysandre Debut, Julien Chaumond, and Thomas Wolf. 2020. DistilBERT, a distilled version of BERT: smaller, faster, cheaper and lighter.

Cicero Nogueira dos Santos, Igor Melnyk, and Inkit Padhi. 2018. Fighting offensive language on social media with unsupervised text style transfer. In *Proceedings of the 56th Annual Meeting of the Association for Computational Linguistics (Volume 2: Short Papers)*, pages 189–194, Melbourne, Australia. Association for Computational Linguistics.

Shardul Suryawanshi, Bharathi Raja Chakravarthi, Pranav Verma, Mihael Arcan, John Philip McCrae, and Paul Buitelaar. 2020. A dataset for troll classification of TamilMemes. In *Proceedings of the WILDRE5– 5th Workshop on Indian Language Data: Resources and Evaluation*, pages 7–13, Marseille, France. European Language Resources Association (ELRA).

Gregor Wiedemann, Eugen Ruppert, and Chris Biemann. 2019. UHH-LT at SemEval-2019 task 6: Supervised vs. unsupervised transfer learning for offensive language detection. In *Proceedings of the 13th International Workshop on Semantic Evaluation*, pages 782–787, Minneapolis, Minnesota, USA. Association for Computational Linguistics.

Gregor Wiedemann, Seid Muhie Yimam, and Chris Biemann. 2020. UHH-LT at SemEval-2020 task 12: Fine-tuning of pre-trained transformer networks for offensive language detection. In *Proceedings of the Fourteenth Workshop on Semantic Evaluation*, pages 1638–1644, Barcelona (online). International Committee for Computational Linguistics.

Thomas Wolf, Lysandre Debut, Victor Sanh, Julien Chaumond, Clement Delangue, Anthony Moi, Pierric Cistac, Tim Rault, Remi Louf, Morgan Funtowicz, Joe Davison, Sam Shleifer, Patrick von Platen, Clara Ma, Yacine Jernite, Julien Plu, Canwen Xu, Teven Le Scao, Sylvain Gugger, Mariama Drame, Quentin Lhoest, and Alexander Rush. 2020. Transformers: State-of-the-art natural language processing. In *Proceedings of the 2020 Conference on Empirical Methods in Natural Language Processing: System Demonstrations*, pages 38–45, Online. Association for Computational Linguistics.

# Hypers@DravidianLangTech-EACL2021: Offensive language identification in Dravidian code-mixed YouTube Comments and Posts

**Charangan Vasantharajan**
Department of Computer Science and Engineering University of Moratuwa
Colombo, Srilanka
Charangan.18@cse.mrt.ac.lk

**Uthayasanker Thayasivam**
Department of Computer Science and Engineering University of Moratuwa
Colombo, Srilanka
rtuthaya@cse.mrt.ac.lk

## Abstract

According to the use of Code-Mixed Offensive contents in social media posts, this study has the focus on such contents in low-resourced Dravidian languages such as Tamil, Kannada, and Malayalam using the bidirectional approach and fine-tuning strategies. Our proposed model got a 0.96 F1-score for Malayalam, 0.73 F1-score for Tamil, and 0.70 F1-score for Kannada based on the benchmark leader-board. Moreover, in the view of multilingual models, our modal ranked $3rd$ and achieved favorable results and confirmed the model as the best among all systems submitted to these shared tasks in these three languages.

## 1 Introduction

The use of social media platforms (e.g., Facebook, Twitter, and YouTube) has become an important activity in the everyday lives of most internet users. The users share their thoughts with multilingual societies in the form of comments and posts on social media. In the last few years, with a proliferation of social media users, posts and comments have become an information form that is simply called **code-mixed** text (Chakravarthi et al., 2020; Androutsopoulos, 2013; Chakravarthi et al., 2019) due to the lack of impressions in a single language when conveying their thoughts online with the multi-linguistic community (Suryawanshi et al., 2020).

Most of the social media platforms encourage users to convey and express their opinions in their preference with a small number of restrictions and intend to collect user comments and posts to provide a customized feed. In addition to this, these collected data are also used for advertising, marketing, and detecting the occurrence of bad activities. It is rather difficult to identify offensive code-mixed content written in a non-native (Roman) script (Rosowsky, 2010). This complexity in such execution of the natural language processing tasks cannot be solved by the technologies developed for a monolingual text (Solorio et al., 2014; Diab et al., 2014) but multilingual models can.

Offensive language identification of code-mixed data on social media platforms is important to identify the movie reviews, product reviews, enable advertisements, monitor political activities, and identify social trends. The code-mixed data always adopts the vocabulary and grammar of multiple languages and generates new user-based content structures (Choudhary et al., 2018). This is challenging for offensive language identification tasks as traditional and unidirectional approaches and lack of dataset result in not capturing the meaning and limits the accuracy of the task.

According to the shared task, this study executed a comment or post level offensive language identification of the code-mixed contents which was collected from YouTube comments and posts on **Dravidian language** pairs (e.g. Tamil-English, Kannada-English, and Malayalam-English). Each of given sentence is annotated with labels as follows: Not-offensive, Offensive Targeted Insult Other, Offensive Targeted Insult Individual, Offensive Targeted Insult Group, not Tamil or not Malayalam or not Kannada, and Offensive Untargeted. This research work proposed a system that uses **M-BERT** which stands for Multilingual-Bidirectional Encoder Representations with Transformers (Devlin et al., 2019), as a pre-trained model and applied fine-tuning strategies as a transfer learning approach to solve the given task.

The rest of the sections in the paper are as follows. Section 2, reviews related experiment works in offensive language identification in three views. Section 3 describes the methodology with system architecture which includes the classification features and transfers learning strategies. The fourth section presents the conducted experiments using



*Proceedings of the First Workshop on Speech and Language Technologies for Dravidian Languages*, pages 195–202
April 20, 2021 ©2021 Association for Computational Linguistics

different approaches and features. Section 5 analyses the results of the proposed system in the benchmark. Benchmark results are discussed in section 6 and finally, the conclusion followed by future research directions.

## 2 Related Work

Due to the code-mixed dataset limitation on the low-resourced languages such as Tamil, Sinhala, Malayalam, and Kannada, there were a few numbers experiments have been done in this area (Jose et al., 2020; Hande et al., 2020; Chakravarthi et al., 2020; Ghanghor et al., 2021b,a; Puranik et al., 2021; Hegde et al., 2021; Yasaswini et al., 2021). Arora (2020) developed a model to identify Hate Speech and Offensive Contents in Dravidian languages (e.g. Tamil-English and Malayalam-English) from the code-mixed comments and posts collected from social media using pre-trained ULMFiT on synthetically generated code-mixed data. Their proposed method achieved 0.88 and 0.91 weight F1-score for code-mixed Tamil-English and Malayalam-English, respectively. On the other hand, some tasks have been done based on dataset creations to provide support for low-resource language identification tasks. To encourage sentiment analysis tasks and overcome the non-availability of the code-mixed dataset in Tamil-English Chakravarthi et al. (2020) created a sentiment-annotated corpus containing 15744 YouTube comments and posts. In addition to this, they examined the benchmark system with various machine learning algorithms such as Logistic Regression (LR), Support Vector Machine (SVM), K-Nearest Neighbour (K-NN), Decision Tree (DT), Random Forest (RF), Multinominal Naive Bayes (MNB), 1DConv-LSTM, BERT Multilingual, DME and CDME. In this task, the Logistic regression, random forest classifiers, and decision trees were provided better results compared to other algorithms. Jose et al. (2020) build a standard corpus for Malayalam-English to increase the sentiment analysis tasks in the code-mixed contents. Thayasivam and Smith (2019) created a newly code-mixed dataset annotated in the sentence and word level collected from Facebook comments, chat history, and from public posts for Sinhala-English language pairs. Hande et al. (2020) explored in Kannada-English by the traditional learning approaches such as Logistic Regression (LR), Support Vector Machine (SVM), Multinomial Naive Bayes (MNB), K-Nearest Neighbors (KNN), Decision Trees (DT), and Random Forest (RF).

In high-resource languages, Priyadharshini et al. (2020) examined methods using Transformer models to predict the named entities in corpus written both in the native script as well as in the Roman script for the English-Hindi language pairs. On the other hand, the explorations for English-Spanish (Solorio et al., 2014), Chinese-English (Lee and Wang, 2015), and English-Bengali (Patra et al., 2018) language pairs were used multiple-classifier based automatic detection approach, unidirectional LSTM, and common generic forms of Deep Learning and Neural Network approaches to perform their identification tasks.

According to the social media explosion, offensive language identification has become an increasingly important task and a few studies have been published on single languages (Thavareesan and Mahesan, 2019, 2020a,b). Malmasi and Zampieri (2017) performed an analysis to separate the general profanity from the hate speech in social media. They presented a supervised classification system that used character n-grams, word n-grams, and word skip grams and their model was able to achieve 80% accuracy on a huge dataset which contained English tweets annotated with three labels, namely, "hate speech (HATE)", "offensive language but no hate speech (OFFENSIVE)", and "no offensive content (OK)". Pitenis et al. (2020) addressed the problem of offensive language identification for the Greek language by created their annotated corpus using comments retrieved from Twitter Posts and experimented with seven different classification models: Pooled GRU (Plum et al., 2019), Stacked LSTM with Attention (Plum et al., 2019), LSTM and GRU with Attention (Plum et al., 2019), 2D Convolution with Pooling, GRU with Capsule, LSTM with Capsule and Attention and BERT (Devlin et al., 2019). In this task, LSTM and GRU with Attention performed well compared to all other models in-terms of macro-f1. However, the fine-tuning approach with the BERT-Base Multilingual Cased model did not provide good results.

Based on the above analysis, most of the approaches were unidirectional-based except the works done by (Chakravarthi et al., 2020) and (Pitenis et al., 2020). They used BERT (Devlin et al., 2019) as their bidirectional algorithm but it did not reach the state-of-the-art on code-mixed contents at that time. After a lot of studies and observations, BERT is chosen for this low-resource language experiment as a challenge.

## 3 Methodology

### 3.1 Data Preprocessing

Two data pre-processing techniques followed and kept them as minimal methods to suit all other languages. Emojis play a key role in expressing emotions in the posts and comments of social media (Hettiarachchi and Ranasinghe, 2019). The better approach to deal with emojis is to convert emojis to words so that it is being helpful to preserve information. So converting Emojis into text is the first preprocessing technique. For this purpose, it is used a dictionary of emojis[1] to do this conversation due to the unconfirmed existence of embeddings for emojis in the pre-trained model. After that, it is discarded a list of punctuation that is available in Python's string module from the input text, based on the use case.

### 3.2 BERT Transformer

BERT is a transformer-based, multi-layer, and bidirectional model with an attention mechanism that has the learning ability to contextual relations between words and sub-words in a sequence or text. The default form of the transformer contains two separate objects such as an encoder and a decoder. The encoder reads the input text and the decoder makes predictions for the given classification task (Devlin et al., 2019). BERT overcome the limitation which is in the previous language models (e.g. **word2vec** and **GloVe**) when interpreting context and polysemous words and it effectively performs in monolingual as well as multilingual classifications and leads to the greatest performance increase in the natural language processing task, including Question Answering (SQuAD v1.1), Natural Language Inference (MNLI), and others (Devlin et al., 2019). Apart from the unidirectional language models, transformer encoders read the whole input sequence of words at once. Therefore, BERT is the best bidirectional transformer rather than bidirectional LSTMs and would perform with high accuracy. This behavior leads the transformer model to learn the context of a word from left to right and right to left of the word at the same time (Devlin et al., 2019).

Primarily, the task of this research is multilingual offensive language identification, therefore it is used a pre-trained transformer-based multilingual BERT model (Devlin et al., 2019) and implemented using **HuggingFace**. The pre-trained models are available in the HuggingFace model repository [2]. BERT supports 104 languages including Tamil, Kannada, and Malayalam. It includes approximately 110M parameters with 12-layers, 768 hidden-states, and 12-heads (Gopalan and Hopkins, 2020). Normally, BERT fetches input data in a specific format, with special tokens to mark the beginning ([CLS]) and separation/end of sentences ([SEP]) to mark the end. Furthermore, it is necessary to tokenize the text into tokens that correspond to BERT's vocabulary. For each tokenized sentence, BERT requires input ids, a sequence of integers identifying each input token to its index number in the BERT tokenizer vocabulary. For a given token, its input representation is built by adding the related token, segment, and position embedding (Devlin et al., 2019). A visual representation of the BERT model can be seen in the Figure 1.

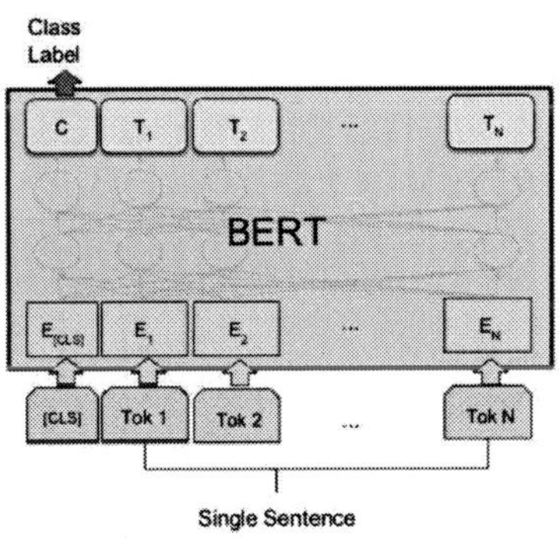


Figure 1: BERT model designed for Text classification tasks for a single sentence input. [CLS] and [SEP] are special and separate tokens.

### 3.3 Fine-tuning

The main idea of the fine-tuning strategies is to load a pre-trained (**bert-base-multilingual-cased**) classification model which is trained on more than the top 100 languages in the largest Wikipedia (Devlin

[1] Bhavika Kanani, 'Text Preprocessing: Handle Emoji & Emoticon', *Machine Learning Tutorials*, 2020, `https://studymachinelearning.com/text-preprocessing-handle-emoji-emoticon/`, (accessed 14 January 2021).

[2] `https://github.com/huggingface/transformers`

et al., 2019), add or remove layers, prepare multiple inputs, and adjust parameters such as a learning rate, the number of epochs, the optimizer, and regularization parameters. According to the recent studies, some fine-tuning strategies have ensured results such as self-ensemble, and language modeling and Hindi, and Bengali. Therefore, this research work examined this strategy to see whether it improves the results for low-resource languages too.

BERT is adopted for the given multilingual offensive language identification task and performs fine-tuning from the pre-trained **bert-base-multilingual-cased** classification model which is trained on more than the top 100 languages with the largest Wikipedia. TFBertModel, the mother of all different BERT classification models[3] is chosen since the task is to classify posts and comments into six distinct classes as above indicated. **BertTokenizerFast** was loaded from the same transformer library[4] to tokenize the input texts and prepare some additional inputs than *input_ids* such as *attention_mask* which leads to performance increase and *token_type_ids*. Dropouts were applied to the BERT layers and passed *TruncatedNormal* distribution as *kernel_initializer* to the output dense layer. Finally, the system was trained on the Tamil, Kannada, and Malayalam languages separately using the training datasets provided by the organizers (Chakravarthi et al., 2021; Jose et al., 2020; Chakravarthi et al., 2020; Hande et al., 2020). The system architecture is shown in Figure 2.

## 4 Experiments

### 4.1 Data

For this study, it is used separate larger datasets with manually annotated labels for training, development, and testing for each language introduced by (Chakravarthi et al., 2021; Jose et al., 2020; Chakravarthi et al., 2020; Hande et al., 2020) as described in section 1. The given dataset was divided into training and validation sets using a 0.8:0.2 split during the training. Dataset statistics and the data visualization according to the labels are shown in the table 1 and Figure 3.

[3]https://huggingface.co/transformers/model_doc/bert.html

[4]https://huggingface.co/transformers/model_doc/bert.html#berttokenizerfast

| Languages | Train | Dev | Test |
|---|---|---|---|
| Tamil | 35139 | 4388 | 4392 |
| Kannada | 6217 | 777 | 778 |
| Malayalam | 16011 | 2000 | 2002 |

Table 1: Dataset statistics according to the languages. As you can see, there is a huge difference in the number of comments and posts between Tamil and the other two languages.

### 4.2 Implementation

Fine-tune was mainly done on the learning rate and the number of epochs of the classification model manually to obtain the best results for the validation set. It is obtained that $5e - 05$ as the best value for the learning rate for the **Adam** optimizer and 50 as the best value for the epochs for all the languages. It took around 1 hour to train the Tamil model due to a large amount of training dataset and other language models took only around 30 minutes. The research model of this study achieved 0.7645, 0.7154, and 0.9634 validation accuracy in Tamil, Kannada, and Malayalam respectively during the training period. After evaluating it by using the development dataset, the testing dataset was used to make predictions.

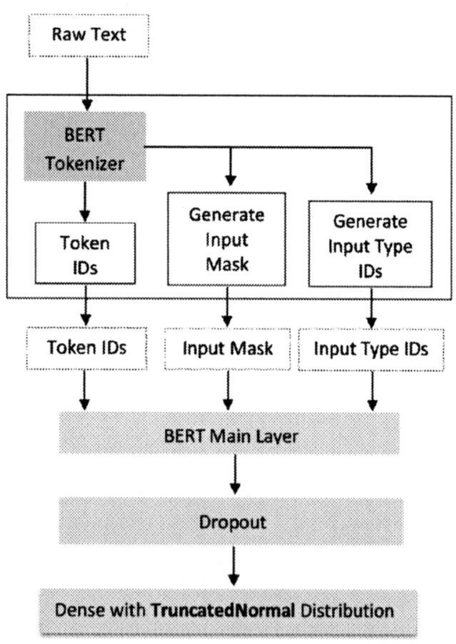


Figure 2: Architecture of our proposed model. BERT Tokenizer converts the word into tokens and generates token ids, input masks, and input type ids according to the input word. The main goal of using an input mask is to gain some performance increase. In addition to the best layer, we added a dropout and pooled output layer.

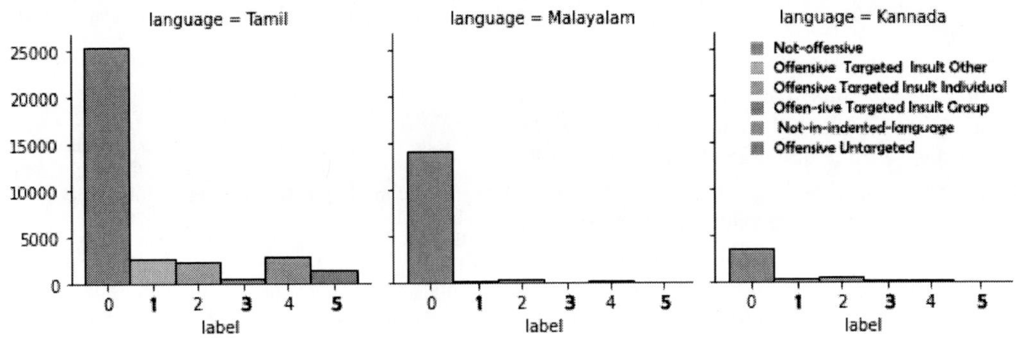


Figure 3: Dataset labels distribution on Tamil, Malayalam, and Kannada code-mixed content. the x-axis 0,1,2,3,4, and 5 indicates Not-offensive, Offensive Targeted Insult Other, Offensive Targeted Insult Individual, Offensive Targeted Insult Group, Not-in-indented-language, and Offensive Untargetede respectively.

## 5 Results and Analysis

Teams are ranked by the weighted average F1 score of their classification system. According to the models which were submitted to all three languages, we have found ourselves as $3^{rd}$ in the order of models. This shows that the research model of this study achieved state-of-the-art results in all three languages. Moreover, table 2 illustrate our ranks in the competition with their weighted Precision, weighted Recall, and weighted F1-score. According to the results published in the benchmark leader-board, the Malayalam, Kannada, and Tamil language models of this study have scored 0.96, 0.70, and 0.73 weighted average F1 scores on the test set and ranked $2^{nd}$ out of 30 participants, $5^{th}$ out of 29 participants, $6^{th}$ out of 31 participants respectively.

Even though the research model of this study got the above rank, the F1-score difference between the first team and **Hypers** is only 1%, 7%, and 6% respectively. Therefore, it is assumed that the proposed model of this study provided better results compared to other models for monolingual languages and also multilingual languages.

| Language | P | R | F1 | Rank |
|---|---|---|---|---|
| Malayalam | 0.96 | 0.96 | 0.96 | 2 |
| Kannada | 0.69 | 0.72 | 0.70 | 5 |
| Tamil | 0.71 | 0.76 | 0.73 | 6 |

Table 2: Leaderboard - Offensive Language Identification in Dravidian Languages-EACL 2021. This shows our ranks in all three languages in the benchmark.

## 6 Discussions

Even with the better F1-scores for all three models, there was some confusion according to the results. F1-score for Malayalam is comparatively higher than the other two models. According to the dataset, the Tamil training set has approximately 35139 posts and comments, in the meantime, Kannada and Malayalam are 6214, and 16011 respectively but given results behaves as opposed to the number of posts and comments in the training sets. It may have happened due to the lack of training of the BERT multilingual based model in the Tamil and Kannada language. Since BERT multilingual model was trained on Wikipedia and analyzed wiki contents[5] and got the total contents in Kannada, Malayalam, and Tamil are 26,769, 71,762, and 134,011 respectively. The lower f1 score for Kannada could be attributed to the less training data. On the contrary, despite having more training data, BERT trained on Tamil and Malayalam performs poorly.

In addition to the above Wikipedia analysis, it was carried out a qualitative analysis to find patterns and observations on the given dataset. Commonly, in the training dataset, more than 80% of the posts and comments were labeled as Not-offensive and the remaining were labeled as other types of labels. The use of English words was minimal although there are many comments and posts which are in the native language but written in Roman script. Therefore, it is assumed that the lack of training in those informal forms of languages led to such results in the benchmark evaluation.

[5] https://meta.wikimedia.org/wiki/List_of_Wikipedias

## 7 Conclusion

Offensive Language Identification in Dravidian Language code-mixed text is one of the most challenging tasks in natural language processing. We have done such a task in this study using BERT with a fine-tuning strategy in the low-resourced languages. In this benchmark, our (**Hypers** team) proposed system got $2^{nd}$, $5^{th}$, $6^{th}$ rankings for the Malayalam, Kannada, and Tamil test set respectively. Finally, it was proved that the BERT system can be used on low-resource languages to the offensive language identification tasks with the best F1- score.

## 8 Future Work

In the future, we are planning to use character-level embedding along with the word embeddings to get a better representation of an input sentence and words. On the other hand, misspelled or other words not appearing in the vocabulary are usually detected and treated as a special unknown token, so this will also help in getting a representation for out-of-vocabulary (OOV) words. Moreover, due to the size of vocabularies, the word embeddings requires a lot of memory to store embeddings, and including word embeddings in a model adds too many parameters to the model, so the computational cost is much higher on it than the character-level model.

Also, it is decided to deal with imbalanced data in the training and development sets by applying oversampling to increase the number of samples for minority classes. It is assumed that the above approaches will increase the model performance.

## 9 Acknowledgments

We would like to thank the EACL organizers for running this interesting shared task and for replying promptly to all our inquiries. We further thank the three anonymous reviewers for their insightful suggestions and feedback.

## References

Jannis Androutsopoulos. 2013. Code-switching in computer-mediated communication. *Pragmatics of Computer-mediated Communication*, pages 667–694.

Gaurav Arora. 2020. Gauravarora@HASOC-Dravidian-CodeMix-FIRE2020: Pre-training ULMFiT on Synthetically Generated Code-Mixed Data for Hate Speech Detection.

Bharathi Raja Chakravarthi, Mihael Arcan, and John P. McCrae. 2019. Comparison of Different Orthographies for Machine Translation of Under-Resourced Dravidian Languages. In *2nd Conference on Language, Data and Knowledge (LDK 2019)*, volume 70 of *OpenAccess Series in Informatics (OASIcs)*, pages 6:1–6:14, Dagstuhl, Germany. Schloss Dagstuhl–Leibniz-Zentrum fuer Informatik.

Bharathi Raja Chakravarthi, Vigneshwaran Muralidaran, Ruba Priyadharshini, and John Philip McCrae. 2020. Corpus creation for sentiment analysis in code-mixed Tamil-English text. In *Proceedings of the 1st Joint Workshop on Spoken Language Technologies for Under-resourced languages (SLTU) and Collaboration and Computing for Under-Resourced Languages (CCURL)*, pages 202–210, Marseille, France. European Language Resources association.

Bharathi Raja Chakravarthi, Ruba Priyadharshini, Navya Jose, Anand Kumar M, Thomas Mandl, Prasanna Kumar Kumaresan, Rahul Ponnusamy, Hariharan V, Elizabeth Sherly, and John Philip McCrae. 2021. Findings of the shared task on Offensive Language Identification in Tamil, Malayalam, and Kannada. In *Proceedings of the First Workshop on Speech and Language Technologies for Dravidian Languages*. Association for Computational Linguistics.

Nurendra Choudhary, Rajat Singh, Ishita Bindlish, and Manish Shrivastava. 2018. Sentiment analysis of code-mixed languages leveraging resource rich languages. *CoRR*, abs/1804.00806.

Jacob Devlin, Ming-Wei Chang, Kenton Lee, and Kristina Toutanova. 2019. BERT: Pre-training of deep bidirectional transformers for language understanding. In *Proceedings of the 2019 Conference of the North American Chapter of the Association for Computational Linguistics: Human Language Technologies, Volume 1 (Long and Short Papers)*, pages 4171–4186, Minneapolis, Minnesota. Association for Computational Linguistics.

Mona Diab, Julia Hirschberg, Pascale Fung, and Thamar Solorio, editors. 2014. *Proceedings of the First Workshop on Computational Approaches to Code Switching*. Association for Computational Linguistics, Doha, Qatar.

Nikhil Kumar Ghanghor, Parameswari Krishnamurthy, Sajeetha Thavareesan, Ruba Priyadharshini, and Bharathi Raja Chakravarthi. 2021a. IIITK@DravidianLangTech-EACL2021: Offensive Language Identification and Meme Classification in Tamil, Malayalam and Kannada. In *Proceedings of the First Workshop on Speech and Language Technologies for Dravidian Languages*, Online. Association for Computational Linguistics.

Nikhil Kumar Ghanghor, Rahul Ponnusamy, Prasanna Kumar Kumaresan, Ruba Priyadharshini, Sajeetha Thavareesan, and Bharathi Raja

Chakravarthi. 2021b. IIITK@LT-EDI-EACL2021: Hope Speech Detection for Equality, Diversity, and Inclusion in Tamil, Malayalam and English. In *Proceedings of the First Workshop on Language Technology for Equality, Diversity and Inclusion*, Online.

Vinay Gopalan and Mark Hopkins. 2020. Reed at SemEval-2020 task 9: Fine-tuning and bag-of-words approaches to code-mixed sentiment analysis. In *Proceedings of the Fourteenth Workshop on Semantic Evaluation*, pages 1304–1309, Barcelona (online). International Committee for Computational Linguistics.

Adeep Hande, Ruba Priyadharshini, and Bharathi Raja Chakravarthi. 2020. KanCMD: Kannada CodeMixed dataset for sentiment analysis and offensive language detection. In *Proceedings of the Third Workshop on Computational Modeling of People's Opinions, Personality, and Emotion's in Social Media*, pages 54–63, Barcelona, Spain (Online). Association for Computational Linguistics.

Siddhanth U Hegde, Adeep Hande, Ruba Priyadharshini, Sajeetha Thavareesan, and Bharathi Raja Chakravarthi. 2021. UVCE-IIITT@DravidianLangTech-EACL2021: Tamil Troll Meme Classification: You need to Pay more Attention. In *Proceedings of the First Workshop on Speech and Language Technologies for Dravidian Languages*. Association for Computational Linguistics.

Hansi Hettiarachchi and Tharindu Ranasinghe. 2019. Emoji powered capsule network to detect type and target of offensive posts in social media. In *Proceedings of the International Conference on Recent Advances in Natural Language Processing (RANLP 2019)*, pages 474–480, Varna, Bulgaria. INCOMA Ltd.

Navya Jose, Bharathi Raja Chakravarthi, Shardul Suryawanshi, Elizabeth Sherly, and John Philip McCrae. 2020. A sentiment analysis dataset for code-mixed Malayalam-English. In *Proceedings of the 1st Joint Workshop on Spoken Language Technologies for Under-resourced languages (SLTU) and Collaboration and Computing for Under-Resourced Languages (CCURL)*, pages 177–184, Marseille, France. European Language Resources association.

Sophia Lee and Zhongqing Wang. 2015. Emotion in code-switching texts: Corpus construction and analysis. In *Proceedings of the Eighth SIGHAN Workshop on Chinese Language Processing*, pages 91–99, Beijing, China. Association for Computational Linguistics.

Shervin Malmasi and Marcos Zampieri. 2017. Detecting hate speech in social media. In *Proceedings of the International Conference Recent Advances in Natural Language Processing, RANLP 2017*, pages 467–472, Varna, Bulgaria. INCOMA Ltd.

Braja Gopal Patra, Dipankar Das, and Amitava Das. 2018. Sentiment Analysis of Code-Mixed Indian Languages: An Overview of SAIL_Code-Mixed Shared Task @ICON-2017. *CoRR*, abs/1803.06745.

Zesis Pitenis, Marcos Zampieri, and Tharindu Ranasinghe. 2020. Offensive language identification in Greek. In *Proceedings of the 12th Language Resources and Evaluation Conference*, pages 5113–5119, Marseille, France. European Language Resources Association.

A Plum, Tharindu Ranasinghe, Constantin Orasan, and R Mitkov. 2019. RGCL at GermEval 2019: offensive language detection with deep learning.

Ruba. Priyadharshini, Bharathi. R. Chakravarthi, Mani. Vegupatti, and John. P. McCrae. 2020. Named entity recognition for code-mixed indian corpus using meta embedding. In *2020 6th International Conference on Advanced Computing and Communication Systems (ICACCS)*, pages 68–72.

Karthik Puranik, Adeep Hande, Ruba Priyadharshini, Sajeetha Thavareesan, and Bharathi Raja Chakravarthi. 2021. IIITT@LT-EDI-EACL2021-Hope Speech Detection: There is always hope in Transformers. In *Proceedings of the First Workshop on Language Technology for Equality, Diversity and Inclusion*. Association for Computational Linguistics.

Andrey Rosowsky. 2010. 'writing it in english': Script choices among young multilingual muslims in the uk. *Journal of Multilingual and Multicultural Development*, 31:163–179.

Thamar Solorio, Elizabeth Blair, Suraj Maharjan, Steven Bethard, Mona Diab, Mahmoud Ghoneim, Abdelati Hawwari, Fahad AlGhamdi, Julia Hirschberg, Alison Chang, and Pascale Fung. 2014. Overview for the first shared task on language identification in code-switched data. In *Proceedings of the First Workshop on Computational Approaches to Code Switching*, pages 62–72, Doha, Qatar. Association for Computational Linguistics.

Shardul Suryawanshi, Bharathi Raja Chakravarthi, Mihael Arcan, and Paul Buitelaar. 2020. Multimodal meme dataset (MultiOFF) for identifying offensive content in image and text. In *Proceedings of the Second Workshop on Trolling, Aggression and Cyberbullying*, pages 32–41, Marseille, France. European Language Resources Association (ELRA).

Sajeetha Thavareesan and Sinnathamby Mahesan. 2019. Sentiment Analysis in Tamil Texts: A Study on Machine Learning Techniques and Feature Representation. In *2019 14th Conference on Industrial and Information Systems (ICIIS)*, pages 320–325.

Sajeetha Thavareesan and Sinnathamby Mahesan. 2020a. Sentiment Lexicon Expansion using Word2vec and fastText for Sentiment Prediction in Tamil texts. In *2020 Moratuwa Engineering Research Conference (MERCon)*, pages 272–276.

Sajeetha Thavareesan and Sinnathamby Mahesan. 2020b. Word embedding-based Part of Speech tagging in Tamil texts. In *2020 IEEE 15th International Conference on Industrial and Information Systems (ICIIS)*, pages 478–482.

Uthayasanker Thayasivam and Ian Smith. 2019. Sinhala-english code-mixed data analysis: A review on data collection process. In *2019 19th International Conference on Advances in ICT for Emerging Regions (ICTer)*, volume 250, pages 1–6.

Konthala Yasaswini, Karthik Puranik, Adeep Hande, Ruba Priyadharshini, Sajeetha Thavareesan, and Bharathi Raja Chakravarthi. 2021. IIITT@DravidianLangTech-EACL2021: Transfer Learning for Offensive Language Detection in Dravidian Languages. In *Proceedings of the First Workshop on Speech and Language Technologies for Dravidian Languages*. Association for Computational Linguistics.

# HUB@DravidianLangTech-EACL2021: Identify and Classify Offensive Text in Multilingual Code Mixing in Social Media

**Bo Huang**
School of Information Science
and Engineering Yunnan University,
Yunnan, P.R. China
hublucashb@gmail.com

**Yang Bai**
School of Information Science
and Engineering Yunnan University,
Yunnan, P.R. China
baiyang.top@gmail.com

## Abstract

This paper introduces the system description of the HUB team participating in Dravidian-LangTech - EACL2021: Offensive Language Identification in Dravidian Languages. The theme of this shared task is the detection of offensive content in social media. Among the known tasks related to offensive speech detection, this is the first task to detect offensive comments posted in social media comments in the Dravidian language. The task organizer team provided us with the code-mixing task data set mainly composed of three different languages: Malayalam, Kannada, and Tamil. The tasks on the code mixed data in these three different languages can be seen as three different comment/post-level classification tasks. The task on the Malayalam data set is a five-category classification task, and the Kannada and Tamil language data sets are two six-category classification tasks. Based on our analysis of the task description and task data set, we chose to use the multilingual BERT model to complete this task. In this paper, we will discuss our fine-tuning methods, models, experiments, and results.

## 1 Introduction and Background

Social media platforms are playing an increasingly important role in people's modern social life. Even applications in academic exchanges and technological dissemination are becoming more and more popular (Sugimoto et al., 2017). In recent years, various offensive comments directed at individuals, groups, races, and countries that have appeared in social media have attracted attention in academic and industrial fields (Zampieri et al., 2019; Davidson et al., 2017). Even more worrying is that offensive comments/posts spread very quickly on social media (Mathew et al., 2019).

As far as the current situation is concerned, the COVID-19 virus is spreading and raging on a global scale. The work of Lyu et al. showed us the age distribution of users who used controversial terms on social media during the COVID-19 virus epidemic, with the total share of the 18-24 and 25-34 age groups being 49% (Depoux et al., 2020). Combining the work of Depoux and others, we can realize that what is more terrifying than the speed and harm of the virus is the public panic caused by rumors and hostile comments on social media (Lyu et al., 2020).

What makes us feel encouraged is that similar issues that are currently appearing on social media have been highly valued in the academic and industrial fields (Ahmad and Murad, 2020). However, the current automation technology is mostly applied to some languages with a large number of users (such as English, Spanish user groups, etc.) (Zahiri and Ahmadvand, 2020; Rangel et al., 2020; Pamungkas et al., 2018). The Dravidian languages were first documented in Tamili (Tamil-Brahmi) script engraved on cave walls in Tamil Nadu's Madurai and Tirunelveli districts in the 6nd century BCE. According to the 14th century Sanskrit text Lilatilakam, which is a grammar of Manipravalam, the spoken languages of modern-day Kerala and Tamil Nadu were identical, and they were referred to as "Dramia" (Tamil). Malayalam split from Tamil after 16th century. The earliest known inscriptions in Sanskrit are from the 1st century BCE, such as the Ayodhya Inscription of Dhana and Ghosundi-Hathibada. Sanskrit borrowed many words and grammatical structure from Tamil, Pali and Prakrit. Tamil languages is one of the longest-surviving classical languages in the world which is older than any surviving language in India.

For Tamil, there few works on sentiment analysis (Thavareesan and Mahesan, 2019, 2020a,b). Combined with our analysis of the negative impact of negative posts/comments in social media, we



*Proceedings of the First Workshop on Speech and Language Technologies for Dravidian Languages*, pages 203–209
April 20, 2021 ©2021 Association for Computational Linguistics

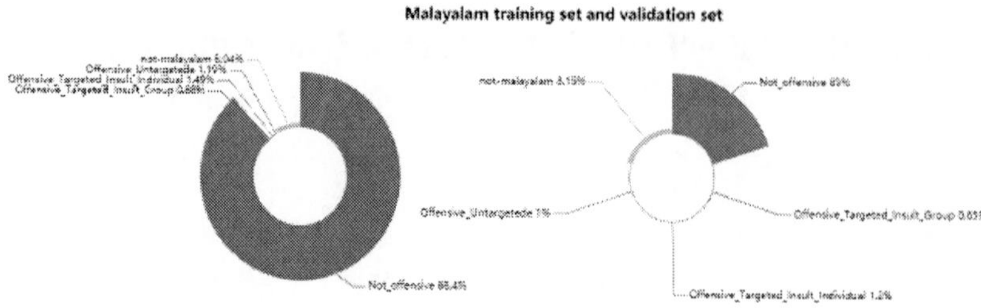


Figure 1: Labels distribution of Malayalam training set and validation set. In the training set, Not offensive: 88.4%, Not Malayalam: 8.04%, Offensive Targeted Insult Individual: 1.49%, Offensive Untargetede: 1.19%, Offensive Targeted Insult Group: 0.88%. In the validation set, Not offensive: 89%, Not Malayalam: 8.15%, Offensive Targeted Insult Individual: 1.2%, Offensive Untargetede: 1%, Offensive Targeted Insult Group: 0.65%.

believe that it is very meaningful and necessary to study the task of Offensive Language Identification in Dravidian Languages-EACL 2021[1] (Chakravarthi et al., 2021). The dataset in the task is the corpus obtained by Chakravarthi and others from social media comments/posts. Use this corpus to create the Dravidian Languages code-mixed dataset for Tamil-English, Malayalam-English, and Kannada-English (Chakravarthi et al., 2020a,b; Hande et al., 2020). Code-mixing is mixing of two or more languages in the conversation (Jose et al., 2020; Priyadharshini et al., 2020; Mandl et al., 2020). What we need to accomplish is to design an automated system and enter a Youtube comment into the system. Then let the system automatically detect which of the categories Not-offensive, Offensive-untargeted, Offensive-targeted-individual, Offensive-targeted-group, Offensive-targeted-other, or Not-in-indented-language the comment content should be classified into. There is usually a lot of noise in the text of social media comments. Also, the data set for this task is text with code mixed types. Combining these characteristics, we chose to use the pre-trained language model multilingual BERT that achieved excellent results in tasks in the natural language processing field to complete this task (Pires et al., 2019). Regarding the problem of code-mixing language, we try to quote Tf-Idf to alleviate the adverse effect of code-mixing on the result. In the next part 3 and part 4, we will introduce our methods and experiments in the task in detail.

[1]https://dravidianlangtech.github.io/2021/

## 2 Related Work

Recently, various issues arising on online social media platforms on the Internet have been receiving attention from many parties. Mossie et al. showed us that they use deep learning methods to process some posts on social media. Their purpose is to predict the target groups that may be subjected to hate attacks. This work provides a very valuable reference for relevant governments and organizations to formulate measures to protect vulnerable groups (Mossie and Wang, 2020). Williams et al. use data science methods to analyze the connection between data from crime, census, and Twitter, revealing to us that hate crime in the digital age is a complete process, not a discrete event (Williams et al., 2020). Velásquez et al. used mathematical analysis and modeling methods to detect and evaluate malicious content related to COVID-19 on online social media. Obtained the critical point of the virus spreading at multiple levels (Velásquez et al., 2020).

Vidgen et al. used machine learning methods to perform a quantitative analysis of whether Islamophobic hate speech in social media may be strong or weak (Vidgen and Yasseri, 2020). The appearance of a large number of fake news on social media has induced hostile comments to a certain extent. To detect fake news in social networks, Zhou et al. proposed a theory-driven fake news detection model. This method investigates fake news from multiple levels, involving lexical semantics, social psychology, and supervised learning method models. The contribution of this work is not only to increase the recognition rate of fake news but also to enhance the interpretability of fake news. What is more worthy of our attention is that the method of Zhou et al. can also detect bad news early when the content information is limited (Zhou et al., 2020).

## 3 Data And Methods

### 3.1 Data Description and Analysis

The task description shows us that the data used in the task comes from some comments and posts on YouTube. The three data sets include training and validation sets composed of code mixed languages. The three code mixed languages are mainly Tamil, Malayalam, and Kannada. The label distribution probabilities in the training set and validation set of the three different code mixed languages provided by the task organizer are very similar. There are five different types in the Malayalam dataset labels, the Tamil data sets, and Kannada data sets are six different types of labels. Compared with the Malayalam language, an "Offensive Targeted Insult Other" label is added. Also, in the three different Dravidian language data sets, the data volume distribution of different tags is very unbalanced. This unbalanced data label distribution is most prominent on the Malayalam dataset. The proportion of "Not offensive" labels in the Malayalam language data set is 88.4%, and the sum of the other four labels only accounts for 21.6%.

In addition to the above-mentioned feature of label ratio distribution, another feature of the data set of this task is code-mixing. Code mixing means that the text in a piece of text may contain two or more languages. Also, since the data set comes from comments/posts on social media, there are many special symbols and emojis in the text. These data characteristics are all difficult points we need to face.

### 3.2 Methods

Combining our analysis and understanding of task description and task data set, we choose to develop our system based on multilingual BERT. Because as far as we know, the multilingual corpus used by multilingual BERT in the pre-training stage includes Malayalam, Tamil, and Kannada[2]. The structure of multilingual BERT is the same as that of BERT. The difference is that a corpus with a richer variety of languages than BERT is used in the pre-training phase. These corpora involve more than 100 text corpora of different language types. Therefore, the multilingual BERT has a strong advantage in cross-language. In the previous content, we have analyzed the characteristics of code mixed text, so we try to use the Tf-Idf algorithm to weight the output of multilingual BERT. We hope that using this method can reduce the impact of code-mixing on the results.

In our system, in the first step, we input text data into the multilingual BERT model, and also process the same text data using the Tf-Idf algorithm. In the second step, we take the output of the last layer of(last_layer_output) the multilingual BERT, and then use the Tf-Idf algorithm to get the text encoding and the last_layer_output to do the weighting operation. We can get a shape that is the same as the output of the last_layer_output. We call it the weighted_output. In the third step, we input the last_layer_output and weighted_output into the same CNN block and use two different linear classifiers(Classifier_0, Classifier_1) to classify the results. The last step is to perform arithmetic average operation(Mean) on the results of the two different linear classifiers into the system Finally output the result. We provide the code implementation of our system[3].

## 4 Experiment and Results

### 4.1 Data Preprocessing

Regarding this part of the data preprocessing, we mainly use the Tf-Idf algorithm to get weighted_output. To ensure that the shape of the text encoding processed by the Tf-Idf algorithm is the same as the shape of (last_layer_output), we delete the part of the text encoding that exceeds the maximum sentence length, and for the text encoding less than the maximum sentence length, we perform zero-padding operations.

### 4.2 Experiment setting

The BERT-base-multilingual-cased pre-training language model we use in our system is from the version released by Hugging Face[4]. The CNN block is composed of Conv2d convolution. The convolution kernel uses three different sizes of 3, 4, and 5. Use the maximum pooling operation and the activation function to select ReLU. Finally, the three convolution results of different sizes are

[2]https://github.com/google-research/bert/blob/master/multilingual.md

[3]https://github.com/Hub-Lucas/hub-at-offensive-2021

[4]https://huggingface.co/bert-base-multilingual-cased/tree/main

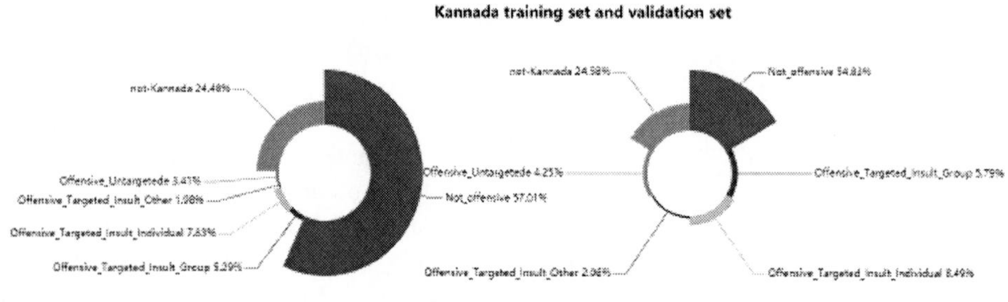


Figure 2: Labels distribution of Kannada training set and validation set. In the training set, Not offensive: 57.01%, Not Kannada: 24.48%, Offensive Targeted Insult Individual: 7.83%, Offensive Targeted Insult Group: 5.29%, Offensive Untargetede: 3.41%, Offensive Targeted Insult Other: 1.98%. In the validation set, Not offensive: 54.83%, Not Kannada: 24.58%, Offensive Targeted Insult Individual: 8.49%, Offensive Targeted Insult Group: 5.79%, Offensive Untargetede: 4.25%, Offensive Targeted Insult Other: 2.06%.

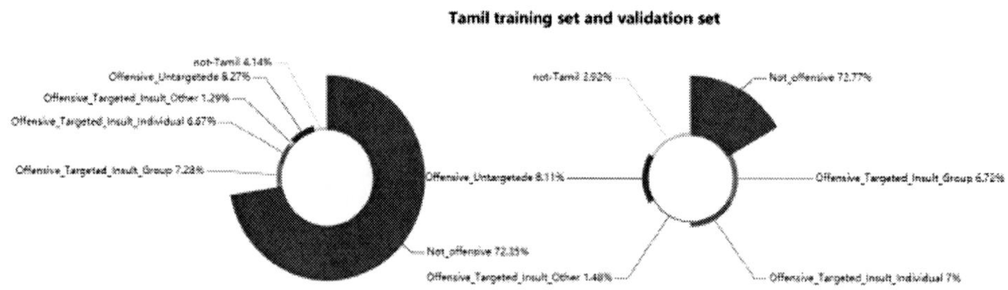


Figure 3: Labels distribution of Tamil training set and validation set.
In the training set, Not offensive: 72.23%, Offensive Untargetede: 8.27%, Offensive Targeted Insult Group: 7.28%, Offensive Targeted Insult Individual: 6.67%, Not-Tamil: 4.14%, Offensive Targeted Insult Other: 1.29%.
In the validation set, Not offensive: 72.77%, Offensive Untargetede: 8.11%, Offensive Targeted Insult Group: 6.72%, Offensive Targeted Insult Individual: 7%, Not Tamil: 3.92%, Offensive Targeted Insult Other: 1.48%.

| Language | F1 | Precision | Recall |
|---|---|---|---|
| Malayalam | 0.91 | 0.91 | 0.92 |
| Tamil | 0.78 | 0.78 | 0.79 |
| Kannada | 0.70 | 0.71 | 0.73 |

Table 1: The results of our model and method on the validation set. The validation set data is provided by the task organizer team.

| Language | F1 | Precision | Recall |
|---|---|---|---|
| Our Malayalam | 0.91 | 0.89 | 0.93 |
| Our Tamil | 0.74 | 0.73 | 0.78 |
| Our Kannada | 0.64 | 0.65 | 0.69 |

Table 2: The results of our model and method on the test set. The score of the test set comes from the ranking list announced by the task organizer team.

stitched together (256+256+256), the output dimension of the CNN block is 768 dimensions. The loss function of the two different classifiers is the CrossEntropyLoss function provided by PyTorch. In the experiment, we adjust the parameters according to the scores of different language data sets on the validation set.

- **Malayalam data set**: The epoch, batch size, maximum sequence length, and learning rate for the data set are 5, 32, 70, and 3e-5, respectively.
- **Kannada data set**: The epoch, batch size, maximum sequence length, and learning rate for the data set are 4, 32, 80, and 4e-5, respectively.
- **Tamil data set**: The epoch, batch size, maximum sequence length, and learning rate for the data set are 5, 32, 70, and 2e-5, respectively.

### 4.3 Analysis of Results

The task evaluation index specified by the task organizer team in the task description is the weighted average F1 score. The leaderboard finally announced by the task organizer not only has the ranking of each team, but also the F1 score, Precision, and Recall of the results submitted by each team.

| Language | F1 | Precision | Recall |
|---|---|---|---|
| Top1 Malayalam | 0.97 | 0.97 | 0.97 |
| Top1 Tamil | 0.78 | 0.78 | 0.78 |
| Top1 Kannada | 0.73 | 0.78 | 0.75 |

Table 3: The results of the Top1 team in the test set. The score of the test set comes from the ranking list announced by the task organizer team.

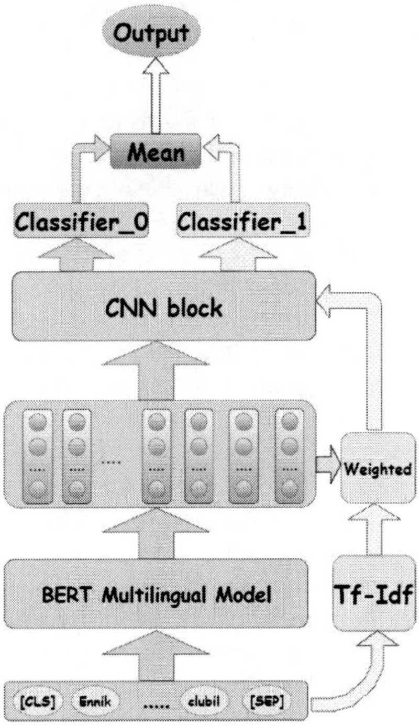

Figure 4: The model structure we used in this task.

Comparing our result score on the Malayalam test set and the result score on the Malayalam data validation set are very close. This shows that our training on the Malayalam language data set is normal. On the Kannada data and Tamil data, there is a large gap between our test set score and the validation set score. This result is likely to be overfitting during the training process. Because the Malayalam data set also has data imbalance, and the result score of the validation set of Malayalam is very close to the result score of the test set. This shows that our result scores on Kannada data and Tamil data are likely to be caused by the model overfitting. By comparing the scores of three different language test data sets, we can see that the prediction results of the two test sets of Tamil and Kannada are compared with the scores submitted by the top1 team, and there is a large gap.

## 5 Conclusion

On the three different language data sets provided by the task organizer, we combined the Tf-Idf algorithm and the output of the multilingual BERT model and introduced the CNN block as a shared layer. Experimental results prove that our conjecture is feasible, but our method needs to be improved. Especially to eliminate the over-fitting phenomenon in the training phase. When we rechecked our work, we also discovered our omissions. On the Kannada and Tami data sets, the verification set and the test set are different in the setting of the maximum sentence length. At the same time, our model has many areas that can be improved. For example, the use of classifiers and the replacement of CNN blocks are areas that we can try to optimize in future work. Stop words and some special symbols can be deleted in data preprocessing. Try to use data enhancement and other methods on the problem of data imbalance. We also hope that our system and methods can give other teams that pay attention to such tasks some inspiration and reference. In future work, we will not only improve our methods and systems but also continue to pay attention to related code-mixing fields progress.

## References


Araz Ramazan Ahmad and Hersh Rasool Murad. 2020. The impact of social media on panic during the covid-19 pandemic in iraqi kurdistan: online questionnaire study. *Journal of Medical Internet Research*, 22(5):e19556.

Bharathi Raja Chakravarthi, Navya Jose, Shardul Suryawanshi, Elizabeth Sherly, and John Philip McCrae. 2020a. A sentiment analysis dataset for code-mixed Malayalam-English. In *Proceedings of the 1st Joint Workshop on Spoken Language Technologies for Under-resourced languages (SLTU) and Collaboration and Computing for Under-Resourced Languages (CCURL)*, pages 177–184, Marseille, France. European Language Resources association.

Bharathi Raja Chakravarthi, Vigneshwaran Muralidaran, Ruba Priyadharshini, and John Philip McCrae. 2020b. Corpus creation for sentiment analysis in code-mixed Tamil-English text. In *Proceedings of the 1st Joint Workshop on Spoken Language Technologies for Under-resourced languages (SLTU) and Collaboration and Computing for Under-Resourced Languages (CCURL)*, pages 202–210, Marseille, France. European Language Resources association.

Bharathi Raja Chakravarthi, Ruba Priyadharshini, Navya Jose, Anand Kumar M, Thomas Mandl, Prasanna Kumar Kumaresan, Rahul Ponnusamy, Hariharan V, Elizabeth Sherly, and John Philip McCrae. 2021. Findings of the shared task on Offensive Language Identification in Tamil, Malayalam, and Kannada. In *Proceedings of the First Workshop on Speech and Language Technologies for Dravidian Languages*. Association for Computational Linguistics.

Thomas Davidson, Dana Warmsley, Michael Macy, and Ingmar Weber. 2017. Automated hate speech detection and the problem of offensive language. In *Proceedings of the International AAAI Conference on Web and Social Media*, volume 11.

Anneliese Depoux, Sam Martin, Emilie Karafillakis, Raman Preet, Annelies Wilder-Smith, and Heidi Larson. 2020. The pandemic of social media panic travels faster than the covid-19 outbreak.

Adeep Hande, Ruba Priyadharshini, and Bharathi Raja Chakravarthi. 2020. KanCMD: Kannada CodeMixed dataset for sentiment analysis and offensive language detection. In *Proceedings of the Third Workshop on Computational Modeling of People's Opinions, Personality, and Emotion's in Social Media*, pages 54–63, Barcelona, Spain (Online). Association for Computational Linguistics.

Navya Jose, Bharathi Raja Chakravarthi, Shardul Suryawanshi, Elizabeth Sherly, and John P. McCrae. 2020. A Survey of Current Datasets for Code-Switching Research. In *2020 6th International Conference on Advanced Computing and Communication Systems (ICACCS)*, pages 136–141.

Hanjia Lyu, Long Chen, Yu Wang, and Jiebo Luo. 2020. Sense and sensibility: Characterizing social media users regarding the use of controversial terms for covid-19. *IEEE Transactions on Big Data*.

Thomas Mandl, Sandip Modha, Anand Kumar M, and Bharathi Raja Chakravarthi. 2020. Overview of the HASOC Track at FIRE 2020: Hate Speech and Offensive Language Identification in Tamil, Malayalam, Hindi, English and German. In *Forum for Information Retrieval Evaluation*, FIRE 2020, page 29–32, New York, NY, USA. Association for Computing Machinery.

Binny Mathew, Ritam Dutt, Pawan Goyal, and Animesh Mukherjee. 2019. Spread of hate speech in online social media. In *Proceedings of the 10th ACM conference on web science*, pages 173–182.

Zewdie Mossie and Jenq-Haur Wang. 2020. Vulnerable community identification using hate speech detection on social media. *Information Processing & Management*, 57(3):102087.

Endang Wahyu Pamungkas, Alessandra Teresa Cignarella, Valerio Basile, Viviana Patti, et al. 2018. 14-exlab@ unito for ami at ibereval2018: Exploiting lexical knowledge for detecting misogyny in english and spanish tweets. In *3rd Workshop on Evaluation of Human Language Technologies for Iberian Languages, IberEval 2018*, volume 2150, pages 234–241. CEUR-WS.

Telmo Pires, Eva Schlinger, and Dan Garrette. 2019. How multilingual is multilingual bert? *arXiv preprint arXiv:1906.01502*.

Ruba Priyadharshini, Bharathi Raja Chakravarthi, Mani Vegupatti, and John P. McCrae. 2020. Named Entity Recognition for Code-Mixed Indian Corpus using Meta Embedding. In *2020 6th International Conference on Advanced Computing and Communication Systems (ICACCS)*, pages 68–72.

Francisco Rangel, Anastasia Giachanou, Bilal Ghanem, and Paolo Rosso. 2020. Overview of the 8th author profiling task at pan 2020: Profiling fake news spreaders on twitter. In *CLEF*.

Cassidy R Sugimoto, Sam Work, Vincent Larivière, and Stefanie Haustein. 2017. Scholarly use of social media and altmetrics: A review of the literature. *Journal of the Association for Information Science and technology*, 68(9):2037–2062.

Sajeetha Thavareesan and Sinnathamby Mahesan. 2019. Sentiment Analysis in Tamil Texts: A Study on Machine Learning Techniques and Feature Representation. In *2019 14th Conference on Industrial and Information Systems (ICIIS)*, pages 320–325.

Sajeetha Thavareesan and Sinnathamby Mahesan. 2020a. Sentiment Lexicon Expansion using Word2vec and fastText for Sentiment Prediction in Tamil texts. In *2020 Moratuwa Engineering Research Conference (MERCon)*, pages 272–276.

Sajeetha Thavareesan and Sinnathamby Mahesan. 2020b. Word embedding-based Part of Speech tagging in Tamil texts. In *2020 IEEE 15th International Conference on Industrial and Information Systems (ICIIS)*, pages 478–482.

Nicolás Velásquez, R Leahy, N Johnson Restrepo, Yonatan Lupu, R Sear, N Gabriel, Omkant Jha, and NF Johnson. 2020. Hate multiverse spreads malicious covid-19 content online beyond individual platform control. *arXiv preprint arXiv:2004.00673*.

Bertie Vidgen and Taha Yasseri. 2020. Detecting weak and strong islamophobic hate speech on social media. *Journal of Information Technology & Politics*, 17(1):66–78.

Matthew L Williams, Pete Burnap, Amir Javed, Han Liu, and Sefa Ozalp. 2020. Hate in the machine: anti-black and anti-muslim social media posts as predictors of offline racially and religiously aggravated crime. *The British Journal of Criminology*, 60(1):93–117.

Sayyed M Zahiri and Ali Ahmadvand. 2020. Crab: Class representation attentive bert for hate speech identification in social media. *arXiv preprint arXiv:2010.13028*.

Marcos Zampieri, Shervin Malmasi, Preslav Nakov, Sara Rosenthal, Noura Farra, and Ritesh Kumar. 2019. Predicting the type and target of offensive posts in social media. *arXiv preprint arXiv:1902.09666*.

Xinyi Zhou, Atishay Jain, Vir V Phoha, and Reza Zafarani. 2020. Fake news early detection: A theory-driven model. *Digital Threats: Research and Practice*, 1(2):1–25.

# HUB@DravidianLangTech-EACL2021: Meme Classification for Tamil Text-Image Fusion

**Bo Huang**
School of Information Science
and Engineering Yunnan University,
Yunnan, P.R. China
hublucashb@gmail.com

**Yang Bai**
School of Information Science
and Engineering Yunnan University,
Yunnan, P.R. China
baiyang.top@gmail.com

## Abstract

This article describes our system for task DravidianLangTech - EACL2021: Meme classification for Tamil. In recent years, we have witnessed the rapid development of the Internet and social media. Compared with traditional TV and radio media platforms, there are not so many restrictions on the use of online social media for individuals and many functions of online social media platforms are free. Based on this feature of social media, it is difficult for people's posts/comments on social media to be strictly and effectively controlled like TV and radio content. Therefore, the detection of negative information in social media has attracted attention from academic and industrial fields in recent years. The task of classifying memes is also driven by offensive posts/comments prevalent on social media. The data of the meme classification task is the fusion data of text and image information. To identify the content expressed by the meme, we develop a system that combines BiGRU and CNN. It can fuse visual features and text features to achieve the purpose of using multi-modal information from memetic data. In this article, we discuss our methods, models, experiments, and results.

## 1 Introduction and Background

The meme is a kind of multimedia document based on image level, which is a picture containing text. Netizens can express their feelings, opinions, interests, and so on through it (Yus, 2018a). The meme is an image with some kind of subtitle text embedded in the image pixels. In the past few years, emoticons have become very popular and used in many different contexts, especially young people (Oriol Sabat et al., 2019). However, this form is also used to produce and spread hate speech in the form of black humor. The meme is a term proposed by biologist Richard Dawkins. It was used to describe the flow, flow, mutation, and evolution of culture and is a means of cultural resistance to genes (Milner, 2012). But the meaning of this term has changed in our public life. In social media, Meme is a kind of self-media work, which is produced and spread by the majority of Internet users through social media networks (Castaño Díaz, 2013). Negative information detection on the Internet has become a core social challenge. Nowadays, the detection of negative information in social media has become more and more intelligent (Chatzakou et al., 2017; Pfeffer et al., 2014).

However, due to the multimodal nature of memes, it is difficult to be intelligently identified whether it is aggressive (Suryawanshi et al., 2020a). Especially in India, some recent memes containing hate messages have threatened people's lives several times (Suryawanshi et al., 2020b). Due to the large population and the mixing of multiple languages, a large number of Indian memes are difficult to monitor due to the lack of intelligent systems for specific languages. This adds another serious challenge to the problem of memetic classification. In this work, we participated in the shared task of memetic classification in Tamil (Suryawanshi and Chakravarthi, 2021). The Indian state of Tamil Nadu, as well as two independent countries, Singapore and Sri Lanka, speak Tamil as their official language. Tamil was the first Indian classical language to be listed as such, and it is still one of the world's oldest classical languages. Dravidian civilisations are believed to have flourished in the Indus Valley civilization (3,300–1,900 BCE), which was situated in the Northwestern Indian subcontinent, this period is considered as second Sangam period in Tamil. Tamil is India's oldest language. Tamil, Pali, and Prakrit all added words, texts, and grammar to Sanskrit. We are committed to making our contribution to the identification of Tamil memetic classification.



*Proceedings of the First Workshop on Speech and Language Technologies for Dravidian Languages*, pages 210–215
April 20, 2021 

## 2 Related Work

In theory, a meme is an example of a large number of humorous words on the Internet, copied or modified, and then spread to other users. But sometimes some information in Internet memes can bring a negative impact (Yus, 2018b). Compared with the propagation speed of memes on the Internet, the research progress of memes is much slower. The work of Wang et al. showed us that the combination of text and vision can help identify popular memetic descriptions (Wang and Wen, 2015). The automatic meme generation system implemented by Vyalla et al. based on the transformer model can allow users to generate memes of their choice (Vyalla and Udandarao, 2020). Compared with the text field, there is less research on sentiment analysis on memetic data. In recent years, deep learning technology has attracted the attention of researchers, especially in sentiment analysis tasks that are significantly better than traditional methods. Zhang et al. used deep learning techniques for sentiment analysis on text datasets (Zhang et al., 2018) and Poria et al. used deep learning models for sentiment analysis on image and video datasets (Poria et al., 2017a). The work of Sabat found that visual modalities provide more information in hate memetic detection than language modalities (Sabat et al., 2019). Suryawanshi and others shared with us their data sets and methods for detecting offensive content in multimodal memetic data sets (Suryawanshi et al., 2020a). Kumar et al. (Kumar et al., 2020) used a multimodal approach to determine the sentiment of a meme.

The method of using both text and visual information to improve performance has also proven to be effective (Guillaumin et al., 2010; Zahavy et al., 2016). Generally speaking, the fusion strategy of text information and visual information can be divided into two methods (Corchs et al., 2019). On the one hand, some models use feature-level fusion methods, where text input sources or image input sources are processed to extract a set of features. Then, the feature set is put together for the final decision (Atrey et al., 2007; Wang et al., 2018). On the other hand, other models perform complete processing of each input source and perform fusion at the decision-making level (Atreya V et al., 2013; Poria et al., 2017b). The result we submitted was predicted using the second strategy.

## 3 Data And Methods

### 3.1 Data Description and Analysis

The training set provided by the task organizer is mainly divided into two types of data, one is a text data set, and the other is a picture data set. There are 2300 pieces of text data in the text data set. The proportion of "Not Troll" text data and "Troll" text data to the total data volume are 44% and 56%, respectively. The text content of some of the text data is "No Captions". This situation means that no text annotations in the Tamil language appear on the meme picture corresponding to this text data. Such meme pictures without text annotations are not many in the dataset. The other text data is the text appearing on the corresponding meme picture. We present the text data set in the training set provided by the task organizer in a word cloud diagram. It is not difficult to see that in these text data, the most frequent words are mainly demonstrative pronouns and some modal particles.

The work of Suryawanshi et al. on the task data set shows us the source of the training set of 2969 meme images that we used in the training phase (Suryawanshi et al., 2020b; Suryawanshi and Chakravarthi, 2021). The proportions of the number of pictures marked as "Not Troll" and the number of pictures marked as "Troll" in the total number of meme picture datasets are 0.66 and 0.34 respectively. Regardless of whether there are texts in the meme pictures, the content of these meme pictures can also express the information of "Troll" and "Not Troll". These meme pictures mainly come from many popular social media platforms (such as YouTube, Facebook, WhatsApp, Instagram, etc.). So the size and style of the pictures are also different. From the comparison between the entire text data and the meme picture data, the relationship between them is not one-to-one. It is not difficult to find that their numbers are not equal. This data distribution feature is not good information for us.

### 3.2 Methods

Combine our analysis and understanding of task description and data set. Our system must process text data while also processing meme image data. Therefore, we choose to use the BiGRU artificial neural network and CNN artificial neural network capable of processing text data as the basic components of our system model. BiGRU can learn the contextual semantic information in the

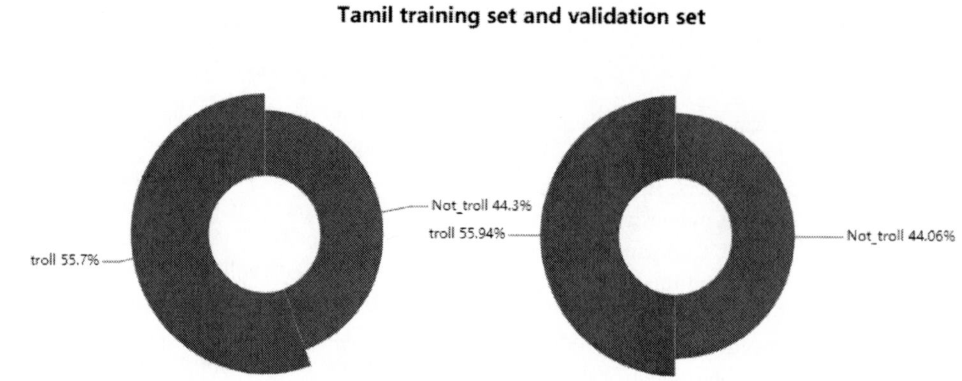


Figure 1: Labels distribution of Tamil training set and validation set. In the training set, Troll: 55.7%, Not troll: 44.3%. In the validation set, Troll: 55.94%, Not troll:44.06%.

Figure 2: No text annotations in the Tamil language appear on the meme picture.

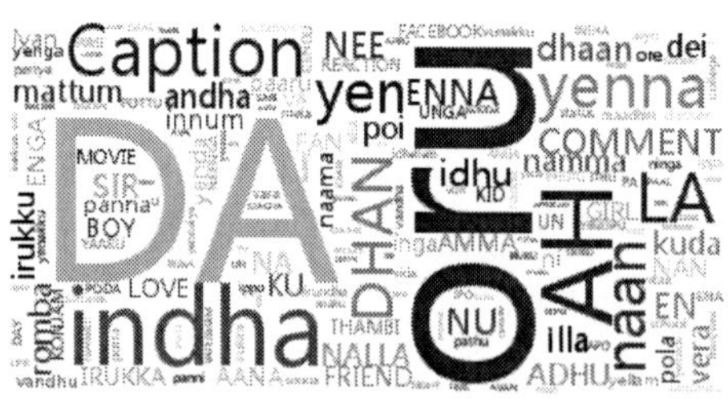


Figure 3: The word cloud image of the text training set is provided by the task organizer. The word "Caption" can not be used as reference information, because it mainly comes from the annotation of the text data, not the text content that appears in the meme picture.

text through the encoded-word vectors. CNN can learn the information in the picture through convolution operation and pooling operation. We use stacking to combine BiGRU and CNN blocks to form the overall architecture of our system.

The CNN block is mainly composed of three two-dimensional convolutional layers and three maximum pooling layers. The size of the convolution kernel is selected as 2. After getting the image processed by the third convolutional layer(Conv2d_2) and the third pooling layer(MaxPooling2D_2), the multi-dimensional tensor is converted into a low-latitude tensor through a straightening(Flatten) operation. Then, the result obtained in the previous step is used as the input of the two dense layers(Dense_0, Dense_1). Finally, the output result of the CNN block is obtained.

Text data We use the Tamil pre-training language vector provided by fasttext[1] to encode the text data (Grave et al., 2018). Then input the encoded text vector into the BiGRU network to obtain the output result of the BiGRU network. Next, input the BiGRU result from the previous step into the Dense layer to get the final output of the BiGRU block. Connect the output result of the CNN block and the output result of the BiGRU block to obtain a new tensor. Finally, input this new tensor into the Dense layer to get the final result of the model. The final effect that our system model needs to achieve is to merge text and image data information. We

[1]https://fasttext.cc/docs/en/crawl-vectors.html

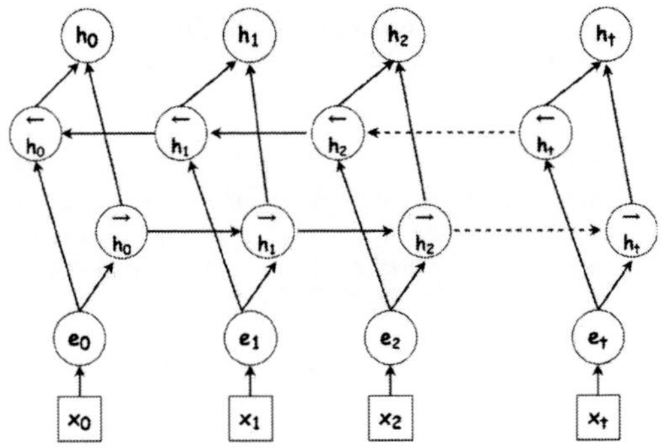


Figure 4: BiGRU structure and data flow.

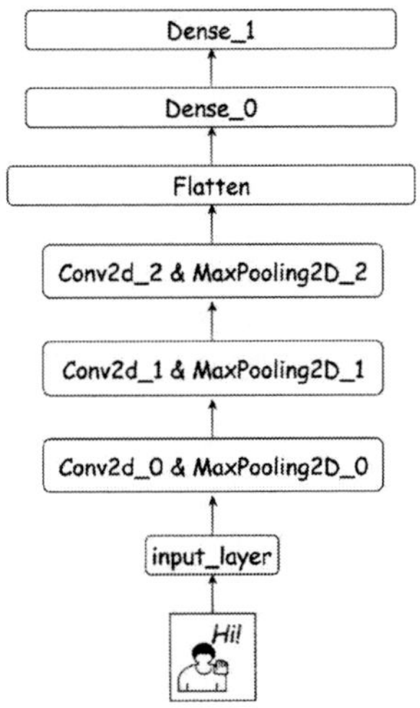


Figure 5: The CNN block in our system.

provide the code implementation of our system[2].

## 4 Experiment and Results

### 4.1 Data Preprocessing

The work in the data preprocessing stage is mainly for text data. We split the text training set released by the task organizer into a new text training set and a text verification set under the premise of ensuring the same data distribution. The text data is divided by spaces to get each word, and then encoded using the fasttext we mentioned in the Methods section. Use the results predicted by the model on the validation set to evaluate our model system and adjust the parameters of the model system. For meme image data, we set their size uniformly to (300, 300).

[2]https://github.com/Hub-Lucas/hub-at-meme

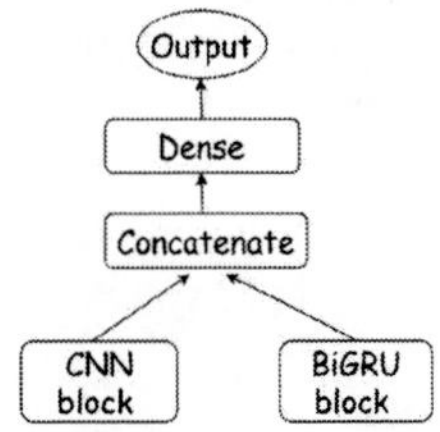


Figure 6: The CNN block, BiGRU block, and Dense layer together constitute the main part of our system.

| Language | F1 Score | Precision | Recall |
|---|---|---|---|
| Top1 results | 0.55 | 0.57 | 0.6 |
| Our results | 0.4 | 0.5 | 0.54 |
| Validation set | 0.50 | 0.52 | 0.56 |

Table 1: The result score of the top1 team on the test set. We submit the test set prediction result score. The score of our system on the validation set.

### 4.2 Experiment setting

In our experiment, the optimizer uniformly uses Adam optimizer. Because Adam uses momentum and adaptive learning rate to speed up convergence. The number of BiGRU layers is set to 2, and the word embedding vector uses 300 dimensions. epoch, learning rate, and batch seize are set to 10, 0.003, and 32 respectively. The activation function used between the three layers in the CNN block is Relu. The activation function used by the dense layer in BiGRU is Softmax. Connect the results in the CNN block and the BiGRU block as the input of the classifier (Dense layer). Use the classifier to get the output result. Figure 6 shows the architecture of our system.

### 4.3 Analysis of Results

The leaderboard results announced by the task organizer are ranked using the weighted average F1 score. At the same time, the Precision and Recall scores of all participants' submission results will be announced on the leaderboard. Table 1 shows the final result of our system model on the test set, the result score of the top1 team's system on the test set, and the result score of our model on the validation set. Comparing the scores in the table, the results of my system on the validation set are quite different from the results on the test set. There is also a gap between the result score of my system on the test set and the top1 result score. Our team solution ranked 9th in the final leaderboard. The number of data sets we can use is not large, and we randomly select a part of them as the verification set. The result of this is that there are fewer data sets that can be used to train the model. There is no restriction on overfitting in our model. These are the shortcomings of our system.

## 5 Conclusion

This article introduces the method and model system used by our team in the Meme classification for the Tamil shared task. We use a text and image fusion scheme to detect memetic categories in the Tamil language environment. We analyzed the deficiencies of our system. These shortcomings are what we need to improve in our future work. We also have a lot of room for improvement in methods and systems. For example, in image processing, we can try some other network models such as MobileNet (Howard et al., 2017), ResNext(He et al., 2016), etc. Some pre-trained language models in text processing.

Considering that meme pictures can quickly spread on Internet social media and can express negative information across languages, we determined that dealing with similar issues in social media is very valuable and meaningful. Similar issues that exist in social media in some small-language communities should also deserve our attention and study. In addition to improving our models and methods in future work, we will continue to pay attention to the research and development of memetic analysis.

## References


Pradeep K Atrey, Mohan S Kankanhalli, and John B Oommen. 2007. Goal-oriented optimal subset selection of correlated multimedia streams. *ACM Transactions on Multimedia Computing, Communications, and Applications (TOMM)*, 3(1):2–es.

Arjun Atreya V, Yogesh Kakde, Pushpak Bhattacharyya, and Ganesh Ramakrishnan. 2013. Structure cognizant pseudo relevance feedback. In *Proceedings of the Sixth International Joint Conference on Natural Language Processing*, pages 982–986, Nagoya, Japan. Asian Federation of Natural Language Processing.

Carlos Mauricio Castaño Díaz. 2013. Defining and characterizing the concept of internet meme. *Ces Psicología*, 6(2):82–104.

Despoina Chatzakou, Nicolas Kourtellis, Jeremy Blackburn, Emiliano De Cristofaro, Gianluca Stringhini, and Athena Vakali. 2017. Mean birds: Detecting aggression and bullying on twitter. In *Proceedings of the 2017 ACM on web science conference*, pages 13–22.

Silvia Corchs, Elisabetta Fersini, and Francesca Gasparini. 2019. Ensemble learning on visual and textual data for social image emotion classification. *International Journal of Machine Learning and Cybernetics*, 10(8):2057–2070.

Edouard Grave, Piotr Bojanowski, Prakhar Gupta, Armand Joulin, and Tomas Mikolov. 2018. Learning word vectors for 157 languages. In *Proceedings of the International Conference on Language Resources and Evaluation (LREC 2018)*.

Matthieu Guillaumin, Jakob Verbeek, and Cordelia Schmid. 2010. Multimodal semi-supervised learning for image classification. In *2010 IEEE Computer society conference on computer vision and pattern recognition*, pages 902–909. IEEE.

Kaiming He, Xiangyu Zhang, Shaoqing Ren, and Jian Sun. 2016. Deep residual learning for image recognition. In *Proceedings of the IEEE conference on computer vision and pattern recognition*, pages 770–778.

Andrew G Howard, Menglong Zhu, Bo Chen, Dmitry Kalenichenko, Weijun Wang, Tobias Weyand, Marco Andreetto, and Hartwig Adam. 2017. Mobilenets: Efficient convolutional neural networks for mobile vision applications. *arXiv preprint arXiv:1704.04861*.

Akshi Kumar, Kathiravan Srinivasan, Wen-Huang Cheng, and Albert Y Zomaya. 2020. Hybrid context enriched deep learning model for fine-grained sentiment analysis in textual and visual semiotic modality social data. *Information Processing & Management*, 57(1):102141.

Ryan M Milner. 2012. *The world made meme: Discourse and identity in participatory media*. Ph.D. thesis, University of Kansas.

Benet Oriol Sabat, Cristian Canton Ferrer, and Xavier Giro-i Nieto. 2019. Hate speech in pixels: Detection of offensive memes towards automatic moderation. *arXiv e-prints*, pages arXiv–1910.

Jürgen Pfeffer, Thomas Zorbach, and Kathleen M Carley. 2014. Understanding online firestorms: Negative word-of-mouth dynamics in social media networks. *Journal of Marketing Communications*, 20(1-2):117–128.

Soujanya Poria, Erik Cambria, Devamanyu Hazarika, Navonil Majumder, Amir Zadeh, and Louis-Philippe Morency. 2017a. Context-dependent sentiment analysis in user-generated videos. In *Proceedings of the 55th annual meeting of the association for computational linguistics (volume 1: Long papers)*, pages 873–883.

Soujanya Poria, Erik Cambria, Devamanyu Hazarika, Navonil Majumder, Amir Zadeh, and Louis-Philippe Morency. 2017b. Context-dependent sentiment analysis in user-generated videos. In *Proceedings of the 55th Annual Meeting of the Association for Computational Linguistics (Volume 1: Long Papers)*, pages 873–883, Vancouver, Canada. Association for Computational Linguistics.

Benet Oriol Sabat, Cristian Canton Ferrer, and Xavier Giro-i Nieto. 2019. Hate speech in pixels: Detection of offensive memes towards automatic moderation. *arXiv preprint arXiv:1910.02334*.

Shardul Suryawanshi and Bharathi Raja Chakravarthi. 2021. Findings of the shared task on Troll Meme Classification in Tamil. In *Proceedings of the First Workshop on Speech and Language Technologies for Dravidian Languages*. Association for Computational Linguistics.

Shardul Suryawanshi, Bharathi Raja Chakravarthi, Mihael Arcan, and Paul Buitelaar. 2020a. Multimodal meme dataset (multioff) for identifying offensive content in image and text. In *Proceedings of the Second Workshop on Trolling, Aggression and Cyberbullying*, pages 32–41.

Shardul Suryawanshi, Bharathi Raja Chakravarthi, Pranav Verma, Mihael Arcan, John Philip McCrae, and Paul Buitelaar. 2020b. A dataset for troll classification of TamilMemes. In *Proceedings of the WILDRE5– 5th Workshop on Indian Language Data: Resources and Evaluation*, pages 7–13, Marseille, France. European Language Resources Association (ELRA).

Suryatej Reddy Vyalla and Vishaal Udandarao. 2020. Memeify: A large-scale meme generation system. In *Proceedings of the 7th ACM IKDD CoDS and 25th COMAD*, pages 307–311.

William Yang Wang and Miaomiao Wen. 2015. I can has cheezburger? a nonparanormal approach to combining textual and visual information for predicting and generating popular meme descriptions. In *Proceedings of the 2015 Conference of the North American Chapter of the Association for Computational Linguistics: Human Language Technologies*, pages 355–365.

Yaqing Wang, Fenglong Ma, Zhiwei Jin, Ye Yuan, Guangxu Xun, Kishlay Jha, Lu Su, and Jing Gao. 2018. Eann: Event adversarial neural networks for multi-modal fake news detection. In *Proceedings of the 24th acm sigkdd international conference on knowledge discovery & data mining*, pages 849–857.

Francisco Yus. 2018a. Identity-related issues in meme communication. *Internet Pragmatics*, 1(1):113–133.

Francisco Yus. 2018b. Identity-related issues in meme communication. *Internet Pragmatics*, 1(1):113–133.

Tom Zahavy, Alessandro Magnani, Abhinandan Krishnan, and Shie Mannor. 2016. Is a picture worth a thousand words? a deep multi-modal fusion architecture for product classification in e-commerce. *arXiv preprint arXiv:1611.09534*.

Lei Zhang, Shuai Wang, and Bing Liu. 2018. Deep learning for sentiment analysis: A survey. *Wiley Interdisciplinary Reviews: Data Mining and Knowledge Discovery*, 8(4):e1253.

# ZYJ123@DravidianLangTech-EACL2021: Offensive Language Identification based on XLM-RoBERTa with DPCNN

**Yingjia Zhao**
Yunnan University/Yunnan, P.R. China
zyj1309700118@gmail.com

**Xin Tao**
Yunnan University / Yunnan, P.R. China
taoxinwy@126.com

## Abstract

The development of online media platforms has given users more opportunities to post and comment freely, but the negative impact of offensive language has become increasingly apparent. It is very necessary for the automatic identification system of offensive language. This paper describes our work on the task of Offensive Language Identification in Dravidian language-EACL 2021. To complete this task, we propose a system based on the multilingual model XLM-Roberta and DPCNN. The test results on the official test data set confirm the effectiveness of our system. The weighted average F1-score of Kannada, Malayalam, and Tamil language are 0.69, 0.92, and 0.76 respectively, ranked 6th, 6th, and 3rd.

## 1 Introduction

With the development of the information society, people have become accustomed to uploading content on social media platforms in the form of text, pictures, or videos. At the same time, they also comment on the content uploaded by other users and interact with each other, thus increasing the activity of social media platforms (Thavareesan and Mahesan, 2019, 2020a,b). Inevitably, however, some users will post offensive posts or comments. The use of offensive discourse is a kind of impolite phenomenon which has negative effects on the civilization of the network community (Chakravarthi, 2020). It usually has the characteristics of causing conflicts and the purpose of publishing intentionally. The publisher of offensive language may use reproach, sarcasm, swear and other language means to achieve intentional offense, and express a variety of intentions, such as disturbing, provoking, and expressing negative emotions (Chakravarthi and Muralidaran, 2021; Suryawanshi and Chakravarthi, 2021). Most people will take measures to respond to offensive words. The way to respond to the direct conflict of offensive words is mainly rhetorical questions, swear, sarcasm and threat, so as to express dissatisfaction, deny and satirize the other party and provoke the other party. This will further cause conflicts and destroy the harmony of the network environment.

Many social media platforms use a content review process, in which human reviewers check users' comments for offensive language and other infractions, and which comments have been removed from the platform because of the violation (Mandl et al., 2020). It is up to the moderator to decide which comments will be removed from the platform due to violations and which ones will be kept. As the number of network users increases and user activity increases, the manual approach is undoubtedly inefficient. Therefore, the automatic detection and identification of offensive content are very necessary. However, offensive words often depend on the emotions and psychology of the listener, and some seemingly innocuous words can be potentially offensive, and words that often seem offensive are watered down by the emotions of the listener. This kind of language phenomenon is not uncommon in real life, either unintentionally or deliberately used to achieve the speaker's expected purpose, which is a challenging work for the current detection system.

Our team takes part in the shared task of Offensive Language Identification in Dravidian Languages-EACL 2021 (Chakravarthi et al., 2021, 2020a,b; Hande et al., 2020). This is a classification task at the comment/post level. The goal of this task is to identify offensive language content of the code-mixed dataset of comments/posts in Dravidian Languages ( (Tamil-English, Malayalam-English, and Kannada-English)) collected from social media. Tamil language is the oldest language in Indian languages, Malayalam and Kannada evolved



*Proceedings of the First Workshop on Speech and Language Technologies for Dravidian Languages*, pages 216–221
April 20, 2021 ©2021 Association for Computational Linguistics

from Tamil language. For a comment on Youtube, the system must classify it into not-offensive, offensive-untargeted, offensive-targeted-individual, offensive-targeted-group, offensive-targeted-other, or not-in-indented-language.

In our approach, the multilingual model XLM-RoBERTa and DPCNN are combined to carry out the classification task. This method can combine the advantages of the two models to achieve a better classification effect. The rest of the paper is divided into the following parts. In the second part, we introduce the relevant work in this field, which involves offensive language detection and text classification methods. In the third part, we introduce the model structure and the composition of our training data. The fourth part introduces our experimental setup and results. The fifth part is the conclusion.

## 2 Related Work

Due to the harm of offensive language to the network environment, the identification of offensive language has been carried out for a long time. Research so far has focused on automating the decision-making process in the form of supervised machine learning for classification tasks (Sun et al., 2019). As far back as 2012, Chen et al. (2012) proposed a lexical syntactic feature (LSF) framework to detect offensive content in social media, distinguished the roles of derogatory/profane and obscenity in identifying offensive content, and introduced handwritten syntax rules to identify abusive harassment. In contrast to the start-to-end training model, Howard and Ruder (2018)proposed an effective transfer learning method, Universal Language Model Tuning (ULMFIT), which can be applied to any task in natural language processing, and has shown significant results on six text classification tasks. Subsequently, Abdellatif and Elgammal (2020) used the ULMFiT transfer learning method to train forward and backward models on Arabic datasets and ensemble the results to perform an offensive language detection task.

Although English is currently one of the most commonly spoken languages in the world, work is ongoing to identify the offensive language in other languages that are less widely spoken. Pitenis et al. (2020) tested the performance of several traditional machine learning models and deep learning models on an offensive language dataset of Greek, and the best results were achieved with the attention model of LSTM and GRU. Ozdemir and Yeniterzi (2020) ensembled CNN-LSTM, BILSTM-Attention, and BERT three models, combined with pre-trained word embedding on Twitter to complete the identification task of offensive Turkish language, and achieved a good result.

A key challenge in automatically detecting hate speech on social media is to separate hate speech from other offensive languages. Davidson et al. (2017) used the crowd-sourced hate speech lexicon to collect tweets containing hate speech keywords. They trained a multi-class classifier to reliably distinguish hate speech from other offensive languages, and found that racist and homophobic tweets were more likely to be classified as hate speech, but sexist tweets were generally classified as offensive. Razavi et al. (2010) proposed to extract features at different conceptual levels and apply multilevel classification for offensive language detection. The system leverages a variety of statistical models and rule-based patterns, combined with an auxiliary weighted pattern library, to improve accuracy by matching text with its graded entries. Pitsilis et al. (2018) proposed the ensemble of a recursive neural network (RNN) classifier, which combines various characteristics related to user-related information, such as the user's sexist or racist tendencies, and was then fed to the classifier as input along with a word frequency vector derived from the text content.

When there is a large amount of labeled data, increasing the size and parameters of the model will definitely improve the performance of the model.However, when the amount of training is relatively small, the large-scale model may not be able to achieve good results, so solving the problem of model training under the condition of a small amount of target data has become a research hotspot. Sun et al. (2019) proposed a Hierarchical Attention Prototype Network (HAPN) for few-shot text classification, which designed multiple cross-concerns of a feature layer, word layer, and instance layer for the model to enhance the expressive power of semantic space. The model was validated on two standard reference text classification datasets, Fewrel and CSID. Prettenhofer and Stein (2010) built on structural correspondence learning, using untagged documents and simple word translation to induce task-specific, cross-language word correspondence. English was used as the source language and German, French, and Japanese were used as the target language to conduct the experiment in the field of cross-language sentiment classification. Using English data, Ranasinghe and Zampieri (2020) trained the model by applying cross-language contextual word embedding and transfer learning methods, and then predicted the effect of cross-language contextual embedding and transfer learning on this task in less resource-intensive languages such as Bengali, Hindi, and Spanish.

## 3 Data and Methodology

### 3.1 Data description

We count the number of each type of tag in the training set and the validation set, and obtain the data distribution of Not-offensive, offensive-untargeted, offensive-targeted-individual, offensive-targeted-group, offensive-targeted-other, and Not-in-indented-language in Tamil, Malayalam, and Kannada. as shown in Table 1.

### 3.2 Why XLM-RoBERTa

Compared with the original BERT model, XLM-RoBERTa increases the number of languages and the number of training data sets. Specifically, a preprocessed CommonCrawl dataset of more than 2TB based on 100 languages is used to train cross-language representations in a self-supervised manner. This includes generating new unlabeled corpora for low-resource languages and expanding the amount of training data available for these languages by two orders of magnitude. In the fine-tuning period, the multi-language tagging data is used based on the ability of the multi-language model to improve the performance of the down-stream tasks. This enables XLM-RoBERTa to achieve state-of-the-art results in cross-language benchmarks while exceeding the performance of the single-language BERT model for each language. Tune the parameters of the model to address cases where extending the model to more languages using cross-language migration limits the ability of the model to understand each language. The XLM-RoBERTa parameter changes include up-sampling of low-resource languages during training and vocabulary building, generating a larger shared vocabulary, and increasing the overall model to 550 million parameters.

### 3.3 XLM-RoBERTa with DPCNN

In this task, we combined XLM-RoBERTa with DPCNN (Johnson and Zhang, 2017) to make the whole model more suitable for the downstream classification task. DPCNN(Deep Pyramid Convolutional Neural Networks) is a kind of deep word level CNN structure, the calculation amount of each layer of the structure decreases exponentially. DPCNN simply stacks the convolution module and negative sampling layer. The computation volume of the whole model is limited to less than two times the number of convolution blocks. At the same time, the pyramid structure also enables the model to discover long-term dependencies in the text. In a common classification task, the last hidden state of the first token of the sequence (CLS token), namely the original output of XLM-Roberta (Pooler output), is further processed through the linear layer and the tanh activation function for classification purposes. To obtain richer semantic information features of the model and improve the performance of the model, we first processed the output of the last three layers of XLM-RoBERTa through DPCNN, and then concatenate it with the original output of XLM-RoBERTa (Pooler output) to get a new and more effective feature vector, and then input this feature vector into the classifier for classification. As shown in Figure 1.

## 4 Experiment and results

### 4.1 Experiment setting

In this experiment, the pre-training model I used was XLM-RoBERTa-base. After adding the DPCNN module, we began to set the experimental parameters. We set the learning rate as 2e-5, the maximum sequence length is 256, and the gradient steps are set to 4. The batch size is set to 32, as shown in table 2. In the training process, we used five-fold stratified cross-validation to make the proportion of data of each category in each subsample the same as that in the original data and finally obtained the optimal result through the voting (Onan et al., 2016) system, as shown in Figure 2.

### 4.2 Results

After the evaluation by the organizer, we obtained the weighted average F1-score in the three languages, as shown in table 3. Our team's F1-score is 0.69, ranked 6th place for the Kannada language. For the Malayalam language, our team's F1-score

| | Kannada | | Malayalam | | Tamil | |
|---|---|---|---|---|---|---|
| **Label** | Train | Validation | Train | Validation | Train | Validation |
| **Not-offensive** | 3544 | 426 | 14153 | 1779 | 25405 | 3193 |
| **Not-in-indented-language** | 1522 | 191 | 6205 | 163 | 1454 | 172 |
| **offensive-targeted-individual** | 487 | 66 | 239 | 24 | 2343 | 307 |
| **offensive-targeted-group** | 329 | 45 | 140 | 13 | 2557 | 295 |
| **offensive-untargeted** | 212 | 33 | 191 | 20 | 2906 | 356 |
| **offensive-targeted-other** | 123 | 16 | 0 | 0 | 454 | 65 |

Table 1: Train and Validation datasets description.

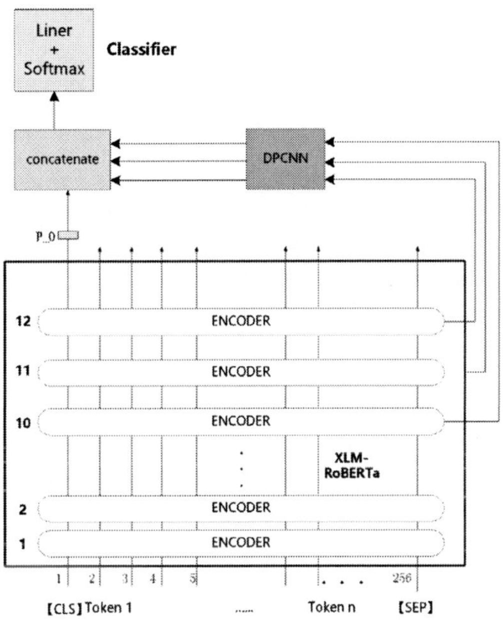


Figure 1: Schematic overview of the architecture of our model

| maximum sequence length | learning rate |
|---|---|
| 256 | 2e-5 |
| **gradient steps** | **batch size** |
| 4 | 32 |

Table 2: Details of the parameters

| | Kan | Mal | Tam |
|---|---|---|---|
| **Best F1-score** | 0.75 | 0.97 | 0.78 |
| **Our Precision** | 0.65 | 0.91 | 0.75 |
| **Our Recall** | 0.74 | 0.94 | 0.77 |
| **Our F1-score** | **0.69** | **0.92** | **0.76** |
| **Rank** | 6 | 6 | 3 |

Table 3: the results of our methods.

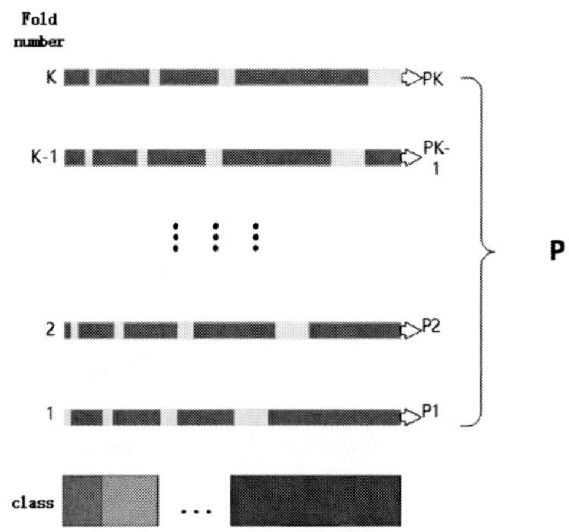


Figure 2: Voting system

is 0.92 ranked 6th place, and for the Tamil language, our team's F1-score is 0.76 ranked 3rd place.

## 5 Conclusion

In this paper, we describe our system in the task of offensive language identification for Tamil, Malayalam, and Kannada language. In this model, the XLM-RoBERTa pre-training model is used to extract semantic information features of the text, and DPCNN is used to further process the output features. At the same time, the hierarchical cross-validation method is used to improve the training effect. The final results show that our model achieves satisfactory performance. In future work, we will try to adjust the structure of the new model, so as to improve its effect more significantly.

## References


Mohamed Abdellatif and Ahmed Elgammal. 2020. Offensive language detection in arabic using ulmfit. In

*Proceedings of the 4th Workshop on Open-Source Arabic Corpora and Processing Tools, with a Shared Task on Offensive Language Detection*, pages 82–85.

Bharathi Raja Chakravarthi. 2020. HopeEDI: A multilingual hope speech detection dataset for equality, diversity, and inclusion. In *Proceedings of the Third Workshop on Computational Modeling of People's Opinions, Personality, and Emotion's in Social Media*, pages 41–53, Barcelona, Spain (Online). Association for Computational Linguistics.

Bharathi Raja Chakravarthi, Navya Jose, Shardul Suryawanshi, Elizabeth Sherly, and John Philip McCrae. 2020a. A sentiment analysis dataset for code-mixed Malayalam-English. In *Proceedings of the 1st Joint Workshop on Spoken Language Technologies for Under-resourced languages (SLTU) and Collaboration and Computing for Under-Resourced Languages (CCURL)*, pages 177–184, Marseille, France. European Language Resources association.

Bharathi Raja Chakravarthi and Vigneshwaran Muralidaran. 2021. Findings of the shared task on Hope Speech Detection for Equality, Diversity, and Inclusion. In *Proceedings of the First Workshop on Language Technology for Equality, Diversity and Inclusion*. Association for Computational Linguistics.

Bharathi Raja Chakravarthi, Vigneshwaran Muralidaran, Ruba Priyadharshini, and John Philip McCrae. 2020b. Corpus creation for sentiment analysis in code-mixed Tamil-English text. In *Proceedings of the 1st Joint Workshop on Spoken Language Technologies for Under-resourced languages (SLTU) and Collaboration and Computing for Under-Resourced Languages (CCURL)*, pages 202–210, Marseille, France. European Language Resources association.

Bharathi Raja Chakravarthi, Ruba Priyadharshini, Navya Jose, Anand Kumar M, Thomas Mandl, Prasanna Kumar Kumaresan, Rahul Ponnusamy, Hariharan V, Elizabeth Sherly, and John Philip McCrae. 2021. Findings of the shared task on Offensive Language Identification in Tamil, Malayalam, and Kannada. In *Proceedings of the First Workshop on Speech and Language Technologies for Dravidian Languages*. Association for Computational Linguistics.

Ying Chen, Yilu Zhou, Sencun Zhu, and Heng Xu. 2012. Detecting offensive language in social media to protect adolescent online safety. In *2012 International Conference on Privacy, Security, Risk and Trust and 2012 International Confernece on Social Computing*, pages 71–80. IEEE.

Thomas Davidson, Dana Warmsley, Michael Macy, and Ingmar Weber. 2017. Automated hate speech detection and the problem of offensive language. In *Proceedings of the International AAAI Conference on Web and Social Media*, volume 11.

Adeep Hande, Ruba Priyadharshini, and Bharathi Raja Chakravarthi. 2020. KanCMD: Kannada CodeMixed dataset for sentiment analysis and offensive language detection. In *Proceedings of the Third Workshop on Computational Modeling of People's Opinions, Personality, and Emotion's in Social Media*, pages 54–63, Barcelona, Spain (Online). Association for Computational Linguistics.

Jeremy Howard and Sebastian Ruder. 2018. Universal language model fine-tuning for text classification. *arXiv preprint arXiv:1801.06146*.

Rie Johnson and Tong Zhang. 2017. Deep pyramid convolutional neural networks for text categorization. In *Proceedings of the 55th Annual Meeting of the Association for Computational Linguistics (Volume 1: Long Papers)*, pages 562–570.

Thomas Mandl, Sandip Modha, Anand Kumar M, and Bharathi Raja Chakravarthi. 2020. Overview of the HASOC Track at FIRE 2020: Hate Speech and Offensive Language Identification in Tamil, Malayalam, Hindi, English and German. In *Forum for Information Retrieval Evaluation*, FIRE 2020, page 29–32, New York, NY, USA. Association for Computing Machinery.

Aytuğ Onan, Serdar Korukoğlu, and Hasan Bulut. 2016. A multiobjective weighted voting ensemble classifier based on differential evolution algorithm for text sentiment classification. *Expert Systems with Applications*, 62:1–16.

Anil Ozdemir and Reyyan Yeniterzi. 2020. Su-nlp at semeval-2020 task 12: Offensive language identification in turkish tweets. In *Proceedings of the Fourteenth Workshop on Semantic Evaluation*, pages 2171–2176.

Zeses Pitenis, Marcos Zampieri, and Tharindu Ranasinghe. 2020. Offensive language identification in greek. *arXiv preprint arXiv:2003.07459*.

Georgios K Pitsilis, Heri Ramampiaro, and Helge Langseth. 2018. Detecting offensive language in tweets using deep learning. *arXiv preprint arXiv:1801.04433*.

Peter Prettenhofer and Benno Stein. 2010. Cross-language text classification using structural correspondence learning. In *Proceedings of the 48th annual meeting of the association for computational linguistics*, pages 1118–1127.

Tharindu Ranasinghe and Marcos Zampieri. 2020. Multilingual offensive language identification with cross-lingual embeddings. *arXiv preprint arXiv:2010.05324*.

Amir H Razavi, Diana Inkpen, Sasha Uritsky, and Stan Matwin. 2010. Offensive language detection using multi-level classification. In *Canadian Conference on Artificial Intelligence*, pages 16–27. Springer.

Shengli Sun, Qingfeng Sun, Kevin Zhou, and Tengchao Lv. 2019. Hierarchical attention prototypical networks for few-shot text classification. In *Proceedings of the 2019 Conference on Empirical Methods in Natural Language Processing and the 9th International Joint Conference on Natural Language Processing (EMNLP-IJCNLP)*, pages 476–485.

Shardul Suryawanshi and Bharathi Raja Chakravarthi. 2021. Findings of the shared task on Troll Meme Classification in Tamil. In *Proceedings of the First Workshop on Speech and Language Technologies for Dravidian Languages*. Association for Computational Linguistics.

Sajeetha Thavareesan and Sinnathamby Mahesan. 2019. Sentiment Analysis in Tamil Texts: A Study on Machine Learning Techniques and Feature Representation. In *2019 14th Conference on Industrial and Information Systems (ICIIS)*, pages 320–325.

Sajeetha Thavareesan and Sinnathamby Mahesan. 2020a. Sentiment Lexicon Expansion using Word2vec and fastText for Sentiment Prediction in Tamil texts. In *2020 Moratuwa Engineering Research Conference (MERCon)*, pages 272–276.

Sajeetha Thavareesan and Sinnathamby Mahesan. 2020b. Word embedding-based Part of Speech tagging in Tamil texts. In *2020 IEEE 15th International Conference on Industrial and Information Systems (ICIIS)*, pages 478–482.

# IIITK@DravidianLangTech-EACL2021: Offensive Language Identification and Meme Classification in Tamil, Malayalam and Kannada

**Nikhil Kumar Ghanghor**[1], **Prameshwari Krishnamurthy,**[2] **Sajeetha Thavareesan** [3], **Ruba Priyadarshini,**[4] **Bharathi Raja Chakravarthi**[5]
[1]Indian Institute of Information Technology Kottayam
[2]University of Hyderbad, India, [3]ULTRA Arts and Science College, Tamil Nadu, India
[4] Eastern University, Sri Lanka, [5] National University of Ireland Galway
nkghanghor18bcs@iiitkottayam.ac.in

## Abstract

This paper describes the IIITK team's submissions to the offensive language identification and troll memes classification shared tasks for Dravidian languages at DravidianLangTech 2021 workshop@EACL 2021. We have used the transformer-based pretrained models along with their customized versions with custom loss functions. State of the art pretrained CNN models were also used for image-related tasks. Our best configuration for Tamil troll meme classification achieved a 0.55 weighted average F1 score, and for offensive language identification, our system achieved weighted F1 scores of 0.75 for Tamil, 0.95 for Malayalam, and 0.71 for Kannada. Our rank on Tamil troll meme classification is 2, and offensive language identification in Tamil, Malayalam, and Kannada is 3, 3 and 4. We have open-sourced our code implementations for all the models across both the tasks on GitHub[1].

## 1 Introduction

With the rise of deep learning in the past decade, we have seen some groundbreaking milestones achieved by various machine learning (ML) models being built over the era. The AlexNet (Krizhevsky et al., 2012) architecture achieved the first significant milestone on ILVRSC challenge, which showed the state of the art results at their time of recording on the image classification tasks. Although transfer learning was proposed much before in the community, it was not used much due to the lack of computational resources. The success of AlexNet reignited the usage of transfer learning (Bozinovski, 2020) which leverages the knowledge gained by the models having parameters of the size of millions to billions and which are being trained over an enormously large dataset can be further use for fine-tuning it over other computer vision tasks to achieve promising results.

Another breakthrough in the community was the release of BERT (Devlin et al., 2019) which was being built upon the transformer architecture (Vaswani et al., 2017) with several innovative training strategies at the time of its release topped the GLUE (Wang et al., 2019) benchmarks. The introduction of BERT paved the ways for the transfer learning on the Natural Language Processing (NLP) tasks. However, one particular issue with these huge pretrained models was that they were most of the times not available for under-resourced languages.

The Offensive Language Identification task aimed to detect the presence of offensive content in texts of such under-resourced languages (Mandl et al., 2020; Chakravarthi et al., 2020b; Ghanghor et al., 2021; Yasaswini et al., 2021; Puranik et al., 2021). The texts were in the native language scripts as well as of code-mixed nature (Chakravarthi, 2020a). Code-mixing means the mixing of two or more languages or language varieties in speech (Priyadharshini et al., 2020; Jose et al., 2020). The Meme Classification task focused on classifying memes into a troll and not a troll. Along with the memes, their extracted captions were also being provided in Tamil native scripts and code-mixed nature (Hegde et al., 2021). All the three languages Kannada, Malayalam and Tamil for which the datasets were being provided across the two tasks are under resourced in nature and belong to Dravidian languages' family (Chakravarthi, 2020b). The Dravidian language family is dated to approximately 4500 years old (Kolipakam et al., 2018). In Jain and Buddhist texts written in Pali and Prakrit in ancient times, they referred to Tamil as Damil, and then Dramil became Dravida and Dravidian. Tamil language family includes Kannada, Telugu, Tulu and Malayalam. The Tamil languages scripts

[1]https://github.com/nikhil6041/OLI-and-Meme-Classification



*Proceedings of the First Workshop on Speech and Language Technologies for Dravidian Languages*, pages 222–229
April 20, 2021 

are first attested in the 580 BCE as Tamili[2] script inscribed on the pottery of Keezhadi, Sivagangai and Madurai district of Tamil Nadu, India (Sivanantham and Seran, 2019). The Dravidian languages have its scripts evolved from Tamili scripts.

In this paper, we showcase our efforts for the two shared tasks on Dravidian languages. We participated in the shared task Offensive Language Identification (Chakravarthi et al., 2021) for Tamil, Malayalam and Kannada. We also participated in the shared task on Tamil Troll Meme Classification (Suryawanshi and Chakravarthi, 2021) task. We have used the Transformer and BERT based models in our work. This paper summarizes our works on the two shared tasks. Each of the following sections is being subdivided further into two sections to detail every aspect of the procedures being worked out on them.

## 2 Related Work

Offensive content detection from texts has been part of some conferences as challenging tasks. Some of the most popular tasks have been part of the SemEval [3] organized by International Workshop on Semantic Evaluation. The tasks covered in SemEval varied from offensive content detection in monolingual corpus to code-mixed corpus collected from social media comments. However, most of these competitions had their tasks on datasets based on English and other high resourced languages from the west. HASOC-Dravidian-CodeMix-FIRE2020 [4] was one such competition being organized for under-resourced languages such as Tamil and Malayalam.

Ranasinghe et al. (2020) at HASOC-Dravidian-CodeMix-FIRE2020 used traditional Machine Learning (ML) methods like Naive Bayes Classifier (NBC) , Support Vector Machines (SVMs) and Random Forest along with the pretrained transformers models like XLM-Roberta (XLMR) (Conneau et al., 2020) and BERT for the offensive content identification in code-mixed datasets ( Tamil-English and Malayalam-English). Arora (2020) at HASOC-Dravidian-CodeMix-FIRE2020 used ULMFit (Howard and Ruder, 2018) to pre-train on a synthetically generated code-mixed dataset and then fine-tuned it to the downstream tasks of text classification.

Meme Classification has been one of the major tasks that various social media platforms aim to solve in the past decade. Various methods have been proposed in order to classify memes. However, it is still an unsolved problem because of its multimodal nature, making it extremely hard to have a system correctly classify the memes (Suryawanshi et al., 2020a). Classification of memes needs a visual and linguistic approach to be followed. Hu and Flaxman (2018) did work similar to memes analysis. They used the Tumblr dataset using memes, which had images with several tags associated with them. They dealt with texts and visual features independently and built a model to predict sentiments behind those pictures with corresponding tags and obtained good results. Using this idea of dealing with different modalities independently, different researchers came forward with different implementations for this problem of memes analysis. This particular problem became a flagship the task of SemEval-2020. The team having the best performance for sentiment analysis was obtained by the (Keswani et al., 2020) where they used several different models for addressing the problem by considering both the modalities and coming up with several combinations using both the modalities.

However, the best performance was given by considering the textual features only using BERT as the architecture for doing so for sentiment analysis of the memes. The overview paper (Sharma et al., 2020) of memotion analysis has summarized the works of the participants and gives a clearer picture of the status of the task of memotion analysis its reporting. Recently Facebook AI conducted hateful memes challenge [5] in 2020 whose winner has achieved the best results using several visual, linguistic transformer models. Zhu (2020) used an ensemble of four different Visual Linguistic models VL-BERT (Su et al., 2020), UNITER (Chen et al., 2020), VILLA (Gan et al., 2020), and ERNIE-Vil (Yu et al., 2020).

## 3 Dataset Description

The competition organizers have released datasets for three different languages namely the Kannada dataset (Hande et al., 2020), Malayalam dataset (Chakravarthi et al., 2020a) and Tamil dataset (Chakravarthi et al., 2020c) languages for the Offen-

[2] This is also called Damili or Dramili or Tamil-Brahmi

[3] https://semeval.github.io/

[4] https://competitions.codalab.org/competitions/25295

[5] https://ai.facebook.com/blog/hateful-memes-challenge-and-data-set/

sive Language Identification shared task. However, for the Meme Classification shared task the dataset (Suryawanshi et al., 2020b) was only released for the Tamil language. The train, dev and test set distributions for both of them are as follows:

| Distribution | Kannada | Malayalam | Tamil |
|---|---|---|---|
| Train | 6,217 | 16,010 | 35,139 |
| Dev | 777 | 1,999 | 4,388 |
| Test | 778 | 2,001 | 4,392 |

Table 1: Offensive Language Dataset Distribution

For the Meme Classification task, the competition organizers have provided us with images and the extracted texts present in them.

| Distribution | Data |
|---|---|
| Train | 2,300 |
| Test | 667 |

Table 2: Meme Dataset Distribution

## 4 Methodology

### 4.1 Offensive Language Identification Task

Analysing the sentiment behind the texts have been one of the central tasks of the NLP community. Over time, many advancements have been made in order to analyse the sentiments behind the texts (Chakravarthi et al., 2020d). However, it is still an unsolved problem because of the linguistic diversity existing across the globe and the requirement of the difference in ways the texts have to be addressed depending upon its nature. Here, by nature, we intend to highlight that in languages like English, the casing of words matters; however, it is not even a thing to consider in languages like Malayalam. There could be many more differences across the languages on similar lines across the languages many details on which can be found on the internet.

Several different techniques which are in existence to address the sentiment analysis problem have been developed over the past years. They encompass from the primitive ML models built upon Bag Of Words (BOW), TF-IDF, and N-grams representations to the neural network models like RNNs having LSTMs (Hochreiter and Schmidhuber, 1997), GRUs (Chung et al., 2014), and BiLSTMs (Schuster and Paliwal, 1997) as their key components to the current models having state of the results on various GLUE benchmarks based upon the popular transformer architecture. We also have word embeddings (Bengio et al., 2003) available for the representations of words in a high dimensional vector space which are being used as a starting component of different neural network models.

We have used several pretrained multilingual models in our works and used them to fine-tune the offensive language identification task. Most of the work has been done by using huggingface transformers library[6]. One key issue with the dataset was the skewness of it. We have used the Negative Log Likelihood (NLL) Loss with class weights, Self Adjusting Dice (Li et al., 2020) (Sadice) loss and applied it to address the class imbalance issues with the customised version of models provided by the transformers library. We have also used the original versions of the models available apart from the customised implementations. We have trained each of the models possible combinations as mentioned above and loss functions with each of the language available in the dataset separately. The multilingual models which we have used are multilingual BERT-cased (mBERT-cased), XLM-Roberta and IndicBERT (Kakwani et al., 2020).

Since the IndicBERT model is comparatively much smaller than mBERT-cased and the XLM-Roberta models we have not tried to develop a customised version for it and went with the original version. There are two different multilingual BERT models available one spans 100 languages, and the uncased version, the other one spans 104 languages and is the cased version. BERT's author's recommendations are to use the cased versions, so we have used it in our implementations. For the XLM-Roberta model, we have gone with the base model, which covers 100 languages. We have added a fully connected layer of 512 neurons on top of the final transformer layer for the customised versions of these models, which gives us 768-dimensional feature vectors as outputs. This fully connected layer is finally followed by a LogSoftmax layer having the number of neurons the same as our output classes. The base layers of the original models in the customised versions of the models were being frozen. The custom models were trained with two different loss functions: one was the Negative Log-Likelihood Loss (NLL Loss) with class weights being applied. The other loss function we have tried is the Sadice Loss. We have reported

[6] https://huggingface.co/transformers/

our results on the development set in Table 3 and the results on the test set are reported at Table 4. The results are being reported in terms of weighted average F1 scores.

### 4.2 Meme Classification Task

With the rise of social media in the past decade, we have observed the raise of memes. However, the meme is not a new word and dates back to 1970s. To better understand memes, we have two different definitions, each of them unique in their way and helps us understand it from two different perspectives.

The first definition[7] says that meme can be an element of a culture or system of behaviour passed from one individual to another by imitation or other non-genetic means. Moreover, the other definition[8] states that meme can be an image, video, and text piece that is typically humorous, copied and spread rapidly by internet users, often with slight variations.

According to researchers, both definitions are equally acceptable and set the required knowledge base to fully understand a meme. As we discuss the type of modality of memes, evident from the definition, the memes are a mixture of modalities with textual and visual contents and audio in videos. Several methods for approaching the multimodal problems spanning from simple unimodal approaches to different ways to concatenating the multiple modalities like fusion and concat.

We have used the unimodal approaches in our work, which has a different model for each different modality. The competition organizers have provided us with images along with the extracted captions from those memes. We list our approach to each of the modalities in the following subsections:

### 4.3 Text Modality

As discussed in Section 4.1, we know there exist several methods for approaching any sentence classification problem. We have used several pretrained multilingual models, namely mBERT-cased , XLM-Roberta and IndicBERT for this problem and fine-tuned them on our dataset. Since the dataset was not suffering from skewness, we went with the models original pretrained versions.

[7]https://www.britannica.com/topic/meme

[8]https://www.lexico.com/definition/meme

### 4.4 Image Modality

Image classification was the task which can be attributed to recoiling the interest in neural networks and bringing the deep learning era because of its exceptional performance in ILVRSC challenges. Image classification techniques have evolved from the usage of Support Vector Machines(SVM) and other primitive machine learning models for classification with handcrafted image features to the LeNEt (Lecun et al., 1998). LeNEt brought CNNs into the picture which proceeded further with AlexNet, ResNet (He et al., 2016), Inception (Szegedy et al., 2014) and other popular architectures giving the state of the art results at their time of introductions and bringing some revolutionary ideas into the picture resulting in pushing the performance each time. These architectures were trained on massive datasets having 100s or even 1000s of classes in them. We have used the ResNet50 and inception architectures with their pretrained weights and fine-tuned them over our classification task.

We have reported our results on the development and test set in Table 5. The results are being reported in terms of weighted average F1 scores.

## 5 Results and Discussion

### 5.1 Offensive Language Identification Task

The task aimed to detect the offensive content in three different languages Tamil, Malayalam and Kannada. We have used the pretrained transformer models checkpoints provided by hugging face transformers library. For the identification task, the original pretrained versions and the customized versions as described in Section 4.1 with NLL Loss and Sadice loss were being used, however, out of all the custom implementations the original versions performed much better when being fine-tuned on our datasets. Across all the models, mBERT-cased and XLMR gave very competitive results across both dev and test sets, which may be attributed to their vast size and training corpus. Although IndicBERT having almost ten times fewer parameters gave almost similar results to mBERT-cased and XLMR. The competitive performance of IndicBERT can be attributed to the fact that it was trained on a corpus having Dravidian languages in a relatively more significant proportion as compared to the other two models where the proportion of the Dravidian languages in the entire training corpus was comparatively lesser. However, the better performance of the XLMR and mBERT-cased

| Model | Tamil | Malayalam | Kannada |
|---|---|---|---|
| mBERT-cased | 0.76 | 0.96 | 0.68 |
| Custom mBERT-cased with NLL loss and Class weights | 0.58 | 0.82 | 0.35 |
| Custom mBERT-cased with Sadice Loss | 0.61 | 0.87 | 0.55 |
| XLMR | 0.76 | 0.94 | 0.67 |
| Custom XLMR with Sadice Loss | 0.61 | 0.84 | 0.39 |
| Custom XLMR with NLL loss and Class weights | 0.64 | 0.84 | 0.10 |
| IndicBERT | 0.74 | 0.94 | 0.63 |

Table 3: Experiments with Offensive Language Identification development dataset

| Model | Tamil | Malayalam | Kannada |
|---|---|---|---|
| mBERT-cased | **0.75** | **0.95** | **0.71** |
| Custom mBERT-cased with NLL loss and Class weights | 0.59 | 0.82 | 0.34 |
| Custom mBERT-cased with Sadice Loss | 0.61 | 0.87 | 0.53 |
| XLMR | 0.75 | 0.93 | 0.71 |
| Custom XLMR with Sadice Loss | 0.61 | 0.83 | 0.39 |
| Custom XLMR with NLL loss and Class weights | 0.64 | 0.83 | 0.09 |
| IndicBERT | 0.73 | 0.93 | 0.67 |

Table 4: Experiments with Offensive Language Identification test dataset

| Model | Dev | Test |
|---|---|---|
| mBERT-uncased | 0.90 | 0.50 |
| mBERT-cased | 0.94 | **0.55** |
| XLMR | 0.93 | 0.54 |
| IndicBERT | 0.85 | 0.50 |
| Inception | 0.78 | 0.53 |
| ResNet | 0.89 | 0.46 |

Table 5: Experiments with Meme Classification dataset

on the task datasets can be attributed to the training objective of these models which evaluates their model's performance on XNLI (Conneau et al., 2018) benchmark thus resulting in their competitive performance when compared to IndicBERT. We have used mBERT-cased for our final submissions across all the three languages as it performed comparatively better on all the three languages dev sets. The one major bottleneck of the model's lower performance across several languages in the offensive language identification task was the skewness of the dataset. The performance can further be improved by having some techniques to generate synthetic text data in order to handle the class imbalance issues. Since the transformer models expect texts as inputs, and each one has their own tokenizers, the generation of synthetic text data is another challenge to improve these models' performance.

### 5.2 Meme Classification Task

The task aimed to detect the troll memes in the Tamil language. Since the memes are multimodal, we have tried several different pretrained unimodal models to deal with each of the modalities. For the image modality, we have used inception and ResNet50 , and for the text modality, we have used mBERT-uncased , mBERT-cased , XLMR and IndicBERT. The competition organizers have provided us with a training set of 2,300 images along with their captions. We used a validation split of 20% on our training set and evaluated all our models on that validation set. Of all the models, text-based models' performance was comparatively better than the image-based models except for ResNet performing better than IndicBERT on dev set. Both XLMR and mBERT-cased performed almost similarly on our dev set, but since mBERT-cased had slightly better performance than XLMR on the dev set we submitted our predictions using the mBERT-cased model. For the meme classification task, the reported results show that even after performing well on dev datasets our models have not performed up to the mark on the test datasets which can be attributed to the fact that memes are of multimodal nature. They cannot be solved only by unimodal approaches.

## 6 Conclusion

We have presented the IIITK submission to Tamil troll meme classification, and offensive language identification shared tasks at DravidianLangTech. We experimented with several different pretrained models for the given datasets with their original and customized architecture and different loss functions. Our best model for Tamil troll meme classification was multilingual BERT-cased, and it gave a weighted average F1 score of 0.55. Our best model for offensive language identification was also multilingual BERT-cased, and it gave weighted average F1 scores of 0.75 for Tamil, 0.95 for Malayalam and 0.71 for Kannada.

## References


Gaurav Arora. 2020. Gauravarora@HASOC-Dravidian-CodeMix-FIRE2020: Pre-training ULMFiT on Synthetically Generated Code-Mixed Data for Hate Speech Detection.

Yoshua Bengio, Réjean Ducharme, Pascal Vincent, and Christian Janvin. 2003. A neural probabilistic language model. *J. Mach. Learn. Res.*, 3(null):1137–1155.

Stevo Bozinovski. 2020. Reminder of the first paper on transfer learning in neural networks, 1976. *Informatica*, 44.

Bharathi Raja Chakravarthi. 2020a. HopeEDI: A multilingual hope speech detection dataset for equality, diversity, and inclusion. In *Proceedings of the Third Workshop on Computational Modeling of People's Opinions, Personality, and Emotion's in Social Media*, pages 41–53, Barcelona, Spain (Online). Association for Computational Linguistics.

Bharathi Raja Chakravarthi. 2020b. *Leveraging orthographic information to improve machine translation of under-resourced languages*. Ph.D. thesis, NUI Galway.

Bharathi Raja Chakravarthi, Navya Jose, Shardul Suryawanshi, Elizabeth Sherly, and John Philip McCrae. 2020a. A sentiment analysis dataset for code-mixed Malayalam-English. In *Proceedings of the 1st Joint Workshop on Spoken Language Technologies for Under-resourced languages (SLTU) and Collaboration and Computing for Under-Resourced Languages (CCURL)*, pages 177–184, Marseille, France. European Language Resources association.

Bharathi Raja Chakravarthi, M Anand Kumar, John Philip McCrae, Premjith B, Soman KP, and Thomas Mandl. 2020b. Overview of the track on HASOC-Offensive Language Identification-DravidianCodeMix. In *Working Notes of the Forum for Information Retrieval Evaluation (FIRE 2020). CEUR Workshop Proceedings. In: CEUR-WS. org, Hyderabad, India*.

Bharathi Raja Chakravarthi, Vigneshwaran Muralidaran, Ruba Priyadharshini, and John Philip McCrae. 2020c. Corpus creation for sentiment analysis in code-mixed Tamil-English text. In *Proceedings of the 1st Joint Workshop on Spoken Language Technologies for Under-resourced languages (SLTU) and Collaboration and Computing for Under-Resourced Languages (CCURL)*, pages 202–210, Marseille, France. European Language Resources association.

Bharathi Raja Chakravarthi, Ruba Priyadharshini, Navya Jose, Anand Kumar M, Thomas Mandl, Prasanna Kumar Kumaresan, Rahul Ponnusamy, Hariharan V, Elizabeth Sherly, and John Philip McCrae. 2021. Findings of the shared task on Offensive Language Identification in Tamil, Malayalam, and Kannada. In *Proceedings of the First Workshop on Speech and Language Technologies for Dravidian Languages*. Association for Computational Linguistics.

Bharathi Raja Chakravarthi, Ruba Priyadharshini, Vigneshwaran Muralidaran, Shardul Suryawanshi, Navya Jose, Elizabeth Sherly, and John P. McCrae. 2020d. Overview of the Track on Sentiment Analysis for Dravidian Languages in Code-Mixed Text. In *Forum for Information Retrieval Evaluation*, FIRE 2020, page 21–24, New York, NY, USA. Association for Computing Machinery.

Yen-Chun Chen, Linjie Li, Licheng Yu, Ahmed El Kholy, Faisal Ahmed, Zhe Gan, Yu Cheng, and Jingjing Liu. 2020. Uniter: Universal image-text representation learning.

Junyoung Chung, Caglar Gulcehre, KyungHyun Cho, and Yoshua Bengio. 2014. Empirical evaluation of gated recurrent neural networks on sequence modeling.

Alexis Conneau, Kartikay Khandelwal, Naman Goyal, Vishrav Chaudhary, Guillaume Wenzek, Francisco Guzmán, Edouard Grave, Myle Ott, Luke Zettlemoyer, and Veselin Stoyanov. 2020. Unsupervised cross-lingual representation learning at scale.

Alexis Conneau, Guillaume Lample, Ruty Rinott, Adina Williams, Samuel R. Bowman, Holger Schwenk, and Veselin Stoyanov. 2018. Xnli: Evaluating cross-lingual sentence representations.

Jacob Devlin, Ming-Wei Chang, Kenton Lee, and Kristina Toutanova. 2019. Bert: Pre-training of deep bidirectional transformers for language understanding.

Zhe Gan, Yen-Chun Chen, Linjie Li, Chen Zhu, Yu Cheng, and Jingjing Liu. 2020. Large-scale adversarial training for vision-and-language representation learning.

Nikhil Kumar Ghanghor, Rahul Ponnusamy, Prasanna Kumar Kumaresan, Ruba Priyadharshini, Sajeetha Thavareesan, and Bharathi Raja Chakravarthi. 2021. IIITK@LT-EDI-EACL2021: Hope Speech Detection for Equality, Diversity, and Inclusion in Tamil, Malayalam and English. In *Proceedings of the First Workshop on Language Technology for Equality, Diversity and Inclusion*, Online. Association for Computational Linguistics.

Adeep Hande, Ruba Priyadharshini, and Bharathi Raja Chakravarthi. 2020. KanCMD: Kannada CodeMixed dataset for sentiment analysis and offensive language detection. In *Proceedings of the Third Workshop on Computational Modeling of People's Opinions, Personality, and Emotion's in Social Media*, pages 54–63, Barcelona, Spain (Online). Association for Computational Linguistics.

K. He, X. Zhang, S. Ren, and J. Sun. 2016. Deep residual learning for image recognition. In *2016 IEEE Conference on Computer Vision and Pattern Recognition (CVPR)*, pages 770–778.

Siddhanth U Hegde, Adeep Hande, Ruba Priyadharshini, Sajeetha Thavareesan, and Bharathi Raja Chakravarthi. 2021. UVCE-IIITT@DravidianLangTech-EACL2021: Tamil Troll Meme Classification: You need to Pay more Attention. In *Proceedings of the First Workshop on Speech and Language Technologies for Dravidian Languages*. Association for Computational Linguistics.

Sepp Hochreiter and Jürgen Schmidhuber. 1997. Long short-term memory. *Neural computation*, 9(8):1735–1780.

Jeremy Howard and Sebastian Ruder. 2018. Universal language model fine-tuning for text classification.

Anthony Hu and Seth Flaxman. 2018. Multimodal sentiment analysis to explore the structure of emotions. *Proceedings of the 24th ACM SIGKDD International Conference on Knowledge Discovery Data Mining*.

Navya Jose, Bharathi Raja Chakravarthi, Shardul Suryawanshi, Elizabeth Sherly, and John P. McCrae. 2020. A Survey of Current Datasets for Code-Switching Research. In *2020 6th International Conference on Advanced Computing and Communication Systems (ICACCS)*, pages 136–141.

Divyanshu Kakwani, Anoop Kunchukuttan, Satish Golla, Gokul N.C., Avik Bhattacharyya, Mitesh M. Khapra, and Pratyush Kumar. 2020. IndicNLPSuite: Monolingual Corpora, Evaluation Benchmarks and Pre-trained Multilingual Language Models for Indian Languages. In *Findings of EMNLP*.

Vishal Keswani, Sakshi Singh, Suryansh Agarwal, and Ashutosh Modi. 2020. IITK at SemEval-2020 Task 8: Unimodal and Bimodal Sentiment Analysis of Internet Memes.

Vishnupriya Kolipakam, Fiona M Jordan, Michael Dunn, Simon J Greenhill, Remco Bouckaert, Russell D Gray, and Annemarie Verkerk. 2018. A Bayesian phylogenetic study of the Dravidian language family. *Royal Society open science*, 5(3):171504.

Alex Krizhevsky, Ilya Sutskever, and Geoffrey E Hinton. 2012. Imagenet classification with deep convolutional neural networks. In *Advances in Neural Information Processing Systems*, volume 25, pages 1097–1105. Curran Associates, Inc.

Yann Lecun, Léon Bottou, Yoshua Bengio, and Patrick Haffner. 1998. Gradient-based learning applied to document recognition. In *Proceedings of the IEEE*, pages 2278–2324.

Xiaoya Li, Xiaofei Sun, Yuxian Meng, Junjun Liang, Fei Wu, and Jiwei Li. 2020. Dice loss for data-imbalanced nlp tasks.

Thomas Mandl, Sandip Modha, Anand Kumar M, and Bharathi Raja Chakravarthi. 2020. Overview of the HASOC Track at FIRE 2020: Hate Speech and Offensive Language Identification in Tamil, Malayalam, Hindi, English and German. In *Forum for Information Retrieval Evaluation*, FIRE 2020, page 29–32, New York, NY, USA. Association for Computing Machinery.

Ruba Priyadharshini, Bharathi Raja Chakravarthi, Mani Vegupatti, and John P. McCrae. 2020. Named Entity Recognition for Code-Mixed Indian Corpus using Meta Embedding. In *2020 6th International Conference on Advanced Computing and Communication Systems (ICACCS)*, pages 68–72.

Karthik Puranik, Adeep Hande, Ruba Priyadharshini, Sajeetha Thavareesan, and Bharathi Raja Chakravarthi. 2021. IIITT@LT-EDI-EACL2021-Hope Speech Detection: There is always hope in Transformers. In *Proceedings of the First Workshop on Language Technology for Equality, Diversity and Inclusion*. Association for Computational Linguistics.

Tharindu Ranasinghe, Sarthak Gupte, Marcos Zampieri, and Ifeoma Nwogu. 2020. WLV-RIT at HASOC-Dravidian-CodeMix-FIRE2020: Offensive Language Identification in Code-switched YouTube Comments.

Mike Schuster and Kuldip Paliwal. 1997. Bidirectional recurrent neural networks. *Signal Processing, IEEE Transactions on*, 45:2673 – 2681.

Chhavi Sharma, Deepesh Bhageria, William Scott, Srinivas PYKL, Amitava Das, Tanmoy Chakraborty, Viswanath Pulabaigari, and Bjorn Gamback. 2020. SemEval-2020 Task 8: Memotion Analysis – The Visuo-Lingual Metaphor!

R Sivanantham and M Seran. 2019. Keeladi: An Urban Settlement of Sangam Age on the Banks of River Vaigai. *India: Department of Archaeology, Government of Tamil Nadu, Chennai*.

Weijie Su, Xizhou Zhu, Yue Cao, Bin Li, Lewei Lu, Furu Wei, and Jifeng Dai. 2020. VL-BERT: Pre-training of Generic Visual-Linguistic Representations.

Shardul Suryawanshi and Bharathi Raja Chakravarthi. 2021. Findings of the shared task on Troll Meme Classification in Tamil. In *Proceedings of the First Workshop on Speech and Language Technologies for Dravidian Languages*. Association for Computational Linguistics.

Shardul Suryawanshi, Bharathi Raja Chakravarthi, Mihael Arcan, and Paul Buitelaar. 2020a. Multimodal meme dataset (MultiOFF) for identifying offensive content in image and text. In *Proceedings of the Second Workshop on Trolling, Aggression and Cyberbullying*, pages 32–41, Marseille, France. European Language Resources Association (ELRA).

Shardul Suryawanshi, Bharathi Raja Chakravarthi, Pranav Verma, Mihael Arcan, John Philip McCrae, and Paul Buitelaar. 2020b. A dataset for troll classification of TamilMemes. In *Proceedings of the WILDRE5– 5th Workshop on Indian Language Data: Resources and Evaluation*, pages 7–13, Marseille, France. European Language Resources Association (ELRA).

Christian Szegedy, Wei Liu, Yangqing Jia, Pierre Sermanet, Scott Reed, Dragomir Anguelov, Dumitru Erhan, Vincent Vanhoucke, and Andrew Rabinovich. 2014. Going deeper with convolutions.

Ashish Vaswani, Noam Shazeer, Niki Parmar, Jakob Uszkoreit, Llion Jones, Aidan N. Gomez, Lukasz Kaiser, and Illia Polosukhin. 2017. Attention is all you need.

Alex Wang, Amanpreet Singh, Julian Michael, Felix Hill, Omer Levy, and Samuel R. Bowman. 2019. GLUE: A Multi-Task Benchmark and Analysis Platform for Natural Language Understanding.

Konthala Yasaswini, Karthik Puranik, Adeep Hande, Ruba Priyadharshini, Sajeetha Thavareesan, and Bharathi Raja Chakravarthi. 2021. IIITT@DravidianLangTech-EACL2021: Transfer Learning for Offensive Language Detection in Dravidian Languages. In *Proceedings of the First Workshop on Speech and Language Technologies for Dravidian Languages*. Association for Computational Linguistics.

Fei Yu, Jiji Tang, Weichong Yin, Yu Sun, Hao Tian, Hua Wu, and Haifeng Wang. 2020. ERNIE-ViL: Knowledge Enhanced Vision-Language Representations Through Scene Graph.

Ron Zhu. 2020. Enhance multimodal transformer with external label and in-domain pretrain: Hateful meme challenge winning solution.

# cs@DravidianLangTech-EACL2021: Offensive Language Identification Based On Multilingual BERT Model

**Shi Chen**
School of Information Science
and Engineering Yunnan University,
chen-s2020@139.com

**Bing Kong**
School of Information Science
and Engineering Yunnan University,
kongbing@ynu.edu.cn

## Abstract

This paper introduces the related content of the task "Offensive Language Identification in Dravidian LANGUAGES-EACL 2021". The task requires us to classify Dravidian languages collected from social media into Not-Offensive, Off-Untargeted, Off-Target-Individual, etc. This data set contains actual annotations in code-mixed text posted by users on Youtube, not from the monolingual text in textbooks. Based on the features of the data set code mixture, we use multilingual BERT and TextCNN for semantic extraction and text classification. In this article, we will show the experiment and result analysis of this task.

## 1 Introduction

One of the manifestations of the rapid development of the Internet is the increasing number of users, which allows more and more people from different languages, different regions, and different cultures to communicate, but the frequent appearance of offensive speech will affect this harmonious atmosphere (Thavareesan and Mahesan, 2019, 2020a,b). This has become a serious problem for users of online communities and social media platforms. In such a multilingual social environment, it has become a serious problem for users of online communities and social media platforms (Jose et al., 2020; Priyadharshini et al., 2020; Chakravarthi et al., 2020c; Mandl et al., 2020).

This task is to identify offensive language content from Dravidian languages (Tamil-English, Malayalam-English, and Kannada-English) collected from social media. The Dravidian civilization of the Indus Valley civilisation (3,300–1,900 BCE) is believed to have flourished in the Northwestern Indian subcontinent (Tamil). The Dravidian languages were first documented in Tamil-Brahmi script engraved on cave walls in Tamil Nadu's Madurai and Tirunelveli districts in the 6th century BCE. Tamil is India's oldest language. Agglutinative languages are Dravidian languages. Subject–object–verb is the word order (SOV). There is a clusivity distinction in most Dravidian languages. All we need to do is to classify it into not-offensive, offensive-untargeted, offensive-targeted-individual, offensive-targeted-group, offensive-targeted-other, or not-in-indented-language.

To further extract semantic information, we adopt a text classification method based on the hierarchical connection between Bert and TextCNN, which is a combined model of Bert and TextCNN. Use multilingual BERT to vectorize each word, obtain the semantic features of the text, and construct the text mapping matrix. Use TextCNN convolutional neural network to perform convolution operation on text mapping matrix, get the output of all or part of the hidden layer, get the semantic feature matrix of the text, then use the pooling algorithm to reduce the dimension of the semantic feature matrix of the text to obtain the semantic feature vector of the text.

## 2 Related Work

Nowadays, offensive, false, and other remarks on social media have become issues that we have to pay attention to. To solve this problem, many scholars have done a lot of research activities.

(Sohn and Lee, 2019) developed multi-channel BERT models for different languages, integrated the hiding function of separate BERT models trained in different languages, and using transfer learning in NLP, the problem of the shortage of labeled data sets can be solved by pre-training the language model. (Shushkevich et al., 2020) proposed a method to solve multiple classification problems within the framework of active language recognition in Twitter. Created a collection of classic



*Proceedings of the First Workshop on Speech and Language Technologies for Dravidian Languages*, pages 230–235
April 20, 2021 

machine learning models including Logistic regression, support vector machines, naive Bayes models, and a combination of Logistic regression and naive Bayes.

It proposed a CNN-gram deep learning architecture (Rizwan et al., 2020) for hate and offensive language detection in social media and compared its performance with the current baseline method, the model shows higher robustness. (Wanner et al., 2003) used the functional template described by Yarowsky to model hate speech as a classification problem to detect hate speech on the Internet. It trained the classifier through semi-supervised machine learning technology (Epstein and Mengibar, 2015), training the classifier to determine if there are potentially offensive terms in the text. (Pitsilis et al., 2018) proposed a detection scheme when distinguishing hateful content on social media. It is a combination of Recurrent Neural Network (RNN) classifiers. It contains various functions related to user-related information and achieves relatively high classification quality.

(Nugroho et al., 2019) used random forest methods to identify Twitter hate speech datasets and compared them with the accuracy results of neural networks and AdaBoost. (Hande et al., 2020) found that in sentiment classification, Logistic regression, random forest classifier, and decision tree performed relatively well, SVM performed poorly, and its heterogeneity was also poor. It used a HateBERT model retrained (Caselli et al., 2020) on RAL-E (offensive and hateful Reddit English data set) for the detection of abusive language and found that HateBERT is r tosuperio the corresponding conventional BERT model. (Paul and Saha, 2020) fine-tuned the BERT and modeled the BERT as a basic neural network. This model can enhance its detection performance and achieve good accuracy at a low computational cost.

(Xi et al., 2018) proposed a deep convolution model that uses unsupervised pre-trained word embedding to classify objectionable text. It used the pre-trained Arabic language model AraBERT in the task of offensive language detection, which (Djandji et al., 2020) showed good performance in classification tasks. (Kokatnoor and Krishnan, 2020) proposed a stack weighted ensemble (SWE) model with five independent classifiers to detect hate speech. (Gambäck and Sikdar, 2017) tried to use deep learning convolutional neural network models and creating CNN models to classify Twitter's hate speech text.

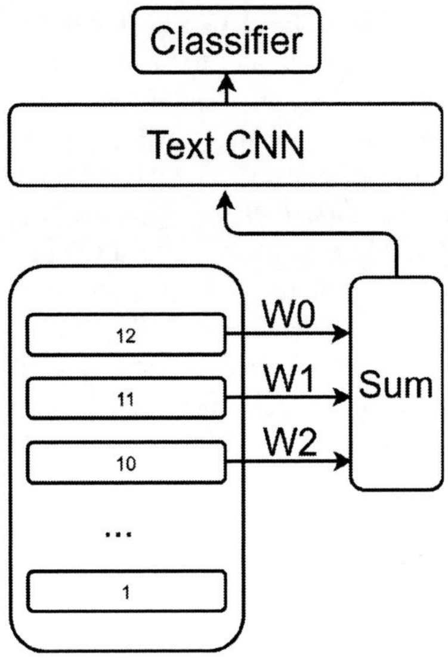


Figure 1: The overall architecture and data flow of our system.

(Mubarak et al., 2020) proposed a systematic method to construct a data set of tweets that do not support specific dialects and topics and use cross-validation to establish offensive language system detection. (Chakravarthi et al., 2020a, 2021) proposed a new gold standard corpus for sentiment analysis of annotated English-language mixed text. (Chakravarthi et al., 2020b) used logistic regression, naive Bayes, decision tree, etc. to code mixed data to classify emotions. Among them, logistic regression and random forest are used in this experiment to get the best results.

## 3 Data

The common feature of the data sets in three different languages is code-mixed. Code-mixed refers to words in multiple different languages that may appear in the same sentence. The data we used in this task is mainly text mixed with English ((Tamil-English, Malayalam-English, and Kannada-English)).

Labels distribution of Malayalam training set and validation set. In the training set, Not offensive: 88.4%, Not Malayalam: 8.04%, Offensive Targeted Insult Individual: 1.49%, Offensive Untargetede: 1.19%, Offensive Targeted Insult Group: 0.88%. In the validation set, Not offensive: 89%, Not Malayalam: 8.15%, Offensive Targeted Insult Individual: 1.2%, Offensive Untargetede: 1%, Offensive Targeted Insult Group: 0.65%.

Labels distribution of Kannada training set and validation set. In the training set, Not offensive: 57.01%, Not Kannada: 24.48%, Offensive Targeted Insult Individual: 7.83%, Offensive Targeted Insult Group: 5.29%, Offensive Untargetede: 3.41%, Offensive Targeted Insult Other: 1.98%. In the validation set, Not offensive: 54.83%, Not Kannada: 24.58%, Offensive Targeted Insult Individual: 8.49%, Offensive Targeted Insult Group: 5.79%, Offensive Untargetede: 4.25%, Offensive Targeted Insult Other: 2.06%.

Labels distribution of Tamil training set and validation set.
In the training set, Not offensive: 72.23%, Offensive Untargetede: 8.27%, Offensive Targeted Insult Group: 7.28%, Offensive Targeted Insult Individual: 6.67%, Not-Tamil: 4.14%, Offensive Targeted Insult Other: 1.29%.
In the validation set, Not offensive: 72.77%, Offensive Untargetede: 8.11%, Offensive Targeted Insult Group: 6.72%, Offensive Targeted Insult Individual: 7%, Not Tamil: 3.92%, Offensive Targeted Insult Other: 1.48%.

The data sets we can use are the training set and validation set in three languages(Tamil, Malayalam, and Kannada) provided by the task organizer team. Code mixing is the main feature of the data set provided by the task organizer. There are five different categories in the Malayalam dataset. Each dataset of Kannada and Tamil has six different categories. There is an imbalance of category labels in the data sets of the three languages.

## 4 Methods

Because the deep learning model can learn the complex distribution characteristics of data through deep artificial neural networks and nonlinearity. Especially the use of deep learning in tasks related to text data has attracted more and more attention(Zhang et al., 2018).

### 4.1 Multilingual BERT

BERT(Bidirectional Encoder Representations from Transformers) is a pre-trained language model method. It uses a plain text corpus to train the artificial neural network in the model. The BERT model can finally solve the most common tasks in NLP (natural language processing) and can achieve state-of-the-art results on many tasks. For example, text sequence labeling, text classification tasks, sentence relationship judgment, text generation tasks.

| Lang | Epoch | Batch | lr | Sent len |
|---|---|---|---|---|
| Kannada | 5 | 32 | 3e-5 | 55 |
| Malayalam | 5 | 32 | 3e-5 | 60 |
| Tamil | 4 | 32 | 4e-5 | 70 |

Table 1: The parameter settings of our system on the training sets of three different languages: Kannada, Malayalam, and Tamil.

It is a language representation model based on Transformer architecture (Vaswani et al., 2017). In the training phase of the model, the model BERT needs to complete the MLM (Masked Language Model) task and the NSP (Next Sentence Prediction) task. The combination of BERT's model structure and its pre-training process makes BERT capable of most NLP tasks. The advantage of BERT is that it is a deep two-way, unsupervised NLP pre-training system. Compared with the previous pre-training model, it learns bidirectional context information in the true sense Its use includes two stages: pre-training and fine-tuning. Generally, we only need to fine-tune the BERT to get good results when completing NLP-related downstream tasks.

The difference between multilingual BERT and BERT that uses other single language pre-training is that it uses a corpus composed of more than 100 different languages in the pre-training phase. The languages supported by the multilingual model are mainly from the top 100 most used languages on Wikipedia. Of course, multi-language models can also complete some single-language tasks, but there may be some gaps in the scores of the BERT pre-trained in a single language. In the model architecture, the multilingual BERT has 12 coding layers and uses a multi-head attention mechanism (a total of 12 heads). These parameters are the same as BERT-base. Therefore, in addition to the advantages of BERT mentioned above, the advantage of multilingual BERT is that it has good cross-language.

### 4.2 TextCNN

The TextCNN artificial neural network was first proposed by Kim et al. in 2014 (Kim, 2014). Compared with the CNN network in the image, the biggest difference of TextCNN is the difference in the input data. It is a text classification model that applies the CNN network. The biggest advantage of TextCNN is that the network structure is simple, which in turn leads to a small number of parameters, a small amount of calculation, and a fast training speed.

The general process of data passing through TextCNN is: first vectorize text data through word embedding, then perform convolution operation on the text converted into vectors, then vector data through the maximum pooling layer, and finally connect the output result to the linear classifier, the layer uses softmax for n classification. Because the convolutional layer and the maximum pooling layer do not activate the vector data, the activation function is usually used after the convolutional layer, such as the Relu function or the Tanh function. Besides, some regularization items are also used, commonly used are dropout, L2, etc.

### 4.3 Our System

TextCNN can use different sizes of convolution kernels to obtain local features of different window sizes in the text vectorized space. The BERT model can obtain true two-way contextual semantic information. We want to obtain both contextual semantic information and local features, so we choose to Combine these two models.

To obtain the top-level semantic information of BERT, we take out the last three layers of BERT output (layer12_output, layer11_output, layer10_output). Then apply weighting effects (W0, W1, W2) on these three output results. Three Different weight values are respectively weighted and sum layer12_output, layer11_output, layer10_output to get weighted_sum_output. Then, input the result of weighted_sum_output into the textCNN network to get a new result. Finally, Input this result into the linear classifier, and the result after linear classification is the final output result of our system.

## 5 Experiment and Results

### 5.1 Experimental details

We use the training set and validation set provided by the task organizer as the input data of our system. As we described in the method introduction section, we take the last three layers of the output of the multilingual BERT model as the input of TextCNN. In TextCNN, the size of the convolution kernel we choose is 2, 3, 4, each of different sizes The number of convolution kernels is 256. Both convolution and pooling are 1-dimensional. The activation function is ReLu. The regularization item is dropout, and the parameter is set to 0.3. Choose different hyperparameters for different language data. The loss function chooses the CrossEntropyLoss function. The parameter setting information can be obtained in Table 1.

| Team/Lang | Precision | Recall | F1 |
|---|---|---|---|
| Top1 Malayalam | 0.97 | 0.97 | 0.97 |
| Our Malayalam | 0.92 | 0.94 | 0.93 |
| Top1 Tamil | 0.78 | 0.78 | 0.78 |
| Our Tamil | 0.74 | 0.75 | 0.74 |
| Top1 Kannada | 0.73 | 0.78 | 0.75 |
| Our Kannada | 0.64 | 0.67 | 0.64 |

Table 2: Our model and the Top1 team on each language data set score on the test set.

### 5.2 Result analysis

The weighted average F1-score is a reference indicator used by task organizers to rank. The scores of the participating teams in Malayalam are generally high. In comparison, the scores of the other two languages are relatively low. Our results are somewhat different from the first place results, especially the scores on the Kannada test set Overall, our system has a certain effect on the text classification task of recognizing code mixture, but there is still a lot of room for improvement.

## 6 Conclusion

For this task, we use multilingual BERT and TextCNN to complete the detection of offensive speech. The above is our description of this task. The result of this task may not be ideal. Therefore, in future work, we try to use new models and improve methods to obtain better results. This task has given us a better understanding of the detection of speech on social media. It not only has an understanding of the importance of the detection of offensive speech but also improved our ability to solve such problems. In the future, we will continue to learn about social media speech detection.

## References


Tommaso Caselli, Valerio Basile, Jelena Mitrović, and Michael Granitzer. 2020. HateBERT: Retraining BERT for Abusive Language Detection in English. *arXiv preprint arXiv:2010.12472.*

Bharathi Raja Chakravarthi, Navya Jose, Shardul Suryawanshi, Elizabeth Sherly, and John Philip McCrae. 2020a. A sentiment analysis dataset for code-mixed Malayalam-English. In *Proceedings of the*

*1st Joint Workshop on Spoken Language Technologies for Under-resourced languages (SLTU) and Collaboration and Computing for Under-Resourced Languages (CCURL)*, pages 177–184, Marseille, France. European Language Resources association.

Bharathi Raja Chakravarthi, Vigneshwaran Muralidaran, Ruba Priyadharshini, and John Philip McCrae. 2020b. Corpus creation for sentiment analysis in code-mixed Tamil-English text. In *Proceedings of the 1st Joint Workshop on Spoken Language Technologies for Under-resourced languages (SLTU) and Collaboration and Computing for Under-Resourced Languages (CCURL)*, pages 202–210, Marseille, France. European Language Resources association.

Bharathi Raja Chakravarthi, Ruba Priyadharshini, Navya Jose, Anand Kumar M, Thomas Mandl, Prasanna Kumar Kumaresan, Rahul Ponnusamy, Hariharan V, Elizabeth Sherly, and John Philip McCrae. 2021. Findings of the shared task on Offensive Language Identification in Tamil, Malayalam, and Kannada. In *Proceedings of the First Workshop on Speech and Language Technologies for Dravidian Languages*. Association for Computational Linguistics.

Bharathi Raja Chakravarthi, Ruba Priyadharshini, Vigneshwaran Muralidaran, Shardul Suryawanshi, Navya Jose, Elizabeth Sherly, and John P. McCrae. 2020c. Overview of the Track on Sentiment Analysis for Dravidian Languages in Code-Mixed Text. In *Forum for Information Retrieval Evaluation*, FIRE 2020, page 21–24, New York, NY, USA. Association for Computing Machinery.

Marc Djandji, Fady Baly, Hazem Hajj, et al. 2020. Multi-task learning using arabert for offensive language detection. In *Proceedings of the 4th Workshop on Open-Source Arabic Corpora and Processing Tools, with a Shared Task on Offensive Language Detection*, pages 97–101.

Mark Edward Epstein and Pedro J Moreno Mengibar. 2015. Classification of offensive words. US Patent App. 14/264,617.

Björn Gambäck and Utpal Kumar Sikdar. 2017. Using convolutional neural networks to classify hate-speech. In *Proceedings of the first workshop on abusive language online*, pages 85–90.

Adeep Hande, Ruba Priyadharshini, and Bharathi Raja Chakravarthi. 2020. KanCMD: Kannada CodeMixed dataset for sentiment analysis and offensive language detection. In *Proceedings of the Third Workshop on Computational Modeling of People's Opinions, Personality, and Emotion's in Social Media*, pages 54–63, Barcelona, Spain (Online). Association for Computational Linguistics.

Navya Jose, Bharathi Raja Chakravarthi, Shardul Suryawanshi, Elizabeth Sherly, and John P. McCrae. 2020. A Survey of Current Datasets for Code-Switching Research. In *2020 6th International Conference on Advanced Computing and Communication Systems (ICACCS)*, pages 136–141.

Yoon Kim. 2014. Convolutional neural networks for sentence classification. *arXiv preprint arXiv:1408.5882*.

S. A. Kokatnoor and B. Krishnan. 2020. Twitter hate speech detection using stacked weighted ensemble (swe) model. In *2020 Fifth International Conference on Research in Computational Intelligence and Communication Networks (ICRCICN)*, pages 87–92.

Thomas Mandl, Sandip Modha, Anand Kumar M, and Bharathi Raja Chakravarthi. 2020. Overview of the HASOC Track at FIRE 2020: Hate Speech and Offensive Language Identification in Tamil, Malayalam, Hindi, English and German. In *Forum for Information Retrieval Evaluation*, FIRE 2020, page 29–32, New York, NY, USA. Association for Computing Machinery.

Hamdy Mubarak, Ammar Rashed, Kareem Darwish, Younes Samih, and Ahmed Abdelali. 2020. Arabic offensive language on twitter: Analysis and experiments. *arXiv preprint arXiv:2004.02192*.

Kristiawan Nugroho, Edy Noersasongko, Ahmad Zainul Fanani, Ruri Suko Basuki, et al. 2019. Improving random forest method to detect hate-speech and offensive word. In *2019 International Conference on Information and Communications Technology (ICOIACT)*, pages 514–518. IEEE.

Sayanta Paul and Sriparna Saha. 2020. Cyberbert: Bert for cyberbullying identification. *Multimedia Systems*, pages 1–8.

Georgios K Pitsilis, Heri Ramampiaro, and Helge Langseth. 2018. Detecting offensive language in tweets using deep learning. *arXiv preprint arXiv:1801.04433*.

Ruba Priyadharshini, Bharathi Raja Chakravarthi, Mani Vegupatti, and John P. McCrae. 2020. Named Entity Recognition for Code-Mixed Indian Corpus using Meta Embedding. In *2020 6th International Conference on Advanced Computing and Communication Systems (ICACCS)*, pages 68–72.

Hammad Rizwan, Muhammad Haroon Shakeel, and Asim Karim. 2020. Hate-speech and offensive language detection in Roman Urdu. In *Proceedings of the 2020 Conference on Empirical Methods in Natural Language Processing (EMNLP)*, pages 2512–2522.

Elena Shushkevich, John Cardiff, Paolo Rosso, and Liliya Akhtyamova. 2020. Offensive language recognition in social media. *Computación y Sistemas*, 24(2).

H. Sohn and H. Lee. 2019. Mc-bert4hate: Hate speech detection using multi-channel bert for different languages and translations. In *2019 International Conference on Data Mining Workshops (ICDMW)*, pages 551–559.

Sajeetha Thavareesan and Sinnathamby Mahesan. 2019. Sentiment Analysis in Tamil Texts: A Study on Machine Learning Techniques and Feature Representation. In *2019 14th Conference on Industrial and Information Systems (ICIIS)*, pages 320–325.

Sajeetha Thavareesan and Sinnathamby Mahesan. 2020a. Sentiment Lexicon Expansion using Word2vec and fastText for Sentiment Prediction in Tamil texts. In *2020 Moratuwa Engineering Research Conference (MERCon)*, pages 272–276.

Sajeetha Thavareesan and Sinnathamby Mahesan. 2020b. Word embedding-based Part of Speech tagging in Tamil texts. In *2020 IEEE 15th International Conference on Industrial and Information Systems (ICIIS)*, pages 478–482.

Ashish Vaswani, Noam Shazeer, Niki Parmar, Jakob Uszkoreit, Llion Jones, Aidan N Gomez, Lukasz Kaiser, and Illia Polosukhin. 2017. Attention is all you need. *arXiv preprint arXiv:1706.03762*.

Leo Wanner, Bernd Bohnet, and Mark Giereth. 2003. Deriving the communicative structure in applied NLG. In *Proceedings of the 9th European Workshop on Natural Language Generation (ENLG-2003) at EACL 2003*.

Jian Xi, Michael Spranger, and Dirk Labudde. 2018. Cnn-based offensive language detection. In *14th Conference on Natural Language Processing KONVENS 2018*, page 125.

Lei Zhang, Shuai Wang, and Bing Liu. 2018. Deep learning for sentiment analysis: A survey. *Wiley Interdisciplinary Reviews: Data Mining and Knowledge Discovery*, 8(4):e1253.

# CUSATNLP@DravidianLangTech-EACL2021:Language Agnostic Classification of Offensive Content in Tweets

**Sara Renjit**
Research Scholar
Department of Computer Science
CUSAT
Kerala, India
sararenjit.g@gmail.com

**Sumam Mary Idicula**
Professor
Department of Computer Science
CUSAT
Kerala, India
sumam@cusat.ac.in

## Abstract

Identifying offensive information from tweets is a vital language processing task. This task concentrated more on English and other foreign languages these days. In this shared task on Offensive Language Identification in Dravidian Languages, in the First Workshop of Speech and Language Technologies for Dravidian Languages in EACL 2021, the aim is to identify offensive content from code mixed Dravidian Languages Kannada, Malayalam, and Tamil. Our team used language-agnostic BERT (Bidirectional Encoder Representation from Transformers) for sentence embedding and a Softmax classifier. The language-agnostic representation based classification helped obtain good performance for all the three languages, out of which results for the Malayalam language are good enough to obtain a third position among the participating teams.

## 1 Introduction

These days, social media platforms support almost all forms of languages for people to communicate. Internet use has increased through the support of language technologies, and code-mixing is common nowadays (Thavareesan and Mahesan, 2019, 2020a,b). With more and more language support, free form communication is possible among people, and as such, comment filtering or evaluating comment content based on its offensiveness to an individual, group, or other forms is an essential task (Jose et al., 2020; Priyadharshini et al., 2020). These platforms also support languages from the Dravidian family (Chakravarthi et al., 2020c; Mandl et al., 2020). As a result, it is necessary to identify offensive content from Tweets in English and all other languages, including code mixed tweets used in these platforms (Hande et al., 2020; Ghanghor et al., 2021b,a).

Dravidian languages are spoken and used in written form by the people in South India and Sri Lanka. This language is also used by a small portion of people in many parts of the world. Dravidian languages are not new, it is almost 4500 years old (Kolipakam et al., 2018), but it remains an under-resourced language (Chakravarthi, 2020). The commonly used languages of this type include Kannada, Malayalam, and Tamil. These are free word order languages and have high agglutinating nature.

Tweet classification based on its offensive content has been challenging over these years. Initially, the focus was on the English language, which is the prime language spoken and used worldwide. Nowadays, its focus is on the low resource languages. The tweets classification is based on different classes, and it can be a binary classification into offensive or not-offensive class. In an alternative way, we can classify tweets based on offensive content, their targeted audience (individual, group, or other), language, and form of insult.

This working note paper discusses the methodology used to identify offensive content from tweets in Kannada, Malayalam, and Tamil. This paper's subsequent sections are as follows: Section 2 discusses the related works based on offensive content identification. Details about the task and the dataset are in Section 3. The methods used for this classification task is in Section 4. We project the results and discuss the observations in Section 5. The last section, Section 6, concludes the working note.

## 2 Related Works

We discuss the works done so far for offensive content classification in this section. It is one of the very relevant topics of concern these days as communication is mostly through online platforms, especially in a pandemic situation like COVID-19 that we face now. Offensive language identifica-



*Proceedings of the First Workshop on Speech and Language Technologies for Dravidian Languages*, pages 236–242
April 20, 2021 ©2021 Association for Computational Linguistics

tion has started with English and other foreign languages, and it has gained its importance concerning other languages, including Dravidian and low resource languages.

Apart from the different forms of offensive content, such as hate speech, abusive language, cyberbullying, cyber-aggression, there are different kinds of offensive content. Zampieri et al. (2019) discuss the different kinds of offensive content classes and a basic definition of the different classes. They proposed a hierarchical model of offensive content in different levels, namely, Level A: Offensive language detection, Level B: Categorization of offensive language, Level C: Offensive language target identification.

The first level (Level A), Offensive language detection, consists of two major classes, namely **Not Offensive**, defined as posts/comments without any offense or profanity and **Offensive** defined as posts with profanity (non-acceptable language) or offense, including insults, threats, and swear words.

The second level (Level B) consists of categorizing offensive language into targeted insult and untargeted class. The **Targeted_Insult** class consists of posts that contain insult to an individual, group, or others. The **Untargeted** class contains posts that are not targeted but have non-acceptable language or swearing.

The third level (Level C) classifies the targets of insults or threats. It is of three types: Individual, Group, and Other. The **Individual (IND)** class has posts that target an individual, may or may not be a named person, also called cyberbullying, whereas the **Group (GRP)** class targets people of the same religion, affiliation, or gender (also referred to as Hate speech). The **Other (OTH)** category targets organizations, situations, events, or issues that do not fall in the above categories. Zampieri et al. (2019) also classified the Offensive Language Identification (OLID) dataset based tweets based on the defined classes using SVM, CNN, BiLSTM, out of which CNN performed better for the three levels of classification.

Offensive language identification has taken place in shared tasks these years. We discuss a few of the notable works here. Apart from the English language, this problem is also being solved in other languages. They predicted offensive content in Bengali, Hindi, and Spanish languages. Pretrained BERT models combined with CNN were used for Arabic, Greek, and Turkish offensive language identification (Safaya et al., 2020).

The significant contributions of offensive language identification from different teams that participated in SemEval, 2020 are discussed in Zampieri et al. (2020). Three sub-tasks corresponding to three levels of the OLID dataset hierarchy were offered for Arabic, Danish, English, Greek, and Turkish languages. German BERT model based on offensive language identification was experimented with for the German language by Risch et al. (2019) as part of GermEval,2019.

## 3 Task Details and Dataset

The shared task on Offensive Language Identification in Dravidian languages aims to identify offensive content from Kannada-English, Malayalam-English, and Tamil-English code-mixed tweet datasets (Chakravarthi et al., 2021). It is an imbalanced multi-class classification at the comment level. The dataset for this task consists of classes, namely,

1. Not_Offensive (NO)
2. Offensive_Targeted_Insult_Group (OTIG)
3. Offensive_Targeted_Insult_Individual (OTII)
4. Offensive_Targeted_Insult_Other (OTIO)
5. Offensive_Untargetede (OU)
6. Not_in_indented_language (not-Malayalam (NM), not-Kannanda (NK), not-Tamil (NT))

| Language | Train | Dev | Test | Total |
|---|---|---|---|---|
| Kannada | 6217 | 777 | 778 | 7772 |
| Malayalam | 16010 | 1999 | 2001 | 20010 |
| Tamil | 35139 | 4388 | 4392 | 43919 |

Table 1: Data statistics for Kannada, Malayalam and Tamil

The dataset statistics for the three languages are shown in Table 1. The average length of each post at sentence level is 1. The dataset includes tweets that are code mixed with the intended language (Kannada, Malayalam, or Tamil) and the English language.

### 3.1 Kannada Dataset

Hande et al. (2020) presented the Kannada-English code mixed dataset collected from YouTube and

| Classes | Kannada | | Malayalam | | Tamil | |
|---|---|---|---|---|---|---|
| | Train | Dev | Train | Dev | Train | Dev |
| Not_Offensive | 3544 | 426 | 14153 | 1779 | 25425 | 3193 |
| Not_in_indented_language | 1522 | 191 | 1287 | 163 | 1454 | 172 |
| Offensive_Targeted _Insult_Group | 329 | 45 | 140 | 13 | 2557 | 295 |
| Offensive_Targeted _Insult_Individual | 487 | 66 | 239 | 24 | 2343 | 307 |
| Offensive_Targeted _Insult_Other | 123 | 16 | 0 | 0 | 454 | 65 |
| Offensive_Untargetede | 212 | 33 | 191 | 20 | 2906 | 356 |

Table 2: Training and Development Dataset for Kannada, Malayalam and Tamil languages

annotated for sentiment analysis and offensive language detection. The dataset statistics for the Kannada language is in Table 2. This dataset has 6217 tweets for training and 777 tweets for development.

### 3.2 Malayalam Dataset

According to Chakravarthi et al. (2020a), systems trained on monolingual data sometimes fail with multilingual data written in non-native scripts. Hence a Malayalam-English code mixed dataset is created, which stands as a gold standard for offensive data identification in Dravidian languages. It helps moderate offensive content in these languages in social media comments or posts. These dataset details are in Table 2, and it has 16010 tweets as training dataset and 1999 tweets as development dataset.

### 3.3 Tamil Dataset

Tamil-English code mixed corpus with sentiment annotations were also developed, and polarities are assigned with an inter-annotator agreement (Chakravarthi et al., 2020b). The Tamil dataset has 35139 tweets for training, 4388 tweets for the development set and its data statistics are in Table 2.

## 4 Methods

Our classification method uses a good sentence representation that is purely language-agnostic in nature. The system design consists of a representation module and a classifier module.

**Representation module** : Efficient sentence embedding for the comments or tweets is derived using the language-agnostic BERT (LaBSE). The comments are in the form of code mixed language scripts written in the non-native script, English, and transliterated form. We have not used any preprocessing technique to make the method more generic and add to the language-agnostic nature.

The language-agnostic BERT uses a masked language model and a translation language model based pretrained encoder. The dual encoder architecture helps to encode source and target sentences separately and feed a combinational function. We obtain the individual embeddings from the [CLS] token's embeddings using a shared BERT encoder. The source and target sentence embeddings comparison using cosine similarity and additive margin softmax loss learn useful cross-lingual embeddings. The architecture of language-agnostic BERT is in Figure 1.

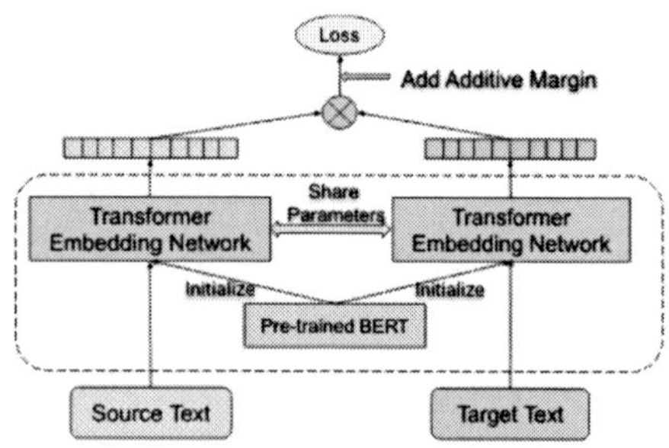


Figure 1: LaBSE model

This approach performed equally well for all the resource-rich languages and resource-poor languages. In zero-shot transfer, it showed above-average performance. This method was evaluated on different corpus like BUCC shared task for parallel sentence extraction, United Nations parallel corpus, Tatoeba corpus for 109 languages, and zero-shot transfer for languages without training data (Feng et al., 2020).

| Class | P | R | F1 | S |
|---|---|---|---|---|
| Not_offensive | 0.69 | 0.78 | 0.73 | 427 |
| Offensive_Targeted _Insult_Group | 0.30 | 0.23 | 0.26 | 44 |
| Offensive_Targeted _Insult_Individual | 0.56 | 0.52 | 0.54 | 75 |
| Offensive_Targeted _Insult_Other | 0.50 | 0.07 | 0.12 | 14 |
| Offensive _Untargetede | 0.00 | 0.00 | 0.00 | 33 |
| not-Kannada | 0.66 | 0.56 | 0.61 | 185 |
| accuracy | | | 0.63 | 778 |
| macro avg | 0.45 | 0.36 | 0.38 | 778 |
| **weighted avg** | **0.62** | **0.63** | **0.62** | **778** |

Table 3: Results for Kannada language in terms of Precision (P), Recall (R), F1-score (F1) and Support (S)

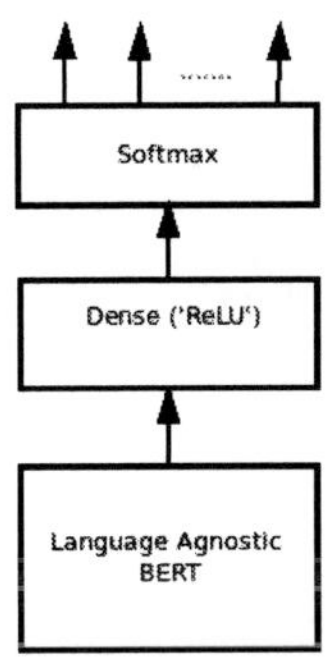


Figure 2: System design

**Classification module** : The embedded representation of sentences are passed through a perceptron based classifier. It is a two-layer classifier with Dense(100) as an input layer with ReLU activation and Dense(5,6) as an output layer with a softmax activation function for multiclass classification. The classifier is trained for 20 epochs with validation data used from the development dataset provided. The same approach is followed for all three languages. The overall system design is shown in Figure 2.

## 5 Results and Observations

This classification task's experimental results are measured in terms of weighted average precision, recall, and F1-score using Scikit-Learn classification report. Weighted average averages the support weighted mean per label [1] and are used when the datasets are highly imbalanced.

### 5.1 Kannada

The classification report for the Kannada language offensive content identification into six classes is in Table 3. We observe that the system is good only at classifying not-offensive classes and comments that do not belong to the Kannada language.

The misclassified instances can be clearly seen through the confusion matrix shown in Table 4. Samples from Offensive_Targeted_Insult_Group, Offensive_Targeted_Insult_Other, Offensive_Untargeted classes are the most misclassified instances.

### 5.2 Malayalam

The results for Malayalam code mixed tweet classification is in Table 7. From the table, we find an above-average performance for the classification of all the classes, resulting in an F1-score of 0.95. This model's better classification F1-score for the Malayalam dataset implies that LaBSE based sentence representations are suitable for Malayalam code mixed texts.

The confusion matrix for Malayalam dataset classification is shown in Table 5. Here we observe that majority of samples from each class are classified correctly which lead to an F1-score of 0.95.

### 5.3 Tamil

For the Tamil language, the classification report for offensive content classification is in Table 8, and we observe above average results only for the not-offensive class and an average value for tweets that do not belong to the Tamil language.

The confusion matrix for Tamil dataset classification is shown in Table 6, from which it is found that Not_offensive and not-Tamil are the only classes classified adequately, which resulted in lesser performance.

### 5.4 Comparison with MBERT

The tweets are encoded with Multilingual BERT (Devlin et al., 2018), bert-base-multilingual-cased, a pretrained encoder with 12 layer, 768 hidden layer size, 12 heads and 110M parameters trained for 104 languages. The same classification module is used. LaBSE based results are compared with the multilingual BERT based classification results in Table 9 in terms of its weighted F1 score. We

[1] https://scikit-learn.org/stable/modules/generated /sklearn.metrics.classification_report.html

| Actual Classes \ Predicted Classes | NO | OTIG | OTII | OTIO | OU | NK |
|---|---|---|---|---|---|---|
| NO | **333** | 11 | 18 | 0 | 20 | 45 |
| OTIG | 23 | **10** | 4 | 1 | 3 | 3 |
| OTII | 23 | 4 | **39** | 0 | 5 | 4 |
| OTIO | 6 | 6 | 0 | **1** | 1 | 0 |
| OU | 25 | 2 | 4 | 0 | **0** | 2 |
| NK | 72 | 0 | 5 | 0 | 4 | **104** |

Table 4: Confusion Matrix for Kannada dataset

| Actual Classes \ Predicted Classes | NO | OTIG | OTII | OU | NM |
|---|---|---|---|---|---|
| NO | **1726** | 3 | 9 | 8 | 19 |
| OTIG | 10 | **12** | 1 | 0 | 0 |
| OTII | 12 | 0 | **14** | 0 | 1 |
| OU | 11 | 0 | 0 | **18** | 0 |
| NM | 29 | 0 | 0 | 0 | **128** |

Table 5: Confusion Matrix for Malayalam dataset

| Actual Classes \ Predicted Classes | NO | OTIG | OTII | OTIO | OU | NT |
|---|---|---|---|---|---|---|
| NO | **2823** | 116 | 79 | 8 | 117 | 47 |
| OTIG | 172 | **60** | 23 | 1 | 29 | 3 |
| OTII | 177 | 28 | **60** | 7 | 26 | 17 |
| OTIO | 46 | 8 | 6 | **1** | 10 | 0 |
| OU | 203 | 37 | 23 | 4 | **93** | 8 |
| NT | 65 | 6 | 4 | 0 | 4 | **81** |

Table 6: Confusion matrix for Tamil dataset

find that the performance of both the models are almost similar with respect to this task.

## 6 Conclusions

In this paper, we used language-agnostic BERT for embedding comments/tweets of any language and identified the different categories of offensive content using a softmax classifier. This model achieved comparatively good results without applying any pre-processing techniques. The quality of the embedding model helps to encode information more effectively. Comparing LaBSE for Kannada, Malayalam, and Tamil language, this embedded representation is more efficient for the Malayalam language and helped improve classification results. Our team was ranked 3rd for the Malayalam language, 11th for the Kannada language, and 9th for the Tamil language in DravidianLangTech 2021, part of EACL, 2021.

## References


Bharathi Raja Chakravarthi. 2020. *Leveraging orthographic information to improve machine translation of under-resourced languages.* Ph.D. thesis, NUI Galway.

Bharathi Raja Chakravarthi, Navya Jose, Shardul Suryawanshi, Elizabeth Sherly, and John Philip McCrae. 2020a. A sentiment analysis dataset for code-mixed Malayalam-English. In *Proceedings of the 1st Joint Workshop on Spoken Language Technologies for Under-resourced languages (SLTU) and Collaboration and Computing for Under-Resourced Languages (CCURL)*, pages 177–184, Marseille, France. European Language Resources association.

Bharathi Raja Chakravarthi, Vigneshwaran Muralidaran, Ruba Priyadharshini, and John Philip McCrae. 2020b. Corpus creation for sentiment analysis in code-mixed Tamil-English text. In *Proceedings of the 1st Joint Workshop on Spoken Language Technologies for Under-resourced languages (SLTU) and Collaboration and Computing for Under-Resourced Languages (CCURL)*, pages

| Class | P | R | F1 | S |
|---|---|---|---|---|
| Not_offensive | 0.97 | 0.98 | 0.97 | 1765 |
| Offensive_Targeted _Insult_Group | 0.80 | 0.52 | 0.63 | 23 |
| Offensive_Targeted _Insult_Individual | 0.58 | 0.52 | 0.55 | 27 |
| Offensive _Untargetede | 0.69 | 0.62 | 0.65 | 29 |
| not-malayalam | 0.86 | 0.82 | 0.84 | 157 |
| accuracy | | | 0.95 | 2001 |
| macro avg | 0.78 | 0.69 | 0.73 | 2001 |
| **weighted avg** | **0.95** | **0.95** | **0.95** | **2001** |

Table 7: Results for Malayalam language in terms of Precision(P), Recall(R), F1-score(F1),and Support (S)

| Class | P | R | F1 | S |
|---|---|---|---|---|
| Not_offensive | 0.81 | 0.88 | 0.85 | 3190 |
| Offensive_Targ _Insult_Group | 0.24 | 0.21 | 0.22 | 288 |
| Offensive_Targ _Insult_Individual | 0.31 | 0.19 | 0.24 | 315 |
| Offensive_Targ _Insult_Other | 0.05 | 0.01 | 0.02 | 71 |
| Offensive _Untargetede | 0.33 | 0.25 | 0.29 | 368 |
| not-Tamil | 0.52 | 0.51 | 0.51 | 160 |
| accuracy | | | 0.71 | 4392 |
| macro avg | 0.38 | 0.34 | 0.35 | 4392 |
| **weighted avg** | **0.67** | **0.71** | **0.69** | **4392** |

Table 8: Results for the Tamil language in terms of Precision(P), Recall(R), F1-score(F1),and Support (S)

| Language | LaBSE | MBERT |
|---|---|---|
| Kannada | 0.62 | 0.68 |
| Malayalam | 0.95 | 0.93 |
| Tamil | 0.69 | 0.68 |

Table 9: Comparison of LaBSE and MBERT encoders in terms of weighted F1-score.


202–210, Marseille, France. European Language Resources association.

Bharathi Raja Chakravarthi, Ruba Priyadharshini, Navya Jose, Anand Kumar M, Thomas Mandl, Prasanna Kumar Kumaresan, Rahul Ponnusamy, Hariharan V, Elizabeth Sherly, and John Philip McCrae. 2021. Findings of the shared task on Offensive Language Identification in Tamil, Malayalam, and Kannada. In *Proceedings of the First Workshop on Speech and Language Technologies for Dravidian Languages*. Association for Computational Linguistics.

Bharathi Raja Chakravarthi, Ruba Priyadharshini, Vigneshwaran Muralidaran, Shardul Suryawanshi, Navya Jose, Elizabeth Sherly, and John P. McCrae. 2020c. Overview of the Track on Sentiment Analysis for Dravidian Languages in Code-Mixed Text. In *Forum for Information Retrieval Evaluation*, FIRE 2020, page 21–24, New York, NY, USA. Association for Computing Machinery.

Jacob Devlin, Ming-Wei Chang, Kenton Lee, and Kristina Toutanova. 2018. Bert: Pre-training of deep bidirectional transformers for language understanding. *arXiv preprint arXiv:1810.04805*.

Fangxiaoyu Feng, Yinfei Yang, Daniel Cer, Naveen Arivazhagan, and Wei Wang. 2020. Language-agnostic bert sentence embedding. *arXiv preprint arXiv:2007.01852*.

Nikhil Kumar Ghanghor, Parameswari Krishnamurthy, Sajeetha Thavareesan, Ruba Priyadharshini, and Bharathi Raja Chakravarthi. 2021a. IIITK@DravidianLangTech-EACL2021: Offensive Language Identification and Meme Classification in Tamil, Malayalam and Kannada. In *Proceedings of the First Workshop on Speech and Language Technologies for Dravidian Languages*, Online. Association for Computational Linguistics.

Nikhil Kumar Ghanghor, Rahul Ponnusamy, Prasanna Kumar Kumaresan, Ruba Priyadharshini, Sajeetha Thavareesan, and Bharathi Raja Chakravarthi. 2021b. IIITK@LT-EDI-EACL2021: Hope Speech Detection for Equality, Diversity, and Inclusion in Tamil, Malayalam and English. In *Proceedings of the First Workshop on Language Technology for Equality, Diversity and Inclusion*, Online.

Adeep Hande, Ruba Priyadharshini, and Bharathi Raja Chakravarthi. 2020. KanCMD: Kannada CodeMixed dataset for sentiment analysis and offensive language detection. In *Proceedings of the Third Workshop on Computational Modeling of People's Opinions, Personality, and Emotion's in Social Media*, pages 54–63, Barcelona, Spain (Online). Association for Computational Linguistics.

Navya Jose, Bharathi Raja Chakravarthi, Shardul Suryawanshi, Elizabeth Sherly, and John P. McCrae. 2020. A Survey of Current Datasets for Code-Switching Research. In *2020 6th International Conference on Advanced Computing and Communication Systems (ICACCS)*, pages 136–141.

Vishnupriya Kolipakam, Fiona M Jordan, Michael Dunn, Simon J Greenhill, Remco Bouckaert, Russell D Gray, and Annemarie Verkerk. 2018. A bayesian phylogenetic study of the dravidian language family. *Royal Society open science*, 5(3):171504.

Thomas Mandl, Sandip Modha, Anand Kumar M, and Bharathi Raja Chakravarthi. 2020. Overview of the

HASOC Track at FIRE 2020: Hate Speech and Offensive Language Identification in Tamil, Malayalam, Hindi, English and German. In *Forum for Information Retrieval Evaluation*, FIRE 2020, page 29–32, New York, NY, USA. Association for Computing Machinery.

Ruba Priyadharshini, Bharathi Raja Chakravarthi, Mani Vegupatti, and John P. McCrae. 2020. Named Entity Recognition for Code-Mixed Indian Corpus using Meta Embedding. In *2020 6th International Conference on Advanced Computing and Communication Systems (ICACCS)*, pages 68–72.

Julian Risch, Anke Stoll, Marc Ziegele, and Ralf Krestel. 2019. hpidedis at germeval 2019: Offensive language identification using a german bert model.

Ali Safaya, Moutasem Abdullatif, and Deniz Yuret. 2020. Kuisail at semeval-2020 task 12: Bert-cnn for offensive speech identification in social media. In *Proceedings of the Fourteenth Workshop on Semantic Evaluation*, pages 2054–2059.

Sajeetha Thavareesan and Sinnathamby Mahesan. 2019. Sentiment Analysis in Tamil Texts: A Study on Machine Learning Techniques and Feature Representation. In *2019 14th Conference on Industrial and Information Systems (ICIIS)*, pages 320–325.

Sajeetha Thavareesan and Sinnathamby Mahesan. 2020a. Sentiment Lexicon Expansion using Word2vec and fastText for Sentiment Prediction in Tamil texts. In *2020 Moratuwa Engineering Research Conference (MERCon)*, pages 272–276.

Sajeetha Thavareesan and Sinnathamby Mahesan. 2020b. Word embedding-based Part of Speech tagging in Tamil texts. In *2020 IEEE 15th International Conference on Industrial and Information Systems (ICIIS)*, pages 478–482.

Marcos Zampieri, Shervin Malmasi, Preslav Nakov, Sara Rosenthal, Noura Farra, and Ritesh Kumar. 2019. Predicting the type and target of offensive posts in social media. In *Proceedings of the 2019 Conference of the North American Chapter of the Association for Computational Linguistics: Human Language Technologies, Volume 1 (Long and Short Papers)*, pages 1415–1420.

Marcos Zampieri, Preslav Nakov, Sara Rosenthal, Pepa Atanasova, Georgi Karadzhov, Hamdy Mubarak, Leon Derczynski, Zeses Pitenis, and Çağrı Çöltekin. 2020. Semeval-2020 task 12: Multilingual offensive language identification in social media (offenseval 2020). In *Proceedings of the Fourteenth Workshop on Semantic Evaluation*, pages 1425–1447.

# IIIT_DWD@EACL2021: Identifying Troll Meme in Tamil using a hybrid deep learning approach

**Ankit Kumar Mishra**[1] and **Sunil Saumya**[2]
[1]Magadh University, Bodh Gaya, Bihar, India
[2]Indian Institute of Information Technology Dharwad, Karnataka, India
ankitmishra.in.com@gmail.com, sunil.saumya@iiitdwd.ac.in

## Abstract

Social media are an open forum that allows people to share their knowledge, abilities, talents, ideas, or expressions. Simultaneously, it also allows people to post disrespectful, trolling, defamation, or negative content targeting users or the community based on their gender, race, religious beliefs, etc. Such posts are available in the form of text, image, video, and meme. Among them, memes are currently widely used to disseminate offensive material amongst people. It is primarily in the form of pictures and text. In the present paper, *troll memes* are identified, which is necessary to create a healthy society. To do so, a hybrid deep learning model combining convolutional neural networks and bidirectional long short term memory is proposed to identify trolled memes. The dataset used in the study is a part of the competition *EACL 2021: Troll Meme classification in Tamil*. The proposed model obtained 10th rank in the competition and reported a precision of 0.52, recall 0.59, and weighted F1 0.3.

## 1 Introduction

Social media has become one of the essential components of our life, thanks to digitization. Over the years, the number of social media users has grown at an exponential pace. According to the survey of *wearesocial*[1], out of around 7.8 billion people worldwide, 3.8 billion people are active social media users (Chakravarthi et al., 2020c; Mandl et al., 2020). They participate in many ways on social media, like posting comments (in the form of text, image, video, audio), online chatting (text, audio, and video ), hosting live events, and so on (Chakravarthi et al., 2020b,a). The information available in these posts is overwhelming and very difficult to manage for users. Therefore, people always look for summarized information available on social media instead of reading the information in the form of text paragraphs. Internet memes are one such summarized version of posts that are attractive, colorful, and extensively being used among the social media community.

An internet meme is a viral concept that alters as it spreads out [2]. It is usually taken as a movie clip or scene with an added subtext that has a modified meaning. As memes contain both image and text information it becomes easier to understand the context. Memes are being used to spread news, sharing knowledge, emotion, ideas, talents, etc. It is also being used by government agencies and industry professionals to disseminate awareness programs, advertise their products, ideas, and so on. At the same time, memes are also extensively being used to spread wrong, hate, or offensive information targeting a particular community based on their color, appearance, gender, religious believes, and so on (Puranik et al., 2021; Hegde et al., 2021; Yasaswini et al., 2021; Ghanghor et al., 2021b,a). Such offensive memes that intend to insult individuals or groups are termed as *troll* memes. Trolling memes can create social media conflicts and influence certain events. It can cause loss of business or ruin somebody's life. Therefore, it is essential to identify such trolling memes and restrict their spread.

There is a number of works proposed in the literature for memes analysis. For example, (Du et al., 2020), proposed a study on the themes contained in the text of memes extracted from Twitter. (Du et al., 2020) performed experiments using a neural network model. They found that thirty percent of memes in their dataset had a political theme and were mostly shared by democrats than repub-

[1]https://wearesocial.com/blog/2020/01/digital-2020-3-8-billion-people-use-social-media

[2]https://whatis.techtarget.com/definition/Internet-meme



*Proceedings of the First Workshop on Speech and Language Technologies for Dravidian Languages*, pages 243–248
April 20, 2021 ©2021 Association for Computational Linguistics

licans. (Zubaidah and Ardelia, 2018) presented a discourse analysis of memes where they found that to understand memes, knowing social content of it is necessary, along with the text and picture. They also concluded that memes can be used for multiple purposes such as humour, sarcasm, identifying feelings, and so on. (Sharma et al., 2020) presented a memotion analysis dataset for categorizing memes into annotated tags namely sentiment, and type of humor that is, sarcastic, humorous, or offensive. (Gomez et al., 2020) proposed a hybrid approach using inception network and long short term memory network for extracting features from image and text respectively to identify hate content in the multimodal dataset. (Suryawanshi et al., 2020a) proposed a multimodal meme dataset (MultiOFF) for offensive content detection. They used an early fusion technique to combine the image and text modality.

As discussed above, most of the existing works have proposed a hybrid approach for tackling image and text present in memes. Moreover, the text language used in those memes was English. The current paper is unique in the sense that it identifies offensive or trolling memes where texts are in the Tamil language. Tamil was the first to be categorized as India's classical language and is one of the world's longest-surviving classical languages. Over 55 percent of the epigraphic inscriptions discovered by the Archaeological Survey of India (about 55,000) are in the Tamil language. In Sri Lanka and on commercial products in Thailand and Egypt, Tamil language inscriptions written in Brahmi script have been found (Chakravarthi and Muralidaran, 2021; Chakravarthi et al., 2021a,b; Thavareesan and Mahesan, 2019, 2020a,b). The dataset used in the paper is a part of the task *EACL 2021:Meme classification for Tamil.* The problem proposed is a binary classification problem where every meme has to be categorized into tags *troll* and *not troll.* The classification model used for this was a hybrid model having 2-layered CNN and Bi-LSTM in parallel[3]. The proposed model on test data reported precision 0.52, recall 0.59, and weighted F1 0.3.

The rest of the article is organized as follows; Section 2 discusses the given task and dimension of the dataset. The methodology of the paper is explained in Section 3. This is followed by experimental results which are explained in Section 4. Finally, Section 5 concludes the paper.

## 2 Task and Data Description

As per the best of our knowledge, this is the first task of identifying offensive *troll* meme in Tamil. The task was proposed in *EACL 2021*. The objective of the task was to classify each meme into two categories *troll* and *not troll* (Suryawanshi and Chakravarthi, 2021; Suryawanshi et al., 2020b). Training and testing dataset of the task was released in a phased manner where initially, training data was released in a folder containing two files; a csv and an image folder. The image folder contained 2300 images out of that 1282 image names were starting with *troll* and other 1080 image names were starting with *not troll.* Based on their naming convention we identified which images belonged to *troll* class or *not troll* class. The csv file contained two fields, image names and their captions (or texts). Similarly, for the test dataset, two files (image folder and csv file) were given to predict the final class label. But, in the test set the image names were not having class information. The total test set count was 667.

## 3 Methodology

To identify *troll* meme in Tamil a hybrid binary classification model is proposed. The detailed flow of the proposed model is shown in Figure 1. The detailed working of the model is discussed in the subsections.

### 3.1 Data Preprocessing

The prepossessing steps were employed in both image and text parts in the given meme data. It was necessary to represent the images and texts into equal length vectors respectively to further use it as an input to the proposed model.

In the caption column of csv file, we checked for missing values and found that for a few images, the caption field was blank. Those missing values were replaced with "0". Then, we performed text cleaning by removing punctuation, extra space from the text. The cleaned texts were then tokenized and encoded into a sequence of token indices. Finally, to make all the texts of equal length, padding was performed with a maximum length of 25 (the average length of sentence in the dataset ).

In the image folder, we fetched each image one by one and performed a few prepossessing steps.

[3]Developed model code repository can be found here: `https://github.com/ankitmishra2232/Troll-memes-classification-in-Tamil-`

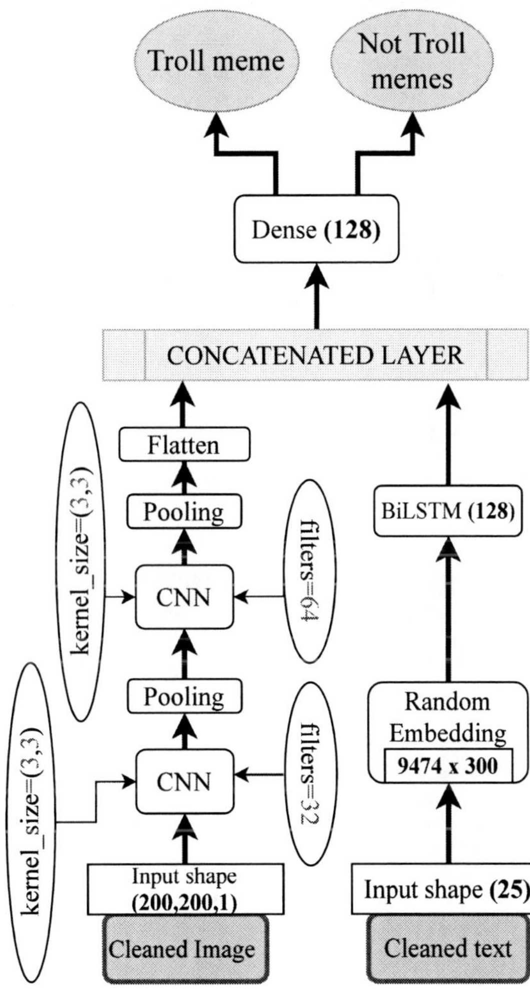


Figure 1: Proposed hybrid model for meme classification

First, we resized each image into an equal shape of a vector (200,200,3). Image processing usually requires a lot of resources. To avoid the resource scarcity problem we converted the colored images into gray-scale. Figure 2 and 3 shows an example of color image and gray-scale image. The gray-scale image was finally applied with denoising steps to make the image smoother and noise-free.

Figure 3: An example of gray-scale image from the dataset

### 3.2 Classification Model

A hybrid parallel deep learning model is developed to extract features from text and image using convolution neural network (CNN) and bidirectional long short term memory (Bi-LSTM) model respectively. The flow diagram of the model is shown in Figure 1. This section discusses the working of text and image models one after the other.

The input to the text model was image caption. For every word in the caption, a one-hot vector is created having a dimension equal to vocabulary size. In our dataset, the vocabulary size was 9474. Therefore, every word was represented in a 9474-dimensional vector. This high dimensional vector contained a single '1' and rest all zeros. The position of '1' in the vector was the word index number obtained while tokenizing the corpus. The input one-hot vector was then passed through an embedding layer that represented them in a 300-dimensional dense vector. The embedded vector obtained from each word was fed to the Bi-LSTM layer having 128 units. The output obtained at the last timestamp (for 25th word) of Bi-LSTM was considered as a feature vector of text.

The input to the image model was the matrix of the gray-scaled image obtained after preprocessing. The shape of the matrix was (200,200,1). The image matrix was passed to the two-layered CNN-pooling layer. In the first CNN layer, 32 filters were used having kernel size (3,3). They performed a two-dimensional convolution on the image matrix and resulted in a feature matrix that was passed through the ReLU activation function. The most prominent features were then pooled from the feature matrix in the window (2,2). The same process was repeated for the second CNN-pooling layer with 64 filters. The feature matrix obtained from the second CNN-pooling layer was converted into a flat vector and considered as the feature vector of the image.

The vectors obtained from image and text were then combined at concatenated layer. Finally, the combined feature was given input to a fully connected dense network which classified each input into *troll* and *not troll*. The training of the model was done for 30 epochs with adam optimizer and binary cross-entropy loss function.

## 4 Result

All models were developed in *Python* using libraries Sklearn, Keras, Pandas, Numpy, and so on. We experimented with different variations of the hybrid settings such as a parallel single-layer CNN-LSTM model, a parallel single layer CNN-CNN model, a parallel single-layer CNN-Bi-LSTM model, a parallel multilayer CNN-LSTM model, a parallel multilayer CNN-CNN model, and a parallel multi CNN layer and single Bi-LSTM layer model. We are reporting here the results of the best model, a parallel multi CNN layer and a single Bi-LSTM layer model for the test dataset. Initially, organizers provided test data without labels. The prediction of each test data was submitted to the competitions. Later, the organizers (*EACL 2021: Troll Meme classification in Tamil*) released the score of the testing data as 0.52 precision, 0.59 Recall, and 0.3 F1 scores. Our model obtained the 10th position in the ranking released by organizers. The 1st ranked model in the competition obtained a precision of 0.57, recall 0.6, and F1-score 0.55. As it is observed, the recall of the current model (0.59) was very close to the recall of the 1st ranked model (0.60). However, the precision of the submitted model (0.52) was a little far from the precision of the best-ranked model (0.59). That means the false positive rate of our model was higher.

## 5 Conclusion and Future work

The current paper identified *troll* Memes in social media platform using a parallel CNN-Bi-LSTM based network. The task was proposed by *EACL 2021* for *troll* Meme classification in Tamil. The proposed model categorised each meme into one of the classes *troll* and *not troll*. The model reported the precision of 0.52, recall 0.59, and F1-score 0.3 on the test dataset. Our model ranked at 10th position in the competition. The best model in the competition reported 0.57 precision, 0.6 recall, and 0.55 F1-score. That means a lot of works has to be done to improve the accuracy of the model. As future work, several transfer learning models can be employed such as VGG-16, ResNet50, inception network, and so on for image and BERT classifiers with a few pre-trained embedding models like GloVe, Word2Vec, FastText, and so on for text processing.

## References


Bharathi Raja Chakravarthi, Navya Jose, Shardul Suryawanshi, Elizabeth Sherly, and John Philip McCrae. 2020a. A sentiment analysis dataset for code-mixed Malayalam-English. In *Proceedings of the 1st Joint Workshop on Spoken Language Technologies for Under-resourced languages (SLTU) and Collaboration and Computing for Under-Resourced Languages (CCURL)*, pages 177–184, Marseille, France. European Language Resources association.

Bharathi Raja Chakravarthi and Vigneshwaran Muralidaran. 2021. Findings of the shared task on Hope Speech Detection for Equality, Diversity, and Inclusion. In *Proceedings of the First Workshop on Language Technology for Equality, Diversity and Inclusion*. Association for Computational Linguistics.

Bharathi Raja Chakravarthi, Vigneshwaran Muralidaran, Ruba Priyadharshini, and John Philip McCrae. 2020b. Corpus creation for sentiment analysis in code-mixed Tamil-English text. In *Proceedings of the 1st Joint Workshop on Spoken Language Technologies for Under-resourced languages (SLTU) and Collaboration and Computing for Under-Resourced Languages (CCURL)*, pages 202–210, Marseille, France. European Language Resources association.

Bharathi Raja Chakravarthi, Ruba Priyadharshini, Shubhanker Banerjee, Richard Saldhana, John Philip McCrae, Anand Kumar M, Parameswari Krishnamurthy, and Melvin Johnson. 2021a. Findings of the shared task on Machine Translation in Dravidian languages. In *Proceedings of the First Workshop on Speech and Language Technologies for Dravidian Languages*. Association for Computational Linguistics.

Bharathi Raja Chakravarthi, Ruba Priyadharshini, Navya Jose, Anand Kumar M, Thomas Mandl, Prasanna Kumar Kumaresan, Rahul Ponnusamy, Hariharan V, Elizabeth Sherly, and John Philip McCrae. 2021b. Findings of the shared task on Offensive Language Identification in Tamil, Malayalam, and Kannada. In *Proceedings of the First Workshop on Speech and Language Technologies for Dravidian Languages*. Association for Computational Linguistics.

Bharathi Raja Chakravarthi, Ruba Priyadharshini, Vigneshwaran Muralidaran, Shardul Suryawanshi, Navya Jose, Elizabeth Sherly, and John P. McCrae. 2020c. Overview of the Track on Sentiment Analysis for Dravidian Languages in Code-Mixed Text. In *Forum for Information Retrieval Evaluation*, FIRE 2020, page 21–24, New York, NY, USA. Association for Computing Machinery.

Yuhao Du, Muhammad Aamir Masood, and Kenneth Joseph. 2020. Understanding visual memes: An empirical analysis of text superimposed on memes shared on twitter. In *Proceedings of the International AAAI Conference on Web and Social Media*, volume 14, pages 153–164.

Nikhil Kumar Ghanghor, Parameswari Krishnamurthy, Sajeetha Thavareesan, Ruba Priyadharshini, and Bharathi Raja Chakravarthi. 2021a. IIITK@DravidianLangTech-EACL2021: Offensive Language Identification and Meme Classification in Tamil, Malayalam and Kannada. In *Proceedings of the First Workshop on Speech and Language Technologies for Dravidian Languages*, Online. Association for Computational Linguistics.

Nikhil Kumar Ghanghor, Rahul Ponnusamy, Prasanna Kumar Kumaresan, Ruba Priyadharshini, Sajeetha Thavareesan, and Bharathi Raja

Chakravarthi. 2021b. IIITK@LT-EDI-EACL2021: Hope Speech Detection for Equality, Diversity, and Inclusion in Tamil, Malayalam and English. In *Proceedings of the First Workshop on Language Technology for Equality, Diversity and Inclusion*, Online.

Raul Gomez, Jaume Gibert, Lluis Gomez, and Dimosthenis Karatzas. 2020. Exploring hate speech detection in multimodal publications. In *Proceedings of the IEEE/CVF Winter Conference on Applications of Computer Vision*, pages 1470–1478.

Siddhanth U Hegde, Adeep Hande, Ruba Priyadharshini, Sajeetha Thavareesan, and Bharathi Raja Chakravarthi. 2021. UVCE-IIITT@DravidianLangTech-EACL2021: Tamil Troll Meme Classification: You need to Pay more Attention. In *Proceedings of the First Workshop on Speech and Language Technologies for Dravidian Languages*. Association for Computational Linguistics.

Thomas Mandl, Sandip Modha, Anand Kumar M, and Bharathi Raja Chakravarthi. 2020. Overview of the HASOC Track at FIRE 2020: Hate Speech and Offensive Language Identification in Tamil, Malayalam, Hindi, English and German. In *Forum for Information Retrieval Evaluation*, FIRE 2020, page 29–32, New York, NY, USA. Association for Computing Machinery.

Karthik Puranik, Adeep Hande, Ruba Priyadharshini, Sajeetha Thavareesan, and Bharathi Raja Chakravarthi. 2021. IIITT@LT-EDI-EACL2021-Hope Speech Detection: There is always hope in Transformers. In *Proceedings of the First Workshop on Language Technology for Equality, Diversity and Inclusion*. Association for Computational Linguistics.

Chhavi Sharma, Deepesh Bhageria, William Paka, Scott, Srinivas P Y K L, Amitava Das, Tanmoy Chakraborty, Viswanath Pulabaigari, and Björn Gambäck. 2020. SemEval-2020 Task 8: Memotion Analysis-The Visuo-Lingual Metaphor! In *Proceedings of the 14th International Workshop on Semantic Evaluation (SemEval-2020)*, Barcelona, Spain. Association for Computational Linguistics.

Shardul Suryawanshi and Bharathi Raja Chakravarthi. 2021. Findings of the shared task on Troll Meme Classification in Tamil. In *Proceedings of the First Workshop on Speech and Language Technologies for Dravidian Languages*. Association for Computational Linguistics.

Shardul Suryawanshi, Bharathi Raja Chakravarthi, Mihael Arcan, and Paul Buitelaar. 2020a. Multimodal meme dataset (multioff) for identifying offensive content in image and text. In *Proceedings of the Second Workshop on Trolling, Aggression and Cyberbullying*, pages 32–41.

Shardul Suryawanshi, Bharathi Raja Chakravarthi, Pranav Verma, Mihael Arcan, John Philip McCrae, and Paul Buitelaar. 2020b. A dataset for troll classification of TamilMemes. In *Proceedings of the WILDRE5– 5th Workshop on Indian Language Data: Resources and Evaluation*, pages 7–13, Marseille, France. European Language Resources Association (ELRA).

Sajeetha Thavareesan and Sinnathamby Mahesan. 2019. Sentiment Analysis in Tamil Texts: A Study on Machine Learning Techniques and Feature Representation. In *2019 14th Conference on Industrial and Information Systems (ICIIS)*, pages 320–325.

Sajeetha Thavareesan and Sinnathamby Mahesan. 2020a. Sentiment Lexicon Expansion using Word2vec and fastText for Sentiment Prediction in Tamil texts. In *2020 Moratuwa Engineering Research Conference (MERCon)*, pages 272–276.

Sajeetha Thavareesan and Sinnathamby Mahesan. 2020b. Word embedding-based Part of Speech tagging in Tamil texts. In *2020 IEEE 15th International Conference on Industrial and Information Systems (ICIIS)*, pages 478–482.

Konthala Yasaswini, Karthik Puranik, Adeep Hande, Ruba Priyadharshini, Sajeetha Thavareesan, and Bharathi Raja Chakravarthi. 2021. IIITT@DravidianLangTech-EACL2021: Transfer Learning for Offensive Language Detection in Dravidian Languages. In *Proceedings of the First Workshop on Speech and Language Technologies for Dravidian Languages*. Association for Computational Linguistics.

Neneng Zubaidah and Irena Ardelia. 2018. A discourse analysis of memes. *Getsempena English Education Journal*, 5(2):58–64.

# Amrita_CEN_NLP@DravidianLangTech-EACL2021: Deep Learning-based Offensive Language Identification in Malayalam, Tamil and Kannada

**Sreelakshmi K, Premjith B and Soman K.P**
Center for Computational Engineering and Networking (CEN)
Amrita School of Engineering, Coimbatore
Amrita Vishwa Vidyapeetham, India
b_premjith@cb.amrita.edu

## Abstract

This paper describes the submission of the team Amrita_CEN_NLP to the shared task on Offensive Language Identification in Dravidian Languages at EACL 2021. We implemented three deep neural network architectures such as a hybrid network with a Convolutional layer, a Bidirectional Long Short-Term Memory network (Bi-LSTM) layer and a hidden layer, a network containing a Bi-LSTM and another with a Bidirectional Recurrent Neural Network (Bi-RNN). In addition to that, we incorporated a cost-sensitive learning approach to deal with the problem of class imbalance in the training data. Among the three models, the hybrid network exhibited better training performance, and we submitted the predictions based on the same.

## 1 Introduction

In recent years, people from all walks of life use social platforms like Twitter, Instagram, Facebook. So, it is demanding to monitor their behavior to avoid violence, hateful and offensive content (Thavareesan and Mahesan, 2019, 2020a,b). Offensive content is any non-verbal or oral communication expressing disparity against a group or person based on their religion, age, sexual orientation, race, gender, nationality, and ethnicity (Chakravarthi and Muralidaran, 2021; Suryawanshi and Chakravarthi, 2021).

A substantial amount of work was done to identify offensive content in English, but much work is not done in Dravidian languages (Chakravarthi et al., 2018, 2019; Chakravarthi, 2020). The Dravidian languages were first documented in Tamili script engraved on cave walls in Tamil Nadu's Madurai and Tirunelveli districts in the 6th century BCE. India being a multilingual country, a lot of people use regional languages along with English. The usage of two languages to communicate is called code-mixing. It is even more challenging to identify hateful content from code-mixed language owing to the non-standard grammar and spelling (Sreelakshmi et al., 2020), (Sreelakshmi et al., 2019), (Sasidhar et al., 2020).

DravidianLangTech-EACL2021 is a task to identify offensive content from code-mixed Tamil-English (Tam-Eng), Malayalam-English (Mal-Eng), and Kannada-English (Kan-Eng). In this task, we came up with a Deep learning model to identify offensive content from Malayalam-English, Tamil-English, and Kannada-English datasets. We employed three different deep learning models for solving the classification problem. A hybrid model that includes a convolutional layer followed by a Bi-LSTM (Graves et al., 2013), (Premjith et al., 2018) and a fully connected network attained the maximum scores while training. Therefore, the labels for the test data were predicted using the aforementioned model.

The rest of the contents are explained in the following sections: Section 2 presents the literature review. Dataset details are provided in Section 3. Section 4 explains the system description, and section 5 relates to experimental details and results. Finally, the work is concluded in Section 6.

## 2 Literature Review

Different abusive and offense language identification problems and shared tasks have been explored in the literature ranging from aggression to cyberbullying, hate speech, toxic comments, and offensive language. Below we discuss each of them briefly.

In 2018, Adithya et.al (Bohra et al., 2018) evolved a dataset consisting of 4500 hate and non-hate code-mixed Hindi-English tweets. The dataset was congregated using Twitter API and annotated by two linguists. Machine learning models like



*Proceedings of the First Workshop on Speech and Language Technologies for Dravidian Languages*, pages 249–254
April 20, 2021 

Random Forest and SVM and handcrafted features like character N-Grams, punctuation count, emoticon count, negation words, word N-Grams were used for classification.

SemEval (Zampieri et al., 2019) conducted three tasks in 2019, of which one task is on offensive and non-offensive comments detection from English tweets. The dataset (OLID) used for the task has 13240 tweets for training and 860 tweets for testing. Several models like Convolutional Neural Networks (CNN), Bidirectional Encoder Representations from Transformers (BERT), Long Short Term Memory (LSTM), LSTM with attention, Embeddings from Language Models (ELMo) were used by various teams. Even basic machine learning models like SVM was a part of the assorted models used.

SemEval 2020 conducted a task on offensive language identification in multilingual languages (OffensEval) such as English, Arabic, Danish, Greek, and Turkish. The same task was also conducted for Indo-European languages in FIRE 2019 (Mandl et al., 2019).

In 2020, FIRE conducted a shared task called Hate Speech and Offensive Content Identification from code-mixed posts in Dravidian languages (Malayalam-English and Tamil-English) (Chakravarthi et al., 2020d; Mandl et al., 2020; Chakravarthi et al., 2020b). Different teams came up with diversified approaches of which include, the work by Gaurav Arora (Arora, 2020). He came up with an approach based on a pretraining ULMFiT on code-mixed data, which are generated synthetically. The code-mixed data was modeled as a Markov process using Markov chains.

## 3 Dataset Description

The dataset (Chakravarthi et al., 2021), (Chakravarthi et al., 2020a), (Chakravarthi et al., 2020c), (Hande et al., 2020) consists of sentences from three code-mixed languages namely Tamil-English, Malayalam-English and Kannada-English. The Kannada-English and Tamil-English dataset have sentences labeled to six classes and, the Malayalam-English dataset has five labels. The labels for each language are given in Table 1 and the dataset statistics is given in Table 2.

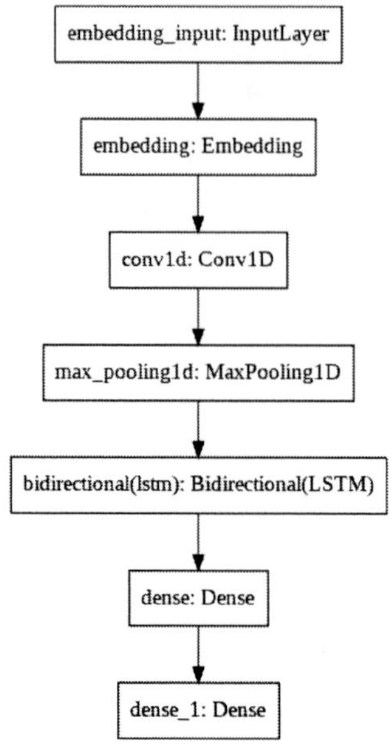


Figure 1: An illustration of the deep learning model submitted to the shared task

## 4 System Description

This section describes the details of the model submitted to the shared task. We have experimented with various deep neural networks for identifying the underlying patterns in the text required for classification.

### 4.1 Preprocessing

The dataset provided for the shared tasks contains words in both native languages (Malayalam, Tamil, and Kannada) and English. The dataset comprises social media texts and hence includes user names, hashtags, and URLs. Since these entities do not contribute much to the classification task, we employed a preprocessing step to remove such entities from the text. In addition to that, the preprocessing step involved steps to remove the punctuation and to lower-case the English characters.

### 4.2 Models

We experimented with different deep learning models for classifying the social media text into different categories. The model which obtained the highest accuracy when tested with the validation data is a hybrid of a 1-D convolution layer, a 1-D max-pooling layer, a Bidirectional-LSTM, and a fully connected network along with another fully connected layer dedicated for classification, and

| Langauge | Label |
|---|---|
| Malayalam-English | Offensive_Targeted_Insult_Group, Offensive_Targeted_Insult_Individual, Offensive_Untargetede, Not_offensive, not-Malayalam |
| Tamil-English | Not_offensive, Offensive_Targeted_Insult_Group, Offensive_Targeted_Insult_Individual, Offensive_Targeted_Insult_Other, Offensive_Untargetede, not-Tamil |
| Kannada-English | Not_offensive, Offensive_Targeted_Insult_Group, Offensive_Targeted_Insult_Individual, Offensive_Targeted_Insult_Other, Offensive_Untargetede, Not_Kannada |

Table 1: Details of the class labels available in the dataset.

| Language | Train set | Valid set | Test set |
|---|---|---|---|
| Mal-Eng | 16010 | 1999 | 2001 |
| Tam-Eng | 35139 | 4388 | 4392 |
| Kan-Eng | 6217 | 777 | 778 |

Table 2: Statistics of the dataset used in the shared task.

is illustrated in Figure 1. The same model is used for all the classification tasks. The other models considered are a network containing one Bi-LSTM layer and another with a Bi-RNN layer.

The cleaned text is fed into the model after another sequence of preprocessing steps which involve the following,

- Tokenization: An "<OOV>" token is used to mark the Out-of-Vocabulary (OOV) words in the test data.
- Translation of words into indexes.
- Padding the sequences with zeros to nake the sequence length equal: Here, maximum sequence length is set to the length of the lengthiest sentence in the dataset. Here, the zeros are padded at the end of the sequences. This padded sequences are fed into the model.

The dataset used for this task is highly imbalanced. To reduce the bias towards the majority class, we applied a cost-sensitive learning approach. This approach computes weights for each class so that the majority class gets minimum weight, and the minority class gets maximum weight. Equation 1 is used for computing the class weights.

$$cw = \frac{N}{N_c} \tag{1}$$

Where $cw$ is the class weight, $N$ is the total number of data points in the corpus, and $N_c$ is the number of sentences in the class $c$.

| Hyperparameter | Value |
|---|---|
| Embedding dimension | 100 |
| Convolution filter size | 128 |
| Convolution kernel size | 5 |
| Activation function at Conv1D layer | ReLU |
| Padding at Conv1D layer | Same |
| Pool size | 5 |
| Padding at the pooling layer | Same |
| No. of neurons in the Bi-LSTM | 32 |
| No. of neurons in the fully connected layer | 32 |
| Activation function at the fully connected layer | ReLU |
| Activation function at the output layer | Softmax |
| Loss | Categorical crossentropy |
| Optimizer | Adam |
| Learning rate | 0.01 |

Table 3: Set of hyperparameters used in building the model.

### 4.3 Hyperparameter Tuning

Hyperparameter tuning is a crucial step in building a deep learning model. The performance of a deep learning model heavily relies on the optimal selection of the hyperparameters. In this model, we chose the hyperparameters from a set of values based on the metrics considered for evaluating the model. The metrics used in this model are accuracy, precision, and recall, and AUC. The hyperparameters were chosen based on the performance of the model on validation data. A grid search method was used to find the optimal hyperparameters from a set of values.

| Model | Accuracy | Precision | Recall | AUC |
|---|---|---|---|---|
| Model-1 | 0.9677 | 0.9241 | 0.9135 | 0.9847 |
| Model-2 | 0.9494 | 0.9420 | 0.7959 | 0.9255 |
| Model-3 | 0.9432 | 0.8613 | 0.8539 | 0.9635 |

Table 4: Training performance of various models experimented for the Malayalam-English data.

| Model | Accuracy | Precision | Recall | AUC |
|---|---|---|---|---|
| Model-1 | 0.8932 | 0.6936 | 0.6438 | 0.8872 |
| Model-2 | 0.8680 | 0.6371 | 0.4829 | 0.8456 |
| Model-3 | 0.8364 | 0.9100 | 0.0207 | 0.8801 |

Table 5: Training performance of various models experimented for the Tamil-English data.

| Model | Accuracy | Precision | Recall | AUC |
|---|---|---|---|---|
| Model-1 | 0.8795 | 0.6951 | 0.4929 | 0.8396 |
| Model-2 | 0.8567 | 0.5767 | 0.5277 | 0.8469 |
| Model-3 | 0.8368 | 0.5113 | 0.4672 | 0.7891 |

Table 6: Training performance of various models experimented for the Kannada-English data.

| Dataset | Precision | Recall | F1-score |
|---|---|---|---|
| Mal-Eng | 0.90 | 0.82 | 0.85 |
| Tam-Eng | 0.64 | 0.62 | 0.62 |
| Kan-Eng | 0.65 | 0.54 | 0.58 |

Table 7: Performance of the model over the test data.

The set of optimal hyperparameters for this model are shown in Table 3. We used the same model for all the tasks and hence didn't change the hyperparameters for individual tasks.

## 5 Results and Discussion

We experimented with three deep learning models for three subtasks in the shared task. The first model, Model-1 is a hybrid of CNN, Bi-LSTM, and a fully connected layer apart from the output layer, the second model, Model-2, has a Bi-LSTM layer, and the third model, Model-3, is made up of a Bi-RNN layer. We used validation data to evaluate the models to identify the best performing model. The performance was measured using metrics such as accuracy, precision, recall, and AUC. Among the three models, the network containing CNN+Bi-LSTM+Dense layers achieved the best scores. Even though all the models exhibited comparable accuracy, the decisive factor was the recall score. The hybrid model performed substantially better than the other two models in terms of recall and precision. Besides that, it is also evident that the hybrid model could use the class weights effectively. This trend is visible in all three tasks. Tables 4, 5, and 6 shows the training performance of the Malayalam-English dataset, Tamil-English dataset and Kannada-English dataset, respectively. We submitted the predictions obtained by Model-1 based on the training performance.

The performance of the submitted model over the testing data is given in Table 7.

## 6 Conclusion

This paper presents the submission of Amrita_CEN_NLP to the shared task at EACL 2021 on Offensive Language Identification from three Dravidian Languages, namely Tamil-English (Tam-Eng), Malayalam-English (Mal-Eng), and Kannada-English (Kan-Eng). Three Deep Learning architectures, such as a hybrid network with a Convolutional layer, a Bidirectional Long Short-Term Memory network (Bi-LSTM) layer, and a fully connected network, a network containing a Bi-LSTM, and another with a BidirectionalRecurrent Neural Network (Bi-RNN) were implemented. The class imbalance problem was solved using the cost-sensitive learning approach. The hybrid of CNN, Bi-LSTM, and a fully-connected layer model gave the highest result of 90% accuracy for Mal-Eng, 64% accuracy for Tam-Eng, and 65% accuracy for kan-Eng.

## References

Gaurav Arora. 2020. Gauravarora@ HASOC-Dravidian-CodeMix-FIRE2020: Pre-training ULM-FiT on Synthetically Generated Code-Mixed Data for Hate Speech Detection. *arXiv preprint arXiv:2010.02094*.

Aditya Bohra, Deepanshu Vijay, Vinay Singh,

Syed Sarfaraz Akhtar, and Manish Shrivastava. 2018. A dataset of hindi-english code-mixed social media text for hate speech detection. In *Proceedings of the second workshop on computational modeling of people's opinions, personality, and emotions in social media*, pages 36–41.

Bharathi Raja Chakravarthi. 2020. *Leveraging orthographic information to improve machine translation of under-resourced languages*. Ph.D. thesis, NUI Galway.

Bharathi Raja Chakravarthi, Mihael Arcan, and John P. McCrae. 2018. Improving wordnets for under-resourced languages using machine translation. In *Proceedings of the 9th Global Wordnet Conference*, pages 77–86, Nanyang Technological University (NTU), Singapore. Global Wordnet Association.

Bharathi Raja Chakravarthi, Mihael Arcan, and John P. McCrae. 2019. WordNet gloss translation for under-resourced languages using multilingual neural machine translation. In *Proceedings of the Second Workshop on Multilingualism at the Intersection of Knowledge Bases and Machine Translation*, pages 1–7, Dublin, Ireland. European Association for Machine Translation.

Bharathi Raja Chakravarthi, Navya Jose, Shardul Suryawanshi, Elizabeth Sherly, and John Philip McCrae. 2020a. A sentiment analysis dataset for code-mixed Malayalam-English. In *Proceedings of the 1st Joint Workshop on Spoken Language Technologies for Under-resourced languages (SLTU) and Collaboration and Computing for Under-Resourced Languages (CCURL)*, pages 177–184, Marseille, France. European Language Resources association.

Bharathi Raja Chakravarthi, M Anand Kumar, John Philip McCrae, Premjith B, Soman KP, and Thomas Mandl. 2020b. Overview of the track on HASOC-Offensive Language Identification-DravidianCodeMix. In *Working Notes of the Forum for Information Retrieval Evaluation (FIRE 2020). CEUR Workshop Proceedings. In: CEUR-WS. org, Hyderabad, India.*

Bharathi Raja Chakravarthi and Vigneshwaran Muralidaran. 2021. Findings of the shared task on Hope Speech Detection for Equality, Diversity, and Inclusion. In *Proceedings of the First Workshop on Language Technology for Equality, Diversity and Inclusion*. Association for Computational Linguistics.

Bharathi Raja Chakravarthi, Vigneshwaran Muralidaran, Ruba Priyadharshini, and John Philip McCrae. 2020c. Corpus creation for sentiment analysis in code-mixed Tamil-English text. In *Proceedings of the 1st Joint Workshop on Spoken Language Technologies for Under-resourced languages (SLTU) and Collaboration and Computing for Under-Resourced Languages (CCURL)*, pages 202–210, Marseille, France. European Language Resources association.

Bharathi Raja Chakravarthi, Ruba Priyadharshini, Navya Jose, Anand Kumar M, Thomas Mandl, Prasanna Kumar Kumaresan, Rahul Ponnusamy, Hariharan V, Elizabeth Sherly, and John Philip McCrae. 2021. Findings of the shared task on Offensive Language Identification in Tamil, Malayalam, and Kannada. In *Proceedings of the First Workshop on Speech and Language Technologies for Dravidian Languages*. Association for Computational Linguistics.

Bharathi Raja Chakravarthi, Ruba Priyadharshini, Vigneshwaran Muralidaran, Shardul Suryawanshi, Navya Jose, Elizabeth Sherly, and John P. McCrae. 2020d. Overview of the Track on Sentiment Analysis for Dravidian Languages in Code-Mixed Text. In *Forum for Information Retrieval Evaluation*, FIRE 2020, page 21–24, New York, NY, USA. Association for Computing Machinery.

Alex Graves, Abdel-rahman Mohamed, and Geoffrey Hinton. 2013. Speech recognition with deep recurrent neural networks. In *2013 IEEE international conference on acoustics, speech and signal processing*, pages 6645–6649. Ieee.

Adeep Hande, Ruba Priyadharshini, and Bharathi Raja Chakravarthi. 2020. KanCMD: Kannada CodeMixed dataset for sentiment analysis and offensive language detection. In *Proceedings of the Third Workshop on Computational Modeling of People's Opinions, Personality, and Emotion's in Social Media*, pages 54–63, Barcelona, Spain (Online). Association for Computational Linguistics.

Thomas Mandl, Sandip Modha, Anand Kumar M, and Bharathi Raja Chakravarthi. 2020. Overview of the HASOC Track at FIRE 2020: Hate Speech and Offensive Language Identification in Tamil, Malayalam, Hindi, English and German. In *Forum for Information Retrieval Evaluation*, FIRE 2020, page 29–32, New York, NY, USA. Association for Computing Machinery.

Thomas Mandl, Sandip Modha, Prasenjit Majumder, Daksh Patel, Mohana Dave, Chintak Mandlia, and Aditya Patel. 2019. Overview of the hasoc track at fire 2019: Hate speech and offensive content identification in indo-european languages. In *Proceedings of the 11th Forum for Information Retrieval Evaluation*, pages 14–17.

B Premjith, KP Soman, and Prabaharan Poornachandran. 2018. A deep learning based Part-of-Speech (POS) tagger for Sanskrit language by embedding character level features. In *FIRE*, pages 56–60.

T Tulasi Sasidhar, B Premjith, and KP Soman. 2020. Emotion Detection in Hinglish (Hindi+ English) Code-Mixed Social Media Text. *Procedia Computer Science*, 171:1346–1352.

K Sreelakshmi, B Premjith, and KP Soman. 2019. Amrita CEN at HASOC 2019: Hate Speech Detection in Roman and Devanagiri Scripted Text. In *FIRE (Working Notes)*, pages 366–369.

K Sreelakshmi, B Premjith, and KP Soman. 2020. Detection of Hate Speech Text in Hindi-English Code-mixed Data. *Procedia Computer Science*, 171:737–744.

Shardul Suryawanshi and Bharathi Raja Chakravarthi. 2021. Findings of the shared task on Troll Meme Classification in Tamil. In *Proceedings of the First Workshop on Speech and Language Technologies for Dravidian Languages*. Association for Computational Linguistics.

Sajeetha Thavareesan and Sinnathamby Mahesan. 2019. Sentiment Analysis in Tamil Texts: A Study on Machine Learning Techniques and Feature Representation. In *2019 14th Conference on Industrial and Information Systems (ICIIS)*, pages 320–325.

Sajeetha Thavareesan and Sinnathamby Mahesan. 2020a. Sentiment Lexicon Expansion using Word2vec and fastText for Sentiment Prediction in Tamil texts. In *2020 Moratuwa Engineering Research Conference (MERCon)*, pages 272–276.

Sajeetha Thavareesan and Sinnathamby Mahesan. 2020b. Word embedding-based Part of Speech tagging in Tamil texts. In *2020 IEEE 15th International Conference on Industrial and Information Systems (ICIIS)*, pages 478–482.

Marcos Zampieri, Shervin Malmasi, Preslav Nakov, Sara Rosenthal, Noura Farra, and Ritesh Kumar. 2019. Semeval-2019 task 6: Identifying and categorizing offensive language in social media (offenseval). *arXiv preprint arXiv:1903.08983*.

# NLP-CUET@DravidianLangTech-EACL2021: Offensive Language Detection from Multilingual Code-Mixed Text using Transformers

**Omar Sharif†, Eftekhar Hossain* and Mohammed Moshiul Hoque†**
†Department of Computer Science and Engineering
*Department of Electronics and Telecommunication Engineering
Chittagong University of Engineering and Technology, Bangladesh
{omar.sharif, eftekhar.hossain, moshiul_240}@cuet.ac.bd

## Abstract

The increasing accessibility of the internet facilitated social media usage and encouraged individuals to express their opinions liberally. Nevertheless, it also creates a place for content polluters to disseminate offensive posts or contents. Most of such offensive posts are written in a cross-lingual manner and can easily evade the online surveillance systems. This paper presents an automated system that can identify offensive text from multilingual code-mixed data. In the task, datasets provided in three languages including Tamil, Malayalam and Kannada code-mixed with English where participants are asked to implement separate models for each language. To accomplish the tasks, we employed two machine learning techniques (LR, SVM), three deep learning (LSTM, LSTM+Attention) techniques and three transformers (m-BERT, Indic-BERT, XLM-R) based methods. Results show that XLM-R outperforms other techniques in Tamil and Malayalam languages while m-BERT achieves the highest score in the Kannada language. The proposed models gained weighted $f_1$ score of $0.76$ (for Tamil), $0.93$ (for Malayalam), and $0.71$ (for Kannada) with a rank of $3^{rd}$, $5^{th}$ and $4^{th}$ respectively.

## 1 Introduction

The exponential increase of offensive contents in social media has become major concern to government organizations and tech companies. It is impossible to identify offensive texts manually from enormous amounts of online contents generated every moment in social media and other online platforms. Therefore, academicians, policymakers and stakeholders are trying to develop robust computational systems to limit the spread of offensive contents using state of the art NLP techniques (Kumar et al., 2020; Akiwowo et al., 2020). In the last few years, several studies have been conducted regarding offensive languages such as hate speech, aggression, toxicity and abusive language. Although most social media users used their regional languages to carry out communication; however, plenty of resources developed in English, Arabic (Mubarak et al., 2017) and other high-resources languages. Lately, people started using code-mixed texts on social media (Jose et al., 2020; Priyadharshini et al., 2020). Linguistic level understanding of the text, complex morphological structure, and lack of training corpora are crucial barriers to classifying code-mixed data. Moreover, the system trained on monolingual data alone may fail to classify code-mixed data because of the texts linguistic level code-switching complexity. This work aims to address the above mentioned problems by contributing the following:

- Prepared transformer-based methods to identify the offensive texts from multilingual (Tamil, Malayalam, Kannada) code-mixed data.
- Perform experiments on the dataset with detail performance and error analysis, thus setting an important baseline to compare in future.

## 2 Related Work

Offensive social media content might trigger objectionable consequences to its user like mental health problem, and suicide attempts (Bonanno and Hymel, 2013). To keep the social media ecosystem, coherent researchers and stakeholders should try to develop computational models to identify and classify offensive contents within a short period. Zampieri et al. (2019a) develop an offensive language identification dataset using hierarchical annotation schema. Three layers of annotation are



*Proceedings of the First Workshop on Speech and Language Technologies for Dravidian Languages*, pages 255–261
April 20, 2021 ©2021 Association for Computational Linguistics

used in the dataset: offensive language detection, categorization of offensive language, and offensive language target identification. SemEval task 6 is organized based on this dataset which had opened interesting research directions (Zampieri et al., 2019b). In early stages, computational models created by using support vector machine, naive Bayes and other traditional machine learning approach (Dadvar et al., 2013). These models performance is not up to the mark as they could not capture the semantic and contextual information in texts. This problem was mitigated with the arrival of word embeddings and recurrent neural networks (Aroyehun and Gelbukh, 2018). Networks like bidirectional LSTMs and GRUs can hold contextual information from both past and future, creating more robust classification systems (Mandl et al., 2019; Chakravarthi et al., 2020c; Mandl et al., 2020). In recent years, transformer-based model such as BERT (Sharif et al., 2021), XLM-R gained more attention to identify and classify offensive texts. These large pre-trained model can classify code-mixed texts of different languages with astonishing accuracy (Hande et al., 2020; Chakravarthi et al., 2020b,a).

## 3 Dataset

In order to detect offensive text from social media, task organizers developed a gold standard corpus. As many social media texts are code-mixed, so system trained on monolingual data fails to classify code-mixed data due to the complexity of code-switching at different linguistic levels in the texts. To address this phenomenon, Chakravarthi et al. (2020b) developed a code-mixed text corpus in Dravidian languages. Corpus has three types of code-mixing texts (Tamil-English, Kannada-English and Malayalam-English). The task aims to implement a system that can successfully detect code-mixed offensive texts. To implement such a system, we utilize the corpus provided by the workshop organizers[1](Chakravarthi et al., 2021). The corpus consists of the text of three different languages, i.e. Tamil, Kannada and Malayalam.

System developed with the different number of train, validation and test examples for each language. The assigned task is a multi-class classification problem where the model has to classify a potential text into one of six predefined classes. These classes are Not offensive (NF), Offensive-Targeted-Insult-Other (OTIO), Offensive-Targeted-Insult-Individual (OTII), Offensive-Targeted-Insult-Group (OTIG), not-Tamil (NT)/not-Malayalam (NM)/not-Kannada (NK), and Offensive-Untargetede (OU). Table 1 shows the number of instances for each class in train, validation and test sets. Datasets are highly imbalanced where a number of instances in NF class is much higher compare to other classes. Before system development, a cleaning process is applied to every dataset. In this phase, unwanted characters, symbols, punctuation, emojis, and numbers are discarded from the texts and thus, a cleaned dataset prepared for each language.

## 4 Methodology

In this part, we briefly describe the methods and techniques employed to address the previous section's problem. First, features are extracted with different feature extraction techniques and

[1]`https://dravidianlangtech.github.io/2021/index.html`

| | **Tamil** | | | **Malayalam** | | | **Kannada** | | |
|---|---|---|---|---|---|---|---|---|---|
| | **Train** | **Valid** | **Test** | **Train** | **Valid** | **Test** | **Train** | **Valid** | **Test** |
| NF | 25425 | 3193 | 3190 | 14153 | 1779 | 1765 | 3544 | 426 | 427 |
| OTIO | 454 | 65 | 71 | - | - | - | 123 | 16 | 14 |
| OTII | 2343 | 307 | 315 | 239 | 24 | 27 | 487 | 66 | 75 |
| OTIG | 2557 | 295 | 288 | 140 | 13 | 23 | 329 | 45 | 44 |
| OU | 2906 | 356 | 368 | 191 | 20 | 29 | 212 | 33 | 33 |
| NT | 1454 | 172 | 160 | - | - | - | - | - | - |
| NM | - | - | - | 1287 | 163 | 157 | - | - | - |
| NK | - | - | - | - | - | - | 1522 | 191 | 185 |
| **Total** | 23962 | 4850 | 2500 | 58500 | 5842 | 1923 | 36009 | 5724 | 2682 |

Table 1: Class wise distribution of train, validation and test set for each language. The acronym used for classes abbreviated in Section 3.

various machine learning (ML) and deep learning algorithms are used for the baseline evaluation. Furthermore, different transformer models, i.e. XLM-R, m-BERT and Indic-BERT, are exploited as well. Figure 1 shows the schematic process of the developed system.

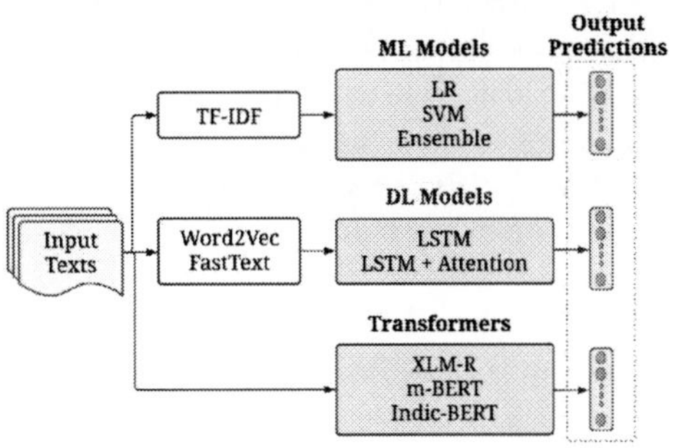


Figure 1: Abstract process of of offensive language detection

**Feature Extraction:** ML and DL algorithms are unable to learn from raw texts. Therefore, feature extraction is required to train the classifier models. For ML methods, tf-idf technique (Tokunaga and Makoto, 1994) is applied to extract the unigram features. On the other hand, Word2Vec (Mikolov et al., 2013) and FastText (Grave et al., 2018) embeddings are used as feature extraction techniques for DL models. Word2Vec implemented using Keras embedding layer with embedding dimension 100 for all languages while pre-trained embedding matrix of each language is utilized for FastText embedding.

**Machine Learning Models** To develop the offensive text detection system, we begin our investigation with traditional ML approaches, including LR and SVM. The ensemble of multiple ML classifiers is also employed to achieve better performance. We use 'lbfgs' optimizer with $C$ value of 0.4, 0.7, and 5 for Tamil, Malayalam and Kannada languages to implement LR. We selected 'linear' SVM and settled $C$ value to 3, 10, and 7. Besides, Decision Tree (DT) and Random Forest (RF) classifiers are incorporated with LR and SVM to construct the ensemble approach. For LR and SVM, the same parameters were retained while 'n_estimators = 100' is used for DT and RF. Majority voting technique is applied to get the prediction from the ensemble method.

**Deep Learning Models** DL algorithms are proven superior over many traditional ML approaches in various classification tasks (Sharif et al., 2020). We employ LSTM and combination of LSTM with Attention-based approach to classify the offensive text to continue the investigations. LSTM is well known for its ability to capture the semantic information as well as long term dependencies. Bidirectional LSTM (BiLSTM) with 100 cells are used to exploit the information from both past and future states. To mitigate the chance of overfitting, a dropout technique utilized with a rate of 0.1. Finally, the output of the BiLSTM layer transferred to a softmax layer for the prediction. However, sometimes all the words in a text do not contribute equally for the classification. To emphasize the words that have a noticeable impact on the input text, we use attention (Vaswani et al., 2017) mechanism. An attention layer of 20 neurons is constructed on the top of a BiLSTM layer. The attention operation applied upon the output of BiLSTM layer and the attention vector passed to a softmax layer for the prediction. We employ the same architectures for all the languages and use 'sparse_categorical_crossentropy' as the loss function. 'Adam' optimizer with learning rate $1e^{-3}$ and batch size 32 is used to train the models for 20 epochs. The best intermediate model is stored by using Keras callbacks.

**Transformer Models** In recent years, transformers have gained popularity for its tremendous performance in almost every aspect of NLP. As our given datasets consist of cross-lingual texts of different languages, we choose three transformers such as XLM-R (Conneau et al., 2020), m-BERT (Devlin et al., 2019), Indic-BERT (Kakwani et al., 2020) to develop our models. XLM-R is a self-supervised training technique for cross-lingual understanding particularly well for low resource languages. On the other hand, m-BERT is a transformer model pre-trained over 104 languages, and Indic-BERT is specifically pre-trained on Indian languages such as Kannada, Tamil, Telugu and Malayalam. These models are culled from Pytorch Huggingface [2] transformers library and fine-tuned on our dataset using ktrain (Maiya, 2020) package. To fine-tune these models, we use ktrain 'fit_onecycle' method with learning rate $2e^{-5}$ for all the languages. We observed that each input text's average length is less than 50

[2]https://huggingface.co/transformers/

words for Kannada and 70 words for Tamil and Malayalam languages. Therefore, to reduce the computational cost, the input texts' maximum size settle to 50 for Kannada and 70 for Tamil and Malayalam. All the models have trained up to 20 epochs with batch size 4 for XLM-R and 12 for m-BERT and Indic-BERT.

## 5 Results and Analysis

This section presents a performance comparison of various ML, DL, and transformer-based offensive text detection models for all the mentioned languages. The superiority of the models is determined based on the weighted $f_1$ score. However, the precision and recall metrics also considered. Table 2 reports the evaluation results of models. The results showed that the ML models ensemble achieved the highest $f_1$ score of 0.73 for the Tamil language. Both SVM and ensemble methods obtained a similar $f_1$ score for Malayalam (0.88) and Kannada (0.48) languages. In contrast, for all the languages, the LR method was poorly performed where a small difference ($< 0.04$) in $f_1$ score value was observed with other ML models. In case of DL techniques, LSTM (with Word2Vec) model obtained comparatively higher $f_1$ score of 0.72, 0.87 and 0.47 than that of provided by LSTM (FastText) modes which are 0.68, 0.86, and 0.45 for Tamil, Malayalam and Kannada languages. However, a combination of LSTM and Attention model shows 0.01 rise amounting to 0.87 and 0.46 respectively for Malayalam and Kannada languages.

Meanwhile, transformer-based models showed outstanding performance for all the languages. For Tamil, Indic-BERT obtained $f_1$ score of 0.74 while both m-BERT and XLM-R exceeds all the previously mentioned models by achieving maximum $f_1$ score of 0.76. Though two models give an identical $f_1$ score, XLM-R is opted as the best model by considering both the precision, recall scores. In Malayalam language, m-BERT and Indic-BERT obtained $f_1$ score of 0.90 and 0.92 respectively. While XLM-R shows a rise of 0.01 and thus beats all the other models. For the Kannada language, both XLM-R and m-BERT outperformed all the previous models obtaining $f_1$ score of 0.71. However, m-BERT is selected as the best model as it outdoes XLM-R concerning precision and recall values.

The results revealed that the transformer-based models performed exceptionally well to accomplish the assigned task for all the languages. Compared to other techniques, the ML models performed moderately while the deep learning models lag than the other models. The possible reason for this weaker performance is the extensive appearance of cross-lingual words in the text. As a result, Word2Vec and FastText embeddings have failed to create the appropriate feature mapping among the words. Thus, LSTM and attention-based models may not find sufficient relational dependencies among the features and performed below the expectation.

### 5.1 Error Analysis

Table 2 showed that XLM-R is the best performing for Tamil and Malayalam languages model, whereas, for Kannada, m-BERT is the best model. To get more insights, we present a detail error analysis of these models. The error analysis is carried out by using the confusion matrix (Figure 2).

| Method | Classifiers | Tamil | | | Malaylam | | | Kannada | | |
|---|---|---|---|---|---|---|---|---|---|---|
| | | P | R | F | P | R | F | P | R | F |
| ML models | LR | 0.76 | 0.65 | 0.69 | 0.88 | 0.84 | 0.86 | 0.52 | 0.44 | 0.47 |
| | SVM | 0.74 | 0.68 | 0.70 | 0.88 | 0.87 | 0.88 | 0.48 | 0.48 | 0.48 |
| | Ensemble | 0.72 | 0.76 | 0.73 | 0.88 | 0.89 | 0.88 | 0.46 | 0.51 | 0.48 |
| DL models | LSTM (Word2vec) | 0.73 | 0.72 | 0.72 | 0.86 | 0.87 | 0.86 | 0.48 | 0.44 | 0.46 |
| | LSTM (Fasttext) | 0.70 | 0.67 | 0.68 | 0.87 | 0.85 | 0.86 | 0.50 | 0.45 | 0.45 |
| | LSTM + Attention | 0.71 | 0.73 | 0.72 | 0.86 | 0.87 | 0.87 | 0.49 | 0.46 | 0.47 |
| Transformers | m-BERT | 0.74 | 0.78 | 0.76 | 0.93 | 0.88 | 0.90 | 0.70 | 0.74 | **0.71** |
| | Indic-BERT | 0.74 | 0.78 | 0.74 | 0.95 | 0.91 | 0.92 | 0.69 | 0.74 | 0.70 |
| | XLM-R | **0.75** | 0.78 | **0.76** | 0.92 | 0.94 | **0.93** | 0.71 | 0.70 | 0.71 |

Table 2: Evaluation results of ML, DL and transformer-based models on the test set. Here P, R, F denotes the precision, recall and weighted $f_1$ score.

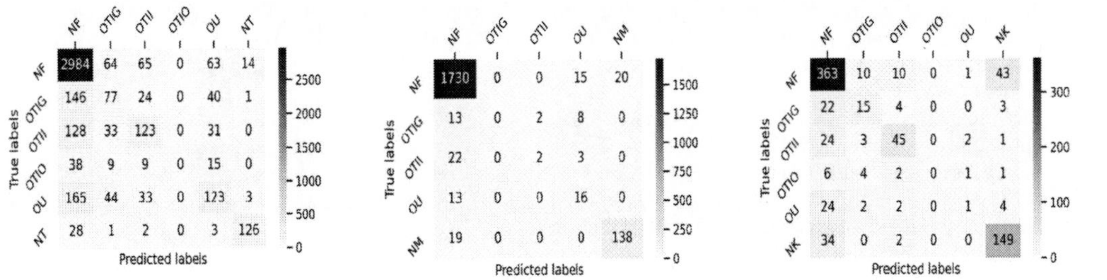


(a) Tamil (b) Malayalam (c) Kannada

Figure 2: Confusion matrix of the best models for each language task

Only NF and NT classes have a high true-positive rate (TPR) while in other classes, texts have mostly misclassified as non-offensive (Figure 2 (a)). However, among all six classes, OTIO got 0% TPR where among 77 texts more than 50% wrongly classified as NF. The high-class imbalance situation might be the reason for this vulnerable outcome. Figure 2 (b) reveals that the model is biased towards NF class. Due to the insufficient number of instances, the model failed to identify none of the 23 OTIG texts. Among 27 OTII texts, only 2 have correctly classified. Meanwhile, we observe that only NF, OTII and NK classes have a high TPR where most of the cases, the model misclassified as NF class (Figure 2 (c)). In contrast, OTIO and OU classes have shown misclassification rate 100% and 97%.

## 6 Conclusion

In this work, we have described and analyzed the system's performance implemented as a participation in the offensive language identification shared task at EACL-2021. Initially, SVM, LR, LSTM, LSTM+Attention models have employed with tf-idf and word embedding features. Results indicate that ML ensemble achieved higher accuracy than DL methods. However, the outcomes are not promising for the available datasets. Code-mixing of multilingual texts might be a reason behind this. We applied transformer-based models to overcome this situation, which provides an astonishing rise in accuracy than ML and DL-based methods. Weighted $f_1$ score increased from 0.73 to 0.76, 0.88 to 0.93 and 0.48 to 0.71 for Tamil, Malayalam and Kannada language respectively. In future, the idea of ensemble technique could be adopted on transformer-based models to investigate the system's overall performance.

## References

Seyi Akiwowo, Bertie Vidgen, Vinodkumar Prabhakaran, and Zeerak Waseem, editors. 2020. *Proceedings of the Fourth Workshop on Online Abuse and Harms*. Association for Computational Linguistics, Online.

Segun Taofeek Aroyehun and Alexander Gelbukh. 2018. Aggression detection in social media: Using deep neural networks, data augmentation, and pseudo labeling. In *Proceedings of the First Workshop on Trolling, Aggression and Cyberbullying (TRAC-2018)*, pages 90–97, Santa Fe, New Mexico, USA. Association for Computational Linguistics.

Rina A Bonanno and Shelley Hymel. 2013. Cyber bullying and internalizing difficulties: Above and beyond the impact of traditional forms of bullying. *Journal of youth and adolescence*, 42(5):685–697.

Bharathi Raja Chakravarthi, Navya Jose, Shardul Suryawanshi, Elizabeth Sherly, and John Philip McCrae. 2020a. A sentiment analysis dataset for code-mixed Malayalam-English. In *Proceedings of the 1st Joint Workshop on Spoken Language Technologies for Under-resourced languages (SLTU) and Collaboration and Computing for Under-Resourced Languages (CCURL)*, pages 177–184, Marseille, France. European Language Resources association.

Bharathi Raja Chakravarthi, Vigneshwaran Muralidaran, Ruba Priyadharshini, and John Philip McCrae. 2020b. Corpus creation for sentiment analysis in code-mixed Tamil-English text. In *Proceedings of the 1st Joint Workshop on Spoken Language Technologies for Under-resourced languages (SLTU) and Collaboration and Computing for Under-Resourced Languages (CCURL)*, pages 202–210, Marseille, France. European Language Resources association.

Bharathi Raja Chakravarthi, Ruba Priyadharshini, Navya Jose, Anand Kumar M, Thomas Mandl, Prasanna Kumar Kumaresan, Rahul Ponnusamy, Hariharan V, Elizabeth Sherly, and John Philip McCrae. 2021. Findings of the shared task on Offensive Language Identification in Tamil, Malayalam, and Kannada. In *Proceedings of the First Workshop on Speech and Language Technologies for Dravidian Languages*. Association for Computational Linguistics.

Bharathi Raja Chakravarthi, Ruba Priyadharshini, Vigneshwaran Muralidaran, Shardul Suryawanshi, Navya Jose, Elizabeth Sherly, and John P. McCrae. 2020c. Overview of the Track on Sentiment Analysis for Dravidian Languages in Code-Mixed Text. In *Forum for Information Retrieval Evaluation*, FIRE 2020, page 21–24, New York, NY, USA. Association for Computing Machinery.

Alexis Conneau, Kartikay Khandelwal, Naman Goyal, Vishrav Chaudhary, Guillaume Wenzek, Francisco Guzmán, Edouard Grave, Myle Ott, Luke Zettlemoyer, and Veselin Stoyanov. 2020. Unsupervised cross-lingual representation learning at scale. In *Proceedings of the 58th Annual Meeting of the Association for Computational Linguistics*, pages 8440–8451, Online. Association for Computational Linguistics.

Maral Dadvar, Dolf Trieschnigg, Roeland Ordelman, and Franciska de Jong. 2013. Improving cyberbullying detection with user context. ECIR'13, page 693–696, Berlin, Heidelberg. Springer-Verlag.

Jacob Devlin, Ming-Wei Chang, Kenton Lee, and Kristina Toutanova. 2019. Bert: Pre-training of deep bidirectional transformers for language understanding.

Edouard Grave, Piotr Bojanowski, Prakhar Gupta, Armand Joulin, and Tomas Mikolov. 2018. Learning word vectors for 157 languages. In *Proceedings of the Eleventh International Conference on Language Resources and Evaluation (LREC 2018)*, Miyazaki, Japan. European Language Resources Association (ELRA).

Adeep Hande, Ruba Priyadharshini, and Bharathi Raja Chakravarthi. 2020. KanCMD: Kannada CodeMixed dataset for sentiment analysis and offensive language detection. In *Proceedings of the Third Workshop on Computational Modeling of People's Opinions, Personality, and Emotion's in Social Media*, pages 54–63, Barcelona, Spain (Online). Association for Computational Linguistics.

Navya Jose, Bharathi Raja Chakravarthi, Shardul Suryawanshi, Elizabeth Sherly, and John P. McCrae. 2020. A Survey of Current Datasets for Code-Switching Research. In *2020 6th International Conference on Advanced Computing and Communication Systems (ICACCS)*, pages 136–141.

Divyanshu Kakwani, Anoop Kunchukuttan, Satish Golla, Gokul N.C., Avik Bhattacharyya, Mitesh M. Khapra, and Pratyush Kumar. 2020. IndicNLPSuite: Monolingual corpora, evaluation benchmarks and pre-trained multilingual language models for Indian languages. In *Findings of the Association for Computational Linguistics: EMNLP 2020*, pages 4948–4961, Online. Association for Computational Linguistics.

Ritesh Kumar, Atul Kr. Ojha, Bornini Lahiri, Marcos Zampieri, Shervin Malmasi, Vanessa Murdock, and Daniel Kadar, editors. 2020. *Proceedings of the Second Workshop on Trolling, Aggression and Cyberbullying*. European Language Resources Association (ELRA), Marseille, France.

Arun S. Maiya. 2020. ktrain: A low-code library for augmented machine learning.

Thomas Mandl, Sandip Modha, Anand Kumar M, and Bharathi Raja Chakravarthi. 2020. Overview of the HASOC Track at FIRE 2020: Hate Speech and Offensive Language Identification in Tamil, Malayalam, Hindi, English and German. In *Forum for Information Retrieval Evaluation*, FIRE 2020, page 29–32, New York, NY, USA. Association for Computing Machinery.

Thomas Mandl, Sandip Modha, Prasenjit Majumder, Daksh Patel, Mohana Dave, Chintak Mandlia, and Aditya Patel. 2019. Overview of the hasoc track at fire 2019: Hate speech and offensive content identification in indo-european languages. In *Proceedings of the 11th Forum for Information Retrieval Evaluation*, FIRE '19, page 14–17, New York, NY, USA. Association for Computing Machinery.

Tomas Mikolov, Ilya Sutskever, Kai Chen, Greg Corrado, and Jeffrey Dean. 2013. Distributed representations of words and phrases and their compositionality.

Hamdy Mubarak, Kareem Darwish, and Walid Magdy. 2017. Abusive language detection on Arabic social media. In *Proceedings of the First Workshop on Abusive Language Online*, pages 52–56, Vancouver, BC, Canada. Association for Computational Linguistics.

Ruba Priyadharshini, Bharathi Raja Chakravarthi, Mani Vegupatti, and John P. McCrae. 2020. Named Entity Recognition for Code-Mixed Indian Corpus using Meta Embedding. In *2020 6th International Conference on Advanced Computing and Communication Systems (ICACCS)*, pages 68–72.

Omar Sharif, Eftekhar Hossain, and Mohammed Moshiul Hoque. 2020. Techtexc: Classification of technical texts using convolution and bidirectional long short term memory network.

Omar Sharif, Eftekhar Hossain, and Mohammed Moshiul Hoque. 2021. Combating hostility: Covid-19 fake news and hostile post detection in social media.

Takenobu Tokunaga and Iwayama Makoto. 1994. Text categorization based on weighted inverse document frequency. In *Special Interest Groups and Information Process Society of Japan (SIG-IPSJ*. Citeseer.

Ashish Vaswani, Noam Shazeer, Niki Parmar, Jakob Uszkoreit, Llion Jones, Aidan N. Gomez, Lukasz Kaiser, and Illia Polosukhin. 2017. Attention is all you need.

Marcos Zampieri, Shervin Malmasi, Preslav Nakov, Sara Rosenthal, Noura Farra, and Ritesh Kumar. 2019a. Predicting the type and target of offensive posts in social media. In *Proceedings of the 2019 Conference of the North American Chapter of the Association for Computational Linguistics: Human Language Technologies, Volume 1 (Long and Short Papers)*, pages 1415–1420, Minneapolis, Minnesota. Association for Computational Linguistics.

Marcos Zampieri, Shervin Malmasi, Preslav Nakov, Sara Rosenthal, Noura Farra, and Ritesh Kumar. 2019b. SemEval-2019 task 6: Identifying and categorizing offensive language in social media (OffensEval). In *Proceedings of the 13th International Workshop on Semantic Evaluation*, pages 75–86, Minneapolis, Minnesota, USA. Association for Computational Linguistics.

# IRLAB-DAIICT@DravidianLangTech-EACL2021: Neural Machine Translation

**Raj Prajapati**
DA-IICT / Gandhinagar, India
prajapatiraj.97@gmail.com

**Vedant Parikh**
DA-IICT / Gandhinagar, India
vedant.parikh.6299@gmail.com

**Prasenjit Majumder**
DA-IICT / Gandhinagar, India
prasenjit.majumder@gmail.com

## Abstract

This paper describes our team's submission of the EACL DravidianLangTech-2021's shared task on Machine Translation of Dravidian languages.We submitted our translations for English to Malayalam , Tamil , and Telugu. The submissions mainly focus on having adequate amount of data backed up by good pre-processing of it to produce quality translations,which includes some custom made rules to remove unnecessary sentences. We conducted several experiments on these models by tweaking the architecture, Byte Pair Encoding (BPE) and other hyperparameters.

## 1 Introduction

We participated in the shared task on Machine Translation in Dravidian languages Dravidian-LangTech, EACL 2021 .The advancement of technology has increased our internet usage and majority of the languages have acclimatised to the growing digital world. However, there are many regional languages which are under-resourced languages and still lack development.One such language family is the Dravidian languages , these languages are majorly spoken in south India ,Nepal, Pakistan, Sri Lanka and South Asia, we have submitted our translations for three language pairs namely:

1. English-Malayalam
2. English-Tamil
3. English-Telugu

Our implementations uses Transformer architecture and for that we have used OpenNMT-py (Klein et al., 2017) framework and BLEU (Papineni et al., 2002) score as the evaluation metric for our translation system.

Our main focus was on proper pre-processing of the data and often we have seen that improper pre-processing has led to horrendous translations. We have done extensive data pre-processing starting basic cleaning of punctuation symbols to language specific script normalization , apart from this we have added some custom rules as well. Which is followed by tokenization , truecasing and byte pair encoding (BPE).

For Indic languages espacially Dravidian langauges we often face the problem of Out of Vocabulary word (OOV) which is taken care by word segmentation using BPE ,so we deal with subwords instead of words.

This paper is arranged as follows : First we describe the task undertaken which is followed by in-depth explanation of the model architecture, then next we have described the experimental setup which includes provided data set information , pre-processing steps and clean data statistics. After that , we describe the experiments conducted on different language pairs and analysis of the results produced. At last we draw some conclusions and propose some future work.

## 2 Task Description

The task focuses on improvement to access and production of information for speakers of Dravidian languages. Due to low resources available , the research community has not developed much of an interest in this domain , the main focus of this task is to promote research in this area and build machine translation systems for native monolingual speakers of these group of languages.

In the era of digitization there is a large population who are not fully connected to the digital world because of their inability to access the digital world in their native language, which is what this task tries to accomplish.

The experiment setup contains the detailed information about our experiments,data and vision.



*Proceedings of the First Workshop on Speech and Language Technologies for Dravidian Languages*, pages 262–265
April 20, 2021 ©2021 Association for Computational Linguistics

## 3 Architecture

### 3.1 Encoder Decoder Frame work

Given two parallel sentences (a , b), the NMT model tries to learn the parameters $\theta$ by maximizing the probability P( b | a ; $\theta$ ) . The Encoder generates a mapping from the input sentence to a hidden set of representations $h$ and the decoder generates a target token $b_t$ using the previously generated target tokens $b_k$ where k<t and source representations $h$.Both encoder and decoder can be individually RNN/LSTM/GRU models as adopted by (Bahdanau et al., 2014) along with that self attention mechanism explained by (Vaswani et al., 2017) which is a vital combination for NMT systems.

### 3.2 Transformers

Introduction of Transformer models has increased the interests of researchers in NMT , transformers have preserved the idea of an encoder - decoder framework , with an addition of attention mechanism as explained in (Vaswani et al., 2017) it increases its worth . Transformer is one of its kind model which only uses self attention mechanisms to generate intermediate representation of input data . Transformers were initially tested on English-French dataset and were pretty successful achieving state of the art results.Unlike English-French language pair, Indian languages are a bit difficult to model because of certain reasons like richness in morphology, free word ordering. So more often we get poor translations.

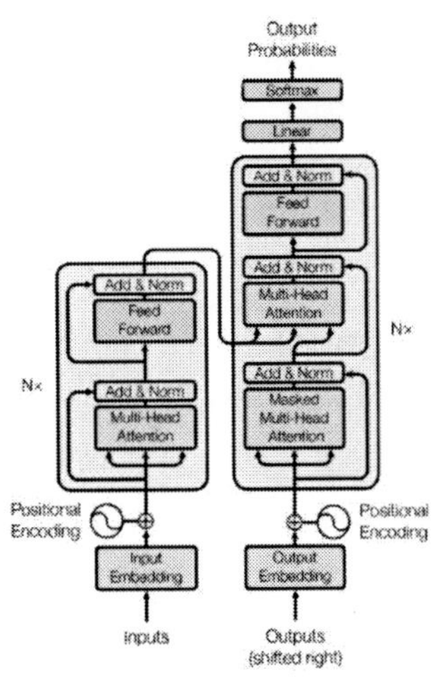


Figure 1: Transformer Architecture from (Vaswani et al., 2017)

| Language Pair | No. of sentences |
|---|---|
| English-Malayalam | 382K |
| Total parallel data | 382K |
| English-Tamil | 28K |
| Additional parallel data | 170K |
| Total parallel data | 198K |
| English-Telugu | 23K |
| Additional parallel data | 95K |
| Total parallel data | 118K |

Table 1: Raw Data Statistics

Figure 1 is the architecture used by almost every recent NMT paper, the biggest challenges in any NMT system are : Missing words , data sparsity . To overcome these challenges subword models were introduced to understand the subwords and how can we utilise them to increase our translation quality. Byte pair encoding is one way to compute subwords , initially introduced as a compression format but has been very efficient in word segmentation.

## 4 Experimental Setup

We have tried to perform experiments on three different language pairs as mentioned in the introduction section. Below mentioned is the detailed explanation of our approaches.

### 4.1 Datasets

Data is the key for any Neural Machine Translation system, this is something which is a driving factor.The language pairs are very resource scarce and the official training data (Chakravarthi et al., 2021) is not sufficient, so we took some additional parallel data as well.

Table 1 contains the data statistics for each language pair we have taken into consideration.

We have taken parallel data for language pairs from different sources. So for English-Tamil pair we have used[1] , similarly for English-Telugu we have used OPUS[2].

### 4.2 Preprocessing

Preprocessing is one of the main steps in any Machine translation system. In our experiment we have perform several steps which are listed below:

[1] http://ufal.mff.cuni.cz/~ramasamy/parallel/html/

[2] http://opus.nlpl.eu/

| Language Pair | No. of sentences |
|---|---|
| English-Malayalam | 380K |
| English-Tamil | 169K |
| English-Telugu | 110K |

Table 2: Cleaned training data statistics

| Language Pair | No. of sentences |
|---|---|
| English-Malayalam | 2K |
| English-Tamil | 1.5K |
| English-Telugu | 1.3K |

Table 3: Cleaned validation data statistics

- The sentences were normalized for punctuation by using Indic NLP Library[3].
- Some of the sentences consists numerical either only in source sentences or target sentences.We removed these sentences from dataset.
- We also removed sentences which contains of repetition of words.
- The words which were not of same language they where transliterated using Indic NLP's transliteration tool.
- Some specific special character(s) were also manually removed from the sentences.
- Many sentences were not aligned properly , so they were removed directly.
- In many sentences either source or target or both sentences were blank, which were also removed.

After all this prepossessing the final data statistics are explained pairwise in Tables 2 and 3 for training and validation.

### 4.3 BPE segmentation

An NMT system relies on mapping each word into a vector space, and we have a word vector corresponding to each word in a fixed vocabulary. The pertaining issues of data scarcity and inability of the system to learn high quality representations for rarely occuring words, (Sennrich et al., 2016) proposed to learn subwords and perform translation at a subword level.Subword segmentation is achieved using Byte Pair Encoding (BPE), by using BPE the vocabulary size is reduced drastically therefore we see a reduction in out-of-vocabulary words error, but it adds an overhead post processing step to convert the subwords back to the original word. We have used google's SentencePiece[4] to perform word segmentations using BPE in which we kept a uniform vocabulary size between 2K and 3K.

| Configuration | Value |
|---|---|
| architecture | transformer |
| word embedding | 512 |
| Encoder depth | 3 |
| Decoder depth | 3 |
| transformer heads | 4 |
| size of FFN | 2048 |
| tranformer dropout attention | 0.1 |
| tranformer dropout FFN | 0.1 |

Table 4: The main model configuration

### 4.4 Metrics

This work used BLEU (Papineni et al., 2002) score as evaluation metrics. A BLEU score compares a machine-translated sentence with the actual reference sentence by matching thier n-grams. The higher the number of n-grams matches, the closer are the two sentences.However, there are several implementations of BLEU available online, we have used multi-bleu[5] script from Mosesdecoder[6].

### 4.5 Modelling

For all the experiments we used OpenNMT-py Klein et al. (2017) toolkit. Table 4 describes the model configuration used in this experiment.

Table 5 describes the training parameters used by us to model data. We validate the model for every 5000 steps on BLEU and perplexity on validation set. We used 2000 as vocab size for English-Malayalam, English-Tamil, Tamil-Telugu and 2500 for English-Telugu language pairs.

[3] https://anoopkunchukuttan.github.io/indic_nlp_library

[4] https://github.com/google/sentencepiece

[5] https://github.com/marian-nmt/moses-scripts/blob/master/scripts/generic/multi-bleu.perl

[6] https://github.com/moses-smt/mosesdecoder

| Parameters | Value |
|---|---|
| maximum sentence length | 80 |
| learning rate | 0.0005 |
| label-smoothing | 0.1 |
| optimizer | Adam |
| learning rate warmup | 8000 |
| training batch size | 12800 tokens |

Table 5: Training Parameters

| Language Pair | BLEU Score |
|---|---|
| English-Malayalam | 24.89 |
| English-Tamil | 7.00 |
| English-Telugu | 15.79 |

Table 6: Results on Validation data

## 5 Results

We made several models with different parameters and vocabulary sizes, Table 6 and Table 7 shows the results produced by the best models in each language pair for validation and test data respectively.

## 6 Conclusion and Future Works

In this paper we describe our submission to Machine Translation for Dravidian Languages (EACL 2021). As the quality of the sentences was not good, we had do a lot of preprocessing steps. So we also added other open source parallel corpora for our training. Our models are performing good on validation data but somewhat good on test data .

For future works, we would like to try pivoting methods and transfer learning methods. We would also like to introduce semantic features such Part of Speech Tags(POS), Named Entity Tags(NER), Lemmas etc. We can also use the language models for feature injection processes. Apart from this, we would also like to employ semi-supervised and unsupervised methods into these language pairs.

| Language Pair | BLEU Score |
|---|---|
| English-Malayalam | 8.43 |
| English-Tamil | 6.04 |
| English-Telugu | 6.25 |

Table 7: Results on Test data

## References


Dzmitry Bahdanau, Kyunghyun Cho, and Yoshua Bengio. 2014. Neural machine translation by jointly learning to align and translate.

Bharathi Raja Chakravarthi, Ruba Priyadharshini, Navya Jose, Anand Kumar M, Thomas Mandl, Prasanna Kumar Kumaresan, Rahul Ponnusamy, Hariharan V, Elizabeth Sherly, and John Philip McCrae. 2021. Findings of the shared task on Offensive Language Identification in Tamil, Malayalam, and Kannada. In *Proceedings of the First Workshop on Speech and Language Technologies for Dravidian Languages*. Association for Computational Linguistics.

Guillaume Klein, Yoon Kim, Yuntian Deng, Jean Senellart, and Alexander Rush. 2017. OpenNMT: Open-source toolkit for neural machine translation. In *Proceedings of ACL 2017, System Demonstrations*, pages 67–72, Vancouver, Canada. Association for Computational Linguistics.

Kishore Papineni, Salim Roukos, Todd Ward, and Wei-Jing Zhu. 2002. Bleu: a method for automatic evaluation of machine translation. In *Proceedings of the 40th Annual Meeting of the Association for Computational Linguistics*, pages 311–318, Philadelphia, Pennsylvania, USA. Association for Computational Linguistics.

Rico Sennrich, Barry Haddow, and Alexandra Birch. 2016. Neural machine translation of rare words with subword units. In *Proceedings of the 54th Annual Meeting of the Association for Computational Linguistics (Volume 1: Long Papers)*, pages 1715–1725, Berlin, Germany. Association for Computational Linguistics.

Ashish Vaswani, Noam Shazeer, Niki Parmar, Jakob Uszkoreit, Llion Jones, Aidan N Gomez, Ł ukasz Kaiser, and Illia Polosukhin. 2017. Attention is all you need. In *Advances in Neural Information Processing Systems*, volume 30. Curran Associates, Inc.

# IRNLP_DAIICT@DravidianLangTech-EACL2021: Offensive Language identification in Dravidian Languages using TF-IDF Char N-grams and MuRIL

**Bhargav Dave**
DA-IICT / Gandhinagar, India
bhargavdave1@gmail.com

**Shripad Bhat**
DA-IICT / Gandhinagar, India
shripadbhat30@gmail.com

**Prasenjit Majumder**
DA-IICT / Gandhinagar, India
prasenjit.majumder@gmail.com

## Abstract

This paper presents the participation of the IRNLP_DAIICT team from Information Retrieval and Natural Language Processing lab at DA-IICT, India in DravidianLangTech-EACL2021 Offensive Language identification in Dravidian languages. The aim of this shared task is to identify Offensive Language from a code-mixed data-set of YouTube comments. The task is to classify comments into Not Offensive (NO), Offensive Untargetede (OU), Offensive Targeted Individual (OTI), Offensive Targeted Group (OTG), Offensive Targeted Others (OTO), Other Language (OL) for three Dravidian languages: Kannada, Malayalam and Tamil. We use TF-IDF character n-grams and pretrained MuRIL embeddings for text representation and Logistic Regression and Linear SVM for classification. Our best approach achieved Ninth, Third and Eighth with weighted F1 score of 0.64, 0.95 and 0.71 in Kannada, Malayalam and Tamil on test dataset respectively. Our code is publicly available here[1].

## 1 Introduction

The emergence of smartphones and widespread access to internet, social media platforms like Facebook, Twitter, YouTube, etc have become increasingly popular. People express their opinions on such platforms on various issues. Due to lack of moderation, a significant amount of offensive content is often posted on these platforms. Since social media is become a indispensable part of our life, the content posted on the social media platforms has great impact on the society. It has been seen recently that offensive and provoking content on these platforms can lead to riots. Hence the moderation of content in these platforms is a very important task. Since the amount of content generated is very high, there is a need to perform automated moderation of the content.

Natural language processing can used to perform automated analysis of text. By identifying and classifying the text content posted, offensive content can be removed and users could be warned. This can help in curbing offensive content online.

The goal of this shared task is to classify offensive language from a code-mixed data-set of comments of Dravidian languages collected from YouTube. Shared task was introduced as six class classification of the YouTube for three Dravidian languages: Kannada, Malayalam and Tamil (Chakravarthi et al., 2021)

Our approaches use TF-IDF character n-grams and MuRIL embeddings for the text representation and Logistic Regression, Linear SVM, Randam Forest for classification.

The rest of this paper is organized as follows. In section we discuss the related work followed by Section 3 which describes the shared task dataset and Methods are presented in Section 4. Results and Analysis is given in final Section 5 and Section 6 present Conclusion.

## 2 Related Work

The identification of hate and offensive Speech in social media is of great importance and receives much attention in the text classification community. Due to the lack of resources and morphological complexity there is a huge demand for research in code-mixed Dravidian languages.

Some of the shared tasks in the recent past are OffensEval (Zampieri et al., 2019, 2020), HateEval(Basile et al., 2019) and HASOC (Mandl et al., 2019, 2020). Among these shared tasks, HASOC 2020 shared task is based on Dravidian languages. In OffensEval (Zampieri et al., 2020), BERT (Devlin et al., 2019), ROBERTa (Liu et al., 2019) and

[1] https://github.com/bhargav25dave1996/IRNLP_DAIICT_DravidianLangTech-EACL2021



*Proceedings of the First Workshop on Speech and Language Technologies for Dravidian Languages*, pages 266–269
April 20, 2021 ©2021 Association for Computational Linguistics

| Label | Kannada | | | Malayalam | | | Tamil | | |
|---|---|---|---|---|---|---|---|---|---|
| | Train | Dev | Test | Train | Dev | Test | Train | Dev | Test |
| NO | 3544 | 426 | 427 | 14153 | 1779 | 1765 | 25425 | 3193 | 3190 |
| OU | 212 | 33 | 33 | 191 | 20 | 29 | 2906 | 356 | 368 |
| OTI | 487 | 66 | 75 | 239 | 24 | 27 | 2557 | 307 | 315 |
| OTG | 329 | 45 | 44 | 140 | 13 | 23 | 2343 | 295 | 288 |
| OTO | 123 | 16 | 14 | - | - | - | 2343 | 172 | 160 |
| OL | 1522 | 191 | 185 | 1287 | 163 | 157 | 1454 | 65 | 71 |
| Total | 6217 | 777 | 778 | 16010 | 1999 | 2001 | 35139 | 4388 | 4392 |

Table 1: Offensive Language Identification Detection shared task Dataset Statistics

ELMo (Peters et al., 2018) were used for offensive language identification. In HASOC (Mandl et al., 2020) Track multilingual transformer based methods like XLM-ROBERTa, mBERT, etc were employed and fine tuned for the task. Other popular techniques were TF-IDF along with Character n-grams combined with machine learning classifiers like Logistic Regression, SVM and XGboost.

## 3 Dataset

Offensive Language Identification shared task organizers provide datasets in three languages Kannada (Hande et al., 2020), Malayalam (Chakravarthi et al., 2020a) and Tamil (Chakravarthi et al., 2020b). Dataset has been curated from Youtube comments using the YouTube Comment Scraper [2]. The number of comments is 28451 in the Kannada dataset, 20198 in the Tamil dataset and 10705 in the Malayalam dataset. Full statistic of dataset given in Table 1

## 4 Methods

For all the YouTube comments we first preprocess the text and then create a text representation and finally classify the text using the machine learning classifiers. Figure 1 illustrates the set of steps used to classify the YouTube comments.

### 4.1 Pre-Processing

Since there is a lot of noise in the social media text we perform the following preprocessing operations. URL's, user mentions of the form @user, emojis, digits, punctuations are removed and the text is lowercased.

[2]https://github.com/philbot9/youtube-comment-scraper

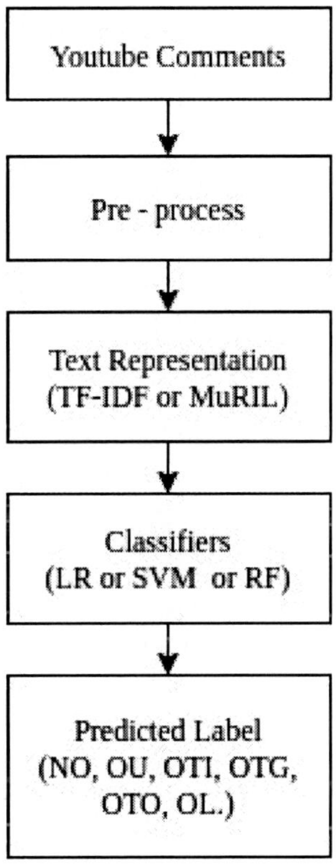


Figure 1: Steps involved in Offensive language identification

### 4.2 Text representation and Classifiers

Representation of the text is one of the fundamental tasks in Natural language processing. We explore two representation techniques: TF-IDF and MuRIL. TF-IDF is a very popular text representation technique which takes into account the frequency of the word in a given document and the number of documents in which a word is present. We employ Scikit-learn TF-IDF vectorizer API for obtaining the text representation. Instead of word based TF-IDF representation we make use of character n-grams based TF-IDF representation so as to effectively capture morphological variations of the words.

MuRIL[3] (Multilingual Representations for Indian Languages) is a transformer based language model trained on 17 Indian languages on self-supervised masked language modeling task. MuRIL training consists of translation and transliteration segment pairs in addition to the standard training used in Multilingual BERT. Pretrained MuRIL model is used to obtain the text representation in the form vectors of 768 dimension.

Logistic Regression (LR), Random Forest (RF), Linear SVM classifiers have been used to perform the classification of the text. Scikit-learn API has been used to implement the classification task. So the six approaches we have used are TF-IDF (Char) + LR, TF-IDF(Char) + SVM, TF-IDF(Char) + RF, MuRIL + LR, MuRIL + SVM, MuRIL + RF for each language.

## 5 Results and Analysis

The submission evaluation on the test data of all the three languages is shown in table tables 2, 3, 4. Our methods achieve Ninth, Third and Eighth rank in Kannada, Malayalam and Tamil respectively. For the Kannada language task, TF-IDF (Char) + LR and TF-IDF (Char) + SVM achieves the best results with weighted F1 score of 0.65 but for ranking task organize consider TF-IDF(char) + RF with weighted F1 score of 0.64. For the Malayalam language task, MuRIL representation of the text with Random Forest classifier (MuRIL + RF) achieves the best weighted F1 score of 0.95. For Tamil language TF-IDF character n-grams representation of the text with Logistic regression classifier ( TF-IDF (Char) + LR) achieves the best results with weighted F1 score of 0.71.

| **Model** | **W-Avg F1-score** |
|---|---:|
| TF-IDF (Char) + LR | **0.65** |
| TF-IDF(Char) + SVM | **0.65** |
| TF-IDF(Char) + RF | 0.64 |
| MuRIL + LR | 0.39 |
| MuRIL + SVM | 0.39 |
| MuRIL + RF | 0.60 |

Table 2: Results for the Kannada on test dataset.

It can be observed that MuRIL is not performing well particularly in case of Kannada and Tamil language but it has help us achieve rank 3 with weighted F1 score of 0.95 in Malayalam. TF-IDF character n-grams representation performs better than MuRIL in Kannada and Tamil. So there is no clear winner in terms of text representation or the classifier across all the three languages. Also, data imbalance problem is prevalent in all three languages making the task more difficult.

| **Model** | **W-Avg F1-score** |
|---|---:|
| TF-IDF (Char) + LR | 0.89 |
| TF-IDF(Char) + SVM | 0.90 |
| TF-IDF(Char) + RF | 0.94 |
| MuRIL + LR | 0.83 |
| MuRIL + SVM | 0.83 |
| MuRIL + RF | **0.95** |

Table 3: Results for the Malayalam on test dataset.

| Model | W-Avg F1-score |
|---|---:|
| TF-IDF (Char) + LR | **0.71** |
| TF-IDF(Char) + SVM | 0.70 |
| TF-IDF(Char) + RF | 0.66 |
| MuRIL + LR | 0.61 |
| MuRIL + SVM | 0.61 |
| MuRIL + RF | 0.63 |

Table 4: Results for the Tamil on test dataset.

## 6 Conclusion

In this paper the details regarding our submission in Offensive Language Identification shared task have been presented. We explored two text representation techniques: TF-IDF character n-grams and MuRIL and conclude that MuRIL works better for Malayalam while TF-IDF works better for other two languages. In future to mitigate the data imbalance problem text augmentation techniques like back translation could be applied to oversample the minority class. Also, other methods like CNN, RNN and fine tuning of Language models could be explored.


## Acknowledgments

We would like to thank the Offensive language identification task organizers for giving us a opportunity to work on a new task. We also like to acknowledge the IRNLP lab at DAIICT, Gandhinagar for their contribution.


[3]https://tfhub.dev/google/MuRIL/1

## References

Valerio Basile, Cristina Bosco, Elisabetta Fersini, Debora Nozza, Viviana Patti, Francisco Manuel Rangel Pardo, Paolo Rosso, and Manuela Sanguinetti. 2019. SemEval-2019 task 5: Multilingual detection of hate speech against immigrants and women in twitter. In *Proceedings of the 13th International Workshop on Semantic Evaluation*, pages 54–63, Minneapolis, Minnesota, USA. Association for Computational Linguistics.

Bharathi Raja Chakravarthi, Navya Jose, Shardul Suryawanshi, Elizabeth Sherly, and John Philip McCrae. 2020a. A sentiment analysis dataset for code-mixed Malayalam-English. In *Proceedings of the 1st Joint Workshop on Spoken Language Technologies for Under-resourced languages (SLTU) and Collaboration and Computing for Under-Resourced Languages (CCURL)*, pages 177–184, Marseille, France. European Language Resources association.

Bharathi Raja Chakravarthi, Vigneshwaran Muralidaran, Ruba Priyadharshini, and John Philip McCrae. 2020b. Corpus creation for sentiment analysis in code-mixed Tamil-English text. In *Proceedings of the 1st Joint Workshop on Spoken Language Technologies for Under-resourced languages (SLTU) and Collaboration and Computing for Under-Resourced Languages (CCURL)*, pages 202–210, Marseille, France. European Language Resources association.

Bharathi Raja Chakravarthi, Ruba Priyadharshini, Navya Jose, Anand Kumar M, Thomas Mandl, Prasanna Kumar Kumaresan, Rahul Ponnusamy, Hariharan V, Elizabeth Sherly, and John Philip McCrae. 2021. Findings of the shared task on Offensive Language Identification in Tamil, Malayalam, and Kannada. In *Proceedings of the First Workshop on Speech and Language Technologies for Dravidian Languages*. Association for Computational Linguistics.

Jacob Devlin, Ming-Wei Chang, Kenton Lee, and Kristina Toutanova. 2019. BERT: Pre-training of deep bidirectional transformers for language understanding. In *Proceedings of the 2019 Conference of the North American Chapter of the Association for Computational Linguistics: Human Language Technologies, Volume 1 (Long and Short Papers)*, pages 4171–4186, Minneapolis, Minnesota. Association for Computational Linguistics.

Adeep Hande, Ruba Priyadharshini, and Bharathi Raja Chakravarthi. 2020. KanCMD: Kannada CodeMixed dataset for sentiment analysis and offensive language detection. In *Proceedings of the Third Workshop on Computational Modeling of People's Opinions, Personality, and Emotion's in Social Media*, pages 54–63, Barcelona, Spain (Online). Association for Computational Linguistics.

Yinhan Liu, Myle Ott, Naman Goyal, Jingfei Du, Mandar Joshi, Danqi Chen, Omer Levy, Mike Lewis, Luke Zettlemoyer, and Veselin Stoyanov. 2019. Roberta: A robustly optimized bert pretraining approach. *arXiv preprint arXiv:1907.11692*.

Thomas Mandl, Sandip Modha, Anand Kumar M, and Bharathi Raja Chakravarthi. 2020. Overview of the hasoc track at fire 2020: Hate speech and offensive language identification in tamil, malayalam, hindi, english and german. In *Forum for Information Retrieval Evaluation*, FIRE 2020, page 29–32, New York, NY, USA. Association for Computing Machinery.

Thomas Mandl, Sandip Modha, Prasenjit Majumder, Daksh Patel, Mohana Dave, Chintak Mandlia, and Aditya Patel. 2019. Overview of the hasoc track at fire 2019: Hate speech and offensive content identification in indo-european languages. In *Proceedings of the 11th Forum for Information Retrieval Evaluation*, FIRE '19, page 14–17, New York, NY, USA. Association for Computing Machinery.

Matthew Peters, Mark Neumann, Mohit Iyyer, Matt Gardner, Christopher Clark, Kenton Lee, and Luke Zettlemoyer. 2018. Deep contextualized word representations. In *Proceedings of the 2018 Conference of the North American Chapter of the Association for Computational Linguistics: Human Language Technologies, Volume 1 (Long Papers)*, pages 2227–2237, New Orleans, Louisiana. Association for Computational Linguistics.

Marcos Zampieri, Shervin Malmasi, Preslav Nakov, Sara Rosenthal, Noura Farra, and Ritesh Kumar. 2019. SemEval-2019 task 6: Identifying and categorizing offensive language in social media (OffensEval). In *Proceedings of the 13th International Workshop on Semantic Evaluation*, pages 75–86, Minneapolis, Minnesota, USA. Association for Computational Linguistics.

Marcos Zampieri, Preslav Nakov, Sara Rosenthal, Pepa Atanasova, Georgi Karadzhov, Hamdy Mubarak, Leon Derczynski, Zeses Pitenis, and Çağrı Çöltekin. 2020. SemEval-2020 task 12: Multilingual offensive language identification in social media (OffensEval 2020). In *Proceedings of the Fourteenth Workshop on Semantic Evaluation*, pages 1425–1447, Barcelona (online). International Committee for Computational Linguistics.

# Hate-Alert@DravidianLangTech-EACL2021: Ensembling strategies for Transformer-based Offensive language Detection

**Debjoy Saha , Naman Paharia , Debajit Chakraborty,**
**Punyajoy Saha, Animesh Mukherjee**
Indian Institute of Technology, Kharagpur, India
sahadebjoy10@iitkgp.ac.in, namanpaharia.27@gmail.com, debajit15@iitkgp.ac.in
punyajoys@iitkgp.ac.in, animeshm@cse.iitkgp.ac.in

## Abstract

Social media often acts as breeding grounds for different forms of offensive content. For low resource languages like Tamil, the situation is more complex due to the poor performance of multilingual or language-specific models and lack of proper benchmark datasets. Based on this shared task "Offensive Language Identification in Dravidian Languages" at EACL 2021, we present an exhaustive exploration of different transformer models, We also provide a genetic algorithm technique for ensembling different models. Our ensembled models trained separately for each language secured the **first** position in Tamil, the **second** position in Kannada, and the **first** position in Malayalam sub-tasks. The models and codes are provided[1].

## 1 Introduction

Social media platforms have become a prominent way of communication, be it for acquiring information or promotion of business[2]. While we cannot deny the positives, there are some ill consequences of social media as well (Thavareesan and Mahesan, 2019, 2020a,b). Bad actors often use different social media platforms by posting tweets/comments that insult others by targeting their culture and beliefs. In social media, such posts are collectively known as offensive language (Chen et al., 2012). To reduce offensive content, different social media platforms like YouTube have laid down moderation policies and employ moderators for maintaining civility in their platforms. Recently, the moderators are finding it difficult to continue the moderation due to the ever-increasing volume of offensive data. Hence, platforms are looking toward automatic moderation systems. For instance, Facebook is proactively removing a large part of the harmful content from its platform, even before the users report them. There are concerns by different policy-makers that these automatic moderation systems may be erroneous[3]. Situation for countries like India is more complex, as courts often face dilemma while interpreting harmful content and social platforms like Facebook are often unable to take necessary actions[4]. Hence, more effort is required to detect and mitigate offensive language in the Indian social media.

Recently, different shared tasks like HASOC 2019[5] have been launched to understand hateful and offensive language in Indian context but it is limited to Hindi and English mostly. A subtask in HASOC 2020[6] (Chakravarthi et al., 2020c; Mandl et al., 2020) aimed to detect offensive posts in a code-mixed dataset (Jose et al., 2020; Priyadharshini et al., 2020). Extending that task further, the organisers of this shared task have put together a large dataset of 43919, 7772, 20010 posts in three Dravidian languages – Tamil, Kannada, Malayalam respectively, to further advance research on offensive posts in these languages (Chakravarthi and Muralidaran, 2021; Chakravarthi et al., 2021a; Suryawanshi and Chakravarthi, 2021). In this paper, we aim to build algorithmic systems that can detect offensive posts. Contributions of our paper are two-fold. First, we investigate how the current state-of-the-art multilingual language models perform on these languages. Second, we demonstrate how we can use ensembling techniques to improve our classification performance.

[1] `https://github.com/Debjoy10/Hate-Alert-DravidianLangTech`

[2] https://www.webfx.com

[3] https://www.forbes.com/

[4] https://www.npr.org

[5] `https://hasocfire.github.io/hasoc/2019/index.html`

[6] Dravidian-codemix-fire2020



*Proceedings of the First Workshop on Speech and Language Technologies for Dravidian Languages*, pages 270–276
April 20, 2021 

| Classifiers | Tamil | | | Kannada | | | Malayalam | | |
|---|---|---|---|---|---|---|---|---|---|
| | Train | Dev | Test | Train | Dev | Test | Train | Dev | Test |
| Not-offensive | 25425 | 3193 | 3190 | 3544 | 426 | 427 | 14153 | 1779 | 1765 |
| Offensive-untargeted | 2906 | 356 | 368 | 212 | 33 | 33 | 191 | 20 | 29 |
| Offensive-targeted-individual | 2343 | 307 | 315 | 487 | 66 | 75 | 239 | 24 | 27 |
| Offensive-targeted-group | 2557 | 295 | 288 | 329 | 45 | 44 | 140 | 13 | 23 |
| Offensive-targeted-other | 454 | 65 | 71 | 123 | 16 | 14 | - | - | - |
| Not-in-indented-language | 1454 | 172 | 160 | 1522 | 191 | 185 | 1287 | 163 | 157 |
| Total | 35139 | 4388 | 4392 | 6217 | 777 | 778 | 16010 | 1999 | 2001 |

Table 1: Dataset statistics for languages Tamil, Kannada and Malayalam for all splits Train, Dev and Test

## 2 Related Work

Offensive language has been studied in the research community for a long time, One of the earliest studies (Chen et al., 2012) tried to detect offensive users by using lexical syntactic features generated from their posts. Although, they provided an efficient framework for future research, their dataset was small for any conclusive evidence. Davidson et al. curated one of the largest dataset containing both offensive and hate speech. The authors found that one of the issues with their best performing models was that they could not distinguish between hate and offensive posts. In order to mitigate this, subsequent research (Pitsilis et al., 2018) tried to use deep learning to identify offensive language in English and found that recurrent neural networks (RNNs) are quite effective this task. Recently, the research community has begun to focus on offensive language detection in other low resourced languages like Danish (Sigurbergsson and Derczynski, 2019), Greek (Pitenis et al., 2020) and Turkish (Çöltekin, 2020). In the Indian context, the HASOC 2019 shared task (Mandl et al., 2019) was a significant effort in that direction, where the authors developed a dataset of hate and offensive posts in Hindi and English. The best model in this competition used an ensemble of multilingual transformers, fine-tuned on the given dataset (Mishra and Mishra, 2019). In Dravidian part of HASOC 2020, Renjit and Idicula used an ensemble of deep learning and simple neural networks to identify offensive posts in Manglish (Malayalam in roman font).

Transformer based language models are becoming quite popular in the past few years. Recently, different multilingual models like XLM-RoBERTa (Conneau et al., 2019), multilingual-BERT (Devlin et al., 2018), MuRIL [7] and Indic-BERT (Conneau et al., 2019) have been introduced to facilitate NLP research in different languages. Often in different machine learning pipeline, ensembling different classification outcomes helps in getting better performance (Alonso et al., 2020; Renjit and Idicula, 2020; Mishra and Mishra, 2019). Rather than selecting the models for the ensemble manually, genetic algorithms (GA) are used to optimise the weights of different classifiers, to improve the ensemble performance on the development set. GA-based ensembling techniques have previously been used in the hate speech domain for architecture and hyperparamter search Madukwe et al. (2020).

## 3 Dataset description

The shared task on Offensive Language Identification in Dravidian Languages-EACL 2021 (Chakravarthi et al., 2021b) is based on a post classification problem with an aim to moderate and minimise offensive content in social media. The objective of the shared task is to develop methodology and language models for code-mixed data in low-resource languages, as models trained on monolingual data fail to comprehend the semantic complexity of a code-mixed dataset.

**Dataset:** The Dravidian offensive code-mixed language dataset is available for Tamil (Chakravarthi et al., 2020b), Kannada (Hande et al., 2020) and Malayalam (Chakravarthi et al., 2020a). The data provided is scraped entirely from the YouTube comments of a multilingual community where code-mixing is a prevalent phenomenon. The dataset contains rows of text and the corresponding labels from the list not-offensive, offensive-untargeted, offensive-targeted-individual, offensive-targeted-group, offensive-targeted-other, or not-in-indented-language. Final evaluation score was calculated using weighted F1-score metric on a held-out test dataset.

We present the dataset statistics in Table 1. Please note that the Malayalam split of the dataset

[7] https://tfhub.dev/google/MuRIL/1

contained no instances of 'Offensive-targeted-other' label, so classification is done using 5 labels only, instead of the original six labels. In order to understand the amount of misspelt and code-mixed words, we compare with an existing pure language vocabulary available in the Dakshina dataset (Roark et al., 2020). We find the proportion of out-of-vocabulary (OOV) words (including code-mixed, English and misspelt words) in the dataset as 85.55%, 84.23% and 83.03% in Tamil, Malayalam and Kannada respectively.

## 4 Methodology

In this section, we discuss the different parts of the pipeline that we followed to detect offensive posts in this dataset.

### 4.1 Machine learning models

As a part of our initial experiments, we used several machine learning models to establish a baseline performance. We employed random forests, logistic regression and trained them with TF-IDF vectors. The best results were obtained on ExtraTrees Classifier (Geurts et al., 2006) with 0.70, 0.63 and 0.95 weighted F1-scores on Tamil, Kannada and Malayalam respectively. As we will notice further, these performances were lower than single transformer based model. Hence, the simple machine learning models were not used in the subsequent analysis.

### 4.2 Transformer models

One of the issues with simple machine learning models is the inability to learn the context of a word based on its neighbourhood. Recent transformer based architectures are capable of capturing this context, as established by their superior performance in different downstream tasks. For our purpose, we fine-tuned different state-of-the-art multilingual BERT models on the given datasets. This includes XLM-RoBERTa (Conneau et al., 2019), multilingual-BERT (Devlin et al., 2018)[8], Indic BERT and MuRIL[9]. We also pretrain XLM-Roberta-Base on the target dataset for 20 epochs using Masked Language Modeling, to capture the

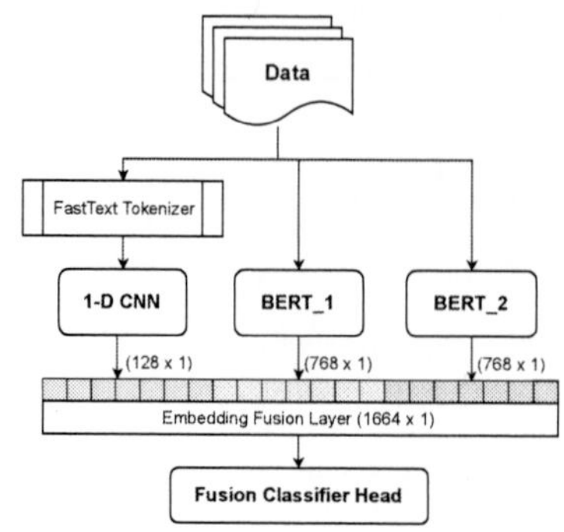


Figure 1: Our fusion model architecture for two BERT models. Note that $768 \times 1$ embedding sizes are used for the BERT-base models. Embeddings size of $1024 \times 1$ is used for BERT-large models.

semantics of the code-mixed corpus. This additional pretrained BERT model was also used for fine-tuning. In addition, all models were fine-tuned separately using unweighted and weighted cross-entropy loss functions (Mannor et al., 2005). For training, we use HuggingFace (Wolf et al., 2019) with PyTorch (Paszke et al., 2019). We use the Adam adaptive optimizer (Loshchilov and Hutter, 2019) with an initial learning rate of 1e-5. Training is stopped by early stopping if macro-F1 score of the development split of the dataset does not increase for 5 epochs.

### 4.3 Fusion models

Convolution neural networks are able to capture neighbourhood information more effectively. One of the previous state-of-the-art model to detect hate speech was CNN-GRU (Zhang et al., 2018), We propose a new BERT-CNN fusion classifier where we train a single classification head on the concatenated embeddings from different BERT and CNN models. BERT models were initialised with the fine-tuned weights in the former section and the weights were frozen. The number of BERT models in a single fusion model was kept flexible with maximum number of models fixed to three, due to memory limitation. For the CNN part, we use the 128-dim final layer embeddings from CNN models trained on skip-gram word vectors using FastText (Bojanowski et al., 2017)[10]. FastText vectors worked the best among other word embeddings like LASER (Artetxe and Schwenk, 2019). For the fusion classifier head, we use a feed-forward neural

[8]XLM-Roberta-Base, 270M parameters, trained on data from 100 languages; Multilingual-BERT-Base, 179M parameters, trained on data from the top 104 languages.

[9]Originally released by Google, MuRIL (Multilingual Representations for Indian Languages) is a BERT model pre-trained on code-mixed data from 17 Indian languages `https://huggingface.co/simran-kh/muril-cased-temp`

[10]`https://fasttext.cc/docs/en/unsupervised-tutorial.html`

| Classifiers | Tamil | | Kannada | | Malayalam | |
|---|---|---|---|---|---|---|
| | Dev | Test | Dev | Test | Dev | Test |
| XLMR-base (A) | 0.77 | 0.76 | 0.69 | 0.70 | 0.97 | 0.96 |
| XLMR-large | **0.78** | **0.77** | 0.69 | 0.71 | **0.97** | **0.97** |
| XLMR-C (B) | 0.76 | 0.76 | **0.70** | **0.73** | **0.97** | **0.97** |
| mBERT-base (C) | 0.73 | 0.72 | 0.69 | 0.70 | 0.97 | 0.96 |
| IndicBERT | 0.73 | 0.71 | 0.62 | 0.66 | 0.96 | 0.95 |
| MuRIL | 0.75 | 0.74 | 0.67 | 0.67 | 0.96 | 0.96 |
| DistilBERT | 0.74 | 0.74 | 0.68 | 0.69 | 0.96 | 0.95 |
| CNN | 0.71 | 0.70 | 0.60 | 0.61 | 0.95 | 0.95 |
| CNN + A + C | 0.78 | 0.76 | 0.71 | 0.70 | **0.97** | **0.97** |
| CNN + A + B | **0.78** | **0.77** | 0.71 | 0.71 | **0.97** | **0.97** |
| CNN + B + C | 0.77 | 0.76 | **0.71** | **0.72** | **0.97** | **0.97** |

Table 2: Weighted F1-score comparison for transformer, CNN and fusion models on Dev and Test splits (XLMR-C refers to the custom-pretrained XLM-Roberta-Base Classifier).

| ModelSets | Tamil | | Kannada | | Malayalam | |
|---|---|---|---|---|---|---|
| | Dev | Test | Dev | Test | Dev | Test |
| Trans | 0.80 | 0.78 | 0.74 | 0.73 | 0.98 | 0.97 |
| F-models | 0.79 | 0.77 | 0.73 | 0.73 | 0.98 | 0.97 |
| R-models | 0.79 | 0.78 | 0.75 | 0.74 | 0.97 | 0.97 |
| **Overall** | **0.80** | **0.78** | **0.75** | **0.74** | **0.98** | **0.97** |

Table 3: Weighted-F1 score comparison for GA-weighted ensemble for transformers category, Fusion models(F-models) and Random seed models(R-models)

network having four layers with batch normalization (Ioffe and Szegedy, 2015) and dropout (Srivastava et al., 2014) on the final layer. The predictions were generated from a softmax layer of dimension equal to the number of classes. We present the details of the pipeline in Figure 1.

### 4.4 Ensembling strategies

Ensemble of different models often turn out better predictors than using a single classifier. Standard prediction averaging ensembles will not perform well, since some models might be weak predictors in the mix of different models. One of the strategies to reduce the influence of weak models is using weights for different models based on their performance. Genetic algorithm (GA) based techniques (Madukwe et al., 2020) are one of the popular ways to set the weights of different models in an ensemble. Our approach is similar to that introduced in Zhou et al. (2001), except that instead of selecting the models with the highest weights for the final ensemble, we directly use the weights to compute the weighted average ensemble.

Another issue with neural networks is the performance is dependent on the initial random seeds. With pretrained models like BERT, most of the weights are fixed only in the final layer (classification head). Past research (McCoy et al., 2020) has shown that even the initialisation of this final layer can affect the final performance by large margins. Hence, we take 10 different random seeds to train the models and then pass all the models to the GA pipeline. We perform this operation for two of the best models in Table 2.

## 5 Results and conclusion

We observe that among the individual transformer models, the best performance is obtained using XLM-RoBERTa-large (XLMR-large) in the Tamil dataset and Custom XLM-RoBERTa-base (XLMR-C) in the Kannada dataset. For Malayalam dataset, both the former models perform similarly. The higher performance of XLM-RoBERTa (Artetxe and Schwenk, 2019) models can be attributed to the fact that they are pretrained using a parallel corpus (same corpus in different languages). Further pretraining with our dataset helps in further improvement of the performance in the Kannada dataset. We did not use the XLM-R large model further due to limited GPU space. Next, we note the performance of the fusion models, which perform almost similarly across different combinations.

When we use different random seeds, the performance of multilingual BERT models varied around 2-3% across different languages. For XLM-RoBERTa models the variation was more (around 15-20%). Table 3 shows the ensemble performance of different categories of models and all the models combined. GA-optimised weighted ensembling improves the final model scores by a 1-2% across datasets of different languages which finally helped us to rank higher in the leader board.

In this shared task, we evaluated different transformer based architectures and introduced different ensembling strategies. We found that XLM-RoBERTa models usually perform better than other transformer models, although their performance is highly variable across different random seeds. GA based ensembling helps us in further improving the models. Our immediate next step will be to investigate the reason behind lower performance of IndicBERT and MuRIL which are specifically trained for Indian context.

## References


Pedro Alonso, Rajkumar Saini, and György Kovács. 2020. Hate speech detection using transformer ensembles on the hasoc dataset. In *International Conference on Speech and Computer*, pages 13–21. Springer.

Mikel Artetxe and Holger Schwenk. 2019. Massively multilingual sentence embeddings for zero-shot cross-lingual transfer and beyond. *Transactions of the Association for Computational Linguistics*, 7:597–610.

Piotr Bojanowski, Edouard Grave, Armand Joulin, and Tomas Mikolov. 2017. Enriching word vectors with subword information. *Transactions of the Association for Computational Linguistics*, 5:135–146.

Bharathi Raja Chakravarthi, Navya Jose, Shardul Suryawanshi, Elizabeth Sherly, and John Philip McCrae. 2020a. A sentiment analysis dataset for code-mixed Malayalam-English. In *Proceedings of the 1st Joint Workshop on Spoken Language Technologies for Under-resourced languages (SLTU) and Collaboration and Computing for Under-Resourced Languages (CCURL)*, pages 177–184, Marseille, France. European Language Resources association.

Bharathi Raja Chakravarthi and Vigneshwaran Muralidaran. 2021. Findings of the shared task on Hope Speech Detection for Equality, Diversity, and Inclusion. In *Proceedings of the First Workshop on Language Technology for Equality, Diversity and Inclusion*. Association for Computational Linguistics.

Bharathi Raja Chakravarthi, Vigneshwaran Muralidaran, Ruba Priyadharshini, and John Philip McCrae. 2020b. Corpus creation for sentiment analysis in code-mixed Tamil-English text. In *Proceedings of the 1st Joint Workshop on Spoken Language Technologies for Under-resourced languages (SLTU) and Collaboration and Computing for Under-Resourced Languages (CCURL)*, pages 202–210, Marseille, France. European Language Resources association.

Bharathi Raja Chakravarthi, Ruba Priyadharshini, Shubhanker Banerjee, Richard Saldhana, John Philip McCrae, Anand Kumar M, Parameswari Krishnamurthy, and Melvin Johnson. 2021a. Findings of the shared task on Machine Translation in Dravidian languages. In *Proceedings of the First Workshop on Speech and Language Technologies for Dravidian Languages*. Association for Computational Linguistics.

Bharathi Raja Chakravarthi, Ruba Priyadharshini, Navya Jose, Anand Kumar M, Thomas Mandl, Prasanna Kumar Kumaresan, Rahul Ponnusamy, Hariharan V, Elizabeth Sherly, and John Philip McCrae. 2021b. Findings of the shared task on Offensive Language Identification in Tamil, Malayalam, and Kannada. In *Proceedings of the First Workshop on Speech and Language Technologies for Dravidian Languages*. Association for Computational Linguistics.

Bharathi Raja Chakravarthi, Ruba Priyadharshini, Vigneshwaran Muralidaran, Shardul Suryawanshi, Navya Jose, Elizabeth Sherly, and John P. McCrae. 2020c. Overview of the Track on Sentiment Analysis for Dravidian Languages in Code-Mixed Text. In *Forum for Information Retrieval Evaluation*, FIRE 2020, page 21–24, New York, NY, USA. Association for Computing Machinery.

Y. Chen, Y. Zhou, S. Zhu, and H. Xu. 2012. Detecting offensive language in social media to protect adolescent online safety. In *2012 International Conference on Privacy, Security, Risk and Trust and 2012 International Confernece on Social Computing*, pages 71–80.

Ying Chen, Yilu Zhou, Sencun Zhu, and Heng Xu. 2012. Detecting offensive language in social media to protect adolescent online safety. In *2012 International Conference on Privacy, Security, Risk and Trust and 2012 International Confernece on Social Computing*, pages 71–80. IEEE.

Çağrı Çöltekin. 2020. A corpus of turkish offensive language on social media. In *Proceedings of the 12th Language Resources and Evaluation Conference*, pages 6174–6184.

Alexis Conneau, Kartikay Khandelwal, Naman Goyal, Vishrav Chaudhary, Guillaume Wenzek, Francisco Guzmán, Edouard Grave, Myle Ott, Luke Zettlemoyer, and Veselin Stoyanov. 2019. Unsupervised cross-lingual representation learning at scale. *arXiv preprint arXiv:1911.02116*.

Thomas Davidson, Dana Warmsley, Michael Macy, and Ingmar Weber. 2017. Automated hate speech detection and the problem of offensive language. In *Proceedings of the International AAAI Conference on Web and Social Media*, volume 11.

Jacob Devlin, Ming-Wei Chang, Kenton Lee, and Kristina Toutanova. 2018. Bert: Pre-training of deep bidirectional transformers for language understanding. *arXiv preprint arXiv:1810.04805*.

Pierre Geurts, Damien Ernst, and Louis Wehenkel. 2006. Extremely randomized trees. *Mach. Learn.*, 63(1):3–42.

Adeep Hande, Ruba Priyadharshini, and Bharathi Raja Chakravarthi. 2020. KanCMD: Kannada CodeMixed dataset for sentiment analysis and offensive language detection. In *Proceedings of the Third Workshop on Computational Modeling of People's Opinions, Personality, and Emotion's in Social Media*, pages 54–63, Barcelona, Spain (Online). Association for Computational Linguistics.

Sergey Ioffe and Christian Szegedy. 2015. Batch normalization: Accelerating deep network training by reducing internal covariate shift. In *International conference on machine learning*, pages 448–456. PMLR.

Navya Jose, Bharathi Raja Chakravarthi, Shardul Suryawanshi, Elizabeth Sherly, and John P. McCrae. 2020. A Survey of Current Datasets for Code-Switching Research. In *2020 6th International Conference on Advanced Computing and Communication Systems (ICACCS)*, pages 136–141.

Ilya Loshchilov and Frank Hutter. 2019. Decoupled weight decay regularization.

K. J. Madukwe, X. Gao, and B. Xue. 2020. A ga-based approach to fine-tuning bert for hate speech detection. In *2020 IEEE Symposium Series on Computational Intelligence (SSCI)*, pages 2821–2828.

Thomas Mandl, Sandip Modha, Anand Kumar M, and Bharathi Raja Chakravarthi. 2020. Overview of the HASOC Track at FIRE 2020: Hate Speech and Offensive Language Identification in Tamil, Malayalam, Hindi, English and German. In *Forum for Information Retrieval Evaluation*, FIRE 2020, page 29–32, New York, NY, USA. Association for Computing Machinery.

Thomas Mandl, Sandip Modha, Prasenjit Majumder, Daksh Patel, Mohana Dave, Chintak Mandlia, and Aditya Patel. 2019. Overview of the hasoc track at fire 2019: Hate speech and offensive content identification in indo-european languages. In *Proceedings of the 11th forum for information retrieval evaluation*, pages 14–17.

Shie Mannor, Dori Peleg, and Reuven Rubinstein. 2005. The cross entropy method for classification. In *Proceedings of the 22nd International Conference on Machine Learning*, ICML '05, page 561–568, New York, NY, USA. Association for Computing Machinery.

R Thomas McCoy, Junghyun Min, and Tal Linzen. 2020. Berts of a feather do not generalize together: Large variability in generalization across models with similar test set performance. In *Proceedings of the Third BlackboxNLP Workshop on Analyzing and Interpreting Neural Networks for NLP*, pages 217–227.

Shubhanshu Mishra and Sudhanshu Mishra. 2019. 3idiots at hasoc 2019: Fine-tuning transformer neural networks for hate speech identification in indo-european languages. In *FIRE (Working Notes)*, pages 208–213.

Adam Paszke, Sam Gross, Francisco Massa, Adam Lerer, James Bradbury, Gregory Chanan, Trevor Killeen, Zeming Lin, Natalia Gimelshein, Luca Antiga, et al. 2019. Pytorch: An imperative style, high-performance deep learning library. *arXiv preprint arXiv:1912.01703*.

Zeses Pitenis, Marcos Zampieri, and Tharindu Ranasinghe. 2020. Offensive language identification in greek. *arXiv preprint arXiv:2003.07459*.

Georgios K Pitsilis, Heri Ramampiaro, and Helge Langseth. 2018. Detecting offensive language in tweets using deep learning. *arXiv preprint arXiv:1801.04433*.

Ruba Priyadharshini, Bharathi Raja Chakravarthi, Mani Vegupatti, and John P. McCrae. 2020. Named Entity Recognition for Code-Mixed Indian Corpus using Meta Embedding. In *2020 6th International Conference on Advanced Computing and Communication Systems (ICACCS)*, pages 68–72.

Sara Renjit and Sumam Mary Idicula. 2020. Cusatnlp@hasoc-dravidian-codemix-fire2020:identifying offensive language from manglishtweets.

Brian Roark, Lawrence Wolf-Sonkin, Christo Kirov, Sabrina J. Mielke, Cibu Johny, Isin Demirsahin, and Keith Hall. 2020. Processing south asian languages written in the latin script: the dakshina dataset.

Gudbjartur Ingi Sigurbergsson and Leon Derczynski. 2019. Offensive language and hate speech detection for danish. *arXiv preprint arXiv:1908.04531*.

Nitish Srivastava, Geoffrey Hinton, Alex Krizhevsky, Ilya Sutskever, and Ruslan Salakhutdinov. 2014. Dropout: A simple way to prevent neural networks from overfitting. *Journal of Machine Learning Research*, 15(56):1929–1958.

Shardul Suryawanshi and Bharathi Raja Chakravarthi. 2021. Findings of the shared task on Troll Meme Classification in Tamil. In *Proceedings of the First Workshop on Speech and Language Technologies for Dravidian Languages*. Association for Computational Linguistics.

Sajeetha Thavareesan and Sinnathamby Mahesan. 2019. Sentiment Analysis in Tamil Texts: A Study on Machine Learning Techniques and Feature Representation. In *2019 14th Conference on Industrial and Information Systems (ICIIS)*, pages 320–325.

Sajeetha Thavareesan and Sinnathamby Mahesan. 2020a. Sentiment Lexicon Expansion using Word2vec and fastText for Sentiment Prediction in Tamil texts. In *2020 Moratuwa Engineering Research Conference (MERCon)*, pages 272–276.

Sajeetha Thavareesan and Sinnathamby Mahesan. 2020b. Word embedding-based Part of Speech tagging in Tamil texts. In *2020 IEEE 15th International Conference on Industrial and Information Systems (ICIIS)*, pages 478–482.

Thomas Wolf, Lysandre Debut, Victor Sanh, Julien Chaumond, Clement Delangue, Anthony Moi, Pierric Cistac, Tim Rault, Rémi Louf, Morgan Funtowicz, et al. 2019. Huggingface's transformers: State-of-the-art natural language processing. *arXiv preprint arXiv:1910.03771*.

Ziqi Zhang, D. Robinson, and Jonathan Tepper. 2018. Detecting hate speech on twitter using a convolution-gru based deep neural network.

Zhi-Hua Zhou, Jian-Xin Wu, Yuan Jiang, and Shi-Fu Chen. 2001. Genetic algorithm based selective neural network ensemble. In *Proceedings of the 17th International Joint Conference on Artificial Intelligence - Volume 2*, IJCAI'01, page 797–802, San Francisco, CA, USA. Morgan Kaufmann Publishers Inc.

# TrollMeta@DravidianLangTech-EACL2021: Meme classification using deep learning

**Manoj Balaji J**
BITS, Pilani
manojbalaji1@gmail.com

**Chinmaya HS**
Cambridge Institute of Technology, Bengaluru
chinmayasbhat4@gmail.com

## Abstract

Memes act as a medium to carry one's feelings, cultural ideas, or practices by means of symbols, imitations, or simply images. Whenever social media is involved, hurting the feelings of others and abusing others are always a problem. Here we are proposing a system, that classifies the memes into Troll or Non-Troll memes . The system implements resnet-50, a deep residual neural network architecture.

## 1 Introduction

Social media are the interactive platforms that are in and around the daily life of most of the people (Thavareesan and Mahesan, 2019, 2020a,b). Memes has become integral part of daily life and they play a crucial role in sociopolitical, cultural and behaviour of the people (a P K et al., 2020). Memes are not only media for conveying information or disrupting the socio-political situation but, they serve as the main source of sharing humour and laughter. Internet humour can create a logical bonding between people and can act as a common platform for like minded people (Laineste and Voolaid, 2017). Memes with colorful/even much dull background powered by splashy texts can create amazing sense of humour (a P K et al., 2020; Laineste and Voolaid, 2017).

On the other hand, meme trolling is considered as online activism (a P K et al., 2020), creating awareness and new kind of marketing too. Troll is a person who starts the flame of insulting/ upsetting the feelings of another person on internet. This can be done by posting messages in the online community such as social media or even in private chats. Trolling has caused in one's personal and professional life even (Bishop, 2013). The content in any mainstream media are closely monitored but, for social media there are no such monitoring systems. Internet has opened the road to post anything and everything on social platforms. Offensive content memes are spreading the emotion of fear, misguided phobia and they are misleading the population as they spend most of their time on the internet(Suryawanshi et al., 2020a).

Considering the psychological, socio-political and social impacts of memes, especially memes we are proposing a deep learning based meme classifier that can differentiate the trolling one's from non-trolling counterparts.

## 2 Related Works

Suryawanshi et al. (2020a) in their work stated the importance of meme classification/filtering. Their work included the dataset of memes that contains 2000+ annotated images with captions. Their work showed a path towards importance of monitoring social media about the postings from regional languages.

Bishop (2013) discussed the application of criminal procedure over the internet bully's and insulting one's feelings over the internet. Memes not only contain text data, but the visual appearance should also be considered, Smitha et al. (2018) proposed a technique to extract text data from images and analysing the emotions on the image and later classifying them into one of the 6 predefined classes, and they concluded that the work helps to understand the behaviour of the community and information for any further data analysis (Smitha et al., 2018).

Suryawanshi et al. (2020b) observed that the offensive contents are not only in the form of text but, they can also be offensive in visual aspect. Therefore they proposed a technique to classify this multimodel memes, which uses a stacked LSTM + VGG16 model.

## 3 Dataset

The dataset used here, 'Tamil Troll Memes' dataset, which was made available by Suryawanshi et al. (2020a). The dataset contained total of 2,969 im-



*Proceedings of the First Workshop on Speech and Language Technologies for Dravidian Languages*, pages 277–280
April 20, 2021 ©2021 Association for Computational Linguistics

ages of memes, most which contained text embedded images.

Figure 1: Sample memes from TamilMemes dataset with Latin transcripted or Tamil text

## 4 Methodology

Residual networks are playing a crucial role in image classification. They find a way to overcome the gradient loss, which are a major problem in deep neural networks. Residual networks, which uses residue from the previous layers to prevent loss of gradients due to depth of the network (Suryawanshi and Chakravarthi, 2021).

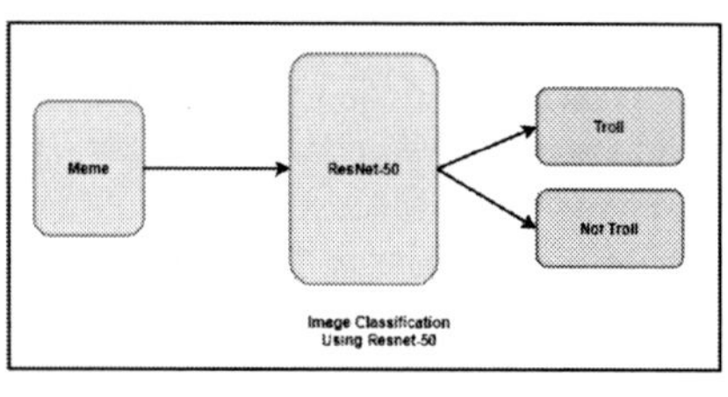


Figure 2: Proposed system architecture (ResNet 50) that distinguishes troll from not troll Tamil memes

Here we are using a deep residual neural network based on resnet architecture. The architecture has 50 layers, with which the network can grasp the features from different parts and levels of the image. The images are resized to 64x64, with all three color channels, are fed into the algorithm, which then passed to sub-sequent layers of the neural network to finally give the output. Softmax activation in the last layer gives the probability value for each class and class with max probability is selected as output. We used fastai library, with which we are able to train our model much faster(He et al., 2015). The framework provides easy to access layered API architecture, which has the APIs to access most of the deep learning algorithms. Pause and train architecture(Howard and Gugger, 2020) helps to improve the control over model training as one can have a look at loss, accuracy and other parameters. Manual early stopping mechanism helps to monitor the model improvement easily(Howard and Gugger, 2020) which is integrated as a part of fastai library, which employs cycle training that allows to monitor each cycle and freeze the weights if required.

## 5 Results and Evaluation

The work was performed to classify the memes in to trolling and non-trolling. The resnet-50 model which was trained on the dataset containing 2349 images belonging to two different classes, for 50 epochs.

The variation of loss and accuracy for image classification are shown in the figure below.

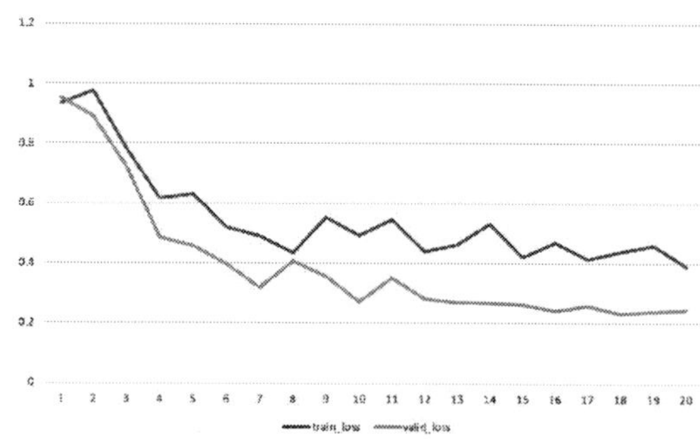


Figure 3: Graph showing variation of loss during the course of training. (Blue line shows decrease in training loss and orange line shows the variation of validation loss)

To analyze the results of the model, a confusion matrix was constructed, and the weighted f1 is calculated. The model trained with Binary Cross Entropy loss function for 10 cycles with imagenet weights and performed with the following results,

The values for validation are more than that of training, even though it looks like overfitting the values remained same for the K-fold validation also, therefore the model is not overfitting over a set of data but it suffers lack of data, which we think can be improved with accumulation of data from different sources.

|  | precision | recall | F1-score | support |
|---|---|---|---|---|
| Train | 0.87 | 0.87 | 0.87 | 1840 |
| Val | 0.92 | 0.92 | 0.92 | 460 |
| Test | 0.45 | 0.41 | 0.48 |  |

Table 1: Evaluation values for training, validation and test (weighted avg. values)

However the values in the test are much lesser compared to that of training and validation, which can be result of model overfitting.

## 6 Limitations

During the course of work we faced many challenges and observed some limitations. It is hard to identify sarcasm. Most of the times text and the expression in the image contradict each other and create a wave of sarcasm. An example of such meme is where a character is associated with "Ahaan". This is highly contextual as this was part of a Tamil movie comedy scene.

The text/caption in the image is in Tamil but written in Italic, and mixture of Tamil and English will also pose a huge problem while building the model.

## 7 Conclusion

Memes poses as a medium which are powerful enough to disrupt politics, induce and spread humour. In the mean time they are capable of causing considerable harm to socio-political and personal health of individuals via trolls. Our work, meme classification using deep learning sheds light towards filtering the memes to trolling and non-trolling ones with training weighted f1 of 0.87, validation weighted f1 of 0.92 and overall testing accuracy of 0.48. There's work needed to be done as a part of building model with better generalization.

The work helped us to understand the impacts and effects of the memes in day today life of the people and how they evolved to be an integral part of the internet and social media.

## 8 Future Work

The work carried out here proposes the method to classify memes based only on images, but the future work is intended to consider both text and image from the memes. In simple words, it includes, extracting text from images, emotion detection using some NLP technique, combining the results with image classification model to form a hybrid model that can classify the emotions more efficiently.

## References


Jonathan Bishop. 2013. The effect of de-individuation of the internet troller on criminal procedure implementation: An interview with a hater. *International Journal of Cyber Criminology*, 7:28.

Kaiming He, Xiangyu Zhang, Shaoqing Ren, and Jian Sun. 2015. Deep residual learning for image recognition.

Jeremy Howard and Sylvain Gugger. 2020. Fastai: A layered api for deep learning. *Information*, 11(2):108.

L. Laineste and Piret Voolaid. 2017. Laughing across borders: Intertextuality of internet memes. *The European Journal of Humour Research*, 4:26–49.

Abdul Rasheed a P K, Carmel Maria, and Anju Michael. 2020. Social media and meme culture: A study on the impact of internet memes in reference with 'kudathai murder case'.

E. S. Smitha, S. Sendhilkumar, and G. S. Mahalaksmi. 2018. Meme classification using textual and visual features. In *Computational Vision and Bio Inspired Computing*, pages 1015–1031, Cham. Springer International Publishing.

Shardul Suryawanshi and Bharathi Raja Chakravarthi. 2021. Findings of the shared task on Troll Meme Classification in Tamil. In *Proceedings of the First Workshop on Speech and Language Technologies for Dravidian Languages*. Association for Computational Linguistics.

Shardul Suryawanshi, Bharathi Raja Chakravarthi, Mihael Arcan, and Paul Buitelaar. 2020a. Multimodal meme dataset (MultiOFF) for identifying offensive content in image and text. In *Proceedings of the Second Workshop on Trolling, Aggression and Cyberbullying*, pages 32–41, Marseille, France. European Language Resources Association (ELRA).

Shardul Suryawanshi, Bharathi Raja Chakravarthi, Pranav Verma, Mihael Arcan, John Philip McCrae, and Paul Buitelaar. 2020b. A dataset for troll classification of TamilMemes. In *Proceedings of the WILDRE5– 5th Workshop on Indian Language Data: Resources and Evaluation*, pages 7–13, Marseille, France. European Language Resources Association (ELRA).

Sajeetha Thavareesan and Sinnathamby Mahesan. 2019. Sentiment Analysis in Tamil Texts: A Study on Machine Learning Techniques and Feature Representation. In *2019 14th Conference on Industrial and Information Systems (ICIIS)*, pages 320–325.

Sajeetha Thavareesan and Sinnathamby Mahesan. 2020a. Sentiment Lexicon Expansion using Word2vec and fastText for Sentiment Prediction in Tamil texts. In *2020 Moratuwa Engineering Research Conference (MERCon)*, pages 272–276.

Sajeetha Thavareesan and Sinnathamby Mahesan. 2020b. Word embedding-based Part of Speech tagging in Tamil texts. In *2020 IEEE 15th International Conference on Industrial and Information Systems (ICIIS)*, pages 478–482.

# Maoqin @ DravidianLangTech-EACL2021: The Application of Transformer-Based Model

**Maoqin Yang**
School of Information Science and Engineering
Yunnan University, Yunnan, P.R. China
1695157605@qq.com

## Abstract

This paper describes the result of team-Maoqin at DravidianLangTech-EACL2021. The provided task consists of three languages (Tamil, Malayalam, and Kannada), I only participate in one of the language task-Malayalam. The goal of this task is to identify offensive language content of the code-mixed dataset of comments/posts in Dravidian Languages (Tamil-English, Malayalam-English, and Kannada-English) collected from social media. This is a classification task at the comment/post level. Given a Youtube comment, systems have to classify it into Not-offensive, Offensive-untargeted, Offensive-targeted-individual, Offensive-targeted-group, Offensive-targeted-other, or Not-in-indented-language. I use the transformer-based language model with BiGRU-Attention to complete this task. To prove the validity of the model, I also use some other neural network models for comparison. And finally, the team ranks 5th in this task with a weighted average F1 score of 0.93 on the private leader board.

## 1 Introduction

Offensive language refers to direct or indirect use of verbal abuse, slander, contempt, ridicule, and other means to infringe or damage the dignity, spiritual world, and mental health of others. It will seriously affect the mental state of others, disrupt work, the life and learning order of others, and seriously pollute the public opinion environment of the entire network(Schmidt and Wiegand, 2017).

Due to the development of the Internet and the popularity of anonymous comments, many offensive languages have spread on the Internet and caused trouble to relevant personnel (Thavareesan and Mahesan, 2019, 2020a,b). Relevant organizations should take measures to prevent this from happening. It is unrealistic to judge whether online sentences are completely offended by humans. Therefore, mechanical methods must be used to distinguish whether the language is offensive. The task is to directly test whether the system can distinguish offensive language in Dravidian languages. Dravidian languages are a group of languages spoken by 220 million people, predominantly in southern India and northern Sri Lanka, but also in other areas of South Asia. The Dravidian languages were first recorded in Tamili script inscribed on cave walls in Tamil Nadu's Madurai and Tirunelveli districts in the 6th century BCE. The Dravidian languages are closely related languages the are under-resourced (Chakravarthi, 2020).

Existing deep learning and pre-training models have achieved good results on other tasks(Zampieri et al., 2019), so I use the deep learning method to deal with the related task. According to the latest related research progress, the transformer-based language model has become my preferred model. Because the pre-trained and fine-tuned transformers-based models have shown excellent performance in many NLP problems, such as sentiment classification and automatic extraction of text summaries. So I choose ALBERT(Lan et al., 2019) as my basic model in this task. To get a more effective and higher accuracy model, BiGRU combined with attention. To prove the effectiveness of this model, I have also done comparative experiments with other neural networks. In this task, my model is an effective way to perform well. To obtain as much effective information as possible from the limited data, I also use the 5-fold cross-validation method. my model achieves the desired result.

The rest of this article is structured as follows. Section 2 introduces related work. Model and data preparation are described in Section 3. Experiments and evaluation are described in Section 4. Section 5 describes the results of my work. The conclusions and future work are drawn in Section 6.



*Proceedings of the First Workshop on Speech and Language Technologies for Dravidian Languages*, pages 281–286
April 20, 2021 ©2021 Association for Computational Linguistics

## 2 Related Work

There are many competitions about offensive language detection(such as HASOC (Chakravarthi et al., 2020c; Mandl et al., 2020) and TRAC (Kumar et al., 2018)), and many corresponding methods have been produced. People often tend to abstract this task into a text classification task (Howard and Ruder, 2018).

Text classification is called extracting features from original text data and predicting the category of text data based on these features. In the past few decades, many models for text classification have been proposed (Qian, 2020).

From the 1960s to the 2010s, text classification models based on shallow learning dominated. Shallow learning means statistical-based models such as Naive Bayes (NB), K Nearest Neighbors (KNN)(Cover and Hart, 1967) and Support Vector Machines (SVM). Compared with earlier rule-based methods, this method has obvious advantages in accuracy and stability. However, these methods still require functional design, which is time-consuming and expensive. In addition, they usually ignore the natural order structure or context information in the text data, which makes learning the semantic information of words difficult. Since the 2010s, text classification has gradually changed from a shallow learning model to a deep learning model. Compared with methods based on shallow learning, deep learning methods avoid the manual design of rules and functions and automatically provide semantically meaningful representations for text mining. Therefore, most of the text classification research work is based on DNN(Yu et al., 2013), which is a data-driven method with high computational complexity. Few studies have focused on shallow learning models to solve the limitations of computation and data.

The shallow learning model speeds up the text classification speed, improves the accuracy, and expands the application range of shallow learning.

The shallow learning method is a type of machine learning. It learns from data, which is a predefined function that is important to the performance of the predicted value. However, element engineering is an arduous and giant job. Before training the classifier, we need to collect knowledge or experience to extract features from the original text. The shallow learning method trains the initial classifier based on various text features extracted from the original text. For small data sets, under the limitation of computational complexity, shallow learning models generally show better performance than deep learning models. Therefore, some researchers have studied the design of shallow models in specific areas of data replacement.

Deep learning consists of multiple hidden layers in a neural network(Aroyehun and Gelbukh, 2018), has higher complexity, and can be trained on unstructured data. The deep learning architecture can directly learn feature representations from the input without excessive manual intervention and prior knowledge. However, deep learning technology is a data-driven method that usually requires a lot of data to achieve high performance. And the self-attention-based model can bring some inter-word interpretability to DNN, but the comparison with the shallow model does not explain why and how it works.

| Set | Total number |
|---|---|
| train | 16010 |
| development | 1999 |
| test | 2001 |

Table 1: The number of sentences in each set.

## 3 Methodology and Data

An overall framework and processing pipeline of my solution are shown in Figure 1.

In my job, I use the ALBERT model as my base model and take BiGRU-Attention behind it. My model is shown in Figure 2.

### 3.1 Data Preparation

This is a comment/post level classification task. Given a Youtube comment (Chakravarthi et al., 2020b,a, 2021; Chakravarthi and Muralidaran, 2021), the system has to classify it into one of the five categories mentioned in the *Abstract* section. For this task, the available sentences including 16010 training sentences, 1999 development sentences, and 2001 testing sentences. The label distribution is very uneven(Not-offensive label accounts 88.4%. The label with the second largest number is not-malayalam, which accounts for only 0.08% of the total. And there are relatively fewer labels in other categories.)The number of sentences for each domain is listed in Table 1.

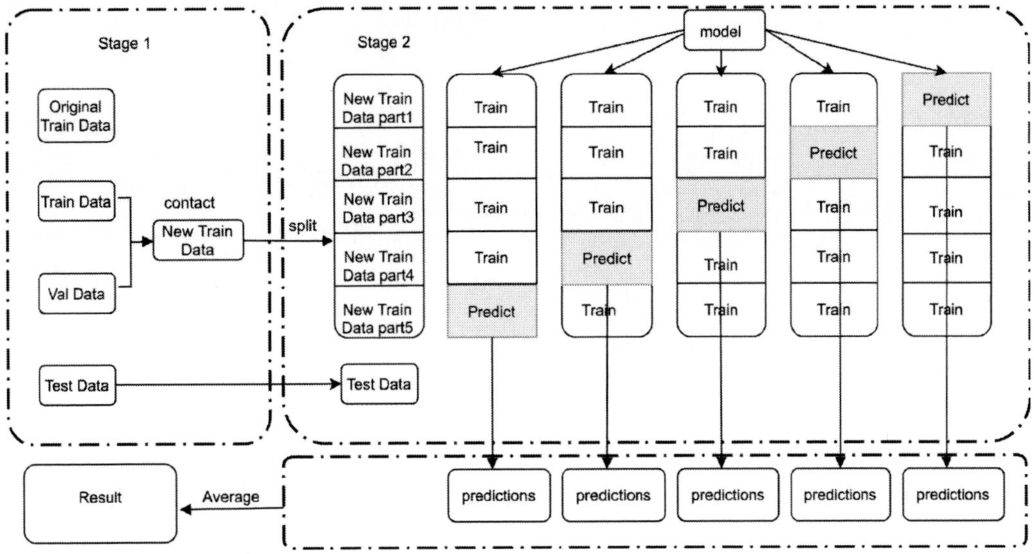


Figure 1: An overall framework

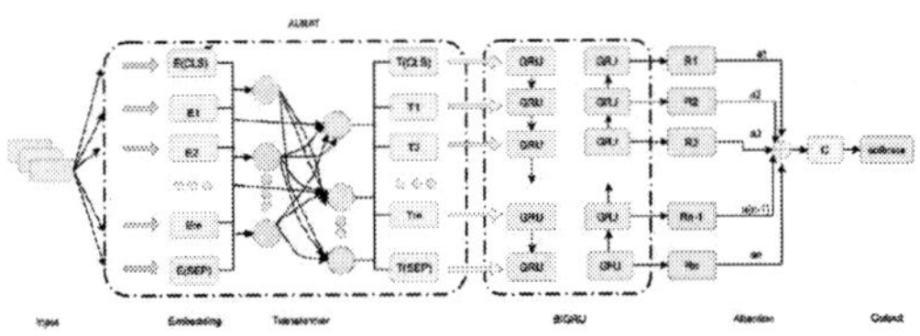

Figure 2: The architecture of the model, where the $E[CLS]$ and $E[SEP]$ are added at the beginning and end of each instance respectively, which can separate different sentences. The format is as follows: $[CLS]$+sentence+$[SEP]$.

### 3.2 ALBERT

The ALBERT model belongs to transformer-based language models. The ALBERT model is improved on the basis of Bidirectional Encoder Representations for Transformers(BERT)(Devlin et al., 2018) model. It has designed a parameter reduction method to reduce memory consumption by changing the result of the original embedding parameter $P$ (the product of the vocabulary size $V$ and the hidden layer size $H$).

$$V * H = P \rightarrow V * E + E * H = P \quad (1)$$

$E$ represents the size of the low-dimensional embedding space. In BERT, $E = H$. While in ALBERT, $H >> E$, so the number of parameters will be greatly reduced. At the same time, the self-supervised loss is used to focus on the internal coherence in the construction of sentences. The ALBERT model implements three embedding layers: word embedding, position embedding, and segment embedding. The token embedding layer predicts each word as a fixed-size vector. Position embedding is used to retain position information, use a vector to randomly initialize each position, add model training, and finally obtain an embedding containing position information. Segment embedding helps BERT distinguish between paired input sequences.

### 3.3 BiGRU-Attention

The BiGRU-Attention model(Cover and Hart, 1967) is divided into three parts: text vector input layer, hidden layer, and output layer. Among them, the hidden layer consists of three layers: the BiGRU layer, the attention layer, and the Dense layer (fully connected layer). I set the output of the ALBERT model as the input. After receiving the input, it uses the BiGRU neural network layer to extract features of the deep-level information of the text firstly. Secondly, it uses the attention layer to assign corresponding weights to the deep-level information of the extracted text. Finally, the text feature information with different weights is put into the softmax function layer for classification. The structure of the BiGRU-Attention model is shown in Figure 3.

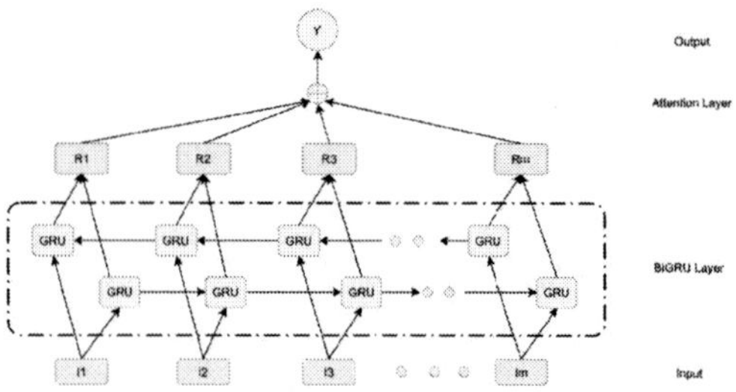


Figure 3: The structure of the BiGRU-Attention model. The $I1, I2...Im$ represent the output of the ALBERT layer and the $R1, R2...Rm$ represent the output of the BiGRU layer and will be input to the Attention layer.

| **Model** | ALBERT(Base) |
|---|---|
| **train step** | 2501 |
| **learning rate** | 2e-5 |
| **batch size** | 32 |
| **epoch** | 5 |

Table 2: The parameter configuration of ALBERT.

## 4 Experiment

In this task, I use the ALBERT model to pre-train the task. For the ALBERT model, the main hyper-parameters I pay attention to are the training step size, batch size and learning rate. The parameters of my model are shown in Table 2.

I have obtained good performance using the ALBERT-BASE.[1] model. Considering that BiGRU-Attention can capture contextual information well and extract text information features more accurately(Radford et al., 2018), I add it after ALBERT. I use the development data set to verify the performance of the models. The standard of judgment is a weighted F1-score, and this standard is the judgment standard used for my task. Table3 lists the results of various models described previously. The best performance is in bold. My model gets the best performance of 0.93. As shown in the table my model can greatly improve the performance and my overall approach achieved 5th place on the final leader board.

## 5 Results

The output of the classification result is shown in Figure 4. We can see that the label of $Offensive - Targeted - Insult - Other$, $Offensive - Targeted - Insult - Individual$, and $Offensive - Targeted - Insult - Group$ is zero. $Not - Offensive$ labels account for the majority, accounting for 91.15% of the total number of labels. The $Not - Malayalam$ labels account for the second most significant 7.5% of the total. Offensive-Untargeted labels are the least, only about 1%. This may be due to data imbalance ($Not - Offensive$ labels in the training set account for about 88% of the total) resulting in only three categories being identified.

[1]https://huggingface.co/albert-base-v2

| **Model** | **F1** |
|---|---|
| ALBERT(Base) | 0.919 |
| BERT(Base) | 0.912 |
| RoBERTa(Base) | 0.920 |
| BERT(Base)+BiGRU-Attention | 0.928 |
| **Mine(ALBERT+BiGRU-Attention)** | **0.930** |

Table 3: Results of comparative experiments.

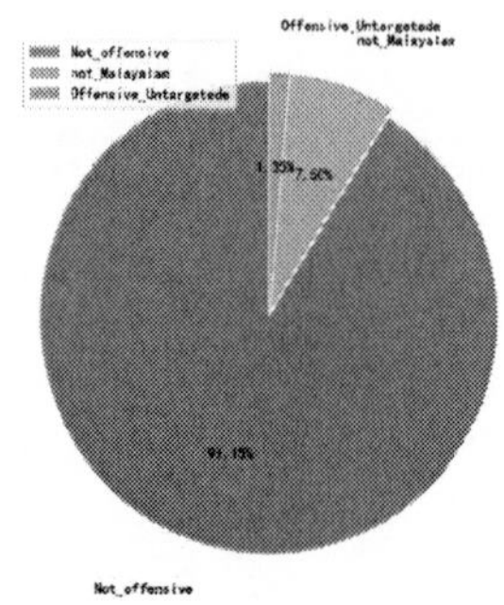

Figure 4: The classification result

## 6 Conclusion and Future Work

In this paper, I present my result on Offensive Language Identification in Dravidian Languages-EACL 2021 which includes three tasks of different languages. For this task, I regard it as a multiple classification task, I use the BiGRU-Attention based on the ALBERT model to complete, and my model works very well. I also summarized the possible reasons for classifying only three types of labels. At the same time, I also use some other neural networks for comparative experiments to prove that my model can obtain excellent performance. The result shows that my model ranks 5th in the Malayalam task.

Due to the continuous development of the definition of offensive information on the Internet, it is difficult to accurately describe the nature of this information only from the perspective of data mining, which makes it impossible to model this information effectively. In the future, I will use methods based on multidisciplinary discovery to guide model learning. These models are more likely to use limited data to learn more effective models. At the same time, I will also consider whether I can use other transfer learning models to perform better on multi-classification tasks.

## References


S. T. Aroyehun and A. Gelbukh. 2018. Aggression detection in social media: Using deep neural networks, data augmentation, and pseudo labeling. *Proceedings of the First Workshop on Trolling, Aggression and Cyberbullying (TRAC-2018)*, pages 90–97.

Bharathi Raja Chakravarthi. 2020. *Leveraging orthographic information to improve machine translation of under-resourced languages*. Ph.D. thesis, NUI Galway.

Bharathi Raja Chakravarthi, Navya Jose, Shardul Suryawanshi, Elizabeth Sherly, and John Philip McCrae. 2020a. A sentiment analysis dataset for code-mixed Malayalam-English. In *Proceedings of the 1st Joint Workshop on Spoken Language Technologies for Under-resourced languages (SLTU) and Collaboration and Computing for Under-Resourced Languages (CCURL)*, pages 177–184, Marseille, France. European Language Resources association.

Bharathi Raja Chakravarthi and Vigneshwaran Muralidaran. 2021. Findings of the shared task on Hope Speech Detection for Equality, Diversity, and Inclusion. In *Proceedings of the First Workshop on Language Technology for Equality, Diversity and Inclusion*. Association for Computational Linguistics.

Bharathi Raja Chakravarthi, Vigneshwaran Muralidaran, Ruba Priyadharshini, and John Philip McCrae. 2020b. Corpus creation for sentiment analysis in code-mixed Tamil-English text. In *Proceedings of the 1st Joint Workshop on Spoken Language Technologies for Under-resourced languages (SLTU) and Collaboration and Computing for Under-Resourced Languages (CCURL)*, pages 202–210, Marseille, France. European Language Resources association.

Bharathi Raja Chakravarthi, Ruba Priyadharshini, Navya Jose, Anand Kumar M, Thomas Mandl, Prasanna Kumar Kumaresan, Rahul Ponnusamy, Hariharan V, Elizabeth Sherly, and John Philip McCrae. 2021. Findings of the shared task on Offensive Language Identification in Tamil, Malayalam, and Kannada. In *Proceedings of the First Workshop on Speech and Language Technologies for Dravidian Languages*. Association for Computational Linguistics.

Bharathi Raja Chakravarthi, Ruba Priyadharshini, Vigneshwaran Muralidaran, Shardul Suryawanshi, Navya Jose, Elizabeth Sherly, and John P. McCrae. 2020c. Overview of the Track on Sentiment Analysis for Dravidian Languages in Code-Mixed Text. In *Forum for Information Retrieval Evaluation*, FIRE 2020, page 21–24, New York, NY, USA. Association for Computing Machinery.

Cover and Hart. 1967. Nearest neighbor pattern classification.

J. Devlin, M.-W. Chang, K. Lee, and K. Toutanova. 2018. Bert: Pre-training of deep bidirectional transformers for language understanding. arXiv:1810.04805.

Jeremy Howard and Sebastian Ruder. 2018. Universal language model fine-tuning for text classification. arXiv:1801.06146.

R. Kumar, A. K. Ojha, S. Malmasi, and M. Zampieri. 2018. Benchmarking aggression identification in social media. *Proceedings of the First Workshop on Trolling, Aggression and Cyberbullying (TRAC-2018)*, pages 1–11.

Zhenzhong Lan, Mingda Chen, Sebastian Goodman, Kevin Gimpel, and Piyush Sharma. 2019. Albert: A lite bert for self-supervised learning of language representations. arXiv:1909.11942. Version 6.

Thomas Mandl, Sandip Modha, Anand Kumar M, and Bharathi Raja Chakravarthi. 2020. Overview of the HASOC Track at FIRE 2020: Hate Speech and Offensive Language Identification in Tamil, Malayalam, Hindi, English and German. In *Forum for Information Retrieval Evaluation*, FIRE 2020, page 29–32, New York, NY, USA. Association for Computing Machinery.

Qu Qian. 2020. A review of the latest text classification 2020-the development of text classification from shallow to deep from 1961 to 2020.

Alec Radford, Karthik Narasimhan, Tim Salimans, and Ilya Sutskever. 2018. Improving language understanding with unsupervised learning. *Technical report, OpenAI.*

A. Schmidt and M. Wiegand. 2017. A survey on hate speech detection using natural language processing. *Proceedings of the Fifth International workshop on natural language processing for social media*, (1):1–10.

Sajeetha Thavareesan and Sinnathamby Mahesan. 2019. Sentiment Analysis in Tamil Texts: A Study on Machine Learning Techniques and Feature Representation. In *2019 14th Conference on Industrial and Information Systems (ICIIS)*, pages 320–325.

Sajeetha Thavareesan and Sinnathamby Mahesan. 2020a. Sentiment Lexicon Expansion using Word2vec and fastText for Sentiment Prediction in Tamil texts. In *2020 Moratuwa Engineering Research Conference (MERCon)*, pages 272–276.

Sajeetha Thavareesan and Sinnathamby Mahesan. 2020b. Word embedding-based Part of Speech tagging in Tamil texts. In *2020 IEEE 15th International Conference on Industrial and Information Systems (ICIIS)*, pages 478–482.

Dong Yu, Michael L. Seltzer, Jinyu Li, Jui-Ting Huang, and Frank Seide. 2013. Feature learning in deep neural networks - studies on speech recognition tasks. arXiv:1301.3605.

M. Zampieri, S. Malmasi, P. Nakov, and S. Rosenthal. 2019. Predicting the type and target of offensive posts in social media. arXiv:1902.09666.

# Simon @ DravidianLangTech-EACL2021: Meme Classification for Tamil with BERT

**Qinyu Que**
School of Information Science and Engineering,
Yunnan University, Yunnan, P.R. China
1309487642@qq.com

**Abstract**

In this paper, we introduce the system for the task of meme classification for Tamil, submitted by our team. In today's society, social media has become an important platform for people to communicate. We use social media to share information about ourselves and express our views on things. It has gradually developed a unique form of emotional expression on social media – meme. The meme is an expression that is often ironic. This also gives the meme a unique sense of humor. But it's not just positive content on social media. There's also a lot of offensive content. Meme's unique expression makes it often used by some users to post offensive content. Therefore, it is very urgent to detect the offensive content of the meme. Our team uses the natural language processing method to classify the offensive content of the meme. Our team combines the BERT model with the CNN to improve the model's ability to collect statement information. Finally, the F1-score of our team in the official test set is 0.49, and our method ranks 5th.

## 1 Introduction

Everything has two sides, and information technology is no exception. On the one hand, the rapid development of information technology makes it easy for people to communicate and discuss on social platforms (Thavareesan and Mahesan, 2019, 2020a,b). On the other hand, the rapid development of information technology has also led to the proliferation of offensive content on the Internet (Chakravarthi et al., 2021; Chakravarthi and Muralidaran, 2021; Chakravarthi et al., 2020a; Mandl et al., 2020). Meme makes people like it because of its unique sense of humor. This also allows meme to spread rapidly on social media. But these memes don't just contain positive content. Some memes also contain offensive content. With the rapid growth of offensive content, hateful content, and offensive content on the Internet, the detection of offensive content on Meme has become more and more important. The meme is special. Different people have different perceptions of its content. Some memes are only accessible to a certain group of people, and others don't get the true meaning of these memes. This also makes people unclear about the offensive content in Meme, and also increases the difficulty of detecting the offensive content in Meme. The meme usually consists of pictures and text. Our team uses a natural language processing method to detect offensive content in the meme. We do the classification for Memes in Tamil language.

Tamil is a Dravidian language spoken by the Tamil people of South Asia as their first language (Chakravarthi et al., 2018). For over 2600 years, Tamil literature has been recorded. Tamil has the oldest non-Sanskritic Indian literature in any Indian language. Tamil was the first Indian classical language to be listed, and it is one of the world's oldest classical languages. There are 12 vowels, 18 consonants, and one special character, the aytam, in the present Tamil script. The vowels and consonants merge to form 216 compound characters, for a total of 247 (12 + 18 + 1 + (12 x 18) characters (Chakravarthi et al., 2020b). In Tamil, suffixes are used to denote noun class, number, and case, as well as verb tense and other grammatical categories. In comparison to Sanskrit, which is the standard for most Aryan languages, Tamil's standard metalinguistic terminology and scholarly vocabulary is Tamil. Tamil is under-resourced languages (Chakravarthi, 2020).

## 2 Related Work

Many researchers have made efforts to detect offensive language. As people communicate more and



*Proceedings of the First Workshop on Speech and Language Technologies for Dravidian Languages*, pages 287–290
April 20, 2021 

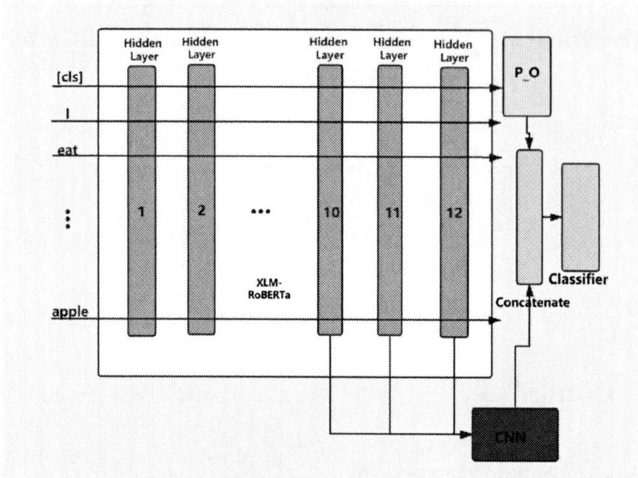


Figure 1: The description of the model used for this task

more online, the detection of hateful content and offensive language has become necessary. Content published in traditional media such as newspapers and television is heavily censored. But people are often free to express their opinions on the new social media platforms. Troll memes disrupt the user's communication experience on these platforms. Nascimento et al. (Reddy and Vasu, 2002) believe that people can communicate without face to face in social networks. So people don't know each other's point of view and background. People abuse anonymous nature of the internet by using offensive language. This greatly accelerates the spread of offensive language. Nascimento et al. classified the Brazilian grape language text into hate languages. They used data sets from the Brazilian 55chan Imageboard. They used three classifiers for classification, with the best F1-score being 0.955. The meme is a regional language, and the expression in communication is that only some people can know the specific meaning of a certain meme. This characteristic of meme makes its offensive language have a specific target group. There has been an increase in Islamophobic comments on social media platforms. It ostracized Muslims in the community. B. Vidgen' team built a model that could distinguish between Islamophobia (Ross et al., 2017). This model can divide content into strongly Islamophobic content, weakly Islamophobic content, and non-Islamophobic content. The targeted groups are not only Muslims, but also immigrant groups and Jewish groups (Vidgen and Yasseri, 2020; Bilewicz et al., 2013; Finkelstein et al., 2018; Djuric et al., 2015). In recent years, developments in the field of detecting offensive content have contributed to many problems (Bohra et al., 2018; Jurgens et al., 2019; Caselli et al., 2020; Fortuna et al., 2019).

| Label | Train set | Test set |
|---|---|---|
| troll | 1282 | 395 |
| Not_troll | 1018 | 272 |

Table 1: Class distribution for TamilMemes dataset

## 3 Methodology and Corpus

### 3.1 Data Description

Competition organizers provides dataset with text and image as features(Suryawanshi et al., 2020; Suryawanshi and Chakravarthi, 2021). Because our team uses natural language processing to identify offensive content. We used the text portion of the dataset. The text portion of the dataset contains two types of tags, one troll, and the other Not_troll. The tag troll represents a meme that has provocative or offensive content. The Not_troll tag indicates that the meme has no offensive or provocative content. The detailed contents of the dataset are shown in Table 1.

### 3.2 Model Description

We reviewed the results of recent competitions and found that participants who used pre-trained language models scored highly on many of the tasks. For example, in the Hate Speech and Offensive Content Identification in Indo-European

| Hyper-parameter | Value |
|---|---|
| dropout | 0.5 |
| learning rate | 1e-5 |
| epoch | 10 |
| per gpu train batch size | 32 |
| gradient accumulation steps | 8 |

Table 2: The hyper-parameters settings used to train the XLM-Roberta on the TamilMemes dataset

Languages(HASOC[1]) competition, many contestants using the BERT model rank high. And in the competition, many players adopted the fine-tuned BERT(Devlin et al., 2019) model method to complete the task. In our model, we use XLM-Roberta(Conneau et al., 2020) as our pre-processing model. The XLM-Roberta model is a multilingual processing model. It can handle text in 100 languages. Compared with the BERT model, the XLM-Roberta model greatly increases the amount of data to be trained. XLM-Roberta has no prediction for the next sentence. Our team fine-tuned the superstructure of the XLM-Roberta model to enhance the semantic collection capability of XLM-Roberta. The specific model is shown in Figure 1. In the first step, we get the pooler output of XLM-Roberta (P_O). For classification tasks, the output of XLM-Roberta(pooler output) is obtained by its last layer hidden state of the first token of the sequence (CLS token) further processed by a linear layer and a Tanh activation function. Second, we combine the output of the last three hidden layers of XLM-Roberta with CNN (Simonyan and Zisserman, 2014). Finally, we concatenate the CNN output with the pooler output of XLM-Roberta and put it into the classifier.

## 4 Experiment and Results

Our team uses the stratified 5-fold cross-validation to divide the training sets provided by the competition organizer into new training sets and validation sets. Our pre-training model is from XLM Roberta - Base [2]. We put the hyper-parameters used in the experiment in Table 2. Finally, Our method rankings 5th in this task, and the F1-score is 0.49.

## 5 Conclusion

This paper describes the model and results used by the Simon team in the meme classification task. This model is a fine-tuned XLM-Roberta model, which improves the ability of the model to obtain sentence information. The datasets used for this competition are slightly unbalanced. This also affects the final result of the model. Our team will continue to improve the model to achieve better results. The code is available online.[3]

[1] https://competitions.codalab.org/competitions/26027

[2] https://huggingface.co/xlm-roberta-base

[3] https://https://github.com/queqinyu/EACL

## References


Michal Bilewicz, Miko?Aj Winiewski, Miros?Aw Kofta, and Adrian Wójcik. 2013. Harmful ideas, the structure and consequences of anti-semitic beliefs in poland. *Political Psychology*, 34(6):821–839.

Aditya Bohra, Deepanshu Vijay, Vinay Singh, Syed S. Akhtar, and Manish Shrivastava. 2018. A dataset of hindi-english code-mixed social media text for hate speech detection. In *Proceedings of the Second Workshop on Computational Modeling of People's Opinions, Personality, and Emotions in Social Media*.

Tommaso Caselli, Valerio Basile, Jelena Mitrovi, Inga Kartoziya, and Michael Granitzer. 2020. I feel offended, don't be abusive! implicit/explicit messages in offensive and abusive language. In *Proceedings of the Twelfth International Conference on Language Resources and Evaluation (LREC 2020)*.

Bharathi Raja Chakravarthi. 2020. *Leveraging orthographic information to improve machine translation of under-resourced languages*. Ph.D. thesis, NUI Galway.

Bharathi Raja Chakravarthi, Mihael Arcan, and John P. McCrae. 2018. Improving wordnets for under-resourced languages using machine translation. In *Proceedings of the 9th Global Wordnet Conference*, pages 77–86, Nanyang Technological University (NTU), Singapore. Global Wordnet Association.

Bharathi Raja Chakravarthi and Vigneshwaran Muralidaran. 2021. Findings of the shared task on Hope Speech Detection for Equality, Diversity, and Inclusion. In *Proceedings of the First Workshop on Language Technology for Equality, Diversity and Inclusion*. Association for Computational Linguistics.

Bharathi Raja Chakravarthi, Ruba Priyadharshini, Navya Jose, Anand Kumar M, Thomas Mandl, Prasanna Kumar Kumaresan, Rahul Ponnusamy, Hariharan V, Elizabeth Sherly, and John Philip McCrae. 2021. Findings of the shared task on Offensive Language Identification in Tamil, Malayalam, and Kannada. In *Proceedings of the First Workshop on Speech and Language Technologies for Dravidian Languages*. Association for Computational Linguistics.

Bharathi Raja Chakravarthi, Ruba Priyadharshini, Vigneshwaran Muralidaran, Shardul Suryawanshi, Navya Jose, Elizabeth Sherly, and John P. McCrae. 2020a. Overview of the Track on Sentiment Analysis for Dravidian Languages in Code-Mixed Text. In *Forum for Information Retrieval Evaluation*, FIRE 2020, page 21–24, New York, NY, USA. Association for Computing Machinery.

Bharathi Raja Chakravarthi, Navaneethan Rajasekaran, Mihael Arcan, Kevin McGuinness, Noel E. O'Connor, and John P. McCrae. 2020b. Bilingual lexicon induction across orthographically-distinct under-resourced Dravidian languages. In *Proceedings of the 7th Workshop on NLP for Similar Languages, Varieties and Dialects*, pages 57–69, Barcelona, Spain (Online). International Committee on Computational Linguistics (ICCL).

Alexis Conneau, Kartikay Khandelwal, Naman Goyal, Vishrav Chaudhary, and Veselin Stoyanov. 2020. Unsupervised cross-lingual representation learning at scale. In *Proceedings of the 58th Annual Meeting of the Association for Computational Linguistics*.

Jacob Devlin, Ming-Wei Chang, Kenton Lee, and Kristina Toutanova. 2019. BERT: Pre-training of deep bidirectional transformers for language understanding. In *Proceedings of the 2019 Conference of the North American Chapter of the Association for Computational Linguistics: Human Language Technologies, Volume 1 (Long and Short Papers)*, pages 4171–4186, Minneapolis, Minnesota. Association for Computational Linguistics.

Nemanja Djuric, Zhou Jing, Robin Morris, Mihajlo Grbovic, and Narayan Bhamidipati. 2015. Hate speech detection with comment embeddings. In *the 24th International Conference*.

Joel Finkelstein, Savvas Zannettou, Barry Bradlyn, and Jeremy Blackburn. 2018. A quantitative approach to understanding online antisemitism.

Paula Fortuna, Joo Rocha Da Silva, Juan Soler-Company, Leo Wanner, and Sérgio Nunes. 2019. A hierarchically-labeled portuguese hate speech dataset. In *Proceedings of the Third Workshop on Abusive Language Online*.

David Jurgens, Eshwar Chandrasekharan, and Libby Hemphill. 2019. A just and comprehensive strategy for using nlp to address online abuse.

Thomas Mandl, Sandip Modha, Anand Kumar M, and Bharathi Raja Chakravarthi. 2020. Overview of the HASOC Track at FIRE 2020: Hate Speech and Offensive Language Identification in Tamil, Malayalam, Hindi, English and German. In *Forum for Information Retrieval Evaluation*, FIRE 2020, page 29–32, New York, NY, USA. Association for Computing Machinery.

Reddy and Vasu. 2002. Perverts and sodomites: homophobia as hate speech in africa. *Southern African Linguistics Applied Language Studies*, 20(3):163–175.

Björn Ross, Michael Rist, Guillermo Carbonell, Benjamin Cabrera, Nils Kurowsky, and Michael Wojatzki. 2017. Measuring the reliability of hate speech annotations: The case of the european refugee crisis.

Karen Simonyan and Andrew Zisserman. 2014. Very deep convolutional networks for large-scale image recognition. *Computer Science*.

Shardul Suryawanshi and Bharathi Raja Chakravarthi. 2021. Findings of the shared task on Troll Meme Classification in Tamil. In *Proceedings of the First Workshop on Speech and Language Technologies for Dravidian Languages*. Association for Computational Linguistics.

Shardul Suryawanshi, Bharathi Raja Chakravarthi, Pranav Verma, Mihael Arcan, John Philip McCrae, and Paul Buitelaar. 2020. A dataset for troll classification of TamilMemes. In *Proceedings of the WILDRE5– 5th Workshop on Indian Language Data: Resources and Evaluation*, pages 7–13, Marseille, France. European Language Resources Association (ELRA).

Sajeetha Thavareesan and Sinnathamby Mahesan. 2019. Sentiment Analysis in Tamil Texts: A Study on Machine Learning Techniques and Feature Representation. In *2019 14th Conference on Industrial and Information Systems (ICIIS)*, pages 320–325.

Sajeetha Thavareesan and Sinnathamby Mahesan. 2020a. Sentiment Lexicon Expansion using Word2vec and fastText for Sentiment Prediction in Tamil texts. In *2020 Moratuwa Engineering Research Conference (MERCon)*, pages 272–276.

Sajeetha Thavareesan and Sinnathamby Mahesan. 2020b. Word embedding-based Part of Speech tagging in Tamil texts. In *2020 IEEE 15th International Conference on Industrial and Information Systems (ICIIS)*, pages 478–482.

Bertie Vidgen and Taha Yasseri. 2020. Detecting weak and strong islamophobic hate speech on social media. *Journal of E-Government*, 17(1):66–78.

# Bitions@DravidianLangTech-EACL2021: Ensemble of Multilingual Language Models with Pseudo Labeling for Offence Detection in Dravidian Languages

**Debapriya Tula***, **Prathyush Potluri***, **Shreyas MS**,
**Sumanth Doddapaneni**, **Pranjal Sahu**, **Rohan Sukumaran**, **Parth Patwa**
IIIT Sri City, India
debapriya.t17@iiits.in

## Abstract

With the advent of social media, we have seen a proliferation of data and public discourse. Unfortunately, this includes offensive content as well. The problem is exacerbated due to the sheer number of languages spoken in these platforms and the multiple other modalities used for sharing offensive content (images, gifs, videos and more). In this paper, we propose a multilingual ensemble based model that can identify offensive content targeted against an individual (or group) in low resource Dravidian language. Our model is able to handle code-mixed data as well as instances where the script used is mixed (for instance, Tamil and Latin). Our solution **ranked number one** for Malayalam dataset and ranked 4th and 5th for Tamil and Kannada, respectively. The code is available at `github.com/Debapriya-Tula/EACL2021-DravidianTask-Bitions`.

## 1 Introduction

Online communication has helped break a lot of barriers in terms of time, distance and ease of communication. The number of active Internet users has grown rapidly over the last few years. The ease of sharing content and the lack of automatic systems for monitoring them, has led to a great increase in the amount of offensive and hate speech in the open internet. Hate speech is often targeted towards a group of people or individuals hurting their identity, beliefs or sentiments. Owing to the ease of access and lack of monitoring, Individuals tend to misuse this freedom to hurl abuses and cause disharmony in the community. It is therefore important to address this issue. Social media is easily accessible by a larger domain of people and the scale of open internet restricts us from manually monitoring social media content, at scale. This calls for the need of automatic systems for identification of hate/offensive speech.

The style of data on open internet also plays a major role in the understanding of data. The language structure is often missing and people tend to make use of words from different languages, ultimately resulting in code-switched data (Barman et al., 2014; Patwa et al., 2020). The problem is exacerbated as people use words from different written scripts, mixing both latin script and native script (*Devanagri, Dravidian, Mandarin etc*) from the language. A unified model which can understand a multitude of these scripts can play a major role in understanding the discourse in open internet data and conducive to creating a safer virtual environment.

Majority of the research work in NLP has been predominantly in English (Bender, 2019; Hu et al., 2020). And the multilingual models currently available are trained on a multitude of languages making it hard to fine-tune for downstream tasks like Sentiment analysis, Text classification etc. on low-resource languages. Our work addresses this issue by employing pseudo labelling and ensemble based techniques.

The importance of the issue and the challenges posed, calls for novel ideas for offensive language detection. Owing to this many workshops (Waseem et al., 2017; Akiwowo et al., 2020) and shared tasks (Kumar et al., 2018, 2020; Chakravarthi et al., 2021), have been conducted to address the problem at hand.

In this paper, we present our system for the task of offensive language identification in Dravidian languages. We make use of multilingual BERT based models with pseudo labelling and

*Equal contribution.



*Proceedings of the First Workshop on Speech and Language Technologies for Dravidian Languages*, pages 291–299
April 20, 2021 ©2021 Association for Computational Linguistics

ensemble strategies to achieve 1st rank out out 30 participants on Malayalam data. Our models perform equally well on the Kannada (5th rank) and Tamil (4th rank) dataset as well.

## 2 Related Works

Ever since social media platforms started gaining popularity, the problem of detecting offensive language has existed. Many researchers have worked to develop different ways that automate the process to tackle the issue. Authors in (Fortuna and Nunes, 2018) have discussed the intricacy hate speech concept and its conclusive potential for societal impact, specifically in online communities and digital media platforms.

Detection of profanity and hate speech in tweets and comments has been a part of many shared tasks(Kumar et al., 2018, 2020; Chakravarthi et al., 2021; Patwa et al., 2021). The SemEval 2019 task 9 (Zampieri and Others, 2019b), aimed at identification of offensive and non-offensive comments in English tweets. It used the OLID dataset (Zampieri and Others, 2019a) which has 14000 tweets annotated using a hierarchical annotation model. OffensEval 2020 (Zampieri et al., 2020) was a profanity identification task presented in SemEval 2020. It was conducted for 5 languages (multilingual) language, namely English, Arabic, Danish, Greek, and Turkish.

Many researchers have tried to solve hate speech, offense and aggression detection using Deep Learning techniques like CNNs, LSTMs, etc. (Aroyehun and Gelbukh, 2018; Risch and Krestel, 2018; Mahata et al., 2019). Some researchers have also tried using Machine Learning algorithms for the same (Safi Samghabadi et al., 2018; Datta et al., 2020). Recently Language models like BERT (Devlin et al., 2018) have become very popular for this problem (Gupta et al., 2021; Safi Samghabadi et al., 2020; Risch and Krestel, 2020; Wiedemann et al., 2020).

There have been attempts at developing models for hate speech detection in English, Hindi-German (Mandl et al., 2019) and Italian (Corazza et al., 2020) have emerged, but not many works for Dravidian code-mix languages. Nevertheless, attempts are underway to accelerate advancements in NLP in Dravidian languages (Chakravarthi et al., 2021, 2020c), have emerged. Methods like LSTMs (Mahata et al., 2020), Transformer (Dowlagar and Mamidi, 2021) etc. have been previously tried to detect offense in dravidian languages.

## 3 Data

There are three datasets for the three languages that we consider: Kannada (Hande et al., 2020), Malayalam (Chakravarthi et al., 2020a), and Tamil (Chakravarthi et al., 2020b). The six class labels in the Kannada and Tamil data are:

- Not Offensive - (NO)
- Not Native - (NN)
- Offensive Individual - (OI)
- Offensive Group - (OG)
- Offensive Untargeted - (OU)
- Offensive Other - (OO)

All classes mentioned above except 'Offensive Other' are the classes in the Malayalam data set. The distribution of the data is described in Table 1 for all three classes. In total there are 5936 samples for Kannada, 11695 samples for Malayalam and 34898 samples for Tamil.

The majority class in all three languages is the 'Not Offensive' class. This accounts for 56.97% of the samples in Kannada, 88.77% of the samples in Malayalam and 72.25% of the samples in Tamil data.

Another important fact to note is the skewness in the data. The dataset is extremely skewed toward the non-offensive class and in order to overcome this challenge we make use of class weighting by penalising more for the under-represented classes. This is discussed in detail in the next section.

Table 2 shows a list of the most frequent words for each language for each class. We often see the same native word written in different ways in English. The word "your" in Kannada is written as ನಿನ್/ನಿನ್ನ/ ನಿಮ್/ ನಿಮ್ಮ/nin/ninna (singular) and nim/nimma (plural). From manual analysis it is clear that there are a lot of stop-words in the most frequent words.

Number of samples in training data

| Class | Kannada | Malayalam | Tamil |
|---|---|---|---|
| NO | 3382 | 10382 | 25215 |
| NN | 1407 | 882 | 1447 |
| OI | 486 | 171 | 2338 |
| OG | 327 | 106 | 2550 |
| OU | 212 | 154 | 2894 |
| OO | 122 | - | 454 |
| Total | 5936 | 11695 | 34898 |

Table 1: Data distribution of the three datasets.

## 4 Methods

This section describes our solution for the Offensive Language Detection Task. It is divided into 4 sub-sections viz, Models, Class-weighting, Pseudo-labelling and Ensemble. A look at the data provided for the task calls for a multi-lingual approach, as it has both Latin script and text in the native language.

### 4.1 Models

We leverage two transformer-based models viz, DistilmBERT (multilingual) and Indic-BERT, and a non-transformer based model, ULMFiT (Howard and Ruder, 2018) for the task.

#### 4.1.1 DistilmBERT

DistilBERT (Sanh et al., 2019) has the same general architecture as BERT (Devlin et al., 2018), with the number of layers reduced by a factor of 2. A triple loss combines language modelling, distillation and cosine-distance losses to leverage the inductive biases of large models learnt during pre-training. With a 40% reduction in the size of the BERT, the DistilBERT retains 97% of its language understanding capabilities while being 60% faster. Inspired by the efficacy of the performance of DistilBERT[1], we use a distilled version of the BERT base multilingual model (mBERT-base) called the *DistilBERT-base-multilingual-model*. We use the cased model as the data is code-mixed with English (the only case sensitive language in the corpora). The model was pre-trained on the concatenation of Wikipedia in 104 different languages including Tamil, Malayalam and Kannada. DistilmBERT is twice as fast as mBERT-base based on the comparisons done by HuggingFace[1].

#### 4.1.2 ULMFiT

The ULMFiT (Universal Language Model Fine-tuning for Text Classification) (Howard and Ruder, 2018) is an effective transfer learning method which achieves the state of the art results on various NLP tasks with the help of novel techniques like a) gradual unfreezing: beginning from the final most significant layer, one layer per epoch is unfrozen and is fine-tuned; b) discriminative fine-tuning: higher learning rate is used for the final layer and is lowered one by one to the first layer; c) slanted triangular learning rates: scheduler based learning rate approach which gradually propels the learning rate until it reaches it's maximum and then gradually reduces it. The ULMFiT is based on a 3-layer encoder and decoder based architecture of AWD-LSTM or the averaged stochastic gradient descent weight dropped LSTM. Training the ULMFiT can be broken down into three major tasks: Firstly, pre-training a language model on a Wikipedia-based corpus. Then, following an unsupervised approach, fine-tuning the language model to the target task and finally in a supervised approach, adding new classifier layers and fine-tuning the classifier to the actual task.

#### 4.1.3 IndicBERT

IndicBERT (Kakwani et al., 2020) is an ALBERT based model trained exclusively on Indian languages. The model is pre-trained on 11 Indian languages and English using the standard Masked Language Modelling (MLM) objective. The model is pre-trained on news-articles, magazines and blog posts. Since the number of pre-training languages is much less compared to mBERT and includes only indic-languages, we explore IndicBERT with the intuition that it would better represent the three Indian languages at hand.

### 4.2 Class Weighting

Due to the class imbalance in the data, we use an inverse weighting strategy to penalize the under-represented classes more in the loss function. We also use **focal loss**(Lin et al., 2017) that can be considered as an improved version of the Cross-Entropy loss, that handles class

[1]https://huggingface.co/distilbert-base-multilingual-casedmodel-card

| | Kannada | Malayalam | Tamil |
|---|---|---|---|
| Not Offensive | super, song, sir, guru, bro | oru, like, trailer, ഒരു, padam, ഈ | Like, Thala, Vera, Mass, படம் |
| Not Native | super, song, sir, guru, bro | like, fans, movie, fan, trailer | hai, movie, like, ki, me, ka |
| Offensive Individual | @nandi, parthasarathi, ನಿನ್ / nin, ನಿಮ್ಮ / nim, gowda, sule | oru, padam, ഈ, ee, ആണ് | da, ah, la, padam, trailer, like |
| Offensive Group | movie, fans, dislike, tiktok, like | dislike, fans, trailer, padam, പടം | da, padam, la, oru, ah, nu |
| Offensive untargeted | movie, ge, ಅಂತ, e, nam, song | dislike, trailer, oru, adicha, like | da, la, trailer, ah, dislike |
| Offensive Other | tiktok, guru, movie, e, na, madi | - | da, la, padam, trailer, like |

Table 2: Most frequent words

imbalance by assigning more weights to hard examples and down-weighting easy examples.

### 4.3 Pseudo Labelling

Pseudo-labelling is a semi-supervised learning technique where the model is first trained over the small set of labelled examples available. This model is then used to approximate the labels on the test set and this newly labelled data is used together with the train set for further training the model. This results in a considerable increase in performance.

### 4.4 Ensemble

Ensembling of models have shown to have better performance in a multitude of tasks. The principle behind ensemble models is to leverage the various representations learnt by multiple (weak) learners/models to built a more robust model. Here, in this paper, we make use of a fairly simple, yet efficient form of ensembling. The output probability distributions from the models (DistilmBERT and ULMFiT) were added up, thereby making a new probability distribution. This was further converted to the required label using one-hot encoding.

## 5 Experiment

We describe the experiments that we perform. All the models are trained on google colab[2]. The code is available publicly[3].

### 5.1 DistilmBERT

We use DistilmBERT tokenizer which has a vocabulary size of 110k. A max sequence of 128 is used for truncating the input text and shorter sequences are padded with special tokens. The model uses a batch size of 8 for training. Adam optimizer with a learning rate of 1e-8 is used for optimizing the weights. The model is trained for 10 epochs.

### 5.2 ULMFiT

For the ULMFiT method, we follow the implementation provided by Arora (2020). The authors here pre-train ULMFiT on synthetically generated code mixed data which was created using a Markov model on preprocessed and transliterated versions of Wikipedia articles. Through transfer learning, the authors fine-tune the pre-trained ULMFiT model for the downstream task of hate speech detection[4]. We use the pretrained tokenizers (pre-trained using Google's Sentence Piece[5]) and language model provided in (Arora, 2020) for our task [6][7][8]. For each one of the 3 language sub-tasks, we split the training data into train-validation splits in the ratio of 80:20. For fine-tuning of the language model, the drop-out multiplicity is set to 0.3 with a batch size of 16. The model is trained for 1 epoch with the learning rate of 1e-2 with just the last layer unfreezed. After unfreezing all layers, The mode is fine-tuned for 5 epochs with a learning rate of 1e-3.

### 5.3 IndicBERT

For pre-processing we use the indicBERT tokenizer with a vocabulary size of 200k. The input sequences are truncated to a max length of 200 and padding is used for the shorter sequences. IndicBERT per-trained weights are used for fine-tuning the task. An additional fully connected layer with a dropout of 0.3 is used on top of the AlBERT model. We use a batch size of 32 for training and batch size 16 for validation. The optimization algorithm of choice was Adam with a learning rate of 1e-5.

In all the three models, to address the class

[2]https://colab.research.google.com/

[3]github.com/Debapriya-Tula/EACL2021-DravidianTask-Bitions

[4]https://sites.google.com/view/dravidian-codemix-fire2020/overview

[5]https://github.com/google/sentencepiece

[6]https://github.com/goru001/nlp-for-manglish

[7]https://github.com/goru001/nlp-for-tanglish

[8]https://github.com/goru001/nlp-for-kannada

| Language | Model | precision | Recall | f1-score |
|---|---|---|---|---|
| Tamil | ULMFiT | 0.72 | 0.77 | 0.73 |
| | ULMFiT (PL) | 0.72 | **0.78** | 0.73 |
| | DistilmBERT | 0.75 | 0.77 | 0.76 |
| | DistilmBERT (CW) | 0.74 | 0.76 | **0.76** |
| | DistilmBERT (FL) | 0.75 | 0.77 | 0.75 |
| | E [DistilmBERT (CW)+ULMFiT] | **0.75** | 0.77 | 0.76 |
| Kannada | ULMFiT | 0.67 | 0.69 | 0.67 |
| | ULMFiT(PL) | 0.67 | 0.70 | 0.67 |
| | DistilmBERT | 0.68 | 0.69 | 0.68 |
| | DistilmBERT (CW) | 0.67 | 0.69 | 0.68 |
| | DistilmBERT (FL) | 0.68 | 0.69 | 0.69 |
| | IndicBERT | 0.59 | 0.59 | 0.59 |
| | IndicBERT (CW) | 0.65 | 0.66 | 0.65 |
| | E [DistilmBERT (CW)+ULMFiT] | **0.692** | **0.705** | **0.697** |
| Malayalam | ULMFiT | 0.95 | 0.95 | 0.95 |
| | ULMFiT (PL) | 0.95 | 0.95 | 0.95 |
| | DistilmBERT | 0.96 | 0.97 | 0.96 |
| | DistilmBERT (CW) | 0.96 | 0.96 | 0.96 |
| | DistilmBERT (FL) | 0.96 | 0.96 | 0.96 |
| | IndicBERT | 0.95 | 0.91 | 0.92 |
| | IndicBERT (CW) | 0.95 | 0.92 | 0.93 |
| | E [DistilmBERT (CW)+ULMFiT] | **0.965** | **0.966** | **0.965** |

Table 3: Weighted Precision, Recall, f1-scores using all methods for the 3 languages on the validation set. Abbreviations used: Pseudo-labelled (**PL**), Class-weighted (**CW**), Focal loss (**FL**), Ensemble of model X and Y(**E**[**X, Y**])

| Language | Model | precision | recall | f1-score |
|---|---|---|---|---|
| Tamil | E [DistilmBERT(CW+PL)+ULMFiT (PL)] | 0.74 | 0.77 | 0.75 |
| Kannada | | 0.69 | 0.72 | 0.70 |
| Malayalam | | 0.97 | 0.97 | 0.97 |

Table 4: weighted Precision, Recall, f1-scores for the 3 languages using our best model on the test set

imbalance issue, we use class weighting where each class has been weighted inversely by the number of samples in the class. We also try to address the imbalance using focal loss (Lin et al., 2017), which however was not as effective as class-weighting w.r.t. improving performance for the under-represented classes.

For DistilmBERT and ULMFiT, we implement pseudo labelling. The trained model is used to make predictions on the unseen test set. These predictions along with the original train set was used to train a new model. Thus proving to be a good data augmentation strategy.

The outputs from DistilmBERT and ULMFiT are used for a soft voted ensemble strategy. We discard the indicBERT model from the ensemble due to poor results. The ensembling strategy of our best system is shown in figure 1.

## 6 Results

All the results for all experiments are reported in Table 3. Similar experiments were carried out in all the languages. The base model of ULMFiT on Malayalam gives an accuracy of 0.95 but the performance on under-represented classes was poor. DistilmBERT proved to be better on the data giving an f1-score of 0.965.

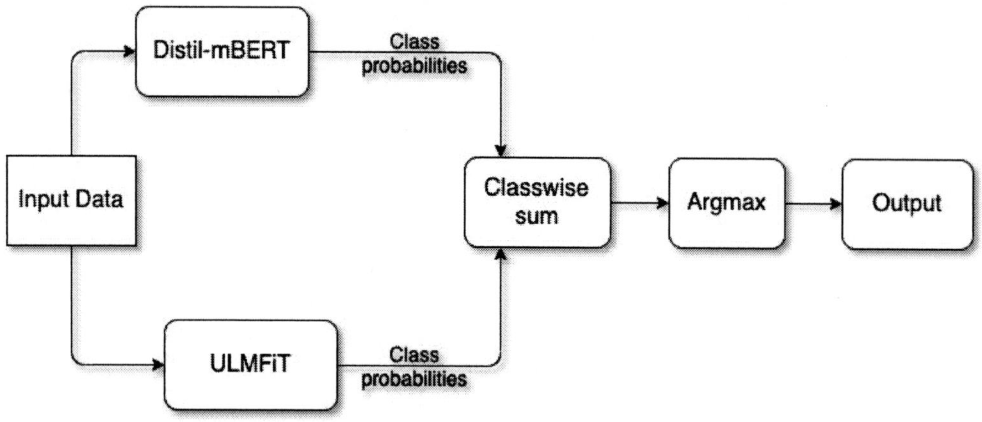


Figure 1: The input data is passed through an ensemble of DistilmBERT and ULMFiT. The aggregate of probability distributions of these models is the final prediction vector and the arg max of the probability vector is the final prediction.

Overall looking at all the results in table 3, class-weighting helps the model perform better on the under-represented classes thereby improving the overall performance of the model. Focal loss was also used to account for class imbalance the results with focal loss in DistilmBERT can be found in table 3.

Having different models which are pre-trained on different types of data, we ensembled our model predictions from ULMFit and DistilmBERT which boosted our model f1-score from 0.65 to 0.697 on Kannada data.

We observe that the DistilmBERT performs better than the ULMFiT (with and without pseudo-labelling). Its better performance can be attributed to the truly bidirectional nature of BERT (Sanh et al., 2019) based models. Secondly, BERT based models use transformers at their heart and hence do not suffer from long dependency issues. The use of the class-weighting scheme and focal loss (Lin et al., 2017) help to better represent the under-represented classes. It can be seen that the focal loss approach performs better than the naive class-weighting. But empirical results show that using focal loss led to much lower precision and recall for the minority classes than class-weighting. For example, for the Malayalam dataset, the precision and recall obtained using class-weighting were greater by 19% and 10% respectively than using focal loss. This is an interesting observation which we believe needs further experimentation for validation.

Overall our unified model which uses class-weighting, pseudo labelling and ensemble methods was the best performing model on Malayalam testset with an f1-score of 0.97. Our model was also in the top 5 best performing models for both Tamil and Kannada with f1-scores of 0.75 (4th place) and 0.70 (5th place).

## 7 Conclusion and Future Work

In this paper, we proposed an ensemble model utilising pseudo labelling to effectively detect offensive statements in Dravidian languages, namely Kannada, Malayalam and Tamil. We show competitive results on all three languages with first rank for Malayalam and within top-5 for Kannada and Tamil. Pre-trained multi-lingual model worked best for our use case as knowledge from similar language families was used across all the languages. In future research, we will consider synthetically creating new code-mixed data for each language and the usage of language specific tokenizers for the multi-lingual models.

## References


Seyi Akiwowo, Bertie Vidgen, Vinodkumar Prabhakaran, and Zeerak Waseem, editors. 2020. *Proceedings of the Fourth Workshop on Online Abuse and Harms*. Association for Computational Linguistics.

Gaurav Arora. 2020. Gauravarora@ hasoc-dravidian-codemix-fire2020: Pre-training ulmfit on synthetically generated code-mixed data for hate speech detection. *arXiv preprint arXiv:2010.02094*.

Segun Taofeek Aroyehun and Alexander Gelbukh. 2018. Aggression detection in social media: Using deep neural networks, data augmentation, and pseudo labeling. In *Proceedings of the First Workshop on Trolling, Aggression and Cyberbullying (TRAC-2018)*. Association for Computational Linguistics.

Utsab Barman, Amitava Das, Joachim Wagner, and Jennifer Foster. 2014. Code mixing: A challenge for language identification in the language of social media. In *Proceedings of the First Workshop on Computational Approaches to Code Switching*. Association for Computational Linguistics.

Emily Bender. 2019. The benderrule: On naming the languages we study and why it matters. *The Gradient*.

Bharathi Raja Chakravarthi, Navya Jose, Shardul Suryawanshi, Elizabeth Sherly, and John Philip McCrae. 2020a. A sentiment analysis dataset for code-mixed Malayalam-English. In *Proceedings of the 1st Joint Workshop on Spoken Language Technologies for Under-resourced languages (SLTU) and Collaboration and Computing for Under-Resourced Languages (CCURL)*. European Language Resources association.

Bharathi Raja Chakravarthi, Vigneshwaran Muralidaran, Ruba Priyadharshini, and John Philip McCrae. 2020b. Corpus creation for sentiment analysis in code-mixed Tamil-English text. In *Proceedings of the 1st Joint Workshop on Spoken Language Technologies for Under-resourced languages (SLTU) and Collaboration and Computing for Under-Resourced Languages (CCURL)*. European Language Resources association.

Bharathi Raja Chakravarthi, Ruba Priyadharshini, Navya Jose, Anand Kumar M, Thomas Mandl, Prasanna Kumar Kumaresan, Rahul Ponnusamy, Hariharan V, Elizabeth Sherly, and John Philip McCrae. 2021. Findings of the shared task on Offensive Language Identification in Tamil, Malayalam, and Kannada. In *Proceedings of the First Workshop on Speech and Language Technologies for Dravidian Languages*. Association for Computational Linguistics.

Bharathi Raja Chakravarthi, Ruba Priyadharshini, Vigneshwaran Muralidaran, Shardul Suryawanshi, Navya Jose, Elizabeth Sherly, and John P. McCrae. 2020c. Overview of the track on sentiment analysis for dravidian languages in code-mixed text. In *Forum for Information Retrieval Evaluation*, FIRE 2020, page 21–24. Association for Computing Machinery.

Michele Corazza, Stefano Menini, Elena Cabrio, Sara Tonelli, and Serena Villata. 2020. A multilingual evaluation for online hate speech detection. *ACM Trans. Internet Technol.*, 20(2).

Anisha Datta, Shukrity Si, Urbi Chakraborty, and Sudip Kumar Naskar. 2020. Spyder: Aggression detection on multilingual tweets. In *Proceedings of the Second Workshop on Trolling, Aggression and Cyberbullying*.

Jacob Devlin, Ming-Wei Chang, Kenton Lee, and Kristina Toutanova. 2018. Bert: Pre-training of deep bidirectional transformers for language understanding. *arXiv preprint arXiv:1810.04805*.

Suman Dowlagar and Radhika Mamidi. 2021. Cmsaone@dravidian-codemix-fire2020: A meta embedding and transformer model for code-mixed sentiment analysis on social media text.

Paula Fortuna and Sérgio Nunes. 2018. A survey on automatic detection of hate speech in text. *ACM Comput. Surv.*, 51(4).

Ayush Gupta, Rohan Sukumaran, Kevin John, and Sundeep Teki. 2021. Hostility detection and covid-19 fake news detection in social media.

Adeep Hande, Ruba Priyadharshini, and Bharathi Raja Chakravarthi. 2020. KanCMD: Kannada CodeMixed dataset for sentiment analysis and offensive language detection. In *Proceedings of the Third Workshop on Computational Modeling of People's Opinions, Personality, and Emotion's in Social Media*. Association for Computational Linguistics.

Jeremy Howard and Sebastian Ruder. 2018. Universal language model fine-tuning for text classification. *arXiv preprint arXiv:1801.06146*.

Junjie Hu, Sebastian Ruder, Aditya Siddhant, Graham Neubig, Orhan Firat, and Melvin Johnson. 2020. Xtreme: A massively multilingual multi-task benchmark for evaluating cross-lingual generalisation. In *International Conference on Machine Learning*, pages 4411–4421. PMLR.

Divyanshu Kakwani, Anoop Kunchukuttan, Satish Golla, Gokul N.C., Avik Bhattacharyya, Mitesh M. Khapra, and Pratyush Kumar. 2020. IndicNLPSuite: Monolingual corpora, evaluation benchmarks and pre-trained multilingual language models for Indian languages. In *Findings of the Association for Computational Linguistics: EMNLP 2020*. Association for Computational Linguistics.

Ritesh Kumar, Guggilla Bhanodai, Rajendra Pamula, and Maheshwar Reddy Chennuru. 2018. TRAC-1 shared task on aggression identification: IIT(ISM)@COLING'18. In *Proceedings of the First Workshop on Trolling, Aggression and Cyberbullying (TRAC-2018)*. Association for Computational Linguistics.

Ritesh Kumar, Atul Kr. Ojha, Shervin Malmasi, and Marcos Zampieri. 2020. Evaluating aggression identification in social media. In *Proceedings of the Second Workshop on Trolling, Aggression and Cyberbullying*. European Language Resources Association (ELRA).

Tsung-Yi Lin, Priya Goyal, Ross Girshick, Kaiming He, and Piotr Dollár. 2017. Focal loss for dense object detection. In *Proceedings of the IEEE international conference on computer vision*, pages 2980–2988.

Debanjan Mahata, Haimin Zhang, Karan Uppal, Yaman Kumar, Rajiv Ratn Shah, Simra Shahid, Laiba Mehnaz, and Sarthak Anand. 2019. MIDAS at SemEval-2019 task 6: Identifying offensive posts and targeted offense from Twitter. In *Proceedings of the 13th International Workshop on Semantic Evaluation*. Association for Computational Linguistics.

Sainik Kumar Mahata, Dipankar Das, and Sivaji Bandyopadhyay. 2020. Junlp@dravidian-codemix-fire2020: Sentiment classification of code-mixed tweets using bi-directional rnn and language tags.

Thomas Mandl, Sandip Modha, Prasenjit Majumder, Daksh Patel, Mohana Dave, Chintak Mandlia, and Aditya Patel. 2019. Overview of the hasoc track at fire 2019: Hate speech and offensive content identification in indo-european languages. In *Proceedings of the 11th Forum for Information Retrieval Evaluation*, FIRE '19. Association for Computing Machinery.

Parth Patwa, Gustavo Aguilar, Sudipta Kar, Suraj Pandey, Srinivas PYKL, Björn Gambäck, Tanmoy Chakraborty, Thamar Solorio, and Amitava Das. 2020. Semeval-2020 task 9: Overview of sentiment analysis of code-mixed tweets. In *Proceedings of the 14th International Workshop on Semantic Evaluation (SemEval-2020)*. Association for Computational Linguistics.

Parth Patwa, Mohit Bhardwaj, Vineeth Guptha, Gitanjali Kumari, Shivam Sharma, Srinivas PYKL, Amitava Das, Asif Ekbal, Shad Akhtar, and Tanmoy Chakraborty. 2021. Overview of constraint 2021 shared tasks: Detecting english covid-19 fake news and hindi hostile posts. In *Proceedings of the First Workshop on Combating Online Hostile Posts in Regional Languages during Emergency Situation (CONSTRAINT)*. Springer.

Julian Risch and Ralf Krestel. 2018. Aggression identification using deep learning and data augmentation. In *Proceedings of the First Workshop on Trolling, Aggression and Cyberbullying (TRAC-2018)*. Association for Computational Linguistics.

Julian Risch and Ralf Krestel. 2020. Bagging BERT models for robust aggression identification. In *Proceedings of the Second Workshop on Trolling, Aggression and Cyberbullying*. European Language Resources Association (ELRA).

Niloofar Safi Samghabadi, Deepthi Mave, Sudipta Kar, and Thamar Solorio. 2018. RiTUAL-UH at TRAC 2018 shared task: Aggression identification. In *Proceedings of the First Workshop on Trolling, Aggression and Cyberbullying (TRAC-2018)*. Association for Computational Linguistics.

Niloofar Safi Samghabadi, Parth Patwa, Srinivas PYKL, Prerana Mukherjee, Amitava Das, and Thamar Solorio. 2020. Aggression and misogyny detection using BERT: A multi-task approach. In *Proceedings of the Second Workshop on Trolling, Aggression and Cyberbullying*. European Language Resources Association (ELRA).

Victor Sanh, Lysandre Debut, Julien Chaumond, and Thomas Wolf. 2019. Distilbert, a distilled version of bert: smaller, faster, cheaper and lighter. *arXiv preprint arXiv:1910.01108*.

Zeerak Waseem, Wendy Hui Kyong Chung, Dirk Hovy, and Joel Tetreault, editors. 2017. *Proceedings of the First Workshop on Abusive Language Online*. Association for Computational Linguistics.

Gregor Wiedemann, Seid Muhie Yimam, and Chris Biemann. 2020. UHH-LT at SemEval-2020 task 12: Fine-tuning of pre-trained transformer networks for offensive language detection. In *Proceedings of the Fourteenth Workshop on Semantic Evaluation*. International Committee for Computational Linguistics.

Marcos Zampieri, Preslav Nakov, Sara Rosenthal, Pepa Atanasova, Georgi Karadzhov, Hamdy Mubarak, Leon Derczynski, Zeses Pitenis, and Çağrı Çöltekin. 2020. SemEval-2020 task 12: Multilingual offensive language identification in social media (OffensEval 2020). In *Proceedings of the Fourteenth Workshop on Semantic Evaluation*. International Committee for Computational Linguistics.

Marcos Zampieri and Others. 2019a. Predicting the type and target of offensive posts in social media. In *Proceedings of the 2019 Conference of the North American Chapter of the Association for Computational Linguistics: Human Language Technologies, Volume 1 (Long and Short Papers)*. Association for Computational Linguistics.

Marcos Zampieri and Others. 2019b. SemEval-2019 task 6: Identifying and categorizing offensive language in social media (OffensEval). In *Proceedings of the 13th International Workshop on Semantic Evaluation*. Association for Computational Linguistics.

# NLP-CUET@DravidianLangTech-EACL2021: Investigating Visual and Textual Features to Identify Trolls from Multimodal Social Media Memes

**Eftekhar Hossain*, Omar Sharif† and Mohammed Moshiul Hoque†**
†Department of Computer Science and Engineering
*Department of Electronics and Telecommunication Engineering
Chittagong University of Engineering and Technology, Bangladesh
{eftekhar.hossain, omar.sharif, moshiul_240}@cuet.ac.bd

## Abstract

In the past few years, the meme has become a new way of communication on the Internet. As memes are the images with embedded text, it can quickly spread hate, offence and violence. Classifying memes are very challenging because of their multimodal nature and region-specific interpretation. A shared task is organized to develop models that can identify trolls from multimodal social media memes. This work presents a computational model that we have developed as part of our participation in the task. Training data comes in two forms: an image with embedded Tamil code-mixed text and an associated caption given in English. We investigated the visual and textual features using CNN, VGG16, Inception, Multilingual-BERT, XLM-Roberta, XLNet models. Multimodal features are extracted by combining image (CNN, ResNet50, Inception) and text (Long short term memory network) features via early fusion approach. Results indicate that the textual approach with XLNet achieved the highest weighted $f_1$-score of 0.58, which enabled our model to secure $3^{rd}$ rank in this task.

## 1 Introduction

With the Internet's phenomenal growth, social media has become a platform for sharing information, opinion, feeling, expressions, and ideas. Most users enjoy the liberty to post or share contents in such virtual platforms without any legal authority intervention or moderation (Thavareesan and Mahesan, 2019, 2020a,b). Some people misuse this freedom and take social platforms to spread negativity, threat and offence against individuals or communities in various ways (Chakravarthi, 2020). One such way is making and sharing troll memes to provoke, offend and demean a group or race on the Internet (Mojica de la Vega and Ng, 2018). Although memes meant to be sarcastic or humorous, sometimes it becomes aggressive, threatening and abusive (Suryawanshi et al., 2020a). Till to date, extensive research has been conducted to detect hate, hostility, and aggression from a single modality such as image or text (Kumar et al., 2020). Identification of troll, offence, abuse by analyzing the combined information of visual and textual modalities is still an unexplored research avenue in natural language processing (NLP). Classifying memes from multi-model data is a challenging task since memes express sarcasm and humour implicitly. One meme may not be a troll if we consider only image or text associated with it. However, it can be a troll if it considers both text and image modalities. Such implicit meaning of memes, use of sarcastic, ambiguous and humorous terms and absence of baseline algorithms that take care of multiple modalities are the primary concerns of categorizing multimodal memes. Features from multiple modalities (i.e image, text) have been exploited in many works to solve these problems (Suryawanshi et al., 2020a; Pranesh and Shekhar, 2020). We plan to address this issue by using transfer learning as these models have better generalization capability than the models trained on small dataset. This work is a little effort to compensate for the existing deficiency of assign task with the following contributions:

- Developed a classifier model using XLNet to identify trolls from multimodal social media memes.
- Investigate the performance of various transfer learning techniques with the benchmark experimental evaluation by exploring visual, textual and multimodal features of the data.



*Proceedings of the First Workshop on Speech and Language Technologies for Dravidian Languages*, pages 300–306
April 20, 2021 ©2021 Association for Computational Linguistics

## 2 Related Work

In the past few years, trolling, aggression, hostile and abusive language detection from social media data has been studied widely by NLP experts (Kumar et al., 2020; Sharif et al., 2021; Mandl et al., 2020). Majority of these researches carried out concerning the textual information alone (Akiwowo et al., 2020). However, a meme existence can be found in a basic image, text embedded in image or image with sarcastic caption. Very few researches have investigated both textual and visual features to classify meme, troll, offence and aggression. Suryawanshi et al. (2020a) developed a multimodal dataset to identify offensive memes. Authors have combined text and image both modalities to detect an offensive meme. Their model obtained $f_1$-score of 0.50 in a multimodal setting with LSTM and VGG16 network. A unimodal framework utilized the image features to detect offensive content in image (Gandhi et al., 2019). A multimodal framework is proposed by (Pranesh and Shekhar, 2020) to analyze the underlying sentiment of memes. They used VGG19 model pre-trained on ImageNet and bidirectional encoder representations from transformers (BERT) language model to capture both textual and visual features. Wang and Wen (2015) have combined visual and textual information to predict and generate a suitable description for memes. Du et al. (2020) introduced a model to identify the image with text (IWT) memes that spread hate, offence or misinformation. (Suryawanshi et al., 2020b) built a dataset 'TamilMemes' to detect troll from memes. In 'TamilMemes' text is embedded in the image, each image is labelled as either 'troll' or 'not-troll'. To perform classification, the authors utilized image-based features, but their method did not achieve credible performance.

## 3 Task and Dataset Descriptions

Meme as the troll is an image that has offensive or sarcastic text embedded into it and intent to demean, provoke or offend an individual or a group (Suryawanshi et al., 2020b). An image itself can also be a troll meme without any embedded text into it. In this task, we aim to detect troll meme from an image and its associated caption. Task organizers[1] provided a dataset of troll memes for Tamil language (Suryawanshi and Chakravarthi, 2021). The dataset contains two parts: an image with embedded Tamil code-mixed text, and a caption. Each instance of the dataset labelled as either 'troll' and 'not-troll'. Dataset divided into train, validation and test sets. Statistics of the dataset for each class given in table 1. Dataset divided into train, validation and test sets. Dataset is imbalanced where several data in the 'troll' class is much higher than the 'not-troll' class.

| Data Sets | Troll | Not-Troll |
|---|---|---|
| Train | 1026 | 814 |
| Valid | 256 | 204 |
| Test | 395 | 272 |
| Total | 1677 | 1290 |

Table 1: Dataset summary

Participants are allowed to use image, caption or both to perform the classification task. We used image, text, and multimodal (i.e., image + text) features to address the assigned task (detail analysis is discussed in Section 4).

## 4 Methodology

The prime concern of this work is to classify trolling from the multimodal memes. Initially, the investigation begins with accounting only the images' visual features where different CNN architectures will use. The textual features will consider in the next and apply the transformer-based model (i.e. m-BERT, XLM-R, XLNet) for the classification task. Finally, we investigate the effect of combined visual and textual features and compare its performance with the other approaches. Figure 1 shows the abstract view of the employed techniques.

### 4.1 Visual Approach

A CNN architecture is used to experiment on visual modality. Besides the pre-trained models, VGG16 and Inception are also employed for the classification task. Before feeding into the model, all the images get resized into a dimension of $150 \times 150 \times 3$.

**CNN:** We design a CNN architecture consists of four convolution layers. The first and second layers contained 32 and 64 filters, while 128 filters are used in third and fourth layers. In all layers, convolution is performed by $3 \times 3$ kernel and used

[1] https://competitions.codalab.org/competitions/27651

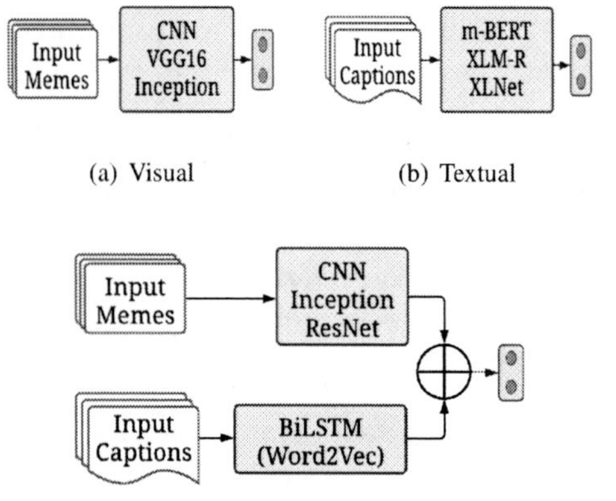


(a) Visual (b) Textual

(c) Multimodal

Figure 1: Abstract process of troll memes classification

the Relu non-linearity function. To extract the critical features max pooling is performed with $2 \times 2$ window after every convolution layer. The flattened output of the final convolution layer is feed to a dense layer consisting of 512 neurons. To mitigate the chance of overfitting a dropout layer is introduced with a dropout rate of 0.1. Finally, a sigmoid layer is used for the class prediction.

**VGG16:** A CNN architecture (Simonyan and Zisserman, 2015) is pre-trained on over 14 million images of 1000 classes. To accomplish the task, we froze the top layers of VGG16 and fine-tuned it on our images with adding one global average pooling layer followed by an FC layer of 256 neurons and a sigmoid layer which is used for the class prediction.

**Inception:** We fine-tuned the InceptionV3 (Szegedy et al., 2015) network on our images by freezing the top layers. A global average pooling layer is added along with a fully connected layer of 256 neurons, followed by a sigmoid layer on top of these networks.

In order to train the models, 'binary_crossentropy' loss function and 'RMSprop' optimizer is utilized with learning rate $1e^{-3}$. Training is performed for 50 epochs with passing 32 instances in a single iteration. For saving the best intermediate model, we use the Keras callback function.

### 4.2 Textual Approach

Various state-of-the-art transformer models are used including m-BERT (Devlin et al., 2018), XLNet (Yang et al., 2019), and XLM-Roberta (Conneau et al., 2019) to investigate the textual modality. We selected 'bert-base-multilingual-cased', 'xlnet-base-cased', and 'xlm-Roberta-base' models from Pytorch Huggingface[2] transformers library and fine-tuned them on our textual data. Implementation is done by using Ktrain (Maiya, 2020) package. For fine-tuning, we settled the maximum caption length 50 and used a learning rate of $2e^{-5}$ with a batch size 8 for all models. Ktrain 'fit_onecycle' method is used to train the models for 20 epochs. The early stopping technique is utilized to alleviate the chance of overfitting.

### 4.3 Multimodal Approach

To verify the singular modality approaches effectiveness, we continue our investigation by incorporating both visual and textual modality into one input data. Various multimodal classification tasks adopted this approach (Pranesh and Shekhar, 2020). We have employed an early fusion approach (Duong et al., 2017) instead of using one modality feature to accept both modalities as inputs and classify them by extracting suitable features from both modalities. For extracting visual features, CNN is used, whereas bidirectional long short term memory (BiLSTM) network is applied for handling the textual features. Different multimodal models have been constructed for the comparison. However, due to the high computational complexity, incorporating transformer models with CNN-Image models has not experimented within the current work.

**CNNImage + BiLSTM:** Firstly, CNN architecture is employed to extract the image features. It consists of four convolutional layers consisting of 32, 64, 128, and 64 filters with a size of $3 \times 3$ in $1^{st}$-$4^{th}$ layers. Each convolutional layer followed by a maxpool layer with a pooling size of $2 \times 2$. An FC layer with 256 neurons and a sigmoid layer is added after the flatten layer. On the contrary, Word2Vec (Mikolov et al., 2013) embedding technique applied to extract features from the captions/texts. We use the Keras embedding layer with embedding dimension 100. A BiLSTM layer with 128 cells is added at the top of the embedding layer to capture long-term dependencies from the texts. Finally, the output of the BiLSTM layer is passed to a sigmoid layer.

[2]https://huggingface.co/transformers/

After that, the two constructed models' output layers are concatenated together and created a new model.

**Inception + BiLSTM:** We combined the pre-trained Inception and BiLSTM network for the classification using both modalities. The inception model is fetched from Keras library and used it as a visual feature extractor. By excluding the top layers, we fine-tuned it on our images with one additional FC layer of 256 neurons and a sigmoid layer. For textual features, similar BiLSTM architecture is employed (Described in CNNImage + BiLSTM). The Keras concatenation layer used two models output layers and combined them to create one model.

**ResNet50 + BiLSTM:** Pretrained residual network (ResNet) (He et al., 2015) is employed to extract visual features. The model is taken from Keras library. To fine-tuned it on our images, the final pooling and FC layer of the ResNet model is excluded. Afterwards, we have added a global average pooling layer with a fully connected layer and a sigmoid layer at the ResNet model's top. To extract the textual features identical BiLSTM network is employed (Described in CNNImage + BiLSTM). In the end, the output layer of the two models is concatenated to create one combined model.

In all cases, the output prediction is obtained from a final sigmoid layer added just after the concatenation layer of a multimodal model. All the models have compiled using 'binary_crossentropy' loss function. Apart from this, we use 'Adam' optimizer with a learning rate of $1e^{-3}$ and choose the batch size of 32. The models are trained for 50 epochs utilizing the Keras callbacks function to store the best model.

## 5 Result and Analysis

This section presents a comparative performance analysis of the different experimental approaches to classify the multimodal memes. The superiority of the models is determined based on the weighted $f_1$-score. However, other evaluation metrics like precision and recall are also considered in some cases. Table 2 shows the evaluation results of different approaches on the test set. The outcome reveals that all the models (i.e. CNN, VGG16, and Inception) developed based on the imaging modality obtained approximately same $f_1$-score of 0.46. However, considering both precision (0.625) and recall (0.597) score, only Inception model performed better than the other visual models. On the other hand, models that are constructed based on textual modality show a rise of $10 - 12\%$ in $f_1$ score than the visual approach. In the textual approach, m-BERT and XLM-R achieved $f_1$-score of 0.558 and 0.571 respectively. However, XLNet outperformed all the models by obtaining the highest $f_1$-score of 0.583. For comparison, we also perform experiment by combining both modality features into one model. In case of multimodal approach, CNNImage + BiLSTM model obtained $f_1$-score of 0.525 while ResNet + BiLSTM model achieved a lower $f_1$- score (0.47) with a drops of 6%. Compared to that Inception + BiLSTM model achieved the highest $f_1$-score of 0.559. Though two multimodal models (CNNImage + BiLSTM and Inception + BiLSTM) showed better outcome than visual models, they could not beat the textual model's performance (XLNet). Though it is skeptical that XLNet (monolingual model) outperformed multilingual models (m-BERT and XLM-R), the possible reason might be the provided captions in English.

From the above analysis, it is evident that visual models performed poorly compared to the other approaches. The possible reason behind this might be due to the overlapping of multiple images in all the classes. That means the dataset consists of many memes with the same visual content with different captions in both classes. Moreover, many images do not provide any explicit meaningful information to conclude whether it is a troll or not-troll meme.

### 5.1 Error Analysis

A detail error analysis is performed on the best model of each approach to obtain more insights. The analysis is carried out by using confusion matrices (Figure 2). From the figure 2 (a), it is observed that among 395 troll memes, Inception + BiLSTM model correctly classified 324 and misclassified 71 as not-troll. However, this model's true positive rate is comparatively low than the true negative rate as it identified only 72 not-troll memes correctly and wrongly classified 200 memes. On the other hand, in the visual approach, the Inception model showed outstanding performance by detecting 392 troll memes correctly from 395. However, the model

| Approach | Classifiers | Precision | Recall | $f_1$-score |
|---|---|---|---|---|
| Visual | CNN | 0.604 | 0.597 | 0.463 |
| | VGG16 | 0.526 | 0.588 | 0.461 |
| | Inception | 0.625 | 0.597 | 0.458 |
| Textual | m-BERT | 0.574 | 0.597 | 0.558 |
| | XLM-R | 0.578 | 0.597 | 0.571 |
| | XLNet | 0.592 | 0.609 | **0.583** |
| Multimodal | CNNImage + BiLSTM | 0.551 | 0.585 | 0.525 |
| | ResNet50 + BiLSTM | 0.669 | 0.603 | 0.471 |
| | Inception + BiLSTM | 0.571 | 0.594 | 0.559 |

Table 2: Performance comparison of different models on test set.

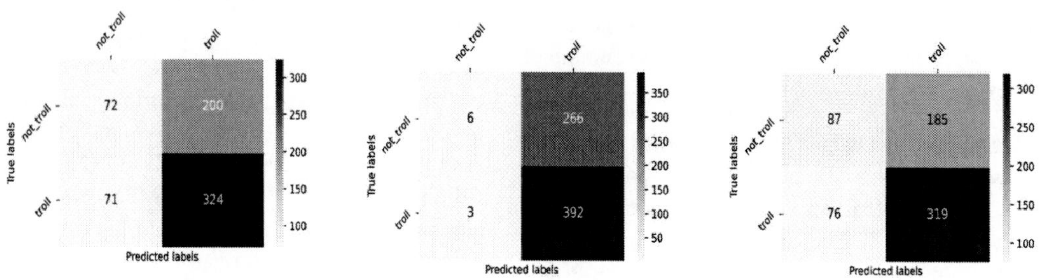


(a) Inception+BiLSTM

(b) Inception

(c) XLNet

Figure 2: Confusion Matrix of the best model in each approach (a) Multimodal (b) Visual (c) Textual

confused in identifying not troll memes as it correctly classified only 6 memes and misclassified 266 from a total 272 not-troll memes. Meanwhile, figure 2 (c) indicates that among 272 not-troll memes, XLNet correctly classified only 87. In contrast, among 395, the model correctly identified 319 troll memes.

The above analysis shows that all models get biased towards the troll memes and wrongly classified more than 70% memes as the troll. The probable reason behind this might be the overlapping nature of the memes in all classes. Besides, many memes do not have any embedded captions which might create difficulty for the textual and multimodal models to determine the appropriate class. Moreover, we observed that most of the missing caption memes were from troll class which might be a strong reason for the text models to incline towards the troll class.

## 6 Conclusion

This work present the details of the methods and performance analysis of the models that we developed to participate in the meme classification shared task at EACL-2021. We have utilized visual, textual and multimodal features to classify memes into the 'troll' and 'not troll' categories. Results reveal that all the visual classifiers achieve similar weighted $f_1$-score of 0.46. Transformer-based methods capture textual features where XLNet outdoes all others by obtaining 0.58 $f_1$-score. In the multimodal approach, visual and textual features are combined via early fusion of weights. $F_1$ score rose significantly after adding textual features in CNN and Inception models. Only BiLSTM method is applied to extract features from the text in this approach. In future, it will be interesting to see how the models behave if transformers use in place of BiLSTM. An ensemble of transformers might also be explored in case of textual approach.

## References


Seyi Akiwowo, Bertie Vidgen, Vinodkumar Prabhakaran, and Zeerak Waseem, editors. 2020. *Proceedings of the Fourth Workshop on Online Abuse and Harms*. Association for Computational Linguistics, Online.

Bharathi Raja Chakravarthi. 2020. HopeEDI: A multilingual hope speech detection dataset for equality, diversity, and inclusion. In *Proceedings of the Third Workshop on Computational Modeling of People's Opinions, Personality, and Emotion's in Social Media*, pages 41–53, Barcelona, Spain (Online). Association for Computational Linguistics.

Alexis Conneau, Kartikay Khandelwal, Naman Goyal, Vishrav Chaudhary, Guillaume Wenzek, Francisco Guzmán, Edouard Grave, Myle Ott, Luke Zettlemoyer, and Veselin Stoyanov. 2019. Unsupervised cross-lingual representation learning at scale. *CoRR*, abs/1911.02116.

Jacob Devlin, Ming-Wei Chang, Kenton Lee, and Kristina Toutanova. 2018. BERT: pre-training of deep bidirectional transformers for language understanding. *CoRR*, abs/1810.04805.

Yuhao Du, Muhammad Aamir Masood, and Kenneth Joseph. 2020. Understanding visual memes: An empirical analysis of text superimposed on memes shared on twitter. *Proceedings of the International AAAI Conference on Web and Social Media*, 14(1):153–164.

Chi Thang Duong, Remi Lebret, and Karl Aberer. 2017. Multimodal classification for analysing social media.

Shreyansh Gandhi, Samrat Kokkula, Abon Chaudhuri, Alessandro Magnani, Theban Stanley, Behzad Ahmadi, Venkatesh Kandaswamy, Omer Ovenc, and Shie Mannor. 2019. Image matters: Scalable detection of offensive and non-compliant content / logo in product images.

Kaiming He, Xiangyu Zhang, Shaoqing Ren, and Jian Sun. 2015. Deep residual learning for image recognition.

Ritesh Kumar, Atul Kr. Ojha, Bornini Lahiri, Marcos Zampieri, Shervin Malmasi, Vanessa Murdock, and Daniel Kadar, editors. 2020. *Proceedings of the Second Workshop on Trolling, Aggression and Cyberbullying*. European Language Resources Association (ELRA), Marseille, France.

Arun S. Maiya. 2020. ktrain: A low-code library for augmented machine learning.

Thomas Mandl, Sandip Modha, Anand Kumar M, and Bharathi Raja Chakravarthi. 2020. Overview of the HASOC Track at FIRE 2020: Hate Speech and Offensive Language Identification in Tamil, Malayalam, Hindi, English and German. In *Forum for Information Retrieval Evaluation*, FIRE 2020, page 29–32, New York, NY, USA. Association for Computing Machinery.

Tomás Mikolov, Ilya Sutskever, Kai Chen, Greg Corrado, and Jeffrey Dean. 2013. Distributed representations of words and phrases and their compositionality. *CoRR*, abs/1310.4546.

Raj Ratn Pranesh and Ambesh Shekhar. 2020. Memesem: A multi-modal framework for sentimental analysis of meme via transfer learning.

Omar Sharif, Eftekhar Hossain, and Mohammed Moshiul Hoque. 2021. Combating hostility: Covid-19 fake news and hostile post detection in social media.

Karen Simonyan and Andrew Zisserman. 2015. Very deep convolutional networks for large-scale image recognition.

Shardul Suryawanshi and Bharathi Raja Chakravarthi. 2021. Findings of the shared task on Troll Meme Classification in Tamil. In *Proceedings of the First Workshop on Speech and Language Technologies for Dravidian Languages*. Association for Computational Linguistics.

Shardul Suryawanshi, Bharathi Raja Chakravarthi, Mihael Arcan, and Paul Buitelaar. 2020a. Multimodal meme dataset (MultiOFF) for identifying offensive content in image and text. In *Proceedings of the Second Workshop on Trolling, Aggression and Cyberbullying*, pages 32–41, Marseille, France. European Language Resources Association (ELRA).

Shardul Suryawanshi, Bharathi Raja Chakravarthi, Pranav Verma, Mihael Arcan, John Philip McCrae, and Paul Buitelaar. 2020b. A dataset for troll classification of TamilMemes. In *Proceedings of the WILDRE5– 5th Workshop on Indian Language Data: Resources and Evaluation*, pages 7–13, Marseille, France. European Language Resources Association (ELRA).

Christian Szegedy, Vincent Vanhoucke, Sergey Ioffe, Jonathon Shlens, and Zbigniew Wojna. 2015. Rethinking the inception architecture for computer vision. *CoRR*, abs/1512.00567.

Sajeetha Thavareesan and Sinnathamby Mahesan. 2019. Sentiment Analysis in Tamil Texts: A Study on Machine Learning Techniques and Feature Representation. In *2019 14th Conference on Industrial and Information Systems (ICIIS)*, pages 320–325.

Sajeetha Thavareesan and Sinnathamby Mahesan. 2020a. Sentiment Lexicon Expansion using Word2vec and fastText for Sentiment Prediction in Tamil texts. In *2020 Moratuwa Engineering Research Conference (MERCon)*, pages 272–276.

Sajeetha Thavareesan and Sinnathamby Mahesan. 2020b. Word embedding-based Part of Speech tagging in Tamil texts. In *2020 IEEE 15th International Conference on Industrial and Information Systems (ICIIS)*, pages 478–482.

Luis Gerardo Mojica de la Vega and Vincent Ng. 2018. Modeling trolling in social media conversations. In *Proceedings of the Eleventh International Conference on Language Resources and Evaluation (LREC-2018)*, Miyazaki, Japan. European Languages Resources Association (ELRA).

William Yang Wang and Miaomiao Wen. 2015. I can has cheezburger? a nonparanormal approach to combining textual and visual information for predicting and generating popular meme descriptions. In *Proceedings of the 2015 Conference of the North American Chapter of the Association for Computational Linguistics: Human Language Technologies*, pages 355–365, Denver, Colorado. Association for Computational Linguistics.

Zhilin Yang, Zihang Dai, Yiming Yang, Jaime G. Carbonell, Ruslan Salakhutdinov, and Quoc V. Le. 2019. Xlnet: Generalized autoregressive pretraining for language understanding. *CoRR*, abs/1906.08237.

# SJ_AJ@DravidianLangTech-EACL2021: Task-Adaptive Pre-Training of Multilingual BERT models for Offensive Language Identification

**Sai Muralidhar Jayanthi**
Language Technologies Institute
Carnegie Mellon University
sjayanth@cs.cmu.edu

**Akshat Gupta**
Electrical and Computer Engineering
Carnegie Mellon University
akshatgu@andrew.cmu.edu

## Abstract

In this paper we present our submission for the EACL 2021-Shared Task on Offensive Language Identification in Dravidian languages. Our final system is an ensemble of mBERT and XLM-RoBERTa models which leverage task-adaptive pre-training of multilingual BERT models with a masked language modeling objective. Our system was ranked 1st for Kannada, 2nd for Malayalam and 3rd for Tamil. [1]

## 1 Introduction

The task of offensive language identification aims to identify offensive language used in social media texts, which could be in the form of threats, abusive language, insults (Zampieri et al., 2020; Chakravarthi, 2020). Social media platforms like Twitter, Facebook, YouTube are now mediums where a large number of people interact and express their opinions. Conflicts and target abuses are common on social media platform. Offensive language detection is a form of social media monitoring which is best done by building computational models and automatic methods due to the large stream of data involved.

Code-Switching[2] is a phenomenon common in bilingual and multilingual communities where words from two (or more) languages are used in the same sentence (Sitaram et al., 2019; Priyadharshini et al., 2020; Jose et al., 2020) and is very commonly used for social media interactions. Thus it is vital to build models that are able to process code-switched data for the relevant social media tasks. Previous shared tasks in the domain of offensive language identification have focused on identifying offensive language in English (Zampieri et al., 2019), Arabic, Greek, Danish and Turkish (Zampieri et al., 2020). The datasets used for this shared task in Dravidian languages are characterized by code-mixing.

Pretrained BERT models (Devlin et al., 2018) and their multilingual versions– mBERT and XLM-RoBERTa (Conneau et al., 2019) have produced state of the art results in multiple tasks. These models have also been used to built best performing sentiment analysis systems in various shared tasks for code-mixed datasets (Patwa et al., 2020; Chakravarthi et al., 2020d; Mandl et al., 2020; Chakravarthi et al., 2020b). In this paper we present our submission for the Shared Task on Offensive Language Identification in Dravidian languages. We employ task-adaptive pre-training with a Masked Language Modeling objective and ensemble predictions from mBERT and XLM-RoBERTa models for our final submission.

## 2 Dataset

The dataset statistics for the task of Offensive Language Identification in Malayalam (Chakravarthi et al., 2020a), Tamil (Chakravarthi et al., 2020c) and Kannada (Hande et al., 2020) are shown in Table 1. The class-wise training dataset statistics are shown in Table 2. Hande et al. (2020) outlines a brief about the data collection procedure and some baselines. We see that the datasets are highly imbalanced.[3]

| Language | Split | | |
|---|---|---|---|
| | Train | Dev | Test |
| Kannada | 6217 | 777 | 778 |
| Tamil | 35139 | 4388 | 4392 |
| Malayalam | 16010 | 1999 | 2001 |

Table 1: Dataset statistics

[1] Code and pretrained models are available at github.com/murali1996/eacl2021-OffensEval-Dravidian.

[2] Interchangeably used with the term code-mixing

[3] More details of the task can be found at https://competitions.codalab.org/competitions/27654



*Proceedings of the First Workshop on Speech and Language Technologies for Dravidian Languages*, pages 307–312
April 20, 2021 

| Class | Language | | |
|---|---|---|---|
| | Kannada | Tamil | Malayalam |
| Not-{language} | 1522 | 1454 | 1287 |
| Not_offensive | 3544 | 25425 | 14153 |
| Offensive_Targeted_Insult_Individual | 487 | 2343 | 239 |
| Offensive_Targeted_Insult_Group | 329 | 2557 | 140 |
| Offensive_Targeted_Insult_Other | 123 | 454 | 0 |
| Offensive_Untargetede | 212 | 2906 | 191 |
| Total Training Data | 6217 | 35139 | 16010 |

Table 2: Class-wise training data statistics

## 3 Modeling

In this section, we describe the different techniques and models that were used in developing offensive language classifiers. We use two popular transformer architecture based models- Multilingual BERT (Devlin et al., 2019) and XLM-RoBERTa (Conneau et al., 2020) as our backbone models. Inspired by some of the recent works on Hindi-English codemixed datasets, such as Khanuja et al. (2020) and Aguilar et al. (2020), we develop solutions based on language model pretraining and transliteration. We additionally evaluate the usefulness of representation fusion on all the three task datasets.

### 3.1 Architectures

Motivated by the successes of BERT model and its underlying Masked Language Modeling (MLM) pretraining strategy (Devlin et al., 2019), several derivatives evolved over the last couple of years. In this task, since the datasets contain texts in English, Tamil, Kannada and Malayalam in their native scripts as well as in Romanized form, we identify two suitable BERT based models for creating offensive identification classifiers.

Multilingual-BERT[4], aka. mBERT, is based on BERT architecture but pretrained with Wikipedias of 104 different languages including English, Tamil, Kannada and Malayalam. In this work, we specifically use the *cased* version of mBERT[5]. mBERT is pretrained on textual data from different languages with a shared architecture and a shared vocabulary, due to which there is a possible representation sharing across native and transliterated text forms. Corroborating it, Pires et al. (2019) presented its superior zero-shot abilities for an NER task in Hinglish.

XLM-RoBERTa, on the other hand, is also a transformer based model but is pretrained on Common Crawl data[6]. The common crawl data consists of textual data both in native scripts as well as in romanized script for some of the languages. Among the three languages in this task, only Tamil has Romanized data in the Common Crawl.

Given a stream of text as input, mBERT splits the text into sub-words by using WordPiece tokenization, whereas XLM-RoBERTa uses SentencePiece tokenization strategy. The sub-tokens are then appended with terminal markers such as `[CLS]` and `[SEP]`, indicating the start and end of the input stream, as shown below.

$$[CLS], w_1, w_2, ..., w_n, [SEP]$$

Popularized by BERT, the representation corresponding to the `[CLS]` token in the output layer is utilized for multi-class classification via a softmax layer. We utilize the same methodology in this work. While there are alternative choices for obtaining sentence-level representations, such as *sentence-transformers*[7], we leave their evaluation for future work. We obtain results with this setup and consider them as our baselines.

In an attempt to understand the usefulness of character embeddings when augmented with representations from BERT-based models, we develop a fusion architecture. In this architecture, we first obtain sub-word level representations from mBERT or XLM-RoBERTa models. We then convert them back to word-level representations by averaging the representations of sub-tokens of a given word. If a word is not split into sub-tokens, we use its representation as the word's representations. For every batch of training data, we keep track of words and their corresponding sub-tokens for the purpose of averaging. In a parallel, we also pass character-level embedding sequences through a Bidirectional-LSTM for every word. The hope is that the character-level BiLSTM helps to capture different variations in word patterns due to Romanization, especially useful in the context of social media text.

Once we obtain word-level representations from both character-level BiLSTM as well as BERT-based models, we concatenate the representations at word-level and pass them through a word-level Bidirectional-LSTM. The representation of the last word at the output of BiLSTM is then used for classification.

[4]https://github.com/google-research/bert/multilingual.md
[5]https://huggingface.co/transformers/multilingual.html
[6]http://data.statmt.org/cc-100/
[7]https://github.com/UKPLab/sentence-transformers

| Model | Input Text | F1 / Acc (Dev Split) | | |
|---|---|---|---|---|
| | | Kannada | Tamil | Malayalam |
| Baselines | | | | |
| mBERT | as-is | 67.30 / 70.79 | 76.79 / 79.01 | 95.77 / 96.10 |
| XLM-RoBERTa | | 68.70 / 71.56 | 76.28 / 78.19 | 94.12 / 94.85 |
| Task-adaptive pretraining | | | | |
| mBERT | as-is | 68.40 / 72.07 | 76.95 / 78.87 | 96.58 / 96.75 |
| XLM-RoBERTa | | 69.66 / 72.72 | 77.10 / 78.83 | 96.28 / 96.55 |
| Transliteration | | | | |
| mBERT | romanized | 68.84 / 72.07 | 75.16 / 78.49 | 95.72 / 95.80 |
| XLM-RoBERTa | | 67.73 / 71.17 | 75.73 / 78.08 | 94.18 / 95.00 |
| Fusion Architecture (w/ char-BiLSTM) | | | | |
| XLM-RoBERTa | as-is | 69.79 / 72.97 | 75.51 / 77.87 | 95.78 / 96.05 |
| Ensemble (Task-adaptive pretraining)) | | | | |
| mBERT | as-is | 70.30 / 74.00 | 76.94 / 79.67 | 96.76 / 97.00 |

Table 3: Results on all three languages of the task. *as-is* implies the text is inputted without any preprocessing.

### 3.2 Training Methodologies

In this section, we discuss some techniques to tailor mBERT and XLM-ROBERTa models for the task of offensiveness identification in Dravidian languages.

**MLM Pretraining:** Both the backbone models are pretrained with their respective corpora using Masked Language Modeling (MLM) objective–given a sentence, the model randomly masks 15% of the tokens in the input stream, runs the masked stream through several transformer layers, and then has to predict the masked tokens. Doing so helps the model to learn bi-directional contextual representations, unlike LSTM (Hochreiter and Schmidhuber, 1997) based language modeling.

Recent works such as Gururangan et al. (2020) showed that a second phase of pretraining (called domain-adaptive pretraining) with in-domain data can lead to performance gains. Relevant in the realm of codemixing NLP, Khanuja et al. (2020) and Aguilar et al. (2020) have shown that such a domain-adaptive pretraining can improve performances for classification tasks in Hinglish. They curated a corpora with millions of entries consisting of codemixed Hinglish in Romanized form. Once the multilingual BERT-based models are trained with such data, they utilized those models for downstream tasks. Their downstream tasks generally contained only texts in Romanized form. Gururangan et al. (2020) have further shown that adapting the models to the task's unlabeled data (called task-adaptive pretraining) improves performance even after domain-adaptive pretraining.

However, we identify few challenges in order to directly adopt ideologies from the related works to our task at hand. Firstly, the datasets provided for each language in this task consists of texts in English, native script of that language and its transliterated form. Thus, in order to convert everything into Romanized form, we need an accurate transliterator tool. Moreover, even if such a oracle transliterator exists, there could be challenges related to word normalization due to peculiarity of a given language's usage in social media platforms. Secondly, obtaining large amounts of Malayalam-English or Kannada-English code-mixed data for the purpose of pretraining is not readily feasible due to scarcity of relevant public datasets. Thus, we resort to only task-adaptive pretraining.

Some ideas towards curating corpora for domain-adaptive pretraining could be using machine translation datasets which have fair amounts of code-mixing or by adopting semi-supervised code-mixed data creation techniques (Gupta et al., 2020). Alternate approaches could be developing techniques for efficient representation-sharing between words from native script and their Romanized forms, similar to works such as Chaudhary et al. (2020). We leave these explorations to future work.

**Transliteration:** In order to evaluate the performance of mBERT and XLM-RoBERTa models when inputted with only Romanized script, we first transliterate the task datasets. To this end, we identify `indic-trans`[8] as the transliterator. While task-adaptive pretraining could also be conducted with transliterated texts, we leave this exploration to future work.

[8] https://github.com/libindic/indic-trans

| Model | Input Text | F1 / Acc (Dev Split) | | |
|---|---|---|---|---|
| | | Kannada | Tamil | Malayalam |
| mBERT (run-1) | as-is | 69.88 / 73.49 | 76.04 / 78.30 | 96.48 / 96.65 |
| XLM-RoBERTa (run-1) | | 69.72 / 72.59 | 76.80 / 79.40 | 95.80 / 96.25 |
| mBERT (run-2) | as-is | 68.67 / 72.72 | 76.58 / 79.17 | 96.50 / 96.70 |
| XLM-RoBERTa (run-2) | | 68.39 / 71.69 | 76.20 / 79.03 | 96.30 / 96.70 |
| mBERT (run-3) | as-is | 66.28 / 70.91 | 76.30 / 79.54 | 96.04 / 96.55 |
| XLM-RoBERTa (run-3) | | 69.08 / 71.94 | **77.86** / 78.71 | 96.17 / 96.30 |
| Ensemble (Mode) | as-is | **70.30 / 74.00** | 76.94 / **79.67** | **96.76 / 97.00** |

Table 4: Ensemble results on all three languages. *as-is* implies the text is inputted without any preprocessing.

## 4 Experiments

**Dataset and Metrics:** The number of training and validation examples for each language are presented in Table 1. Table 2 presents the class-wise distribution of the training data. As observed, the distribution is skewed with the dominant class being *Not_offensive*. In this work, we experiment with all three languages presented in the shared task. We use F1 and Accuracy as evaluation metrics[9].

**Implementation details:** For the purpose of training and validation, the corresponding data splits are utilized. Since gold labels for test sets were not previously available, different techniques were compared using evaluations on the validation set itself. For the purpose of task-adaptive pretraining using MLM objective, we combine the train and validation splits of the task data for training BERT models, and utilize test split of the task data for testing MLM pretraining. Due to compute resource limitations, we trim longer sentences to 300 characters (including spaces) and always use a batch size of 8. We do not perform any preprocessing on the text so as to allow for a generalized evaluation across the different datasets in the task.

We use Huggingface library (Wolf et al., 2020) for implementation of our backbone models. Specifically, we use `bert-base-multilingual-cased` and `xlm-roberta-base` models. For experiments related to representation fusion, we implement the BiLSTM models in PyTorch (Paszke et al., 2019). During task specific training for offensive classification, we optimize using the BertAdam[10] optimizer for models with a BERT component and with Adam (Kingma and Ba, 2014) optimizer for the remainder. These optimizers are used with default parameter settings. All experiments are conducted for 5 epochs and we pick the best model using the dev set. We use a hidden size of 128 for character-level BiLSTM and a size of 256 for word-level BiLSTM. We add dropouts with 0.40 rate at the outputs of both BiLSTMs.

**Ensemble:** For the final submission, we create a *majority voting* ensemble of 6 models– 3 of mBERT and 3 of XLM-RoBERTa– based on task-adaptive pretraining technique. Table 4 shows the results of various runs and the ensemble scores across all three languages.

**Discussion:** We observe that task-adaptive pretraining improves performance (1-2% absolute) in case of both the BERT-based models, with major gains obtained for Malayalam dataset (upto 2% absolute improvement). We also observe that the baseline performances are retained when the input text is fully Romanized, thereby opening up scope for future research along the direction of domain-adaptive pretraining. We also observe that the representation fusion helps in some datasets and degrades performance in others. However, we believe that more evaluation needs to be conducted to ascertain the usefulness of such fusion.

## 5 Conclusions

In this paper, we present our submission for EACL-2021 Shared Task on Offensive Language Identification in Dravidian languages. Our system was an ensemble of 6 different mBERT and XLM-RoBERTa models fine-tuned for the task of offensive language identification. The BERT models were pre-trained on given datasets in Malayalam, Tamil and Kannada. Our system ranked 1st for Kannada, 2nd for Malayalam and 3rd for Kannada. We also proposed a fusion-architecture to leverage character-level, subword-level and word-level embedding to improve performance.

[9]sklearn.metrics.classification_report.html

[10]github.com/cedrickchee/pytorch-pretrained-BERT

## References


Gustavo Aguilar, Sudipta Kar, and Thamar Solorio. 2020. LinCE: A Centralized Benchmark for Linguistic Code-switching Evaluation. In *Proceedings of The 12th Language Resources and Evaluation Conference*, pages 1803–1813, Marseille, France. European Language Resources Association.

Bharathi Raja Chakravarthi. 2020. HopeEDI: A multilingual hope speech detection dataset for equality, diversity, and inclusion. In *Proceedings of the Third Workshop on Computational Modeling of People's Opinions, Personality, and Emotion's in Social Media*, pages 41–53, Barcelona, Spain (Online). Association for Computational Linguistics.

Bharathi Raja Chakravarthi, Navya Jose, Shardul Suryawanshi, Elizabeth Sherly, and John Philip McCrae. 2020a. A sentiment analysis dataset for code-mixed Malayalam-English. In *Proceedings of the 1st Joint Workshop on Spoken Language Technologies for Under-resourced languages (SLTU) and Collaboration and Computing for Under-Resourced Languages (CCURL)*, pages 177–184, Marseille, France. European Language Resources association.

Bharathi Raja Chakravarthi, M Anand Kumar, John Philip McCrae, Premjith B, Soman KP, and Thomas Mandl. 2020b. Overview of the track on HASOC-Offensive Language Identification-DravidianCodeMix. In *Working Notes of the Forum for Information Retrieval Evaluation (FIRE 2020). CEUR Workshop Proceedings. In: CEUR-WS. org, Hyderabad, India.*

Bharathi Raja Chakravarthi, Vigneshwaran Muralidaran, Ruba Priyadharshini, and John Philip McCrae. 2020c. Corpus creation for sentiment analysis in code-mixed Tamil-English text. In *Proceedings of the 1st Joint Workshop on Spoken Language Technologies for Under-resourced languages (SLTU) and Collaboration and Computing for Under-Resourced Languages (CCURL)*, pages 202–210, Marseille, France. European Language Resources association.

Bharathi Raja Chakravarthi, Ruba Priyadharshini, Vigneshwaran Muralidaran, Shardul Suryawanshi, Navya Jose, Elizabeth Sherly, and John P. McCrae. 2020d. Overview of the Track on Sentiment Analysis for Dravidian Languages in Code-Mixed Text. In *Forum for Information Retrieval Evaluation*, FIRE 2020, page 21–24, New York, NY, USA. Association for Computing Machinery.

Aditi Chaudhary, Karthik Raman, Krishna Srinivasan, and Jiecao Chen. 2020. Dict-mlm: Improved multilingual pre-training using bilingual dictionaries.

Alexis Conneau, Kartikay Khandelwal, Naman Goyal, Vishrav Chaudhary, Guillaume Wenzek, Francisco Guzmán, Edouard Grave, Myle Ott, Luke Zettlemoyer, and Veselin Stoyanov. 2019. Unsupervised cross-lingual representation learning at scale. *arXiv preprint arXiv:1911.02116.*

Alexis Conneau, Kartikay Khandelwal, Naman Goyal, Vishrav Chaudhary, Guillaume Wenzek, Francisco Guzmán, Edouard Grave, Myle Ott, Luke Zettlemoyer, and Veselin Stoyanov. 2020. Unsupervised cross-lingual representation learning at scale. *Proceedings of the 58th Annual Meeting of the Association for Computational Linguistics.*

Jacob Devlin, Ming-Wei Chang, Kenton Lee, and Kristina Toutanova. 2018. Bert: Pre-training of deep bidirectional transformers for language understanding. *arXiv preprint arXiv:1810.04805.*

Jacob Devlin, Ming-Wei Chang, Kenton Lee, and Kristina Toutanova. 2019. BERT: Pre-training of deep bidirectional transformers for language understanding. In *Proceedings of the 2019 Conference of the North American Chapter of the Association for Computational Linguistics: Human Language Technologies, Volume 1 (Long and Short Papers)*, pages 4171–4186, Minneapolis, Minnesota. Association for Computational Linguistics.

Deepak Gupta, Asif Ekbal, and Pushpak Bhattacharyya. 2020. A semi-supervised approach to generate the code-mixed text using pre-trained encoder and transfer learning. In *Findings of the Association for Computational Linguistics: EMNLP 2020*, pages 2267–2280, Online. Association for Computational Linguistics.

Suchin Gururangan, Ana Marasović, Swabha Swayamdipta, Kyle Lo, Iz Beltagy, Doug Downey, and Noah A. Smith. 2020. Don't stop pretraining: Adapt language models to domains and tasks. *Proceedings of the 58th Annual Meeting of the Association for Computational Linguistics.*

Adeep Hande, Ruba Priyadharshini, and Bharathi Raja Chakravarthi. 2020. KanCMD: Kannada CodeMixed dataset for sentiment analysis and offensive language detection. In *Proceedings of the Third Workshop on Computational Modeling of People's Opinions, Personality, and Emotion's in Social Media*, pages 54–63, Barcelona, Spain (Online). Association for Computational Linguistics.

Sepp Hochreiter and Jürgen Schmidhuber. 1997. Long short-term memory. *Neural Computation*, 9(8):1735–1780.

Navya Jose, Bharathi Raja Chakravarthi, Shardul Suryawanshi, Elizabeth Sherly, and John P. McCrae. 2020. A Survey of Current Datasets for Code-Switching Research. In *2020 6th International Conference on Advanced Computing and Communication Systems (ICACCS)*, pages 136–141.

Simran Khanuja, Sandipan Dandapat, Anirudh Srinivasan, Sunayana Sitaram, and Monojit Choudhury. 2020. GLUECoS: An evaluation benchmark for code-switched NLP. In *Proceedings of the 58th Annual Meeting of the Association for Computational Linguistics*, pages 3575–3585, Online. Association for Computational Linguistics.

Diederik P. Kingma and Jimmy Ba. 2014. Adam: A method for stochastic optimization.

Thomas Mandl, Sandip Modha, Anand Kumar M, and Bharathi Raja Chakravarthi. 2020. Overview of the HASOC Track at FIRE 2020: Hate Speech and Offensive Language Identification in Tamil, Malayalam, Hindi, English and German. In *Forum for Information Retrieval Evaluation*, FIRE 2020, page 29–32, New York, NY, USA. Association for Computing Machinery.

Adam Paszke, Sam Gross, Francisco Massa, Adam Lerer, James Bradbury, Gregory Chanan, Trevor Killeen, Zeming Lin, Natalia Gimelshein, Luca Antiga, Alban Desmaison, Andreas Kopf, Edward Yang, Zachary DeVito, Martin Raison, Alykhan Tejani, Sasank Chilamkurthy, Benoit Steiner, Lu Fang, Junjie Bai, and Soumith Chintala. 2019. Pytorch: An imperative style, high-performance deep learning library. In H. Wallach, H. Larochelle, A. Beygelzimer, F. d'Alché-Buc, E. Fox, and R. Garnett, editors, *Advances in Neural Information Processing Systems 32*, pages 8024–8035. Curran Associates, Inc.

Parth Patwa, Gustavo Aguilar, Sudipta Kar, Suraj Pandey, Srinivas PYKL, Björn Gambäck, Tanmoy Chakraborty, Thamar Solorio, and Amitava Das. 2020. Semeval-2020 task 9: Overview of sentiment analysis of code-mixed tweets. *arXiv e-prints*, pages arXiv–2008.

Telmo Pires, Eva Schlinger, and Dan Garrette. 2019. How multilingual is multilingual BERT? In *Proceedings of the 57th Annual Meeting of the Association for Computational Linguistics*, pages 4996–5001, Florence, Italy. Association for Computational Linguistics.

Ruba Priyadharshini, Bharathi Raja Chakravarthi, Mani Vegupatti, and John P. McCrae. 2020. Named Entity Recognition for Code-Mixed Indian Corpus using Meta Embedding. In *2020 6th International Conference on Advanced Computing and Communication Systems (ICACCS)*, pages 68–72.

Sunayana Sitaram, Khyathi Raghavi Chandu, Sai Krishna Rallabandi, and Alan W Black. 2019. A survey of code-switched speech and language processing. *arXiv preprint arXiv:1904.00784*.

Thomas Wolf, Lysandre Debut, Victor Sanh, Julien Chaumond, Clement Delangue, Anthony Moi, Pierric Cistac, Tim Rault, Remi Louf, Morgan Funtowicz, Joe Davison, Sam Shleifer, Patrick von Platen, Clara Ma, Yacine Jernite, Julien Plu, Canwen Xu, Teven Le Scao, Sylvain Gugger, Mariama Drame, Quentin Lhoest, and Alexander Rush. 2020. Transformers: State-of-the-art natural language processing. In *Proceedings of the 2020 Conference on Empirical Methods in Natural Language Processing: System Demonstrations*, pages 38–45, Online. Association for Computational Linguistics.

Marcos Zampieri, Shervin Malmasi, Preslav Nakov, Sara Rosenthal, Noura Farra, and Ritesh Kumar. 2019. Semeval-2019 task 6: Identifying and categorizing offensive language in social media (offenseval). *arXiv preprint arXiv:1903.08983*.

Marcos Zampieri, Preslav Nakov, Sara Rosenthal, Pepa Atanasova, Georgi Karadzhov, Hamdy Mubarak, Leon Derczynski, Zeses Pitenis, and Çağrı Çöltekin. 2020. Semeval-2020 task 12: Multilingual offensive language identification in social media (offenseval 2020). *arXiv preprint arXiv:2006.07235*.

# SSNCSE_NLP@DravidianLangTech-EACL2021: Offensive Language Identification on Multilingual Code Mixing Text

**B. Bharathi & Agnusimmaculate Silvia A**
Department of CSE
Sri Siva subramaniya Nadar College of Engineering
Kalavakkam - 603110
bharathib@ssn.edu.in
agnusimmaculate18011@cse.ssn.edu.in

## Abstract

Social networks made a huge impact in almost all fields in recent years. Text messaging through the Internet or cellular phones has become a major medium of personal and commercial communication. Everyday we have to deal with texts, emails or different types of messages in which there are a variety of attacks and abusive phrases. It is the moderator's decision which comments to remove from the platform because of violations and which ones to keep but an automatic software for detecting abusive languages would be useful in recent days. In this paper we describe an automatic offensive language identification from Dravidian languages with various machine learning algorithms. This is work is shared task in DravidanLangTech-EACL2021. The goal of this task is to identify offensive language content of the code-mixed dataset of comments/posts in Dravidian Languages ( (Tamil-English, Malayalam-English, and Kannada-English)) collected from social media. This work explains the submissions made by SSNCSE_NLP in DravidanLangTech-EACL2021 Code-mix tasks for Offensive language detection. We achieve F1 scores of 0.95 for Malayalam, 0.7 for Kannada and 0.73 for task2-Tamil on the test-set.

## 1 Introduction

Social media has become an important tool to connect the people all over the world. This is because it allows its users to share the content they want quickly, efficiently and in real-time. However, user-created content shared on social media is not always organized by the rules. In fact, nowadays, content written in an offensive language has become widespread on social media (Chakravarthi and Muralidaran, 2021; Chakravarthi et al., 2021; Suryawanshi and Chakravarthi, 2021). Offensive language is defined as message which contains insulting or threatening expressions written by one person to another (Chakravarthi et al., 2020d; Mandl et al., 2020). The severity of this problem is increasing each day; consequently, it is very important to deal with this problem in terms of government policy, social media terms and policies and online community plans (Chakravarthi et al., 2020b). At this stage, there is a need for effective methods. Social media generates a large amount of data daily as mentioned above. Therefore, it is very difficult to manually determine offensive language on the social media even by an expert. Some words that have multiple meanings that could be offensive to some people from some places. There is an increasing demand for offensive language identification on social media texts which are largely code-mixed (Chakravarthi, 2020).

Code-mixing is a prevalent phenomenon in a multilingual community and the code-mixed texts are sometimes written in non-native scripts (Jose et al., 2020; Priyadharshini et al., 2020). Systems trained on monolingual data fail on code-mixed data due to the complexity of code-switching at different linguistic levels in the text (Chakravarthi et al., 2018, 2019). This shared task on Offensive Language Identification in Dravidian Languages-EACL 2021 presents a new gold standard corpus for offensive language identification of code-mixed text in Dravidian languages (Tamil-English, Malayalam-English, and Kannada-English). A recorded Tamil writing has been archived for more than 2600 years (Thavareesan and Mahesan, 2019, 2020a,b). The oldest time of Tamil writing, Sangam writing, is dated from ca. 600 BC – AD 300. It has the most established surviving writing among Dravidian languages. Over 55% of the epigraphical engravings (around 55,000) found by the Archeological Survey of India are in the Tamil language.

The remainder of the paper is organized as fol-



*Proceedings of the First Workshop on Speech and Language Technologies for Dravidian Languages*, pages 313–318
April 20, 2021 

| Task description | Class label | Train-set | Dev-set | Test-set |
|---|---|---|---|---|
| Tamil-code mixed | Not_offensive | 25425 | 3193 | 3190 |
| | Offensive_Untargeted | 2906 | 356 | 368 |
| | Offensive_Targeted_Insult_Group | 2557 | 309 | 315 |
| | Offensive_Targeted_Insult_Individual | 2343 | 295 | 288 |
| | not-Tamil | 1454 | 172 | 160 |
| | Offensive_Targeted_Insult_Other | 454 | 65 | 71 |
| Malayalam-code mixed | Not_offensive | 14153 | 1779 | 1765 |
| | not-malayalam | 1287 | 163 | 157 |
| | Offensive_Targeted_Insult_Individual | 239 | 24 | 29 |
| | Offensive_Untargeted | 191 | 20 | 27 |
| | Offensive_Targeted_Insult_Group | 140 | 13 | 23 |
| Kananda-code mixed | Not_offensive | 3544 | 426 | 427 |
| | not-Kannada | 1522 | 191 | 185 |
| | Offensive_Targeted_Insult_Individual | 487 | 66 | 75 |
| | Offensive_Targeted_Insult_Group | 329 | 45 | 44 |
| | Offensive_Untargetede | 212 | 33 | 33 |
| | Offensive_Targeted_Insult_Other | 123 | 16 | 14 |

Table 1: Data Distribution

lows. Section 2 discusses the related work on offensive language identification task. The dataset about the shared task is described in Section . Section 4 outlines the features and machine learning algorithms used for this task. Results are discussed in Section 5. Section 6 concludes the paper.

## 2 Related work

Offensive language identification for Greek language is described in (Pitenis et al., 2020). This paper uses different machine learning and deep learning models to for offensive language identification task with Offensive Greek Tweet Dataset. Multilingual offensive language identification using cross lingual embeddings with transfer learning is carried out in (Puranik et al., 2021; Hegde et al., 2021; Yasaswini et al., 2021; Ghanghor et al., 2021b,a). In (Razavi et al., 2010), flame detection approach which extracts features at different conceptual levels and applies multilevel classification for flame detection was described. Arabic offensive language identification task was described in (Alakrot et al., 2018). The survey of offensive language identification task is explained in (Pradhan et al., 2020). Machine learning approach for detecting offensive language identification on Twitter data is carried out in (Gaydhani et al., 2018).

## 3 Data-set Analysis and Preprocessing

The goal of this task is to identify offensive language content of the code-mixed dataset of comments/posts in Dravidian Languages ( (Tamil-English, Malayalam-English, and Kannada-English)) collected from social media(Chakravarthi et al., 2021, 2020a,c; Hande et al., 2020). The comment/post may contain more than one sentence but the average sentence length of the corpora is 1. Each comment/post is annotated at the comment/post level. This dataset also has class imbalance problems depicting real-world scenarios. The dataset containing YouTube comments with class labels such as Not-offensive, offensive-untargeted, offensive-targeted-individual, offensive-targeted-group, offensive-targeted-other, or Not-in-indented-language. The train-set, dev-set and test-set distribution with class-wise distribution is shown in Table 1. There is a clear imbalance in the data-set distribution. This could cause a bias towards a particular class and the model trained on this data-set would be more inclined towards the dominant class.

## 4 Experimental setup and features

For feature extraction, the n-gram model and BERT embedding model are experimented upon. As the content of the comments is a mix of Dravidian language grammar in Roman lexicons along with English grammar, it becomes challenging to find

| Features | Classifier | Precision | Recall | F1-score |
|---|---|---|---|---|
| Tfidf | Random forest | 0.77 | 0.75 | 0.66 |
| Tfidf | K-nearest | 0.69 | 0.75 | 0.70 |
| Tfidf | Adaboost | 0.62 | 0.74 | 0.65 |
| Tfidf | Decision tree classifier | 0.66 | 0.66 | 0.67 |
| Count vec | Random forest | 0.74 | 0.75 | 0.66 |
| Count vec | MLP classifier | 0.74 | 0.76 | 0.75 |
| BERT | MLP classifier | 0.71 | 0.72 | 0.69 |

Table 2: Performance of the proposed approach of Tamil-English code mixed text using dev data

| Features | Classifier | Precision | Recall | F1-score |
|---|---|---|---|---|
| Tfidf | k-nearest | 0.91 | 0.91 | 0.91 |
| Tfidf | MLP | 0.97 | 0.97 | 0.97 |
| Tfidf | SVM | 0.87 | 0.75 | 0.81 |
| Countvec | k-nearest | 0.90 | 0.91 | 0.91 |
| Countvec | MLP | 0.97 | 0.97 | 0.97 |
| Countvec | SVM | 0.96 | 0.96 | 0.96 |
| BERT | MLP classifier | 0.95 | 0.87 | 0.85 |

Table 3: Performance of the proposed approach of Malayalam-English code mixed text using dev data

pre-trained models for this context. So a simple n-gram approach is considered. Also, the advancements done by the transformer model for pre-training and the availability of multilingual trained models encourage to experiment with BERT pre-trained embeddings. In the proposed approach, TFIDF, Count vectorizer and BERT embeddings were extracted from the input text. Then the extracted features were trained with different machine learning models such as K-nearest neighbour, MLP classifier, random forest classifier, Ada boost classifier, decision tree classifier and voting classifier etc. The experiments were conducted for Tamil-English, Malayalam-English, and Kannada-English data sets and best models obtained for these tasks were used to generate the scores for the test-set.

## 5 Observations

### 5.1 Tamil-English dataset

The features such as TFIDF, Count vectorizer and BERT embeddings were extracted from the youtube comments specified in Tamil-English code mixed text. The extracted features were trained with different machine learning models and the models are evaluated using the development data and results are tabulated in Table 2.

From the Table 2, count vectorizer feature with MLP classifier is giving the F1-score of 0.75.

### 5.2 Malayalam-English dataset

The features such as TFIDF, Count vectorizer and BERT embeddings were extracted from the youtube comments specified in Malayalam-English code mixed text. The extracted features were trained with different machine learning models and the models are evaluated using the development data and results are tabulated in Table 3.

From the Table 3, count vectorizer feature with MLP classifier is giving the F1-score of 0.97.

### 5.3 Kannada-English dataset

The features such as TFIDF, Count vectorizer and BERT embeddings were extracted from the youtube comments specified in Kannada-English code mixed text. The extracted features were trained with different machine learning models and the models are evaluated using the development data and results are tabulated in Table 4.

From the Table 3, count vectorizer feature with MLP classifier is giving the F1-score of 0.69.

Three runs were submitted using the Tamil-English, Malayalam-English, and Kannada-English code mixed text. The results of the runs were tabulated in Table in 5.

From Table 5, it has been noted that the performance of the proposed system is better for

| Features | Classifier | Precision | Recall | F1-score |
|---|---|---|---|---|
| Tfidf | k-nearest | 0.63 | 0.65 | 0.63 |
| Tfidf | MLP | 0.68 | 0.70 | 0.68 |
| Tfidf | SVM | 0.68 | 0.73 | 0.69 |
| Countvectorizer | k-nearest | 0.62 | 0.65 | 0.62 |
| Countvectorizer | MLP | 0.69 | 0.71 | 0.69 |
| Countvectorizer | SVM | 0.67 | 0.69 | 0.68 |
| SentenceTransformer | MLP classifier | 0.67 | 0.65 | 0.64 |

Table 4: Performance of the proposed approach of Kannada-English code mixed text using dev data

| Dataset | Precision | Recall | F1-score | Rank |
|---|---|---|---|---|
| Tam-Eng | 0.74 | 0.73 | 0.73 | 6 |
| Mal-Eng | 0.95 | 0.96 | 0.95 | 3 |
| Kan-Eng | 0.71 | 0.74 | 0.70 | 5 |

Table 5: Performance of the proposed approach using test data

Malayalam-English code mixed text.

## 6 Conclusion

There is an increasing demand for offensive language identification on social media texts which are largely code-mixed. The goal of this task is to identify offensive language content of the code-mixed dataset of comments/posts in Dravidian Languages ( (Tamil-English, Malayalam-English, and Kannada-English)) collected from social media. In the proposed work, the basic TFIDF and count vectorizer features are giving better performance when compared to sentence embeddings. The examples are not sufficient to train the deep learning models. The machine learning models are giving better performance than the deep learning models.

## References


Azalden Alakrot, Liam Murray, and Nikola S. Nikolov. 2018. Towards accurate detection of offensive language in online communication in arabic. *Procedia Computer Science*, 142:315 – 320. Arabic Computational Linguistics.

Bharathi Raja Chakravarthi. 2020. *Leveraging orthographic information to improve machine translation of under-resourced languages*. Ph.D. thesis, NUI Galway.

Bharathi Raja Chakravarthi, Mihael Arcan, and John P. McCrae. 2018. Improving wordnets for under-resourced languages using machine translation. In *Proceedings of the 9th Global Wordnet Conference*, pages 77–86, Nanyang Technological University (NTU), Singapore. Global Wordnet Association.

Bharathi Raja Chakravarthi, Mihael Arcan, and John P. McCrae. 2019. WordNet gloss translation for under-resourced languages using multilingual neural machine translation. In *Proceedings of the Second Workshop on Multilingualism at the Intersection of Knowledge Bases and Machine Translation*, pages 1–7, Dublin, Ireland. European Association for Machine Translation.

Bharathi Raja Chakravarthi, Navya Jose, Shardul Suryawanshi, Elizabeth Sherly, and John Philip McCrae. 2020a. A sentiment analysis dataset for code-mixed Malayalam-English. In *Proceedings of the 1st Joint Workshop on Spoken Language Technologies for Under-resourced languages (SLTU) and Collaboration and Computing for Under-Resourced Languages (CCURL)*, pages 177–184, Marseille, France. European Language Resources association.

Bharathi Raja Chakravarthi, M Anand Kumar, John Philip McCrae, Premjith B, Soman KP, and Thomas Mandl. 2020b. Overview of the track on HASOC-Offensive Language Identification-DravidianCodeMix. In *Working Notes of the Forum for Information Retrieval Evaluation (FIRE 2020). CEUR Workshop Proceedings. In: CEUR-WS. org, Hyderabad, India.*

Bharathi Raja Chakravarthi and Vigneshwaran Muralidaran. 2021. Findings of the shared task on Hope Speech Detection for Equality, Diversity, and Inclusion. In *Proceedings of the First Workshop on Language Technology for Equality, Diversity and Inclusion*. Association for Computational Linguistics.

Bharathi Raja Chakravarthi, Vigneshwaran Muralidaran, Ruba Priyadharshini, and John Philip McCrae. 2020c. Corpus creation for sentiment analysis in code-mixed Tamil-English text. In *Proceedings of the 1st Joint Workshop on Spoken Language Technologies for Under-resourced languages (SLTU) and Collaboration and Computing *for Under-Resourced Languages (CCURL)*, pages 202–210, Marseille, France. European Language Resources association.

Bharathi Raja Chakravarthi, Ruba Priyadharshini, Navya Jose, Anand Kumar M, Thomas Mandl, Prasanna Kumar Kumaresan, Rahul Ponnusamy, Hariharan V, Elizabeth Sherly, and John Philip McCrae. 2021. Findings of the shared task on Offensive Language Identification in Tamil, Malayalam, and Kannada. In *Proceedings of the First Workshop on Speech and Language Technologies for Dravidian Languages*. Association for Computational Linguistics.

Bharathi Raja Chakravarthi, Ruba Priyadharshini, Vigneshwaran Muralidaran, Shardul Suryawanshi, Navya Jose, Elizabeth Sherly, and John P. McCrae. 2020d. Overview of the Track on Sentiment Analysis for Dravidian Languages in Code-Mixed Text. In *Forum for Information Retrieval Evaluation*, FIRE 2020, page 21–24, New York, NY, USA. Association for Computing Machinery.

Aditya Gaydhani, Vikrant Doma, Shrikant Kendre, and Laxmi Bhagwat. 2018. Detecting hate speech and offensive language on twitter using machine learning: An n-gram and tfidf based approach.

Nikhil Kumar Ghanghor, Parameswari Krishnamurthy, Sajeetha Thavareesan, Ruba Priyadharshini, and Bharathi Raja Chakravarthi. 2021a. IIITK@DravidianLangTech-EACL2021: Offensive Language Identification and Meme Classification in Tamil, Malayalam and Kannada. In *Proceedings of the First Workshop on Speech and Language Technologies for Dravidian Languages*, Online. Association for Computational Linguistics.

Nikhil Kumar Ghanghor, Rahul Ponnusamy, Prasanna Kumar Kumaresan, Ruba Priyadharshini, Sajeetha Thavareesan, and Bharathi Raja Chakravarthi. 2021b. IIITK@LT-EDI-EACL2021: Hope Speech Detection for Equality, Diversity, and Inclusion in Tamil, Malayalam and English. In *Proceedings of the First Workshop on Language Technology for Equality, Diversity and Inclusion*, Online.

Adeep Hande, Ruba Priyadharshini, and Bharathi Raja Chakravarthi. 2020. KanCMD: Kannada CodeMixed dataset for sentiment analysis and offensive language detection. In *Proceedings of the Third Workshop on Computational Modeling of People's Opinions, Personality, and Emotion's in Social Media*, pages 54–63, Barcelona, Spain (Online). Association for Computational Linguistics.

Siddhanth U Hegde, Adeep Hande, Ruba Priyadharshini, Sajeetha Thavareesan, and Bharathi Raja Chakravarthi. 2021. UVCE-IIITT@DravidianLangTech-EACL2021: Tamil Troll Meme Classification: You need to Pay more Attention. In *Proceedings of the First Workshop on Speech and Language Technologies for Dravidian Languages*. Association for Computational Linguistics.

Navya Jose, Bharathi Raja Chakravarthi, Shardul Suryawanshi, Elizabeth Sherly, and John P. McCrae. 2020. A Survey of Current Datasets for Code-Switching Research. In *2020 6th International Conference on Advanced Computing and Communication Systems (ICACCS)*, pages 136–141.

Thomas Mandl, Sandip Modha, Anand Kumar M, and Bharathi Raja Chakravarthi. 2020. Overview of the HASOC Track at FIRE 2020: Hate Speech and Offensive Language Identification in Tamil, Malayalam, Hindi, English and German. In *Forum for Information Retrieval Evaluation*, FIRE 2020, page 29–32, New York, NY, USA. Association for Computing Machinery.

Zesis Pitenis, Marcos Zampieri, and Tharindu Ranasinghe. 2020. Offensive language identification in Greek. In *Proceedings of the 12th Language Resources and Evaluation Conference*, pages 5113–5119, Marseille, France. European Language Resources Association.

Rahul Pradhan, Ankur Chaturvedi, Aprna Tripathi, and Dilip Sharma. 2020. *A Review on Offensive Language Detection*, pages 433–439.

Ruba Priyadharshini, Bharathi Raja Chakravarthi, Mani Vegupatti, and John P. McCrae. 2020. Named Entity Recognition for Code-Mixed Indian Corpus using Meta Embedding. In *2020 6th International Conference on Advanced Computing and Communication Systems (ICACCS)*, pages 68–72.

Karthik Puranik, Adeep Hande, Ruba Priyadharshini, Sajeetha Thavareesan, and Bharathi Raja Chakravarthi. 2021. IIITT@LT-EDI-EACL2021-Hope Speech Detection: There is always hope in Transformers. In *Proceedings of the First Workshop on Language Technology for Equality, Diversity and Inclusion*. Association for Computational Linguistics.

Amir H. Razavi, Diana Inkpen, Sasha Uritsky, and Stan Matwin. 2010. Offensive language detection using multi-level classification. In *Advances in Artificial Intelligence*, pages 16–27.

Shardul Suryawanshi and Bharathi Raja Chakravarthi. 2021. Findings of the shared task on Troll Meme Classification in Tamil. In *Proceedings of the First Workshop on Speech and Language Technologies for Dravidian Languages*. Association for Computational Linguistics.

Sajeetha Thavareesan and Sinnathamby Mahesan. 2019. Sentiment Analysis in Tamil Texts: A Study on Machine Learning Techniques and Feature Representation. In *2019 14th Conference on Industrial and Information Systems (ICIIS)*, pages 320–325.

Sajeetha Thavareesan and Sinnathamby Mahesan. 2020a. Sentiment Lexicon Expansion using Word2vec and fastText for Sentiment Prediction in Tamil texts. In *2020 Moratuwa Engineering Research Conference (MERCon)*, pages 272–276.

Sajeetha Thavareesan and Sinnathamby Mahesan. 2020b. Word embedding-based Part of Speech tagging in Tamil texts. In *2020 IEEE 15th International Conference on Industrial and Information Systems (ICIIS)*, pages 478–482.

Konthala Yasaswini, Karthik Puranik, Adeep Hande, Ruba Priyadharshini, Sajeetha Thavareesan, and Bharathi Raja Chakravarthi. 2021. IIITT@DravidianLangTech-EACL2021: Transfer Learning for Offensive Language Detection in Dravidian Languages. In *Proceedings of the First Workshop on Speech and Language Technologies for Dravidian Languages*. Association for Computational Linguistics.

# JUNLP@DravidianLangTech-EACL2021: Offensive Language Identification in Dravidian Langauges

**Avishek Garain**[1] Jadavpur University, India

**Atanu Mandal**[2] Jadavpur University, India

**Sudip Kumar Naskar**[3] Jadavpur University, India

{[1]avishekgarain, [2]atanumandal0491}@gmail.com, [3]sudipkumar.naskar@jadavpuruniversity.in

## Abstract

Offensive language identification has been an active area of research in natural language processing. With the emergence of multiple social media platforms offensive language identification has emerged as a need of the hour. Traditional offensive language identification models fail to deliver acceptable results as social media contents are largely in multilingual and are code-mixed in nature. This paper tries to resolve this problem by using IndicBERT and BERT architectures, to facilitate identification of offensive languages for Kannada-English, Malayalam-English, and Tamil-English code-mixed language pairs extracted from social media. The presented approach when evaluated on the test corpus provided precision, recall, and F1 score for language pair Kannada-English as 0.62, 0.71, and 0.66, respectively, for language pair Malayalam-English as 0.77, 0.43, and 0.53, respectively, and for Tamil-English as 0.71, 0.74, and 0.72, respectively.

## 1 Introduction

Social media platforms like question answering platforms, collaborative projects, social networks, news platforms provide discussion area for users, where content moderators are engaged to keep respectful conversations (Thavareesan and Mahesan, 2019, 2020a,b). Moderators assure that the platform's discussion rules are adhered to, including the prohibition of offensive languages. Moderators implement these rules by partly or entirely removing user comments.

Typically, platform rules are available to the user in the form of guidelines. However, all user doesn't follow the rules while commenting on a post. An increase of end-users in social platforms leads to the increasing number of comments that make the moderator restless to identify offensive and non-offensive. To intercept the circumstances recent trends of identification of offensive language have become a scientific asset (Chakravarthi et al., 2020c; Chakravarthi, 2020).

In the context of Natural Language Processing (NLP), offensive language identification is a classification task that is aimed to identify and minimize offensive contents in social media (Mandl et al., 2020). There have been advancements in this domain of research both in industrial and academia with increasing access to larger and richer social media data over the years. India is a linguistically diverse country with 22 official languages with common languages used being English and Hindi. There has been a mixing of cultures and languages over the years thus leading to an increasing demand for offensive language identification on social media texts which are largely code-mixed.

Code-mixing refers to a prevalent phenomenon which exists in a multilingual community and the code-mixed texts are sometimes written in non-native scripts. Any System which is trained on monolingual datasets miserably fails when exposed to code-mixed data due to the complexity of code-switching at different linguistic levels in the text (Jose et al., 2020; Priyadharshini et al., 2020).

Many researcher has proposed many different approaches to achieve the state-of-the-art results in code-mixing scenarios during the recent years. Author (Mathur et al., 2018) has solved the problem of classification of the tweets in Hindi-English Offensive Tweet (HEOT) dataset using transfer learning in which author has employed Convolutional Neural Networks as pre-trained on tweets in English followed by retraining on Hinglish tweets. HEOT dataset consists of Hindi-English code switched language into three classes nonoffensive, abusive and hate-speech. The author (Bohra et al., 2018) proposes a supervised classification system that detects hate speech in the text using various character level, word level, and lexicon based features



*Proceedings of the First Workshop on Speech and Language Technologies for Dravidian Languages*, pages 319–322
April 20, 2021 ©2021 Association for Computational Linguistics

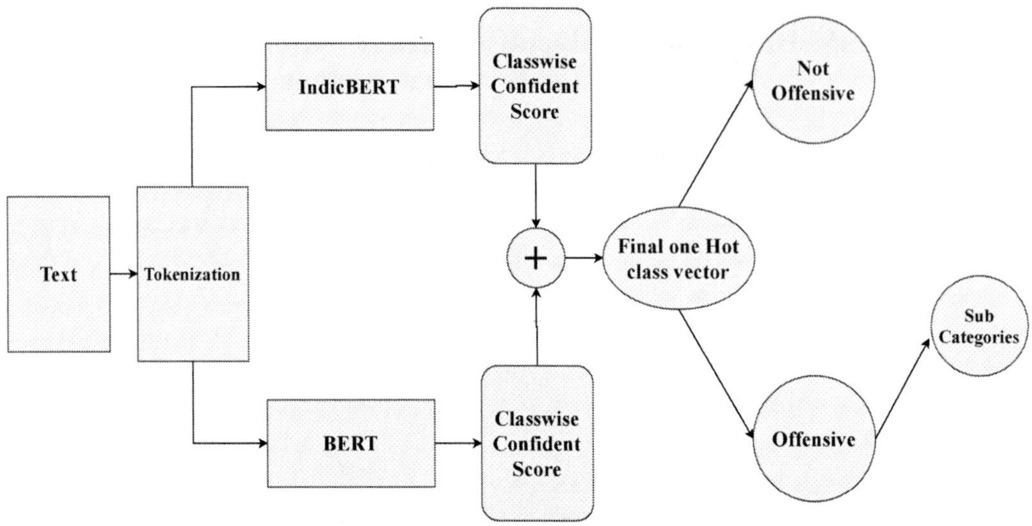


Figure 1: Framework for Offensive Language Identification

whereas (Santosh and Aravind, 2019) dealt the task of identification of hate speech and offensive language from code-mixed social media text using two architecture namely sub-word level LSTM model and Hierarchical LSTM model with attention based on phonemic sub-words. Another real-world issue dataset have been released by the authors (Hande et al., 2020) who have introduced Kannada CodeMixed Dataset (KanCMD). The dataset is a multi-task learning dataset for sentiment analysis and offensive language identification. The KanCMD dataset highlights two real-world issues from the social media text. Firstly, it contains actual comments in code mixed text posted by users on YouTube social media, rather than in monolingual text from the textbook. Secondly, it has been annotated for two tasks, namely sentiment analysis and offensive language detection for under-resourced Kannada language. Hence, KanCMD was meant to stimulate research in under-resourced Kannada language on real-world code-mixed social media text and multi-task learning. Our proposed system is yet to explore the dataset.

This paper aims to solve this research problem by using generalized Deep learning architectures named IndicBERT (Kakwani et al., 2020) and BERT (Devlin et al., 2019). The goal of this task is to identify offensive language content of the code-mixed dataset of comments or posts in Dravidian Languages collected from social media. The code-mixed language for the task was Tamil-English (Chakravarthi et al., 2020b), Malayalam-English (Chakravarthi et al., 2020a), and Kannada-English (Hande et al., 2020) provided by DravidianLangTech-2021 (Chakravarthi et al., 2021). The working system is available in GitHub[1].

The rest of the paper has been organized as follows. Section 2 describes the data that was used to build the proposed Offensive Language Identification system. Section 3 describes the proposed model used to build the system and will be followed by the evaluation of the model in section 4.

## 2 Data

The shared task organized by DravidianLangTech-2021 provided the gold standard corpus for offensive language identification of code-mixed text for three different sets Tamil-English, Malayalam-English, and Kannada-English in Dravidian languages.

The dataset was collected from social media. The average sentence length of comment or post of the corpora is 1. Each comment or post is annotated at the comment or post level. Depicting the real-life scenarios the corpora was provided with class imbalance problem. The corpora has 6 output labels: Not offensive, Offensive untargeted, Offensive targeted individual, Offensive targeted group, Offensive targeted other, or Not in indented language.

[1]https://github.com/garain/EACL21-system

## 3 Framework

Every sentence is a sequence of words. For a code-mixed scenarios, these words from different languages might have no proper boundary to separate them. Our goal was to first classifying the texts to the primary category which are either Offensive or not offensive. Thereafter, if the texts were identified to be offensive, then further classification was done for sub categories which are targeted insult individual, targeted insult group or targeted insult other. We considered the whole task as a multi-label classification problem. The overall methodology is shown in Figure 1.

The training corpus was first tokenized and the required tags were inserted. Then the tokenized data was fed to the IndicBERT and BERT models. We make use of pre-trained vectors for initializing the mentioned models and then fine-tuned using the training corpus. The IndicBERT model supports various Indic languages. Therefore for each language pair a seperate model had to be trained with corresponding language settings. The confidence scores for each class obtained from the IndicBERT model and the regular BERT model are then concatenated to give the final scores for each of the classes. The score array is converted to a 1-D array in one-hot vector format containing 1's depicting not offensive category and 0's depicting offensive category, which was further classified for rest of the sub categories.

The output vector consisted of the following labels in order:

- Not - offensive
- Offensive - Untargeted
- Offensive - Targeted Insult Individual
- Offensive - Targeted Insult Group
- Offensive - Targeted Insult Other
- Not in indented language

If the output vector had '1' for the first class, then rest of the classes were converted to '0' else the maximum among the classes leaving the first class was converted to '1'. Finally the corresponding label is given as output.

## 4 Evaluation

Offensive language identification was evaluated using Sklearn Classification Report (Pedregosa et al., 2011). Performance was measured in terms of Precision, Recall and F1-Score across all the classes. The result of the evaluation are shown in Table 1.

| **Language Pair** | **Precision** | **Recall** | **F1 score** |
|---|---|---|---|
| Kannada English | 0.62 | 0.71 | 0.66 |
| Malayalam English | 0.77 | 0.43 | 0.54 |
| Tamil English | 0.71 | 0.74 | 0.72 |

Table 1: Results for all the Language pairs by Team JUNLP

## 5 Conclusion

In the current work, we attempted to solve the problem of Offensive Language Identification, while participating in the DravidianLangTech-2021 shared task. Our system was based on ensemble of IndicBERT model and generic BERT model using multi-label classification approach. Our system when evaluated by the organizers earned F1 score of 0.66, 0.54, and 0.72 for Kannada-English, Malayalam-English, and Tamil-English Language Pair, respectively. As future work, we would like to increase this data, and use other state-of-the-art Neural Network architecture to improve the performance. Also we would like to evaluate with the dataset released by author (Hande et al., 2020).

## References


Aditya Bohra, Deepanshu Vijay, Vinay Singh, Syed Sarfaraz Akhtar, and Manish Shrivastava. 2018. A dataset of hindi-english code-mixed social media text for hate speech detection. In *Proceedings of the second workshop on computational modeling of people's opinions, personality, and emotions in social media*, pages 36–41.

Bharathi Raja Chakravarthi. 2020. HopeEDI: A multilingual hope speech detection dataset for equality, diversity, and inclusion. In *Proceedings of the Third Workshop on Computational Modeling of People's Opinions, Personality, and Emotion's in Social Media*, pages 41–53, Barcelona, Spain (Online). Association for Computational Linguistics.

Bharathi Raja Chakravarthi, Navya Jose, Shardul Suryawanshi, Elizabeth Sherly, and John Philip McCrae. 2020a. A sentiment analysis dataset for code-mixed Malayalam-English. In *Proceedings of the 1st Joint Workshop on Spoken Language Technologies for Under-resourced languages (SLTU) and Collaboration and Computing for Under-Resourced Languages (CCURL)*, pages 177–184, Marseille, France. European Language Resources association.

Bharathi Raja Chakravarthi, Vigneshwaran Muralidaran, Ruba Priyadharshini, and John Philip McCrae. 2020b. Corpus creation for sentiment analysis in code-mixed Tamil-English text. In *Proceedings of the 1st Joint Workshop on Spoken Language Technologies for Under-resourced languages (SLTU) and Collaboration and Computing for Under-Resourced Languages (CCURL)*, pages 202–210, Marseille, France. European Language Resources association.

Bharathi Raja Chakravarthi, Ruba Priyadharshini, Navya Jose, Anand Kumar M, Thomas Mandl, Prasanna Kumar Kumaresan, Rahul Ponnusamy, Hariharan V, Elizabeth Sherly, and John Philip McCrae. 2021. Findings of the shared task on Offensive Language Identification in Tamil, Malayalam, and Kannada. In *Proceedings of the First Workshop on Speech and Language Technologies for Dravidian Languages*. Association for Computational Linguistics.

Bharathi Raja Chakravarthi, Ruba Priyadharshini, Vigneshwaran Muralidaran, Shardul Suryawanshi, Navya Jose, Elizabeth Sherly, and John P. McCrae. 2020c. Overview of the Track on Sentiment Analysis for Dravidian Languages in Code-Mixed Text. In *Forum for Information Retrieval Evaluation*, FIRE 2020, page 21–24, New York, NY, USA. Association for Computing Machinery.

Jacob Devlin, Ming-Wei Chang, Kenton Lee, and Kristina Toutanova. 2019. BERT: pre-training of deep bidirectional transformers for language understanding. In *Proceedings of the 2019 Conference of the North American Chapter of the Association for Computational Linguistics: Human Language Technologies, NAACL-HLT 2019, Minneapolis, MN, USA, June 2-7, 2019, Volume 1 (Long and Short Papers)*, pages 4171–4186. Association for Computational Linguistics.

Adeep Hande, Ruba Priyadharshini, and Bharathi Raja Chakravarthi. 2020. KanCMD: Kannada CodeMixed dataset for sentiment analysis and offensive language detection. In *Proceedings of the Third Workshop on Computational Modeling of People's Opinions, Personality, and Emotion's in Social Media*, pages 54–63, Barcelona, Spain (Online). Association for Computational Linguistics.

Navya Jose, Bharathi Raja Chakravarthi, Shardul Suryawanshi, Elizabeth Sherly, and John P. McCrae. 2020. A Survey of Current Datasets for Code-Switching Research. In *2020 6th International Conference on Advanced Computing and Communication Systems (ICACCS)*, pages 136–141.

Divyanshu Kakwani, Anoop Kunchukuttan, Satish Golla, Gokul N.C., Avik Bhattacharyya, Mitesh M. Khapra, and Pratyush Kumar. 2020. IndicNLPSuite: Monolingual corpora, evaluation benchmarks and pre-trained multilingual language models for Indian languages. In *Findings of the Association for Computational Linguistics: EMNLP 2020*, pages 4948–4961, Online. Association for Computational Linguistics.

Thomas Mandl, Sandip Modha, Anand Kumar M, and Bharathi Raja Chakravarthi. 2020. Overview of the HASOC Track at FIRE 2020: Hate Speech and Offensive Language Identification in Tamil, Malayalam, Hindi, English and German. In *Forum for Information Retrieval Evaluation*, FIRE 2020, page 29–32, New York, NY, USA. Association for Computing Machinery.

Puneet Mathur, Rajiv Shah, Ramit Sawhney, and Debanjan Mahata. 2018. Detecting offensive tweets in hindi-english code-switched language. In *Proceedings of the Sixth International Workshop on Natural Language Processing for Social Media*, pages 18–26.

F. Pedregosa, G. Varoquaux, A. Gramfort, V. Michel, B. Thirion, O. Grisel, M. Blondel, P. Prettenhofer, R. Weiss, V. Dubourg, J. Vanderplas, A. Passos, D. Cournapeau, M. Brucher, M. Perrot, and E. Duchesnay. 2011. Scikit-learn: Machine learning in Python. *Journal of Machine Learning Research*, 12:2825–2830.

Ruba Priyadharshini, Bharathi Raja Chakravarthi, Mani Vegupatti, and John P. McCrae. 2020. Named Entity Recognition for Code-Mixed Indian Corpus using Meta Embedding. In *2020 6th International Conference on Advanced Computing and Communication Systems (ICACCS)*, pages 68–72.

TYSS Santosh and KVS Aravind. 2019. Hate speech detection in hindi-english code-mixed social media text. In *Proceedings of the ACM India Joint International Conference on Data Science and Management of Data*, pages 310–313.

Sajeetha Thavareesan and Sinnathamby Mahesan. 2019. Sentiment Analysis in Tamil Texts: A Study on Machine Learning Techniques and Feature Representation. In *2019 14th Conference on Industrial and Information Systems (ICIIS)*, pages 320–325.

Sajeetha Thavareesan and Sinnathamby Mahesan. 2020a. Sentiment Lexicon Expansion using Word2vec and fastText for Sentiment Prediction in Tamil texts. In *2020 Moratuwa Engineering Research Conference (MERCon)*, pages 272–276.

Sajeetha Thavareesan and Sinnathamby Mahesan. 2020b. Word embedding-based Part of Speech tagging in Tamil texts. In *2020 IEEE 15th International Conference on Industrial and Information Systems (ICIIS)*, pages 478–482.

# MUCS@DravidianLangTech-EACL2021:COOLI-Code-Mixing Offensive Language Identification

**F. Balouchzahi**
Dept. of Computer Science,
Mangalore University,
Mangalore - 574199, India
frs_b@yahoo.com

**B. K. Aparna**
Dept. of Computer Science,
Mangalore University,
Mangalore - 574199, India
aparnabk14@gmail.com

**H. L. Shashirekha**
Dept. of Computer Science,
Mangalore University,
Mangalore - 574199, India
hlsrekha@gmail.com

## Abstract

This paper describes the models submitted by the team MUCS for Offensive Language Identification in Dravidian Languages-EACL 2021 shared task that aims at identifying and classifying code-mixed texts of three language pairs namely, Kannada-English (Kn-En), Malayalam-English (Ma-En), and Tamil-English (Ta-En) into six predefined categories (5 categories in Ma-En language pair). Two models, namely, COOLI-Ensemble and COOLI-Keras are trained with the char sequences extracted from the sentences combined with words in the sentences as features. Out of the two proposed models, COOLI-Ensemble model (best among our models) obtained first rank for Ma-En language pair with 0.97 weighted F1-score and fourth and sixth ranks with 0.75 and 0.69 weighted F1-score for Ta-En and Kn-En language pairs respectively.

## 1 Introduction

Along with the increasing developments on social media, social networks, and Internet, the number of people using these are also increasing. The advantage of social media is that users' have the freedom of expressing their opinions without revealing their identity (Thavareesan and Mahesan, 2019, 2020a,b). This feature is exploited by miscreants for spreading offensive messages targeting an individual or a group. These messages will be usually code-mixed texts in native languages mixed with English words but written in Roman script. The texts on social media do not adhere to the rules of any of the languages in which they are written. Hence, the analysis of code-mixed texts is a more challenging task compared to analysis of texts in native scripts because of the inconsistent Romanization conventions and non-standard grammars in code-mixed texts (Riyadh and Kondrak, 2019). These issues have created a demand for analyzing social media text which is becoming important day by day.

Generally, social media analysis and Offensive Language Identification (OLI) is fathomably important for social media platforms to monitor the texts including hateful or offensive content or advertising violence against people, communities, or religions. Many studies have been carried out in this direction to identify offensive content in texts. But, most of these works focus on rich resource languages such as English, Spanish, etc. giving less or no importance for low resource languages such as Kannada, Tamil, Telugu, Malayalam (Chakravarthi et al., 2020c; Mandl et al., 2020). However, most texts in social media are not written in any one language, but a mix of several languages making the OLI task more challenging (Arora, 2020). Further, the task becomes more complex due to the usage of non-native scripts. Indians usually mix English language with their native language and use Roman script mixed with their native language script to post messages. This type of mixing two or more languages in a text is called Code-Mixing (Chakravarthi, 2020; Jose et al., 2020; Priyadharshini et al., 2020). Due to lack of efficient keyboards for native languages or ease of using Roman script and better adaptation of Roman script in software and smartphones, code-mixing texts are increasing day-by-day. To promote analyzing code-mixing texts to identify offensive language posts in Dravidian languages, "Offensive Language Identification in Dravidian Languages" (Chakravarthi et al., 2021) shared task provides texts in three code-mixing language pairs namely, Kannada-English (Kn-En), Malayalam-English (Ma-En), and Tamil-English (Ta-En).

The datasets provided by DravidianLangTech[1]

[1] https://dravidianlangtech.github.io/



*Proceedings of the First Workshop on Speech and Language Technologies for Dravidian Languages*, pages 323–329
April 20, 2021 ©2021 Association for Computational Linguistics

include code-mixing texts labeled into one of six categories namely, "not-offensive, offensive-untargeted, offensive-targeted-individual, offensive-targeted-group, offensive-targeted-other, and not-in-indented-language" ("offensive-targeted-other" is not included for Ma-En language pair). This paper describes the models submitted by team MUCS to "Offensive Language Identification in Dravidian Languages" (Chakravarthi et al., 2021) shared task. The two models COOLI[2]-Ensemble and COOLI-Keras are trained using char sequences extracted from sentences combined with words in the sentences. COOLI-Ensemble is a voting classifier obtained by ensembling three estimators namely, Multi-Layer Perceptron (MLP), eXtreme Gradient Boosting (XGB), and Logistic Regression (LR) that predict a final tag based on a hard majority voting configuration. COOLI-Keras is a simple architecture based on Neural Network (NN) using Keras sequential model.

The rest of paper is organized as follows: Section 2 describes the recent literature on code-mixed text processing, and Section 3 presents details of submitted models followed by the results in Section 4. Conclusion and future plans are given in Section 5.

## 2 Related Work

Researchers have proposed many models for OLI for several languages. However, very few works are reported for OLI task in code-mixed texts. Some of the recent literature related to OLI in Dravidian code-mixed texts (Mandl et al., 2020) are given here: A shared task on OLI conducted by (Mandl et al., 2020), on Dravidian code-mixed texts consists of two message level subtasks namely, subtask A and subtask B. While the focus of subtask A was to classify YouTube comments in Malayalam-English code-mixed texts subtask B focused on the classification of Romanized Twitter comments in Tamil-English and Malayalam-English code-mixed texts. The datasets used in this shared task are described in (Chakravarthi et al., 2020b) (Chakravarthi et al., 2020a).

(Renjit and Idicula, 2020) proposed a binary classification model for subtask B to classify Malayalam-English code-mixed texts into "offensive" and "not offensive" posts. Their model consists of a text processing step which includes removing English stopwords, hashtags, URLs, and emojis, converting text to lower case, and tokenization. Using Keras embedding they represented text as one-hot encoding with 50D and fed it to two LSTM architectures. The first LSTM architecture comprised of an LSTM layer and recurrent dropout (0.2) followed by a dense layer that was configured with sigmoid activation and binary cross-entropy and the second LSTM architecture is same as the first architecture with three dense layers and Relu activation added in between LSTM and dense layer. They obtained 0.53 and 0.48 macro F1-score using first and second architectures respectively.

A Universal Language Model Fine-Tuning (ULMFiT) based on Transfer Learning (TL) approach submitted by (Arora, 2020) trained a language model synthetically for Malayalam –English code-mixed texts using fastai library from Malayalam –English code-mixed data collected from Wikipedia articles in native script as well as the translated and transliterated versions. Fastai library was also used to build final classifiers after a step of fine-tuning the pre-trained language model using training set. They obtained 0.91 and 0.74 weighted F1-score on subtasks A and B respectively.

Another work in this shared task submitted by (Ghanghor et al., 2021) is based on TL and Machine Learning (ML) approaches for subtask A. In addition to the dataset provided by task organizers they used the OLID dataset (Zampieri et al., 2019a), a well-known dataset that has been used in the SemEval-2019 Task 6 (OffensEval) (Zampieri et al., 2019b) in TL model and explored BERT and XLM-ROBERTA by adopting implementation from HuggingFace's transformer models (Wolf et al., 2019). They trained ML classifiers namely, Multinomial Naive Bayes (MNB), Support Vector Machines (SVM), and Random Forest (RF) on vectors obtained from bag-of-words feature engineering method. The reported results illustrate that RF with a 0.93 weighted F1-score outperformed other models. However, XLM-ROBERTA based on TL obtained 0.89 weighted F1-score and $5^{th}$place in subtask A.

## 3 Methodology

The methodology includes two major steps for each proposed models, namely, Feature Extraction and Classification Models. Details of the steps are given below:

2021

[2]COOLI stands for Code-Mixing Offensive Language Identification

| Input text | Extracted features |
|---|---|
| "yuvanvera level ya" (Ta-En) | yu, uv, va, an, n_, _v, ve, er, ra, a_, _l, le, ev, ve, el, l_, _y, ya, yuv, uva, van, an_, _ve, ver, era, ra_, _le, lev, eve, vel, el_, _ya, yuva, uvan, van_, _ver, vera, era_, _lev, leve, evel, vel_, yuvan, uvan_, _vera, vera_, _leve, level, evel_, yuvan_, _vera_, _level, level_, yuvanvera, level, ya |

Table 1: An example of a text and its char sequences

### 3.1 Feature Extraction

The feature extraction module pre-processes the input texts and extracts a set of char sequences and words as features which are then converted to vectors using CountVectorizer[3] library.

Pre-processing includes converting emojis to text (using emoji library[4]), removing punctuations, words of length less than 2, unwanted characters (such as !()-[];:'" ¡¿./?$=% +@*_ ', etc.), and finally converting text to lower case.

The everygrams [5] function of NLTK library is used to generate char sequences of length 2 to 6 from texts and then the extracted char sequences are combined with tokenized words of text. An example of a text and its char sequences are shown in Table 1. The combination of features are converted to vectors using CountVectorizer library and fed to the classification models. Figure 1 shows the Feature Extraction steps in the proposed methodology.

#### 3.1.1 Feature Selection

Text is high dimensional in nature as every word is considered as a feature. The char sequences extracted in feature extraction module adds further to this dimensionality increasing the complexity of the algorithms processing these texts (Shashirekha et al., 2020). Hence, reducing the features becomes important to reduce the complexity of the algorithms. Feature selection has gained importance since it reduces the number of features by eliminating redundant and irrelevant features that is expected to improve the performance of the algorithm (Gao et al., 2017).

Inspired by (Giglou et al., 2019), a feature selection module that consists of three feature selection algorithms namely Chi-Square test, Mutual Information (MI), and F test is adopted from

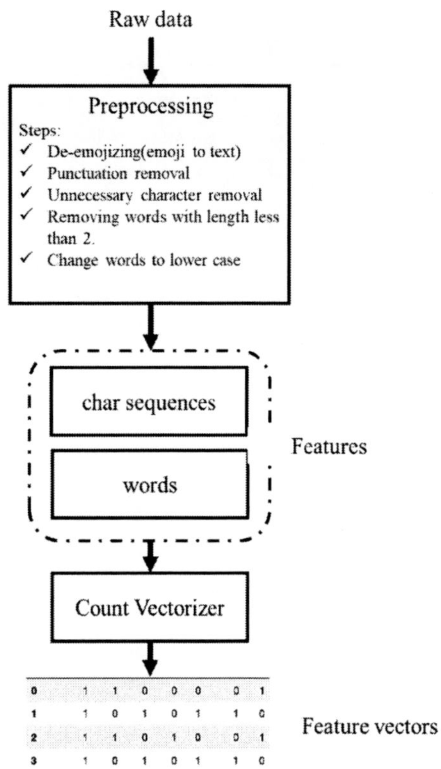


Figure 1: Feature engineering module

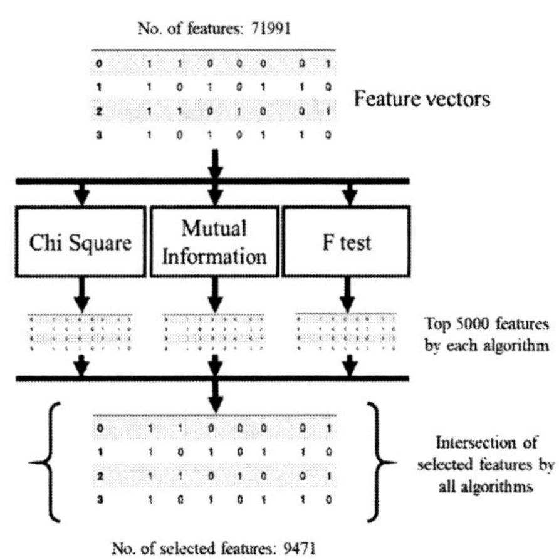


Figure 2: Feature selection module

[3]https://scikit-learn.org/stable/modules/generated/sklearn.feature_extraction.text.CountVectorizer.html

[4]https://pypi.org/project/emoji

[5]https://www.kite.com/python/docs/nltk.everygrams

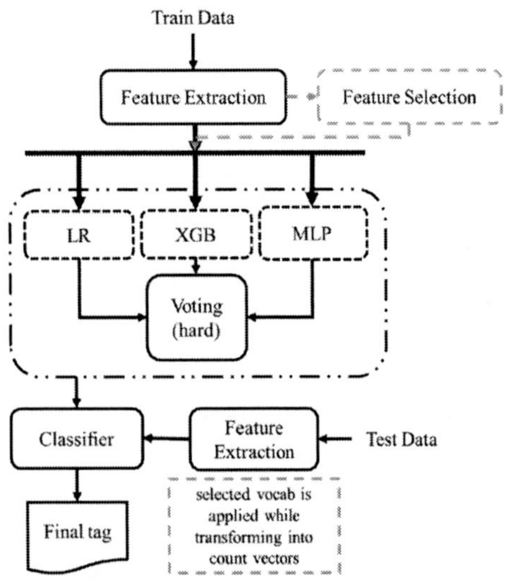


Figure 3: Structure of COOLI-Ensemble model (the dashed lined path is applied only for Kn-En texts)

(Shashirekha et al., 2020). The feature selection module utilizes a statistical measure to assign a score to features and based on these scores features are ranked and top k features are selected (in this case top 5000 features) as most relevant features for further processing.

Each of the three feature selection algorithms are used to select top 5000 ranked features and an intersection of these selected features are considered as final features. Figure 2 gives an overview of feature selection module. This feature selection is applied only for Ka-En code-mixed texts. Figure 2 illustrates that 71991 features get reduced to 9471.

Due to technical problems and limitation on RAM and GPU to process huge datasets in the machine that was used for processing the task, Feature selection algorithms could not be applied for Ta-En and Ma-En texts.

### 3.2 Classification Models

We propose two classification models namely, COOLI-Ensemble and COOLI-Keras which are trained on the features obtained in feature extraction module. The size of obtained vectors that are fed as input to the models depend on datasets and 71,991, 326,628 and 187,810 features were obtained for Ka-En, Ta-En, and Ma-En texts respectively. The proposed models are described below:

#### 3.2.1 COOLI-Ensemble

It is a Voting Classifier (VC) with three sklearn[6] estimators given below:

**Multi-Layer Perceptron[7] (MLP):** is one of the Neural Network (NN) models that are widely used in the field of ML due to its simplicity compared to the recent complex NN models. MLP is also defined as a supplement for feed-forward NN that consists of three types of layers namely, the input layer, output layer, and hidden layer [16].In the proposed model, one layer per type (input layer, hidden layer, and output layer) is used and layer sizes are set to (150, 100, 50) and maximum iteration, activation, solver[8](that specifies the algorithm for weight optimization across the nodes), and random state have been set to 300, Relu, Adam, and 1 respectively.

**eXtreme Gradient Boosting (XGB):** is one of Gradient boosting classifier that use Gradient boosting technique to solve classification and regression problems. The major advantage of "boosting" is producing a robust classifier by converting a set of learners that perform poor (Athanasiou and Maragoudakis, 2017). Adaptive Boosting (AdaBoost), Gradient Boosting (GBM) are other classifiers in boosting family. In this study, XGB classifier from Sklearn with the following configuration is used: max_depth is set to 20, and n_estimators, learning rate, colsample_bytree, gamma, reg_alpha, and objective are set to 80, 0.1, 0.7, 0.01, 4, 'multi: softmax' respectively.

**Logistic Regression (LR):** is one of the most popular binary classifier that is driven from the field of statistics. However, it utilizes the one-vs-rest (OvR) scheme to deal with multi-class classification tasks. LR classifier has been used with default parameters.

Figure 3 represents the structure of COOLI-Ensemble. Features are extracted from the training set as described in feature extraction module and are used to construct the classifier. Features from test data are also extracted using feature extraction module and only those features in the feature set are considered for classification. In case of Ka-En code-mixed texts, feature selection is applied to get reduced feature set. The COOLI-Ensemble is configured as hard voting.

[6]https://scikit-learn.org/stable/

[7]https://scikit-learn.org/stable/modules/generated/sklearn.neural_network.MLPClassifier.html

[8]nnabla.readthedocs.io

### 3.2.2 COOLI-Keras

The feature extraction and feature selection steps described earlier are used to train COOLI-Keras model which is a Keras[9] dense NN architecture adopted from

```
https://www.kaggle.com/ismu94/
tf-idf-deep-neural-net
```

COOLI-Keras model has been trained for 40 epochs with a batch size of 128. The main diference between MLP in COOLI-Ensemble and COOLI-Keras model is in layers and configuration of them. Figure 4 describes the overview of COOLI-Keras model with all NN layers and configurations.

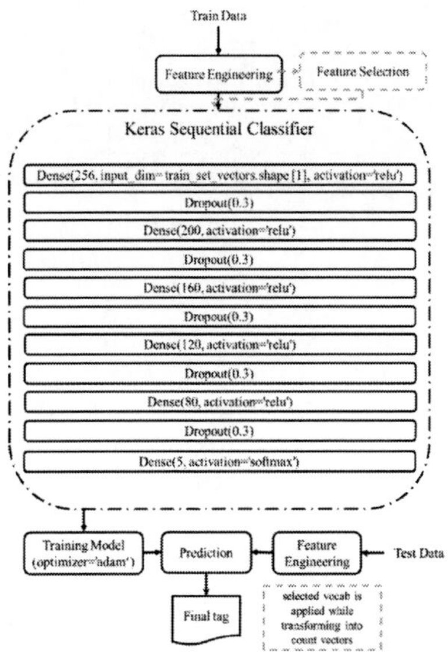


Figure 4: Structure of COOLI-Keras model (the dashed lined path is applied only for Kn-En texts)

## 4 Experimental Results

### 4.1 Datasets

Datasets provided by the organizers for this study includes code-mixed texts in three Language Pairs (LP), namely, Ma-En, Ta-En, Ka-En and the details are given in (Chakravarthi et al., 2021). Texts are distributed into 6 categories, namely, "Not-offensive (NO), offensive-untargeted (OU), offensive-targeted-individual (OTI), offensive-targeted-group (OTG), offensive-targeted-other (OTO), and Not-in-indented-language (NIL)". "offensive-targeted-other" is skipped for Ma-En language pair. The distribution of train, development (Dev.) and test sets is given in Table 2.

Statistics of the datasets shown in Table 2 illustrates that Ka-En texts are less than other two language pairs and it can affect the performance of the proposed models. Further, all datasets are imbalanced. However, as the percentage of imbalance sounds to be less in Ma-En dataset and also having more text in Malayalam native script, it is expected that the proposed models performs better for this dataset compared to other two datasets.

| Train Set | | | |
|---|---|---|---|
| **tag** | Ma-En | Ka-En | Ta-En |
| **NO** | 14153 | 3544 | 25425 |
| **OU** | 1287 | 1522 | 1454 |
| **OTI** | 140 | 329 | 2557 |
| **OTG** | 239 | 487 | 2343 |
| **OTO** | 191 | 212 | 2906 |
| **NIL** | - | 123 | 454 |
| **Dev. Set** | | | |
| **tag** | Ma-En | Ka-En | Ta-En |
| **NO** | 1779 | 426 | 3193 |
| **OU** | 163 | 191 | 172 |
| **OTI** | 13 | 45 | 295 |
| **OTG** | 24 | 66 | 307 |
| **OTO** | 20 | 33 | 356 |
| **NIL** | - | 16 | 65 |
| **Test Set** | | | |
| **tag** | Ma-En | Ka-En | Ta-En |
| **NO** | 1765 | 427 | 3190 |
| **OU** | 157 | 185 | 160 |
| **OTI** | 23 | 44 | 288 |
| **OTG** | 27 | 75 | 315 |
| **OTO** | 29 | 33 | 368 |
| **NIL** | - | 14 | 71 |

Table 2: Datasets for each Language Pairs

#### 4.1.1 Results

The results obtained for each model on the test set of each language pairs are evaluated by weighted Precision, Recall, and F1-score using Sklearn.metrics library. For Ka-En language pair the models are constructed with Feature Selection (with FS) and without Feature Selection (No FS).

The results obtained by COOLI-Ensemble (along with obtained ranks) and COOLI-Keras

[9]https://keras.io/

| COOLI-Ensemble | | | | | |
|---|---|---|---|---|---|
| Language Pair | | P | R | F1 | Rank |
| **Ma-En** | | **0.97** | **0.97** | **0.97** | **1** |
| **Ta-En** | | **0.74** | **0.77** | **0.75** | **4** |
| **Ka-En** | **With FS** | **0.68** | **0.72** | **0.69** | **6** |
| | No FS | 0.68 | 0.71 | 0.68 | - |
| **COOLI-Keras model** | | | | | |
| Language Pairs | | P | R | F1 | |
| Ma-En | | 0.96 | 0.96 | 0.96 | |
| Ta-En | | 0.73 | 0.74 | 0.73 | |
| Ka-En | With FS | 0.68 | 0.72 | 0.69 | |
| | No FS | 0.68 | 0.68 | 0.68 | |

Table 3: Results of proposed models

models are shown in Table 3 and the results illustrate that COOLI-Ensemble model (best among our models) outperformed COOLI-Keras model for Ma-En and Ta-En language pairs. However, the performance on Kn-En language pair by both the models remains more or less the same. Further, it can be observed that both the models with feature selection for KA-En dataset performed slightly better compared to other models with all the features. Hence, applying feature selection module for rest of language pairs could improve their performance. As it was expected both models performed better for Ma-En texts due to nature of dataset that includes more number of texts in Malayalam native script that results in distinguishing of not Malayalam texts.

## 5 Conclusion and Future Work

This paper describes the two models, COOLI-Ensemble and COOLI-Keras submitted for "Offensive Language Identification in Dravidian Languages-EACL 2021" shared task to classify code-mixed text in Tamil-English, Malayalam-English, and Kannada-English. The analysis of results shows that COOLI-Ensemble (best among our models) on a feature set of char sequences, and words outperformed COOLI-Keras model for both Ma-En and Ta-En language pairs and also obtained first rank for Ma-En language pair with 0.97 weighted F1-score and fourth and sixth ranks with 0.75 and 0.69 weighted F1-score for Ta-En and Kn-En language pairs respectively. The results also illustrate that feature selection applied on Ka-En texts slightly improved the performance of models. As a future work, we planned to explore different feature sets and feature selection models along with various learning approaches to process code-mixed texts.

## References

Gaurav Arora. 2020. Gauravarora@ HASOC-Dravidian-CodeMix-FIRE2020: Pre-training ULM-FiT on Synthetically Generated Code-Mixed Data for Hate Speech Detection. *arXiv preprint arXiv:2010.02094.*

Vasileios Athanasiou and Manolis Maragoudakis. 2017. A novel, gradient boosting framework for sentiment analysis in languages where nlp resources are not plentiful: a case study for modern greek. *Algorithms*, 10(1):34.

Bharathi Raja Chakravarthi. 2020. *Leveraging orthographic information to improve machine translation of under-resourced languages.* Ph.D. thesis, NUI Galway.

Bharathi Raja Chakravarthi, Navya Jose, Shardul Suryawanshi, Elizabeth Sherly, and John Philip McCrae. 2020a. A sentiment analysis dataset for code-mixed Malayalam-English. In *Proceedings of the 1st Joint Workshop on Spoken Language Technologies for Under-resourced languages (SLTU) and Collaboration and Computing for Under-Resourced Languages (CCURL)*, pages 177–184, Marseille, France. European Language Resources association.

Bharathi Raja Chakravarthi, Vigneshwaran Muralidaran, Ruba Priyadharshini, and John Philip McCrae. 2020b. Corpus creation for sentiment analysis in code-mixed Tamil-English text. In *Proceedings of the 1st Joint Workshop on Spoken Language Technologies for Under-resourced languages (SLTU) and Collaboration and Computing for Under-Resourced Languages (CCURL)*, pages 202–210, Marseille, France. European Language Resources association.

Bharathi Raja Chakravarthi, Ruba Priyadharshini, Navya Jose, Anand Kumar M, Thomas Mandl, Prasanna Kumar Kumaresan, Rahul Ponnsamy, Hariharan V, Elizabeth Sherly, and John Philip McCrae. 2021. Findings of the shared task on Offensive Language Identification in Tamil, Malayalam, and Kannada. In *Proceedings of the First Workshop on Speech and Language Technologies for Dravidian Languages*. Association for Computational Linguistics.

Bharathi Raja Chakravarthi, Ruba Priyadharshini, Vigneshwaran Muralidaran, Shardul Suryawanshi, Navya Jose, Elizabeth Sherly, and John P. McCrae. 2020c. Overview of the Track on Sentiment Analysis for Dravidian Languages in Code-Mixed Text. In *Forum for Information Retrieval Evaluation*, FIRE 2020, page 21–24, New York, NY, USA. Association for Computing Machinery.

Weihao Gao, Sreeram Kannan, Sewoong Oh, and Pramod Viswanath. 2017. Estimating mutual information for discrete-continuous mixtures. *arXiv preprint arXiv:1709.06212.*

Nikhil Kumar Ghanghor, Rahul Ponnusamy, Prasanna Kumar Kumaresan, Ruba Priyadharshini, Sajeetha Thavareesan, and Bharathi Raja Chakravarthi. 2021. IIITK@LT-EDI-EACL2021: Hope Speech Detection for Equality, Diversity, and Inclusion in Tamil, Malayalam and English. In *Proceedings of the First Workshop on Language Technology for Equality, Diversity and Inclusion*, Online.

Hamed Babaei Giglou, Mostafa Rahgouy, Taher Rahgooy, Mohammad Karami Sheykhlan, and Erfan Mohammadzadeh. 2019. Author profiling: Bot and gender prediction using a multi-aspect ensemble approach. In *CLEF (Working Notes)*.

Navya Jose, Bharathi Raja Chakravarthi, Shardul Suryawanshi, Elizabeth Sherly, and John P. McCrae. 2020. A Survey of Current Datasets for Code-Switching Research. In *2020 6th International Conference on Advanced Computing and Communication Systems (ICACCS)*, pages 136–141.

Thomas Mandl, Sandip Modha, Anand Kumar M, and Bharathi Raja Chakravarthi. 2020. Overview of the HASOC Track at FIRE 2020: Hate Speech and Offensive Language Identification in Tamil, Malayalam, Hindi, English and German. In *Forum for Information Retrieval Evaluation*, FIRE 2020, page 29–32, New York, NY, USA. Association for Computing Machinery.

Ruba Priyadharshini, Bharathi Raja Chakravarthi, Mani Vegupatti, and John P. McCrae. 2020. Named Entity Recognition for Code-Mixed Indian Corpus using Meta Embedding. In *2020 6th International Conference on Advanced Computing and Communication Systems (ICACCS)*, pages 68–72.

Sara Renjit and Sumam Mary Idicula. 2020. CUSATNLP@ HASOC-Dravidian-CodeMix-FIRE2020: Identifying Offensive Language from ManglishTweets. *arXiv preprint arXiv:2010.08756*.

Rashed Rubby Riyadh and Grzegorz Kondrak. 2019. Joint approach to deromanization of code-mixed texts. In *Proceedings of the Sixth Workshop on NLP for Similar Languages, Varieties and Dialects*, pages 26–34.

H. L. Shashirekha, M. D. Anusha, and Nitin S. Prakash. 2020. Ensemble model for profiling fake news spreaders on twitter. In *Working Notes of CLEF 2020 - Conference and Labs of the Evaluation Forum, Thessaloniki, Greece, September 22-25, 2020*, volume 2696 of *CEUR Workshop Proceedings*. CEUR-WS.org.

Sajeetha Thavareesan and Sinnathamby Mahesan. 2019. Sentiment Analysis in Tamil Texts: A Study on Machine Learning Techniques and Feature Representation. In *2019 14th Conference on Industrial and Information Systems (ICIIS)*, pages 320–325.

Sajeetha Thavareesan and Sinnathamby Mahesan. 2020a. Sentiment Lexicon Expansion using Word2vec and fastText for Sentiment Prediction in Tamil texts. In *2020 Moratuwa Engineering Research Conference (MERCon)*, pages 272–276.

Sajeetha Thavareesan and Sinnathamby Mahesan. 2020b. Word embedding-based Part of Speech tagging in Tamil texts. In *2020 IEEE 15th International Conference on Industrial and Information Systems (ICIIS)*, pages 478–482.

Thomas Wolf, Lysandre Debut, Victor Sanh, Julien Chaumond, Clement Delangue, Anthony Moi, Pierric Cistac, Tim Rault, Rémi Louf, Morgan Funtowicz, et al. 2019. HuggingFace's Transformers: State-of-the-art natural language processing. *arXiv preprint arXiv:1910.03771*.

Marcos Zampieri, Shervin Malmasi, Preslav Nakov, Sara Rosenthal, Noura Farra, and Ritesh Kumar. 2019a. Predicting the type and target of offensive posts in social media. *arXiv preprint arXiv:1902.09666*.

Marcos Zampieri, Shervin Malmasi, Preslav Nakov, Sara Rosenthal, Noura Farra, and Ritesh Kumar. 2019b. Semeval-2019 task 6: Identifying and categorizing offensive language in social media (offenseval). *arXiv preprint arXiv:1903.08983*.

# indicnlp@kgp at DravidianLangTech-EACL2021: Offensive Language Identification in Dravidian Languages

**Kushal Kedia**
IIT Kharagpur
kushal.k@iitkgp.ac.in

**Abhilash Nandy**
IIT Kharagpur
nandyabhilash@gmail.com

## Abstract

The paper presents the submission of the team indicnlp@kgp to the EACL 2021 shared task "Offensive Language Identification in Dravidian Languages". The task aimed to classify different offensive content types in 3 code-mixed Dravidian language datasets. The work leverages existing state of the art approaches in text classification by incorporating additional data and transfer learning on pre-trained models. Our final submission is an ensemble of an AWD-LSTM based model along with 2 different transformer model architectures based on BERT and RoBERTa. We achieved weighted-average F1 scores of 0.97, 0.77, and 0.72 in the Malayalam-English, Tamil-English, and Kannada-English datasets ranking $1^{st}$, $2^{nd}$, and $3^{rd}$ on the respective tasks.

## 1 Introduction

Offensive language identification is a natural language processing (NLP) text classification task where the goal is to moderate and reduce objectionable social media content. There has been a rapid growth in offensive content on social media and users from different ethnicities and cultures worldwide. A significant portion of offensive content is specifically targeted at various individuals and minority & ethnic groups. Consequently, the identification and classification of these different kinds of foul language are receiving increased importance. Dravidian languages like Kannada, Malayalam, and Tamil (Chakravarthi, 2020) are low-resourced, making this task challenging. Training embeddings of words has previously been a common approach employed in text classification tasks. However, transfer learning approaches in deep learning (Mou et al., 2016) have been shown unsuccessful or requiring extensive collections of in-domain documents to produce strong results (Dai and Le, 2015).

Code-mixing is a prevalent practice in a multilingual culture, and code-mixed texts are often written in native scripts. Due to code-switching complexity at multiple linguistic levels, systems trained on monolingual data can fail on code-mixed data. While multilingual versions of transformer models have been shown to perform remarkably well, even in zero-shot settings (Pires et al., 2019), a zero-shot transfer may perform poorly or fail altogether (Søgaard et al., 2018). This is when the target language, here code-mixed Dravidian data, is different from the source language, mainly monolingual in English. In our work, we tackle these problems by exploiting additional datasets for fine-tuning our models and using effective transfer learning techniques. Our code and experiments are available on GitHub[1] for reproducing our models.

## 2 Task Description and Datasets

This task aims to classify offensive language material gathered from social media from a set of code-mixed posts in Dravidian Languages. The systems have to classify each post into one of the six labels:

- not offensive
- untargeted offense
- offense targeted at an individual
- offense targeted at a group
- offense targeted at someone else
- not in intended language

There is also a significant class imbalance in all the datasets representing a real-world situation. This shared task presents a new gold standard corpus for offensive language identification of code-mixed

[1] https://github.com/kushal2000/Dravidian-Offensive



*Proceedings of the First Workshop on Speech and Language Technologies for Dravidian Languages*, pages 330–335
April 20, 2021 ©2021 Association for Computational Linguistics

text in three Dravidian languages: Tamil-English (Chakravarthi et al., 2020b), Malayalam-English (Chakravarthi et al., 2020a), and Kannada-English (Hande et al., 2020). The Malayam dataset does not contain the *offense targeted at someone else* tag. The posts can contain more than one sentence, but the average number of sentences is 1. The Tamil and Malayalam datasets are considerably large, containing over $30k$ and $20k$ annotated comments, while the Kannada dataset is relatively smaller with almost $8k$ annotations. Apart from the dataset supplied by the organizers, we also use a monolingual English Offensive Language Identification Dataset (OLID) (Zampieri et al., 2019a) used in the SemEval-2019 Task 6 (OffensEval) (Zampieri et al., 2019b). The dataset contains the same labels as our task datasets except for the *not in intended language* label. The one-to-one mapping between the labels in OLID and its large size of $14k$ tweets makes it suitable for aiding the transfer learning detailed in Section 3.3.

## 3 Methods

A variety of methods are experimented on our datasets to provide a complete baseline. In Section 3.1, we describe our implementation of three traditional machine learning classifiers; Multinomial Naive Bayes, Linear Support Vector Machines (SVM), and Random Forests. These approaches work well on small datasets and are more computationally efficient than deep neural networks. Their performance is similar to the later sections described in the absence of pretraining and additional data. In Section 3.2, our Recurrent Neural Network (RNN) models are explained. We have compared an LSTM model, using word-level embeddings trained from scratch, to an ULMFiT model, an effective transfer learning approach for language models. Finally, in Section 3.3, we discuss transformer architectures using their cross-lingual pretrained models, which can be data-intensive during fine-tuning but provide the strongest results.

### 3.1 Machine Learning Classifiers

**Dataset Preprocessing** We preprocess the datasets by removing punctuation, removing English stop words, removing emojis, and lemmatizing the English Words. The Natural Language Toolkit library (Bird and Loper, 2004) was used for lemmatization and removing stop words. The word vocabulary is constructed, and vocabulary-length vectors containing each word's counts are used to represent each input. Based on each word's Mutual Information scores, feature selection is done to reduce the vocabulary size.

**Hyperparameters** For all three models, the number of words selected using the top Mutual Information scores was varied from 1000 to the length of the vocabulary. Further hyperparameters were specific to the SVM and Random Forest. The random state, the regularisation parameters, and max iterations were tuned for the SVM, and the number of decision trees used was the only hyperparameter in the case of random forests.

### 3.2 RNN Models

**Vanilla LSTM** To set a baseline for an RNN approach, we build word embeddings from scratch using just the individual datasets. For this, we selected the top $32,000$ occurring words in each dataset for one-hot encoding, which is passed through an embedding layer to form 100-dimension word vectors. A spatial dropout of $0.2$ followed by a single LSTM cell and a final softmax activation forms the rest of the model. While the results for larger datasets are marginally better than the previous section, they are worse than the transfer learning approach.

**ULMFiT** Transfer learning has been shown to perform well in text classification tasks. Usually, language models are trained on large corpora, and their first layer, i.e., the word embeddings, are fine-tuned on specific tasks. This approach has been a very successful deep learning approach in many state of the art models. (Mikolov et al., 2013) However, Howard and Ruder, 2018 argue that we should be able to do better than randomly initializing the remaining parameters of our models and propose *ULMFiT: Universal Language Model Fine-tuning for Text Classification*. For the Dravidian languages in this task, the problem of in-domain data collection for effective transfer is also significant, especially in hate speech domains. ULMFiT provides a robust framework for building language models from moderate corpora and fine-tunes them on our specific tasks.

**Language Models & Corpora** We make use of language models open-sourced by the team *gauravarora* (Arora, 2020) in the shared task at HASOC-Dravidian-CodeMix FIRE-2020 (Mandl et al., 2020). They build their corpora for language modeling from large sets of Wikipedia articles. For

Tamil & Malayalam languages, they also generate code-mixed corpora by obtaining parallel sets of native, transliterated, and translated articles and sampling sentences using a Markov process, which has transition probabilities to 3 states; native, translated, and transliterated. For Kannada, only a native script corpus is available, and we had to transliterate our code-mixed dataset to Kannada to match their language model. The models are based on the Fastai (Howard and Gugger, 2020) implementation of ULMFiT. Pre-trained tokenizers and language models are available on Github. [2] [3] [4]

**Preprocessing & Model Details** Basic preprocessing steps included lower-casing, removing punctuations and mentions. Subword tokenization using unigram segmentation is implemented, which is reasonably resilient to variations in script and spelling. The tokenization model used is SentencePiece[5]. The language model is based on an AWD-LSTM (Merity et al., 2018), a regular LSTM cell with additional parameters related to dropout within the cell. The text classification model additionally uses two linear layers followed by a softmax on top of the language model. To tackle the difference in distributions of the target datasets and the pretraining corpora, ULMFiT proposes using 1) *discriminative fine-tuning*, i.e, layers closer to the last layer have higher learning rates, 2) *slanted triangular learning rates* which increase aggressively during the start of training and then decay gradually and 3) *gradual unfreezing*, i.e, instead of learning all layers of the model at once, they are gradually unfrozen starting from the last layer. The combination of these techniques leads to robust transfer learning on our datasets.

### 3.3 Transformer Models

In recent years, transformer networks like the Bidirectional Encoder Representation from Transformer (BERT) (Devlin et al., 2019) and its variant RoBERTa (Liu et al., 2019) have been used successfully in many offensive language identification tasks. For our work, we use the already pre-trained cross-lingual versions of these models available in the HuggingFace[6] library. Specifically, we use the *bert-base-multilingual-cased* model, mBERT trained on cased text in 104 languages from large

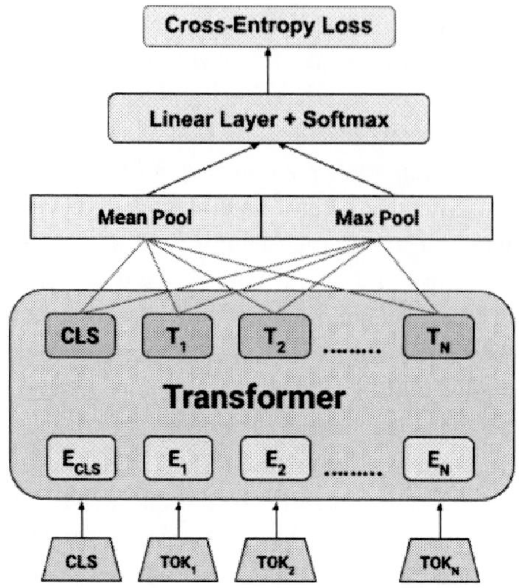


Figure 1: Transformer Model Architecture

Wikipedia articles, and the *xlm-roberta-base* model, XLM-R (Conneau et al., 2020) trained on 100 languages, using more than two terabytes of filtered CommonCrawl data. Both of these models were originally trained on a masked language modeling objective, and we fine-tune them on our specific downstream text classification tasks.

**Transfer Learning** The transfer learning approach's core principle is to use a pre-trained transformer model for training a classification model on a resource-rich language first, usually English, and transfer the model parameters to a less resource-rich language. For this approach, we concatenate all three code-mixed datasets as well as the OLID dataset. Our results do not change significantly on the transliteration of all datasets to Roman script. The *not in intended language* label is also removed for fine-tuning on the combined dataset since this label does not represent the same meaning across the datasets. We then use these learned model weights replacing the final linear layer to include the additional removed label *not in intended language*. This fine-tuning approach is shown to increase the performance of various scarce-resourced languages such as Hindi and Bengali.

**Model Architecture** We restrict the maximum length of the input sentences to be 256 by truncation and zero-padding. As shown in Fig 1, using the contextual embeddings from the last hidden states of all tokens in the sentence, we build a vector representation by concatenating the max pooling and mean pooling of these hidden states. Corre-

[2] github.com/goru001/nlp-for-tanglish
[3] github.com/goru001/nlp-for-manglish
[4] github.com/goru001/nlp-for-kannada
[5] github.com/google/sentencepiece
[6] https://huggingface.co/

spondingly, the dimension of the final sentence representation is 1536 x 1 . This is passed through a linear layer with a dropout of 0.3. The learning rate for all fine-tuning was fixed as $2e^{-5}$ and batch size was 32. The only preprocessing step before feeding the input to the transformer tokenizers was replacing emojis with their English language description. This is done because the tokenizers might not recognize the emojis, but they contain useful information about the sentence's sentiment.

## 4 Experiments and Results

This task's assessment metric is Weighted-F1, which is the F1 score weighted by the number of samples in all the classes. The datasets are divided into train, validation, and test sets in an approximately 8:1:1 ratio. The test labels are hidden and only available to us after the evaluation phase is over. We strictly train our models on the train set using the validation set scores for hyperparameter tuning. We have reported the results of our various models on the validation set. The average-ensemble of our top three performing models is submitted finally, and we also report its scores on the validation and test set using the scores we are ranked with on the task leader board.

| Model | T | M | K |
|---|---|---|---|
| Random Forest | 0.69 | 0.94 | 0.62 |
| Naive Bayes | 0.74 | 0.94 | 0.64 |
| Linear SVM | 0.74 | 0.95 | 0.65 |

Table 1: Weighted-F1 scores for ML models on Tamil (T), Malayalam (M) and Kannada (K) datasets.

Table 1 showcases the scores we have obtained for standard machine learning algorithms. Out of the three traditional machine learning algorithms, the Linear SVM model is best across all three datasets. The results in Table 2 summarize our RNN approaches where ULMFiT is markedly superior. The performance of our transformer models detailed in Table 3 considers two settings, one without transfer learning and one with transfer learning using the OLID and other Dravidian code-mixed datasets in conjunction.

The results on the validation set of our transfer-learned XLM-R model are the best across all 3 datasets and are followed closely by the transfer learned multilingual BERT model and the ULMFiT model. We finally submit an average ensemble of these three models, and our results on the validation

| Model | T | M | K |
|---|---|---|---|
| Vanilla LSTM | 0.74 | 0.95 | 0.64 |
| ULMFiT | 0.76 | 0.96 | 0.71 |

Table 2: Weighted-F1 scores for RNN models on Tamil (T), Malayalam (M) and Kannada (K) datasets.

| Model | T | M | K |
|---|---|---|---|
| mBERT | 0.74 | 0.95 | 0.66 |
| XLM-R | 0.76 | 0.96 | 0.67 |
| mBERT (TL) | 0.75 | 0.97 | 0.71 |
| XLM-R (TL) | 0.78 | 0.97 | 0.72 |

Table 3: Weighted-F1 scores for transformers on Tamil (T), Malayalam (M) and Kannada (K) datasets. TL indicates transfer learning using OLID and other datasets.

set and the test set used in the final task evaluation are also enlisted in Table 4 below.

| Model | T | M | K |
|---|---|---|---|
| avg-Ensemble (V) | 0.78 | 0.97 | 0.73 |
| avg-Ensemble (T) | 0.77 | 0.97 | 0.72 |

Table 4: Final weighted-F1 scores using average ensembling on Tamil (T), Malayalam (M) and Kannada (K) validation (V) and test (T) datasets.

## 5 Conclusion

This paper describes various approaches for offensive language identification in three code-mixed English-Dravidian language datasets. We also discuss the final system submitted by the indic-nlp@kgp team, which ranks first, second, and third on the competition's three tasks. The benefit of pre-trained language models was shown by the significant improvement in results using a robust transfer learning framework (ULMFiT) compared to a vanilla LSTM model trained from scratch. Transformer networks' performance also improved when all the Dravidian language datasets were combined. This suggests that learning from one Dravidian language may help in zero-shot or few-shot transfer to other new Dravidian languages. In future works, we wish to explore these effects in more detail.

## References

Gaurav Arora. 2020. Gauravarora@HASOC-Dravidian-CodeMix-FIRE2020:Pre-training ULM-FiT on Synthetically Generated Code-Mixed Data for Hate Speech Detection. In *FIRE-2020 (Working Notes)*. CEUR, Hyderabad, India.

Steven Bird and Edward Loper. 2004. NLTK: The natural language toolkit. In *Proceedings of the ACL Interactive Poster and Demonstration Sessions*, pages 214–217, Barcelona, Spain. Association for Computational Linguistics.

Bharathi Raja Chakravarthi. 2020. *Leveraging orthographic information to improve machine translation of under-resourced languages*. NUI Galway.

Bharathi Raja Chakravarthi, Navya Jose, Shardul Suryawanshi, Elizabeth Sherly, and John Philip McCrae. 2020a. A sentiment analysis dataset for code-mixed Malayalam-English. In *Proceedings of the 1st Joint Workshop on Spoken Language Technologies for Under-resourced languages (SLTU) and Collaboration and Computing for Under-Resourced Languages (CCURL)*, pages 177–184, Marseille, France. European Language Resources association.

Bharathi Raja Chakravarthi, Vigneshwaran Muralidaran, Ruba Priyadharshini, and John Philip McCrae. 2020b. Corpus creation for sentiment analysis in code-mixed Tamil-English text. In *Proceedings of the 1st Joint Workshop on Spoken Language Technologies for Under-resourced languages (SLTU) and Collaboration and Computing for Under-Resourced Languages (CCURL)*, pages 202–210, Marseille, France. European Language Resources association.

Alexis Conneau, Kartikay Khandelwal, Naman Goyal, Vishrav Chaudhary, Guillaume Wenzek, Francisco Guzmán, Edouard Grave, Myle Ott, Luke Zettlemoyer, and Veselin Stoyanov. 2020. *Unsupervised Cross-lingual Representation Learning at Scale*. Association for Computational Linguistics.

Andrew M Dai and Quoc V Le. 2015. Semi-supervised sequence learning. In *Advances in Neural Information Processing Systems*, volume 28, pages 3079–3087. Curran Associates, Inc.

Jacob Devlin, Ming-Wei Chang, Kenton Lee, and Kristina Toutanova. 2019. BERT: Pre-training of deep bidirectional transformers for language understanding. In *Proceedings of the 2019 Conference of the North American Chapter of the Association for Computational Linguistics: Human Language Technologies, Volume 1 (Long and Short Papers)*, pages 4171–4186, Minneapolis, Minnesota. Association for Computational Linguistics.

Adeep Hande, Ruba Priyadharshini, and Bharathi Raja Chakravarthi. 2020. KanCMD: Kannada CodeMixed dataset for sentiment analysis and offensive language detection. In *Proceedings of the Third Workshop on Computational Modeling of People's Opinions, Personality, and Emotion's in Social Media*, pages 54–63, Barcelona, Spain (Online). Association for Computational Linguistics.

Jeremy Howard and Sylvain Gugger. 2020. Fastai: A layered api for deep learning. *Information*, 11(2):108.

Jeremy Howard and Sebastian Ruder. 2018. Universal language model fine-tuning for text classification. In *Proceedings of the 56th Annual Meeting of the Association for Computational Linguistics (Volume 1: Long Papers)*, pages 328–339, Melbourne, Australia. Association for Computational Linguistics.

Yinhan Liu, Myle Ott, Naman Goyal, Jingfei Du, Mandar Joshi, Danqi Chen, Omer Levy, Mike Lewis, Luke Zettlemoyer, and Veselin Stoyanov. 2019. Roberta: A robustly optimized bert pretraining approach.

Thomas Mandl, Sandip Modha, Anand Kumar M, and Bharathi Raja Chakravarthi. 2020. Overview of the HASOC Track at FIRE 2020: Hate Speech and Offensive Language Identification in Tamil, Malayalam, Hindi, English and German. In *Forum for Information Retrieval Evaluation*, FIRE 2020, page 29–32, New York, NY, USA. Association for Computing Machinery.

Stephen Merity, Nitish Shirish Keskar, and Richard Socher. 2018. Regularizing and optimizing LSTM language models. In *International Conference on Learning Representations*.

Tomas Mikolov, Ilya Sutskever, Kai Chen, Greg S Corrado, and Jeff Dean. 2013. Distributed representations of words and phrases and their compositionality. In *Advances in Neural Information Processing Systems*, volume 26, pages 3111–3119. Curran Associates, Inc.

Lili Mou, Zhao Meng, Rui Yan, Ge Li, Yan Xu, Lu Zhang, and Zhi Jin. 2016. How transferable are neural networks in NLP applications? In *Proceedings of the 2016 Conference on Empirical Methods in Natural Language Processing*, pages 479–489, Austin, Texas. Association for Computational Linguistics.

Telmo Pires, Eva Schlinger, and Dan Garrette. 2019. How multilingual is multilingual BERT? In *Proceedings of the 57th Annual Meeting of the Association for Computational Linguistics*, pages 4996–5001, Florence, Italy. Association for Computational Linguistics.

Anders Søgaard, Sebastian Ruder, and Ivan Vulić. 2018. On the limitations of unsupervised bilingual dictionary induction. In *Proceedings of the 56th Annual Meeting of the Association for Computational Linguistics (Volume 1: Long Papers)*, pages 778–788, Melbourne, Australia. Association for Computational Linguistics.

Marcos Zampieri, Shervin Malmasi, Preslav Nakov, Sara Rosenthal, Noura Farra, and Ritesh Kumar. 2019a. Predicting the type and target of offensive posts in social media. In *Proceedings of the 2019 Conference of the North American Chapter of the Association for Computational Linguistics: Human Language Technologies, Volume 1 (Long and Short Papers)*, pages 1415–1420, Minneapolis, Minnesota. Association for Computational Linguistics.

Marcos Zampieri, Shervin Malmasi, Preslav Nakov, Sara Rosenthal, Noura Farra, and Ritesh Kumar. 2019b. SemEval-2019 task 6: Identifying and categorizing offensive language in social media (OffensEval). In *Proceedings of the 13th International Workshop on Semantic Evaluation*, pages 75–86, Minneapolis, Minnesota, USA. Association for Computational Linguistics.

# SSNCSE_NLP@DravidianLangTech-EACL2021: Meme classification for Tamil using machine learning approach

**B. Bharathi & Agnusimmaculate Silvia A**
Department of CSE
Sri Siva subramaniya Nadar College of Engineering
Kalavakkam - 603110
bharathib@ssn.edu.in
agnusimmaculate18011@cse.ssn.edu.in

## Abstract

Social network is the place for the creation or sharing of information, ideas or other forms of expression among people. This exchange of information may contain offensive, trolling or malicious contents targeting users or communities. The memes is one of the way to include trolling. A meme is an image or video that represents the thoughts and feelings of a specific audience. The challenge of dealing with memes is that they are region-specific and their meaning is often obscured in humour or sarcasm. A meme is a form of media that spreads an idea or emotion across the internet. The multi modal nature of memes, postings of hateful memes or related events like trolling, cyberbullying are increasing day by day. Memes make it even more challenging since they express humour and sarcasm in an implicit way, because of which the meme may not be offensive if we only consider the text or the image. In this paper we proposed a approach for meme classification for Tamil language that considers only the text present in the meme. This work explains the submissions made by SSNCSE_NLP in DravidanLangTech-EACL2021 task for meme classification in Tamil language. We achieve F1 scores of 0.50 using the proposed approach using the test-set.

## 1 Introduction

More recently, as memes and GIFs dominate the social feeds; typo-graphic visual content has become a considerable element of social media. 'Meme' is a viral image or video often altered by internet users for humorous effect. These convey human expressions but with a wide range of emotions, and often require context to fully understand humor and sarcasm. "Sarcasm is a type of sentiment where people express their negative feelings using positive or intensified positive words in the text (Bharti et al., 2016)". The meme classification is handled by considering both the linguistic features as well as visual features. This task will be considered as multi modal approach. The approaches of natural language processing and computer vision are to be used for the meme classification task. Using this idea, a model has to be designed which deals with the challenges associated with the semantic nature of text and image, and performs classification on the emotional responses obtained.

Tamil language is official language of Tamil Nadu, Singapore, and Sri Lanka (Chakravarthi, 2020b,a; Chakravarthi and Muralidaran, 2021). From the 6th century BCE to the 3rd century CE, the Sangam (koodal) period encompassed ancient Tamil Nadu, Kerala, and portions of Sri Lanka (then known as Tamilakam). It was named after the illustrious Madurai-based Sangam (koodal) academies of poets and scholars. Tamil was the first Indian classical language to be listed as classical language, and it is one of the world's oldest classical languages still in use by common people. Inscriptions in the Tamil language written in Tamili (Tamil-Bharmi) script have been found in Sri Lanka, Thailand, and Egypt. This work explains the submissions made by SSNCSE_NLP in DravidanLangTech-EACL2021 task for meme classification in Tamil language.

The remainder of the paper is organized as follows. Section 2 discusses the related work on meme classification and related tasks using text and images. The dataset about the shared task is described in Section . Section 4 outlines the features and machine learning algorithms used for this task. Results are discussed in Section 5. Section 6 concludes the paper.

## 2 Related work

Researchers experimented with few approaches used in the text sentiment classification task as well



*Proceedings of the First Workshop on Speech and Language Technologies for Dravidian Languages*, pages 336–339
April 20, 2021 

as emotion classification task using images. Sentiment analysis from the text is essential in understanding the idea behind the meme. The authors of (Wang and Wen, 2015) concentrate on generating meme descriptions through non parametric estimation approaches which uses lexical features, POS features, named-entity features, frame-semantics features and dependency triples. In (Amalia et al., 2018), the memes are classified by applying image processing and OCR Tesseract which are combined with Naïve Bayes Algorithm. The survey of using visual linguistic information used for meme classification, image capationed are discussed in (Afridi et al., 2020). The MultiOFF multimodal meme data set for offensive content detection data set was developed by (Suryawanshi et al., 2020a) (Suryawanshi et al., 2020b). Most of the research work on meme classification uses both linguistic and visual features for better performance. In our proposed approach, only text based features were used. The proposed work have been described in the next section.

## 3 Data-set Analysis

The data set given by the shared task organizers contains the image file and transcriptions present in the image file. All the image files are in jpeg format and have text embedded on them in the Tamil language (Suryawanshi et al., 2020c),(Suryawanshi and Chakravarthi, 2021). Later, each meme has been annotated by three annotators (native speakers) in troll or not_troll class. The class label (troll or not_troll) of the data is embedded in the filename. E.g. A meme with filename "troll_0.jpg" has a label "troll", similarly, "Not_troll_0.jpg" has label Not_troll. Further, the transcription of captions for each file is given in the data set. The data distribution of train and test set is given in Table 1

Table 1: Data distribution for meme classification in Tamil

| Class label | Train set | Test set |
|---|---|---|
| Troll | 1282 | 395 |
| Not troll | 1018 | 272 |

## 4 Experimental setup and features

From the given text transcription, n-gram and TFIDF and BERT embeddings are extracted as features. As the content of the memes is a mix of Dravidian language grammar in Roman lexicons along with English grammar, it becomes challenging to find pre-trained models for this context. So a simple n-gram approach is considered. Also, the advancements done by the transformer model for pre-training and the availability of multilingual trained models encourage to experiment with BERT pre-trained embeddings.

The extracted features are used to train machine learning models such as Multi-Layer Perceptron, Random Forest, K-nearest neighbour, and the performance of these models are compared. For shared task for meme classification is provided only with training set. To analyze the performance of the proposed approach, 5 fold cross validation is used. The metrics such as accuracy and weighted average F1 score are analyzed. The machine learning model implementations and the metrics of comparison is used from Scikit-learn [1].

### 4.1 Count and TFIDF n-grams

As the data-set consists of sentences in Tamil as well few colloquial words. So the n-gram model trained from scratch is considered for the tasks and this strategy has shown good results with HI-EN and BN-HI-EN datasets (Mishra et al., 2018). Basic count-based and Term Frequency Inverse Document Frequency-based models are compared for feature extraction. The char TFIDF is calculated as explained in equation 1.

For each char $t$ in a document $d$ from the document set $D$ TD-IDF is calculated as:
$N$ is the total number of documents.

$$tfidf(t, d, D) = tf(t, d).idf(t, D) \quad (1)$$

where

$$tf(t, d) = log(1 + freq(t, d)) \quad (2)$$

$$idf(t, D) = log(Ncount(d\epsilon D : t\epsilon d)) \quad (3)$$

Different character n-gram are constructed with n-gram range varying from 1 to 7. Out of which n-gram range of 1-5 showed good results for meme classification task in Tamil.

### 4.2 BERT Embedding

The memes are given in Tamil language with few colloquial words. For experimental purpose BERT multilingual model is used for this task. BERT multilingual model trained on a large corpus from 104 different languages (Devlin et al., 2018), which

[1]https://scikit-learn.org/stable/

includes Malayalam, Tamil, and English could be considered. A fixed dimension embedding is generated by sentence-transformers, with the pre-trained base-multilingual-cased model implementation as explained in (Reimers and Gurevych, 2020).

These embeddings are then used to classify as Troll or Not-troll by training a machine learning model. Different models such as Random Forest, K-nearest, and Multi Layer Perceptron (MLP) are compared, out of which the MLP with 512 hidden layers, generated the best results.

## 5 Observations

The output from n-gram embedding is a sparse matrix of high dimension. And as the total number of training samples is limited, it is observed that the Random Forest model and MLP model is producing the same performance for this task. Whereas the embedding generated by the BERT model is of 512 dimensions for each meme. The model comparison based on train-set evaluation for the meme classification and cross-validation with k = 5 is shown in table 2. As we can see that the overall performance of the TFIDF model is slightly better than the sentence transformers. This maybe is due to the difference in the base corpus the BERT model is trained on, which is conflicting with the given colloquial Tamil corpus. Whereas the TFIDF and the Count vectorization yielded similar results because of the short length of the meme and containing varied usage of words by different users. The performance of the cross validation scores for the different machine learning approaches are tabulated in Table 2.

Table 2: Cross validation scores of the meme classification task using different machine learning approaches

| Features | Classifiers | Acc |
|---|---|---|
| Tfidf | MLP | 89 |
| Tfidf | Random forest | 89 |
| Tfidf | K-nearest | 88 |
| Count-vec | MLP | 89 |
| Count-vec | Random forest | 87 |
| Count-vec | K-nearest | 86 |
| Sent. Transformer | MLP | 85 |

From the Table 2, it has been noted that Tfidf and n-gram features giving almost the same performance. The sentence transformer is slightly lower performance than the others, this may be because of the colloquial words used in the transcription.

Performance of the test set is given in Table 3. In Table 3, the results of other participating teams are listed.

Table 3: Performance of the meme classification task using test set

| Team | Precision | Recall | F1 |
|---|---|---|---|
| Codewithzichao | 0.57 | 0.60 | 0.55 |
| IIITK | 0.56 | 0.59 | 0.54 |
| NLP@CUET | 0.55 | 0.58 | 0.52 |
| SSNCSE_NLP | 0.58 | 0.60 | 0.50 |
| Simon_work | 0.53 | 0.58 | 0.49 |
| TrollMeta | 0.45 | 0.41 | 0.48 |
| UVCE-IIITT | 0.60 | 0.60 | 0.46 |
| cean | 0.53 | 0.57 | 0.43 |
| HUB | 0.50 | 0.54 | 0.40 |
| iiit_dwd | 0.52 | 0.59 | 0.30 |

## 6 Conclusion

A meme is a form of media that spreads an idea or emotion across the internet. Memes make it even more challenging since they express humour and sarcasm in an implicit way, because of which the meme may not be offensive if we only consider the text or the image. In this paper we proposed a approach for meme classification for Tamil language that considers only the text present in the meme. Tfidf and n-gram features given slightly better performance than the sentence embeddings. We achieve F1 scores of 0.50 using the proposed approach using the test-set. Meme classification performance can be increased by considering visual features also.

## References


Tariq Habib Afridi, Aftab Alam, Muhammad Numan Khan, Jawad Khan, and Young-Koo Lee. 2020. A multimodal memes classification: A survey and open research issues.

A. Amalia, A. Sharif, F. Haisar, D. Gunawan, and B. B. Nasution. 2018. Meme opinion categorization by using optical character recognition (ocr) and naïve bayes algorithm. In *2018 Third International Conference on Informatics and Computing (ICIC)*, pages 1–5.

S.K. Bharti, B. Vachha, R.K. Pradhan, K.S. Babu, and S.K. Jena. 2016. Sarcastic sentiment detection in tweets streamed in real time: a big data approach. *Digital Communications and Networks*, 2(3):108–121. Advances in Big Data.

Bharathi Raja Chakravarthi. 2020a. HopeEDI: A multilingual hope speech detection dataset for equality, diversity, and inclusion. In *Proceedings of the Third Workshop on Computational Modeling of People's Opinions, Personality, and Emotion's in Social Media*, pages 41–53, Barcelona, Spain (Online). Association for Computational Linguistics.

Bharathi Raja Chakravarthi. 2020b. *Leveraging orthographic information to improve machine translation of under-resourced languages*. Ph.D. thesis, NUI Galway.

Bharathi Raja Chakravarthi and Vigneshwaran Muralidaran. 2021. Findings of the shared task on Hope Speech Detection for Equality, Diversity, and Inclusion. In *Proceedings of the First Workshop on Language Technology for Equality, Diversity and Inclusion*. Association for Computational Linguistics.

Jacob Devlin, Ming-Wei Chang, Kenton Lee, and Kristina Toutanova. 2018. Bert: Pre-training of deep bidirectional transformers for language understanding. *arXiv preprint arXiv:1810.04805*.

Pruthwik Mishra, Prathyusha Danda, and Pranav Dhakras. 2018. Code-mixed sentiment analysis using machine learning and neural network approaches.

Nils Reimers and Iryna Gurevych. 2020. Making monolingual sentence embeddings multilingual using knowledge distillation. *arXiv preprint arXiv:2004.09813*.

Shardul Suryawanshi and Bharathi Raja Chakravarthi. 2021. Findings of the shared task on Troll Meme Classification in Tamil. In *Proceedings of the First Workshop on Speech and Language Technologies for Dravidian Languages*. Association for Computational Linguistics.

Shardul Suryawanshi, Bharathi Raja Chakravarthi, Mihael Arcan, and Paul Buitelaar. 2020a. Multimodal meme dataset (MultiOFF) for identifying offensive content in image and text. In *Proceedings of the Second Workshop on Trolling, Aggression and Cyberbullying*, pages 32–41, Marseille, France. European Language Resources Association (ELRA).

Shardul Suryawanshi, Bharathi Raja Chakravarthi, Mihael Arcan, and Paul Buitelaar. 2020b. Multimodal meme dataset (MultiOFF) for identifying offensive content in image and text. In *Proceedings of the Second Workshop on Trolling, Aggression and Cyberbullying*, pages 32–41, Marseille, France. European Language Resources Association (ELRA).

Shardul Suryawanshi, Bharathi Raja Chakravarthi, Pranav Verma, Mihael Arcan, John Philip McCrae, and Paul Buitelaar. 2020c. A dataset for troll classification of TamilMemes. In *Proceedings of the WILDRE5– 5th Workshop on Indian Language Data: Resources and Evaluation*, pages 7–13, Marseille, France. European Language Resources Association (ELRA).

William Yang Wang and Miaomiao Wen. 2015. I can has cheezburger? a nonparanormal approach to combining textual and visual information for predicting and generating popular meme descriptions. In *Proceedings of the 2015 Conference of the North American Chapter of the Association for Computational Linguistics: Human Language Technologies*, pages 355–365, Denver, Colorado. Association for Computational Linguistics.

# MUCS@ - Machine Translation for Dravidian Languages using Stacked Long Short Term Memory

**Asha Hegde**
Dept of Computer Science
Mangalore University
hegdekasha@gmail.com

**Ibrahim Gashaw**
Dept of Computer Science
Mangalore University
ibrahimug1@gmail.com

**H. L. Shashirekha**
Dept of Computer Science
Mangalore University
hlsrekha@gmail.com

## Abstract

The Dravidian language family is one of the largest language families in the world. In spite of its uniqueness, Dravidian languages have gained very less attention due to scarcity of resources to conduct language technology tasks such as translation, Parts-of-Speech tagging, Word Sense Disambiguation etc. In this paper, we, team MUCS, describe sequence-to-sequence stacked Long Short Term Memory (LSTM) based Neural Machine Translation (NMT) models submitted to "Machine Translation in Dravidian languages", a shared task organized by EACL-2021. The NMT models are applied for translation using English-Tamil, English-Telugu, English-Malayalam and Tamil-Telugu corpora provided by the organizers. Standard evaluation metrics namely Bilingual Evaluation Understudy (BLEU) and human evaluations are used to evaluate the model. Our models exhibited good accuracy for all the language pairs and obtained 2[nd] rank for Tamil-Telugu language pair.

## 1 Introduction

Human being is a social entity and they love to communicate with each other and live together from ancient times. They communicate with each other through different means of communication and exchange their data/information/thoughts with each other. Initially, sign language was the means of communication and it was used to exchange thoughts with each other, but now, in this era of technology, there are many ways to communicate out of which language plays a major role. There are more than thousands of languages used all over the world, even in India, due to different religion, culture and tradition. Among Indian languages Dravidian is a language family consisting of four long literary languages, namely, Tamil, Kannada, Telugu and Malayalam along with Tulu and Kodava which are small literary languages. All these languages except Kodava have their own script. Further, these languages consists of 80 different dialects[1] namely Brahui, Kurukh, Malto, Kui, Kuvi, etc. Dravidian Languages are mainly spoken in southern India, Sri Lanka, some parts of Pakistan and Nepal by over 222 million people (Hammarström et al., 2017). It is thought that Dravidian languages are native to the Indian subcontinent and were originally spread throughout India[1]. Tamil have been distributed to Burma, Indonesia, Malaysia, Fiji, Madagascar, Mauritius, Guyana, Martinique and Trinidad through trade and emigration. With over two million speakers, primarily in Pakistan and two million speakers in Afghanistan, Brahui is the only Dravidian language spoken entirely outside India (Ethnologue)[2]. Rest of the Dravidian languages are extensively spoken inside India and by south Indians settled throughout the world. These languages share similar linguistic features and few of them are listed below (Unnikrishnan et al., 2010):

- Verbs have a negative as well as an affirmative voice.
- Root word can be extended using one or more suffixes or prefixes according to the comfort level of the speaker.
- Phonology of all Dravidian languages follow similar strategy.
- Though these languages follow Subject-Object-Verb word order, they are considered as free word order languages as meaning of the sentence will not change when the word order is changed.

[1] https://www.shh.mpg.de/870797/dravidian-languages
[1] https://www.mustgo.com/worldlanguages/dravidian-language-family
[2] http://self.gutenberg.org/articles/eng/Languages_of_Pakistan



*Proceedings of the First Workshop on Speech and Language Technologies for Dravidian Languages*, pages 340–345
April 20, 2021 

- Gender classification is made based on suffix.
- Nouns are declined, showing case and number.
- These languages have their own alphabets related to the Devanagari alphabet that is used for Sanskrit.

Though these languages have rich collection of resources, they are still considered as under-resourced languages[4] due to the availability of very less digital resources and tools. Most of the south Indians speak/understand only their native language as a means of communication. Further, because of migration people need to learn the local languages to survive. In this regard, Language Translation (LT) technology gains importance as it provides the easy means of communication between people when language barrier is a major issue. Various LT technologies are available, namely, manual translation or human translation, Machine aided translation and automatic translation or Machine Translation (MT). As MT is fast, inexpensive, reliable and consistent compared to other LT technologies, they are gaining popularity.

### 1.1 Machine Translation Approaches

MT is an area in Natural Language Processing and does translation of information from one natural language to another natural language by retaining the meaning of source context. Initially, MT task was treated with dictionary matching techniques and upgraded slowly to rule-based approaches (Dove et al., 2012). In order to address information acquisition, corpus-based methods have become popular and bilingual parallel corpora have been used to acquire knowledge for translation (Britz et al., 2017). Hybrid MT approaches have also become popular along with corpus-based approaches, as these approaches promise state-of-the-art performance.

The recent shift to large-scale analytical techniques has led to substantial changes in the efficiency of MT. It has attracted the attention of MT researchers through a corpus based approach. NMT has now become an important alternative to conventional Statistical Machine Translation based on phrases (Patil and Davies, 2014). It is the task of translating text from one natural language (source) to another natural language (target) using the most popular architectures namely Encoder-Decoder, Sequence-to-Sequence or Recurrent Neural Network (RNN) models (Sutskever et al., 2014). In addition, all parts of the neural translation model are trained jointly (end-to-end) to optimise translation efficiency unlike traditional translation systems (Bahdanau et al., 2014). In an NMT system, a bidirectional RNN, known as encoder is used to encode a source sentence and another RNN known as decoder is used to predict the target language terms. With multiple layers, this encoder-decoder architecture can be built to improve the translation performance of the system. The rest of the paper is organized as follows: Related work is presented in Section 2 followed by Methodology and Dataset in Section 3. Experiments and Results are given in Section 4 and the paper concludes in Section 5.

## 2 Related Work

Many attempts are being carried out by the researchers to give special attention for Dravidian language family and several researches have made noticeable work in this direction (Chakravarthi et al., 2019a). NMT is a promising technique to establish sentence level translation and suitable preprocessing techniques will share their contribution for better performance. Observing this (Choudhary et al., 2018) have applied Byte Pair Encoding (BPE) for their model to resolve Out-of-Vocabulary problem. They used EnTam V2.0 dataset that contains English-Tamil parallel sentences. Their model exhibited improvement in BLEU score of 8.33 for Bidirectional LSTM+Adam (optimizer) + Bahdanau (attention) + BPE + word Embedding. Multi-modal multilingual MT system utilizing phonetic transcription was implemented by (Chakravarthi et al., 2019b) using under-resourced Dravidian languages. As a part of this work they have released MMDravi - a Dravidian language dataset that comprises of 30,000 sentences. They have conducted both Statistical Machine Translation (SMT) and NMT and the NMT model outperformed SMT in terms of Bilingual Evaluation Under Study (BLEU) score. (Pareek et al., 2017) have proposed a novel Machine Learning based translation approach for Kannada-Telugu Dravidian language pair considering wikipedia dataset. Further, they considered English-Kannada and English-Telugu language pairs for illustrating the efficacy of their model. They have proposed n-grams based connecting phrase extraction and these extracted

[4]https://en.unesco.org/news/towards-world-atlas-languages

phrases are trained in multilayered neural network. For testing, the phrases are extracted from test dataset and alignment score is computed and then these phrases are used for post-processing. They have observed a considerable accuracy of 91.63%, 90.65% and 88.63% for English-Kannada, English-Telugu and Kannada-Telugu, respectively. Dictionary based MT for Kannada to Telugu is developed by (Sindhu and Sagar, 2017) and as a part of this work, a bilingual dictionary with 8000 words is developed. Providing suffix mapping table at the tag level, this model uses dictionary for translating word by word without giving much attention on the correlation between words and has shown more than 50% accuracy.

## 3 Methodology

Though many attempts are being carried out to develop MT system for Dravidian languages, development of full fledged MT system for Dravidian languages is an open ended problem as these languages are agglutinative and morphologically rich (Chakravarthi, 2020). In the proposed work, sequence-to-sequence stacked LSTM is used to build the translation system using the dataset provided by the organizers[5].

### 3.1 Sequence-to-Sequence Architecture

Sequence-to-sequence architecture is basically used for response generation and it is suitable when source and target sentences are almost of same length. Further, it is used to find the relationship between two distinct language pairs in MT model. This architecture consists of two parts, namely, i) the encoder that accepts the text of the source language as input and generates its intermediate representation and (ii) the decoder that generates the output based on the encoding vector and previously generated words. Since, the model utilises the source representation information and the previously generated words to predict the next-word, this distributed representation allows the sequence-to-sequence model to generate appropriate mapping between the input and the output (Li et al., 2016). Therefore, this model has shown good performance compared to conventional statistical MT systems and rule based MT systems. Suppose, S is source consisting of n sentences $s_1$, $s_2$, $s_3$, ... , $s_n$ and R is target. Encoder transforms source sentences into fixed dimension vectors $A_{s1}$,$A_{s2}$, $A_{s3}$, ... , $A_{sn}$ and the decoder uses conditional probability to produce the predicted sentences $b_1$, $b_2$, $b_3$, ... , $b_n$ word-by-word. While decoding, next word is predicted using previously predicted word vectors and source sentence vectors in equation 1 and equation 2 is derived from the equation 1. Each term in the distribution is represented with a softmax over all the words in the vocabulary (Neubig, 2017).

$$P(R\,|S) = P(R\,|A_{s1}, A_{s2}, ..., A_{sn}) \quad (1)$$

$$P(R\,|S) = P(b_1, b_2, ....b_n; s_1, s_2, ..., s_n) \quad (2)$$

### 3.2 Stacked Long Short Term Memory

LSTM is an RNN architecture used to address the issues of RNN, namely, long term dependence and gradient disappearance. Like RNN, LSTM has a chain like system, but the structure of the repeating module is distinct from RNN (Tai et al., 2015). LSTM has the ability to add and remove information to the cell state by carefully regulating the structure called gates. There are four gates in a module in place of a single neural network layer. Forget gate is the first gate that shows one of the major features of LSTM network. It helps in determining the portion that should be forgotten by the network. In this architecture, forgetting is as important as learning. If network is able to forget unimportant information and just retain important details, this will reduce the memory requirement of the system. Next gate is based on sigmoid layer and known as input gate that helps to determine which values are changed by the system. This gate is useful in deciding the role of current layer by choosing the right inputs to improve learning. The third gate is a input modulation gate (tanh) that generates a new candidate value vector that could be added in the same module to the state. Finally, the fourth gate ie., output gate determines the production. This is also a function of *tanh* that produces the state for the next modules.

Conventional LSTM model has single hidden LSTM layer followed by a standard feed forward output layer whereas the stacked LSTM model has multiple LSTM layers along with multiple hidden layers. Stacking of LSTM makes the model more deeper, more accurate and gives the correct meaning of deep learning (Barone et al., 2017). In recent years, stacked LSTM model is becoming a stable approach for problems with sequence prediction. A stacked LSTM architecture can be described as

[5]https://dravidianlangtech.github.io/2021/index.html

**Table 1:** Details of the given dataset used for training and validating the model

| Corpus name | # of parallel sentences used for training | # of parallel sentences used for validation | # of words |
|---|---|---|---|
| English-Telugu | 23,222 | 2000 | 13,05,105 |
| English-Tamil | 28,417 | 2000 | 17,44,747 |
| English-Malayalam | 3,82,868 | 2000 | 2,55,97,816 |
| Tamil-Telugu | 17,155 | 2000 | 9,40,921 |

LSTM model comprised of multiple LSTM layers. The LSTM layer above provides a sequence output rather than a single value output to the LSTM layer below, specifically, one output per input time step rather than one output for all input time steps (Barone et al., 2017). This information is shown in Figure 1 and it consists of two LSTM layers namely Layer 1 and Layer 2. Further, in Figure 1 $X_i$ is the encoder input, $Y_i$ is the decoder input and $Z_i$ is the predicted sequence (decoder output) obtained using multilayered LSTM architecture.

### 3.3 Dataset

In MT, dataset and preparation of the dataset for training the translation model play a major role. To perform successful translation, this data preparation process should be carried out at different levels. In this work, we have used English-Telugu, English-Tamil, English-Malayalam and Tamil-Telugu the dataset. Details of the dataset are shown in Table 1.

### 3.4 Dataset Preprocessing

Insights of the dataset makes the translation task more effective and efficient. As many sentences in the datasets were duplicated both in train and test sets, it becomes essential to clean, analyse and correct the dataset before using it for the translation experiments. It was also observed that few sentences are repeated more than 5 times and this confuses the model to learn and recognise various new characteristics and overfits the model by leading to wrong output. Train and test set containing the same sentences may give better prediction for test set but poor prediction for new sentences. To resolve these problems, unique sentences are selected from the corpus. Further, duplication of sentences with same source and target text are removed to avoid uncertainty during training. Null lines cause mapping issues while training the corpora for translation. Hence, null lines and extra spaces are removed . The remaining parallel text is considered for building the translation model.

**Table 2:** Hyper parameters used in sequence-to-sequence stacked LSTM model

| Hyper Parameters used | Values |
|---|---|
| latent dimension | 512 |
| optimizer | adam |
| learning rate | 0.001 |
| dropout | 0.03 |
| epochs | 100 |
| batch size | 128 |

## 4 Experiments and Result

Sequence-to-Sequence stacked LSTM model is used to build translation model for the given dataset. This model is developed with multiple layers to enhance learning ability of the model. Further, in this work we used one-hot encoding embedding technique for both source and the target text. The experiments are conducted in Google Colab to resolve resource issues during translation and is conducted for various hyper parameter values and best values are shown in Table 2.

### 4.1 Result

In this work, translation is carried out separately for the given corpora, namely, English-Tamil, English-Telugu, English-Malayalam and Tamil-Telugu. Further, this model is evaluated using BLEU as well as human evaluation against gold dataset which is provided by the organizers and performance measure of the models are as shown in Table 3. Though there are many challenges with the test dataset, considerable results are obtained for all the corpora.

### 4.2 Analysis

In this work, Tamil-Telugu translation model achieved $2^{nd}$ rank with a BLEU score of 0.43. Further, the models exhibited BLEU scores of 1.66, 0.29 and 0.48 for English-Tamil, English-Telugu and English-Malayalam corpora respectively. In this sequence-to-sequence model, number of LSTM layers is varied to get better translation performance and for 3 LSTM layers models achieved good accuracy. When the number of LSTM layers is increased beyond this break even

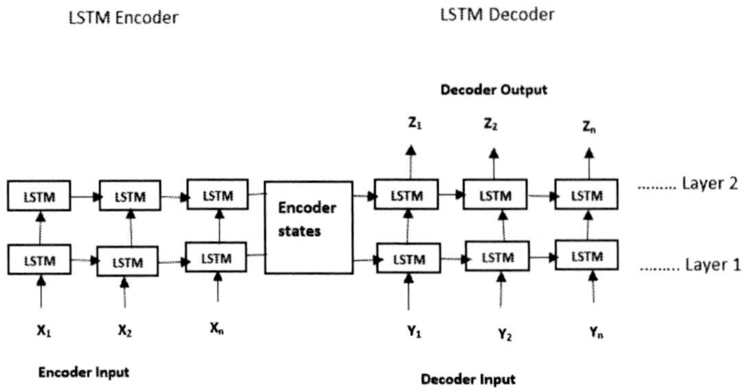


**Figure 1:** Stacked LSTM architecture with two layers

**Table 3:** Performance measure of Sequence-to-Sequence stacked LSTM model

| Corpus Name | Validation Accuracy | Validation Loss | BLEU Score |
|---|---|---|---|
| English-Tamil | 37.77 | 1.04 | 1.66 |
| English-Telugu | 32.87 | 1.32 | 0.29 |
| English-Malayalam | 42.55 | 0.88 | 0.48 |
| **Tamil-Telugu** | **33.26** | **1.27** | **0.43** |

point performance of the models started decreasing.

This sequence-to-sequence stacked LSTM models have exhibited considerable BLEU score as the size of the corpora is small to conduct efficient translation. The morphological richness and agglutinativeness of the language pairs used in translation increases the translation complexity. In addition, test sets provided for these tasks are challenging due to the presence of special characters. Further, long sentences, duplicate sentences and null lines in the test sets had their share to the translation complexities.

## 5 Conclusion and Future Work

This paper describes the models submitted to "Machine Translation in Dravidian languages" shared task to perform translation of English-Tamil, English-Telugu, English-Malayalam and Tamil-Telugu language pairs. A close analysis of the corpora is carried out before performing the preprocessing and the corpora are found challenging to establish translation. Though all the corpora belong to low-resource languages and being rich in morphology, this sequence-to sequence stacked LSTM model exhibits the satisfactory results for all the corpora. All the models exhibited considerable performance and our model obtained 2nd rank for Tamil-Telugu language pair. In future, we would like to explore different NMT techniques that helps to translate low-resource languages efficiently.

## References

Dzmitry Bahdanau, Kyunghyun Cho, and Yoshua Bengio. 2014. Neural machine translation by jointly learning to align and translate. *arXiv preprint arXiv:1409.0473*.

Antonio Valerio Miceli Barone, Jindřich Helcl, Rico Sennrich, Barry Haddow, and Alexandra Birch. 2017. Deep architectures for neural machine translation. *arXiv preprint arXiv:1707.07631*.

Denny Britz, Anna Goldie, Minh-Thang Luong, and Quoc Le. 2017. Massive exploration of neural machine translation architectures. *arXiv preprint arXiv:1703.03906*.

Bharathi Raja Chakravarthi. 2020. *Leveraging orthographic information to improve machine translation of under-resourced languages*. Ph.D. thesis, NUI Galway.

Bharathi Raja Chakravarthi, Mihael Arcan, and John P McCrae. 2019a. Comparison of different orthographies for machine translation of under-resourced dravidian languages. In *2nd Conference on Language, Data and Knowledge (LDK 2019)*. Schloss Dagstuhl-Leibniz-Zentrum fuer Informatik.

Bharathi Raja Chakravarthi, Ruba Priyadharshini, Bernardo Stearns, Arun Jayapal, S Sridevy, Mihael Arcan, Manel Zarrouk, and John P McCrae. 2019b. Multilingual multimodal machine translation for Dravidian languages utilizing phonetic transcription. In *Proceedings of the 2nd Workshop on Technologies for MT of Low Resource Languages*. European Association for Machine Translation.

Himanshu Choudhary, Aditya Kumar Pathak, Rajiv Ratan Saha, and Ponnurangam Kumaraguru. 2018. Neural machine translation for English-Tamil. In *Proceedings of the Third Conference on Machine Translation: Shared Task Papers*, pages 770–775.

Catherine Dove, Olga Loskutova, and Ruben de la Fuente. 2012. What's your pick: RbMT, SMT or hybrid. In *Proceedings of the tenth conference of the Association for Machine Translation in the Americas (AMTA 2012). San Diego, CA*.

Harald Hammarström, Robert Forkel, and Martin Haspelmath. 2017. Glottolog 3.0. *Max Planck Institute for the Science of Human History*.

Xiaoqing Li, Jiajun Zhang, and Chengqing Zong. 2016. Towards zero unknown word in neural machine translation. In *IJCAI*, pages 2852–2858.

Graham Neubig. 2017. Neural machine translation and sequence-to-sequence models: A tutorial. *arXiv preprint arXiv:1703.01619*.

Piyush Kumar Pareek, K Swathi, Puneet Shetteppanavar, et al. 2017. An efficient machine translation model for Dravidian language. In *2017 2nd IEEE International Conference on Recent Trends in Electronics, Information & Communication Technology (RTEICT)*, pages 2101–2105. IEEE.

Sumant Patil and Patrick Davies. 2014. Use of google translate in medical communication: evaluation of accuracy. *Bmj*, 349:g7392.

DV Sindhu and BM Sagar. 2017. Dictionary based machine translation from Kannada to Telugu. In *IOP conference series: materials science and engineering*, volume 12182.

Ilya Sutskever, Oriol Vinyals, and Quoc V Le. 2014. Sequence to sequence learning with neural networks. In *Advances in neural information processing systems*, pages 3104–3112.

Kai Sheng Tai, Richard Socher, and Christopher D Manning. 2015. Improved semantic representations from tree-structured long short-term memory networks. *arXiv preprint arXiv:1503.00075*.

P Unnikrishnan, PJ Antony, and KP Soman. 2010. A novel approach for English to South Dravidian language statistical machine translation system. *the International Journal on Computer Science and Engineering*, 2(8):2749–2759.

# OffTamil@DravideanLangTech-EACL2021: Offensive Language Identification in Tamil Text

**Disne Sivalingam**
Eastern University, Sri Lanka
disnesiva777@gmail.com

**Sajeetha Thavareesan**
Eastern University, Sri Lanka
sajeethas@esn.ac.lk

## Abstract

In the last few decades, Code-Mixed Offensive texts are used penetratingly in social media posts. Social media platforms and online communities showed much interest on offensive text identification in recent years. Consequently, research community is also interested in identifying such content and also contributed to the development of corpora. Many publicly available corpora are there for research on identifying offensive text written in English language but rare for low resourced languages like Tamil. The first code-mixed offensive text for Dravidian languages are developed by shared task organizers which is used for this study. This study focused on offensive language identification on code-mixed low-resourced Dravidian language Tamil using four classifiers (Support Vector Machine, random forest, k- Nearest Neighbour and Naive Bayes) using $\chi^2$ feature selection technique along with BoW and TF-IDF feature representation techniques using different combinations of n-grams. This proposed model achieved an accuracy of 76.96% while using linear SVM with TF-IDF feature representation technique.

## 1 Introduction

Offensive language is the key concern of technical companies nowadays due to exponential growth in number of internet users around the world and since these people are from different culture, race, religion, origin, gender and nationality (Chakravarthi et al., 2021). Internet gives more freedom to people to express their opinions freely in different forms such as blogs, forums and social media platforms (e.g., Facebook, Twitter, and YouTube) (Suryawanshi and Chakravarthi, 2021). It is noted that the usage of social media among the people has increased rapidly since last decade (Hande et al., 2020). People can express their opinion in a positive way as well as negative way (Chakravarthi and Muralidaran, 2021). So the offensive comments are now avoidable in those platforms, the problem has to be solved. It has a negative impact on society and individuals (Puranik et al., 2021; Hegde et al., 2021; Yasaswini et al., 2021; Ghanghor et al., 2021b,a). There are huge amount of researches are found in identifying the offensive words in English language. There are so many publicly available corpora in English language.

People from multilingual society will add comments and reviews with the mixing of vocabulary and syntax of multiple languages in the same sentence (Priyadharshini et al., 2020; Jose et al., 2020). So it is a big challenge to identify the offensive words from the Dravidian languages (Mandl et al., 2020; Chakravarthi et al., 2020c). With a history stretching back to 600 BCE, the Tamil language is one of the world's longest-surviving classical languages. Poetry, especially Sangam literature, which is made up of poems written between 600 BCE and 300 CE, dominates Tamil literature. All the Dravidian languages evolved from Tamil language. The first attempt to create this offensive language has done by Chakravarthi et al. (2020b). We used code-mixed texts from the YouTube reviews as a corpus. In this paper, we proposed a method using linear SVM with $chi^2$ feature selection based approach to find offensive language in Tamil language (Thavareesan and Mahesan, 2019, 2020a,b).

The rest of the paper is organised as follows. Section 2 describes related works. Section 3 presents proposed method. Section 4 presents experimental setup and the results. Finally, discussion and conclusion are in Section 5.



*Proceedings of the First Workshop on Speech and Language Technologies for Dravidian Languages*, pages 346–351
April 20, 2021 ©2021 Association for Computational Linguistics

## 2 Related work

Detecting offensive language is not an easy task. Many researchers has proposed many methods and algorithms to detect offensive language content on the web.

Alakrot et al. (2018) trained a Support Vector Machine (SVM) classifier using world-level features (with and without preprocessing), SVM (with and without the normalisation), n-gram level features. They used Arabic language corpus which was pre-processed with tokenization, filtering and normalisation. Their classifier achieved an accuracy of 90.05 upon using 10-fold cross-validation. It has been observed that the n-gram features improves the classifier's performance. On the contrary, the combination of stemming and n-gram features harms precision.

Ibrohim and Budi (2018) used machine learning approach with simple word n-gram and character n-gram features and trained Naïve Bayes, Support vector machine, and Random Forest Decision Tree Classifiers. Discussed abusive language detection in the Indonesian language corpus. 10-fold cross validation technique is used to evaluate the classification result. If the corpus labeled with three classes(non-abusive language, abusive language but not offensive and offensive language) Naïve bayes classifier with the combination of word unigram and bi-grams features gives the best result 70.06% of F1-score. If the corpus labeled with two classes(abusive language or non-abusive language) then all the classifiers gives higher results. The have Concluded that the classifying into three classes is more difficult than just classifying abusive language or non-abusive language.

Waseem and Hovy (2016) analyzed the impact of various extra-linguistic features in conjunction with character n-grams for hate speech detection. Corpus is normalized for pre-processing. Uni grams, bi grams, tri grams and four grams were Collected for each tweets. Logistic regression classifier and 10-fold cross validation were used to test the influence of various features on prediction. Found that character n-grams of length up to 4 along with gender as an additional feature provides the best results.

Nayel and Shashirekha (2019) In this research they have used corpus in three languages (English, Germany and Hindi). TF-IDF vectors has been computed for all the posts in the training set. For pre-processing all un-informative tokens such as urls, digits and special characters have been removed from all the posts. Trained using linear classifier, SVM and MLP classifier, tested with 5-fold cross-validation approach. Classified as three tasks as A, B and C respectively. Unlabeled instance into one of the two predefined categories classified for task A, unlabeled instance into one of the three predefined categories classified for task B and same instance into one of the two predefined categories classified for task C. Concluded that for English language SVM outperforms for all three tasks. For German language MLP out performs for task A and B. For Hindi language MLP outperforms for task A and SVM gives better results for task B.

Chakravarthi et al. (2020b) created a corpus containing 15744 YouTube comments and posts as a code-mixed dataset. Following classifiers are used to classify the corpus Support Vector Machine(SVM), Logistic Regression (LR), k-Nearest Neighbour (k-NN), Decision tree, Random Forest, Multinomial Naive Bayes,BERT Multilingual, 1DConv-LSTM, DME, CDME. They have concluded that Random Forest classifier, Logistic regression and decision tree gives the best results.

Chakravarthi et al. (2020a)analysed in code-mixed Dravidian text from social media that aims at classifying YouTube comments. The hundred and nineteen teams partici-pated in the task, and a total of 32 teams for Tamil and 28 teams Malayalam submitted the results.They trained on the unbalanced dataset. The methods proposed by participants ranged from traditional machine learning models with features based approaches to using state-of-the-art embedding methods in deep learning models.The best performing run achieved weighted F1-score of 0.65 and 0.74 for Tamil and Malayalam respectively.

## 3 Methodology

Offensive language identification aims to identify the offensive text written in Tamil language. In this paper we experimented a method using four classifiers and $\chi^2$ feature selection technique to identify the offensive text written in Tamil documents. The overall framework of Offensive language identification is shown in Figure 1.

The methodology applied in this research is divided into four parts. Subsection 3.1 describes the corpus used, subsection 3.2 describes the preprocessing applied, subsection 3.3 describes the feature selection and representation techniques and

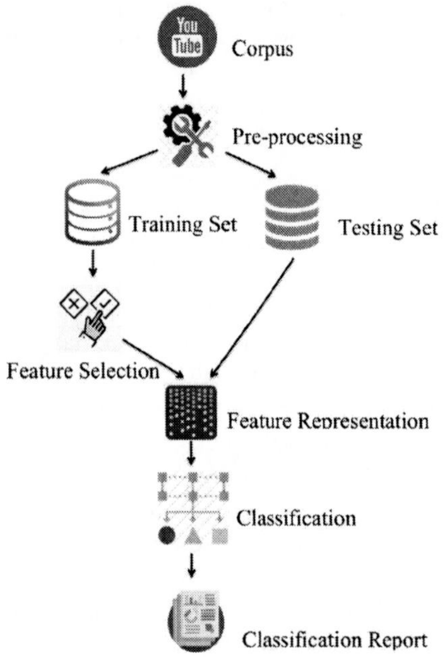


Figure 1: Overall framework of Offensive Language Identification

the subsection 3.4 describes classifiers used.

### 3.1 Corpus

Offensive language identification is a natural language processing (NLP) task which aims to moderate and minimise offensive content in social media. It is an active research area in both fields: academic and industry. There is an increasing demand for offensive language identification on social media texts written in code-mixed. Code-mixing is the text written in two or more languages or language varieties in speech. The shared task Organized by *dravidianlangtech* presents a new gold standard corpus for offensive language identification of code-mixed text in Dravidian languages such as Tamil-English (Chakravarthi et al., 2020b), Malayalam-English (Chakravarthi et al., 2020a) and Kannada-English (Hande et al., 2020). As far as we know, this is the first shared task on offensive language identification in Dravidian languages. The goal of this task is to identify offensive language content of the code-mixed corpus of comments in Dravidian Languages collected from social media. This task aims to classify the given comment into Not-offensive, offensive-untargeted, offensive-targeted-individual, offensive-targeted-group, offensive-targeted-other, or Not-in-indented-language. Description of corpus used for this research is shown in Table 1 and Table 2.

| Label | Tamil |
|---|---|
| Not offensive | 25,425 |
| Not in indented language | 1,454 |
| Offensive-Targeted-Insult-Individual | 2,343 |
| Offensive Targeted Insult Group | 2,557 |
| Offensive Targeted Insult Other | 454 |
| Offensive Untargeted | 2,906 |

Table 1: Class distribution of Tamil corpus.

| Language | Train | Dev | Test |
|---|---|---|---|
| Tamil | 35139 | 4388 | 4392 |

Table 2: Corpus statistic of Tamil.

### 3.2 Pre-processing

In the pre-processing phase all un-informative tokens such as symbols, numbers, URLs and non-Tamil words in other language fonts are removed.

### 3.3 $\chi^2$ Feature Selection and Representation

A $\chi^2$ test is used in statistics to test the independence of two events which is used as the feature selection method in this proposed method. Given the data of two variables, we can get observed count O and expected count E. $\chi^2$ measures how expected count E and observed count O deviates each other.

BoW and TF-IDF are used as the feature representation techniques in this proposed method. BoW is used to represent the number of times a word appears in a comment. Equation of BoW is shown in Equation 1.

$$\texttt{BoW} = \texttt{No. of times word w occurred} \quad (1)$$

TF-IDF is the multiplication of Term Frequency (TF) and Inverse Document Frequency (IDF) scores whereas TF algorithm is the ratio of number of times the word appeared in a comment compared to the total number of words in that comment and IDF is a scoring of how rare the word is across comments.

$$\texttt{TF} = \frac{\texttt{No. of times w appeared in a document}}{\texttt{Total no. of words in that comment}} \quad (2)$$

| Classifier | BoW | TF-IDF |
|---|---|---|
| k-Nearest Neighbour | 75.34 | 74.73 |
| Linear SVM | 75.57 | 75.62 |
| Logistic Regression | 31.22 | 41.82 |
| Random Forest | 75.34 | 73.66 |

Table 3: Results of feature-set-1 with BoW and TF-IDF

| Feature set | 50 | 100 | 500 | 1000 | 1500 | 2000 | 2500 | 3000 | 3500 |
|---|---|---|---|---|---|---|---|---|---|
| Feature-Set-1 | 74.77 | 75.39 | 75.57 | 75.93 | 76.17 | 76.16 | 76.14 | **76.48** | 75.98 |
| Feature-Set-2 | 74.77 | 75.07 | 75.59 | 75.59 | 75.57 | 75.93 | 76.19 | **76.25** | 75.18 |
| Feature-Set-3 | 74.77 | 74.93 | 75.58 | 75.24 | 75.34 | 75.73 | 76.16 | **76.18** | 74.78 |

Table 4: Results of linear SVM with BoW

| Feature set | 50 | 100 | 500 | 1000 | 1500 | 2000 | 2500 | 3000 | 3500 | 4000 |
|---|---|---|---|---|---|---|---|---|---|---|
| Feature-Set-1 | 74.77 | 74.68 | 75.61 | 76.2 | 76.12 | 76.25 | 76.55 | 76.19 | **76.96** | 76.34 |
| Feature-Set-2 | 74.64 | 74.59 | 74.77 | 75.09 | 75.84 | 76.09 | 76.23 | 76.28 | **76.78** | 76.12 |
| Feature-Set-3 | 74.51 | 74.48 | 74.65 | 74.92 | 75.56 | 75.68 | 76.01 | 76.25 | **76.74** | 75.88 |

Table 5: Results of linear SVM with TF-IDF

$$\texttt{IDF(w)} = \frac{\texttt{No. of comments}}{\texttt{No. of comments containing word w}} \quad (3)$$

### 3.4 Training the Classifier

In this training phase the classifiers such as linear Support Vector Machine(SVM), random forest, k-Nearest Neighbour (k-NN) and Naive Bayes are used along with BoW and TF-IDF feature representation techniques using different combination of n-grams.

Firstly, we selected the most relevant features using $\chi^2$ feature selection technique and represented them using BoW and TF-IDF feature representation techniques. We used different combinations of uni gram, bi gram and tri grams of words in training corpus to create the vocabulary of the proposed method. We used three feature sets to experiment this proposed method. They are listed below:

- Feature-Set-1: Word Uni gram.
- Feature-Set-2: Word Uni gram and bi gram.
- Feature-Set-3: Word Uni gram, bi gram and tri gram.

These three feature sets are represented using BoW and TF-IDF feature representation techniques and trained using four classifiers mentioned above. We performed six experiments per each classifier. Moreover, we have repeated these six experiments for linear SVM by selecting varying number of features using $\chi^2$ feature selection technique.

### 3.5 Evaluation

Evaluation of these experiments are performed by calculating accuracy as in equation 4.

$$\texttt{Acc} = \frac{\texttt{No. of correctly classified comments}}{\texttt{Total no. of comments in the Corpus}} \times 100 \quad (4)$$

## 4 Experimental Setup and Results

Test results of Feature-Set-1 with BoW and TF-IDF feature representation techniques of four classifiers are listed in Table 3.

It is observed that from the table that linear SVM performs better than other three classifiers for this corpus while using Feature-Set-1. Therefore we continued our experiments using linear SVM.

Results of BoW feature representation technique with varying values of features for all three feature sets are shown in Table 4.

Test results of linear SVM with TF-IDF feature representation technique are shown in Table 5

## 5 Discussion and Conclusion

In this paper we proposed $\chi^2$ feature selection technique based Offensive language identification method. We compared results of four classifiers and observed that linear SVM outperformed all other classifiers tested here. Moreover we have checked the influence of different feature sets and found that Feature-Set-1 performs better than other two feature sets for both feature representation techniques. Another finding of this research is that we can be able to get better results with least number of features while using $\chi^2$ feature selection technique. The highest accuracy of 76.96% is obtained while using TF-IDF feature representation with linear SVM. More over we obtained highest accuracy while using 3500 features as vocabulary for both BoW and TF-IDF feature representation techniques.

## References


Azalden Alakrot, Liam Murray, and Nikola S Nikolov. 2018. Towards accurate detection of offensive language in online communication in arabic. *Procedia computer science*, 142:315–320.

Bharathi Raja Chakravarthi, Navya Jose, Shardul Suryawanshi, Elizabeth Sherly, and John Philip McCrae. 2020a. A sentiment analysis dataset for code-mixed Malayalam-English. In *Proceedings of the 1st Joint Workshop on Spoken Language Technologies for Under-resourced languages (SLTU) and Collaboration and Computing for Under-Resourced Languages (CCURL)*, pages 177–184, Marseille, France. European Language Resources association.

Bharathi Raja Chakravarthi and Vigneshwaran Muralidaran. 2021. Findings of the shared task on Hope Speech Detection for Equality, Diversity, and Inclusion. In *Proceedings of the First Workshop on Language Technology for Equality, Diversity and Inclusion*. Association for Computational Linguistics.

Bharathi Raja Chakravarthi, Vigneshwaran Muralidaran, Ruba Priyadharshini, and John Philip McCrae. 2020b. Corpus creation for sentiment analysis in code-mixed Tamil-English text. In *Proceedings of the 1st Joint Workshop on Spoken Language Technologies for Under-resourced languages (SLTU) and Collaboration and Computing for Under-Resourced Languages (CCURL)*, pages 202–210, Marseille, France. European Language Resources association.

Bharathi Raja Chakravarthi, Ruba Priyadharshini, Navya Jose, Anand Kumar M, Thomas Mandl, Prasanna Kumar Kumaresan, Rahul Ponnusamy, Hariharan V, Elizabeth Sherly, and John Philip McCrae. 2021. Findings of the shared task on Offensive Language Identification in Tamil, Malayalam, and Kannada. In *Proceedings of the First Workshop on Speech and Language Technologies for Dravidian Languages*. Association for Computational Linguistics.

Bharathi Raja Chakravarthi, Ruba Priyadharshini, Vigneshwaran Muralidaran, Shardul Suryawanshi, Navya Jose, Elizabeth Sherly, and John P. McCrae. 2020c. Overview of the Track on Sentiment Analysis for Dravidian Languages in Code-Mixed Text. In *Forum for Information Retrieval Evaluation*, FIRE 2020, page 21–24, New York, NY, USA. Association for Computing Machinery.

Nikhil Kumar Ghanghor, Parameswari Krishnamurthy, Sajeetha Thavareesan, Ruba Priyadharshini, and Bharathi Raja Chakravarthi. 2021a. IIITK@DravidianLangTech-EACL2021: Offensive Language Identification and Meme Classification in Tamil, Malayalam and Kannada. In *Proceedings of the First Workshop on Speech and Language Technologies for Dravidian Languages*, Online. Association for Computational Linguistics.

Nikhil Kumar Ghanghor, Rahul Ponnusamy, Prasanna Kumar Kumaresan, Ruba Priyadharshini, Sajeetha Thavareesan, and Bharathi Raja Chakravarthi. 2021b. IIITK@LT-EDI-EACL2021: Hope Speech Detection for Equality, Diversity, and Inclusion in Tamil, Malayalam and English. In *Proceedings of the First Workshop on Language Technology for Equality, Diversity and Inclusion*, Online.

Adeep Hande, Ruba Priyadharshini, and Bharathi Raja Chakravarthi. 2020. KanCMD: Kannada CodeMixed dataset for sentiment analysis and offensive language detection. In *Proceedings of the Third Workshop on Computational Modeling of People's Opinions, Personality, and Emotion's in Social Media*, pages 54–63, Barcelona, Spain (Online). Association for Computational Linguistics.

Siddhanth U Hegde, Adeep Hande, Ruba Priyadharshini, Sajeetha Thavareesan, and Bharathi Raja Chakravarthi. 2021. UVCE-IIITT@DravidianLangTech-EACL2021: Tamil Troll Meme Classification: You need to Pay more Attention. In *Proceedings of the First Workshop on Speech and Language Technologies for Dravidian Languages*. Association for Computational Linguistics.

Muhammad Okky Ibrohim and Indra Budi. 2018. A dataset and preliminaries study for abusive language detection in indonesian social media. *Procedia Computer Science*, 135:222–229.

Navya Jose, Bharathi Raja Chakravarthi, Shardul Suryawanshi, Elizabeth Sherly, and John P. McCrae. 2020. A Survey of Current Datasets for Code-Switching Research. In *2020 6th International Conference on Advanced Computing and Communication Systems (ICACCS)*, pages 136–141.

Thomas Mandl, Sandip Modha, Anand Kumar M, and Bharathi Raja Chakravarthi. 2020. Overview of the HASOC Track at FIRE 2020: Hate Speech and Offensive Language Identification in Tamil, Malayalam, Hindi, English and German. In *Forum for*

*Information Retrieval Evaluation*, FIRE 2020, page 29–32, New York, NY, USA. Association for Computing Machinery.

Hamada A Nayel and HL Shashirekha. 2019. Deep at hasoc2019: A machine learning framework for hate speech and offensive language detection. In *FIRE (Working Notes)*, pages 336–343.

Ruba Priyadharshini, Bharathi Raja Chakravarthi, Mani Vegupatti, and John P. McCrae. 2020. Named Entity Recognition for Code-Mixed Indian Corpus using Meta Embedding. In *2020 6th International Conference on Advanced Computing and Communication Systems (ICACCS)*, pages 68–72.

Karthik Puranik, Adeep Hande, Ruba Priyadharshini, Sajeetha Thavareesan, and Bharathi Raja Chakravarthi. 2021. IIITT@LT-EDI-EACL2021-Hope Speech Detection: There is always hope in Transformers. In *Proceedings of the First Workshop on Language Technology for Equality, Diversity and Inclusion*. Association for Computational Linguistics.

Shardul Suryawanshi and Bharathi Raja Chakravarthi. 2021. Findings of the shared task on Troll Meme Classification in Tamil. In *Proceedings of the First Workshop on Speech and Language Technologies for Dravidian Languages*. Association for Computational Linguistics.

Sajeetha Thavareesan and Sinnathamby Mahesan. 2019. Sentiment Analysis in Tamil Texts: A Study on Machine Learning Techniques and Feature Representation. In *2019 14th Conference on Industrial and Information Systems (ICIIS)*, pages 320–325.

Sajeetha Thavareesan and Sinnathamby Mahesan. 2020a. Sentiment Lexicon Expansion using Word2vec and fastText for Sentiment Prediction in Tamil texts. In *2020 Moratuwa Engineering Research Conference (MERCon)*, pages 272–276.

Sajeetha Thavareesan and Sinnathamby Mahesan. 2020b. Word embedding-based Part of Speech tagging in Tamil texts. In *2020 IEEE 15th International Conference on Industrial and Information Systems (ICIIS)*, pages 478–482.

Zeerak Waseem and Dirk Hovy. 2016. Hateful symbols or hateful people? predictive features for hate speech detection on twitter. In *Proceedings of the NAACL student research workshop*, pages 88–93.

Konthala Yasaswini, Karthik Puranik, Adeep Hande, Ruba Priyadharshini, Sajeetha Thavareesan, and Bharathi Raja Chakravarthi. 2021. IIITT@DravidianLangTech-EACL2021: Transfer Learning for Offensive Language Detection in Dravidian Languages. In *Proceedings of the First Workshop on Speech and Language Technologies for Dravidian Languages*. Association for Computational Linguistics.

# Codewithzichao@DravidianLangTech-EACL2021: Exploring Multimodal Transformers for Meme Classification in Tamil Language

**Zichao Li**
School of Software and Microelectronics, Peking University, China
lizichao@pku.edu.cn

## Abstract

This paper describes our submission to shared task on Meme Classification for Tamil Language. To address this task, we explore a multimodal transformer for meme classification in Tamil language. According to the characteristics of the image and text, we use different pre-trained models to encode the image and text so as to get better representations of the image and text respectively. Besides, we design a multimodal attention layer to make the text and corresponding image interact fully with each other based on cross attention. Our model achieved 0.55 weighted average F1 score and ranked first in this task.

## 1 Introduction

In recent years, with the prosperity of social media platforms, memes have gradually become a part of online communication. Therefore, it is essential to detect whether memes are offensive to individuals or organizations to ensure the diversity and sustainability of content on the Internet. It it a challenging task to classify whether memes are troll or not. In addition, there has been a lot of work currently focused on English (Truong and Lauw, 2019; Xu et al., 2019; Cai et al., 2019), but little work has been done for Tamil language.

Shared task on Meme Classification for Tamil Language fills this gap. The goal of this shared task is to detect whether memes which are collected from social media platforms are troll or not. Each meme has been annotated with troll or not troll class. Furthermore, a transcription of captions in Latin script for both Tamil is embedded in each image. This is a multimodal classification task that given the image and text pair, systems have to classify this pair into troll or not troll class.

In this paper, we explore a multimodal transformer for meme classification on Tamil language. According to the characteristics of the image and text, we use different pre-trained models to encode the image and text so as to get better representations of the image and text respectively. Besides, due to the particularity of social media text, in many cases we can only understand the meaning of text through the corresponding image, so it is essential to make the text and corresponding image interact fully with each other. To tackle this issue, we design a multimodal attention layer based on cross attention. Our model took first place in this task.

| Class | Train | Test |
|---|---|---|
| troll | 1282 | 395 |
| not troll | 1018 | 272 |

Table 1: Statistics of the train and test datasets.

## 2 Data

The data we used is provided by the organizers of shared task on Meme Classification in Tamil Language (Suryawanshi et al., 2020; Suryawanshi and Chakravarthi, 2021). There are 2300 samples in the training data. The specific statistics of the data are shown in Table 1.

### 2.1 Text Preprocessing

There are two methods used to preprocess social media text as follow:

- **Noise removal:** Emojis and extra blanks in the training data are removed in advance. Experimental results show that removing these noise can improve the performance of our model. The maximum sequence size is 256.
- **Tokenization:** Texts are tokenized using the sentencepiece toolkit[1] and converted to the corresponding IDs through the vocabulary of XLM-RoBERTa (Conneau et al., 2020).

[1] https://github.com/google/sentencepiece



*Proceedings of the First Workshop on Speech and Language Technologies for Dravidian Languages*, pages 352–356
April 20, 2021 

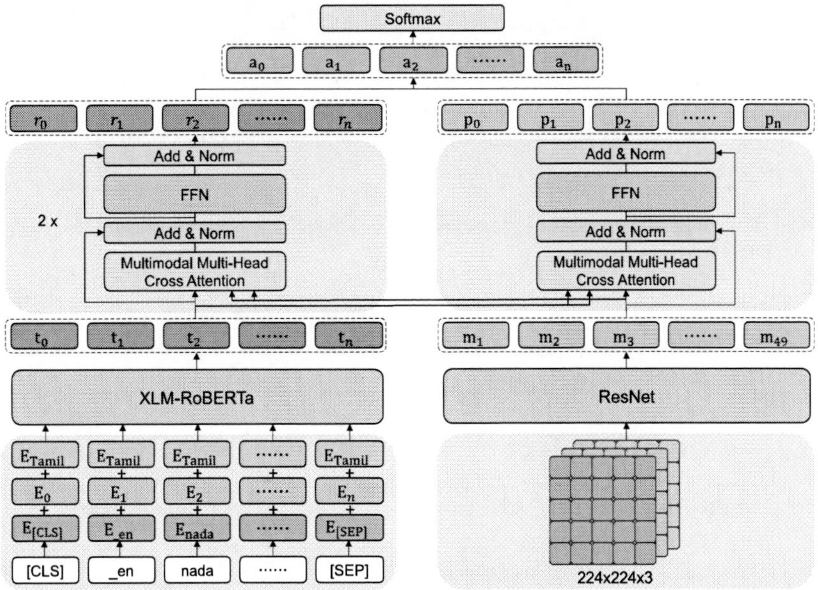


Figure 1: Our model architecture.

### 2.2 Image Preprocessing

Similar to the image preprocessing method in ImageNet (Deng et al., 2009), each image is cropped and scaled so that the dimension size of each image is 224×224×3.

## 3 Proposed Model

In this section, we will present our model for meme classification on Tamil language. Our model is mainly divided into three layers: encoding layer, multimodal attention layer and prediction layer. Encoding layer is used to obtain word representations and image representations. Multimodal attention layer is used to make the text and corresponding image interact fully with each other. Prediction layer is used to get the probabilities of all classes. Overall model architecture is shown in Figure 1.

### 3.1 Encoding Layer

**Text Encoding:** Compared with RNN such as LSTM (Hochreiter and Schmidhuber, 1997) or GRU (Chung et al., 2014), the pre-trained language model like XLM-RoBERTa can learn better contextual representations of text and also helps in fighting vanishing and exploding gradient descent. Therefore, we use XLM-RoBERTa as the encoder of the social media text. Given a sentence $X = \{x_i\}_{i=0}^{n}$, where $n$ is equal to 256 and $x_i$ is the sum of token embedding, position embedding and language embedding of token at position $i$ and the dimension size of $x_i$ is $d$, we can obtain contextual representation $T = \{t_i\}_{i=0}^{n}$ for each word:

$$T = XLM\text{−}RoBERTa(X). \quad (1)$$

**Image Encoding:** Since ResNet (He et al., 2016) is currently the most widely used image feature extraction network, we use ResNet with 152 layers as the encoder of the image to extract the features for each image $I \in R^{224\times224\times3}$. The output of the last layer which is denoted as $\hat{M} = \{\hat{m}_i\}_{i=1}^{49}$ is used to represent an image:

$$\hat{M} = ResNet(I). \quad (2)$$

Besides, we use a linear transformation to make the dimension size of the image representations consistent with the word representations: $M = W_M^T \hat{M}$, where $W_M \in R^{2048*d}$ and the length of $M$ is 49.

### 3.2 Multimodal Attention Layer

This layer is the core of our model. Due to the particularity of social media text, although we have obtained representations of the image and text respectively, in many cases we can only understand the meaning of text through the corresponding image, so it is essential to make the text and corresponding image interact fully with each other. To tackle this issue, we designed a multimodal attention layer based on cross attention (Tsai et al., 2019).

| Team | Metric | Precision | Recall | F1-score |
|---|---|---|---|---|
| Codewithzichao | weighted avg | **0.57** | **0.60** | **0.55** |
| IIITK | weighted avg | 0.56 | 0.59 | 0.54 |
| NLP@CUET | weighted avg | 0.55 | 0.58 | 0.52 |
| SSNCSE_NLP | weighted avg | 0.58 | 0.60 | 0.50 |
| Simon_work | weighted avg | 0.53 | 0.58 | 0.49 |

Table 2: Top-5 of the official leader-board in shared task for meme classification in Tamil language. Systems are ordered by weighted average F1 score.

| Model | Metric | Precision | Recall | F1-score |
|---|---|---|---|---|
| Our submission | weighted avg | **0.57** | **0.60** | **0.55** |
| w/o Multimodal Attention Layer | weighted avg | 0.56 | 0.59 | 0.54 |

Table 3: Ablation study of our model in the test dataset. w/o means without.

**Multimodal Multi-Head Cross Attention:** Similar to multi-head self attention used in Transformer (Vaswani et al., 2017), multimodal multi-head cross attention (**MMHCA**) has three input vectors: $Q = \{w_i\}_{i=1}^{n_Q}$, $K = \{w_i\}_{i=1}^{n_K}$, $V = \{w_i\}_{i=1}^{n_V}$, where $w_i$ refers to a $d$ dimension vector and $n_K$ is equal to $n_V$. Attention results are defined as:

$$Attn_i(Q_i, K_i) = softmax(\frac{(W_{Q_i}Q_i)(W_{K_i}K_i^T)}{\sqrt{d/m}}) \quad (3)$$

$$V_i^{attn} = Attn_i(Q_i, K_i)(W_{V_i}V_i) \quad (4)$$

$$MMHCA(Q, K, V) = [V_1^{attn}; ...; V_m^{attn}]. \quad (5)$$

**Attentive Word Representations:** To obtain word representations for each image, we use MMHCA, which take M as queries and T as keys and values. The attentive word representations are defined as :

$$\hat{R} = LN(M + MMHCA(M, T, T)); \quad (6)$$

$$R = LN(\hat{R} + FFN(\hat{R})), \quad (7)$$

where LN is the layer normalization (Ba et al., 2016) and FFN is the feed-forward network. We use MMHCA again to obtain final attentive word representations.

**Attentive Image Representations:** To obtain image representations for each word, we use MMHCA, which take T as queries and M as keys and values. The attentive image representations are defined as :

$$\hat{P} = LN(M + MMHCA(T, M, M)); \quad (8)$$

$$P = LN(\hat{P} + FFN(\hat{P})). \quad (9)$$

| Hyper-parameters | Value |
|---|---|
| Batch size | 8 |
| Epoch | 50 |
| Learning rate | 2e-5 |
| Gradient clipping | 0.25 |
| Dropout rate | 0.2 |

Table 4: Hyper-parameters of our model.

After obtaining attentive word representations and attentive image representations, we concatenate them as the output of this layer: $A = [R; P]$.

### 3.3 Prediction Layer

To classify each image and text pair, we feed $A$ to a average-over-time pooling layer and then use softmax to get the probabilities of all classes:

$$Z = AvgPool(A); \quad (10)$$

$$P(y|X, I) = softmax(WZ + b), \quad (11)$$

where $A$ is the output of multimodal attention layer. We use focal loss (Lin et al., 2017) to train our model:

$$L = -\sum_{\{X,I\} \in S} \alpha(1 - P(y|X, I))^{\gamma} \log P(y|X, I), \quad (12)$$

where $S$ refers to the train dataset.

## 4 Experiment and Results

### 4.1 Experimental Settings

We use Pytorch (Paszke et al., 2017) and HuggingFace's transformers (Wolf et al., 2020) to implement our model. We use XLM-RoBERTa and

ResNet-152 as encoders for the text and image, respectively. We use mixed precision training based on Apex library[2]. AdamW (Loshchilov and Hutter, 2019) optimizer is used to optimize our model with a learning rate at 2e-5. We use 5-fold cross validation to obtain better performance. We use adversarial training (i.e. FGM (Goodfellow et al., 2015)) to further improve the robustness and generalization ability of our model. We list all hyper-parameters of our model in Table 4. we conduct the experiments on NVIDIA Tesla T4 GPUs. Our code is available at Github[3].

### 4.2 Results and Ablations

The top five results in this task have been shown in Table 2. Our model achieved 0.55 weighted average F1 score and ranked first. Besides, our result is 0.01 higher than the second.

In addition, to prove the effectiveness of multimodal attention layer, we conduct the ablation experiment. The ablation result is shown in Table 3. When multimodal attention layer is removed, the final result drops by 0.01, which indicates that multimodal attention layer is considerably useful.

## 5 Conclusion

In this paper, we present a multimodal transformer for meme classification on Tamil language. Using ResNet and XLM-RoBERTa for the image and text, we obtain better representations of the image and text. Besides, we design a multimodal attention layer to make the text and corresponding image interact fully with each other. Finally, our model took first place in this task which demonstrates the effectiveness of our model. In future research, we will explore ways to better filter irrelevant information in the image and text to obtain better performance.

[2]https://github.com/NVIDIA/apex

[3]https://github.com/codewithzichao/Multimodal-Transformers

## References


Jimmy Ba, J. Kiros, and Geoffrey E. Hinton. 2016. Layer normalization. *ArXiv*, abs/1607.06450.

Yitao Cai, Huiyu Cai, and Xiaojun Wan. 2019. Multimodal sarcasm detection in twitter with hierarchical fusion model. In *Proceedings of the 57th Annual Meeting of the Association for Computational Linguistics*, pages 2506–2515, Florence, Italy. Association for Computational Linguistics.

Junyoung Chung, Çaglar Gülçehre, KyungHyun Cho, and Yoshua Bengio. 2014. Empirical evaluation of gated recurrent neural networks on sequence modeling. *CoRR*, abs/1412.3555.

Alexis Conneau, Kartikay Khandelwal, Naman Goyal, Vishrav Chaudhary, Guillaume Wenzek, Francisco Guzmán, Edouard Grave, Myle Ott, Luke Zettlemoyer, and Veselin Stoyanov. 2020. Unsupervised cross-lingual representation learning at scale. In *Proceedings of the 58th Annual Meeting of the Association for Computational Linguistics*, pages 8440–8451, Online.

J. Deng, W. Dong, R. Socher, L. Li, Kai Li, and Li Fei-Fei. 2009. Imagenet: A large-scale hierarchical image database. In *2009 IEEE Conference on Computer Vision and Pattern Recognition*, pages 248–255.

Ian J. Goodfellow, Jonathon Shlens, and Christian Szegedy. 2015. Explaining and harnessing adversarial examples. *CoRR*, abs/1412.6572.

Kaiming He, Xiangyu Zhang, Shaoqing Ren, and Jian Sun. 2016. Deep residual learning for image recognition. In *Proceedings of the IEEE Conference on Computer Vision and Pattern Recognition (CVPR)*.

Sepp Hochreiter and Jürgen Schmidhuber. 1997. Long short-term memory. *Neural Computation*, 9(8):1735–1780.

Tsung-Yi Lin, Priya Goyal, Ross Girshick, Kaiming He, and Piotr Dollar. 2017. Focal loss for dense object detection. In *Proceedings of the IEEE International Conference on Computer Vision (ICCV)*.

I. Loshchilov and F. Hutter. 2019. Decoupled weight decay regularization. In *ICLR*.

Adam Paszke, S. Gross, Soumith Chintala, G. Chanan, E. Yang, Zachary Devito, Zeming Lin, Alban Desmaison, L. Antiga, and A. Lerer. 2017. Automatic differentiation in pytorch. In *NIPS-W*.

Shardul Suryawanshi and Bharathi Raja Chakravarthi. 2021. Findings of the shared task on Troll Meme Classification in Tamil. In *Proceedings of the First Workshop on Speech and Language Technologies for Dravidian Languages*. Association for Computational Linguistics.

Shardul Suryawanshi, Bharathi Raja Chakravarthi, Pranav Verma, Mihael Arcan, John Philip McCrae, and Paul Buitelaar. 2020. A dataset for troll classification of TamilMemes. In *Proceedings of the WILDRE5– 5th Workshop on Indian Language Data: Resources and Evaluation*, pages 7–13, Marseille, France. European Language Resources Association (ELRA).

Quoc-Tuan Truong and Hady W. Lauw. 2019. Vistanet: Visual aspect attention network for multimodal sentiment analysis. *Proceedings of the AAAI Conference on Artificial Intelligence*, 33(01):305–312.

Yao-Hung Hubert Tsai, Shaojie Bai, Paul Pu Liang, J. Zico Kolter, Louis-Philippe Morency, and Ruslan Salakhutdinov. 2019. Multimodal transformer for unaligned multimodal language sequences. In *Proceedings of the 57th Annual Meeting of the Association for Computational Linguistics (Volume 1: Long Papers)*, Florence, Italy.

Ashish Vaswani, Noam Shazeer, Niki Parmar, Jakob Uszkoreit, Llion Jones, Aidan N Gomez, Ł ukasz Kaiser, and Illia Polosukhin. 2017. Attention is all you need. In *Advances in Neural Information Processing Systems*, volume 30, pages 5998–6008.

Thomas Wolf, Lysandre Debut, Victor Sanh, Julien Chaumond, Clement Delangue, Anthony Moi, Pierric Cistac, Tim Rault, Rémi Louf, Morgan Funtowicz, Joe Davison, Sam Shleifer, Patrick von Platen, Clara Ma, Yacine Jernite, Julien Plu, Canwen Xu, Teven Le Scao, Sylvain Gugger, Mariama Drame, Quentin Lhoest, and Alexander M. Rush. 2020. Transformers: State-of-the-art natural language processing. In *Proceedings of the 2020 Conference on Empirical Methods in Natural Language Processing: System Demonstrations*, pages 38–45, Online.

Nan Xu, Wenji Mao, and Guandan Chen. 2019. Multi-interactive memory network for aspect based multimodal sentiment analysis. *Proceedings of the AAAI Conference on Artificial Intelligence*, 33(01):371–378.

# DLRG@DravidianLangTech-EACL2021: Transformer based approach for Offensive Language Identification on Code-Mixed Tamil

**Ratnavel Rajalakshmi, B. Yashwant Reddy, Lokesh Kumar**
School of Computer Science and Engineering,
Vellore Institute of Technology, Chennai
rajalakshmi.r@vit.ac.in

## Abstract

Internet advancements have made a huge impact on the communication pattern of people and their life style. People express their opinion on products, politics, movies etc. in social media. Even though, English is predominantly used, nowadays many people prefer to tweet in their native language and sometimes by combining it with English. Sentiment analysis on such code-mixed tweets is challenging, due to large vocabulary, grammar and colloquial usage of many words. In this paper, the transformer based language model is applied to analyse the sentiment on Tanglish tweets, which is a combination of Tamil and English. This work has been submitted to the the shared task on DravidianLangTech-EACL2021. From the experimental results, it is shown that an $F_1$ score of 64% was achieved in detecting the hate speech in code-mixed Tamil-English tweets using bidirectional transformer model.

## 1 Introduction

Recent advancements in the Internet technologies and the usage of smart phones changed the behaviour of communication pattern among the people of all walks of life. Many people use the social media to post their opinion about various domains, including politics, movies, sports etc. This has led to a sharp increase in offensive posts and hate speech targeted towards an individual or a group or women. Recently, the trend of using Code-Mixed language for tweets has increased, in which the words/phrases from more than one Language is used to express their feelings (Chakravarthi et al., 2020a; Chakravarthi, 2020a; Hande et al., 2020). Many research works have been reported for identifying the Hate Speech in English / German tweets using mono-lingual models (Rajalakshmi and Reddy, 2019), but limited works are performed for under-resourced languages like Tamil (Thavareesan and Mahesan, 2019, 2020a,b). The Third Tamil Sangam Period is the period of history from c. 6th century BCE[1] to c. 3rd century CE of ancient Tamil Nadu, Kerala and parts of Sri Lanka (then known as Tamilakam) (Sivanantham and Seran, 2019). The Tamilakam (Puranuru 168. 18) referred to the whole ancient Tamil-speaking territory in the Old Tamil language, approximately equivalent to the area known today as southern India, consisting of the regions of the present-day Indian states of Tamil Nadu, Kerala, parts of Andhra Pradesh, parts of Karnataka, and also known as Eelam in northern Sri Lanka. Tamil language is the oldest language in India, all the Dravidian languages evolved from Tamil language [2] (Chakravarthi and Muralidaran, 2021; Suryawanshi and Chakravarthi, 2021; Chakravarthi et al., 2021a,b).

The machine learning algorithms with hand-crafted features are not sufficient to capture the semantic information from these multi-lingual tweets. This has made the researchers to move towards the Sequence Models which have proven capability to capture the semantic Information from the data using the Transformer Architecture. Among the Sequence Models, Bi-Directional Encoder Representation from Transformer(BERT) has gained more popularity because of its ability to capture the semantic relationship from both the directions of text and suitable method for understanding context-heavy sentences (Ghanghor et al., 2021b,a; Puranik et al., 2021; Hegde et al., 2021; Yasaswini et al., 2021). In this research work, we have studied the effectiveness of BERT to identify hate speech in the code-mixed tweets. This work is submitted for the shared task on DravidianLangTech, the first workshop on Speech and Language Technologies for

[1]Iron Age - Early Historic Transition in South Indian Appraisal

[2]Tamil-language



*Proceedings of the First Workshop on Speech and Language Technologies for Dravidian Languages*, pages 357–362
April 20, 2021 

Dravidian Languages at EACL 2021. This paper is organized as follows: Related works are presented in Section 2 followed by the proposed methodology in Section 3. Experimental details are discussed in Section 4 followed by the Conclusion in Section 5.

## 2 Related Works

Sentiment analysis on social media tweets is an important problem being studied for various reasons like identifying the opinion of people about a product, movie or sports etc. Extracting the sentiments from the tweets is a challenging task, as the users give their comments explicitly or implicitly. (Soubraylu and Rajalakshmi, 2020) performed sentiment analysis on movie reviews and proposed a method to determine the explicit opinions by combining the advantages of Convolution Neural Networks with the Bidirectional Long Short Memory. The task of identifying the implicit opinions from the tweets is more challenging and many works are reported to address the same. A detailed survey is presented in (Ganganwar and Rajalakshmi, 2019).

Many research works are reported in the literature for hate speech detection in social media tweets. (Corazza et al., 2020) studied this problem in multi-lingual context and evaluated their deep learning and machine leaning approaches on three different languages viz., English, German and Italian. In a study by (Rani et al., 2020) on code-mixed Hindi tweets, the performance of CNN is found to be better than the linear classifiers such as SVM. (Rajalakshmi and Reddy, 2019) proposed an ensemble based approach for detecting hate speech in Hindi and German languages. To process the multi-lingual queries quickly, differentiating Code-Mixing and Code borrowing is important (Chakravarthi et al., 2018, 2019b,a, 2020c; Chakravarthi, 2020b). For this, a relevance based metric is proposed by (Rajalakshmi and Agrawal, 2017) to rank the borrowing likeliness of the words in Hindi-English tweets. Code-mixing is common among many bi-lingual speakers (Priyadharshini et al., 2020; Jose et al., 2020) and to identify hate speech in Tamil-English tweets, a corpus is created by (Chakravarthi et al., 2020a). The overview of the different approaches to address this issue is presented in (Chakravarthi et al., 2020b; Mandl et al., 2020). A novel methodology has been proposed by (Sainik Kumar Mahata and Bandyopadhyay, 2020) by combining BLSTM with language tags to identify the hate speech in Tanglish tweets. (Devlin et al., 2018) proposed a new language model Bidirectional Encoder Representations from Transformers (BERT) that is suitable for many NLP tasks. BERT is simple and can be fine-tuned for various downsteam task in NLP. In this work, we have applied BERT for the task of identifying the hate speech in code-mixed Tamil-English tweets.

## 3 Methodology

The objective of this shared task is to identify the hate speech in the code-mixed Tamil-English tweets that contain any one of the following 6 category labels viz., Not-Offensive, Offensive-TargetedGroup, Offensive-Targeted-Individual, Offensive-TargetedOther, Offensive-Untargeted and not-Tamil. The data distribution among the categories is not uniform and 72% of them are not-offensive tweets with the remaining tweets split among the other categories with 7%, 6%, 1%, 8% and 4% respectively. As part of this task, the training and validation set were released with 35,139 and 4388 labelled tweets that followed the same distribution as mentioned above.

The code-mixed Tanglish tweets contain both Tamil and English words and phrases. So, we have converted the Tamil words into English terms by using Tamil to English Mapping Corpus. We have utilized NLTK(Natural Language Tool Kit) package in python to clean the data. For any classification task, the pre-processing steps are important which helps to improve the classifier performance. We have performed some of the cleaning steps like stop word removal,lemmatization and removed the special characters. For example, after pre-processing, the tweet

> "@Bala sundar ayyo sorry...antha line ah clarify pannama vittutu irukan[:drowsy]ok na solran( en appavum indha grant work ku vanthurukkaru,neenga en appava paakala pola....en appavukku munnadiye ipdi enna affront panra maathri kevi kettu asinga paduthuringa nu solraaru[:yeah][:yeah] ' chiiiii karumam podinnngggg... asingama vaila vanthurum...."

is converted into

> "bala sundar ayyo sorry antha line ah clarify pannama vittutu irukandrowsyok na solran en appavum indha grant

work ku vanthurukkaruneenga en appava paakala pola en appavukku munnadiye ipdi enna affront panra maathri kevi kettu asinga paduthuringa nu solraaruyeahyeah chi karumam poding asingama vaila vanthurum."

For any classification task, suitable vector representation need to be chosen that can capture the relationship between the terms in multiple aspects. After the pre-processing step, we have used (Pennington et al., 2014) Glove for obtaining vector representation of the words. The reason to choose Glove embedding is that, it has the ability to capture the linguistic similarity among the words. In this method, the cosine similarity metric has been employed to find the nearest neighbour, which helps in revealing the rare and relevant terms from the corpus. By this method, we could obtain the interesting patterns among the words and their relationship in a better way.

The data set has 6 categories of tweets viz., Not Offensive (25425), Offensive Targeted Insult Group (2557) , Offensive Targeted Insult Individual (2343), Offensive Targeted Insult Other (454), Offensive Untargeted (2906) and not-Tamil (1454) with imbalanced distribution. As this data set is highly imbalanced, we have applied SOUP(Similarity-based Oversampling and Undersampling Pre-processing) (Janicka et al., 2019). In this technique, the number of minority class samples are increased and the number of majority class samples are decreased to make the data set a balanced one. This is performed by removing the most unsafe examples until a desired class cordinality is obtained. The calculation of the safe level is done by using the Heterogeneous Value difference metric (HVDM). By this method, the multi-class imbalance problem is solved and then we used this balanced data for performing classification task. After applying SOUP the samples of all the classes are balanced.

To determine the sentiment expressed in the multi-lingual tweet, we have also applied the BERT model (Devlin et al., 2018). BERT is the language representation model that extracts the context from the input sentence from both the directions. To capture semantic and linguistic features from the given sentence, a bidirectional encoder representation is applied. In general, tweets may have one or more sentences. BERT has the ability to consider these input sentences into a single sequence that can unambiguously result in a better input representation. BERT embeddings are effective compared to other language models, as it combines the token embedding, segment embedding and positional embedding. Another advantage is that, pre-training of BERT combines both Masked Language Model (MLM) and Next Sequence Prediction (NSP). The pre-trained BERT can be fine-tuned to suit the downstream tasks. By adding a classification layer, BERT can be be used for this task of Hate speech identification in code-mixed Tamil-English tweets.

Unlike GloVe, that deals with word-like tokens, BERT considers the word-pieces which are segmented input units. The out-of-vocabulary tokens are also avoided when we use BERT language model. Compared to other language models, we have chosen BERT as it is possible to capture the context in a bidirectional way and efficient than the single directional models. The multi-head attention is applied to identify the key terms that are more important in determining the sentiment of the sentence expressed in Tamil. Considering the baseline models, such as LSTM, BLSTM, the BERT based model performed well on the validation data set. The fine-tuned model was used to predict the sentiment on the released test set. The details of experiments and the results are reported in the next section.

## 4 Results and Discussion

To study the performance of the proposed method, we have conducted the experiments on the released Code-mixed Tamil-English tweets. All the experiments were carried on a workstation with Intel Xeon Quad Core Processor, 32 GB RAM, NVIDIA Quadro P4000 GPU 8GB. For implementation, we have used Python 3, scikit-learn with NLTK library. For the base line experiments, we have tried with different vector representatiosn like TF-IDF and Glove with machine learning techniques. In order to capture the linguistic terms that contribute more to identify the hate speech, we have tried deep learning technique (BERT) with attention mechanism. We have applied BERT and fine-tuned the parameters. The following parameters were fixed, based on its better performance on the validation set. The experiments were conducted with a learning rate of $3e-5$, batch size of 4 with 5 epochs. We have obtained the validation accuracy of 65% for these parameters. We have applied the obtained best model, on the test set and we could achieve the

| Label | Precision | Recall | F-1 |
|---|---|---|---|
| Not Offensive | 0.79 | 0.78 | 0.78 |
| Offensive Targeted Insult Group | 0.14 | 0.14 | 0.14 |
| Offensive Targeted Insult Individual | 0.00 | 0.00 | 0.00 |
| Offensive Targeted Insult Other | 0.00 | 0.00 | 0.00 |
| Offensive Untargeted | 0.21 | 0.38 | 0.27 |
| not-Tamil | 0.99 | 0.5 | 0.66 |
| Accuracy | 0.63 | | |
| Macro-Average | 0.36 | 0.30 | 0.31 |
| Weighted-Average | 0.65 | 0.63 | 0.64 |

Table 1: Performance of the proposed approach

same 63% accuracy. The obtained results for different classes are presented in Table 1. With the BERT based model, the weighted average precision, recall and $F_1$ values of 0.65, 0.63 and 0.64 have been achieved. It could be observed that, the classifier is able to differentiate the non-offensive and non-Tamil classes alone and could not correctly identify the hate-speech tweets in code-mixed Tamil-English text. As mentioned in Section 3, the data set is highly skewed with more than 75% samples from non-offensive category, the model could not generalize well for the other categories. We are trying to address this issue of multi-class imbalance in the future work by combining other techniques to improve the performance.

## 5 Conclusion

The social media plays an important role in reflecting people's opinion on different issues. This work focused on identifying the hate speech posted in social media that contains code-mixed Tamil-English tweets, and is submitted to the DravidianLangTech-EACL2021 shared task. To capture the linguistic terms with higher contextual awareness, we have used BERT language model for this task. From the experiments, it is shown that, an $F_1$ score of 64% has been achieved using this bidirectional transformer based model. The data set is highly skewed, hence suitable techniques for addressing the multi-class imbalance will be explored in future.

## 6 Acknowledgement

The authors would like to thank the management of Vellore Institute of Technology, Chennai for providing the support to carry out this work. Also, the authors thank the Science and Engineering Research Board, Govt. of India for their financial support (ECR/2016/000484).

## References

Bharathi Raja Chakravarthi. 2020a. HopeEDI: A multilingual hope speech detection dataset for equality, diversity, and inclusion. In *Proceedings of the Third Workshop on Computational Modeling of People's Opinions, Personality, and Emotion's in Social Media*, pages 41–53, Barcelona, Spain (Online). Association for Computational Linguistics.

Bharathi raja Chakravarthi. 2020b. *Leveraging orthographic information to improve machine translation of under-resourced languages*. Ph.D. thesis, NUI Galway.

Bharathi Raja Chakravarthi, Mihael Arcan, and John P. McCrae. 2018. Improving wordnets for under-resourced languages using machine translation. In *Proceedings of the 9th Global Wordnet Conference*, pages 77–86, Nanyang Technological University (NTU), Singapore. Global Wordnet Association.

Bharathi Raja Chakravarthi, Mihael Arcan, and John P McCrae. 2019a. Comparison of different orthographies for machine translation of under-resourced dravidian languages. In *2nd Conference on Language, Data and Knowledge (LDK 2019)*. Schloss Dagstuhl-Leibniz-Zentrum fuer Informatik.

Bharathi Raja Chakravarthi, Mihael Arcan, and John P. McCrae. 2019b. WordNet gloss translation for under-resourced languages using multilingual neural machine translation. In *Proceedings of the Second Workshop on Multilingualism at the Intersection of Knowledge Bases and Machine Translation*, pages 1–7, Dublin, Ireland. European Association for Machine Translation.

Bharathi Raja Chakravarthi and Vigneshwaran Muralidaran. 2021. Findings of the shared task on Hope Speech Detection for Equality, Diversity, and Inclusion. In *Proceedings of the First Workshop on Language Technology for Equality, Diversity and Inclusion*. Association for Computational Linguistics.

Bharathi Raja Chakravarthi, Vigneshwaran Muralidaran, Ruba Priyadharshini, and John Philip McCrae. 2020a. Corpus creation for sentiment analysis in code-mixed Tamil-English text. In *Proceedings of the 1st Joint Workshop on Spoken Language Technologies for Under-resourced languages (SLTU) and Collaboration and Computing for Under-Resourced Languages (CCURL)*, pages 202–210, Marseille, France. European Language Resources association.

Bharathi Raja Chakravarthi, Ruba Priyadharshini, Shubhanker Banerjee, Richard Saldhana, John Philip McCrae, Anand Kumar M, Parameswari Krishnamurthy, and Melvin Johnson. 2021a. Findings of the shared task on Machine Translation in Dravidian languages. In *Proceedings of the First Workshop on Speech and Language Technologies for Dravidian Languages*. Association for Computational Linguistics.

Bharathi Raja Chakravarthi, Ruba Priyadharshini, Navya Jose, Anand Kumar M, Thomas Mandl, Prasanna Kumar Kumaresan, Rahul Ponnusamy, Hariharan V, Elizabeth Sherly, and John Philip McCrae. 2021b. Findings of the shared task on Offensive Language Identification in Tamil, Malayalam, and Kannada. In *Proceedings of the First Workshop on Speech and Language Technologies for Dravidian Languages*. Association for Computational Linguistics.

Bharathi Raja Chakravarthi, Ruba Priyadharshini, Vigneshwaran Muralidaran, Shardul Suryawanshi, Navya Jose, Elizabeth Sherly, and John P. McCrae. 2020b. Overview of the track on Sentiment Analysis for Dravidian Languages in Code-Mixed Text. *Forum for Information Retrieval Evaluation.*

Bharathi Raja Chakravarthi, Navaneethan Rajasekaran, Mihael Arcan, Kevin McGuinness, Noel E. O'Connor, and John P. McCrae. 2020c. Bilingual lexicon induction across orthographically-distinct under-resourced Dravidian languages. In *Proceedings of the 7th Workshop on NLP for Similar Languages, Varieties and Dialects*, pages 57–69, Barcelona, Spain (Online). International Committee on Computational Linguistics (ICCL).

Michele Corazza, Stefano Menini, Elena Cabrio, Sara Tonelli, and Serena Villata. 2020. A multilingual evaluation for online hate speech detection. *ACM Transactions on Internet Technology*, pages 1–24.

Jacob Devlin, Ming-Wei Chang, Kenton Lee, and Kristina Toutanova. 2018. Bert: Pre-training of deep bidirectional transformers for language understanding. *arXiv preprint arXiv:1810.04805.*

Vaishali Ganganwar and R. Rajalakshmi. 2019. Implicit aspect extraction for sentiment analysis: A survey of recent approaches. *Procedia Computer Science*, 165:485–491.

Nikhil Kumar Ghanghor, Parameswari Krishnamurthy, Sajeetha Thavareesan, Ruba Priyadharshini, and Bharathi Raja Chakravarthi. 2021a. IIITK@DravidianLangTech-EACL2021: Offensive Language Identification and Meme Classification in Tamil, Malayalam and Kannada. In *Proceedings of the First Workshop on Speech and Language Technologies for Dravidian Languages*, Online. Association for Computational Linguistics.

Nikhil Kumar Ghanghor, Rahul Ponnusamy, Prasanna Kumar Kumaresan, Ruba Priyadharshini, Sajeetha Thavareesan, and Bharathi Raja Chakravarthi. 2021b. IIITK@LT-EDI-EACL2021: Hope Speech Detection for Equality, Diversity, and Inclusion in Tamil, Malayalam and English. In *Proceedings of the First Workshop on Language Technology for Equality, Diversity and Inclusion*, Online.

Adeep Hande, Ruba Priyadharshini, and Bharathi Raja Chakravarthi. 2020. KanCMD: Kannada CodeMixed dataset for sentiment analysis and offensive language detection. In *Proceedings of the Third Workshop on Computational Modeling of People's Opinions, Personality, and Emotion's in Social Media*, pages 54–63, Barcelona, Spain (Online). Association for Computational Linguistics.

Siddhanth U Hegde, Adeep Hande, Ruba Priyadharshini, Sajeetha Thavareesan, and Bharathi Raja Chakravarthi. 2021. UVCE-IIITT@DravidianLangTech-EACL2021: Tamil Troll Meme Classification: You need to Pay more Attention. In *Proceedings of the First Workshop on Speech and Language Technologies for Dravidian Languages*. Association for Computational Linguistics.

Małgorzata Janicka, Mateusz Lango, and Jerzy Stefanowski. 2019. Using information on class interrelations to improve classification of multiclass imbalanced data: A new resampling algorithm. *International Journal of Applied Mathematics and Computer Science*, 29:769–781.

Navya Jose, Bharathi Raja Chakravarthi, Shardul Suryawanshi, Elizabeth Sherly, and John P. McCrae. 2020. A Survey of Current Datasets for Code-Switching Research. In *2020 6th International Conference on Advanced Computing and Communication Systems (ICACCS)*, pages 136–141.

Thomas Mandl, Sandip Modha, Anand Kumar M, and Bharathi Raja Chakravarthi. 2020. Overview of the HASOC Track at FIRE 2020: Hate Speech and Offensive Language Identification in Tamil, Malayalam, Hindi, English and German. In *Forum for Information Retrieval Evaluation*, FIRE 2020, page 29–32, New York, NY, USA. Association for Computing Machinery.

Jeffrey Pennington, Richard Socher, and Christopher D. Manning. 2014. Glove: Global vectors for word representation. In *Empirical Methods in Natural Language Processing (EMNLP)*, pages 1532–1543.

Ruba Priyadharshini, Bharathi Raja Chakravarthi, Mani Vegupatti, and John P. McCrae. 2020. Named Entity Recognition for Code-Mixed Indian Corpus using Meta Embedding. In *2020 6th International Conference on Advanced Computing and Communication Systems (ICACCS)*, pages 68–72.

Karthik Puranik, Adeep Hande, Ruba Priyadharshini, Sajeetha Thavareesan, and Bharathi Raja Chakravarthi. 2021. IIITT@LT-EDI-EACL2021-Hope Speech Detection: There is always hope in Transformers. In *Proceedings of the First Workshop on Language Technology for Equality, Diversity and Inclusion*. Association for Computational Linguistics.

R. Rajalakshmi and Rohan Agrawal. 2017. Borrowing likeliness ranking based on relevance factor. In *Proceedings of the Fourth ACM IKDD Conferences on Data Sciences*, CODS '17, New York, NY, USA. Association for Computing Machinery.

R Rajalakshmi and B Yashwant Reddy. 2019. Dlrg@ hasoc 2019: An enhanced ensemble classifier for hate and offensive content identification. In *FIRE (Working Notes)*, pages 370–379.

Priya Rani, Shardul Suryawanshi, Koustava Goswami, Bharathi Raja Chakravarthi, Theodorus Fransen, and John Philip McCrae. 2020. A Comparative Study of Different State-of-the-Art Hate Speech Detection Methods in Hindi-English Code-Mixed Data. In *Proceedings of the Second Workshop on Trolling, Aggression and Cyberbullying*, pages 42–48, Marseille, France. European Language Resources Association (ELRA).

Dipankar Das Sainik Kumar Mahata and Sivaji Bandyopadhyay. 2020. JUNLP@Dravidian-CodeMix-FIRE2020: Sentiment Classification of Code-Mixed Tweets using Bi-Directional RNN and Language Tags. *Forum for Information Retrieval Evaluation*.

R Sivanantham and M Seran. 2019. Keeladi: An Urban Settlement of Sangam Age on the Banks of River Vaigai. *India: Department of Archaeology, Government of Tamil Nadu, Chennai*.

Sivakumar Soubraylu and Ratnavel Rajalakshmi. 2020. Hybrid convolutional bidirectional recurrent neural network based sentiment analysis on movie reviews. *Computational Intelligence*, pages 1–23.

Shardul Suryawanshi and Bharathi Raja Chakravarthi. 2021. Findings of the shared task on Troll Meme Classification in Tamil. In *Proceedings of the First Workshop on Speech and Language Technologies for Dravidian Languages*. Association for Computational Linguistics.

Sajeetha Thavareesan and Sinnathamby Mahesan. 2019. Sentiment Analysis in Tamil Texts: A Study on Machine Learning Techniques and Feature Representation. In *2019 14th Conference on Industrial and Information Systems (ICIIS)*, pages 320–325.

Sajeetha Thavareesan and Sinnathamby Mahesan. 2020a. Sentiment Lexicon Expansion using Word2vec and fastText for Sentiment Prediction in Tamil texts. In *2020 Moratuwa Engineering Research Conference (MERCon)*, pages 272–276.

Sajeetha Thavareesan and Sinnathamby Mahesan. 2020b. Word embedding-based Part of Speech tagging in Tamil texts. In *2020 IEEE 15th International Conference on Industrial and Information Systems (ICIIS)*, pages 478–482.

Konthala Yasaswini, Karthik Puranik, Adeep Hande, Ruba Priyadharshini, Sajeetha Thavareesan, and Bharathi Raja Chakravarthi. 2021. IIITT@DravidianLangTech-EACL2021: Transfer Learning for Offensive Language Detection in Dravidian Languages. In *Proceedings of the First Workshop on Speech and Language Technologies for Dravidian Languages*. Association for Computational Linguistics.

**Association for Computational Linguistics**
209 N. Eighth Street
Stroudsburg, Pennsylvania 18360

ISBN 978-1-7138-2959-1

CURRAN ASSOCIATES INC.
proceedings.com